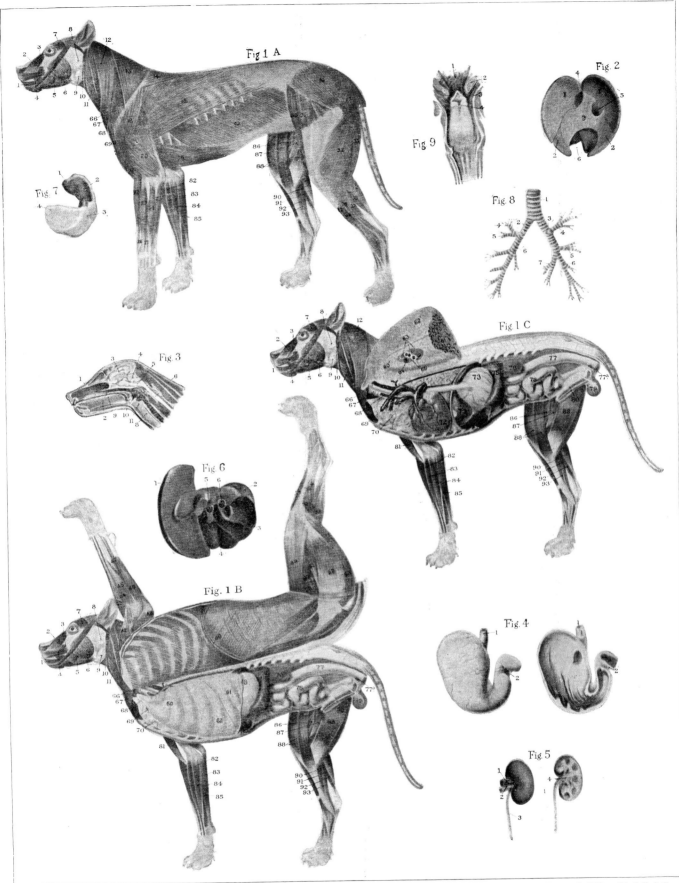

ANATOMY OF THE DOG.

These diagrams (reproduced at a reduction of one half from the originals) show the entire organism of the dog.
Fig. 1A, the muscular system. Fig. 1B, the nearside of the dog opened up to display the lung and abdomen. Fig. 1C, the lung raised, giving a view of the aorta and heart. Fig. 2, lungs. Fig. 3, section of head. Fig. 4, stomach. Fig. 5, kidney. Fig. 6, liver. Fig. 7, spleen. Fig. 8, trachea and bronchi. Fig. 9, larynx. References to the numbers will be found where the various parts are referred to in this Encyclopaedia.

HUTCHINSON'S
DOG
ENCYCLOPÆDIA

An invaluable work of international importance (alphabetically arranged for easy reference) on breeds of dogs of every country, with full veterinary advice in cases of accidents or ailments, etc., on their care and home treatment, contributed by the most eminent authorities

Edited by WALTER HUTCHINSON

M.A., F.R.G.S., F.R.S.A., F.R.A.I., F.Z.S., BARRISTER-AT-LAW

VOLUME I — A to Fo

containing

**1168 Black-and-White Illustrations
20 Colour and Art Plates**

Leading Contributors to this Volume include

SIR FREDERICK HOBDAY, C.M.G., F.R.C.V.S., ETC., MAJOR HAMILTON KIRK, M.R.C.V.S., G. HOROWITZ, B.SC. (ANT.), LT.-COL. HESELTINE, CAPT. E. A. V. STANLEY, E. C. ASH, W. P. PYCRAFT, F.Z.S., A. CROXTON SMITH, G. MORTIMER SMITH, AND MANY OTHER EXPERTS

1934-1935

PRINTED IN
GREAT BRITAIN,
AT THE ANCHOR
PRESS, TIPTREE,
::   ESSEX   ::

VOLUME I : ERRATA

PAGE **xii.**—Caption to lower illustration, line 2 : For "Fräulein" read "Frau"; "President of the Austrian Kennel Club, 1933" should be deleted. The President in 1933 was Dr. Karl Witzelhuber.

,, **xxviii.**—Caption to lower illustration : "President of the Yugoslavian Women's Kennel Club, 1933" should be deleted.

,, **2.**—Column 2, line 2 from bottom : "solution of" should be deleted.

,, **12.**—Column 1, line 6 : For Ch. "Sirdar of Ghazni" read Ch. "Asri-Havid of Ghazni".

,, **16.**—Column 1, ten lines from bottom : For "See CAPE HUNTING DOG" read "See SOUTH AFRICAN HUNTING DOG".

,, **33.**—Column 1, line 1 : For "Alsatian Hound" read "Alsatian Wolf-dog".

,, **41.**—Caption to top illustration, heading : For "The Belgian Alsatian" read "A Belgian Alsatian-type". Line 1 : For "Alsatian" read "Sheepdog". Caption to centre illustration : For "The French Alsatian" read "A French Alsatian-type".

,, **48.**—Caption to upper series of photographs, line 1 : For "Mr. Arnold Brotherton" read "Mr. Stanley J. Porter". The Alsatian depicted is the bitch "Keeper-of-the-Door".

107.—Caption to illustration, line 1 : For "of Mrs. N. E. Elms's breeding" read "of Miss D. White's breeding".

,, **139.**—Under each illustration read "By courtesy of E. C. Ash".

,, **156.**—Column 1, line 14 : For "See POISONS" read "See SEPTICAEMIA".

,, **190.**—Column 1, second line from bottom : For "See ALCOHOL" read "See STIMULANTS".

,, **199.**—Column 1, lines 36 and 37. These lines should be deleted.

,, **201.**—Column 2, line 24 : For "See ALBUMINURIA" read "See URINE".

,, **230.**—For "at the end of the nineteenth century" read "early twentieth century".

,, **240.**—Captions to left-hand illustrations should be transposed.

,, **260.**—Column 1, line 9 : For "affected" read "effected".

,, **270.**—Column 2, lines 3 and 4 : For "Roy Uhor" and "Call Uhor" read "Roy Mohr" and "Calla Mohr", respectively. Column 2, line 23 : For "Callarnchor" read "Calla Mohr".

,, **273.**—Column 1, line 1 : For "Skye" read "Ose".

,, **278.**—Column 1, eighteenth line from bottom : For "yellow" read "greyish-white".

,, **281.**—Caption to bottom left-hand illustration : For "Brocaire Righorn Ruadh" and "Brocaire Jurk" read "Brocaire Righim Ruadh" and "Brocaire Jura" respectively.

Also, line 3 of caption, for "heavier" read "stronger".

PAGE **323.**—Caption to left-hand centre illustration : Delete word "good".

,, **334.**—Caption to bottom illustration, line 1 : For "Cocker" read "Clumber".

,, **340.**—Captions to bottom left and bottom centre illustrations : For "Fairholme Rally" read "Galtrees May", and vice versa.

,, **342.**—Caption to illustration, line 2 : For "Mr. H. S. Lloyd" read "Mr. S. W. Bloxham".

,, **343.**—Caption to topmost illustration, heading : Delete "Ch." Same caption, lines 1 and 2 : For "strain" read "Kennel". Caption to right centre illustration : For "Invader of Ware" read "Ch. 'Invader of Ware'."

,, **344.**—Caption to illustration, line 1 : For "Ch. 'Ivador', Ch. 'Lucky Star' and Ch. 'Whoopee'" read "Ch. 'Invader', 'Lucky Star' and 'Whoopee'." Also for "Mr. Lloyd's breeding" read "Mr. Lloyd's Kennel".

,, **407.** opposite ; caption to plate, line 2 : For "Miss E. V. Barnes" read "Miss Clay".

,, **417.**—Caption to illustration : For "curly" read "long-haired".

,, **419.**—Caption to illustration : For "Miniature Long-haired" read "Wire-haired".

,, **424.**—Caption to lower illustration, line 1 : For "Miss Stephenson" read "Miss Stephens".

,, **429.**—Caption to lower illustration, line 1 : For "Miss E. V. Barnes" read "Mrs. Wigglesworth's".

,, **432.**—Caption to illustration : For "Miss Barnes'" read "Mrs. Eggo's".

,, **452.**—Caption to upper illustration, line 1 : For "The Misses Loughreys'" read "Miss A. N. Hartley's".

,, **456.**—Caption to illustration, line 2 : For "Miss E. S. M. Branfoot" read "Miss Adelcron".

,, **458.**—Caption to illustration : For "Revis of Rotherwood" read "Silver Cloud".

,, **468.**—Column 1, line 29 : For "presence" read "detection". Column 1, line 4 from bottom : For "hiccup" read "hiccough".

,, **500.**—Caption to illustrations, line 1 : For "At top" read "Below". Line 2 : For "second" read "upper".

,, **514.**—Caption to bottom illustration, heading : For "germ" read "parasite".

,, **524.**—Caption to top illustration : For "Bacot" read "Buscot".

,, **525.**—For "Piek" read "Peik" : For "bred by Mr. Holmes" read "owned by".

,, **538.**—Caption to bottom illustration : For "Spaniel" read "Setter".

,, **566.**—Nine lines from bottom : For "enterotomy" read "enterectomy"

Photo by]   A ROYAL PRIZE WINNER.   *[London News Agency.*

"Claus of Seale", the Prince of Wales's Alsatian, with the Challenge Cup won at the Crystal Palace in 1931. Alsatians are famed
as watch dogs and are much used in police work.

Introduction

By Professor Sir FREDERICK HOBDAY, C.M.G., F.R.C.V.S.

Dr.Vet.Med.h.c. (Zurich), Principal and Dean of the Royal Veterinary College, London, Honorary Veterinary Surgeon to H.M. the King.

THE fact that there are something like four million dog licences
issued annually in this country is evidence of the affection of the
British nation for its canine friends, for whose welfare they thus
take up the responsibility equally when ill or when in good health. I
and the other members of my profession have a very special interest in
this, and it is for that reason I have pleasure in recommending this
Encyclopaedia.

That it fills a real need, and fills it well, will, I am sure, be the opinion
of its readers, for not only are the pages that follow pleasing to look upon,
but they are also—and I know from my own perusal of them—full of
sound advice and instructive suggestions.

My special province is of course the veterinary side of this, and I do
not pretend to speak with authority of breeds and shows. We of the
veterinary profession treat not only champions worth hundreds of pounds
but, just as in a hospital for human beings the poor and needy go for
treatment, so to the Royal Veterinary College Hospital there are brought
animals who are ailing and who receive all the curative attention of which
our institution is capable. The Poor Out-Patients Department alone
passed nearly 14,000 individual patients through its portals in 1933, and
a perusal of this canine encyclopaedia will bring home to its readers the
importance of this subject and the amount of commercial assets involved.

The majority of ailments to which a dog is heir is set out in alpha-
betical order and dealt with in an authoritative and yet simple manner ;
and, since prevention is better than cure, every dog-lover will be the
richer in knowledge as to the best way to care for his animal, and this
means many more healthy and, therefore, happy dogs.

One of the facts we can write down to the credit of our own generation
is the tremendous increase in the affection shown towards animals.

By courtesy of]   *[the proprietors of
"Punch".*
DOG TOBY.
Perhaps the best-known member
of the canine race in England.
Mr. Punch's dog.

A

I suppose ever since the ancient Egyptian walked his flagged pathway a dog trotted at man's heels but the animal has not always been given a square deal. There have been ages when he knew little but cruelty. Indeed, only in comparatively recent years has he come into his own as man's chief friend among the animals.

In the same degree veterinary science has advanced. There may not be a sufficiency of skilled vets in the country, but students are being trained as rapidly as possible at the London College and at colleges in other centres—and that these will be thoroughly efficient is sufficiently indicated by the fact that the Matriculation entrance examinations are exactly of the same standard as for the medical student : i.e. five years for the Diploma alone.

In the meantime one is genuinely interested in every step that is taken towards educating the general public in those general principles which help to keep our dumb animals healthy and can be quickly applied in case of illness. This Encyclopaedia is a very efficient and very worthy effort to give practical help to the owner in that direction. The information it contains is up to

(Continued on page v.)

Photo by]   [Sport and General.

THE BULLDOG : EMBLEM OF BRITAIN.

The Bulldog was used for the baiting of bulls, hence the type of head which allowed the dog to hold on to the bull and continue to breathe. The Bulldog, Mr. F. E. Read's "Hero of Maida", shown in the photograph, has won numerous prizes.

TWO ROYAL FRIENDS.

Closely related to Scottish, West Highland and Skye Terriers, Cairns were first recognized as a separate breed in 1909, and have since gained universal popularity. "Cora" and "Jaggs" are the favourite pets of H.R.H. The Prince of Wales.

Princess Alice with Prince Albert's favourite Greyhound.

"Saved". The Landseer Newfoundland dog brings a child from the water.

FAMOUS DOG PAINTINGS BY LANDSEER.

Edwin Landseer, the artist who designed the lions of Trafalger Square, was the most famous animal painter of the Victorian age. Modern critics have objected to the sentimentality of his treatment.

INTRODUCTION—*(continued)*.

date and written in such a way that it is to be hoped it will be well understood.

A glance will assure the reader of its general attractiveness in method of appeal. Those who

and other illustrations from all parts of the world.

That information about every type of dog known in all countries has been gathered together and so lucidly and attractively presented is an achievement which should make its appeal to every dog-

Photo] [*Sport and General.*

THE CURLY-COATED BREED OF IRELAND.

Irish Water Spaniels were first bred by Justin M'Carthy about 1834, but although in 1893 they were becoming popular as a Show breed they never made the headway expected. They are excellent sporting dogs and their closely curled hair makes them impervious to weather conditions. Here we have Captain M. J. H. Anwyl's "Thunder of Lligwy"

contribute articles about the breeds, about shows the history and other fascinating matters connected with dogs are all experts in their various branches, and what they have to say is illustrated by thousands of splendid photographs

lover, whether he be owner of an animal which he wishes to care for and train as a potential champion or confines his affection to the lovable little nondescript that puts its muzzle on its master's foot in front of the home fire.

Scott Langley
1933

Drawn by]   A NOTED SPORTING BREED.   [Nina Scott-Langley.

The name "Spaniel" suggests that the breed first came from Spain and there seems no reason to doubt that the Peninsula was the place of their origin. In the seventeenth century there were two kinds only, the Land and Water Spaniel, but in recent times many varieties have been evolved.

A SCOTTISH TERRIER.

These dogs have been bred for over a century. Scottish Terrier is the correct name for this breed, though it is often erroneously described as an Aberdeen Terrier.

A MEMBER OF CHINESE SOCIETY.

From the seventh century A.D., when the first Pekingese is said to have been presented to one of the first T'ang Emperors, until 1860, Pekingese were seldom seen outside the Royal Palaces of China. In that year Admiral Lord John Hay brought the first specimens back to England, but in changed surroundings the breed still claims the pampered luxury of its royal ancestors.

THE SAMOYED.

This breed, which comes from the arctic regions and is used by the natives for pulling their sledges in the area of the Ob and Zenesi, are here seen in harness on a snow-covered road in England.

Photo]   *[E.N.A.*

TERRIER.

Of all the breeds of dogs, because it fits well into the small home and because of its sporty nature, the Terrier is now the most universally popular. Fräulein Dorothea Wieck, of the German Theatrical Kennel Club, is shown with a Terrier friend.

In Praise of Dog: An Appreciation

BY GILBERT FRANKAU

HOW did Dog first come to Man?
You will not find this in any history book that I know; I very much doubt whether you will even find it in this Encyclopaedia, where all else about Dog is so clearly revealed. The poet, however, will tell you. And most convincingly, in words ever so much better than any I can hope to write.

"Hear and attend and listen" says the poet, "for this befell and behappened and became and was, O my Best Beloved, when the Tame animals were wild. . . .

"Of course the Man was wild too. He didn't even begin to be tame till he met the woman, and she told him that she did not like living in his wild ways. She picked out a nice dry cave, instead of a heap of wet leaves to lie down in; and she strewed clean sand on the floor, and she

it a nice fire of wood at the back of the Cave. . . .

"Out in the Wet Wild Woods all the wild animals gathered together where they could see the light of the fire a long way off and they wondered what it meant. . . .

"Then Wild Horse stamped with his wild foot and said, 'O my Friends and O my Enemies, why have the Man and the Woman made that great light in that great Cave, and what harm will it do us?'

"Wild Dog lifted up his wild nose and smelled the smell of the roast mutton, and said, 'I will go up and see, and look, and say; for I think it is good. . . .'

"When Wild Dog reached the mouth of the Cave he lifted up the dried horse-skin with his nose and sniffed the beautiful smell of the roast mutton, and the Woman, looking at the blade-bone,

Photo |E.N.A.

A COURSING EPISODE—TAKING A GATE.

Owing to popularity of coursing even in ancient times Greyhounds are probably the oldest breed of dogs in existence. They **were** certainly used in ancient times. Lord Orford was famous for his Greyhound experiments and no dog of to-day exists free from Lord Orford's Greyhound blood.

heard him, and said, 'Here comes the first. Wild Thing out of the Wild Woods, what do you want ?'"

And after that Rudyard Kipling tells how Wild Dog ate roasted mutton-bone, and crawled into the Cave, and laid his head on the Woman's lap, and said, "O my Friend and Wife of my

THE WATER DOG OF AMERICA.
The Chesapeake dog is one of the few genuine American breeds which has also gained a certain popularity in Canada. It takes the place of the English retriever.

Friend, I will help your man to hunt through the day, and at night I will guard your Cave."

A poet's dream, that story of the "Firstest Friend". Symbolism, as they call it in our modern phraseology. Not at all the kind of scientific truth you will read in

(Continued on p. xv.)

Photo]　　　　　　　　　　　　　　　　　　　　　　　　　[E.N.A.
AN AUSTRIAN GREAT DANE.
German Boarhounds, or Great Danes, were used for hunting boars in Germany and were kept in England before the 18th century In the picture is seen a Harlequin Great Dane with Fräulein Hilda Tressler-Wagner, President of the Austrian Kennel Club, 1933.

A LONG-HAIRED DACHSHUND.

In their native Germany Dachshunds are used as their name implies to hunt badgers, their curiously shaped front feet being specially adapted for digging.   The dog shown in the picture is seen with its owner, Fräulein Friedl Czepa, of Vienna, who is said to have paid £250 for it to a London dealer.

Photo | *[Sport and General.*

WELL OVER !

Contrary to general belief Pekingese are game and energetic dogs and if not unduly pampered will show surprising agility. **"Tai Tu of Alderbourne"**, belonging to Mrs. Ashton Cross, proves his ability as a jumper by easily clearing a tennis net.

IN PRAISE OF DOG—
(continued.)

the pages that follow this.

Yet what is truth? Surely not alone the skeleton of anatomical fact ? And what is Dog if he be not the symbol of that first friendship between Man and the Wild which our poet describes ?

Quot homines, tot sententiae ! I have known some men, and some women

Photo]   *[E.N.A*
READY TO HELP.
It is by no means a happy experience to have to be saved by a dog. Here we have one pulling a boy out of the sea.

Curiously, that deprivation lasted until I was four-and twenty. Till then, barring a canary or so and a brace of doves (both of whom laid eggs for a surprised nursery), I had never owned any living thing of my own

Yet stay. Am I quite right about this ? Doesn't memory recall—even as these words flow from my pen—the

also, who disliked Dog. George Moore was one such. And my own mother happened to be another of them.

But dog-haters are exceptional ; I could almost write "freakish" ; and their freakish hate is seldom inherited. The most fanatical dog-lover I ever knew, for instance, was a dog-hater's child —myself, deprived—the only deprivation I ever suffered by parental authority—of canine companionship

wraith of a Fox-terrier in pursuit of that stripling who was myself, clad in an outrageous waistcoat of green checked with white and yellow, as he galloped the wild wetwoods of Frankfort-on-the-Maine ?

Yes, memory is right there. Such a Fox-terrier there was—and his name "X". He was called that in memory of the first paper for which I ever wrote (and which I also owned) at Eton in the long-ago days of the Great Queen.

Photo]   *[Sport and General.*
A NOTED GERMAN BREED.
There are three types of Dachshund—the smooth, the wire-coated, and the long-haired, all of which are extremely intelligent and make excellent companions. Here are three smooth-coated members of a famous kennel "Kailora", "Karzaire", and "Karzador", the property of Miss F. E. Dixon.

Photo]   [E.N.A.
STRANGE FRIENDSHIPS.
Here we have a dog, cat and pony, the dog helping
the cat to get on the pony's back

That paper went the way of most Eton ephemerals ; and its namesake did not return with me to England.

But how I came by my dog, "X", and to whom I gave him when I left Frankfort, escapes me down the mists of the years.

Better do I remember his successor —a thin sad-faced Dane, bought all unwisely, who lingered but a little while before he licked my hand for the last time, and turned his head away, and passed to the Good Hunting and the Better Biscuits.

"Never again will I love Dog," I said to myself, as every dog-lover has said to himself on some such desolate day. Yet consolation came swiftly, and from that very mother who could not "abide the beasts" herself.

She left the choice to me—and that time, having a little more knowledge, I chose well.

Expensively too ! Grandiosely ! So that I shall never forget the commotion of that day when there presented himself to the astonished clerks of my City offices, the tiger-tamer from the North ; and,

following him, gentle as a lamb on his burnished chain, Dog of Dogs.

"Grim Tiger," his name was. "From Axwell Kennels by the northern main, Where the cropped Porthos throats a prizeless growl, His line is traced through Redgrave's noblest strain," as you may read if you care for the lesser author.

And in appearance my "Grim Tiger" lived up to his name.

But for all his size—even at six months' old he occupied most of the taxi in which he and I fared to the station—a less tigerish Brindle never lived. My Pamela and my Ursula, then mere babies, played with him from the first ; and neither to them nor to any, baby or grown-up, did he ever do the least injury—though his python of a tail, merely beginning to wag, would often sweep my suburban tea-table clear ; and on one occasion, walking and leaping his loose-box door early, he swiped the entire suburban butter-and-egg ration, standing tall as a man to the kitchen window-sill for the steal. (Continued on page xix.)

Photo]   [E.N.A
AFTER THE ELECTRIC HARE.
Track racing in pursuit of an electrically moved hare, a sport introduced
from America after the close of the Great War, has given an enormous
impetus to the breeding of Greyhounnds.

REMARKABLE SPECIMEN OF GREAT DANE.

The Great Dane is one of the largest breeds, and the dogs often attain a weight of 150 lbs. or more. The Great Dane relies for its beauty upon the proportions of the whole rather than on any particular point. The fine specimen shown in the picture is a Champion of U.S.A., the property of Miss Maureen O'Sullivan. The ears are cropped, an operation not performed in this country.

Photo] GRIFFON BRUXELLOIS. *[Sport and General.*

A popular toy breed that is said to have originated by a York shire Terrier and Irish Terrier cross.

PHU-QUOC DOG OF CHINA.

A variety only occasionally seen in Britain. It may possibly have Greyhound blood in its ancestry.

Photo] BOSTON TERRIER. *[Fall.*

The Boston Terrier is the most popular breed in the U.S.A. It is indeed the national breed. A relation of the French Bulldog.

MALTESE TERRIER.

The Maltese Terrier, though named after the famous breed of ancient times, has been evolved in its present form in Britain and other countries.

LHASSA TERRIERS.

This breed was only recently introduced into England from Lhassa. It is long-coated and hardy.

Photo] MINIATURE POODLES. *[Sport and General.*

Poodles probably originated in France. The coat grows from a fluff to become a cord and is clipped and shaven.

DOGS THE WORLD OVER

IN PRAISE OF DOG—(continued)

Those were the days before the dog-destroying motor-car

"Grim" would accompany my walk to the station of a morning, find his way home alone, and alone return to meet me of an evening, waiting patiently for me on those rare occasions when I failed to catch the 6.35 from Cannon Street. For he had a sense of time which is often not given to humans; and perhaps this made him doubly precious to one who has always lived by the clock.

Of a week-end we would roam together—five-and-thirty miles sometimes. And at holiday-time he was never far behind any horse's heels.

"Nick Carter and his blood-'ound," rude little boys of those days used to call after us. But for "Grim's" sake my vanity bore even with that.

I loved him, you see! Yet I cannot pretend that my love for "Grim" was altogether shared in a modest household, whose sofa would only just accommodate his wet carcass stretched at doggy ease to dry perfumedly before the fire. Maybe also—and if so let it be a lesson to others—for the dog-bore can be even as the golf-bore to the wife of his bosom—I voiced my love too loudly and too often.

The cost of "Grim's" keep, moreover, was a constant bone of contention on "bill-nights". Neither did it escape wifely notice that the grooming of "Grim", with curry-comb, brush and shammy leather took time which a single-handed gardener might better have employed among his flowers.

Nevertheless, my passion for "Grim" remained un-shakable until Fate again sent me from England; and I was forced to find him another home

Photo'   *E.N.A*

AN AUSTRIAN SCHNAUZER.
The Schnauzer is a German breed claimed to be a sheep dog, though some say it is a Terrier
It is pepper and salt coloured in even proportions.

Only a temporary home, I hoped. But on my return to England, War came between.

He lived apart from me after that, to a ripe old age, and very happily as I am glad to think, in a great house which I still visit ; and when his Time came, he, also, passed on.

One likes to imagine that Dog passes on. It was so in Homer's day, when heroes dreamed of their

Photo]   [E.N.A.

FRENCH BULLDOG.

It is agreed that the French Bulldog is, as the name implies, a French breed, although opinion has it that the original stock from which the French Bulldog was made came from England. It is an active, muscular, and intelligent breed. Signorina Vera Salvotti, here shown with her dog, was President of the Italian Women's Kennel Club in 1933.

shadowy companionship in the Elysian Fields. It is so still when our same poet who symbolized his first coming can write, of Woman Dog this time :

> She did not know that she was dead,
> But, when the pang was o'er,
> Sat down to wait her Master's tread
> Upon the Golden Floor,
> With ears full-cock and anxious eyes
> Impatiently resigned ;
> But ignorant that Paradise
> Did not admit her kind.

Yet for that particular Woman Dog, even

Paradise broke its rules. So that, in the end we read :

> Then flew Dinah from under the chair,
> Into his arms she flew—
> And licked his face from chin to hair—
> And Peter passed them through.

And who, being a dog-lover, does not agree that Saint Peter was right ?

For man's desire that his dog should also be remembered when he himself has passed over, is as old as civilization's self. You will find Dog on the walls of the first troglodytes—just as you will find him on the stelæ of Assur-bani-pal. Because Dog alone of all the beasts and all the birds and all the creeping things can give us a comradeship so nearly human that it is almost divine.

Sentiment, this. Sentimentality if you will. Yet where should we be in this age when most men, and most women too, worship the Brass Idol of Efficiency, without a little sentiment and even a little sentimentality. Are we to live only by statistics and celluloid in a house furnished with nothing but chromium steel chairs ? Perish the thought.

Sentimentality apart, however, Dog has many practical uses and qualities. Who better to watch over us while we sleep ? Who better to warn us against fire or thieves ? Who better to lead us blind through the streets of the city ? Who better to beg for us when the open eyes are hard ?

Consider, next, Dog for Sport. Consider Gun-Dog. Consider Hound, whether he help you to chase proud Fox, or humble Hare, or lordly Stag. Some there are—Galsworthy, also a great dog-lover, was one of them—who would have no more of blood-sports.

But it will be a sad day, I think, for Britain, when no man with good red blood in his veins rides out to Ranksborough Gorse of a winter's morning ; when no whip cracks in Owston Woods ; when no horn twangs, and never a knee tightens against a saddle-flap, and no Ravager, leaping first through quick-set, gives tongue, till twenty couple of black-white-and-tan pour after, and a

(Continued on page xxiii.)

WEST HIGHLAND TERRIER—AN ARTIST'S IMPRESSION.

The fact that Scotland was the natural home of the badger, the fox, and the otter partially accounts for the evolving of short-legged breeds in that country.   The original West Highland White was a white Cairn destroyed on account of its colour.   West Highlanders are one of the most vivacious breeds and every look and attitude is expressive of intelligence and activity.

SCOTTISH TERRIER.

Although clearly of Cairn ancestry the exact origin of the Scottish Terrier is a mystery.   All that is known is that it was made, presumably, in the towns of Scotland.   The breed is very popular on the Continent, the one illustrated being a prizewinner in Berlin.

IN PRAISE OF DOG—
(continued).

pack you could cover with a pocket handkerchief is away on a breast-high scent down Gartree Hill.

And it was a sad day for England, I think, when the first machine-reaper swept the stubbles clean ; and all men began to learn how much easier it is to sit on a shooting-stick than to tramp the roots.

Photo courtesy of]   THE DOG IN 2000 B.C.   *["Antiquity."*
The Egyptian Hound as depicted on the tomb of Ptahheteh Sakkara

quartering the roots ahead of me, to see him standing to his point (are those the right words ?—I hope so) to approach, that first hammer-gun cocked, one's young eyes clear even if one's young hand was a trifle unsteady.

Few boys learn to shoot that way nowadays, I believe.

Yet the Pointer is still with us. And if you, meeting Gun-dog for the first

My own first shooting memory is also a dog memory. And what a thrill it was to see Dog time, will only watch him in the ring, or better still at a Field Trial, your eyes will be opened

Photo]   THE LONG-HAIRED VARIETY OF THE GERMAN BADGER DOG.   *[Sport & General*
Long-haired Dachshunds have been known in Germany for well over a hundred years, but are still not as popular as the short-coated variety. Two distinguished dogs are shown in the picture, Miss K. E. Allinson's "Kalje of Bromholm" and "Gamester of Bromholm".

SHEEP DOGS TRIALS.

Sheep Dog Trials take place all over Great Britain and the dogs show great intelligence in driving and penning the sheep. The work needs no little control of all natural instincts. Collies and cross-bred Collies are chiefly used for this purpose.

to the First Lesson of those who would be dog-worthy.

For the First Lesson of those who would be worthy of Dog is that Puppy-Dog must be taught obedience —seeing that without discipline he can become, like the human puppy he so much resembles not Perfect Companion, but Perfect Pest.

This is a hard lesson, yet a very necessary one. Puppy-dog *does* need discipline. Moreover, he is far happier, like puppy human, under a reasonable system of obedience than when left altogether to his own desires.

Many dog-owners, especially many women

(Continued on page xxvii.)

CAIRN TERRIER.

Cairns are very affectionate and intelligent and make splendid companions. They are smaller than Scottish Terriers, the ideal weight being about 14 lbs. Here we have H.R.H. Princess de Chimay et de Caraman with her Cairn.

GRIFFON BRUXELLOIS.

These dogs need plucking to give them the coat and appearance so much desired. They were first introduced into England about 1894. This dog is said to be the most extravagant dog in the world, the property of Mme. Landing of France.

Photo, [Sport and General.

WIRE-HAIRED FOX TERRIERS.

Authorities seem to agree that the wire-haired black and tan was Britain's first Terrier, and there can be little doubt that the Wire-haired Fox Terrier owes its origin to it. A few years ago the smooth Fox Terriers were far more prized than their rough-coated relations, but recently the wire-haired has come into its own and now this engaging companion is by far the most popular of all Terriers. The two shown here are "Petwick Courtesan" and "Petwick Cointreau", bred by Mr. H. L. Cottrill.

[Photo] SKYE TERRIER. [E.N.A.

There is a legend that the Skye Terriers originated from certain Spanish white dogs rescued by the inhabitants of Skye from the wrecked Galleons of the Armada. A description by Dr. Johnson of a visit to Skye suggests that they were then used for hunting foxes. The above illustration is of the noted "Miss Penny", property of Mme. Raymonde Latour.

[Photo] GRIFFON BRUXELLOIS AND WIRE-HAIRED TERRIER. [E.N.A.

One of the favourite toy breeds and one of the most popular Terriers are here shown together. Owing to its long hair the Griffon is even lighter than it appears, six pounds being a fair average weight. The two dogs illustrated are shown with their American owner, Miss Daisy Holmes, a well-known exhibitor in Sweden.

IN PRAISE OF DOG—
(continued).

dog-owners, will find this lesson more than hard. Many will deny it altogether—just as they will deny that old maxim, "Spare the rod and spoil the child". But if you are real dog-lover you will know the stark truth of it—just as you will know how wrong it is to keep Dog solely for your own sport, your own safety, or your own selfish pleasure.

Photo]   *[E.N.A*
A WORLD-FAMOUS KENNEL.
St. Bernards with some of the monks of the famous hospice amid the Swiss snows.

possibly he requires knowledge even more than love.

A hundred dogs die, a thousand are irretrievably ruined, by lack of knowledge, for every one that suffers through actual cruelty. I have never seen an unhappy dog in the kennels of a good breeder. But I have seen many such—and many more who make the lives of their human neighbours a burden—in the average home.

Man cannot possess any living creature, even a canary, without some responsibility. And least of all can he so possess Dog.

Dog requires far more than just a little water, just a little food, just a little straw or maybe a soft cushion to lie on. He requires, as human beings require, both love and knowledge. And

Dog with a knowledgeable owner, for instance, does not bark except to give warning. His habits, properly inculcated during puppyhood, are just as clean as his master's—and his characteristics often very much better if it comes to that. Dog with such an owner does not steal. He does not over-eat himself. Neither does he run riot, whether

Photo]   *[Sport and General*
TERRIER RACING.
Though lacking the speed and popular appeal of Greyhounds, Terriers may be trained to race and will provide exciting sport.
Dandie Dinmonts, seen in training in the photograph are a suitable breed for racing purposes.

it be after Woman Dog, or humans, or merely sheep.

So be wise; and do not spare the whip to him when young.

A brutal idea, you say. Surely, say you, Dog, in these days of universal liberty, also deserves some freedom. But you are wrong. Because Dog, unlike human being, has no intrinsic desire for his own free will.

He is happiest as your slave. He can be happy even on a chain; though for myself I abhor the chain, and would insist on every man or woman who possesses Dog housing him properly—either

KING CHARLES' SPANIELS.
Though King Charles II did not introduce, he did much to popularise, the breed. The King would often be seen by the populace striding among the trees of St. James's Park feeding his Spaniels.

in the home where he rightly belongs, or else in a proper kennel with a warm sleeping compartment and an open yard from which he can look out, as he loves to look out, on the world of men and women passing by.

But I have not been asked to write a homily on dog-keeping. Those who seek knowledge or advice will find it abundantly in the pages which follow. My task is not the expert's. It is the amateur's. I come, if I may paraphrase Shakespeare, to praise Dog and not to dissect him. Yet

(Continued on page xxxi.)

Photo]　　　　　　　　　　　　　　　　　　　　　　　　　[E.N.A.
GREYHOUNDS AS PETS.
President of the Yugoslavian Women's Kennel Club, 1933 : Mlle. Ossy Rondje photographed with two of her Greyhounds.

Photo. *Altieri.*

HUNTING WITH SEALYHAMS.

Though Hounds have been immemorially preferred to Terriers by the hunting community, the smaller dogs have their sporting instincts fully developed and when properly trained will do excellent work. The dogs shown in the picture are Captain Jocelyn Lucas' mixed pack of Sealyhams and Jack Russel Terriers.

Photo]   [E.N.A.   Photo]   [E.N.A.   Photo]   [E.N.A.

THREE AMONG THE WORLD'S HIGHEST-PRICED PETS.

"Jo-Jo", with his owner, Mme. Mesrity, won the first French Bulldog Derby before he was sold to America for £2,350.   £1,420 was paid by Mrs. Maria Habig, of New York, for one West Highland Terrier, which her daughter is shown holding.   Winner of Gold Medals at the National Shows of seven countries—Fräulein Ilse Huttich's dog "Mucky".

Photo   [Sport and General.

AUSTRALIAN TERRIERS.

The breed of Australian Terriers, a twentieth-century introduction into Britain, is derived from the English Black-and-Tan, the original Cairn and the Yorkshire Terrier. The colour is grey-and-tan. Miss R. Rodocanachi's "Judy of Toovak" and "Sally of Toovak".

Photo]   [*Sport and General*

DINNER-TIME.

And taken very seriously by these one-month-old Spaniel pups near Godalming. Surrey.

IN PRAISE OF DOG—

(continued).

surely his praises have already been sung enough, surely my task is almost superfluous in these days, and in this country where Dog is no longer the pariah, and where even Mongrel Dog is rapidly ceasing to exist!

Our human world may be turning either towards or away from democracy. But the dog-world is turning more and more towards aristocracy. The *mésalliances*, the cross-breeds of a mere century

Photo]   [*Sport and General*.

CH. "NIGHT WATCHMAN".

A very fine example of the Bulldog.

ago—bulldog and bull-terrier among them—have already reached the peerage. And this is a true Reformation. Because the more Dog is pedigree Dog, the better it will be for him, the more he will be honoured and the more he will be prized.

People who sneer at the pedigree dog, people who believe that old cliché about the mongrel being more intelligent, are themselves only mongrel dog-lovers. If you can afford no other dog, by all means buy one with a blot upon

DALMATIANS.

Introduced originally from the territory which gives them their name, Dalmatians used to be very popular as carriage-dogs in the days before motor-cars. Apart from their heads and colouring they are very like Pointers. Dr. Wheeler-O'Bryen's "Florrie", "Linacre", and "Abernethy" are shown in the above photo.

his canine escutcheon. Any Dog is better than no Dog. But if you have the money, patronize breed.

In the pages which are to follow you will find hundreds of breeds of Dog, and each one adapted to some especial human requirement.

If your ambitions be grandiose, as mine were once grandiose, here are Stag-hound and Elk-hound, Great Dane, and Mastiff for you. If you shoot, if you hunt, and even if you fish—(yes, I know a Labrador who watches every cast and is worth ten landing-nets)—here are aristocratic servitors beyond counting.

If you crave to be protected by another, here is Airedale, here is Alsatian, here is Bull-terrier

his "stop" ought to be. All I want is Dog, a pal to go for walks with in summer-time, a pal to lie across my feet by the fire of a winter's evening. To blazes with you and your canine aristocracy."

Yet you are wrong, my friend. And—if I may be forgiven just one more tiny homily—I will tell you why.

The thoroughbred dog, bought from a good kennel, is—for one thing—usually the healthiest dog. For another thing—coming as he does from a long line of disciplined ancestors—he is almost inevitably the cleanest dog. And quite apart from all practical considerations, he is inevitably the handsomest dog.

Photo]   *[Sport and General.*

LABRADOR RETRIEVING FROM WATER.

Experiments in evolving a perfect retrieving dog had long been made in England, but it was not until the strain of a black coated dog from Labrador was introduced about 1850 that success was reached. The result was the fine black smooth-coated Retriver now known as the Labrador. Ch. "Bramshaw Bob", bred by Lorna, Countess Howe.

(whom also I have loved) and a whole host more. If you would merely be warned to protect yourself, here are smaller breeds innumerable, Scotties and Bedlingtons, Cairns and Sealyhams, terriers of every shape and colour who can not only bark, but, at need, bite. While if you need—and this perhaps is all that seventy per cent of dog-lovers really do need—nothing more than companionship, why then the whole Debrett of Dogdom here lies open to your choice.

"But I am not a snob," you say. "So what do I care whether my dog comes to me with a Kennel Club certificate? What do I care whether his ears are cocked as they should be cocked, whether his colour be the right colour, or his tail the right length, or his "stop" where judges say

While—if I may conclude with the material as I began with the poetic aspect of Dogdom—those who buy pedigree dogs, even though they cannot afford champions, are actually helping British Industry and to keep British workpeople employed.

The breeding of pedigree dogs, whether for home use or for export, is one of our most flourishing little industries. It must continue to flourish. And every real dog-lover should help it along.

That is one of two reasons why I have enjoyed writing this preface.

And my other reason?

Sheer sentimentality, I am afraid! Because the writing of it has brought back the memory of my old friend "Grim".

Photo]   *[Blades*
Mrs. Knox's Irish Wolfhound "Duke of
Raikeshill".

Photo]   *[Thos. Fail.*
Two fine Bedlington Terriers, "Tommy Precious of
Simonside" and "Jackanapes of Simonside".

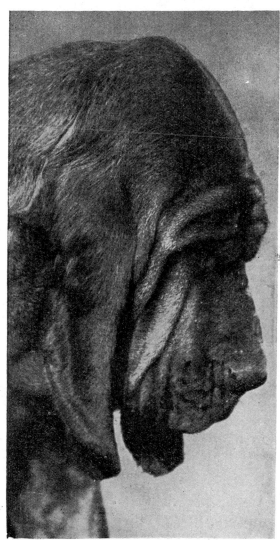

Photo]   *[Country Life.*
Mrs. Edmund's noted champion Bloodhound,
"Ledburn Banner."

Photo]   *[Country Life.*
Mrs. Manooch's Chow Chow "Choonam
Jerry Mee."

CONTRASTS IN HEADS.

C

HIS MAJESTY THE KING'S CLUMBER SPANIEL.

H.M. King George V, like the majority of his subjects, inherited a love of dogs.   He has an excellent kennel of Labrador Retrievers and Clumber Spaniels.
The above is his "Sandringham Sparks", a dog not only of the best working type but also His Majesty's constant companion when out with the guns.

Hutchinson's
Popular and Illustrated
DOG
Encyclopaedia

A

Abdomen.—The abdomen is the largest cavity in the body and contains most of the visceral organs, such as the stomach, intestines, liver, kidneys, and the bladder when this is distended with urine.

The abdomen is bounded above by the spinal column and muscles ; in front by the diaphragm ; below and each side by the abdominal muscles and partly by ribs ; and behind by the pelvis.

the mammary glands, and in dogs the penis. Owing to its normal deficiency of hair growth, the abdominal wall generally is the area selected for irradiation with ultra-violet rays, as their absorption by the skin can occur without hindrance in this region.

ABNORMALITIES OF.—The abdominal surface is quite frequently the seat of vesicles and pustules, sometimes as a symptom accompanying

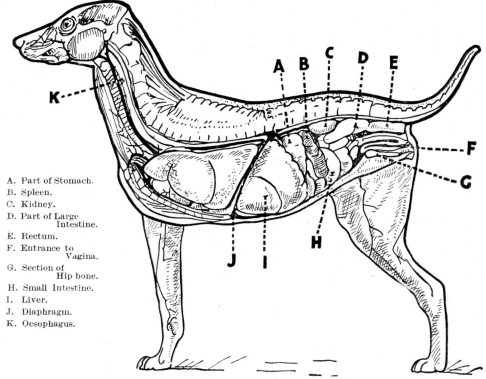

A. Part of Stomach.
B. Spleen.
C. Kidney.
D. Part of Large Intestine.
E. Rectum.
F. Entrance to Vagina.
G. Section of Hip bone.
H. Small Intestine.
I. Liver.
J. Diaphragm.
K. Oesophagus.

ABDOMEN OF THE DOG.

Very obviously, as so many organs are accommodated in this cavity, the pains and diseases which can arise therefrom are very numerous and varied, and reference concerning any one of them must be made to the appropriate paragraph. The general public quite frequently makes the serious mistake of naming the stomach when really alluding to the abdomen. The stomach is not the abdomen, but merely one of its contents, and the term "stomach-ache" should in reality mean pain in the stomach and not pain in some other abdominal organ.

Below the abdominal wall are found, in bitches,

distemper in young dogs. These eruptions are not uncommonly seen even when the dog is apparently healthy in every other way. In such cases one might conclude that the lesions are either the forerunner of an attack of distemper to follow, or are the only manifestation of a very mild existing infection, or of some dietetic upset. Excoriation, redness, soreness, and sometimes small pustules may also arise on the abdominal surface in male dogs in consequence of continuous dribbling of urine.

Quite commonly, in very young puppies, one may discern a small circular elevation or distension in the exact position of the navel. This is due to

I

a defect in the abdominal muscle at that point, and is, in fact, anumbilical hernia. (*See under* HERNIA.)

Abnormal distension of the abdomen may arise from quite a number of causes, notably from ascites (or abdominal dropsy), tumour formation, pregnancy, flatulence, enlargement of the liver or spleen, engorgement of the stomach with food, ventral hernia, etc. Young puppies badly infested with worms are often said to be "pot-bellied". For a fuller description of these various conditions, reference will appear under the appropriate headings.

Aberdeen Terrier. (*See* SCOTTISH TERRIER.)

Abortion.—A term used to signify the expulsion of the fœtus before full term, i.e. premature delivery. This is an accident which is common enough among human beings, cattle, and horses, but is of rare occurrence in the canine species. Puppies may be born a few days before expiry of their full term and prove to be robust, healthy animals, but such instances could hardly be included under the term "abortion". A true abortion entails the expulsion of a still-born fœtus, or of one so immature that post-natal life is impossible.

It not infrequently happens that a bitch may be accidentally served by a sire of a breed much larger than her own. In such a case her owner might contemplate the possibilities of procuring an early abortion in order to obviate the eventual surgical removal of whelps which otherwise might never be born in a normal manner.

This is very difficult of accomplishment without seriously endangering the life of the mother, and no useful purpose will be served by detailing intricate operations which amateurs could not perform.

CAUSES.—Premature parturition may be induced by such accidents as impacts with vehicles, severe frights, high jumps, kicks, or other violence ; and uterine, febrile or debilitating diseases. The same factors may be responsible for death of the pups *in utero* without premature delivery.

Prevention may be accomplished by taking care to exclude all possibility of shocks, violence or excessive exercise in the case of in-whelp bitches, and to ensure that the latter are well fed and unable to pick up any kind of poison such as may be laid as bait for vermin. No bitch should be served unless she herself is fully matured and in robust health.

Abrasion indicates a loss of epithelial cells, or a rubbing-off of the outermost layer of skin or mucous membrane. The skin commonly suffers

from abrasions, and, whilst blood may be drawn, there is no penetration of the whole thickness of the skin. Treatment adopted is that used for ordinary wounds, i.e. antiseptic lotions and cleanliness. Bandaging is unnecessary and probably retards scab formation.

Abscess.—A localized collection of pus in a cavity formed by the disintegration of tissues. Two kinds are recognized, viz. hot and cold. The acute or hot variety is one running a relatively short course, causing perhaps some amount of fever and a painful local inflammation. The cold or chronic abscess is detected, when superficial, only by the gradual swelling and softening of the part affected. It is of slow development and usually gives rise to little or no pain.

CAUSES.—Blows, bites, scratches, or other mechanical violence ; the entry to the tissues (internal or external) of pus-producing germs ; debility, with its usual accompaniment of low resistance of the blood to infections. Tuberculosis and distemper are frequently complicated by the formation of abscesses in various parts of the body.

SYMPTOMS.—These will depend primarily upon the situation of the abscess. For instance, if the latter is on the flap of the ear, the dog shakes its head or holds it on one side, and the ear gradually swells and becomes very hot and tender. If on a leg, the animal will be lame and refuse to allow the limb to be touched. Acute abscesses are always accompanied by heat, pain, and swelling, though whilst the pus is in the early stage of formation one may find it difficult to distinguish the condition from a severe contusion or bruise. A ripening abscess, when pressed, will be found to yield slightly to touch, or feel elastic. It is then said to be "pointing" or fluctuating.

TREATMENT.—A suspected abscess should be liberally bathed or fomented with hot water to induce its speedy maturation, a result which is also attained, though perhaps not always so easily, by the frequent application of hot bread-poultices. When the swelling "points" it will be perceived that one spot will feel softer than all others. At this point the surgeon introduces his knife (a special sharp-pointed knife), and with one swift cut opens up the cavity. It is highly advisable that a veterinary surgeon should perform this operation, simple though it may seem, as it is quite possible to injure underlying tissues or sever important nerves or arteries, and thus involve permanent damage.

All pus must be gently expelled through the opening so made—a performance which gives great and immediate relief. The cavity should be syringed out with a warm solution of antiseptic solution, and the edges of the wound kept apart

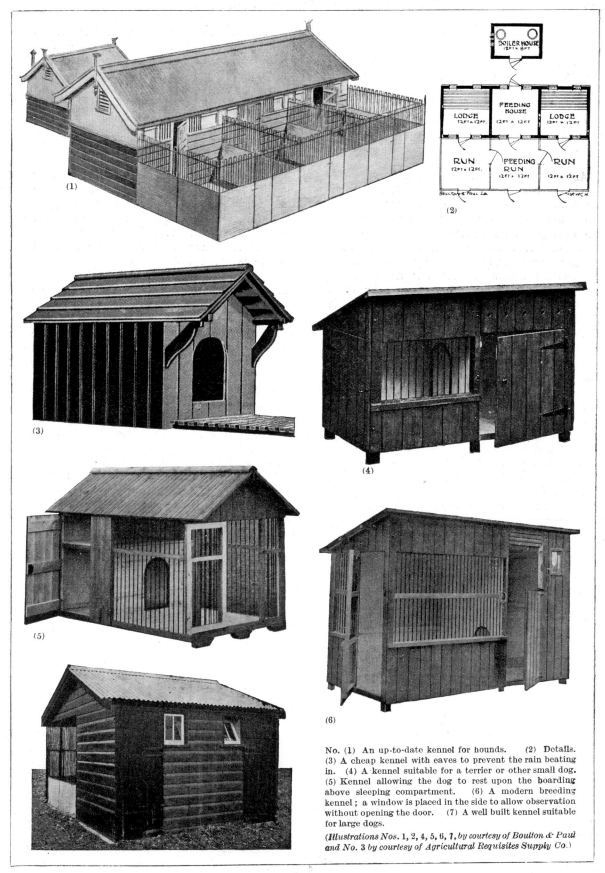

No. (1) An up-to-date kennel for hounds.   (2) Details.
(3) A cheap kennel with eaves to prevent the rain beating
in.   (4) A kennel suitable for a terrier or other small dog.
(5) Kennel allowing the dog to rest upon the boarding
above sleeping compartment.   (6) A modern breeding
kennel ; a window is placed in the side to allow observation
without opening the door.   (7) A well built kennel suitable
for large dogs.

(Illustrations Nos. 1, 2, 4, 5, 6, 7, by courtesy of Boulton & Paul
and No. 3 by courtesy of Agricultural Requisites Supply Co.)

by a small wad of cotton-wool to prevent early union.

Severe or repeated abscesses will usually cause great weakness or debility, and the patient will need a course of tonics such as syrup of phosphates of iron, etc., etc., for a fortnight or three weeks. This should be coupled with a liberal meat diet, a sufficiency of exercise, and exposure to the sun's rays.

Acarus.—A very small, and sometimes micro-scopic, creature belonging to the natural order *Acarina*. Cheese mites, the red harvest mites, and those mites which are the cause of sarcoptic and demodectic mange, are examples of members of this family. There are mites, too, which inhabit exclusively the ear, and set up, by their irritation, a condition known as auricular acariasis. It follows that skin diseases which owe their origin to these acari must be classed among the parasitic skin diseases, in contradistinction to those which arise in quite a different way, such as eczema, acne, etc. The former are contagious, whilst the latter, being due to blood impurity, are not. (*See* EAR DISEASES, AND MANGE.)

Accidents.—The accidents which befall the dog are usually due to fights with other members of his species, or encounters with moving vehicles. Many thousands of dogs must be "run-over" annually, and a fair proportion of them are undoubtedly killed outright. Those which escape with their lives frequently sustain fractures, dislocations (or both), loss of teeth or internal haemorrhage. In connection with the latter possibility, it is really remarkable how a dog which appears to have sustained no other injury whatsoever evinces every symptom of crushed liver, kidneys, or other internal organ. The writer has proved the truth of this assertion by post-mortem examination in many instances ; and yet the body has revealed no trace even of sub-cutaneous bruising. (*See* INTERNAL HAEMORRHAGE.) One would do well to suspect that internal bleeding is taking place if a dog is picked up, after an accident, showing all signs of collapse, such as extreme pallor of the gums, rapid respiration feeble pulse, inability to stand, etc. No time should then be lost in securing the services of a veterinary surgeon ; and meanwhile, as a first-aid measure, give some brandy in water, or strong coffee. Keep the animal absolutely quiet, and raise the hindquarters slightly above the level of the head.

Fractured bones are not by any means always easy of detection, and slight dislocations may even be more elusive ; thus if a dog shows marked lameness or other evidence of pain, an examination

by a qualified man will serve to put the owner's mind at ease, or at least to dispel his doubts. Of recent years there has been a tremendous development in the use of X-rays for animals, and where a surgeon cannot definitely decide upon the nature of an injury he should be permitted resort to radiography in the best interests of both owner and animal. (*See* FRACTURES AND DIS-LOCATIONS.) The injuries resulting from fights will be dealt with under WOUNDS.

Occasionally dogs become seriously burned by indulging in their fondness for the kitchen fire, the actual injury being usually caused by a kettle of boiling water becoming spilled upon them. Such burns, together with those arising from contact with acids and other chemicals, will be discussed under the general heading—BURNS.

Accommodation of the Dog.—In these days of enlightenment it would seem superfluous to dilate upon the question of housing the dog ; and yet great numbers of people appear not to have the least idea of even the rudiments of a dog's requirements in this respect.

The sympathy one may feel for the poor captive yard-dog, which is provided with nothing more comfortable than an old barrel, is often only out-weighed by the contempt with which one regards the perpetrator of such callousness. It is no uncommon sight to see a mud-bedraggled, shiver-ing and unhappy dog living in conditions of abject misery, exposed to frost, north winds or rain alike, and afforded no more protection than can be ob-tained from an open-ended barrel—often without bedding or a waterproof covering. The sloping sides of a barrel make it impossible for a dog to sleep or rest in comfort, and when rain percolates through the top, an animal's dejection is complete. Sometimes such a barrel, or even a well-made kennel, is thoughtlessly placed in a passage such as may exist between two houses, with the result that the guard-dog is almost perpetually in a draught.

OUTDOOR DOGS.—If a dog must be kept out of doors it is only right and fair that provision for its comfort should be the owner's first thought. Quite apart from the humanity of the case, every-thing obviously should be done to preserve health and happiness, if one would obtain the best and most economical results.

When it is decided that a dog must live out of doors, one must accommodate the animal either in a good outhouse or in a weatherproof, roomy, and draughtless kennel. The latter should be so situated that it will be exposed to the maximum amount of sunshine all the year round, although in the case of a small portable kennel, considera-tion would have to be paid to the desirability or otherwise of leaving it for many hours in the heat of a blazing summer sun.

Doors or windows should face south or south-west in order that the bitterly cold winds from east and north should not penetrate into the interior. A kennel should not be situated in a hollow where water can collect, or dampness be ever prevalent : nor should it, as a rule, be beneath a tree.

Portable kennels should have a floor raised above the ground, an outside awning as protection against the hot sun or driving rain, and a low bar across the bottom of the door to hinder the piecemeal escape of the bedding. The interior dimensions should be sufficiently high and wide to permit the inmate to stand up or stretch out comfortably.

The necessity for regular cleansing and disinfection of the interior must not be forgotten, and to facilitate this it would be very convenient if the roof were removable.

PERMANENT QUARTERS.—Where more pretentious or non-portable kennels are contemplated the construction of some efficient drainage system will probably have to be included—especially if it is proposed to house a number of animals in the building. Such drains should be properly trapped to prevent the emanation of injurious gases therefrom. Built-up kennels should have concrete yards attached, to which the dogs would have access, and provision should be made in their construction for rapid disposal of surface water.

Both in the sleeping apartment and yard, it is desirable to provide a wooden dais upon which the dog may lie without coming in contact with the cold concrete floor. Many people consider that prolonged contact with a cold floor is conducive of rheumatism, chills, and even rickets. The truth of this belief is very debatable, but in any case it is a wise and humane precaution to provide an alternative, and rely in some measure upon an animal's intuition as to what is best for itself.

The average dog owner in founding a kennel for breeding purposes, or even in purchasing a single home for a companion dog, will probably consult a firm of leading kennel manufacturers who can be thoroughly relied upon as to what is most suitable to his requirements and pocket. Kennels may, of course, be purchased or built in every conceivable shape or size, and at all prices, according to the simplicity or complexity of their specification. Thus it is not proposed to occupy valuable space or time in describing the details of these structures, for such information is readily obtainable from the makers' catalogues.

As to lighting and heating, it is usually possible to run an electric cable from the owner's dwelling to outdoor kennels for these dual purposes, and where electricity is obtainable it is by far the healthiest and safest mode of warming a kennel. Radiators are now obtainable which show no glow and which would be incapable even of igniting petrol if the latter were thrown in contact. If gas is utilized, great care must be exercised to screen the flame with wire guards, which precaution pertains also to oil stoves, anthracite, and other methods of heating.

INDOOR DOGS.—The smallest breeds of dogs are usually accommodated inside the owner's house and, strangely enough, not infrequently on the owner's bed. Nobody but the most ignorant or inhuman would think of housing a delicate toy dog out of doors, but there seems no possible reason why they should share a person's own bed. Viewed from every aspect, such a procedure can only be condemned.

Indoor dogs can be made very comfortable by the provision of a wooden box, or basket, placed in some draughtless corner and suitably lined with hygienic bedding.

If such a dog is intended as a guard for the house, it should not be confined to any particular room, but should have the liberty of the whole building, since nobody can foresee where a burglar will attempt his entrance. For the comfort and happiness of the inmates of a house, however, it is imperative that the dog shall be clean in its habits, and this can only be encouraged by allowing the dog regular access to the outside.

Nothing pretentious or elaborate in the way of a kennel is required for the indoor dog, but it must be large enough to accommodate the animal and should be located in a dry, warm, and well-ventilated place, out of everybody's way. Indeed, nothing is more useful than an orange box or a wooden soap box half filled with "egg shavings", for if parasites or contagious diseases make their appearance, the whole lot can be burnt and replaced with a brand new box for a few pence.

The room in which a dog sleeps should be furnished with linoleum rather than with a carpet.

Acidity.—A term somewhat loosely applied, but indicating generally that the blood, or one or more of the secretions from various parts of the body, contains an unusually high percentage of acids when compared with the normal. The gastric secretion of the dog is markedly acid and necessarily so. (*See* STOMACH, DYSPEPSIA.) The blood should have an alkaline reaction (*see* RHEUMATISM), as also should the bitch's milk, but occasionally these reactions become acid and give rise to ill health in both mother and offspring. (For vaginal acidity, *see* BREEDING.)

Acid Milk. (*See* MILK.)

Photo]   [E.N.A.
TWO CHAMPION AFFENPINSCHERS OF AUSTRIA.

Aconite.—The tincture prepared from the plant *Aconitum Napellus*, or Monkshood, is commonly used by dog breeders and others for the relief of painful and inflammatory surface conditions, such as bruises and swellings of all kinds, but particularly inflamed and swollen mammary glands. Given internally it is a febrifuge, and lessens the force and frequency of the pulsations. In the hands of the layman, however, it is not an agent which can safely be recommended on account of its highly poisonous nature. It is readily absorbed by the skin, and if applied to the milk glands there is often a great risk of little puppies sucking it off. Given internally, its administration is accompanied with some risk owing to its very depressant effect upon the cardiac and respiratory centres. Even half a grain of the alkaloid "aconitine" given to a thirty-pound dog has caused death in one hour. Generally, therefore, the use of aconite is not advised unless a veterinary surgeon prescribes the exact dose and method of administration.

Should poisoning occur, the stomach should at once be washed out with a pump. Then a teaspoonful of brandy in water may be given. Camphor in oil, ether or digitalis, should then be injected hypodermically to sustain the heart. Massage and warmth must be applied.

Adrenal Glands. — The adrenal glands are two in number, situated one in front of each kidney. They are very minute, but are of extreme im-

portance in consequence of the secretion they pour into the blood stream, and without which life is impossible. The active principle of this secretion is known as adrenalin, or suprarenin, and it is so powerful that only 1 part in 1,000 is required for the preparation of the commercial solutions sold on the market. It is largely believed among medical and veterinary men, that the meekness or aggressiveness of individuals is closely connected with the amount of adrenal hormone circulating in their respective blood streams. Thus, a mild, frightened and defenceless individual would be thought to have a marked deficiency of the secretion ; whilst a person who easily loses his temper, abounds in courage and even aggressiveness, is credited with possessing well-developed adrenals productive of an abundant secretion.

Medically applied, adrenalin exerts remarkable specific effects directed mainly to the raising of blood pressure, and thus is of great value in warding off shock or collapse of an individual. Applied to cut or injured blood-vessels, or torn wounds, its rapid styptic effect is at once appreciated, for haemorrhage is either stopped altogether or greatly lessened. Very inflamed and swollen mucous surfaces are quickly robbed of their fiery and sore appearance after being swabbed with a solution of adrenalin.

It may be given, too, in cases of gastric hæmorrhage, for which purpose it is, of course, swallowed.

A GERMAN AFFENPINSCHER.
A dog of the late nineteenth century.

Affenpinscher.—At the end of the nineteenth century the Affenpinscher was specially

Photo]   [E.N.A.
ANOTHER CHAMPION AFFENPINSCHER.
Affenpinschers, or "Monkey Terriers", are a small wire-haired toy breed, not unlike the Griffon Bruxellois.

THE AIREDALE.

The Airedale is the largest terrier in the world and is certainly one of the most popular of breeds. Here Mrs. Scott-Langley depicts an Airedale waiting for his master, and ready to be off. It is interesting to note how nearly the show-points of this dog resemble those of the Welsh Terrier.

recommended as a suitable dog for ladies. It will be seen from the illustration to be somewhat like the Griffon, but rather larger than this breed and longer-haired, the hair being very hard.

The head is rounded and the muzzle fairly short, and the beard is important. The nose is black and must be clearly seen from amongst the hair that surrounds it.

Afghan Hound. The Afghan Hound, as the name may seem to imply, is not confined to Afghanistan in its origin, as the breed is to be found in large numbers all along the Borderland and Northern India, where it is also known as the Barakzai, Kurram Valley Hound.

There is really no doubt that the Afghan Hound is one of the most ancient breeds in the world;

THE AFGHAN HOUND.
This interesting relation to the Saluki, the dog of Arabia, is larger and stronger and with a much heavier coat. It is used with hawks in its native country. This excellent specimen is Mrs. Prude's "Marica of Babergh".

It was usual to crop the ears to a point, and to have them standing up in a similar way to the ears of the Pinscher. But, as will be seen in the photos, the ears are entirely hidden in the long upstanding hair. The eyes were large and round but greatly concealed by the face hair.

The variety, which may or may not have Skye Terrier in its make, has never been taken up in England. At one time the breed was popular as a toy-dog on the Continent

so old, in fact, that the Afghan Shikaris claim that this was the breed favoured by Noah, and taken into the Ark with him. How far this may be true, history does not say, but there is every evidence that the type has not changed with centuries. "Yet no man knoweth whence they came, but there they are and there they stay."

It is well known that the native chiefs and hunters highly prize their respective strains and guard them with jealous care. While they definitely

THE SALUKI HEAD.

The Saluki head resembles that of the Afghan. This study of "Amhersti Darius" bred by the Hon. Florence Amherst, shows the type that later brought the Greyhound into being.

like the tangible proceeds from the sale of some favourite hound, their "affection" for the animal has been known not infrequently to provoke the late owner to reacquire the sold animal by the simple process of theft !

It is said that an Afghan has bluer blood in its veins than any other dog in the world. Its pedigree runs back centuries before the Christian era.

Portraits of its ancestors appear engraved upon cuneiform pillars and tablets.

The Afghan in its native country is utilized to guard sheep and cattle, also for other purposes such as hunting deer and the smaller wild animals, and it has been known to attack and kill a leopard and panther. The hounds usually hunt in couples. Their uses go even further, which give quite a different conception to which the breed is used in India, as an eye-witness, writing under the nom-de-plume of "Mali", gives the following interesting account of a visit which he paid to the North-West Frontier of India :

"Chaman, you must know, is one of our principal posts on the North-West Frontier. A former Commander-in-Chief decreed that a post should be established at Chaman to be fed by a light railway from Quetta. Two mud forts guard the railway station, one on each side ; each fort is manned by one company of Indian infantry, and one squadron native mounted levies and *by dogs.*

"What strikes the newcomer entering either of the forts at any hour of the day is the large, extraordinary-looking creatures sprawling all over the place, fast asleep. In size and shape they somewhat resemble a large Greyhound, but such slight resemblance is dispelled by the tufts with which all are adorned : some having tufted ears, others tufted feet, and others, again, possessing tufted tails.

"They are known as Baluchi Hounds, and they get their daily food ration from the commissariat babu ; he is the only permanent resident of the fort. They will have no truck with any stranger, white or black.

"When 'Retreat' sounds, the pack awakes, yawns, pulls itself together, and solemnly marches out to take up positions close to the newly arrived night guard. *They appear to be under no leadership,* yet as the patrols are told off a couple of dogs attach themselves to each patrol, and they remain with their respective patrols till

A YOUTHFUL CHAMPION.

The extraordinary feet of the Afghan, built to run on the sand, are clearly shown in this picture of Mrs. T. S. Couper's eleven-months-old champion "Garrymhor Souriya".

Photo]
[*Sport and General.*

A HEAD STUDY.

The Afghan Hound is often known as the Barukhzy. The name is that of the Royal Family of Afghanistan.
Above is a typical head—Mrs. M. Wood's "Westmell Tamasar".

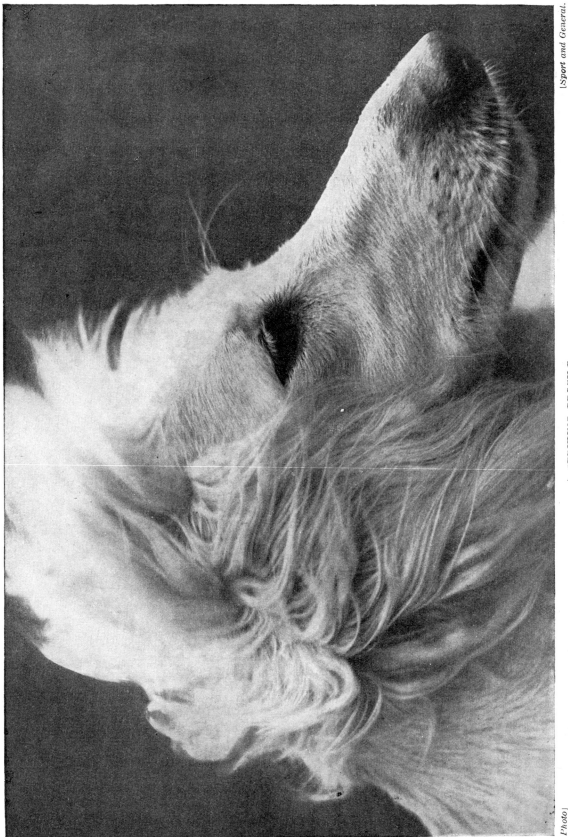

A STRIKING PROFILE.

The Afghan Hound is mainly found in the neighbourhood of Cabul and Balkh, and great care is taken of the variety in order to keep it constant in type.
Mrs. J. Chesterfield-Cooke's "Rupmati of Zemi" displays here the real beauty of the breed.

Photo]   [*Country Life.*

TWO MATRONS OF THE AFGHAN BREED.
Although little is known of the Afghan, it is said that in the history
of India of the sixteenth century mention is made of the importation
of these dogs. Down to modern times the breed has maintained its
ancient characteristics.

'reveille' next morning. Between a deep ditch and wall of the fort is a narrow path. Throughout the night, this path is patrolled by successive couples of dogs. Immediately one couple has completed the circuit of the walls and arrives back at the main gate, another couple starts out.

"When it is remembered that these extraordinary hounds have never had any training whatsoever, that their duties are absolutely self-imposed—for no human being has the slightest control over them—the perfection of their organization and the smoothness with which they carry out their tasks make mere man gasp!"

After detailing several other interesting incidents on the Afghan frontier connected with these hounds, the writer concludes :

"I have a deep respect for those 'hounds of Chaman'—I always shall have."

Up to 1914, the Afghan Hound was practically unknown in this country, but an occasional specimen was brought over and looked upon as a great curiosity. One of the first of these was "Mustapha", an Afghan owned by the Shah of Persia.

Actually the first Afghan to come before the British public was the hound "Zardin", which was exhibited at the Kennel Club Championship Show in 1907 by Mrs. Barff, taking first prize in the Foreign Dog class. So much, indeed, was the interest taken in this dog, that Queen Alexandra expressed a wish to see him. "Zardin" was afterwards taken as the accepted model of the perfect Afghan Hound, and the Standard of Points of the Afghan Hound Association was fixed from him. His embalmed body can be seen in the British Museum.

Soon after its introduction the Afghan grew into favour, not only because of its beauty and picturesque appearance, but also because of its many excellent qualities as a companion and guard.

Mrs. Amps must be regarded as the pioneer of the breed in this country, when she brought back with her from her kennels in Cabul the famous Ch. "Sirdar of Ghazni" and "Khan of Ghazni". Ch. "Sirdar's" progeny has been the foundation of most of the principal kennels in this country. He is undoubtedly one of the finest specimens of his breed, and has done more to popularize it than any other Afghan. Another well-known imported hound which helped to establish the breed was Ch. "Buckmal".

With the advent of several good bitches from Afghanistan into this country, the breed steadily made great progress, and from a few hounds entered in the early championship shows the entries

Photo]   [*Sport and General.*

MAJOR BELL MURRAY'S FAMOUS TRIO.
On the rocks of Afghanistan some of these dogs are depicted in drawings of great
age, yet not until 1920 did they find popularity outside their native country.

rapidly increased until it became one of the principal attractions of our leading championship shows.

The honour of attaining a championship in the three highest entries which the breed had received up to 1934 goes to Mrs. Phyllis Robson's Ch. "Sirdar of Ghazni", a son of Ch. "Sirdar". Other well-known champion dogs are Ch. "Badshat of Ainsdart" (later sent to America) and the late Ch. "Ashna of Ghazni", both sons of Ch. "Sirdar".

Bitches which have played an important part in the progress of the breed are Ch. "Alfreda" and her two daughters, Ch. "Sirfreda" and Ch.

days, should have a liberal supply of raw meat daily.

In disposition, the Afghan is, naturally, bold and courageous, but it is very much a one-man dog, and for this reason it often shows timidity in the presence of strangers, which is more apparent than real, as it is the outcome of the care and seclusion in which the dog was originally kept.

The Afghan varies in colour from almost white with a black mask to almost pure black. The rich golden-reds with the fawn feathering are among the most popular, but there is no bar to colour. Brindles and black-and-tans both find favour with many breeders.

The whole appearance of the dog should give the

Photo]   [Sport and General.
'RAJA THE SECOND".
The speed, courage, and power of negotiating rocks are remarkable in these dogs, for they are accustomed to face the rough conditions of the countryside when hunting. Major Bell Murray's "Raja the Second" is a fine type.

"Garrymhor Souriya": the latter attained her championship when under 14 months old and established a record. There must also be mentioned Ch. "Marika of Baberbach", Ch. "Nusk-ki of Ruritania", and Ch. "Mahaprajapati of Geufron".

The breed is now popular in America and on the Continent, and several well-known British winners have been exported.

The question of breeding presents no greater difficulties than the breeding of any other hound, but they are most particular feeders and require more thought and care in this respect than many other breeds. As the Afghan has a natural tendency to hunt for its food and kill, it is always desirable that the nursing mother, after the first two or three

impression of strength and activity, combining speed with power. As the hound is largely used for hunting over very rough and mountainous ground, a compact, well-coupled body, rather than a body on Greyhound lines, is essential.

A good average height for a dog is 27 inches and about 2 inches less for a bitch.

The Afghan Hound Association have drawn up a Standard of Points, which is set out below, and which give an excellent description of the hound. This Association was formed several years ago to further the interest of the breed, and it is largely due to their influence that classes for the breed are now provided at most of the leading championship shows in this country.

THE AFGHAN OF OTHER DAYS.

Major Mackenzie, about 1888, was the leading authority on this breed, and these two pictures (left, Mr. F. Carter's "Rajah II": right, Mackenzie's "Khulm") show the type of dog as he said it ought to be. It is interesting to compare these specimens with the present-day variety.

A NOTED KENNEL.

Miss Denyer, one of the original breeders of Afghan Hounds, is seen here with some typical examples of the breed.

[Photo]

[Sport and General.

A STUDY IN COAT.

At one of the most important shows in England, known as the Southern Counties Canine Show, a team of Afghans, the property of Mrs. M. E. Till, were much admired. They are here seen in full coat.

STANDARD OF POINTS.

HEAD.—Skull long and not too narrow, with prominent occiput. Foreface long, with punishing jaws and little stop, mouth level. Nose usually black, liver no disqualification in lighter-coloured dogs. Eyes: dark preferred, golden colour no disqualification. Ears long, heavily feathered and carried close to the head, which is surmounted by long top-knot of hair.

NECK.—Long, strong, with a proud carriage of the head.

SHOULDERS.—Long and sloping, well set back, well muscled and strong.

BACK.—Well muscled the whole length, falling slightly away to the stern. Loin: straight, broad and rather short. Hip joints rather prominent and wide: a fair spring of ribs and good depth of chest.

FORELEGS.—Straight, well-boned, elbows rather straight.

FEET.—Large. Toes very long, well arched and heavily feathered.

HINDQUARTERS.—Powerful and long, with plenty of bend to hock and stifle, and well under the dog.

TAIL.—Set on low and carried "gaily", with a ring at the end: sparsely feathered.

COAT.—Long, of very fine texture on the ribs, fore and hind quarters and flanks. From the shoulders backward, along the top of the back, the hair is short and close. Hair long from the eyes backward, with a distinct silky topknot; on foreface hair is short as on the back. Ears and legs well feathered.

ANY COLOUR.

HEIGHT.—Dogs 27 to 29 inches. Bitches 2 to 3 inches smaller.

The whole appearance of the dog should give the impression of strength and activity, combining speed with power.

The object of the dog is to hunt its quarry over very rough and mountainous ground, a country of crags and ravines. For this a compact and well-coupled dog is necessary rather than a long-loined racing dog whose first quality is speed.

EXPRESSION.—Dignified, aloof, and intelligent.

In motion his head and tail are carried high; springy gait.

There is a marked variation in both the texture and the quality of an Afghan's coat. This is largely due to climatic and atmospheric conditions. A cold climate produces a thick coat, sometimes corded; a hot climate results in little or no coat in some cases. For the most part, the coats in this country are of a soft and silky texture; but few instances of the corded variety have been seen,

Photo]　　　　　　　　　　　　　　　*[Fall.*

THE AFGHAN MUZZLE.
The attenuated muzzle of the breed is well exemplified in this head study.
Except for the Saluki, no dog has so fine a muzzle.

as this texture seems largely confined to high altitudes, and colder climates.

To keep an Afghan in show condition one must be prepared to have patience and to devote a certain amount of time each day to its grooming and care of its coat. Good food, plenty of exercise and fresh air, and an avoidance of over-bathing is all that is required to keep the hound in healthy show condition.

From personal experience many agree that the Afghan is a most delightful and fascinating breed, as he is gifted with great intelligence and is a devoted and faithful companion.

The quaint appearance of the dog invariably attracts attention, with its long silky coat and heavy feathering, which so much resembles the "chaps" of a cowboy that one often hears small boys remark, "Here come the cowboy dogs !"

It has been said that the Afghan has somewhat of an unruly nature and with a tendency to chase and hunt, but this is largely due to want of proper training in early youth, as the hounds live in perfect harmony with poultry, pigeons, horses, cattle, and sheep.

Although the Afghan Hound is not recognized as a coursing dog, in the strictest sense of the word, it was tried out in 1933 with Salukis after hares. In each instance the Afghan proved quicker to sight the hare and showed an astonishing turn of speed. The trials proved so successful that an Afghan Hound Coursing Club was immediately projected.

breed, and although it is very possible that a breed of hairless dog might be evolved by selection, no such thing has been accomplished, and the present hairless dogs can only be looked upon as freaks due to the absence of certain bodies in their blood. It is found that these dogs are lacking in teeth formation. Some, too, are crested, that is to say, have developed topknots—an interesting fact when it is considered that the human race is also practically hairless except for the head, where hair develops to a considerable length. Specimens of hairless dogs have often been kept both in private collections and also in the London Zoological Gardens and elsewhere.

Many suggestions are made as to the cause of this extraordinary condition, and it may be that it is due entirely to a lack of a food constituent or to the climatic conditions of the country affecting dogs which have a pre-disposition towards hairlessness. To try and discover an explanation of this hairlessness, and also account for it, some examples of these dogs in the Zoological Gardens in London have been carefully examined and every channel has been searched for any difference in their physiology but without result. It may be that in the future ardent fanciers will produce a hairless breed.

Photo]   *[Ralph Robinson.*
ABYSSINIAN SAND DOG.

These freak dogs claim to be a particular breed, but are found on examination to have something lacking in their blood which prevents normal development of hair and teeth. It is doubtful if they should be accepted as a separate variety.

African Hunting Dog. (*See* CAPE HUNTING DOGS.)

African (Abyssinian) Sand Dog.—From time to time hairless dogs have been met with in various parts of the world and introduced into this country as Sand Dogs, Chinese Hairless Dogs, Turkish Hairless Dogs, etc. They vary in colour from mottled or black to white and pink of various shades. Although attempts have been made to suggest that these dogs constitute a definite

Age: AVERAGE ATTAINED.—Puppyhood endures until the age of twelve months, although by law a puppy has to be licensed at the age of six months. The majority of breeds may be said to have reached maturity at one year old, the exceptions being the largest breeds, which are probably not fully and finally developed until they have nearly attained their second year. (*See also* OESTRUM.)

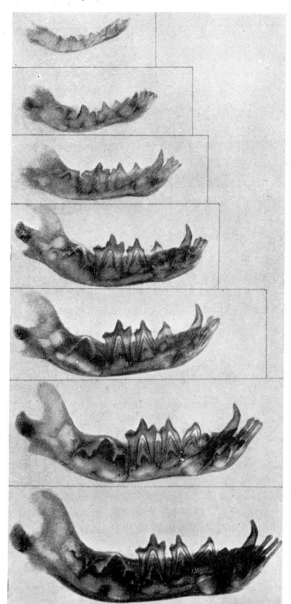

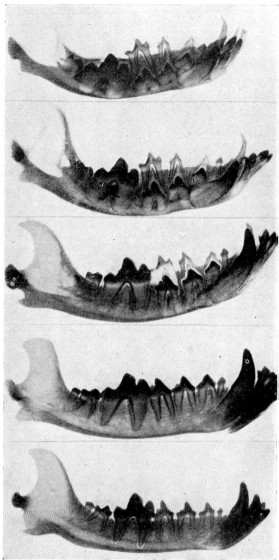

Twelve radiographs of puppies' lower teeth, from age four days to maturity: showing progress of calcification.

A DOG'S AGE AS SHOWN BY THE TEETH.

This is a photo-micrograph of a small section of a dog's tooth which is almost fully mature
The dog, in this case, is aged two years.

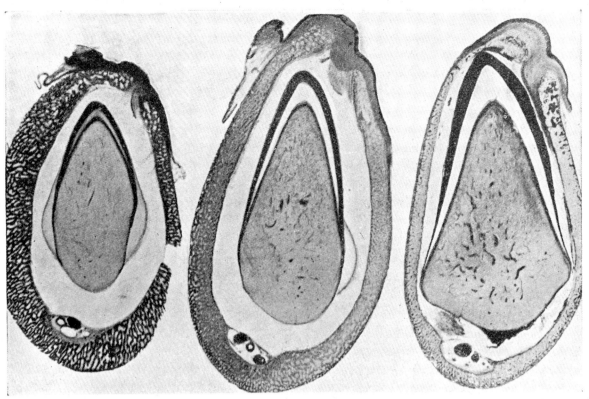

Sectional views of three lower molars at ages (from left to right) of two, four and nine weeks.

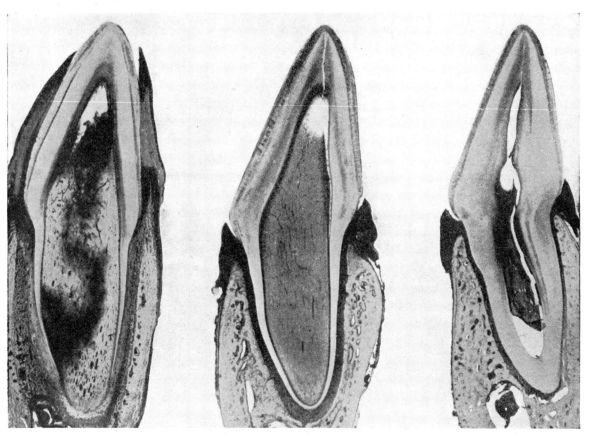

PHOTO-MICROGRAPHS OF TEETH, SHOWING AGE.

The lower picture is a continuation of the upper, and shows the teeth at the ages of 19 (the two left photos) and 27 weeks. The development of the teeth is clearly marked. Later the sharp points wear, giving further indication of the dog's age.

Provided that a dog has been reared and cared for in a rational manner, its average length of life will be about twelve years.

Environment, exercise, feeding and general hygiene, all exert their influence upon the length of an animal's life.

AGE: SIGNS OF ADVANCING.—After twelve months of age, dogs become more sensible, are usually cleaner in habits, and often over their juvenile ailments, such as distemper, to which the majority of survivors will have acquired an immunity. These are reasons why it is preferable to purchase a dog of twelve months or more, than a young puppy.

There are no very decided indications of a dog's age after puppyhood, except that with advancing age the teeth gradually lose their pearly whiteness and show progressive wear of the points and biting edges. Generally, one can perceive a yellowish discolouration beginning from the gums and working towards the tips after two and a half to three years of age. The density of the discolouration and the degree of wear both increase with age, though certain influences may exist which exert considerable modification of the normal appearance.

For instance, a dog taught or encouraged to retrieve stones would very soon exhibit a quite abnormal amount of wear of its teeth. A like effect would be produced by the habitual gnawing of bones, though, of course, to a less extent. On the other hand, the teeth of dogs which are allowed few bones and subsist mainly upon soft foods are much earlier subjected to deposits of tartar, decay, or pyorrhoea.

A sign of old age observed in dogs is the appearance of white hairs about the muzzle, particularly on black dogs, or those with black faces. These white hairs are frequently found on dogs which have reached the age of only four years. Generally, however, their appearance is not noted until after about six years of age, though there is no hard and fast rule. A very old dog will, in addition, show a faint cloudiness of the lens of the eyes indicating the onset of impairment of vision. This

does not, as a rule, become manifest until about the eighth or ninth year, though it may in some be observed very much earlier, or in others may not appear at all.

Although the majority of dogs may die in their eleventh or twelfth year, one not infrequently finds dogs of eight years of age showing all the evidences of senile decay, such as urinary incontinence

Photo]   [*Fall.*

THE AIREDALE.

Mrs. Ohm's Airedale "Balam Hill Brunette". The Airedale is the largest terrier in the world and is considered to be a "one man's" dog. Here we have a head study of this popular breed.

rheumatism, emaciation, asthma, chronic constipation, foul body odour, defective hearing and vision, tumour formation, and loss of agility, followed soon after by death.

AGE: TO TELL THE.—Since the function of dog's teeth is not to grind but to cut and tear, it follows that their surfaces do not approximate in the same manner as is observed in the case of the horse; and there is little loss of their substance by

SAVING LIFE.

Life-saving is one of the attributes of the Airedale character, and one is here seen being trained to carry out that duty.

normal wear throughout life. In consequence, there are no very definite indications of a dog's age to be gleaned from a picture presented by its teeth. A general idea of age can, however, be judged by remembering the following facts : the puppy cuts its first teeth at from four to six weeks old.

From this time onward there is little to be observed except the growth of the milk teeth, until the age of about four months is reached, when permanent teeth commence to make their appearance. By the sixth or seventh month dentition is usually complete, i.e. all milk teeth have been displaced by permanent ones. Temporary teeth may be distinguished from permanent by the fact that they are more slender and sharp, and are of a bluish-white or diluted milk colour, as contrasted with the ivory-like and more solid-looking tooth of the adult dog.

When the animal has attained "a full month" it is in possession of forty-two teeth, twenty of which are in the upper jaw and twenty-two in the lower jaw. Up to the age of two or three years there is little change ; then, however, one may discern commencing wear of opposed surfaces, and a brownish discolouration of the incisors and canines notably near the gums

These features become accentuated as time goes on, until at about six or seven years (varying in individuals

we note the appearance of the symptoms of senile decay already mentioned in the previous paragraph.

Notwithstanding the apparent absence of deleterious influences, however, it is not uncommon to find dogs showing many or all of the signs of senile decay at about six or seven years of age. In fact, it is calculated by some people that the length of a dog's life may be determined by multiplying the period of its maturation by seven.

On the other hand, several instances have come to the writer's notice of dogs having reached the ripe old age of twenty years and, in at least two cases. twenty-five years.

Airedale Terrier. — Airedales have a world-wide vogue, and wherever they once get transplanted their popularity is lasting. Specimens of the race have gone to high honours, even to the highest awards, over all other more ancient breeds, to the winning of trophies for absolute "best in the show". This occurred several times during the writer's judging trip to India a few years ago ; and also in the United States during his judging engagements.

Photo]   [Fall.

MATADOR MANDARIN".

A champion Airedale that was purchased for a few shillings (it is said) as a pet and later won several championships

A SPLENDID HEAD.

Head and shoulder study of a perfect specimen of the ever-popular Airedale breed. Note the cubist effect of muzzle.

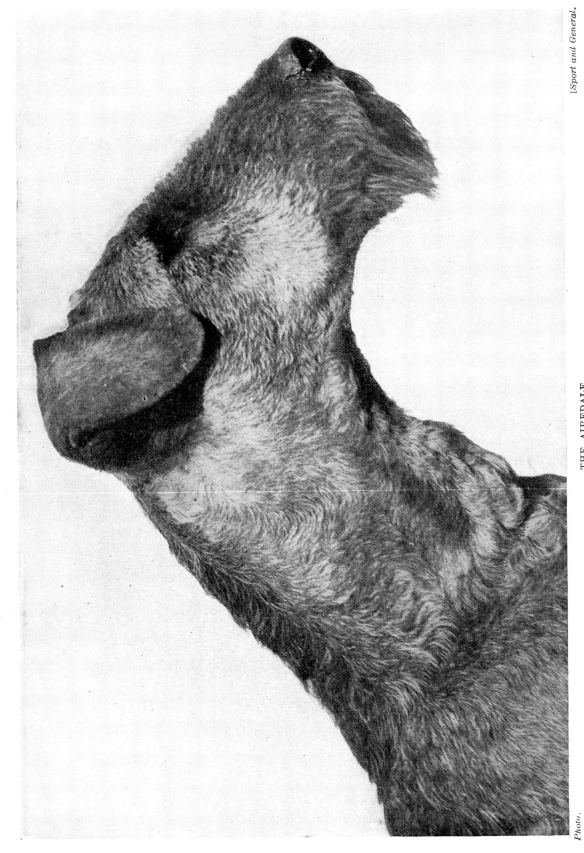

Photo, [*Sport and General.*

THE AIREDALE.

Ch. "Cotsford Topsail", a noted Airedale Terrier with a remarkable head, also suggesting the desired coat and the way such a dog is trimmed and prepared for a show.

By courtesy of]   *[E. C. Ash*

PIONEER OF THE AIREDALE BREED.

"Young Tanner" shows what an Airedale was in the early days of its history. This is Mr. Tatham's dog. Its mother was "Burn's Music", but the father was unknown. It lived about 1882.

Many handsome specimens of both sexes were acquired by the breed-lovers over there for record sums, and £500 to almost twice that sum were prices not at all out of the ordinary.

The breed has long been held in high favour by the armies of European and Asiatic countries, being easy to train and, once trained, showing great determination of character and devotion to duty, and almost superhuman intelligence, chiefly in carrying despatches on the field of battle and finding the wounded. In fact, the dog's intelligence was so high in the latter respect that they became a source of embarrassment to the Japanese victors during the Russo-Japanese War by always finding and directing to the Russians first and the Japanese soldiers last, for the Airedale's power of scent is remarkable.

Historically considered, there is not a great deal of background, but the Airedale's ancestors were without any sort of doubt highly-bred dogs and bred for certain sporting purposes. His origin cannot be traced back like the Mastiff's for hundreds of years, for the Mastiff is probably the descendant of the Molassian dog.

It is pretty certain that the Airedale as such emerged about seventy years ago ; at that time there were many sportsmen living in the valleys of the Aire and Wharfedale very fond of otter-hunting ; and others, whose means did not permit of keeping a couple or more of Otter Hounds, kept a working strain of Ratting Terrier larger than the Fox Terrier. These dogs were all workers and devoted to their owners, who usually spent their Sundays hunting rats, digging out rabbits, and bolting foxes. Some brilliant brain evolved the idea of crossing these working-terriers with the Otter Hound, thus obtaining weight and substance to tackle larger foes and a formidable

guard to person and property while retaining all sporting attributes.

In a few years Bingley—which gave them their first name—became alive with them. Then the Irish Terrier, and probably the Welsh Terrier, were introduced, and gradually the type and size became set, and the Birmingham National Show recognized them as Airedale or Waterside Terriers, taking the first name, very sensibly, from the place of their origin. As Airedales simply, their history started in 1884, when the famous "Keighley Crack" won at the Kennel Club Show of that year, and their separate classification came two years later in the Stud Book. Since then the breed has never looked back.

The genius for breeding—that prerogative of the British race in livestock—set to work to breed out the houndy ears, light eyes, long back, and splay feet—bad qualities which came from the Otter Hound—with such success that in a few years the Airedale Terrier's appearance vied with that of any other terrier breed. The point has often been raised : Is he not too big for his classification as a terrier ? And it must be conceded that there is good reason for this objection. However, his great terrier character won him his place in that classification, and all attempts to place him in any other division were strongly resisted.

For the one-man-one-dog man he cannot be beaten, for his qualities of friendship, carrying with them infinite protection for his master and all that belong to his master, are illimitable. For the gun

Photo   *[Hedges.*

FAMOUS AIREDALE.

Ch. "Gowerton Minx", one of the best specimens of the breed in England. She has the longest head ever seen on a bitch. She can be taken as what a breeder should endeavour to obtain.

he is an excellent retriever, and his setting and pointing are simply superb. For big duck he is to be preferred to Cockers and Springers, as no weight bothers him ; and his speed in the water is far in advance of the breeds named. In appearance he is as handsome as possible. He is a sahib to his master and family and a natural enemy to burglars.

By courtesy of]   [Lt.-Col. E. H. Richardson.
COURAGE.
Airedales have been trained for many years as police dogs, and here Lt.-Col. E. H. Richardson is teaching a member of his noted kennel to face revolver fire.

His gay, bright, debonair demeanour is enormously heartening while on a country walk, and the style in which he returns to heel when ordered, and sometimes, when a suspicious tramp hoves into view, without being ordered, is something to be marvelled at.

It will not be amiss if now we study the standard.

SKULL.—Should be long and flat, not too broad between the ears, and narrowing slightly to the eyes. It should be well balanced, with only little apparent difference between skull and foreface

the skull free from wrinkles, with stop hardly visible ; cheeks level and free from fullness ; foreface must be well filled up before the eyes. There should be no duskiness or falling away abruptly below the eyes ; a little delicate chiselling should keep appearance from wedginess and plainness.

UPPER AND LOWER JAWS.—Should be deep, powerful, strong, and muscular ; teeth strong and level, being capable of closing together like a vice. Strength of foreface is a great point in the Airedale, but no excess development of the jaw to give a rounded appearance or full appearance to the cheeks is desirable. Lips should be tight and the nose black.

EYES.—Should be dark in colour, small, not prominent, full of terrier character, keenness and intelligence.

EARS.—V-shaped, with a carriage rather to the side of the head, not pointing to the ears, as in the case of the Fox Terrier. A pendulous ear hanging dead by the side of the skull like the Foxhound is a bad fault.

NECK.—Clean, muscular, of good length, gradually widening to the shoulders, and entirely free from throatiness. The skin should be tight and not loose.

SHOULDERS.—Should be long, laid back, and sloping obliquely into the back. Chest deep, but not broad.

BODY.—Back short, strong, straight and level, with no slackness observable. Loins muscular. Well-sprung ribs. In a short-coupled dog whose ribs are well up there is little space between ribs and hips, otherwise the dog will be long in couplings and slack.

HINDQUARTERS.—Should be long and muscular, with no drop. Thighs long and powerful, with apparent second thigh stifles well bent, not turned in or out. Hocks will let down, not turned in or out, but parallel with each other when viewed from behind.

TAIL.—Should be set on high and carried gaily, but not curled over the back ; of fair length, and strong

LEGS.—Perfectly straight as to forelegs, with good, hard, straight bone of great substance. Elbows should be perpendicular to the body, working free of the sides.

FEET.—Small, round, compact like a cat's, with good depth of pad. Toes a little arched, not turning in or out.

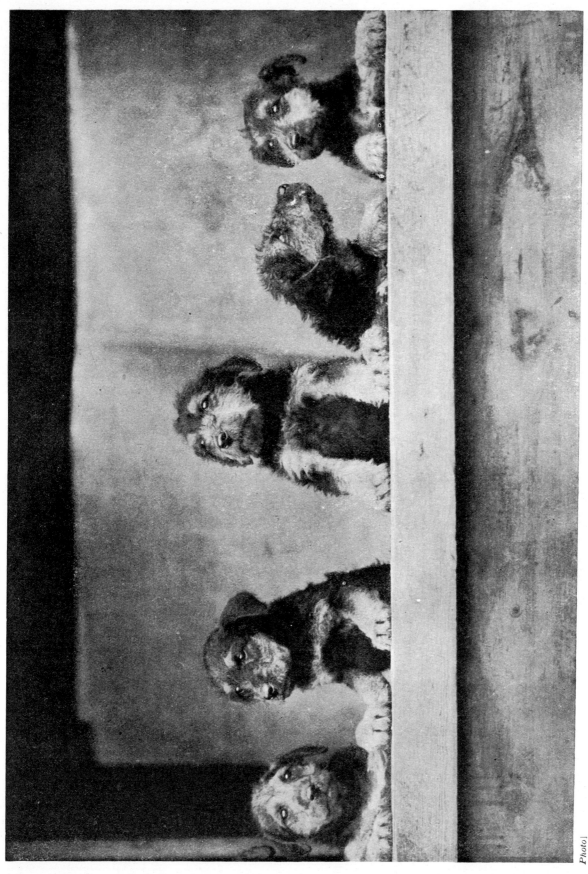

Photo]

AIREDALE PUPPIES. Special attention is drawn to the heavy muzzle of the second dog from the right —an outstanding feature of the breed.

The strong legs and feet and typical head of the young Airedale are seen in this attractive group.

The Airedale, taught to track a thief, follows the quarry to his hiding-place.

.Photos]

Here the dog in training is seen preventing an intruder from escaping.

[Sport & General.

AIREDALES AS TRACKERS.

COAT.—A very important feature in a dog which will take to water like a duck. It must be harsh, dense, and wiry ; rugged but not ragged. It should lie straight and close, covering the dog well all over the body and legs. There should be an oily thick undercoat, which enables them to stand any amount of work in cold water. A curly coat is undesirable, but one with a slight wave is much less so, as such coats are always the correct texture.

COLOUR.—The head and ears, with the exception of dark markings each side of the skull, should be a rich hard tan, the ears being a darker shade than the rest. The legs, up to the thighs and elbows, also tan. The body to be black or hard

train by reason of its intelligence and docility.

He is by instinct a perfectly mannered dog in the house ; very unobtrusive ; will lie in a selected corner and be perfectly mum until strange footsteps impinge on his consciousness—and then comes the deep thunder of his voice, telling to all whom it may concern that a stranger seeks attention.

Tramps dislike the Airedale excessively. They know perfectly well the menace of his voice ; so much so that they give a wide berth to the house where they know an Airedale is kept.

The training is simple for this purpose ; the command from the owner to "Keep him, Peter," will ensure the dog not attacking the man, but he

Photo]   [*Sport and General.*
A USEFUL LITTER.
Airedale puppies after they have left their mother are, if well reared, strong and lusty youngsters. Above is a hearty litter at feeding-time.

grizzle ; the latter is generally of the hardest texture.

SIZE.—45 pounds is the ideal weight for dogs ; bitches a little less. Height from 23 to 24 inches, taken, of course, from the top of the shoulders ; bitches an inch less.

GENERAL APPEARANCE.—The whole effect is that of a muscular, active, fairly cobby terrier, without a suspicion of legginess and undue length of barrel. In galloping he moves like a racehorse—not, as has often been said, like a hackney, which would be a blemish. His movement a dream of motion, he looks exactly what he is—a gentleman and a sportsman.

It is not proposed to include a scale of points, for they are useless as a guide—in fact, a delusion and a snare for beginners on taking up a breed.

This breed is perhaps the easiest of all to

will not let him stir until told to lie down by his master.

He can kill rats as fast as you can wink, so the only education required when a puppy is to let an adult kill those caught in traps and he will learn in a few lessons to kill without being himself bitten. He is easily broken to ferrets : a little not-too-near proximity when young is all that is required, and then when ferrets are put in rabbit- or rat-holes he will soon be *au fait* to the fact that the ferrets are his allies and not enemies.

BREEDING.—Airedales are natural whelpers and rarely does the bitch require helping. The average litter is eight to ten, and, unless trouble is expected through the bitch going over her time, the best plan is to let her severely alone, or with a glance to see that the whelps are comfortably around their mother. A few hours after whelping the dam should be taken out for short exercise, as it is imperative that the afterbirth should come away or high fever and worse may occur.

On the third day the pups' tails should be docked. The fashion is now to take off one-third. Push the skin of the tail back and take off one-third with not too sharp a knife ; also, with a pair of curved surgical scissors, take off with an upward motion any dew claws that may be on their legs, back or front, and sometimes both. No further attention is necessary, as the dam will keep the ends clean, and the pups, if docked at three days, will hardly know that it has been done, as the tails are simply gristle at that age, and there will be very little bleeding. A member of the family should be requisitioned to take the mother for a walk while the docking is being done ; it will not distress the whelps at all, but it will the dam.

If the pups are intended for show, they should be kept, if possible, for six months, when it will be quite simple to tell which are the most likely (if any) good enough for show purposes.

The history of the breed is full of tragical happenings for the breeder who has sold his puppies at too early an age, for young stock improve in the most amazing manner during the first six months, and many a breeder has had the vexing experience of selling a puppy for a few guineas which has afterwards turned out champion.

The breeder who lacks experience will receive a shock when he first views the litter, for with the exception of a tiny tan spot on the cheeks and a trifle on the feet they will be born absolutely black.

Do not breed from a weakly parent either

side, and never, if your object is high-class show stock, breed from inferior parents. The stud dog who is mostly a champion is never above a stud fee of £5 5s. ; most of them are less, so there is no excuse for thrift, and no profit in it.

The dam should be up to the breed's standard weight, hash-jacketed, plenty of bone and substance ; strong, short back, with powerful, galloping hindquarters, the latter being of first-class importance, for it means, when present, perfect movement and soundness. Never breed from parents who are not absolutely sound fore and aft.

The dam should possess good shoulders and a long, reaching neck, and well-set-in ears, not too large. Light eyes should never be bred from. If once in a strain it is almost impossible to breed them out. Straight fronts are a *sine qua non*. The head should be as good as you can get for a moderate sum with, if possible, length and quality ; but the stud dog usually looks after these important departments by stamping his own image on his progeny.

Photo]   AIREDALE CHARACTERISTICS.   *[Fall*
Size without clumsiness, and keenness of expression, are characteristics of the breed
and these are marked in Mr. Wesley's "Roger Courtier", shown above.

The writer has met many breeders who have studied breeding principles such as the law of heredity, natural variability, and selection, with much intelligence, but nearly always with little profit in so far as breeding outstanding stock is concerned. For the practical truth of the matter is that the small breeder, with a brace of bitches in a backyard, who knows nothing of these laws, almost invariably turns out finer stock, even to consistently breeding champions, than those who spend midnight oil on the theories of Cossar Ewart, Weismann, and Mendel. Telegony most small breeders do believe in, because, as they think, they see the taints that the bitch shows by the first sire to which she bears her first family, and also think they see it again from the bitches of that family when bred again; or, putting it plainly, that puppies often resemble a sire which, though not their sire, has been mated previously with their dam.

The belief has caused many good bitches to be "put down", or never bred from again after an accidental misalliance with a mongrel; but experience teaches the utter falseness of the theory.

Champion sires invariably come from the most prepotent families, so that selection is comparatively easy. It is strongly urged that the bitch should be as good as can possibly be afforded, for the strength of any kennel is in its bitches.

It is a fairly sound theory that two opposite qualities in the sire and dam can balance each other in the resultant litter. If the idea is to correct a long back in the bitch, do not put her to the short-backed dog unless he comes from a family of short-backs. Compensating theories are entire fallacies.

To get the best out of your brood bitch, breed only at alternate seasons. For show stock the best time to breed in our climate is February. The pups will then come in the best time to get the sun on their backs, and also to make progress for the seasonal shows later on.

So far as your brood bitch is concerned, let exercise be your constant endeavour. For grooming, use a dandy-brush once a day. She will do well if kept in a kennel, but better still if kept in the domestic circle, and will pay a thousandfold for the privilege. Do not bathe too often. Dose about once in six weeks for worms, which are mostly present in some form or another. Do not think because she is "merry" in condition she is free from these pests, for no dogs, however kept or fed, are entirely free.

Beyond watching the feet for thorns and suchlike, little more attention is needed.

To come to the time when your breeding efforts are ready for the show-ring, a little forethought and preparation are necessary.

We will take it that the show where your débutant is to prove what he is made of is eight weeks off. Your dog should be stripped of his top coat. Choose your plan of campaign at that period. When his old coat is ready to yield to the pressure

ALBANIAN WOLFHOUND.
This breed, long famous for its extreme ferocity, was known in ancient times. The above is a design of the hound found on an antique Greek vase.

of finger and thumb, take it off from the shoulders to the end of the back, where the tail meets it. Use your hound-glove daily after this.

At three weeks before the show, take the outer coat off the neck down to the shoulders; at two weeks, clean off the shoulders in a like manner and also the skull and cheeks, leaving a little eyebrow on top of the eyes. Do not, until you become expert, touch the whiskers; simply brush them outwards. In time you will be able to tackle this delicate job by thinning them out, as it were. Underneath the throat should also have a little cleaning with thumb and finger. Leave the hair on the legs and hindquarters until you fancy yourself expert. They are, anyway, only fancy touches, and certainly do not carry you far with the Solomon adjudicating. It is simply tidiness which shows the exhibit's general balance. The leg hair should first of all be combed and then brushed with a dandy-brush.

FEEDING.— Super-baked bread, broken up small, with a good soup containing meat and green vegetables, and uncooked minced meat, the latter at least once a day, is recommended.

Albanian Wolfdog.—At the present day much interest is taken in the Alsatian, and it is interesting to consider other dogs of similar type which existed long before the present Alsatian was bred. By similar type it must be understood dogs typically wolf.

Amongst these the extremely ferocious Albanian Wolfdog is one of the most important. It is not so named because of its relationship to the wolf, but because of its use in protecting the flocks from the attack of wild animals.

It plays a very different part in Albania from the British sheep-dog. The latter helps to control the sheep, whilst the Albanian Wolfdog's duty is to drive away marauders.

It was a rule in Albania that warning be given to travellers arriving there that on no account were they to shoot or injure one of these dogs, even if they thought the dog intended to attack them. If the shepherds saw a stranger shoot at their dogs they immediately used their guns on the stranger, being entirely indifferent whether they shot him dead or not.

On account of their reputed ferocity, any of these dogs exhibited cause considerable interest. One by the name of "Arslan" was exhibited at Islington by Frank Buckland, the noted naturalist, and one or two of these dogs were kept at the London Zoo.

Alopecia.—A normal or abnormal baldness or deficiency of hair which may be local or general. The seasonal shedding of the coat each spring and autumn is so complete in some animals as to leave them almost entirely bald. In others, hair falls irregularly, causing unsightly bare patches.

CAUSES.—It originates usually as a result of some debilitating condition such as is produced by distemper and other severe illnesses : gestation ; suckling of puppies ; blood impoverishment ; starvation, etc., etc. It may occur as a result of "in and in" breeding ; or of burns, wounds, or other destruction of hair follicles ; ringworm, mange, eczema, skin parasites; glandular insufficiency such as hypothyroidism ; some interference with the blood or nerve supply of the part ; dandruff ; scalding by discharges and other mechanical or chemical irritants. If a dog ever really recovers from follicular mange, it is extremely likely that areas of its skin will be permanently denuded of hair. There is no permanent baldness, however, following recovery from sarcoptic mange or eczema. Fleas and lice will induce baldness because the dog actually rubs itself bare on the under sides of chairs and other articles of furniture ; perpetual scratching with the hind paws on one area of skin will similarly produce localized alopecia.

Any treatment adopted must depend entirely upon the cause, and if this cannot be ascertained by the owner, a veterinary surgeon should be consulted. As might be expected, a generalized baldness would arise from some constitutional disturbance and should be treated accordingly. This would involve an improvement in general health by the administration of suitable tonics, judicious exercise, exposure to sunlight (real or artificial), attention to the bowels and stimulation of the skin by regular brushing and cleanliness of the coat. When the hair follicles have been actually destroyed as by burns or follicular mange, nothing can again induce the hair to grow ; but if the hair bulbs are intact it is often possible to stimulate them by the use of special lotions.

Localized alopecia has very frequently yielded to ultra-violet irradiation.

Nerve tonics, together with a liberal and nourishing diet, should not be omitted from the list of remedies calculated to cure baldness.

Alpine Mastiff.—This dog, the Alpine Mastiff, is the St. Bernard dog imported into England about 1825 and used to cross with the British Mastiff, to which it was related, as British Mastiffs had been sent to the Hospice to be used in the making of the St. Bernard breed

The Alpine Mastiff was close-cropped—that is to say, the outer ear had been entirely removed, so that its appearance was peculiarly savage—and

ALPINE MASTIFF.

This breed was said to have been made from the English Mastiff that had been introduced into Switzerland at some time previously. It contained, however, to judge from its appearance, the Thibet Mastiff. It is the foundation stock of the present-day St. Bernard dog. The engraving is by Landseer.

seemed very full about the eyes. It had the reputation of being ferocious in disposition.

The public being anxious to see so evil a creation, the owner of one of the imported dogs, "L'Ami", a brindle, sent it on tour in 1829, charging a shilling to view it.

Alpine Spaniel.—The name Alpine Spaniel has been given to the St. Bernard dog and also to a variety of Spaniel said to have existed, at one time, in the area of the Alps, and said by some to be the originator of the present-day Clumber Spaniel. In various old books Alpine Spaniels are mentioned. The only illustration that may be of this breed occurs in a German book printed in 1665, showing William Tell and the apple, and by his side are Spaniels, somewhat of the Clumber type.

Photo] THE HUNGARIAN ALSATIAN. [*E.N.A.*

The Alsatian is popular the world over, and although many people are prejudiced against it, yet its loyalty and devotion to its owner are proverbial. The above photograph is of Mme. Maria Lazar with her famous companion.

REMARKABLE INTELLIGENCE.

The Alsatian is so noted for its intelligence that we are hardly surprised at whatever it may do.
Mrs. J. Giffard's "Crumstone Flora P.D." is seen, at a demonstration, opening a door by undoing the catch.

Alsatian Hound.—One of the most popular of the Non-Sporting breeds, under which heading it is classified in the Kennel Club's Register, the Alsatian stands alone in its appeal to a wide section of dog lovers on account of its sterling qualities combined with its wonderful potentialities for work. It is faithful, courageous and intelligent, and in appearance is strong and alert, with great nobility of carriage. One thing which stamps it as apart from other breeds of dogs is its movement, or "gait" : a long-reaching, effortless, smooth, tireless trot, which is peculiar to the breed, and which is invaluable to it in its natural vocation of sheep herding.

It is common knowledge that the breed is of

with which it came into favour, and its eventual meteoric rise to one of the foremost breeds of the day, is probably without parallel in canine history.

Just after the War, a few ardent enthusiasts banded together and decided to form a Club, at the same time selecting a name for the breed. It was agreed to give the breed the name of Alsatian Wolfdog, and in 1919 The Alsatian Wolfdog Club was formed. The latter half of the title, of course, originated from the resemblance to the wolf, and the former half was a compromise, for to have called the breed German at that time would have sounded its death-knell. The title has since been curtailed to the one word "Alsatian". Opinions

Photo]   [*Sport and General*

ON GUARD.

It has been said with every reason that no more ferocious dog exists, when it is desired that it should be ferocious, than the Alsatian, and that it has an immense sense of duty. It would certainly take a brave man to face Mr. H. W. J. Steven's "Lady Unwin", left to guard his attaché-case.

German origin, and in that country it is known as the deutsche Schäferhunde (German Shepherd Dog) ; but it may not be generally known that a few specimens were exhibited in this country under the name of German Sheep Dogs, in classes for Foreign Dogs, before the War. It was not until after the War, however, that the breed attained popularity over here ; many members of our fighting forces, having seen these dogs working with the French Army, took a fancy to them, and brought specimens back to this country with them on their return. They were then known as French Police Dogs. It soon became evident that the breed was destined to be popular : but the rapidity

vary as to whether any wolf blood was introduced into the breed, but, if so, it was so far back that it could have no bearing on our present-day animals. The majority of the original importations were wolf-greys or sables, but later the black-and-tans became increasingly popular, and to-day these are in a very great majority. At the present time the black-and-tans are mostly in demand by the exhibiting side of the Fancy, whilst the greys are more sought after as companions. One has not far to seek for the exhibitor's preference for black-and-tans, for this colour catches the eye much more than the grey ; and it is often said that it takes an outstanding grey to beat a good black-and-tan.

In 1923 a band of working enthusiasts formed The Alsatian Sheep, Police and Army Dog Society, which devoted itself entirely to the working side ; and in 1932 it was thrown open to embrace all breeds interested in Obedience and Working Trials when it was renamed The Associated Sheep, Police and Army Dog Society. Working Trials are held twice yearly under its auspices, and amongst those which have achieved the distinction of becoming Working Trial Champions are two British-bred Alsatians.

The year 1924 saw the inauguration of the Alsatian League of Great Britain, with which was later incorporated The Alsatian Wolfdog Club,

Wales has exhibited with marked success both in Breed Classes and in Obedience.

The Alsatian went on from success to success, and became one of the fads of fashion. Entries at shows, too, were enormous, and in 1926 it headed the list of registrations for the year at the Kennel Club with 8,058 registrations, over 200 ahead of its nearest competitor. About this time the breed reached the zenith of its fame, and then settled down after these "boom" years to enjoy its present position as one of our most popular breeds.

In the early days the majority of the breeding stock originally was imported from Germany,

A NOTED WINNER.

Ch. "Erich v. Zuchtgut of Picardy" has the letters PH., SuchH., HGH., Sch.H., Zpr. behind his name, which mean that he holds some of the most important honours in the Alsatian trials, apart from his championship. The Picardy kennel is one of the most famous in Europe.

thus forming that stronghold of Alsatiandom in this country, The Alsatian League and Club of Great Britain, which is the premier organization, as well as the oldest, devoting itself to the interests of the breed over here, and numbering amongst its members many distinguished names. Foremost amongst these is His Royal Highness the Prince of Wales, who did the Alsatian League and Club of Great Britain the signal honour of consenting to become an Honorary Member. His Royal Highness is not the only member of the Royal Family to own an Alsatian, for his two brothers, their Royal Highnesses Prince Henry and Prince George, both own one. H.R.H. the Prince of

although France and other European countries also supplied a certain number ; but at the present time most of our stock is British bred, although there are a few breeders who still continue to import new blood from Germany from time to time. On the exhibition side, type is much more even than it was ; and an enormous change for the better has taken place in the character or "temperament" of the dogs, many of which were pitifully shy, even to being afraid of their own shadows, as the saying is. Breeders very soon realized the disadvantages of this type of character, and promptly set about to remedy matters by making a great effort to breed this undesirable

Drawn by J. Nicolson.]   *[Reproduced by courtesy of Frost and Reed Ltd., Bristol and London.*
ALSATIAN EXPRESSION.
The typical expression of an Alsatian's head is one of keen alertness and understanding. The artist has portrayed
here the half-suspicious look that will change instantly either to friendliness or anger.

A HARD TEST.

One of the most difficult tests that an Alsatian is called upon to do in order to gain high honours is to climb a high wooden barrier carrying a heavy dumb-bell in its mouth. What this means can be appreciated when one realizes that the dumb-bell has to be held clear of the boards whilst climbing.

trait out of the breed, in which laudable endeavour they have been, happily, most successful ; so much so that it is very seldom one sees shyness in the Alsatian nowadays. This was in a large measure brought about by the firm attitude taken up by judges in refusing to award prizes to any exhibit displaying shyness, no matter how good its other points might be.

During the early post-war period the breed met with a great deal of strenuous opposition from other sections of the canine fraternity, who, at that time, were thinking Imperially, and resented the introduction of another foreign breed ; but, despite this, rapid strides were made. The beginning of 1927 marked several incidents which were seized upon by a certain section of the Press as propaganda against the Alsatian Wolfdog, dubbing it half wolf, which was, of course, inaccurate, and was prompted by the name Wolfdog. This was one of the reasons which eventually led to the "Wolfdog" being dropped from the title as being misleading. Notwithstanding these difficulties, this wonderful breed continued to maintain its position ; and it speaks volumes that it survived all the attacks made upon it—attacks which would have written "Finis" to the activities of many another breed. Without a doubt, the interest created by the work in Obedience Classes did much to neutralize the prejudice stirred up, and to-day the Alsatian is in as strong a position as ever.

The breed, in its native environment, is essentially a working dog ; and whilst his real job is herding sheep, he has several other vocations at which he is equally adept. He is largely used in Germany as a police dog ; also as a messenger dog ; as a Red Cross dog ; as a guard dog ; and as a dog for leading the blind. The dogs in that country are specially trained for their respective vocations at establishments provided by the State, and if they pass their course they qualify for training titles, which are entered against their names in the books of the Verein für Schäfer-hunde (the breed Club). These titles will often be found against the names of foreign dogs in pedigrees, and are al-ways shown abbreviated. The following are some of the titles with their equivalents : PH. (Polizeihund), Police Dog ; SchH. (Schutzhund), Defence Dog ; HGH. (Herdenge-brauchshund), Sheep Dog ; BlH. (Blindenfuhrhund), Blind-leading Dog ; PDH. (Polizeidiensthund), Police Service Dog ; KrH. (Kreigshund), War Dog ; and SH. (Sanitatshund), Red Cross Dog.

With the formation of the Alsatian Sheep, Police and Army Dog Society, a few breeders interested in the work-ing side took up training, and Working Trials were held ; but it was not until 1927 that training was taken up generally. In this year, and in subsequent years, various Training Societies were formed, at which members were taught the methods of training ; and a debt of gratitude is owing to those experienced trainers who, by means of lectures and by precept, initiated the novice trainer. A great wave of enthusiasm for training swept through the breed, and very soon Obedience Classes became a feature of most shows. These classes created an enormous amount of interest, not only amongst Alsatianists and owners of other breeds

Photo]   *[E.N.A.*
THE MESSENGER.
Dogs proved not only their courage, but their devotion to duty, in the Great War. The Alsatian was well known at the Front and saved many lives carrying messages through every sort of obstruction and danger, including even poison gas. This is "Tilp", of the French Infantry.

but also amongst the general public ; and they were the means of introducing many new recruits to the ranks of Alsatiandom. Not only this, but owners of quite a number of other breeds have taken up training, and now compete in these classes which were inaugurated by Alsatianists.

In this country, the Alsatian is sometimes used for sheep work, although not to any great extent ; many members of the Police Force own Alsatians, the country police finding them invaluable on their lonely beats. Many Alsatians have a flair for tracking, although, up to now, few opportunities have arisen for them to test their prowess in this direction. There are several instances on record in which Alsatians have been used successfully as gundogs ; and quite a number have appeared in cabaret shows and on the music halls, and have astonished the audiences by their sagacity. On the films too, they have delighted thousands by their clever work, and such names as "Rin-Tin-Tin",

FRIENDLINESS.

So much is said of the ferocity of the Alsatian that it is pleasing to be able to show two of the breed "off duty", with their friendly charm clearly depicted in their expressions.

"Greatheart", and "Peter the Great" are household words The latest innovation in England is the Blind-leading movement, on behalf of which a broadcast appeal was made over the wireless by Mr. Christopher Stone, realizing more than £750. The training for leading the blind is a long and costly business ; it costs about £80 to train each dog, but, when trained, they are absolutely reliable. A special trainer has been obtained from abroad, where an intensive study has been made of the subject, and several blind men now possess a trained Alsatian to lead them about, which is done with perfect safety through crowds and traffic. The Alsatian shows especial aptitude for this type of work, and the humanitarian aspect of it has increased the popularity enjoyed by this versatile breed.

Touching on the exhibition side, classes are provided for Alsatians at practically all Dog Shows ; and in this, and other respects, the interests of the breed are in the main looked

ALERTNESS.

A handsome group of high-class Alsatians, all attention for the word of command. The centre dog was described as the most intelligent animal of his class and generation

after by the leading breed Club: The Alsatian League and Club of Great Britain, upon whose list of judges may be found the names of the foremost authorities on the breed in this country.

American dog lovers fell victims to the charm of this ubiquitous breed, which is in a very strong position over there; and many famous dogs from Europe have crossed the "herring pond" to make their homes in the New World. German Shepherd Dog is the cognomen under which they are known there, and under that name, or its equivalent, they are known in nearly every other country except Great Britain, where, in spite of repeated requests from the German Club's headquarters that the name should be changed to German Shepherd Dog, the title Alsatian has been retained. In the Irish Free State the combined title of "Alsatian or German Shepherd Dog" is used. The breed is represented in most parts of the world, and has made rapid strides in India, China, and Japan. In Australia the fear that they would mate with the Dingo or wild dog led to a certain amount of difficulty and caused the authorities to place a restriction on them: but in spite of these exceptional circumstances the breed has many advocates in the great Island Continent. There is no gainsaying the fact that it has proved itself a universal favourite.

Appended is the standard of points of the breed drawn up by the Alsatian League and Club of Great Britain:

GENERAL APPEARANCE. — The general appearance of the Alsatian is a well-proportioned dog, showing great suppleness of limb, neither massive nor heavy, but at the same time free from any suggestion of weediness. It must not approach the Greyhound type. The ideal height (measured to the shoulder) is not less than 22 inches in bitches and 24 inches in dogs and not more than 26 inches in either sex. The body, rather long, is strong boned, with plenty of muscle. obviously

Photo]   *Fox.*

A REMARKABLE HEAD STUDY.

The colouring of an Alsatian varies considerably, and whilst the wolf shades are thought by many people to be the most attractive, others prefer dogs marked with black, and it is a popular belief that such dogs are less wolf-like in their character.

A HANDFUL.

Although there is always a risk in exercising dogs with horses because of the possibility of a kick, Miss Thelma Evans, a leading
breeder of Alsatians, is seen taking some young dogs out for a run well in control.

capable of endurance and speed and of quick and sudden movement. Its method of locomotion is a tireless, long striding gait, and all its movements should be entirely free from stiltiness. The whole dog and its expression give the impression of perpetual vigilance, strong fidelity, lively, and ever watchful, alert to every sight and sound, nothing escaping its attention, showing no fear, but with a decided suspiciousness towards strangers—in striking contra-distinction to the immediate friendliness of some breeds—possessing highly developed senses, a vivid mentality, and plenty of temperament, strongly individualistic and showing unique powers of intelligence. Three of its most outstanding traits are its incorruptibility, its discernment, and its ability to think for itself.

THE HEAD.—The head is proportionate to the size of the body, long, lean, and clean-cut, broad at the back of the skull, but without coarseness, tapering to the nose with only a slight stop between the eyes. The skull is slightly domed and the top of the nose should be parallel to the forehead. The cheeks must not be full or in any way prominent, and the whole head,

THE BELGIAN ALSATIAN.
The type of Alsatian found in Belgium varies somewhat from the German type, as will be seen by comparing these pictures. They have slightly differently shaped heads and are not so strongly built.

THE FRENCH ALSATIAN.
The French variety is again of a different type from either the German, British, or Belgian breeds It is less wolf-like and more dog-like.

when viewed from the top, should be much in the form of a V, well filled in under the eyes. There should be plenty of substance in foreface, with a good depth from top to bottom. A long, narrow, show Collie or Borzoi head is a serious fault.

THE MUZZLE.—The muzzle is strong and long, and while tapering to the nose it must not be carried to such an extreme as to give the appearance of being overshot. It must not show any weakness, or be snipy or lippy. The lips must be tight-fitting and clean. The nose should be black whatever colour the dog may be. A pink or liver-coloured nose is a bad fault.

THE TEETH.—The teeth should be sound and strong, gripping with a scissor-like action, the lower incisors just behind but touching the upper. To be undershot or overshot is a bad fault.

THE EYES.—The eyes are almond shaped, of average size, as nearly as possible matching the surrounding coat but darker rather than lighter in shade, and placed to look straight forward. They must not be in any way bulging or prominent, and must show a lively, alert, and highly intelligent expression.

THE EARS.—The ears should be of moderate size, but rather large than small, broad at the base and pointed at the tips, placed rather high on the

Photos]　　　　　　　　　　　　　[by courtesy of E. C. Ash.
THE GERMAN ALSATIAN.
A famous specimen of the year 1907. Note the strong and solid build and the shape of the feet and tail. The hindquarters are wolf-like, while in the fore portion the dog is more recognizable.

Photo]   *[Sport and General.*

A VARIATION.

That the Alsatian varies in type may be gauged from the above photograph, which shows Mrs. Leslie Thornton's "Southdown Aurea" that
has a head very different from the head of the German specimen on the
previous page and those illustrated on other pages.

skull and carried erect—all adding to the alert
expression of the dog as a whole. It should be
noted, in case novice breeders may be misled, that
in Alsatian dog puppies the ears often hang until
the age of six months and sometimes longer,
becoming erect with the replacement of the milk
teeth.

THE NECK.—The neck should be strong, fairly
long, with plenty of muscle, fitting gracefully into
the body, joining the head without
sharp angles and free from throatiness.

THE FOREQUARTERS.—In the
forequarters the shoulders should
slope well back, the ideal being
that a line drawn through the
centre of the shoulder-blade should
form a right angle with the
humerus when the leg is perpendicular to the ground. Upright
shoulders are a bad fault. They
should show plenty of muscle,
which is quite distinct from, and
must not be confused with, coarse
or loaded bone, which is a fault.
The shoulder-bone should be clean.
The forelegs should be perfectly
straight, viewed from front, but
the pastern should show a slight
angle with the forearm when regarded from the side. Too great
an angle denotes weakness, and
while carrying plenty of bone it
should be of good quality. Anything approaching the massive bone
of the Newfoundland, for example,
is a decided fault.

THE HINDQUARTERS.—The hindquarters should show breadth and
strength, the loins being broad and
strong, the rump rather long and
sloping, and the legs, when viewed from
behind, must be quite straight, without
any tendency to cow-hocks, or bow-
hocks, which are an extremely serious
fault. The stifles are well turned and
the hocks strong and well let down.
The ability to turn quickly is a necessary
asset to the Alsatian, and this can only
be got by a good length of thigh bone
and leg. and by the bending of the
hock.

BODY PROPERTIES.—The body is
muscular, the back is broadish and
straight, rather long, but strong-boned
and well developed. The belly shows a
waist without being tucked up. There
should be a good depth of brisket or
chest, and that should not be too broad. The
sides are flat compared to some breeds, and
while the dog must not be barrel ribbed, it must
not be so flat as to be actually slabsided. While
quick in movement and speedy, the Alsatian is
not a greyhound in any way. As giving an idea
of the body proportions, it may be added that the
length of body from the front point of the breast-
bone in a straight line to the buttocks should be

Photo]   *[Sport and General.*

CONTROL.

The ease with which an Alsatian can be controlled may be seen from this picture of
five adult dogs, grouped together, posing at their mistress's command.

[*Alfieri.*

PERFORMING ALSATIANS.

The Alsatian is quite fearless, and "Coona", the property of Miss Kelly, will jump through a ring of fire without any hesitation. It may be added that "Coona" was trained entirely by Miss Kelly.

[*Photo*]

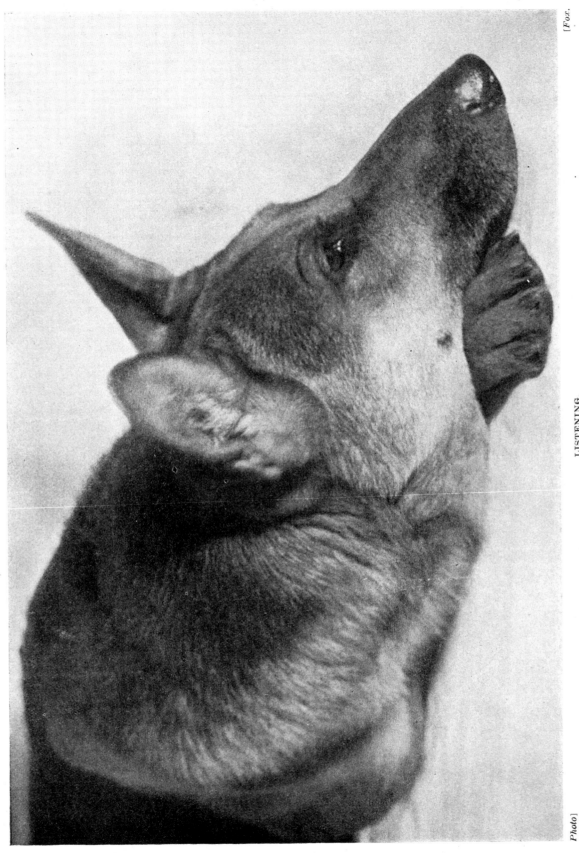

Photo]

[*Fox.*

LISTENING.

This somewhat unusual study of an Alsatian is representative of the animal's readiness for action even when resting. The listening expression is very nearly human. The eye may appear drowsy, but the ears are pricked, acutely sensitive to the slightest sound.

greater than the height to the shoulder as is 10 to 9. Short-backed dogs with high legs should be discarded. A weak back is a decided fault.

THE GAIT.—The gait should be supple, smooth and long reaching, carrying the body along with a minimum of up and down movement.

THE TAIL.—The tail during rest should hang in a slight curve. During movement and excitement it will be raised, but under no circumstances should the tail be carried past a vertical line drawn through the root. The tails with curls and pronounced hooks are faulty.

THE FEET.—The feet should be round and short, the toes strong, slightly arched and held close together. The pads should be hard, the nails short and strong. Dewclaws are neither a fault nor a virtue, but are better removed as they are liable to spoil the gait.

THE COAT.—The coat is smooth, but it is at the same time a double coat. The under-coat is woolly in texture, thick and close, and to it the animal owes its characteristic resistance to cold. The outer-coat is also close, each hair straight, hard, and lying flat, so that it is rain-resisting. Under the body, to behind the legs, the coat is longer, and forms near the thigh a mild form of breeching. On the head (including the inside of the ears), to the front of the legs and feet, the hair is short. Along the neck it is longer and thicker, and in winter approaches a form of ruff. A coat either too long or too short is a fault. As an average, the hairs on the back should be from $1\frac{1}{8}$ inches to $2\frac{1}{8}$ inches in length. The lack of heavy under-coat is a grave fault.

THE COLOUR.—The colour of the Alsatian Dog has no effect on its character or on its fitness for work, and so colour is, in reason, a secondary

Photo] CAPTURED. *[E.N.A.*

For a dog to leap up against a house and seize hold of a man's leg as shown in this photograph, just as the man was about to clamber into a window, is an astonishing feat which shows to what a high degree of usefulness an Alsatian can be trained.

consideration. It may be brown, iron-grey, cinder-grey, fawn, black or black-and-tan, etc. Colour in itself must not influence judicial decisions. The definite colour of puppies cannot be determined until arrival of the upper coat. White should be debarred in Alsatian Dogs, as it makes the animal much too conspicuous for its legitimate work.

SCALE OF POINTS

Nature and Expression	20
General Appearance ..	15
Gait	15
Bone	7
Back	7
Coat	5
Hindquarters ..	7
Forequarters	7
Chest	7
Feet	5
Head	5
Total	100

TRAINING.—The Alsatian is accepted as one of the most intelligent dogs in the world and is a combination of nobleness, strength and brain, which has won him fame as the canine star of the film world, so it must be remembered that in training the Alsatian you are commencing with a dog that already possesses a "brain", and the success almost entirely depends upon the schooling, and more so on the schoolmaster (trainer) himself.

One of the most important factors in training is that the trainer shall himself possess patience, kindness, perseverance and firmness ; and it is up to the trainer to first of all study himself and make a special note always to keep these very important points in his mind when training. A dog trained by a trainer possessing the above essentials is a hundred per cent better than one trained by brutality. The first dog will work for you with perfect happiness and reliability, whereas the second dog works out of sheer fear of his trainer, resulting very often in the treacherous

Photo]   *[Sport and General.*

HELPING THE BLIND.

Mr. J. H. Burt, the first owner of an Alsatian trained to help the blind, is seen holding on to the special harness that has been devised for this particular purpose, so that the unseeing man is sensitive to the very slightest movement on the part of the dog and therefore able to sense what the dog is thinking.

type, especially when out of sight of the trainer.

Before actually commencing to train your dog it is essential that you study his temperament and peculiarities, make a pal of him and let him know that you are his best friend, by having an understanding between you, thus instilling confidence.

In training an Alsatian it is accepted as a fact that very seldom are mistakes made by the dog himself; in nearly all cases it is found that the mistakes are made by the trainer through the lack of patience, neglecting errors, etc., but if your dog is trained correctly you will find that he very seldom makes mistakes. When he does, immediately punish him by slightly smacking him, just hard enough to make him understand he has erred, or by scolding him in harsh tones, but under no circumstances must you be brutal, kicking him or using a stick. Also never smack your dog on his head (ears). One of the best ways to show him you are annoyed is by speaking to him sharply.

In view of the fact that the Alsatian is exceedingly sensitive and has a wonderful hearing, never shout your words of command.

Here are some very important things you must not do. Never give him a meal before training, never play with him during training, never hurry your exercises. The trainer who commences should go through to the end of the training himself, and never let another party take over.

When your dog has done his exercise correctly, it is always wise to use kind words to him, such as "good boy", also give him a tit-bit; this at once conveys to the dog that he has done the right thing. Patting a dog and kindness mean a great deal. In your words of command always select simple words of command, such as "sit", "lie", "place", "fetch", etc. etc., and never try to train your dog another exercise until he can do the last exercise correctly.

If you carry out these instructions, and use the methods already written, you will find training a very interesting and fascinating business, on which when completed you will look back with pleasure and feel very proud of your dog when taking him out.

Now that you have decided and selected a suitable place for your dog in your house (or kennel), take him and show him his new quarters, at the same time giving the word of command, "place", simultaneously gently press him down and repeat this exercise until the dog understands. Each time, as soon as you have got the dog down in his place, walk away from him, all the time facing him, and when he attempts to move again

Photo]   *[Sport and General.*

THE COMPETITIVE SPIRIT.

The Alsatian breeders are so interested in the training of dogs that it has become usual to run inter-area matches. Here is the winning team which won with a margin of fifteen and a half points, together with the Cup thus obtained, when in 1933 the South of England beat the North of England.

"Musket"

F T DAWS. /30

THE BASSET HOUND.

The characteristics of the Basset head—the drooping lower eyelid typical of the Hound family, the large ears and the flews—are strikingly depicted in this handsome plate, painted by one of our leading animal artists, F. T. Daws. It is a study from life of "Musket", an outstanding member of the noted Walhampton Pack.

repeat your word of command, "place". A little patience here is required.

Now that your dog has a name and understands where his "place" (or sleeping accommodation) is, call him by his name and introduce his collar and leash by placing this on him and taking him out for a walk and teaching him to walk at heel. In this exercise it is best to use a short lead, always walking your dog on your left. At first he will most likely drag behind or pull in front, but he will soon get tired of this and no doubt be very glad to walk peacefully alongside you. Each time the dog drags or pulls, check by giving the lead a sharp pull, each time commanding him to heel correctly, always seeing that his head is just in front of your left leg, that is, his body should be in line with your body.

"Rola v. Haus Schutting" is the type of Alsatian matron likely to breed the finest stock. Attention is drawn to the body shape and the general expression shown by her. She is owned by Major J. Y. Baldwin, D.S.O.

Your dog being able to walk out at heel with you, your next exercise is to train him to stop. This is a simple exercise, and all you have to do is to take him out walking and suddenly stop yourself, giving the dog a sharp pull on the lead, at the same time commanding "stop". Repeat this exercise until the dog will obey.

We now come to the "sit" exercise. Place the dog in front of you standing up, hold his head with one hand and press down his loins with the other hand, at the same time giving him the command "sit". When he is sitting, slowly walk away from him (facing him all the time) and command "stay". If he moves, repeat the exercise, until accomplished. This is a very trying exercise, in which a great deal of patience is required. Do not attempt any other training; let the dog understand one exercise at a time, and each day as you advance take him through the previous exercises to which you have accustomed him.

The "lie down" exercise comes next; it is most important that you use the words "lie down" very distinctly when commanding the dog to do so. In this exercise you get your dog on the "sit" position in front of your-

self, then place your hand on his neck, press slowly, at the same time pulling out his legs in front; repeat this two or three times and you will discover that the dog soon begins to understand what you desire of him.

The next exercise is what is known as the "recall". This is a very important command. Take the animal out on a long training lead, send

"Dominant of Picardy", also the property of Major J. Y. Baldwin shows the type of Alsatian that is wanted the world over, combining agility with strength and body fitness. The Picardy kennels are well known.

By courtesy of]　　　　　　　　　　　　　　　　　　　　　[Arnold Brotherton, Esq.

HOW TO TRAIN ALSATIANS.

On this page are specially taken photographs of Mr. Arnold Brotherton, the founder of the Northern Alsatian Club, putting his dog through a course of training.　Above photos are *Left :* At Heel.　*Centre :* Through the Hoop.　*Right :* The Recall.　All the exercises are described in the accompanying article.

him away from you in any direction he likes, and give the command "halt".　Then call him (name and "heel"), and as soon as the dog obeys you, make him sit down in front of you, give him a tit-bit and pat him.　Should the dog not obey your command, repeat, and on the word of command "come", or "halt", pull the lead sharply at the time your command is being given ; bring the dog and make him "sit" in front of you. where he must remain until you have given another command such as "heel".　The dog should then go to your left side and sit there until you are ready to walk away.　Another good method to "recall" is to throw a dumb-bell or ball, call him back and allow him to keep the dumb-bell or ball in his mouth until you take it from him ; but on every occasion the dog is recalled he must always "sit" in front of you waiting further orders

To train a dog to jump, one of the best methods is to place a stick or board between your doorway or gate, place the dog on the other side and give the word "jump" or "hop", at the same time giving him help with the lead.　Do not make the jump too high, just high enough for him to leap over with comfort.　When you have trained him to obey your command you can increase the

jump, but never allow him to take very high jumps, as the landing may prove fatal.

To "guard" is a necessity.　A simple way is to keep the dog in the house at night quietly, get a friend to approach the house loud enough for the dog to take notice, then encourage your dog to "fetch-em" until he barks.

One of the most important exercises is the 'refusal of food" and "picking up" food.　A dog should never be allowed to take food from strangers or pick up food in the street or field, or any other place but at home.　Walk the dog out in the ordinary way, meet a friend and let him offer the dog a tit-bit ; immediately the dog attempts to take it command him, "don't touch", and pull him away.　Let him have another tempting offer from your friend, and if the dog again attempts to, scold him.　Repeat this.

"Picking up" food, etc.　Get some tempting pieces of raw meat, stuff them with mustard or any strong sauce, place one piece on the floor, then take your dog out casually until he attempts to pick up the meat. When he has got a mouthful and tasted the mustard, scold him and smack him gently until he will refuse to lock at anything other than what is given to him.

Pho'o]　　　　　　　　　　[S. & G.
FINDING BY SCENT.

Photo]　　　　　　　　　　[S. & G.
OVER THE HURDLES.

Photo] TWO FAMOUS DOGS IN FAMOUS SURROUNDINGS. [*Harris.*

The Alsatian is the popular dog of the world and can be found in homes of all kinds.   Here we see "Monch" and "Mars of Waterston,"
two Alsatians, the property of Major Carter, A.D.C. to Sir William Marshall in Mesopotamia, at the well-known house
"Waterston Manor", which was the setting of Thomas Hardy's famous novel *Far from the Madding Crowd* (the home of Bathsheba).

Alteratives are chemical and vegetable substances which appear to increase the efficiency of the various organs of the body, thus tending to check sluggishness and probably aid the expulsion of poisonous products through the normal channels. No precise description can be given of the manner in which they affect tissue changes, but definite results have nevertheless been observed to follow their discreet administration. Nitrate of potash, calcium sulphide, antimony sulphide, flowers of sulphur, and ginger are among those which have been commonly prescribed. Dogs looking poor, out of coat and condition, or debilitated after severe illnesses, etc., are those to which alterative mixtures are generally given.

Amaurosis.—(*See* BLINDNESS.)

Amputation.—The surgical severance from the body of a limb or part of a limb is not infrequently performed on dogs in order that the animal may not only retain its good health but may even remain alive. Amputation is the last resort of the surgeon when he finds, in consequence of severe accidents, that the injury to bones or tissues is so extensive and complete that there is no hope whatever of ultimate healing. After compound comminuted fractures, or severe burns, gangrene is not rarely a sequel, and apart from the hopelessness of retaining a useful leg, there may be danger of a further spread of gangrene in an upward direction. The surgeon attending the case must be the sole arbiter of what should be the best and safest course to adopt, and if the constitutional symptoms are such as give cause for anxiety, he may then advise amputation of all the dead and crushed portions, in order to save as much as possible of the remainder. Occasionally amputation becomes a necessity in consequence of frost-bite, cancer, or blood-poisoning.

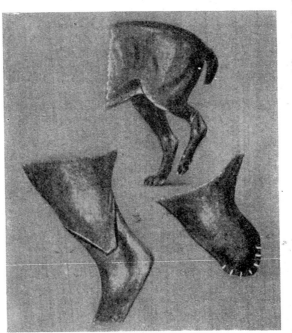

From Hobday's "Surgical Diseases of the Dog and Cat".]
[By courtesy of Messrs. Baillière, Tindall & Cox

Diagrams showing a fractured leg, the flap incision and the sutured flap after amputation

Owners of dogs are often very repugnant at first to the idea of amputation, but dogs so readily adapt themselves to running on three legs that one generally finds such owners are ultimately grateful for an operation which permitted them to retain their dog alive and happy. Furthermore, valuable breeding animals may often remain quite useful for that purpose.

Anaemia.—A condition in which the blood is deficient either in quantity or quality.

CAUSES.—A general quantitative deficiency may be due to an accident or to an operation entailing loss of blood, whilst local anaemia may arise from the interference of the passage of blood to some particular part or organ through the pressure of a growth, or some other mechanical obstruction; or from an alteration of the balance of blood pressure, as may be observed when animals (suffering from abdominal ascites) have large quantities of fluid withdrawn. A localized anaemia of the brain results. Nutritional diseases, or those entailing great wasting and debility, starvation, or exhaustive demands on stud dogs or brood bitches, are usually responsible for alteration of the quality of the blood.

SYMPTOMS.—When an excessive quantity of blood has been lost, the dog loses control of his balance his mucous membranes are exceedingly pale and his pulse is thin, rapid and weak. There will be a general lassitude or lack of energy. An increased rapidity of respiration will be noted upon the least exertion, and to walk upstairs will sometimes cause a good deal of respiratory distress.

TREATMENT.—The first thing to be done is to ascertain, if possible, the cause of the malady, because to remove the cause is better than to apply palliatives. If the origin of the attack is a mystery, one must then adopt measures which are known to increase the quality or quantity of blood. First and foremost is the affordance of a liberal supply of the most valuable foods, taking care that the complete diet shall be a mixture which includes all or most of the known vitamins. Raw meat, raw milk, a portion of biscuit, and a teaspoonful of cod-liver oil and of liquid extract of malt should be given daily, whilst warmth, ventilation, a maximum of sunlight, faultless hygiene, and avoidance of constipation are absolutely essential adjuvants. As for medicinal measures, the most favoured is the internal administration of some iron salt, either alone or in combination with other salts.

Anaesthesia.—Anaesthesia is the artificially induced loss of sensibility, or a localized loss of sensation. There is general anaesthesia and local anaesthesia. It is of passing interest to learn that anaesthetics were practically unheard of before the year 1800, and when one considers that no veterinary surgeon in these days would contemplate any but the most trivial operation without invoking the aid of some kind of numbing agent, it must be a source of wonderment as to what happened to afflicted humans and animals alike prior to A.D. 1800. In reality, it often would be physically impossible to perform many of the painful operations upon highly strung or vicious animals which to-day are painlessly performed, and with the utmost confidence and ease of mind. It is perhaps more surprising to know that the general use of chloroform or ether dates back only thirty-five years Such a routine measure has its use now become, that an Act of Parliament was passed in 1919 making it illegal for certain specified operations to be undertaken without

Photo]   [*Harris.*

AT KNOWLE MANOR.
A delightful picture of Lady Sackville with her Alsatian Dog in the grounds of Knowle Manor, the historic
and picturesque family seat in Kent.

the prior application of general or local anaesthetics. (*See* ANIMALS (ANAESTHETICS) ACT (1919).)

The veterinary profession, however, needed no coercion in this matter, as they were among the first to realize the extreme value of such agents ; for not only was the patient unperturbed, mentally and physically, but its insensible and immobile state rendered possible, as nothing else could, the performance of the most intricate and daring operations requiring a high degree of skill.

GENERAL ANAESTHESIA is considered requisite when the proposed operation is likely to be very painful, protracted or extensive, or when absolute immobility is of paramount importance. The agent most frequently employed is chloroform, which dogs can tolerate very well. Where there are evidences of heart disease, however, it is generally wiser to administer either pure ether or A.C.E. mixture. The latter is a mixture of absolute alcohol 1 part, chloroform 2 parts, and ether 3 parts. Recently, some veterinary surgeons have reported very favourably upon a method in which oxygen gas is driven through chloroform.

When dogs receive a hypodermic injection of morphia about half an hour prior to the application of the chloroform mask, it is found that they need considerably less chloroform to induce surgical anaesthesia. Morphia must not, however, be administered if any septic process is in evidence. In some cases the morphia injection produces such a deep narcosis that it is deemed advisable to dispense with chloroform inhalations, and the operation may be conducted with equal facility and less risk.

Chloroform anaesthesia progresses in three stages, commencing with excitability, when the animal sometimes attempts to yelp and struggles violently. This is followed by a stage of depression, when it merely whimpers and quivers, though still conscious to any painful external stimulus, such as pricking the legs or pinching the toes. Finally, complete unconsciousness supervenes, as evinced by an absence of all reflexes and complete relaxation of all voluntary muscles.

In unfortunate instances, there may be a fourth or paralytic stage, when not only are all voluntary muscles paralysed, but involuntary muscles become similarly affected. One alludes here to the heart and respiratory muscles, and frequently there is no premonitory sign that such is about to happen. In some cases, however, a careful observer would have noted that respiration had become weaker and more rapid.

During the last year or two new additions have been added to the list of general anaesthetics, notably avertin and nembutal. They possess a very distinct advantage over inhalation methods in that avertin is administered per rectum, and nembutal per os. The use of a mask over the face is thus avoided, and very obviously this is of considerable importance in those instances where the operation is to be performed on the face or in the mouth. Avertin, injected per rectum, will produce complete anaesthesia in about seven minutes, which endures approximately two to three hours. Nembutal is administered by the mouth, and in the case of really vicious dogs it can be concealed in a piece of meat, and a very satisfactory deep narcosis, if not complete anaesthesia, may be produced in about one hour. The very great advantage pertaining to the use of either of these drugs is that there is an entire absence of apprehension on the part of the patient.

LOCAL ANAESTHESIA means the insensibility to pain in local areas, and may be induced in a variety of ways. Freezing a part, by spraying it with ether vapour, or ethyl chloride, will rob it of all sensation, and is a method sometimes employed for the opening of serous abscesses on the ear flap.

Local anaesthesia may be accomplished by the subcutaneous injection of a solution of cocaine around the area to be operated upon, or directly over the nerves supplying that area. Owing to the toxic nature of cocaine, however, this drug has largely been supplanted by chemical substitutes such as novocaine, eucaine, stovaine, and many others. Novocaine is an excellent substitute, having only one-third the toxicity of cocaine and inducing complete anaesthesia in two or three minutes, which lasts about an hour. Cocaine is still the most effective substance for instilling into the eye, as it exerts absolutely no preliminary irritation of mucous membranes.

There are some instances in which it would be highly dangerous to administer a general anaesthetic, and yet an operation is imperative. In these cases it is surprising what an extreme degree of anaesthesia of large areas can be produced by the injection of local anaesthetics at carefully selected points. For instance, spinal anaesthesia is now being largely adopted for certain cases, the principle of which consists in the injection of anaesthetic solutions directly into the spinal canal. The effect is to paralyse all sensation in those parts which derive their nerve supply posterior to the point of injection. It is possible, therefore, to rob an animal of all sensation in its hind legs, loins, pelvis and abdomen generally, whilst retaining full consciousness. Abdominal operations, leg or tail amputations, or operations connected with dystokia (difficult labour) may all be undertaken under spinal anaesthesia. The method has so far mostly been carried out in cattle practice, and has not as yet received much attention by canine surgeons.

For partial anaesthesia of the gastric mucous membrane, for the subjection of continuous vomiting, or to prevent a dog from throwing up worm pills or other medicine, a number of substances are available, chief perhaps among them being chloretone, anaesthesin, cocaine, ice, etc., whilst orthoform and those just mentioned may all be applied to painful surface wounds either as powders or liquids (except ice) to afford an animal relief.

Yet another extremely important use for local anaesthetics is the diagnosis of lameness. One can at least ascertain the seat of the pain by paralysing the sensory nerve fibres supplying discrete areas. For example, if injections about the wrist fail to prevent lameness, then obviously the pain arises above that point, and so forth.

Anal Irritation.—Dogs very frequently are observed to bite at the base of the tail or to rub the anus along the ground and, in acute cases, to turn sharply, cry out, or run away.

CAUSES.—Many people are misled by these antics into believing that the dog is affected with worms. It, in fact, may be so affected. But not infrequently the whole trouble arises from occlusion of the ducts which lead from the anal glands to the outer surface on either side of the anal opening.

Sometimes it is due to actual inflammation of these glands, and, more rarely, to the caking of faeces and hair about the anus, owing to negligence on the

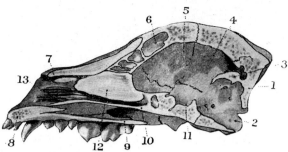

THE SKULL (A LONGITUDINAL SECTION).

The skull is composed of two parts, the cranium (containing the brain) and the framework of the face. It is of interest to note that there are cavities filled only with air, as No. 6 in the diagram. 1. Occipital bone. 2. Foramen magnum, connecting the cranial cavity with the spinal canal. 3. Osseum tentorium. 4 and 5. Cranial cavity for reception of brain. 6. Frontal sinus. 7. Nasal bone. 8. Premaxillary bone. 9. Palatal bone. 10. Vomer, which assists in separation of the two nasal cavities. 11. Nasal septum, separating the two nasal cavities. 12. Turbinate bones, consisting of delicate scrolls of bony tissue. These bones are covered by a vascular mucous membrane, over which the inspired air passes and so becomes warmed and moistened.

This and succeeding diagrams from "Baillière's Atlas of the Dog," by courtesy of Messrs. Baillière, Tindall & Cox.

part of both dog and owner to see that the region is kept clean.

SYMPTOMS.—When trouble arises from the latter cause a very tender condition is set up, resulting sometimes in ulceration of the whole area, stoppage of the bowels, great distress of the dog, and unpleasant odours for the annoyance of the owner. When the ducts have become blocked or the glands are inflamed, an abscess often ensues which causes the part to swell considerably and gives rise to great pain.

TREATMENT of any condition affecting this region is safer left in the hands of a veterinary surgeon, as the dog is always exceedingly "touchy" and often vicious, whilst a decision must be made as to the primary seat of the trouble. Possibly the glands require emptying of their odorous and inspissated contents, by the application of lateral pressure between finger and thumb. Or an abscess may require lancing, and great care must be exercised in its performance lest the "anal ring" might be injured, or a fistula set up. Constipation should be countered, and a local anaesthetic applied to the inflamed area.

Motile segments of tapeworms, and worms of the round variety getting into the rectum, will set up an itching, to allay which, of course, the obvious remedy is a saline lavage and the administration of a vermifuge.

Anal pruritus (itching) of unknown origin will frequently yield to exposure to ultra-violet irradiation.

Anasarca.—A generalized dropsical condition of the body, or, in other words, an accumulation of serous fluid in the cellular tissues of the body. It is due usually to defective action of the heart or kidneys

Anatomy is the study or description of the structure of the organized body. For the purpose of this work it is unnecessary to give more than a brief description of the parts which collectively form the body of the dog.

First there is a *skeleton* or bony framework composed of the skull; vertebral column (7 bones); backbone divided into dorsal vertebrae (13 bones), and lumbar vertebrae (7 bones); the sacrum (3 bones); the tail (20 vertebrae); the ribs (13 pair); the pelvic skeleton composed of three fused bones

known as ileum, ischium and pubis, on either side of the pelvic cavity, which again is bounded superiorly by the bony sacrum; the two fore limbs, each composed of 30 bones. Of this number, 7 bones are in the wrist or carpus, 5 in the metacarpus, and 14 in the toes or digits. Finally, there are two hind limbs each consisting of 32 bones, 7 of which belong to the hock or ankle. The two extra bones in each hind leg are known as fabellae, and are situated just behind the lower end of the femur.

THE MUSCULAR SYSTEM, imposed upon the skeleton, is a very intricate and cunningly arranged mass of fleshy or muscular fibres which render movement of every kind a practical possibility.

THE NERVOUS SYSTEM, equally complicated, is the controlling force of every movement or function of the entire body. It is made up of the brain and spinal cord, and all the countless nerves running from them to more distant regions of the body. The senses of smell or of touch, sight or taste, are impulses carried via the sensory or afferent nerves to the brain. As a result of the receipt of such impulses, other impulses are sent via the motor or efferent nerves to the limbs and their muscles and to any other tissues concerned. For instance, the application of heat to the foot would cause a sensation to be conveyed to the brain which, in a fraction of time, issues other impulses designed to direct the withdrawal of that foot, or even of the whole body, away from the danger. Thus we see that whilst one set of nerve fibres is concerned solely with muscular activity, another set is allocated exclusively to the conveyance of sensation. There is yet another set, known as the sympathetic nervous system, which functions in regulating the blood supply to the internal organs. This is accomplished by contracting or dilating the blood-vessels supplying these organs, and it is not a function which is under the control of the animal.

The brain is divided into two main parts, viz. cerebrum and cerebellum. The former is by far the larger portion and is concerned mainly in the control of the various organs of the body. The cerebellum, situated immediately behind the cerebrum, is a comparatively small mass of nerve tissue having an important association with balance or the equilibrium of the body.

THE CIRCULATORY SYSTEM is made up of the heart, the anterior and posterior aortae, the arteries, and the veins. This mechanism is charged with the duty of supplying fresh oxygenated blood to every part of the body, in order that the muscles and organs may be

THE SKULL (FROM ABOVE NOS. 1-10 AND BELOW NOS. 11-22). 1 The occipital bone. 2. Interparietal bone. 3. Parietal bone. 4. Squamous temporal. 4A. Zygomatic process of same. 5. Frontal bone. 6 Malar bone 6A. Frontal process of same. 7. Lachrymal. 8. Nasal. 9. Maxilla. 10. Premaxilla. 11. Foramen magnum. 12. Paramastoid bone. 13. Occipital condyle. 14. Tympanic portion of temporal bone. 15. Post glenoid process. 16. Glenoid cavity. 17. Palate bone. 18. Incisor teeth. 19. Canine tooth. 20. Premolar teeth. 21. Anterior palatine foramen 22. Molar teeth

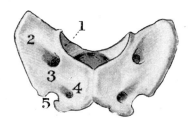

THE ATLAS; THE FIRST BONE OF THE VERTEBRAL COLUMN, ON WHICH THE SKULL PIVOTS (SEEN FROM ABOVE).
1. Articular surface for axis. 2. Wing. 3. Postero-inferior foramen, or transverse foramen. 4. Intervertebral foramen. 5. Intervertebral notch.

nourished and oxygenated continuously. Blood circulation is accomplished in a very wonderful way, and following is a short account of the mechanism.

The heart is, of course, the motive power which is maintained day and night so long as the animal lives. Should the heart cease to pump, then life becomes at once extinct. This vitally important organ is divided, for purposes of description, into four cavities, viz. left ventricle, left auricle, right ventricle and right auricle. Between the auricle and ventricle on the left side are membraneous valves which at once close if any pressure is exerted from a ventricular direction. In other words, blood can pass from an auricle into a ventricle, but not vice versa. A similar anatomy exists on the right side of the heart. It must next be explained that veins are the vessels which collect up used blood from every organ and part of the body (except those in the thorax), and the direction of the dark or venous blood flowing through them is always towards the heart. Minute veins merge into larger ones, and finally all merge into the great vena cava. The latter

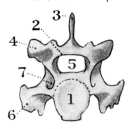

THE SIXTH CERVICAL (OR NECK) VERTEBRA, FROM BEHIND.
1. Posterior articular surface. 2. Dorsal arch. 3. Spinous process. 4. Articular process. 5. Spinal canal. 6. Wing. 7. Vertebral foramen.

leads into the right auricle of the heart, which, having become filled, contracts and drives the blood into the right ventricle. The closure of a valve prevents the blood from returning the same way that it has come. The right ventricle then contracts, the force of which causes the closure of the right auriculo-ventricular valve, and the blood is propelled through the pulmonary artery to the lungs. Here the pulmonary artery ramifies in all directions, finally to form a minute network of vessels which are very closely adjacent with the air cells of the lungs and through the walls of which there is a free interchange of gases. The poisonous products

and gases collected by the blood from distant parts of the body are exchanged in the lungs for pure oxygen which has been inhaled. Thus the dark, impure, or venous blood which has been driven into the lungs becomes cleansed and takes on a bright red hue. The force always following up behind, causes it to continue on through the capillary vessels until, by converging up with others, they become larger and larger and finally become the pulmonary veins, which lead directly into the left auricle of the heart. From here the pure blood is expelled into the left ventricle, which, in turn, forces it into the anterior and the posterior aorta respectively. The anterior aorta conveys it to all parts of the head and neck, whilst the posterior aorta distributes it to the rest of the body.

Again, the arteries become smaller arterioles, arterioles become minute capillaries, capillaries become veins and the whole process is repeated continuously throughout life.

Blood, returning via veins from the digestive organs, not only contains some waste and poisonous products, but also the assimilable food abstracted from the intestines. These veins merge into the big portal vein, which conducts its blood through the entire liver substance, during its passage in which much of its food content is left behind to be dealt with and stored by that organ for the future needs of the body.

THE LYMPHATIC SYSTEM is a network of canals containing a watery fluid known as lymph, the purpose of which is to supply moisture and nourishment to all the cells of the body and to collect from them the products of combustion. The latter, together with fat globules abstracted from the contents of the small intestine, are eventually emptied into the general blood-stream.

If septic or toxic material gain access to the body from an external source, it is at once taken up by the lymph stream and eventually becomes caught up in the nearest lymphatic gland, resulting in a painful swelling.

THE RESPIRATORY SYSTEM comprises the

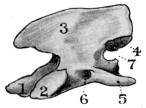

THE AXIS (LEFT LATERAL VIEW); THE SECOND OF THE CERVICAL VERTEBRAE ADJOINING THE ATLAS.
1. Odontoid process. 2. Articular surface for atlas. 3. The spine. 4. Posterior articular process. 5. Transverse process. 6. Transverse foramen. 7. Posterior opening of body, or centrum.

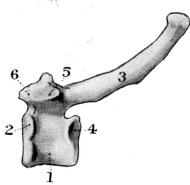

SIDE VIEW OF A THORACIC OR DORSAL VERTEBRA OF WHICH THERE ARE THIRTEEN FORMING THE MAIN PORTION OF THE SPINE.
1. Body. 2. Facet for head of rib. 3. Spinous process. 4. Facet for head of next rib. 5. Facet for tubercle of rib. 6. Transverse process.

A SIDE VIEW OF ONE OF SEVEN CERVICAL VERTEBRAE.
1. Posterior articular surface. 2. Body of the vertebra. 3. Spinous process. 4. Articular surface. 5. Articular facet. 6. Ventral plate. 7. Vertebral foramen.

LEFT SIDE OF A LUMBAR VERTEBRA; THE LUMBARS ARE BETWEEN THE RIBS AND THE PELVIS.
1. Posterior articular surface. 2. Posterior articular process. 3. Spinous process. 4. Anterior articular process. 5. Transverse process.

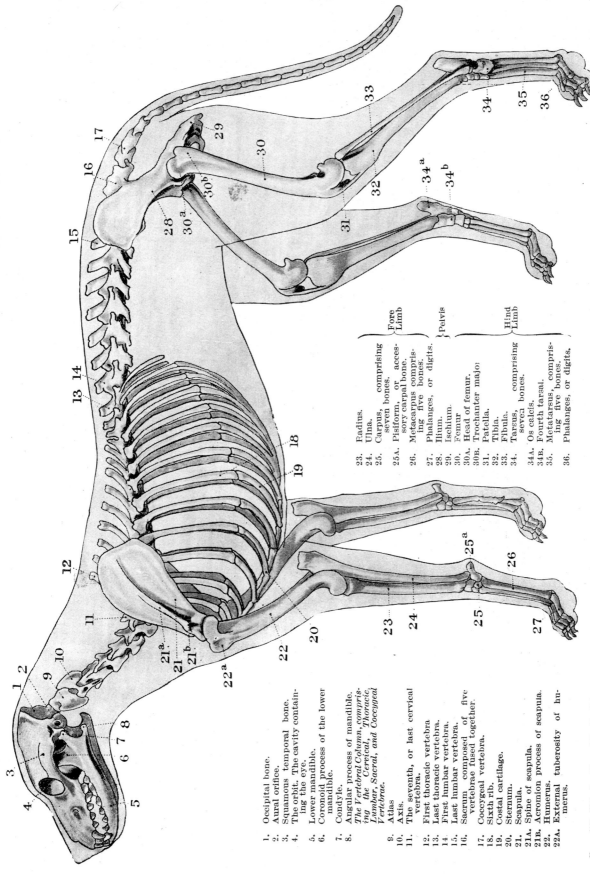

1. Occipital bone.
2. Aural orifice.
3. Squamous temporal bone.
4. The orbit. The cavity containing the eye.
5. Lower mandible.
6. Coronoid process of the lower mandible.
7. Condyle.
8. Angular process of mandible.
 The Vertebral Column, comprising the Cervical, Thoracic, Lumbar, Sacral, and Coccygeal Vertebrae.
9. Atlas
10. Axis.
11. The seventh, or last cervical vertebra.
12. First thoracic vertebra.
13. Last thoracic vertebra.
14. First lumbar vertebra.
15. Last lumbar vertebra.
16. Sacrum composed of five vertebrae fused together.
17. Coccygeal vertebra.
18. Sixth rib.
19. Costal cartilage.
20. Sternum.
21. Scapula.
21A. Spine of scapula.
21B. Acromion process of scapula.
22. Humerus.
22A. External tuberosity of humerus.

23. Radius.
24. Ulna.
25. Carpus, comprising seven bones,
25A. Pisiform, or accessory carpal bone.
26. Metacarpus comprising five bones.
27. Phalanges, or digits. } Fore Limb
28. Ilium.
29. Ischium.
30. Femur. } Pelvis
30A. Head of femur.
30B. Trochanter major.
31. Patella.
32. Tibia.
33. Fibula.
34. Tarsus, comprising seven bones.
34A. Os calcis.
34B. Fourth tarsal.
35. Metatarsus, comprising five bones.
36. Phalanges, or digits, } Hind Limb

From "Bailliere's Atlas of the Dog".]

SKELETON OF A DOG.

[*By courtesy of Messrs. Bailliere, Tindall & Cox.*

The official description of a skeleton is "the bony and cartilaginous framework upon which the soft tissues of the animal body are built". In this lateral view of the skeleton of a dog it is interesting to compare the formation of the bones with those of a man ; the differences are due to the altered distribution of weight of the internal organs when an animal walks upon four feet instead of two.

nostrils, pharynx, larynx, trachea, bronchi, and lungs, through which, during inspiration, air is drawn into the lungs, and expelled during expiration, but in a reverse direction.

As has already been explained, the object of respiration is to supply the blood stream with oxygen, and to remove therefrom the carbon dioxide and other deleterious substances created by the continuous breaking down or combustion of the body tissues. The air so inhaled is filtered and warmed as it passes along the respiratory channels, but it is still further warmed and charged with moisture when exhaled.

Respiration is a muscular effort requiring the assistance of a number of muscles, notably the intercostals, abdominals, and diaphragm. It is by the synchronous contraction of these muscles that the chest cavity is increased in capacity on account of the outward expansion of its walls. Since the thoracic or chest cavity is a vacuum, any increase in ts cubic capacity means that the lungs must follow, and air is drawn in. Air is expelled again by the chest wall and dia-

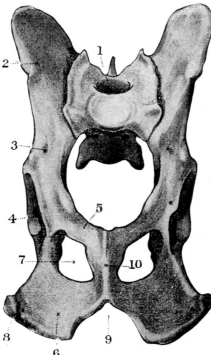

THE PELVIS: A KIND OF 'FRAMEWORK'', MADE UP OF THE FUSION OF SEVERAL BONES AND CONTAINING THE BLADDER, RECTUM, AND OTHER ORGANS WITHIN ITS CAVITY.

1. Body of Sacrum. 2. Ilium. 3. Depression for insertion of rectus femoris muscle. 4. Acetabulum. 5. Pubis. 6. Ischium. 7. Obturator foramen. 8. Tuberosity of ischium. 9. Ischial arch. 10. Symphysis, or line of union of the two hip-bones.

THE EXCRETORY SYSTEM.—The lungs, skin, kidneys, and bowels are the four channels by which waste products are eliminated from the body. So far as the skin is concerned in dogs, sweat glands are not numerous, and perspiration therefore is negligible from their bodies, but they do sweat from the pads of the feet. They make up for this disability by exhaling a great quantity of carbonic-acid gas and soluble poisonous products in the vapour of their respirations. This explains why the dog's mouth is wide open, his tongue hanging out, and his respirations so markedly increased upon exertion. He makes full use too of the kidneys as a channel of elimination, for he seems to miss no opportunity of emptying his bladder in any circumstances.

The bowels, of course, carry off all the insoluble and indigestible fibrous portions of his food, and to speed up this process occasionally is most salutary to health.

THE REPRODUCTIVE SYSTEM consists of testicles, vas deferens, penis, and urethra in the male, and ovaries, fallopian tubes, uterus, and vagina in the female. The two testicles are suspended in a bag known as the scrotum; and the vas deferens is a fine tube which conveys

phragm resuming their former position, thus decreasing the thoracic capacity.

THE DIGESTIVE SYSTEM. —In addition to the mouth, pharynx, gullet, stomach, and bowels, there are other very important organs concerned in the process of digestion. These are teeth, tongue, salivary glands, liver and pancreas. Other organs concerned with digestive processes belong to the excretory system. For a description of the process of digestion, see under that heading.

semen from each testicle into the urethra. The latter is the tubular passage through which urine travels from the bladder, via the penis, to the exterior. The penis is the copulatory organ, which, for the act of coitus has to be erected. The mechanism of erection entails the engorgement of the organ with blood, which, owing to closure of venous valves, is unable to leave. Erection, in the dog, is considerably aided by the normal presence of a long narrow bone in the substance of the penis, known as the os penis.

The female ovaries are two

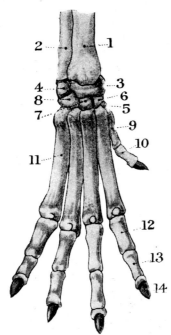

THE CARPUS, OR WRIST; THIS CONSISTS OF SEVEN BONES TO WHICH THE DIGITS ARE AFFIXED.

1. Radius. 2. Ulna. 3. Radial carpal bone (scaphoid). 4. Ulnar carpal bone (semilunar). 5 First carpal. 6. Second carpal. 7. Third carpal. 8. Fourth carpal. 9 and 10. The pollux, or thumb. 11. Metacarpal. 12. First phalanx of the digit. 13. Second phalanx of the digit. 14. Third phalanx of the digit.

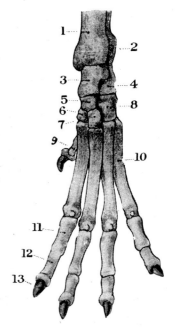

THE TARSUS OR HOCK-JOINT, COMPRISING SEVEN BONES AND CORRESPONDING TO THE HUMAN ANKLE.

1. Tibia. 2. Fibula. 3. Tibial tarsal bone. 4. Fibular tarsal bone. 5. Central tarsal. 6. Second tarsal. 7. Third tarsal. 8. Fourth tarsal. 9. Vestigial phalanx (dew claw). 10. Metatarsal. 11. First phalanx. 12. Second phalanx. 13. Third phalanx.

small ovoid bodies one on either side, and situated close behind the corresponding kidney. There is a connection between each ovary and the uterine horn, on the same side, known as the fallopian tube, and it is along this fine membranous tube that the ripened eggs travel to the womb. The uterus of the bitch is composed of three parts—a body and two horns, the former being short and stumpy and the latter long and narrow. It is in one or both of these horns that the foetuses develop during pregnancy. Posteriorly, the uterine body adjoins the vagina, between the two being a ring of muscular fibres known as the cervix, or os uteri, which normally remains firmly

a clear fluid known as the "aqueous humour". The posterior chamber contains a clear but more viscous fluid called "vitreous humour", and separating the two chambers is the crystalline lens. The iris is a circular diaphragm of muscle fibres placed anteriorly to the lens, and it has the capacity for contracting or expanding, and thus exposing more or less of the lens through its centre aperture or pupil. Under the influence of strong light the circular fibres of the iris contract and reduce the pupil almost to the size of a pinhead, thus preventing an excess of light from reaching the retina at the back of the eye. In subdued light, on the other hand, the circular fibres relax and the radiating fibres contract, with the result that the pupil is widely opened and a maximum amount of light may be permitted to pass to the

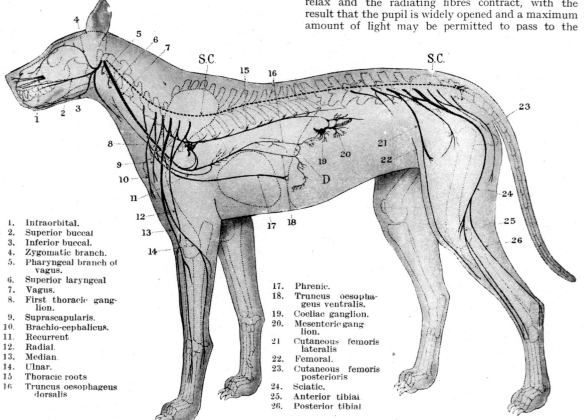

1. Infraorbital.
2. Superior buccal
3. Inferior buccal.
4. Zygomatic branch.
5. Pharyngeal branch of vagus.
6. Superior laryngeal
7. Vagus.
8. First thoracic ganglion.
9. Suprascapularis.
10. Brachio-cephalicus.
11. Recurrent
12. Radial.
13. Median.
14. Ulnar.
15. Thoracic roots
16. Truncus oesophageus dorsalis

17. Phrenic.
18. Truncus oesophageus ventralis.
19. Coeliac ganglion.
20. Mesenteric ganglion.
21. Cutaneous femoris lateralis
22. Femoral.
23. Cutaneous femoris posterioris
24. Sciatic.
25. Anterior tibial
26. Posterior tibial

From 'Bailliere's Atlas of the Dog.'   *[By courtesy of Messrs. Baillière, Tindall & Cox.*

THE NERVOUS SYSTEM WHICH CONTROLS EVERY MOVEMENT AND FUNCTION OF THE BODY.

There are two kinds of nerves—the *sensory* or *afferent*, and the *motor* or *efferent*. The former carry impulses to the brain and control the "five senses": the latter carry impulses outward from the brain to direct the action of the tissues.

closed. The vagina gains access to the exterior at the vulva.

THE SENSORY ORGANS are the eye, nose, ear and tongue. The eye is a highly delicate and specialized organ having a very close attachment with the brain by the optic nerve. Exteriorly it is protected by an upper and lower eyelid, and a third eyelid (known as the haw, or membrana nictitans) which is situated at the inner canthus. All of these move across the eyeball at frequent intervals, to moisten the corneal surface and to remove foreign particles if any are present. The lachrymal gland secretes a fluid which acts as a lubricant for the overlying eyelids.

The eyeball has muscular attachments which permit of its movement in any direction.

The interior of the eyeball is divided into two chambers the anterior and smaller of which contains

interior of the eye. As already mentioned, the optic nerve attaches the eyeball to the brain. The fibres of this nerve terminate anteriorly in the retina, which itself is a layer of nerve tissue, and any impressions received by the retina are transferred to the brain. When the crystalline lens, or the humours, or the glassy corneal surface become, for any reason, opaque, then the image is blurred and eyesight is defective.

The ear is composed of three parts: (a) the cartilaginous external ear, (b) the bony cavity known as the middle ear, and (c) the osseous internal ear closely connected with the brain, to which it transmits sound vibrations via the auditory nerve. The direction of the external ear is downwards and forwards, and the channel in its narrowest portion is curved so that there would be some little difficulty in actually touching the drum or tympanum by the mere act of cleaning out the ear. The drum is a thin membrane which separates the external from the middle ear. Inside the latter are three minute bones which are made to vibrate in consequence of sound waves striking the tympanum. These vibrations are, in turn, transmitted through the fluid of the internal ear, until the nerve impulses are finally picked up by the auditory nerve and impressed upon the brain.

The sense of taste is transmitted to the brain via the fifth and ninth nerves, from groups of nerve endings situated mostly on the tongue surface, but also in various parts of the oral mucous membrane.

Similarly, smells become recognized through stimulation of small olfactory nerve centres situated in the nasal cavities, the sensations being transmitted to the brain via the first or olfactory nerve.

THE TEETH.—A dog has 12 incisor teeth, i.e. three on either side of the mid line in both upper and lower jaws. Next to each outer incisor of both jaws come the large canine teeth, that is to say, one at each corner, making 4 in all. Observing in a backward direction, we next see the premolars, of which a dog has 4 on each side of the upper and lower jaw, making 16. Behind these again are 2 molars on each side of the upper jaw, and 3 each side of the lower jaw, totalling 10 molar teeth. The total number of teeth in an adult dog is therefore 42. The temporary or milk teeth commence erupting at about four weeks of age, and from the age of about four months to seven months these are undergoing gradual substitution by permanent teeth. Permanent dentition is usually complete at about seven months of age.

The two true molars in the upper jaw are not preceded by temporary teeth. The fourth premolar of the upper jaw is the one which is so frequently the cause of "pus in the antrum", for the cure of which extraction of the tooth is the only way. (See also AGE, AND How TO TELL IT.)

THE DUCTLESS GLANDS.—To complete the account of the dog's anatomy we have only now to mention that erstwhile mysterious group of glands styled as "ductless", because no ducts have been discovered in connection with them, designed for the conveyance of their secretions. That they manufacture an internal secretion (or hormone) is undoubted (see HORMONES AND ADRENALS), and it can only be assumed that such products are distributed to other parts of the body via the lymphatic or circulatory systems. The glands under discussion comprise the thyroid, thymus, pituitary, adrenals and spleen. Other glands, such as testicles, ovaries, and mammal, etc., also produce an internal secretion in addition to their external ones, but these will be discussed under the heading of "Hormones".

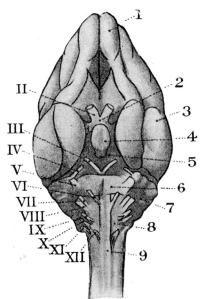

From "Baillière's Atlas of the Dog".]
[By courtesy of Messrs. Baillière, Tindall & Cox.

THE BRAIN AND CRANIAL NERVES.

Being the most important part of the Nervous System, the brain is covered externally by three protective membranes ; in itself it consists of two parts—the Cerebrum, or larger part which controls the organs of the body, and the smaller part, the Cerebellum, which is chiefly concerned with the control of equilibrium. 1. Olfactory bulb. 2. Tuber cinereum. 3. Temporal lobe. 4. Pituitary body. 5. Cerebral peduncle. 6. Pons. 7. Cerebellum. 8. Medulla oblongata. 9. Median fissure and decussation of pyramids. II. Optic nerve. III. Oculomotor. IV. Trochlear. V. Trigeminus. VI. Abducens. VII. Facial. VIII. Auditory. IX. Glosso-pharyngeal. X. Vagus. XI. Spinal accessory. XII. Hypoglossal.

Ancestors and Relatives of the Dog.

—Our records of the evolution of the dog, preserved for us in the form of fossils, leave many gaps yet to be filled ; wherein they compare very unfavourably with the Ungulates, or "hoofed-animals". This is largely explained by the fact that these last lived, as they live now, in herds. Hence they were much more numerous than the animals which preyed on them. And being so much more numerous there were greater chances of their remains being preserved as fossils. Moreover, as at Pikermi, in Greece, large numbers of antelopes, horses, and so on have been dug up, seemingly having been overwhelmed by some great flood, for in a slab of rock at the British Museum of Natural History they can be seen piled one on top of the other.

No such collections of carnivorous animals have ever been found, and for the reasons just stated. But in regard to the dog-tribe, though there are many gaps to be filled, enough fossil material has been preserved for us in these rocks to furnish us with an extremely valuable insight into the early ancestral stages.

We begin the story of what we may call "dogs in the making" with the remains of certain primitive types of animals known to science as "Creodonts". They form the stock which, in due course, gave rise to the carnivores. These creodonts, then, are priceless fossils, for they reveal evidence in this history of the pedigree of the dog which could never have been inferred by the most laborious study of the dogs, wild and domesticated, of to-day.

In this story of the evolution of the dog the teeth play a most important part not only in regard to their number, but also as touching their form. These two items are intimately related to the kind of food which had to be broken up and to the mode of its capture. And in this the dogs have departed less from these ancestral creodonts than the cat-tribe.

The evolution of the dog, as with all other animals, was a slow process, taking millions of years to accomplish. It began to take shape in what the geologists call the Lower and Middle Eocene, both of the Old World and in North America. These forerunners were lowly, carnivorous creatures with a small brain. And as yet they had not developed the "carnassial" teeth just referred to. The dentition, in short, as a whole, resembled that of the flesh-eating marsupials, or pouched animals. Indeed, for many years they were regarded as marsupials. While some were quite small animals, others were as large as lions or bears, and survived in Europe until the beginning of the Miocene period.

When we turn to the Upper Eocene we find the first of the true carnivores, most of them quite small creatures resembling, be it noted, the civet-cats (*Viverridæ*). The civet-cat of to-day has hardly changed since the Upper Eocene

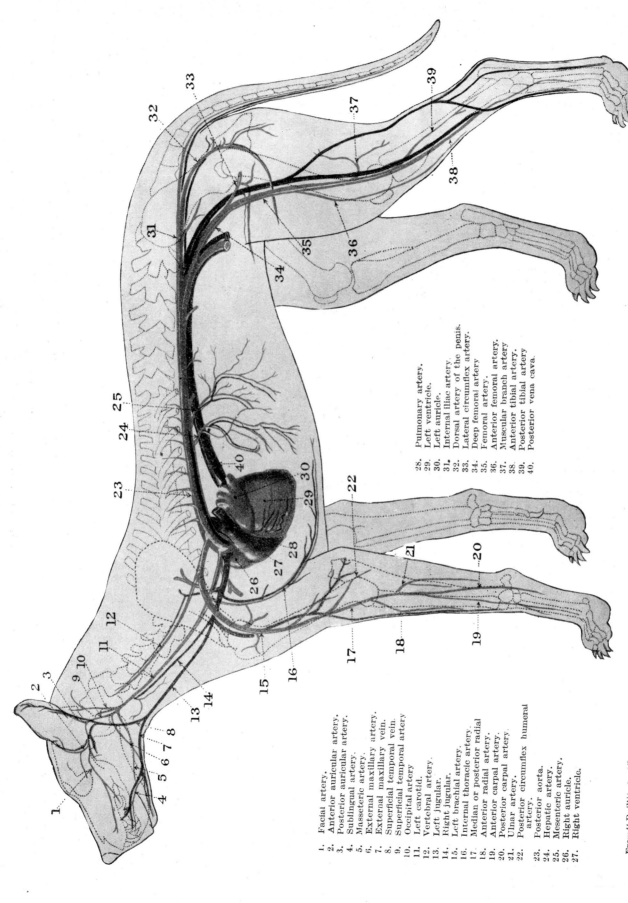

1. Facial artery.
2. Anterior auricular artery.
3. Posterior auricular artery.
4. Sublingual artery.
5. Masseteric artery.
6. External maxillary artery.
7. External maxillary vein.
8. Superficial temporal vein.
9. Superficial temporal artery
10. Occipital artery.
11. Left carotid.
12. Vertebral artery.
13. Left jugular.
14. Right jugular.
15. Left brachial artery.
16. Internal thoracic artery.
17. Median or posterior radial
18. Anterior radial artery.
19. Anterior carpal artery.
20. Posterior carpal artery.
21. Ulnar artery.
22. Posterior circumflex humeral
    artery.
23. Posterior aorta.
24. Hepatic artery.
25. Mesenteric artery.
26. Right auricle.
27. Right ventricle.
28. Pulmonary artery.
29. Left ventricle.
30. Left auricle.
31. Internal iliac artery.
32. Dorsal artery of the penis.
33. Lateral circumflex artery.
34. Deep femoral artery
35. Femoral artery.
36. Anterior femoral artery.
37. Muscular branch artery.
38. Anterior tibial artery.
39. Posterior tibial artery
40. Posterior vena cava.

From "Baillière's Atlas of the Dog".| (*By courtesy of Messrs. Baillière, Tindall & Cox.*

THE VASCULAR OR BLOOD SYSTEM.

This consists of a network of tubes running all over the body, through which the blood is pumped by the heart : it is divided into arteries, capillaries and veins, the last-named returning the "used" blood to the heart for fresh distribution. The blood system fulfils two functions, one being to carry nutritive material to the tissues, the other to carry waste products to the excretory system.

The dog-like hyænas can be traced back to the primitive members of the Family *Viverridæ*, and we find another link between the *Viverridæ* and the *Canidæ* in *Cynodictis*, and allied genera, of the Oligocene, and Upper Eocene of France. It was neither a true civet nor a true dog.

The earliest of these creodonts, it is to be noted, presented many types in the matter of their feeding habits, and this is a most important fact to bear in mind. Some were omnivorous, some insectivorous, and some flesh-eaters. The whole congeries was in a state of flux, ready to specialize along these different lines as occasion offered. And the most important of these forms, in the present connection, was the Family *Miacidæ*, of the Eocene period, from which, undoubtedly, the ancestors of the true carnivora were derived.

Though no complete skeleton of any of these animals has yet been discovered, enough remains have been found to enable us to glean the essential features of this most important and interesting tribe. They were the only members of the creodonts to develop "carnassial", or "shearing-teeth", so conspicuous a feature in the cat- and dog-tribe, and to which reference has already been made. The brain-case was larger than in most of the members of these ancestral types. They had five toes on each foot, but they spread more widely than in the cats and dogs of to-day. The tail was very long and heavy, while the legs were short and also heavy. Moreover, they for the most part walked "flat footed", like a bear, or only partially on the toes, not like the dogs and cats of to-day. Other skeletal peculiarities there were, but these are such as interest the specialist only.

But by the Miocene period wolves, foxes, jackals, and dogs had not only all come into being but they have scarcely changed since.

What agencies determined the rise and development of these several types—the creodonts, civets, hyaenas and bears, and the dogs and cats? The most reasonable explanation seems to be this, that as the numbers of these ancestral types increased, the surplus population spread outwards, into new haunts where the character of the country, and of the food supply, differed. Some, even within the original centre of dispersal, in the competition for food, would, in like manner be

driven to a somewhat different mode of life and choice of food. Their habits, in short, would change, and changes in habit inevitably lead to changes of structure; for they set in motion new stimuli, and the parts affected respond accordingly. Hence the changes in the form of the teeth, the form of the feet, and so on; and even in size. Naturally, such changes are in harmony with the mode of life, for the one shapes the other. Bearing this in mind, the evolution of the different types of wild dog will gain a new interest and a new significance.

The dog-tribe hold an intermediate position between the cat-tribe on the one hand and the bears and their allies on the other.

The wild dogs now living in various parts of the world form a very compact group, closely resembling one another in all their essential structural characters, though presenting conspicuous differences in size and colouration.

The most obvious differences are slight variations in the number of the true molar teeth, which exceed the usual number in the Cape long-eared fox (*Otocyon*) and fall short of it in those strange types *Icticyon* and *Cyon*, to be described presently. There are also slight differences in the number of the toes. Five on the fore-foot and four on the hind are the usual number; but the Cape hunting-dog has only four front toes. The larger species feed on prey which they have chased and killed themselves; the smaller eat garbage, carrion, and insects, as well as fruit and berries, just as did their small fossil ancestors in the days of the creodonts.

Huxley long since divided this group into two parallel series: the Thooids, or wolf-like forms, and the Alopecoids, or fox-like forms. In the former there are large air-sinuses, or cavities in the skull, between the eyes, which are absent in the fox-group, hence their sharper faces. The pupil of the eye is commonly round, when the iris is contracted, in the wolf-group, and vertically elliptical in the fox-group.

The true wolves, the largest members of the tribe, have a wide geographical range, extending over nearly the whole of Europe and Asia, and North America from Greenland to Mexico; but they are not found in South America, or in Africa, where they are replaced by jackals and foxes.

But they are by no means uniform in size and

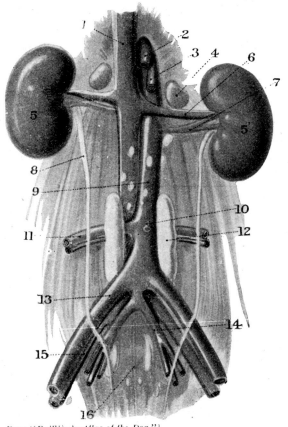

From "Baillière's Atlas of the Dog."
[*By courtesy of Messrs. Baillière, Tindall & Cox*

THE KIDNEYS AND ASSOCIATED STRUCTURES.

The Kidneys lie in the roof of the abdomen, to right and left of the vertebral column; they form an important portion of the excretory system, the other parts of which are the lungs and skin. 1. Posterior vena cava. 2. Hepatic artery. 3. Gastric artery. 4. Suprarenal body. 5 and 5'. Right and left kidney. 6. Renal vein. 7. Renal artery. 8. Ureter. 9. Aorta. 10. Posterior mesenteric artery. 11. Circumflex iliac artery and vein. 12. Mesenteric lymph glands. 13. External iliac artery. 14. Internal iliac artery. 15. External iliac vein. 16. Coccygeal artery

By courtesy of]

NEITHER WOLF NOR FOX.

[*W. P. Pycraft, f Z.S.*

A rare photograph of the Maned-wolf, showing the enormous length of leg and the over-developed ears. Though its habits are little known, wild as it is and avoiding whenever possible all human contacts, the resemblance to the dog family is clear.

Indian Wolf, distinguished by the roundness of his eyes when the iris is contracted, a trait found in several canine tribes.

colouration. This lack of uniformity is of more interest than is apparent at first sight. For it brings home the fact that these superficial characters may change, from various causes, while the more deep-seated structures, like the skeleton, and the digestive and other organs, remain the same in all. Climate and the food supply are important agencies in these changes.

How many different species of wolf there are is a matter of opinion, since what some authorities regard as a distinct species, others call geographical races. But be this as it may, there are at least eight well-marked races, or species. The North American coyote, or prairie-wolf, is one of these ; and the short-legged, and smaller, Japanese wolf is another. The Indian wolf is only slightly smaller than the typical wolf.

The general colouration of the wolf is of a fulvous grey ; white, and occasionally black, specimens are met with. Finally, this animal runs larger, and with longer fur in the colder areas of its range ; and this is especially true of the Thibetan wolves.

The last retreat of wolves in England, where they once abounded, was in the desolate wolds of Yorkshire ; but they seem to have been exterminated during the reign of Henry VII. In Scotland they held their own still longer, the last having been killed in 1680. Their last stronghold was Ireland, where, in Cromwell's time, they were particularly troublesome.

The jackals, which, like the wolf, hunt in packs, and at night, are clearly close allies of the wolf, but are always conspicuously smaller and more brightly coloured. The Common Jackal (*Canis aureus*) range from South-east Europe through South-west Asia to India and Burma, and occur in North Africa, being replaced further south by closely related species.

The origin of our domesticated dogs raises a thorny question as yet undecided. Its early history is lost in the mists of time ; for the dog was one of the first animals to be domesticated by man ; and that subjection began, probably, with Neolithic man, if not earlier. By some the wolf, or the jackal, is held to be the original stock. Others believe it to have originated in the mingling of two or more wild races. But whichever be true, few, if any, other domesticated animals have undergone such an extraordinary amount of variation in size, form and proportions of limbs, ears, and tail as a result of selective breeding by dog-lovers.

It is a moot point as to whether the Australian dog, or Dingo (*q.v.*), should be regarded as a wild dog or as a domesticated race, introduced by the earliest Australian aborigines to enter Australia, and which then became "feral". That is to say, individuals may have escaped, from a by no means perfect control, into the unknown wilds. This seems to be the more likely interpretation, since Australia is the land of marsupials of varied types, and the only doglike member of this stock is the Thylacine, or "Tasmanian wolf". This is curiously dog-like in its general form, but in its colouration, its teeth, and form of reproduction it differs in the strongest possible way from the true dogs, and conforms in every particular with the true marsupials, which stand apart from all other mammals.

The south-east of Asia seems to have formed a second centre of canine evolution, derived, apparently, from the extinct genus *Cynodictis*, an extremely interesting type, whose remains have been found in the Middle Tertiaries both of Europe and the United States, a distribution made possible by an ancient

By courtesy of]　　　　　　　　　　　　　[*W. P. Pycraft, F.Z.S.*

The Wood or Bushdog, originated from Brazil and Guiana and is a particularly interesting specimen, being a link between the living and the prehistoric dog.

THE BEDLINGTON.

(Painted specially for this work by Vere Temple.)

For show purposes the Bedlington Terrier is the most hair-dressed of dogs, with the exception of the Poodle. Its strange appearance is due entirely to the use of scissors and razors. Underneath it all, nevertheless, the Bedlington carries a stout heart, for his original purpose in life was as a sporting dog, and he has a reputation for hard fighting.

ANCESTORS OF THE DOG.

The ancestors of the dog hunted in packs and above is seen a realistic painting by Benjamin Gibbin, who died in 1851, showing wolves attacking deer at the edge of a precipice.   Apart from this interest, it is a fine example of the artist's skill.

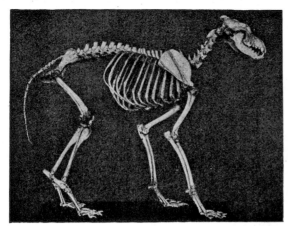 

SIMILARITIES.

On the left is a skeleton of an American Prairie Wolf, and it is interesting to compare it with the one on the right, which is that of an English Retriever.

land-bridge connecting the Old World with the New. This genus includes a number of species mostly not larger than foxes. The teeth bear a close likeness to those of the *Viverridæ* already mentioned, especially in regard to the lower carnassial. There were also other skeletal peculiarities. On this account there seems to be good reason for regarding *Cynodictis* as not far removed from the ancestral types of many *Viverroids* and *Canoids*. And we can carry this blood-relationship still further back, to *Amphicyon* of the Upper Eocene, and Lower Miocene of Europe. It included species as large as a bear. It seems to have had a wide range, and, reaching the New World, gave rise to *Daphaenus* of the Miocene of the United States. It is to be regarded as a generalized dog —a dog in the making—with a leaning towards the bears in the structure of its limbs, for the feet were five-toed, and the gait was plantigrade—that is to say, "flat-footed" like the bears.

But more than this. *Amphicyon*, in its turn, leads to a still larger form *Dinocyon*, from the Middle Miocene of France, wherein the teeth so closely resemble those of the bear-like *Hyaenarctos* as to make it difficult to distinguish between the two.

And now let us return to the wild dogs of the south - east

of Asia, whose lineage appears to be distinct from the dogs of the genus *Canis*. All agree in the absence of the last lower molar. The muzzle is shorter, and the facial profile slightly convex instead of concave. There are also 12 to 14 teats, instead of the normal 10, while there is long hair between the foot-pads. In their general appearance they resemble jackals, and hunt in packs. They range not only through the whole of the Oriental region, but into Central Asia as far as Amurland, the home of *Cyon alpinus*. The best known of these is, perhaps, the Indian "Dhole" (*C. dukhunensis*), which ranges from the forest regions of Peninsula India to Western Thibet. But though the ancestral type seems to have originated in Asia, the group spread westward, as is shown by the fact that remains of this genus are found in the cavern deposits of the Continent.

Another group, for which the name *Lycalopex* has been proposed, is found in South America. It contains eight species of fox-like aspect, and has longer tails than in the typical dogs; they are, however, neither true wolves nor true foxes.

The most remarkable of these is the Maned-wolf (*Canis jubata*), known to the natives as the Aguaraguazu. It is one of the most striking of

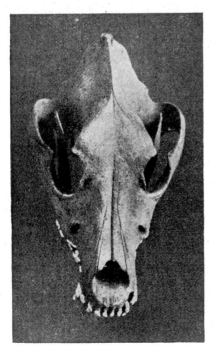

SKULL OF ENGLISH RETRIEVER.

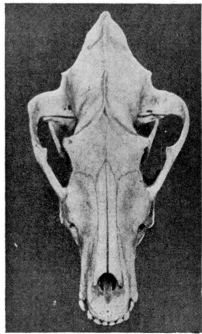

SKULL OF WOLF.

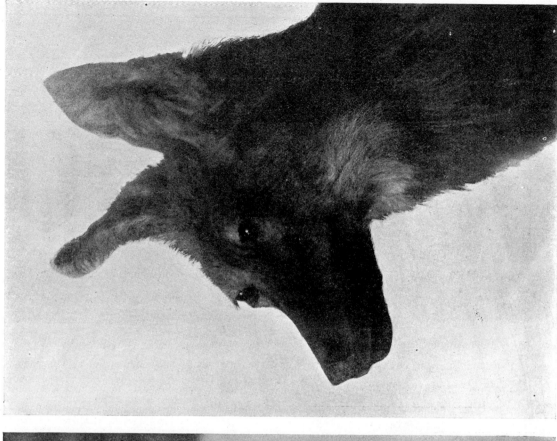

[*Photos*

ARE ALSATIANS CROSS-BRED WOLVES ?

Many people are of the opinion that the Alsatian is a half-bred wolf. Ash tells us in his *Practical Dog Book* that a German breeder crossed dogs and wolves together and exhibited the cross. The wolf cross was therefore made long before the breed was registered, and known as the Wolf Dog. Later, in the early days of the breeding of Alsatians as pedigree dogs, attempts were made to rid the variety of this wolfishness. On this page we have a head of an Alsatian and a head of a Wolf to show the marked resemblance. The Alsatian is Mrs. Leslie Thornton's "Southern Danko".

[*S. & G.*

any of the *Canidæ*; and this on account of the relatively enormous length of the legs and the large ears. The head is more fox-like than wolf-like, and the colour is that of a fox with black legs. It derives its name "maned-wolf" from the long hair on the back and neck; while in the matter of size it agrees with the wolf.

Its range extends from Brazil, into Paraguay and Northern Argentina; and it seems even to extend—though this is not generally known—into the Pampas, where, however, it seems to be rare. It haunts moist regions, concealed during the day in thickets and bushes, venturing forth to hunt in the evenings. Rodents seem to form its principal prey, and some of these are so swift that they successfully evade capture by all other members of the dog-tribe. Birds, reptiles, insects, and even fruit are eaten. It will sometimes attack deer, and even, but very rarely, sheep. The great length of the legs may have come about in response to its mode of life. They would certainly afford the animal a wider

WHITE ARCTIC WOLF

outlook and increase its sprinting powers. As yet, however, but little is known of its habits in its natural haunts, and it is rarely seen in zoological gardens, though one, for a time, was an inmate of the Gardens of the Zoological Society of London.

The Alopecoid, or Fox-group, now claims attention. Some twelve species in all are generally recognized, spread over Eurasia, Africa, and North America. Other authorities recognize fewer species, claiming that many of these are but incipient species or geographical races of the common fox.

The Arctic-fox, and the small and elegant African foxes known as Fennecs, are sufficiently distinct from the typical foxes to merit the specific names which have been given them.

We still seem as far off as ever in our search for the causation of species. Why is it that we meet, on the one hand, with large groups of species all obviously members of one genus—that is to say, all derived from a common stock—and on the other with forms where the genus and species are, so to

THE STORY OF A GREAT BREED

For many generations in early days in the land of Eskimo Dogs and Samoyeds, the natives allowed the dog and the wolf to cross. Although some of the dogs to-day bear strong resemblance to the wolf, they are not wolf-like in character. The above photo shows Mrs. E. G. Quinlan's "Alexis of Iceland," "Mystic of Iceland" and "Prince Sabastian."

speak, combined in one animal ? If more attention was paid to the haunts and habits of living animals, and their inter-relationships with their environment, animate and inanimate, we should probably gain a clearer insight into the problem than is ours at present. The dissecting-table shows us the products of evolution, but we want to be able to lay a finger on evolution at work, and this must be done by the aid of studies in the field.

We have two or three striking examples of a genus and species represented in one animal in the dog-tribe, and they shall be taken now. Let us cite, first of all, the Cape hunting-dog (*Lycaon pictus*) of South and East Africa. In size it is nearly as large as a Mastiff, and its colouration differs most conspicuously from that of any other member of the dog tribe. It is indeed of a very singular character, for it is made up of spots and blotches of white, yellow, and black, very irregularly distributed, and in no two individuals quite the same. Though it hunts in packs, this colouration may afford it concealment when, after hunting, the pack breaks up and its members seek retirement.

Among its many structural peculiarities mention must be made of its teeth, which are more massive and rounded than in the wolf tribe. The skull is shorter and broader, and there are but four toes on each foot. The ears are large, erect and broadly ovate. It is worth noting that a lower jaw was found many years ago in a cave deposit in Glamorganshire, showing that the range of this animal was far wider than now. In *Lycaon* the wolves once so common to Wales must have had a formidable rival, or did their numbers increase as *Lycaon* decreased ?

Another particularly interesting species is the Bush-dog, *Icticyon*, or *Speothos venaticus*, a native of Brazil and Guiana. It is a strange-looking animal, short-faced, and short-eared, and short-legged, and the tail is also short. From the point of view of the evolution of the dog, it is particularly interesting since it serves as a living link with *Temnocyon* of the Miocene of the United States. *Icticyon* is thus indubitably a New World type. Fossil remains of this genus are found in the Pleistocene cavern deposits of Brazil, thus showing that we have in the Bush-dog a "living fossil". Why it has retained so many of its primitive characters while other genera and species have attained to a much higher degree of specialization, and consequent change of form, is still a mystery.

Finally we come to the African Lalande's dog, *Otocyon megalotis*. Here again we have an animal of surpassing interest. It looks like a fox with enormous ears, like those of the Fennecs, but longer on the leg and of a brownish or iron-grey colouration, mottled with yellow ; the outer sides of the leg are black, and the under parts white. From the evolutionist's point of view, however, this animal is of quite peculiar interest, since it has four molars in each jaw. In some specimens, however, there are but three upper molars. In any case, the total number of the teeth is either 46 or 48, a number found in no other mammals outside the marsupials.

Lalande's dog is found in both South and East Africa. It is generally found in open country, hiding among small bushes, and going about in pairs. But it is very wary and difficult to approach.

Here, then, ends the story of the evolution of the dog and the various types we know to-day. There are yet many links in the chain of fossils to be discovered, and these, when found, will fill many puzzling gaps.

The evolution of the domesticated dog is a theme bristling with difficulties, and likely to give rise to endless discussions. If dog-lovers would take up the study of wild dogs they would find many clues to problems which now seem to them insoluble.

THE DINGO.

The history of the Dingo is somewhat of a mystery. It has been said that it developed from domesticated dogs brought into the country, and also that it is a wild dog. One can trace a strong resemblance both to the Wolf and the Alsatian, and when these Dingos are crossed with dogs they become still more typically Alsatian.

Animals (Anaesthetics) Act (1919).

— This Act was designed to prevent the infliction of pain upon animals, by making it illegal for any person to perform the following operations on dogs without the administration of a general anaesthetic :

1. Castration of animals six months old and over.
2. Ovariotomy (excision of the ovaries).
3. Laparotomy (opening of the abdominal cavity).
4. Amputations of the penis, mammae, uterus.
5. Operations for scrotal and inguinal hernia.

It is also illegal to perform the following operations without the employment of a local anaesthetic :

1. Enucleation of the eyeball.
2. Operation for umbilical hernia.
3. Urethrotomy (incision into the urethra).
4. Docking of the tail and clipping or rounding of the ears of animals over six months old.

The penalty for committing an offence under this Act was fixed at a maximum of £5 for the first conviction, but rising to £25, with or without imprisonment, for subsequent offences.

It is obvious that this Act is in sore need of revision if cruelty is to be avoided, for there are scores of very painful operations of which no mention is made in either list, and one must assume that the law would find no fault with their performance without any kind of anaesthesia. Again, it is idle to contend that the docking of the tail or the cutting of the ears of a dog which had reached five months of age, but had not yet qualified under the Act for receipt of an anaesthetic, was not a painful and cruel procedure.

It is fortunate that the veterinary profession needs no guidance from such Acts of Parliament as to whether a proposed operation will be painful at one age or another, and its members realize that easier and better work can be performed upon a docile and immobile patient than upon one shrieking with pain and struggling violently to get away. Yet it is feared that there are persons outside that profession who are not so scrupulous, and for the control of this class we strongly advocate a revision and strengthening of the Act.

Anthelmintics are remedies given for the expulsion of round or tapeworms. (*See* VERMIFUGES VERMICIDES, WORMS.)

Anthrax.—An acute infectious disease caused by the *bacillus anthracis*; very rare in the dog. Cases have, however, occurred as the result of dogs consuming the blood or flesh of other animals which have died of the disease. In dogs, the usual site of the lesions is about the throat, mouth, and bowels, in which there is considerable swelling of the mucous membrane, and sometimes of the whole head, causing an impedance of the respirations, and accompanied by high fever, staggering gait, unconsciousness, and death in from ten to twenty-four hours. Post-mortem examinations, or contact with the dead animal's blood, are highly dangerous to human beings. Anthrax is a scheduled disease under the Contagious Diseases (Animals) Act, and as such it must be notified to the nearest Local Authority immediately it has been diagnosed.

Antidotes.—An antidote is a substance capable of neutralizing the effects of some other substance. Nearly all poisons have their antidotes, and the latter may exert their actions in varying ways. Some change the chemical nature of the poison by uniting with it and forming a harmless compound; others are able to prevent the absorption of the

Photo]   [*S. & G.*

Mrs. P. Leite's Champion Toy Spaniel "Billikin Advocate" is shown here as an illustration of the word "apple-head".

poison, whilst a third class produces entirely opposite effects to those set up by the poison. In a case of poisoning, one is usually not much concerned as to how the antidote works, but wishes rather to obtain a rapid knowledge of the best and most easily accessible remedy. A short list of antidotes against the commoner poisons follows :

AMMONIA.—Give 1 to 2 teaspoonsful of vinegar in equal quantity olive oil or any other oil which is handy. Repeat if necessary. Follow with demulcents such as starch paste, liquid gum, linseed gruel, or glycerine, etc.

ARSENIC.—Hydrated oxide of iron is best, but the average household would not possess any, and the next best antidote is ordinary Blaud's pills. Give 2 or 3 pills at once and then send for a veterinary surgeon. Carbonate of iron may be given, and a drink of lime water, to be followed later by vegetable tonics such as infusion of gentian, etc. Half an hour after the first dose of iron, give an emetic, then repeat the antidote.

ATROPINE.—Emetics : brandy and water, or strong coffee.

BELLADONNA.—Same as atropine.

CANTHARIDES.—Do not give oil in this case, but proceed as for chloride of lime. If morphia or opium are available, give a medicinal dose, i.e. ¼ to 1 gr. of the former, or 5 to 20 drops of tincture of opium. If poisoning has been due to absorption through the skin in consequence of a blistering ointment having been applied, the latter must at once be removed with warm water, soap, and bicarbonate of soda.

CARBOLIC ACID (or any coal tar derivative).—Give an emetic such as a lump of washing soda, and wash it down with half a cup of lime water, or strong tea or coffee ; white of egg, olive oil, milk or cream, or any other similar fatty substance, should be given as soon as possible. If a surgeon can be found, it is desirable that he should use the stomach-pump. A dose of castor oil may be given, followed three or four times in the day by small doses of Epsom salts or Glauber's salt in water.

For slow carbolic poisoning, such as may result from the absorption of dressings applied to the skin or to wounds, the Epsom salt medication is very useful, not forgetting, of course, to remove the offending substances.

CHLORIDE OF LIME.—Do not give acids in this case. Administer an emetic such as washing-soda, and follow with white of egg, milk, starch gruel, or flour and water.

CHLOROFORM.—Fresh air, artificial respiration, massage over the heart, inhalations of ammonia

THE JACKAL

It is worthy of comment that the Greyhound, ancestor of the Saluki, lived in the country in which the jackal represents the wolf and it is a fact that jackals and dogs can be crossed together. It is therefore possible that the Greyhound type may have originated from the jackal.

WOLF CUBS.

The puppies of Alsatians and Wolf Cubs are strikingly alike. In examining this photograph of young wolves it should be borne in mind that in the first cross made between a wolf and a dog, according to one authority, the ears were extremely large.

or amyl nitrite ; carbon dioxide and oxygen gases (if available) to be inhaled ; strychnine, pituitrin, or adrenalin subcutaneously. Keep the body warm.

COAL GAS.—Dogs and cats not infrequently become gassed when left alone in rooms containing gas fires and gas stoves, as quite often they themselves inadvertently turn the taps. Upon discovery, place the animal in fresh air, apply artificial respiration, give brandy or whisky or sal volatile in water ; offer smelling-salts to the nostrils, sponge the back of head and neck with cold water, and telephone for a veterinary surgeon.

IODINE.—Solution of starch followed by boiled barley and its juice.

LEAD SALTS, such as may be ingested with paint. —A purge with a strong dose of Glauber or Epsom salt, say from 1 to 4 teaspoonsful in water or milk ; later a teaspoonful of linseed oil, repeated at four-hour intervals, for three doses. If the poisoning is slow and chronic, iodide of potash should be prescribed for several days.

MERCURY SALTS.—Acute poisoning, such as is produced by the licking of antiseptic dressings, is dealt with by administering a raw egg beaten up with a cupful of milk ; if no egg or milk is obtainable, give flour and water. In ten minutes give an emetic, followed later by more egg, milk, flour or starch. Afterwards the dog should be given drinks of lime-water or milk, and if there appears to be no improvement, give sulphuret of iron or Epsom salt.

MORPHIA.—Strychnine subcutaneously ; strong coffee ; continuous exercise and rousing, massage, cold douches, smelling-salts.

OPIUM.—Emetics followed by an eggspoonful of Condy's Fluid in vinegar. Give a castor-oil purge, and then proceed as for morphia.

PHOSPHORUS (as contained in some rat poisons).— Emetics at once, followed by demulcent drinks such as starch or flour gruel, or liquid gum in which $\frac{1}{2}$ to 1 teaspoonful of turpentine has been added. If there are facilities for washing out the stomach, this should be done after the emetic has acted, a solution of permanganate of potash being used.

STRYCHNINE (as contained in rat and beetle poisons).—Emetics followed by chloral, chloroform or potassium bromide, given by the mouth. If the convulsions have already appeared, the chloroform should be inhaled and morphia injected. Nitrate of potash in large quantities of water should be administered as soon as possible to increase the amount of urine voided, as strychnine is excreted mainly via the kidneys. The convulsions must be kept in check by narcotics or sedatives.

Antiseptics.—The term "antiseptic" literally means "against sepsis". They are substances which have the power to inhibit the growth and development of micro-organisms, and thus to prevent putrefaction. It cannot be too strongly emphasized that antiseptics *do not kill* organisms, and therefore are not disinfectants. This statement, however, may need some qualification, since in some instances a weak solution of a disinfectant may be reduced to the level of an antiseptic, whilst some of the antiseptics, in very strong solution, may acquire germicidal properties. Great heat and excessive cold are each antagonistic to the growth of germs, as also are sunlight, and some of the artificially produced light rays.

There are a huge number and variety of chemicals which may be classed among the antiseptics, but little purpose will be served by enumerating them. It is only necessary to point out that many of them are highly poisonous, and therefore dangerous for use on dogs, since not only is a substance readily absorbed by a dog's skin, but these animals cannot be trusted not to lick their dressing, and in that way poison themselves.

The derivatives of coal tar, such as carbolic acid and lysol, may be classed, along with mercurial salts and iodoform, among the most poisonous of the antiseptics in general use. Boracic acid is probably the weakest of all antiseptics, and, being of a non-irritating nature, it is largely employed as an eye-wash. A 5 per cent solution of common salt is an excellent and safe antiseptic and should be more frequently used by the public, especially as it has the additional recommendation of cheapness. For rapid healing properties, safety of the patient, and strong aseptic powers, few chemicals can surpass the chlorine compounds, of which bleaching powder, liquor sodii chlor., and eusol are typical examples.

Antiseptics are administered internally for bowel medication, among the commonest being bismuth, salol, permanganate of potash and Dimol. Urinary antiseptics, such as urotropine, salol, buchu, etc., are prescribed when septic processes exist in any part of the urinary system.

Anus, Prolapse of.—The protrusion of the rectum through the anal orifice entails, most usually, a simultaneous eversion of the anus itself, and the CAUSE is due, generally, to straining as a consequence either of diarrhoea or constipation. It may appear as an accompaniment of or sequel to enteritis, colitis, or proctitis, and the great majority of cases are encountered among young puppies. It is, curiously enough, a common complication of distemper.

SYMPTOMS.—In a mild case, a small eversion of mucous membrane may be noticed only at the time of defaecation, after which act the mucous membrane returns to its normal position. After it has protruded several times, however, the tendency is for it to stay out, and sooner or later there may ensue the prolapse of a much larger portion ; in fact, the whole of the rectum may prolapse. The appearance is then that of a dark-red sausage-shaped mass hanging from beneath the roof of the tail.

TREATMENT.—In general, it is best that inexpert hands should not attempt to replace these prolapses, as failure to succeed at the first effort only leads to repeated attempts, involving much handling and bruising of the mucous membrane. The quick result of that is an increased inflammation and swelling, often accompanied by small abrasions or wounds, and inducing a serious condition of the bowel. No description will therefore be given of the method of reduction, and the most valuable advice to the layman is to wrap the prolapsed bowel in some oiled cotton wool, which should be retained in position by bandages or a square of clean linen. A surgeon is then sent for, and, pending his arrival, treatment of the underlying cause may be applied, if the latter can be ascertained. Do not apply ice or cold solutions.

Aperients may be described as mild purgatives, or agents which only gently evacuate the bowel of its contents. Castor oil, syrup of buckthorn, syrup of figs, linseed oil, calomel, cascara, etc., are all examples of aperients, if given in medicinal doses. (*See* PURGATIVES.)

These delightful studies of an Australian Terrier made from life for this work by Miss Vere Temple whose animal studies are well known to all Nature lovers.

Aphrodisiac.—This is a drug which excites the sexual impulse, examples being strychnine, cantharides, yohimbine, etc. Dog-breeders possessed of dogs or bitches which habitually evince no desire for the opposite sex are quite often tempted to administer drugs of this nature in the hope that mating will take place in the normal way. It is feared, however, that their efforts are attended generally with indifferent success. Not infrequently the disinclination of an animal for sexual intercourse is due to reasons other than nervous exhaustion or weakness. Some painful abnormality of the genital organs may exist, or the animal may be shy or nervous. However, the resort to any chemical of this nature should be very carefully undertaken, and then as a rule only under the advice of a veterinary surgeon. Many of the aphrodisiacs, such, for instance, as cantharides, are highly irritant to the urinary system and therefore dangerous. It is not rare for nephritis to follow the injudicious use of such agents.

Stimulation of the sex instinct is more safely and scientifically carried out by stimulation of the gonads and other ductless glands by administration of their extracts.

Apoplexy.—A loss of consciousness or of muscular power caused by pressure upon the brain or spinal cord, due perhaps to concussion, fracture of the skull, or the rupture of a local blood-vessel. An apoplectic fit may be caused by intense excitement or exertion, exposure to the sun, a tight collar, or the close air of confined spaces. Well-fed, indolent dogs may suffer from an attack soon after overloading the stomach with indigestible food.

SYMPTOMS.—The animal may seem strange in its manner and then suddenly lose consciousness, which is accompanied by partial or complete paralysis. The preliminary symptoms may be giddiness; trembling; inco-ordinated movements; weak pulse in some cases, or full and bounding in others; stertorous breathing. Champing of the jaws or the frothing of epilepsy are absent; but the eyes may be bloodshot and there may be blindness. It is common for death rapidly to supervene.

TREATMENT.—As first-aid measures, loosen the collar if tight, massage the limbs, apply ice to the head and to the back of the ears and neck. If a surgeon is present, bleeding may be undertaken. Absolute quiet and rest are necessary, and if the pulse is full the head may be raised a little. When consciousness has been regained, and if the pulse is small and weak, some brandy in water may be given. A veterinary surgeon should be summoned at once.

Apple-headed = with top of skull rounded instead of flattened.

Apron = long frill below neck.

Arctic Dogs. (*See* ESKIMO DOGS.)

Areca Nut.—The fruit of the betel-nut tree, and much used among dog owners as an anthelmintic. The powdered nut is astringent, bitter, and insoluble in water. Its specific action is against the tapeworms, having little or no effect on round worms, and in order to ensure success only freshly-ground nut should be administered. Its acrid taste causes most dogs to vomit almost as soon as it is swallowed, thus defeating its object. In order to avoid this annoyance, one is advised either to enclose the dose in a gelatine capsule or anaesthetize the dog's stomach by a preliminary dose of chloretone, anaesthesin, or some other chemical agent capable of numbing the nerve-endings in the gastric mucosa. Quite frequently the liquid extract of areca is prescribed in preference to the fresh nut. Of the powder, one gives about 2 grs. for each pound of the dog's body weight. As it is insoluble in water, a good vehicle to help it down is cod-liver oil, or, indeed, any other kind of oil which is suitable for internal administration.

Arrowroot. (*See* FOODS AND FEEDING.)

Arsenic, Poisoning by.—Arsenic is a potent poison causing gastro-enteritis, and producing such symptoms as continuous retching, vomiting, great uneasiness (evidence of abdominal pain), diarrhoea, staggering gait when gravely poisoned, feeble, rapid pulse, coldness of the extremities, convulsions, and death. The motions may be flecked with blood, as indeed may the vomit, but generally in all cases the defaecations will be dark or black, and very fluid. If arsenic has been established as the cause of the illness, an emetic should be given at once, a useful agent for this purpose being a knob of ordinary washing soda, or some salt and water. If possible, obtain the classical antidote, viz. hydroxide of iron, and give a full medicinal dose every quarter-hour until about eight doses have been given. Carbonate of iron will do as the next best substitute if the hydroxide is unobtainable. Next, the effects of the poison must be treated by administering any kind of demulcent that is handy, such as milk and egg, white of egg, starch gruel, or limewater. If there is great pain a veterinary surgeon will inject a dose of morphia.

Arthritis.—Inflammation of a joint.

CAUSES.—This moderately rare condition in dogs may be caused by tuberculosis, rheumatism, or some other infective disease, but more frequently by injuries such as blows, wrenches, dislocations, or fractures. It is considered that rheumatoid arthritis is a deficiency disease, that is to say, a slow starvation of the animal in connection with B vitamin, and possibly some other of the recognized vitamins.

SYMPTOMS.—The affected joint or joints will be

Photo]   [*S. & G.*
Mr. T. C. Judge Brown's Pomeranian "Vanity Fair", exhibits the "apron" clearly an important characteristic of certain breeds of dogs.

Photo]

FED UP.

[Sport & General.

This photograph of an Australian Terrier suggests the fatigue of a small dog after it has been at a Dog Show for a day or two and explains, perhaps, the reason why few shows are of more than two days' duration, although at one time they continued for a whole week.

tender to touch, show marked puffiness or swelling, some heat, and the animal will be lame on the limb in which the diseased joint is situated. There may be generalized fever, with loss of appetite and a decided aversion to movement.

TREATMENT.—Discover, if possible, the cause, and make sure there is no partial or complete fracture of the bones forming the joint. Bathing the part with hot water will relieve much of the swelling and pain ; or one may apply a warm chemical poultice, provided the long hair is first removed.

Artificial Respiration.   (*See* RESPIRATION.)

Artificial Warmth.   (*See* WARMTH).

Ascarides.   (*See* ROUND WORMS.)

Ascites.   (*See* DROPSY.)

Asphyxia.—The condition arrived at when the respiration and heart action have nearly or entirely ceased. It may be produced by coal-gas poisoning, chloroform, smoke, or other kinds of inhalation, or the obstruction to breathing caused by the presence of swallowed foreign bodies, by abscesses, or new growths, any of which may press upon the respiratory passages. Oedema of the lungs is another and probably far more common cause among canines than are some of the other causes.

SYMPTOMS.—As the cause of the condition is a deficiency of air, and therefore of oxygen, the earliest sign of asphyxia is an increased rapidity of respirations and of pulse. Breathing is eventually a series of gasps ; the animal struggles for breath, then gets weaker and weaker until it is unable to stand. Unconsciousness supervenes, and, finally, death.

TREATMENT.—Seek the cause, and should this be due to coal gas, smoke, or other fumes, the obvious first measure is to remove the dog into pure air. If respirations are very shallow, artificial respiration may be applied, and some stimulating inhalation, such as sal volatile, should be afforded. Keep the dog's body warm by packing hot-water bottles around it, and massage might vigorously be applied over the region of the heart.

Aspirin.—Also known as acetosalicylic acid. It is a very valuable drug for dogs, its particular virtues being its ability rapidly to reduce fever, its specific effect in alleviating the pain of rheumatic conditions, and its soothing action on the nervous system generally. A five-grain tablet may be given, whole or crushed, three times daily to a dog weighing thirty or forty pounds.

Asthma.—A disorder of respiration characterized by severe paroxysms of difficult breathing usually followed by a period of complete relief, with recurrence of the attacks at intervals.

CAUSES.—The distressing symptoms are due to a contraction of the small bronchioles (minute air tubes of the lungs) owing to some deranged condition of the nervous system affecting either directly or reflexly the nerves supplying the muscular fibres of the bronchi and regulating their calibre. Inflammation and swelling of the mucous membranes lining the bronchi and bronchioles, when present, further impede the passage of air into the lungs and account for the gasping for breath and blue discolouration of the visible mucous membranes. Animals having been at rest in a certain atmosphere become attacked if they start running or climbing stairs, or go from one room to a colder one.

SYMPTOMS.—There is increased rapidity and often difficulty of respiration, with wheezing, coughing and sometimes retching. When an attack is severe the animal may fall to the ground gasping, and the paroxysms last from a few minutes to several days.

TREATMENT.—Asthma is frequently incurable, but by the adoption of careful dieting and other prophylactic measures, much discomfort can be spared. As the medicinal remedies likely to be of any service in this distressing complaint would never find a place in any layman's house, the obvious procedure is to call in a veterinary surgeon. Keep the dog in a warm room, and at rest.

Astringents.—These are chemical agents which have the effect of contracting surface tissues when applied to them. If applied to mucous membranes or small injured blood-vessels the result is a diminution of the mucous secretion in the one case, or of loss of blood in the other. Inflamed and sore, or abraded, skin surfaces benefit from the application of astringent solutions because they become hardened and less sensitive to external influences. Healing is promoted and moist lesions become dried. Well-known examples are lead lotion, solutions of alum or zinc, vinegar or other dilute acids, the salts of metals, such as sulphate of copper, perchloride of iron, nitrate of silver, acetate of lead, etc. Ice and cold water are also astringent in their action, as are oak galls, tannic acid, witch-hazel, and many other substances.

Atavism means the inheritance of characters from remote, but not from the immediate, ancestors. If any characteristics which are seen in a puppy resemble those peculiar to its grandparents or great-grandparents, these characters are not imparted by or manifested in the immediate sire and dam. Telegony, on the other hand, indicates the reproduction in the offspring of one sire, of characters derived from a previous sire to whom the mother has borne offspring. It is very questionable indeed if such instances ever occur, as in our experience no authentic cases have ever been encountered, nor could we explain the possibility theoretically. At the same time it is interesting to see what Robert Leighton wrote in his *Book of the Dog* published in 1912. He said : "A dog is to be regarded not only as the offspring of its immediate parents, but also of generations of ancestors, and many are found to be more liable than others to throw back to their remote progenitors. Thus, even in a kennel of related dogs, all of whom are similar in appearance, you may sometimes have a litter of puppies in no visible sense resembling their parents. A white English terrier bitch, for instance, mated with a dog equally white, may have one or more puppies marked with brown or brindle patches. Research would probably show that on some occasion, many generations back, one of the ancestors was crossed with a mate of brindle or brown colouring. But the old-established breeds seldom reveal a throwback, and one of the best indications of a pure strain is that it breeds true to its own type."

If atavism does not exist among pure breeds of dogs, it is indeed hard to explain why it should among impure breeds, and the likeliest explanation of departures in colouring from those of the parents is that there is a promiscuous mating of the bitch, unknown and unsuspected by the owner.

Atavism and telegony might well be regarded as evidence of the transmission of mental impressions, but opinions are greatly divided on this point. If a

Photo]   *[Fall*
It is important to realize that the Australian Terrier is a working dog and must not be mistaken for a plaything. This example shows the hard-bitten appearance of such a dog.

Australian Terrier.—It is of no little interest that in Australia they should have many a variety of terrier resembling very closely some of the best known British breeds, and that this variety should have been brought over to England and introduced into the country by one or two noted people, including Lady Stradbroke of Henham Hall, Suffolk, to whose keen efforts the breed owes much.

Although in Australia many of these terriers are kept, there are two kinds, both of which have been claimed to be the original Australian Terrier. One, however, is really the Sydney Silky Terrier, which differs from the Australian Terrier by its long and silky coat that resembles the English Yorkshire Terrier. The Sydney Silky Terrier is, indeed, the result of a cross between the Skye Terrier and the Yorkshire, and resembles both these clearly, whilst the other Australian Terrier is very much more the type of the Cairn Terrier, so much that some of them might easily be mistaken to be unusual Cairns.

The colour of the AustralianTerrier is blue-and-tan. The coat is rough, and the hair no longer than two inches. It has been said it seems unnecessary to bring this variety into England, but of course this is a matter of opinion ; the more British breeds the better.

The dog should be rather low set, that is to say of short legs. Its body must be broad

pregnant female sees some deformity or other terrible sight, and her offspring, when born, is abnormal in any way, the case is at once quoted as one of transmission of a mental impression. What is present in the offspring is a deformity due to some other cause. In the case of the human species, millions of women see deformities and bear healthy children; and, on the other hand, deformed children may be born in the absence of any such factor. The doctrine of telegony is also regarded as further evidence in favour of transmission of acquirements.

Photo]   *[Ralph Robinson.*
There is always the difficulty in new breeds of keeping the type constant and this picture shows a distinctly different type of Australian Terrier from the one above.

No such actual cases have ever come under our own notice, and we wonder whether these instances which have been cited from time to time are not merely coincidences.

Atrophy means a shrinkage or diminution of some part or organ of the body. It is well exemplified in the shrunken muscles of limbs which have been out of use for some time. For instance, when a fractured bone is set and the whole limb is put out of action, examination of that limb two or three weeks later will reveal that a considerable wastage of muscle has occurred. This is called the "atrophy of inaction". A similar result is often seen after severe blows or other injuries which involve either paralysis of a motor nerve or interference with the blood circulation of a part or area. Lame legs, which are rarely used, thus not infrequently become the seat of localized atrophy. The cause in this case is deficient nutrition, or nerve supply, the same factor which is responsible also for shrinkage of parts that are pressed upon by new growths. Ensure that a good blood circulation is induced by the application of vigorous and regular massage.

Photo]   *[Fall*
Mrs. Herbert Bassett owns a specimen with prick-ears which are less usual than the drop-ear variety.

enough to make it, as the dog fanciers describe it, a compact dog ; at the same time its legs must not be so short as to lose activity. The coat must be hard, in fact it cannot be too hard, and although two inches is given as the required length many of the dogs will be seen to have coats about half an inch longer than this. Breeders are anxious that the coat should not resemble that of the Skye Terrier, hence the reason for being careful as to its length. Too long a coat would spoil the breed altogether.

Australian Terrier dogs should not be too heavy, in fact about 10 or 11 pounds is the weight most desired. Quite a number will be found to weigh more than this, many weighing 13 or 14 pounds, whilst at the other end of the scale some will be found to register only 8 or 9 pounds.

In judging these dogs a long and flat skull is desired. The dog must be full between the eyes, for narrowness will spoil its appearance. On the top of the head is a bunch of "soft hair" known as the "top-knot". The jaw of the Australian Terrier must not be snipy but long and powerful, and there must be no sign of the mouth being overshot, that is to say the upper teeth protruding in front of the lower teeth, or the upper jaw being shorter than the lower jaw. A level mouth is very important.

The nose must be black and on no account may be flesh colour ; a flesh-coloured nose is a definite disqualification for show purposes. No dog may have any white on the chest if it would find favour with the judge.

The eyes are small, intelligent-looking and of a dark colour. Ears should also be small, set straight upon the skull and standing up, that is to say pricked, although drop ears are allowed. The ears must be free from long hair, and although years ago it was customary to cut the ears of this breed no cut ears are to be seen to-day.

Sometimes woolly coats are found amongst Australian Terriers, but this also disqualifies them, and is, therefore, to be avoided.

It is an interesting fact that the neck of the Australian Terrier always appears too long in proportion to its body. Breeders state that the body should also be long in proportion to the head of the dog and should be well ribbed-up, the back being straight. Although in the Scottish Terrier the natural tail is the standard, the Australian Terrier has a docked tail.

The short front legs ought to be perfectly straight and well set up under the body. A slight feather is allowed to the knee. The feet are free from long hair and the toe-nails must be black. If there is one thing more than anything else interesting as to this breed's show limitations it is the fact that dogs with white toe-nails are disqualified, and are therefore not considered to be Australian Terriers ! It seems to most people that disqualification on so minor a detail is hardly necessary.

The hind legs of the Australian Terrier have good strong thighs and the hocks are but slightly bent. On examining the foot it is found to be on the small side, and well padded. There must be no tendency for the foot to spread out as is seen in some other varieties.

The colour of this breed is most important and is divided into two groups. The one, a blue or grey body with tan on legs and tan on the face—the richer the tan the better—with a "top-knot" of blue or silver. In the second example the dog must be of a clear sandy or red colour.

On no account is the Australian Terrier adult allowed to have a black coat, although this is no fault in puppies.

The points of the breed are :

	POINTS
Skull	5
Muzzle and Teeth	10
Eyes and Ears	10
Neck	5
Body	5
Feet and Legs	10
Coat	10
Colour	10
General appearance	10
Total	75

This total of show points is also rather unusual.

Auto-Intoxication.—Poisoning by some un-eliminated toxin generated within the body. The condition is much more common in animals than is generally supposed, and yet there is little difficulty in convincing the public that their own ills may arise from septic foci in their teeth. It is not uncommon to hear that individuals knew no real health until some or nearly all of their teeth had been extracted.

Animals suffer equally from pyorrhoea and diseased teeth, and it is quite feasible that many of their mysterious and undiagnosed ailments may arise from such a source.

Again, there is a condition known as "alimentary toxaemia", a generalized poisoning of the whole body due to the accumulation of intestinal poisons in the blood. This state is brought about by habitual constipation arising from torpidity of the muscular coats of the bowel.

Although, in some such cases, defaecation appears to go on more or less normally, the intestines are in reality never properly emptied, and a post-mortem inspection of the bowels reveals a crusted lining of faeces. Repeated flushings with an enema syringe may bring this away bit by bit, general health improving as the cleansing process becomes complete.

Azara's Dog.—
This fox-like animal
was first described
by Prince Wied as a
dog, but it is hardly
likely that it was
even a wild dog.
It was found, how-
ever, that when
taken young it could
be trained, and
although it would
become friendly
with dogs to which
it was accustomed
it always remained
afraid of a strange
dog. Captured
specimens played
with dogs they knew
quite at ease.

It was first of all
found in the area between Brazil and Tierra de
Fuego and also west of the Andes in Chili.
Because of this it was reported by other explorers
at different times and so was named in some
instances the Tierra de Fuego Dog and in other
cases the Azara's Dog, so that considerable
confusion followed.

It was stated to have lived on sugar-cane and
also on small birds and reptiles. It hunted by
scent, moving slowly with its nose pressed close
to the ground. Being entirely indifferent to

By courtesy of]   *[F. Warne. Ltd.*

AZARA'S DOG.
This was probably the most famous "dog" in the world at one time.
Supposed to be one of the original dogs, it very clearly resembles the fox and
all that can be said of it is, that in its habits it is very dog-like.—(From
Lyddeker's Natural History.)

the approach of
danger when hunt-
ing it was easily
caught by men.

In the summer
these dogs lived a
solitary life hunting
on their own and
sleeping wherever a
suitable hide was
found, and in the
winter it is recorded
that the males and
females slept in the
same nest, dividing
off again in the early
days of the summer.
An illustration taken
from *Lydekker's
Natural History*
shows one of these
animals, and it will
be seen to be extremely foxlike, with a long body,
short legs, and large ears. It has also a bushy tail
of a type which is not found in the domesticated
dog. At various
times Azara's Dogs
were introduced into
Europe and kept in
many Zoological
collections notably
London.

By courtesy of]   *E. C. Ash*

BARBET.
The word Barbet was used to describe dogs accustomed to water in the sporting field. The type varied, and here we have an
example of the Barbet as it was known at the end of the nineteenth century.

B

B = bitch, female.

Bacillus.—A microscopic organism having a rod-like shape. (*See* Bacteria.)

Back, Stiffness of. (*See* Rheumatism; Bruises.) —Stiffness of the back is seen mostly in old dogs and is generally due to muscular rheumatism. It may, in some rare instances, be due to anchylosis (or osseous union) of the dorsal or lumbar vertebrae as a result of localized tuberculosis or arthritis of one or more joints formed by these bones. It may in other cases arise from severe bruising. In practically all cases some relief will be afforded by the application of radiant heat and massage, the dog being housed in a dry, warm, and draughtless kennel or room.

Bacteria are the lowest forms of life and belong to the vegetable kingdom. They are microscopic, and many of them are directly responsible for the dreadful diseases to which animals, no less than human beings, are subject. On the other hand there are numerous bacteria which are not only harmless to animal life, but appear to play a useful rôle in its maintenance. The term "Bacteria" embraces such synonymous words as germs, bacilli, micro-organisms, and microbes.

Some germs are so very minute that at the present time no microscope has been devised which is powerful enough to render them visible. They can pass through the very finest bacterial filters, as is proved by the fact that the solution which has passed through still contains a factor capable of setting up disease when it is inoculated into a susceptible animal. Such an infection has therefore come to be known as an ultra-visible virus. Canine distemper is produced by such a virus; whilst among cattle and other farm animals another one sets up foot-and-mouth disease. Probably measles in human beings, and swine fever among pigs, are also caused by ultra-visible viruses.

Those who study the intensely interesting subject of bacteriology have very definite methods of isolating germs from the animal body, and, by means of suitable stains, are able to classify or name them, in consequence of their shape and other characters as ascertained under the microscope.

For instance, those bacteria which are rod-shaped are known as bacilli, those which are round are called cocci, whilst those with wavy forms are designated as spirilla.

These forms are, in turn, again subdivided, for we find that among the cocci, certain organisms group themselves together in grape-like clusters which is a peculiarity of the staphylococci. Others of them form long chains, and these are known as strepto-cocci. One could go on describing the subdivisions and characteristics of germ life for hours, but further particularization is hardly necessary in a volume of this kind.

Bad-Doer.—Contrary to what some people suppose, a bad-doer is not necessarily an animal which picks over its food without relish or apparent appetite. A dainty feeder is one which seems to need tempting with tasty dishes, taking little at each meal, but keeping up its bodily condition tolerably well and without difficulty. A bad-doer, on the other hand, is a dog which, although it may feed greedily, entirely fails to fill out or look a credit to its owner. In almost every litter—whether of dogs, pigs, or other animals—there is usually a weed, or one which does not thrive, cannot put on flesh, and whose growth and development appear almost at a standstill. It is difficult to account for this phenomenon amongst whelps, but it is certain that a puppy can acquire such a character, after weaning, through a number of circumstances over which it similarly has no control. For instance, it may contract a worm infestation, or rickets, or suppressed distemper, or may be the victim of its owner's ignorance in supplying it with bulky, indigestible and innutritious food, or in depriving it of adequate sunlight, air or exercise. In many cases the writer has observed that the animal which is the bad-doer of the litter is the one which failed properly to suckle its dam. There are many puppies born which seem quite incapable either of finding their mothers' teats or of extracting anything out of them, even though there may be a good supply of milk. Many of such puppies die, one after the other, and the breeder is in despair. Gross feeders among the newly born are not often bad-doers in later life.

Balanitis.—Inflammation of the glans penis is not of frequent occurrence in dogs, and when present might be mistaken for preputial catarrh, which is much more common.

Causes.—Prolonged coitus or some other irritation; phimosis (which see); irritating urine as in diabetes; and specific infections such as distemper. Preputial catarrh is common in old dogs, arising in them, probably, in consequence of a debilitated circulatory system.

Symptoms.—In these conditions there is swelling of the glans or prepuce, whichever may be the seat of affection, and a yellowish purulent discharge drips from the end of the prepuce. The dog calls attention to it by constantly licking the part, or wet stains may be left wherever the animal has rested for any time. There may be redness, swelling and tenderness of the penis or its covering skin, or of both. Balanitis is not of serious consequence, and although frequently attributed to a specific origin, the dog does not suffer from specific gonorrhoea, and the urethra is not implicated. A similar condition may rarely be observed affecting the vulva of the bitch.

Treatment.—The home measures which may be undertaken consist mainly of establishing and maintaining cleanliness of the preputial sac by syringing. Non-irritant antiseptic solutions should be employed, and of course the dog should be kept away from bitches. If recovery does not occur, a veterinary surgeon's advice should be sought.

Baldness. (*See* Alopecia.)

Bandaging.—The application of a bandage to a dog (especially to *some* dogs) is a performance which can only with difficulty be described, and for any person to become proficient thereat a good deal of practice is essential. It is one thing to apply a bandage neatly, but quite another to do so with a conviction that it will *stay* on. Dogs, as a general rule, resent being bandaged, and it is quite certain that if the bandages are not comfortable, every effort will be made with claws and teeth to undo one's good work.

Usually the part to be bandaged is not of uniform dimensions, and the tendency then is for that portion

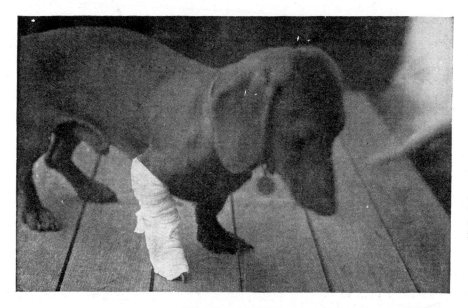

THE CORRECT WAY TO BANDAGE.

This shows the correct method of bandaging a leg. The bandage, which is best made of calico, should be arranged high enough to pass over the elbow joint (though the facility for doing this depends somewhat upon the breed of dog), and must certainly include the foot at its lower end.

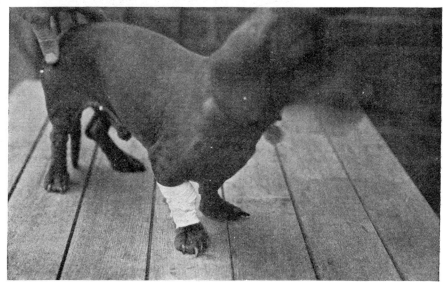

THE WRONG METHOD OF BANDAGING.

This is the wrong method of leg bandaging. Not only is the bandage liable to slip, but it will frequently be found that unless the foot is included, this quickly swells and becomes very painful owing to the interrupted circulation. The knot should always be placed where the dog cannot gnaw it.

TO BANDAGE EARS AND EYES.

To bandage an eye it is necessary to include the rest of the head, as shown, or the calico will tend to slip down the nose. This also applies to bandages for the ears. A further safeguard against an eye-bandage slipping is to make holes through which one or both ears can be passed

of the bandage which surrounds a thick part to slide towards a thin part. Thus it is found by every amateur to be a most difficult task to bandage the thigh of a dog. In ninety-nine cases out of a hundred bandages applied in such a position will fall down to the hock and become useless. Similarly, a bandage round the chest will inevitably slip back to the narrower abdomen or "waist". The tail offers additional difficulty, especially in short-haired and docked dogs, because there is little facility for pulling the bandage reasonably tight or for making it stay in position.

The objects of bandaging are varied, and include provision of support in cases of hernia ; protection of wounds from injury (by the dog) and from dirt and bacteria which might gain access thereto ; to give support to sprains or to sutured wounds ; to keep dressings in position ; and to immobilize limbs or parts of limbs in cases of fracture or dislocation, when movement would be derogatory to resolution.

To give a detailed description of how to bandage every part would occupy great space and would require many diagrams, and we think that, in individual cases, the surgeon attending a case will be better able in a few minutes to demonstrate the method of procedure than we could achieve in as many hours. A few hints, however, would not be out of place. For instance, in bandaging a tail do not employ too wide a bandage ; then, starting at the base of the tail, turn in some of the hairs over each wind of the bandage. This will keep the bandage in position.

In bandaging a leg, it is essential in every case to include the foot, otherwise the foot will swell in an alarming and painful fashion. As regards bandaging the head, advantage can be taken of the dog's collar (suitably tightened) to help keep the bandage in position.

Where some protection is required for parts which are most unsuitable for bandaging, one can substitute the application of a clean linen coat—a method which can be adopted in cases of wounds on the chest wall, abdomen, mammae, back, etc. (*See* COATS.) Alternatively, dressings may be kept in position by the use of strips of adhesive tape crossed over the wound in all directions and stuck to the dog's skin.

Bandages can be made to remain in position here and there with melted pitch, having first effected an attachment between the bandage and the dog's hair. This method is, however, only of service in those instances which do not demand the daily removal of the bandage.

For all wounds which are not aseptic or surgically clean it is generally advised not to apply bandages. The air and light will help considerably to expedite healing, and discharges arising from the initial contamination are able to get away as they form. Surgical wounds, on the other hand, usually are, or should be, aseptic (free of bacteria), and therefore require protection until healing is complete.

Finally, do not pull a bandage tight with every turn or the effect will be to stop cutaneous circulation, and the limb becomes cold, numb, and very uncomfortable. Endeavour not to place the knot just over the wound, nor in a position which renders it an easy matter for the dog to pull it undone with its teeth.

Barakzai or Barukhzy Hound. (*See* AFGHAN HOUND.)

Barbet.—The Barbet in all probability was the forerunner of the modern Poodle, but while the latter has been clipped, the Barbet had a curly coat of unusual stubbornness. This heavy coat was unquestionably developed by reason of the fact that the dog was a water retriever—possibly Nature provided the heavy covering for the purpose of protection. Buffon in 1798 describes the Barbet as having a tight curly coat and in 1792 there is this description : "The tail is truncated or seems cut off in the middle, with long coarse hair." It was essentially a water dog and at one time was greatly in favour. An illustration from an old drawing appears on page 77.

Barley Water. (*See* FOODS AND FEEDING.)

Barrenness.—This term implies inability to breed, which may be due to various causes that make breeding impossible without an operation or other treatment. But this condition is unusual in most kennels, for dogs breed readily. In some instances the word is used incorrectly to describe a temporary condition that will answer to treatment, or is the result of lack of understanding on the part of the owner, who has not taken into consideration the feelings of the animal. Temporary failure to breed may be due to an acid secretion that neutralizes the male germ and thus prevents conception, or it may be due, and more often is, to the female being over-fat. But whilst the inability to breed correctly, known as barrenness, is often incurable, the temporary condition, even after it has existed for some years, may all at once clear away, allowing the female to breed without difficulty, and in some such instances no explanation has been given for this. Mr. E. C. Ash, in *The Book of the Greyhound*, gives an instance in which a noted Greyhound showed no signs of breeding until she was thirteen years old, when she had her first litter, although everything possible had been done to persuade her to breed all through her life. It is interesting to know that, after all such efforts had been discontinued, the owner's wish was fulfilled. (*See also* STERILITY.)

Baskets.—Baskets are seldom ever used for the conveyance of any but the small or toy breeds of dog, and for this purpose they are admirably suited. They are light to carry and permit of a free interchange of air. In purchasing a basket for carrying a dog it is well to select a very stout one, the lid of which cannot be pushed open at either corner by a strong dog which is determined to escape. The roofs or lids of some of these baskets are fitted with waterproof covers to prevent the entry of rain, should the basket be stood in the open in bad weather.

Comfortable basket-beds are obtainable for small breeds, and look quite neat and tidy in any living-apartment. We illustrate a number of varieties and shapes of baskets, and invite readers to study these before purchasing.

This popular type of sleeping basket should be well cushioned for doggie's comfort and safety.

Photo]   *[Sport & General.*

THE BASSET HOUND HURDLING.

Although this breed is not built on lines of a Greyhound and therefore cannot be expected to run at a great speed or to take any prodigious jump, the above photograph shows a Basset Hound leaping a hurdle in a race.

THREE LIGHT AND SENSIBLE DOG BASKETS.
Those at either side are for travelling : the one with the grill-door is the better type. In the centre is a resting-basket, well raised from the ground.

Basset Hound.—It seems strange that a sporting breed of hounds so distinguished and attractive in appearance, so aristocratic, with that sad, reposeful dignity of the head, and so popular amongst sportsmen on the Continent should ever have fallen into disfavour.

The word "Basset" derives from the French adjective "bas", which means "a low thing' or a dwarf.

There are two types of Smooth Basset Hounds in France, and the two strains, the "Le Couteulx", and the "Lane", are named respectively after the two largest breeders in France, Comte le Couteulx and M. Lane, of Frencqueville, near Boos, and they differ mostly in head and eye. The "Lane' Hound has a big prominent eye like a Beagle, with a much thicker skull, whereas the "Le Couteulx'

Hound has that down-faced look, giving a sad expression, brown eye deeply sunk showing a prominent haw, a domed head of considerable length, narrow in comparison to the "Lane" Hound, which is inclined to cheek bumps. or apple-headedness.

Again in France, as in England, there are Rough and Smooth Hounds—the Rough are called "Basset Griffon', and the Smooth "Basset François". They are also classified in three different groups, according to the crookedness of their forelegs. There is the Basset, longest on the leg and almost straight, "Basset à Jambes Droites". the half-crooked-legged hound, "Basset à Jambes demi Tordues' ; and the shortest-legged and most crooked hound, "Basset à Jambes Tordues".

There is a great difference between the Rough

By courtesy of]　　　　　　　　　　　　　　　　　　　　　　　　　[E. C. Ash.
ROUGH AND SMOOTH BASSETS.
There have been in France for many years two distinct types of Basset. They vary mainly in the coat, one being smooth and the other rough. It is difficult, of course, to see the development of the head points in the rough variety. From the illustration it will be noticed that the smooth dog has not such a good head as the Basset shown on page 84. The illustration above is of two of the finest of the breed as they were about the year 1885.

BASSET HOUNDS HUNTING.

The Basset Hound is the shortest legged of all hounds and therefore works very slowly and can be followed on foot, which is one of its advantages. Although never largely kept it is one of the most attractive of the hound family. The names Heseltine and Basset Hound will be for ever united, as the Heseltine family have made the Basset Hound their speciality. The first of these hounds brought into the country were presented to Lord Galway by the Comte de Tournon, who sent him a couple, later to be named "Basset" and "Belle", which in 1867 bred a litter of five. They are described to have been long, low hounds, much like the Dachshund, with crooked forelegs, but with more bone and larger heads than the Beagles of that period. Their colouring resembled that of the Foxhound and their bone formation was also more like a Foxhound's than a Beagle's: The letter describing their arrival is given on page 84.

Photo by]   [Fall.

MODERN BASSET HEAD FORMATION.
The above photograph demonstrates the tendency towards a Bloodhound type of head in the Basset, with enhanced length of ears and wrinkled forehead. "Ragout" belongs to Mrs. Foster Rawlins.

and the Smooth Hounds, and many look upon them as almost a distinct breed. The Smooth is a hound in every sense of the word. He has the manner of a hound, he hunts like a hound, and has a note like a hound, whilst the Rough Hounds hunt more after the manner of a Terrier. They are not so steady, nor are they so pleasurable to the huntsmen to handle. Above all they have not the same wonderful note, which must be heard to be appreciated.

Years ago Brooksby when he first heard a pack of Basset Hounds running in full cry, compared the music of these little hounds to the united packs of the Grafton Pytchley and Bicester

thrown together—"the peal of marriage bells to a tune upon glasses".

The Rough Hounds are not so short on the leg—they can get over the ground quicker and Mr. Willie Mure, who hunted a pack of Rough Hounds from Caldwell, N.B., informed the author that they were not stopped even by stone walls. It is therefore quite understandable that they would account for more hares.

The late Major Godfrey Heseltine, the writer's brother, and himself had a few Rough Hounds in their pack, and some were excellent in their work, but they had a different style of hunting. If they had not been drafted they would have spoilt the pack, so different was their style of hunting.

The first hounds ever brought to this country were presented to Lord Galway, who wrote to Major Godfrey Heseltine on August 26 1925 as follows :

"In July 1866, I was staying at Royat, Puy de Dôme, France, where I met the Marquis de Tournon and his son the Comte de Tournon. The latter promised me a couple of Basset Hounds from his pack, which duly arrived later in the autumn at Serlby. They were a dog and a bitch, and I called them 'Basset' and 'Belle'. They were long, low hounds, shaped much like a Dachshund, with crooked forelegs at the knees, with much more bone and larger heads than our Beagles. They were not the dark tan colour of Dachshunds but the colour of Foxhounds, with a certain amount of white about them. They had deep, heavy bones, more like Foxhounds than Beagles. I mated these two in 1867, and had a litter of five, all of which survive. I remember I called one

Photo by]   [Sport & General.

TWO CHAMPIONS.
In Bassets and Bloodhounds it is extremely difficult to breed good heads with good bodies. An indifferent head is very common. "Walhampton Lynnewood" and "Mulatto", two champion hounds the property of Lt.-Col. Heseltine, have remarkably good heads.

Photo by]

["Country Life."

THE BASSET HOUNDS "LINGUIST" AND "ALICE".

Quite a number of Bassets are exported to other parts of the world from England, which may to-day be said to be the centre of the best Basset stock. The two shown above, the one-time property of Lieut.-Colonel Heseltine, were exported to America.

Photo by]   [*Sport & General*.

A NOTED PACK.

The Wootton Basset Hounds are a well-known pack. Here we see them exercising. Two of the hounds on the right appear to have detected the stale scent of a hare, and one or two of the other hounds are apparently thinking of joining them.

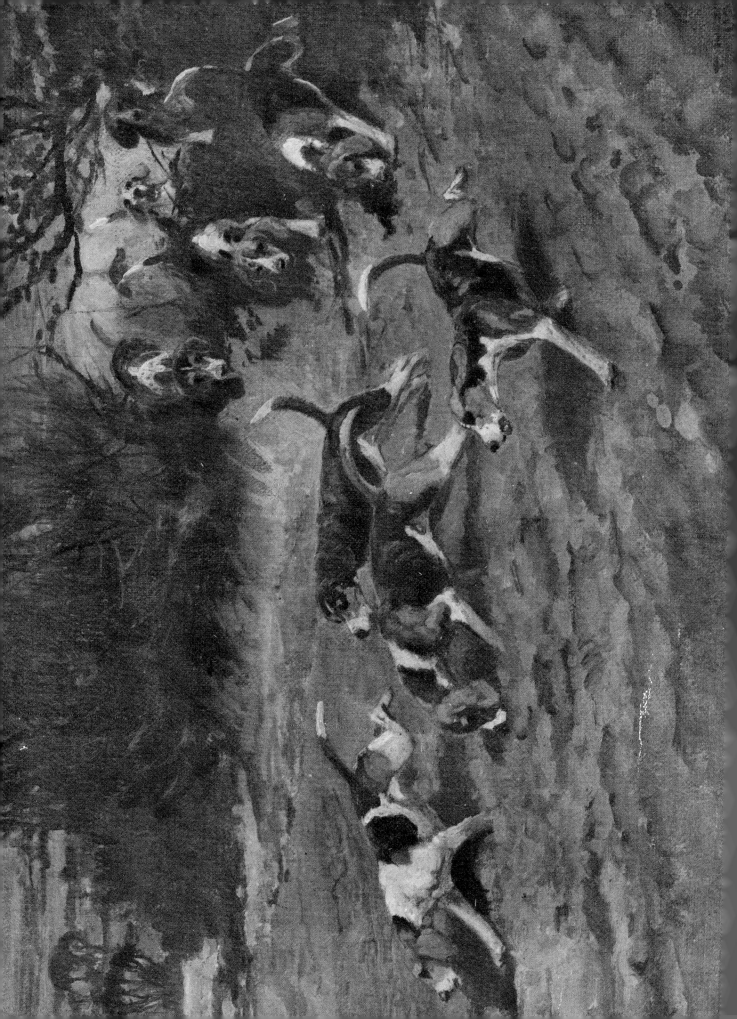

IN FULL CRY.

The breathless joy of the hunt is conveyed in this vivid painting by T. Ivester Lloyd. The pack is in full cry after the quarry, well ahead of the hunt. Mr. Lloyd knows his subject, for not only is he a breeder of Beagles, but has been master of a pack and is recognized as an authority on Hounds in general.

'Bellman'. I sold these three and a half couples to the late Lord Onslow in, I think, 1872, but I am not quite sure of the date.''

In the Winter Dog Show of 1875 at Wolverhampton, the late Sir Everett Millais first exhibited a Hound called "Model", which he procured from the Jardin d'Acclimatation, and this Hound was bred by Comte le Couteulx.

A little later, at the same place, the late Mr. G. R. Krehl bought "Fino de Paris", a Hound far superior to "Model", but which was exhibited with "Model" in Paris in 1874.

In 1877, Lord Onslow procured another couple of Hounds from France, "Fino" and "Finette". From the latter he procured a litter by "Model". It was a bitch from this cross (by "Model" out of Lord Onslow's "Finette"), "Garenne" by name, that the late Sir Everett Millais commenced breeding pure-bred Basset Hounds, and this was in 1878.

Photo]　　　　　　　　　　　　　　[*Fall.*
A sturdy fellow and a good worker, Basset Hound "Patience".

All the best Hounds in England at that time, and for some time later, can trace their parentage to "Fino de Paris", a Hound that stood at stud in 1874 at the Jardin d'Acclimatation, and which the late Mr. G. R. Krehl brought to this country.

From pictures of "Model" and "Fino de Paris" — and judging from them there can be little doubt as to which was the better Hound

The late Queen Alexandra had a small kennel of Rough-haired and Smooth Bassets at Sandringham. The above are some of them.

—"Model" would not compare well with the Hounds of the present day, whereas the same cannot be said of "Fino de Paris". "Model" was flat in skull, with badly hung ears. A French sportsman who visited this country later once said : "If we had known what you could produce from 'Fino de Paris' he would never have left the Jardin d'Acclimatation."

The Kennel Club acknowledged Bassets in their Stud Book by classification in 1883, when there were 10 entries. In 1891 there were 38, and 90 at the Kennel Club's Show in 1896.

In 1886 Mrs. C. C. Ellis bought her first Basset, a small bitch by Ch. "Jupiter", ex "Venus". By mating this bitch with Ch. "Fino VI" in 1887, Ch. "Psyche II" resulted. In 1889 she bred Ch. "Paris", Ch. "Xena", and "Napoleon II" from "Psyche II" by "Forester", and in the same year had another litter from Ch. "Fino VI" and "Venus II". In 1890 Mrs. Ellis bought Ch. "Forester". With these Hounds her kennel at that time was nearly invincible.

In 1886, at a show held at the Aquarium in London, there were 120 entries in the Basset Hound classes, a number which far exceeds anything that we have nowadays; but then, there are many owners of packs in England now (containing many beautiful Hounds) who will not

Photo]　　　　　　　　　　　　[*Sport & General.*
A fine Basset Hound, with well-marked body and extremely short legs, the late Queen Alexandra's "Sandringham Forester".

K

exhibit them, whereas at the time of this show they were in the hands of a very few breeders, who were no doubt interested in promoting the breed. These included H.M. Queen Alexandra, Lord Galway, Mr. G. R. Krehl, Mr. Louis Clement, Sir Everett Millais, Mr. Miles B. Kennedy, Mr. Muirhead, while later on, amongst well-known exhibitors, were Mrs. C. C. Ellis, Mr. Croxton Smith, Mrs. A. M. Lubbock, Marquis Conyngham, Mrs. Tottie, Mr. Musson, Mr. Craven, Col. Christopher, Major Godfrey Heseltine, and others.

Here is the description of points for a Smooth Basset Hound by the late Mr. Krehl, and accepted by the Basset Hound Club: Head, skull, eyes, muzzle, and flews, 15; ears, 15; neck, dewlap, chest, and shoulders, 10; forelegs and feet, 15; back, loins, and hindquarters, 10; stern 5; coat and skin, 10; colour and markings, 15; Basset Hound character and symmetry, 5. Total, 100.

CHARACTER AND SYMMETRY

HEAD.—To begin with, the head is the most distinguishing part of all breeds. The head of the Basset Hound is best when it closest resembles a Bloodhound's. It is long and narrow, with heavy flews, occiput prominent ("la bosse de la chasse"); and forehead wrinkled to the eyes, which should be kind and show the haw.

The general appearance of the head must present high breeding and reposeful dignity; the teeth are small and the upper jaw sometimes protrudes. This is not a fault and is called "bec-de-lièvre".

EARS.—The ears are very long, and when drawn forward falling well over the nose—so long that in hunting they more often actually tread on them —they are set on low and hang loose in folds like drapery; the ends inward curling; in texture thin and velvety.

NECK, ELBOWS, CHEST, BODY.—The neck is powerful, with heavy dewlaps Elbows must not turn out. The chest is deep, full and framed like a man-o'-war. Body long and low.

FORELEGS: FEET. — Forelegs (about four inches) and close fitting to the chest with a crooked knee; the wrinkled angle ends in a massive paw, each toe standing out distinctly.

THE STIFLES: CHARACTER.—The stifles are bent, and the quarters full of muscle, which stands out so that when one looks at the dog from behind it gives him a round, barrel-like effect. This, with the peculiar waddling gait, goes a long way towards Basset character— a quality easily recognized by the judge, and as desirable as terrier character in a Terrier.

STERN. — The stern is coarse underneath, and carried hound fashion

COATS: SKIN.—The coat is short, smooth and fine, and has a gloss on it like that of a racehorse. (To get this appearance, they should be hound-gloved, never brushed.) Skin loose and elastic.

COLOUR.—The colour should be black, white-and-tan; the head, shoulders and quarters a rich tan, and black patches on the back · also sometimes hare-pied.

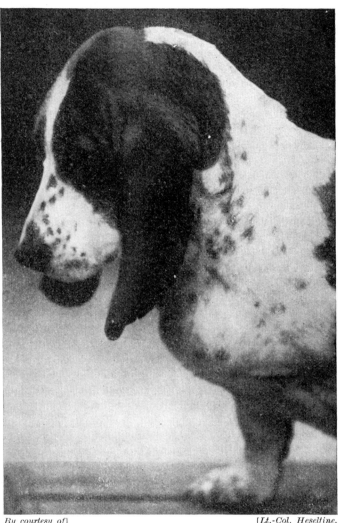

By courtesy of]   *[Lt.-Col. Heseltine.*

A LORD OF THE KENNEL.

There is something noble about the Basset head, and in this example one can see very clearly the evidences of the Bloodhound descent.

Photo]
[*Sport & General.*

A NEW SPORT.

Considering the popularity of Greyhound Racing, it is not altogether surprising that efforts are being made by owners of other breeds to train their animals to the same end.
Here Miss J. Trefusis Forbes tries out her pack of Basset Hounds.

By courtesy of]

[Lt.-Col. Heseltine.

A NOTED CHAMPION.

Major G. Heseltine, owner of Ch. "Walhampton Linguist", shown above, was the great authority on Bassets. He constantly showed and also hunted them. Though, as in the case of all Hounds, owners strive to obtain uniformity in their packs, readers will easily observe how the type varies.

The above description is like "Parson's egg"—it is good in parts ; but the author cannot convince himself that this standard of points, adopted by the B.H.C., tends to improve the breed of a hound.

In 1898 Major Heseltine and the author compiled the following description for the use of their puppy walkers. No doubt there are some who may not agree with their description, just as others take exception to the description accepted by the Basset Hound Club, which description certainly had not the universal approval of its members :

HEAD.—The head should be large, the skull narrow and of good length, the peak being very fully developed, a very characteristic point of the head, which should be free from any appearance of, or inclination to, cheek bumps. It is most perfect when it closest resembles the head of a Bloodhound, with heavy flews and forehead wrinkled to the eyes. The expression when sitting, or when still, should be very sad, full of reposeful dignity. The whole of the head should be covered with loose skin, so loose in fact that when the Hound brings its nose to the ground the skin over the head and cheeks should fall forward and wrinkle sensibly.

JAWS : NOSE.—The nose itself should be strong and free from snipiness, while the teeth of the upper and lower jaws should meet. A pig-jawed Hound, or one that is underhung, is distinctly objectionable.

EARS.—The ears are very long, and when drawn forward folding well over the nose. They are set on the head as low as possible and hang loose in folds like drapery, the ends inward curling, in texture thin and velvety.

EYES.—The eyes should be deeply sunken, showing a prominent haw, and in colour they should be deep brown.

NECK AND SHOULDERS.—The neck should be

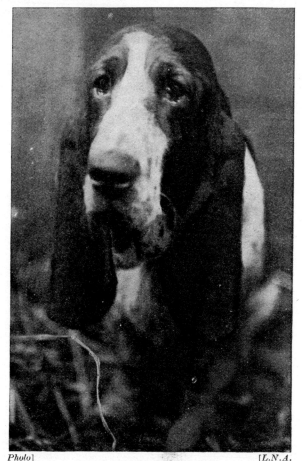

Photo] [*L.N.A.*
WELL KNOWN AT CRUFT'S.
Head study of Major Heseltine's Basset Hound "Walhampton Nightshade", winner of many prizes at Cruft's.

powerful with heavy dewlaps set on sloping shoulders.

FORELEGS.—The forelegs should be short, very powerful, very heavy in bone, close-fitting to the chest, with a crooked knee and wrinkled ankle ending in a massive paw. The Hound must not "be out at elbows", which is a bad fault.

FEET.—He must stand perfectly sound and true on his feet, which should be thick and massive, and the weight of the forepart of the body should be borne equally by each toe of the forefeet so far as it is compatible with the crook of the legs. Unsoundness in legs or feet should absolutely disqualify a Hound from taking a prize.

CHEST AND BODY.—The chest should be deep and full. The body should be long and low and well ribbed up. Slackness of loin, flat-sidedness, or roach or razor back are all bad faults.

HOCKS.—A Hound should not be straight on his hocks, nor should he measure more over his quarters than he does at the shoulders. Cow hocks, straight hocks, or weak hocks are all bad faults

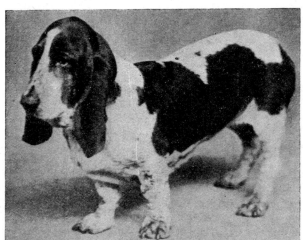

By courtesy of] [*Lt.-Col. Heseltine*
A full-length view of "Walhampton Nightshade".

QUARTERS.—The quarters should be full of muscle, which stand out so that when one looks at the dog from behind it gives him a round, barrel-like effect, with quarters "round as an apple". He should be what is known as "a good dog to follow", and when trotting away from you his hocks should bend well, and he should move true all round.

STERN.—The stern is coarse underneath, and carried "gaily" in Hound fashion, i.e. pothooked.

COLOUR.—No good Hound is a bad colour, so that any recognized Foxhound colour should be acceptable to the judge's eye, and only in the very closest competition should the colour of a Hound have any weight with a judge's decision.

NUMERICAL POINTS OF SMOOTH BASSET HOUND: Head, skull, eyes, muzzle, and flews, 14; ears, 10; neck, dewlaps, chest, and shoulders, 18; forelegs and feet, 18; back, loins, hocks, and hindquarters, 18; stern, 5; coat and skin, 5; colour and markings, 5; Basset Hound character and symmetry, 7. Total, 100.

If the reader will compare the two descriptions he will find many expressions identically the same, for the very reason that the above description is based on that adopted by the Basset Hound Club. The chief difference lies in the stress laid upon absolute soundness in legs and feet, and a more exact description of what is required in shoulders back, loins, hocks, and hindquarters.

The height of a Basset Hound is, in dog hounds, about 13 ins., and in bitches 12 ins., and their weight from 40 to 50 lb. The Hound has really more bone in proportion to its size than any other breed.

Many years ago there was a very strong feeling amongst Basset Hound breeders against unsound Hounds, that is to say Hounds whose forelegs were so bent as to prevent them being fit for use in the field, being awarded a prize in the show ring. In fact the members of the Basset Hound Club were divided in their opinions on the subject. There were those members who kept Hounds for exhibition only, and those who used them for hunting the hare.

Major Heseltine and the writer naturally held very strong views with those members of the latter class; the contention of the former class was that in-breeding a Hound suitable for hunting a hare we should lose type and get Hounds long on the leg. The latter class contended that the hunting members of the Basset Hound Club desired neither of these results. They wished to retain the beautiful type of the head of the "Le Couteulx" Hound, the massive bone, expression, etc., but at the same time improve the back, loins, hindquarters, legs and feet of the Hound then exhibited; least of all did they require him to run any faster than the

sound Hounds then did. If a Basset Hound is really sound on his legs and feet, no matter how short his legs are, he is able to get over the ground a great deal faster than anyone unconnected with the breed would give him credit for.

Many Basset Hound breeders will remember Ch. "Bowman", and Ch. "Louis le Beau", two dog Hounds which, for head properties, could scarcely be surpassed. Yet in both these cases, more especially in that of Ch. "Bowman", their hindquarters were grotesque, they measured two or three inches higher over the rump than they did at the shoulder, were slack in the loin and bad in their hocks, and sired as many prize winners—really well-made, good hunting Hounds—as any Hounds that have ever been exhibited; and that especially applies to Ch. "Louis le Beau".

The "Fino de Paris" and "Forester" blood is of such value that the same may be said of two other Hounds, "Locksley" and "Nicholas", the latter very plain, the former a cripple and very bad in body and legs.

Some of the best and soundest Basset Hounds ever bred came from "Locksley", and it was a matter of extreme regret that not a single dog Hound was to be seen at the Kennel Club Show held at the Crystal Palace in 1905 with the same beautiful type of head as the above-mentioned Hounds.

There has been such improvement since in the breeding of Hounds that there are now very many with beautiful heads, in fact one hound shown since this improvement, "Walhampton Nightshade '31," was considered one of the best Bassets ever bred.

In 1893 Sir Everett Millais found that in-breeding of Hounds was getting so serious that he decided an outcross was absolutely necessary He chose as this outcross the Bloodhound, because the head of the Basset should resemble the Bloodhound. The question of getting the length of leg increase by this cross did not worry him, though it did other breeders.

Sir Everett Millais was convinced he could alter this by breeding in two generations. The first cross was between the Basset Hound "Nicholas" and the Bloodhound "Inoculation". Twelve in all were born, and they were all anatomically nearer the Basset than the Bloodhound; the colour they took after the dam.

The next cross was between Ch. "Forester" and one of the above litter, viz. "Rickey". There were seven puppies born, six of them were tri-colour and one black-and-tan.

The next cross was between "Dulcie", one of the above litter, and "Bowman". They had seven-eighths Basset, one-eighth Bloodhound.

The next cross was the Basset dog "Guignol"

THE FINEST PACK OF ITS DAY.

Major G. Heseltine's pack of Basset Hounds was probably the finest of such packs in the world. The picture gives a meet in 1901 and attention is drawn to the excellence of the bodies and heads of the Hounds.

EVERY ONE A BEAUTY.

Major G. Trestitue's Beagot Pack in 1912 shows an improvement in type over those of 1901. Again attention is drawn to the heads and ears of the Hounds.

and one of the above litter. Six puppies resulted, four tri-colour, one lemon-and-white, and one black-and-tan. They were indistinguishable from the pure Basset, being fifteen-sixteenths Basset and one sixteenth Bloodhound.

Sir Everett Millais gave the author and his brother, Major Godfrey Heseltine, two of these puppies, one a tri-colour dog and one a black-and-tan bitch. They were a bit longer in the leg than those in the Heseltine Pack, but otherwise just like the true Basset ; very sound in legs and feet and wonderful workers. The tri-colour dog was used, but no puppies were ever got from the black-and-tan bitch.

Among the many packs of Basset which have hunted the hare regularly are, Wroxton, Lord North; The Halby Hall, Col. Burns-Hartopp; Greywell Hill, Lt.-Col. Hon. Dudley Carleton (now Lord Dorchester); Dallam Towers, Sir Maurice Bromley Wilson; The Iwerne Minster Pack, hunted by Miss D. Ismay, Mr. V. Fleming's, Lord Tredegars', Wick and District, Winters Hill, West Park, Dale Park, Dalapre, Brighton, Slane, and a few others, and The Walhampton.

Photo]   [B.I P.
A PLEASING STUDY.
Miss Audrey Salisbury, with her father's Basset Hounds, seen at a
Kennel Club Show

The latter pack were started by the purchase of nine and a half couples from Mr. T. Cannon, Junior, of Danebury, and have been hunted regularly since 1890 (with the exception of the war period), until the death of Major Godfrey Heseltine in 1932.

They were, at the time of Major Godfrey Heseltine's death, certainly the finest pack of Bassets in England. They had been bred for work and looks since they were started in 1890. Three times Hounds from France were purchased for an outcross, the last couple in 1920 being "Meteor" by M. Mallort's "Favourite '19" ex his "Minervi", and "Pampeute" by M. Mallort's "Farceur '19" ex M. Verrier's "Gavotte". "Meteor" sired some wonderful hunting Hounds.

The Walhampton Basset Hounds many times won Challenge Prizes for the Champion dog Hound and Bitch, as well as prizes for best in Puppies, also best Couple of Hounds at the Masters of Basset Hounds Association Hound Show at Banbury, besides winning Kennel Club Challenge Certificates on the show bench twenty-seven times since 1921. This proves that the Smooth Basset, if bred on right lines. can be as good at work as in looks.

BASSET GRIFFON OR ROUGH BASSET.—Some of the first Rough Hounds ever exhibited in England were the property of Dr. Seton and the Rev. J. C. Macdona, and the best specimen was a Hound registered in the K.C.S.B. as "Romano"

One of the best collections seen came from France, and was exhibited at Cruft's Show about 1892. The dogs were sent there with a view to sale, and the pick of them were purchased, but the author does not think the top price for any of the Hounds exceeded £35.

Now, Mrs. Tottie bred from Ch. "Tambour", K.C.S.B. 37743, and Ch. "Pervenche", 37741, the celebrated Ch. "Puritan", and his sister "Priscilla".

Ch. "Puritan" was whelped Feb. 6, 1897, and was a Champion by January 25 the following year. He was a splendid Hound, with immense bone, perfectly sound, full of quality, with grand coat, and colour a rich black, tan-and-white. "Puritan" had a coat equal to that of the best of the Smooth variety.

Amongst other breeders of the Rough Basset who had some excellent Hounds were H.M. Queen Alexandra, the Rev. W. Shield, Mr. F. Lowe, Mr. G. R. Krehl, Major H. Jones, and Mr. C. C. Lawrence.

It is to be regretted at the present time that there have been no Rough Basset shown since the war, and it is doubtful if there are many left in England.

STANDARD OF POINTS OF THE ROUGH BASSET
HOUND AS ADOPTED BY THE BASSET HOUND CLUB.

HEAD.—Should be large, the skull narrow but
of good length, the peak well developed. The
muzzle should be strong, and the jaws long and
powerful. A snipy muzzle and weakness of jaw
are objectionable.

EYES.—The eyes should be dark and not prominent.

EARS.—The ears should be set on low, of good
length and not prominent.

NECK.—Should be strong, of good length, and
muscular ; set on sloping shoulders.

BODY.—Should be massive, of good length and
well ribbed up, any weakness or slackness of loin
being a bad fault. The chest should be large and
deep ; the sternum prominent.

FORELEGS. —
Should be short and
powerful, very heavy
in bone, and either
nearly straight or
half crooked. The
elbows should lie
against the sides of
the chest and should
not turn out.

HINDQUARTERS.
—Should be power-
ful and muscular ;
the hindlegs should
be rather longer than
the forelegs, and well
bent at the stifles.

STERN. — Of
moderate length and
carried gaily. It
should be set on
high.

COAT.—Is an ex-
tremely important
point. It should be profuse, thick and harsh to
the touch, with a dense undercoat. The coat may
be wavy.

COLOUR.—Any recognizable Hound colour.

WEIGHT.—Dogs 40–45 lb. : Bitches rather
less.

GENERAL APPEARANCE.—The Rough Basset
should appear a very powerful Hound for his
size, and on short, strong legs. The feet should
be thick, well padded and not open. Body
massive and good length, without slackness of
loin. The expression should be kindly and intelligent. Any unsoundness should disqualify the
Hound.

POINT VALUES.—Head and ears, 20, body,
including hindquarters, 35 ; legs and feet, 20 ;
coat, 15 : Basset character 10. Total 100.

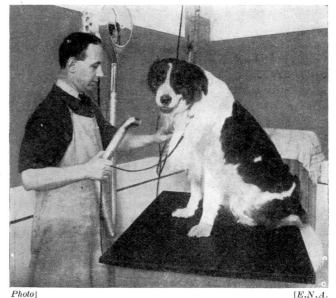

Photo]   *[E.N.A.*
Long-haired dogs are difficult to dry. Electric dryers provide the modern
efficient solution to this problem.

Bat-Ears.—Dogs which have very erect ears, as,
for example, the French Bulldog, are said to be
"bat-eared".

Bathing a Dog.—Opinions often differ very
widely as to the advisability of washing dogs, and as to
whether or not it is risky or even derogatory to the dog.
There seems no manner of doubt, however, that in
certain circumstances a bath is not only salutary but
essential.

There is no doubt that a bathing, properly performed, is an inducement to good health.

OBJECTIONS TO BATHING.—The objections raised
fall, usually, under three heads, viz., risk of the dog
catching cold, reduction of a wiry coat (in the case of
terriers) to one of soft texture, and the difficulty or
trouble sometimes experienced in performing the
task. So far as the first objection is concerned, the
risk is negligible provided ordinary precautions are
taken. For instance, it is quite obvious that the
dog should not only be thoroughly rinsed, but also
thoroughly dried. If
the former is neglect-
ed, then the soap
mats the hair to-
gether, and sets up
areas of dermatitis
beneath the mats,
and, in general, causes
a widespread sore-
ness. If the drying
process is scamped,
then the animal may
take a chill unless it
is vigorously exercised
for a sufficiently long
time.

Now as regards the
objection raised by
owners of wire-haired
dogs who say that
bathing spoils the
coat, they are partly
correct, as wiry hair
is certainly softened,
but only for a limited
and short time.
Probably at the end
of two days the wiry
texture will have re-
turned. For silky-haired dogs this objection is not, of
course, tenable. Concerning the third objection the
reason for this violent resistance, occasionally encountered, is, in most cases, probably traceable to
some malpractice by the owner in the earlier days of
the dog's life. Being put into very hot water is
certainly a terrifying experience, as also is the habit
possessed by some people of ducking the dog's head
when it does not behave quietly. The use, too, of
strong disinfectants, paraffin, and other chemicals in
the water, inducing excoriation or inflammation of
the skin or of the eyes, is not a procedure which a
sensitive dog would readily yield to a second time.

HOW TO BATH A DOG.—The method of dealing
with such a dog as this is first to apply a broad tape
or bandage muzzle around the jaws, tying beneath
the chin in an ordinary granny-knot, and taking the
ends of the tape round the back of the ears, where a
bow is tied. This will prevent the dog from opening
its mouth or biting the operator. The dog's collar
should be tightened to prevent him from slipping it,

Photo] THE SORROWS OF BATH-TIME [Fox
Apparently already burdened with all the woes in the world this Bloodhound seems to think that bathing is the last straw.

THE BEST BEAGLE TYPE.

Here is a true champion of his breed—"Dauntless of Reynalton"—owned by Mrs. N. E. Elms. Time and again in many parts he has carried all before him. He won the 1934 Challenge Certificate at Cruft's. This view shows all his excellent body points and for a closer appreciation of his magnificent head the reader is referred to page 107.

CH. "RINGWOOD".

At the end of the nineteenth century Beagles were often exhibited, and although the head and ears were not as they are to-day on champion dogs, yet, as will be noticed from the above picture, good feet and legs and good bodies were appreciated

and he should be attached by a short chain to a ring or hook in the wall. He cannot then escape or bite; but advantage must never be taken of his defencelessness to subject him to any but the kindest treatment. He is not to be immersed in hot water, but, instead, a pint jug may be used to pour lukewarm water over his coat until he is thoroughly wet to the skin from the tip of the nose to the tip of the tail.

A good liquid soap may then be applied in various areas, followed by vigorous rubbing with the hands. More water and soap may be added as required and a good lather produced. As the cleansing process becomes complete, more and more water is poured over him until all traces of soap have been removed.

The dog is allowed to shake himself, and then receives a vigorous rubbing down with a towel, preferably before a fire.

CHOICE OF A SOAP. — The selection of a soap for the purpose in view is extremely important, as there are some soaps which give an indifferent lather, some which contain an excess of strong soda, and others which contain crude carbolic. Dogs very readily absorb chemicals through their skin, and are rather easily poisoned by carbolic acid and some of the coal-tar preparations which are indiscriminately and thoughtlessly

added to the bath by people ignorant of this fact.

The ideal kind of soap for dogs is a liquid, as there is no waste, no difficulty in its manipulation, and no surplus left in the coat.

The properties one should find in a really good liquid soap are: (1) the production of a profuse and lasting lather; (2) its incapability of harming either hair or skin; (3) its power of dissolving grease and removing every kind of dirt; (4) its destructiveness to fleas, lice and their eggs; and (5) its pleasant aroma.

For alternatives to bathing, see GROOMING; BRUSHES. See also MEDICINAL BATHING.

Battak.—(See SUMATRA BATTAK.)

Beagle.—An ancient breed of small hound, having the usual hound colourings and markings and standing from about twelve to sixteen inches high at the shoulder.

These hounds, though they are quite easily trained as house-dogs and are as jolly little friends by the fireside as they are interesting pals on a walk, are usually bred and used nowadays for beagling, or the organized pursuit of the hare, hounds hunting mainly by scent and followed by the Field on foot.

There is no record of the use of the word "Beagle" in the writings on Venerie before the reign of Henry VII, but there is little doubt that various types of these hounds have existed in the British Isles for many centuries, and it is far from

HEAD IMPROVEMENT.

Two working Beagles, "Reader" and "Ringleader", may be taken as examples of the Hound head and ears which greatly improved the appearance of this breed.

A MOMENT'S RESPITE.

Hounds when hunting get very thirsty, more especially in the early days of the season. They seldom stop to drink, however, when on the scent, but occasionally will slake their thirst during a lull in the proceedings.

improbable that the ancient Greek hounds used for hare-hunting by Xenophon about 350 B.C. (descriptions of which hunts occur in his classic essays, *Cynegeticos*) would be labelled as Beagles to-day.

In Arthur Bryant's *Life of Charles II* it is recorded several times that Charles hunted hares with Beagles on Newmarket Heath.

Some of the oldest prints of the Beagle depict him as having a slimmer build and a sharper nose than have most present-day types, while other sketches show more heaviness and even a certain

the Fox-Beagle of his day as exceptionally lively, as well as light and fleet of foot, and relates how he crossed his Harriers with this type of hound in order to instil into the progeny of the former a greater measure of dash and drive.

The Masters of Harriers' and Beagles' Association has within recent years done a tremendous amount of good work in standardizing and improving Beagle strains.

Present-day Beagles, as was indicated before, must be regarded as composite blends of all the

By courtesy of] [Dr. Jobson-Scott.

A CHECK.

Apparently the hare has passed through a wood and the scent has been lost, the Beagles not knowing which way to go. A Hound on the left side of the picture thinks he has found the scent.

amount of throatiness, and it is quite clear, therefore, that many different types and strains have existed. The present-day types have evolved and been evolved throughout the ages as composite blends, all their best features having been specially chosen for the particular work for which these hounds have been bred.

William Somerville, writing about A.D. 1700, describes the characteristics of the Cotswold Beagle of his day, and relates how he bred some of his best harriers by crossing this type of hound with the old Southern Hound.

A North Country Beagle is also mentioned by writers in the seventeenth century, and is described as faster and nimbler and more slender in outline than was the Cotswold Beagle.

Beckford, writing about A.D. 1750, describes

best strains of a wide and varied ancestry; but most of them can be placed without difficulty in one of the following groups:

(*a*) An almost obsolete group of which the individual members have the appearances and characteristics of miniature editions of the old and now extinct Southern Hound;

(*b*) The rough-haired Welsh Beagle forms a group which is in a class by itself;

(*c*) The largest group includes the majority of present-day Beagles, and these must be regarded as blends of original Beagle blood with Harrier or Foxhound strains, or both;

(*d*) A modern group consists of hounds having the appearances and characteristics of miniature present-day Foxhounds;

(*e*) The Pocket or Rabbit-Beagle forms a

101

small group by itself, has more prominent eyes and other distinctive features, and stands only about ten inches high at the shoulder.

Beagles usually first see the light of day in the month of April or May, and when about four or five months old the puppies are usually sent out "to walk" in the neighbouring farmhouses until the following spring. Thence, at about the age of twelve months, they return to kennels to be trained for their début in October, i.e. when about eighteen months old, at the first Meet of the season.

The staple food of Beagles in kennels is oatmeal porridge. This must be well-cooked and of sufficient consistency to render it, when cooled, capable of being cut into slices like a cake. To these slices are added in the trencher some horse or other flesh, or at times some dog-biscuits or patent food, and the whole is then thoroughly mixed up with warm water. The mixture must not be too sloppy, and should never be served piping-hot.

Each hound is called out to the feeding trough by name, so that the first lesson of each is to know its name. Dainty feeders are given an extra allowance of time, and it is truly marvellous to watch a good or normal feeder practically bolt his food until his once gracefully slender body develops an unseemly bulge in the middle. Nature gave unto the hound a capacious stomach, which in the wild state it was accustomed to fill after each kill; and Nature's method of feeding is the method practised in kennels—that is, to fill the stomach summarily to repletion once in every twenty-four hours.

Beagles in kennels, like other hounds, have a wonderful habit of suddenly bursting forth into song. Each hound, with head raised aloft, as if in praise to its Unknown Creator, in soft and mellow cadences and crescendoes, sings and chants for the very joy of singing. Soulless indeed is he who, even

BEAGLE PUPPIES.
A jolly group of youngsters a few weeks old.

though disturbed in the dead of a still and moonlight night, has not been thrilled by the weirdly wonderful chorus.

In breeding, to bring out and accentuate the best qualities in physical as well as in working characteristics, every care must be taken in the selection of sires and bitches to ensure that neither have in their own or in their more intimate family histories any serious defects which are capable of being transmitted to the next generation. In selecting sires particular attention must be paid to stoutness, strength and amount of bone, as well as to perfection and symmetry of form and hunting qualities in the field. The sire must have a strong firm back, well-sprung ribs, strong loins and hocks close to the ground. In the selection of bitches similar considerations arise, and, though amount of bone is not so essential, perfect field manners are a *sine qua non*.

A Beagle's hunting life is limited as a rule to about seven or eight seasons, though exceptional hounds are able to carry on successfully for even ten or more seasons. It therefore follows that, allowing also for accidental casualties, there must in each season be a replacement of at least a seventh of the pack by new entry, if the pack is to be maintained continuously at the top of its form.

The "points" to be specially considered in a Beagle must be divided into three classes:

(1) Those physical characteristics which can best be seen and judged on the bench or on the flags. There must be, in the first place, perfect symmetry and beauty of form; the height at the shoulder may vary from about twelve to sixteen inches.

The colour of a good Beagle, as of a good horse, is of little importance. The usual hound markings, of varying proportions of black, white-and-tan, occur. Pure black-and-tans, black-and-whites or even pure whites are not uncommon while many

Photo]   [*Sport & General*
A CHAMPION BEAGLE BITCH.
"Bangle", shown here, was exhibited at the Peterborough Hound Show
She was one of the Ampleforth College pack, of Ampleforth Yorkshire.

[Sport & General.

Photo]

A MUDDLED SCENT.

The Worcester Park and Buckland Beagles at Rowgardens Park, Charlwood, are having difficulty in finding the scent. This may possibly be due to the presence of cattle in the background.

IN FULL CRY.

The Master of the West Surrey and Horsell Park keeps up with the pack, watching its behaviour intently. The actions of the Dogs provide him with useful information.

L

[*Photo.*] [*Sport & General.*]

ARRIVING AT THE MEET.

In the olden days packs travelled to the nearer meets on their own feet or in a farm cart, but to-day they are transported by a motor-van specially built for this purpose, allowing adequate ventilation (notice front of van) and affording the men in charge facilities to keep an eye on them. Care is taken to steady the Hounds as they jump down. Those shown are the West Surrey and Horsell Park Beagles.

are badger-pied, hare pied or lemon-pied.

The forelegs should be as straight as arrows and the feet should be round but not too small cat-feet. Good sloping shoulders spell mechanical efficiency and increase staying power. The body of a Beagle should be of moderate length and the back and loins strong, well developed and rather wide. The breast must be amply wide in order to accommodate the heart and lungs, which have of necessity often and for long periods to work at high pressure. Quarters must be well developed and muscular, and pace comes largely from the length and strength of the leg above the hock. The head of a beagle is one of his most characteristic features. It should be small and slightly domed, with a short and sharpish muzzle.

A Beagle's expression must be seen to be even partially appreciated, and no verbal description can fully portray its charm. The somewhat puzzled look is always fascinating, whilst a slight wrinkling of the forehead in some dogs seems to spell a subconscious anxiety, and the patient and steady gaze of all of them an ever-alert expectancy. The whole head is gloriously framed by the most beautifully placed and carefully folded velvety ears. The neck of a Beagle should tend towards slenderness rather than coarseness or throatiness. The stern or tail should be thick and carried well up with a moderate curve over the back.

The characters and temperaments of Beagles are as diverse as are their colours and markings, and though the majority are friendly and good-

By courtesy of]	[*E. C. Ash.*
OLD TYPE BEAGLES.
About 1880 attempts were made to improve the Beagle and to balance the Hound head to a smaller body ; to avoid too short legs and too long bodies, and at the same time to eliminate the Terrier type.

tempered companions they are all liable to exhibit on occasion the most unexpected outbursts of primitive savagery.

To sum up the points which one should look for in a Beagle on the show bench or on the flags they are : Perfect symmetry of build an intelligent and alert expression, a shapely neck, well-balanced shoulders, a compact sturdy body with good depth and width of chest, well-rounded and muscular loins and thighs, and straight well-boned forelegs with perfect cat-feet.

Faults to shudder at in a beagle are straight

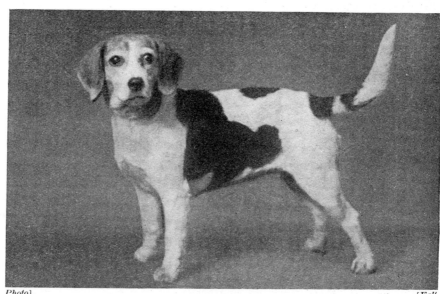

Photo]	[*Fall-*
THE MODERN BEAGLE.
A noted Beagle on the Show Bench is Ch. "Melody of Reynalton", the property of Mrs. Elms, a winner of a Challenge Certificate at Cruft's in 1934.

A FAMOUS PAINTING OF BEAGLES.

Maud Earl painted Miss Oughton's pack of Beagles about 1899, showing the pack discovering the hare when least expecting to find it.

shoulders, flat open splay-feet, short throaty bull-necks, weak thighs, slack loins, flat sides, knock-knees and calf-knees.

(2) Physical characteristics which can to all intents and purposes be judged only when hounds are at work in the field. It is essential that each hound possesses a perfect constitution equal to the strain of the longest day or the sternest chase. Another *sine qua non* of a good hound is a perfect nose, that is, a sense of smell which is as sensitive as it is accurate on the coldest line. One of the greatest joys of beagling is to hear the wondrous burst of melody as a pack crashes off in full cry, in-spiring everyone with the very joy of living. The voice of a good Beagle should therefore be as lovely as it is mellow, and may vary from the true cathedral note of a deep bass to a delightful and soft tenor.

(3) The main working qualities of a good Beagle will now be considered. It is obvious that these can be studied only when hounds are at work in the field. It should be noted that no two Beagles work in exactly the same way at all times. Each has its own temperament and working characteristics, and the main consideration in training a pack of such individualists is to ensure that they act as a solid cohort. Steadiness under all the varying circumstances of weather, soil, the presence of other game, and many other con-fusing eventualities is an essential characteristic

therefore, of a good Beagle, as is a sufficiency of "drive" and "dash".

"Drive" consists in a hound's keeping up a steady and persistent pressure on its quarry undismayed by variations in the quantity and quality of the scent as different crops and soils are traversed, by changes in the direction or force of the wind, by the exe-cution on the part of the hare of its many strata-gems to throw him off the scent, and by the many other diversions of the chase. "Dash," on the other hand, consists of a hound's consciously and boldly flinging forward when difficulties are encountered, sometimes at the expense of over-running the line altogether.

The reverse tendencies of pottering on the line or becoming "tied to the scent" can to a consider-able extent be corrected in early training, but if neglected become irremediable field-faults. In every pack it is a fortunate circumstance that there arise what are called "specialists" These hounds display quite exceptional skill in unravelling special problems in the line of their quarry. Thus, for example, there is the good "road-hound". It is cherished before all others, and lucky indeed is its master-owner who also has some hounds which specialize in working out other problems, e.g those on cold, scentless plough, or over cattle-or-other-animal foiled ground. Among the more common working faults among Beagles is "skirting" or persistently running wide of the line of the hare,

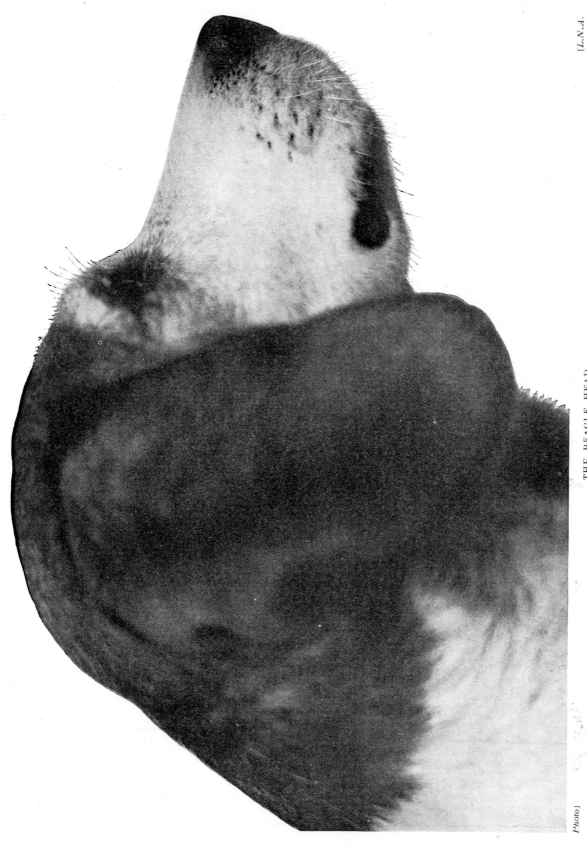

THE BEAGLE HEAD.

Ch. "Dauntless of Reynalton" is one of Mrs. N. E. Elms's breeding. It is interesting to compare this head with that of Ch. "Ringwood" on page 99. It is a fine example of what the head of a modern Beagle should be.

Photo]

[L.N.A.

Photo]   *[Fox.*

ON PARADE.

Like father, like son—a youngster takes stock of some of the best of the South Herts Beagles at the Kennels at Radlett. The reader should notice how much better are the ears of these Hounds than of some of the exhibition type.

and this should invariably be nipped in the bud in early pack-training.

Another unfortunate trait met with in some hounds is a persistent tendency to run "heel-wise", i.e. in a reverse direction to that taken by the hare. This also is amenable to correction if dealt with in early days. "Babbling" is not uncommon among some Beagles, but it has one merit, that it helps to enliven the proceedings, and is not so serious a fault as is the opposite condition, viz. muteness.

It will be readily appreciated in considering hunting qualities that not only must the individuals in the pack be considered, but that the qualities of the pack as a whole must also receive attention. Pack-discipline is therefore of paramount importance. At a draw a good pack should at a sign from the huntsman spread out fanwise with the precision of guardsmen. When running, such a pack, too, will invariably carry "a good head", i.e. there will be no lateral skirting or straggling and no tailing of the pack out behind, but all hounds will be well up as a compact cohort, each hound owning to and carrying the scent and none being a mere follower in the crowd. Even when walking to the Meet or to another draw, a well-disciplined pack will also walk as a compact and orderly body.

"The ancient sport of Beagling" can well be described by all hound-lovers and all lovers of hound-work as one of the purest forms of sport. The Master of Beagles is fortunate in not having to cope with members of his Field who are mere riding enthusiasts. The beagler's primary and, indeed, sole aim, is to watch the work of hounds. Beagling quite rightly entails a salutary amount of physical fitness in its participants, but it is by no means necessary to be a first-class sprinter in order to join in and enjoy the hunt, and quite a lot of the finest hound-work can be seen without going beyond a steady jog-trot.

The quarry of the beagler is usually the Common Brown Hare (*Lepus europoeus occidentalis*); but on the higher hills, such as in Cumberland, Lancashire, etc., the Blue or Mountain Hare (*Lepus variabilis* or *timidus*) is not infrequently met; while in some districts imported specimens of the Dublin variety of Blue Hare (*Lepus timidus lutescens*) occur; and more rarely aberrant types of hares (possibly mere natural variations), such as the speckled hares of the South Downs of Sussex, are hunted.

Most packs of Beagles are nowadays partially or wholly maintained by local clubs or Hunts, and are housed and fed in the Hunt kennels. There are over seventy such Hunts in England and Wales, full particulars of which can be gleaned from the Hunting Directory. It is gratifying to beagling

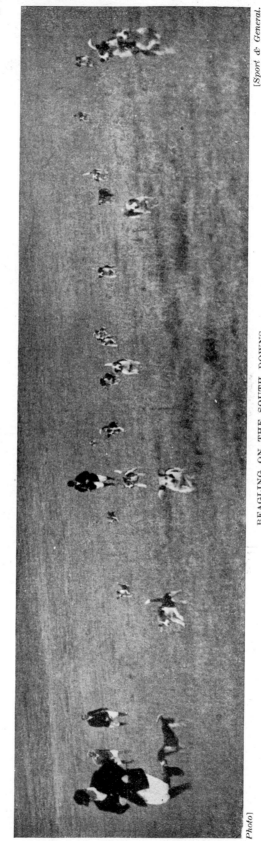

[*Sport & General.*

[*Photo*]

BEAGLING ON THE SOUTH DOWNS.

The Brighton Beagles are crossing the Devil's Dyke, a noted landmark. The Hounds are being moved to fresh ground. Sussex is one of the chief centres of beagling in England and it is a common sight to see the majority of a village's residents following the dogs.

enthusiasts to be able to state that the number of packs shows a progressive increase year by year.

Every beagler must be wholeheartedly a country-lover. Nothing connected with the countryside can be regarded by him as irrelevant in the pursuit of his sport. He must cultivate the closest sympathy with every son of the soil and become in tune with every part of his environment. The seasons, for example, form part and parcel of the background of the sport, and the signs thereof are the daily landmarks in every run. Thus among the autumn tints, patches of burnished

or at a stately mansion, all are varied by the weather settings and other surroundings in which they are staged.

After the ceremony of the Meet has been concluded, at a note or two on the horn, Master, whippers-in, hounds, and Field proceed in orderly procession to the first draw of the day. When the field or meadow to be drawn has been entered, the Master gives the signal to commence and hounds spread out fan-wise in front of him and the whippers-in in line with him, while the Field should align themselves behind. Hounds at once, with

CHECK BY A HEDGE-ROW.

The Ampleforth College Beagles find the trail end in thin air, probably because, working to leeward of the hare, the intervening hedge has spoilt the scent.

copper, of gorgeous shimmering gold, of bronze orange or chrome, stand out and are registered as signposts in every field and dale. Later in the season it is the bare boughs, stark stems, stately tree-trunks, the smooth silvery stems of the beeches and the pale pearly skins of the silver birches which act as guide-posts over the leafy carpets of every woodland. Thence, when spring arrives, every shy little snowdrop, every purple-tinted violet and every pale peeping periwinkle or primrose becomes a landmark and a guidepost in one.

The Meet of Beagles is part of the cream of the sport, and should not on any account be missed. All is joy and all expectancy as hounds are unloaded from the hound-van. No two Meets are ever alike. Whether they take place at a bleak or lonely cross-roads at an hospitable inn or farmhouse

noses to the ground, begin to search for that elusive vapour, the scent of the hare, while it is the duty of the Field as they march forward to search every yard of the ground for a squatting hare : for many a hare prefers to lie doggo and let danger pass her by rather than to spring up at the first sign.

Nowadays it is the custom for hounds to meet at about 11 am., or even later, when the sun is up and the morning scent has largely dissipated, and the usual method of "finding" a hare is for hounds or Field to just come across one and put it up from its "form" or "seat". In former days Meets much more frequently took place soon after dawn and in such circumstances, as fortunately happens also even now after some of the later Meets, the hare is actually tracked by hounds by her line or "drag" to her "form".

[*Dennis Moss.*

A FAMOUS COLLEGE PACK.

Photo]

The Royal Agricultural College at Cirencester has one of the best packs of Beagles in the country. The pack is here seen moving off after a meet outside the College. The Master leads the pack and the Whips form up on three sides to prevent any breaking away. Incidentally, somebody's Sealyham is hurrying up. The Field follows at a distance.

Photo]   *[Sport & General.*

CH. "DAUNTLESS OF REYNALTON".

Although the Beagle is really a hunting dog (hound), quite a number of people exhibit these dogs at Shows. Mrs. N. Elms's Kennel is an important one, and "Dauntless" is its pride.

Photo]   *[Sport & General.*

'CARNAVAL'.

Some Beagles show, even to-day the Terrier ancestry that evolved them from the larger Hound, as the reader will readily notice from this picture.

Photo]   ON THE HEATH.   *[Fox.*

The ordinary Hound used for hunting fox or stag or drag is, as will be noticed from the above picture of exercising, a very much more powerful animal, with a head more like that of a Pointer, and with small ears. The pack is the Aldershot Command Drag Hounds which took part in the Aldershot Tattoos.

A "find" under such conditions as a rule provides some of the most fascinating incidents of hound-work. As soon as hounds hit off the line of a morning drag, all sterns commence to wave in an agitated manner called "feathering" and all noses search the ground as if to the very roots of the grasses for the elusive scent. Thence one of the Nestors of the pack emits a few plaintive whimpers. The pack at once edge towards and "clump" round him and at the same time exhibits increased excitement. Then bursts forth a loudly proclaimed and joyous note of challenge, and soon all are speaking to a line, as they carry it along, till, see! like a bolt from the blue, the hare has sprung from the very centre of the pack. With infinite coolness she has managed to wriggle herself out of her apparently awful predicament and is now off like a streak with every hound screaming with joy as they course her to the first hedgerow. As soon as she disappears through the hedge all

heads have to come down to earth, and thence the pack settle down joyously to hunt the line again.

Now the run has started, and it has been well said that, once a hare gets on the run, it may do anything. It may streak off in a straight line for a mile or two, or it may run only a few fields, before it begins to weave some of its innumerable stratagems. In any event, it tends to work round in a circle or series of circles unless diverted from its chosen course by other dangers. Some of its favourite stratagems are: to weave a maze of tracks, to double back on the line and thence to spring side-wise and "squat" or "clap" until hounds have passed on, to run along the top of a wall or hedge, to "run" a road where scent holds badly, and to swim across or run along a stream or water-course.

The problem for hounds is therefore how to unravel these many stratagems, and for this they must have a sufficiency of time and room, hence

Photo]   POCKET BEAGLE.   *[Sport & General.*

Many years ago a very small Beagle, known as the Pocket Beagle, was evolved; the name implies a Hound sufficiently small to be carried in the pocket. Although the modern Pocket Beagle is not as small as that, yet they are diminutive, as Mrs. Hillyard's dogs show

the Field must ever be on their guard not to press hounds, especially on the days when scent is not of the best and the pace of hounds is slowed down.

Not infrequently hounds actually "check" at such points, as the hare of course intended that they should, and here the keen hound-lover very often comes into a paradise of his own. During a "check" every member of the Field should "stand still and keep quiet", and from such a point of vantage every movement of every hound can be studied and analysed by those of the Field who are well up with the chase. Hounds should be allowed to range around for themselves. They usually range down-wind a bit at first, but very soon turn up-wind again. No movement or sound of any hound is without significance, and the man who knows and understands each hound is thrilled with expectancy as the work of unravelling the hare's tangled line proceeds, until, as at the original "find" after following the morning drag, first breaks out the whimper with the agitated "feathering" of sterns and "clumping" of hounds, then the joyous notes of challenge and later the full-voiced thrilling clamour of the whole pack as they stream off again in full cry on the refound line.

The kill is a short and sharp affair and the natural end to a hunt. With a pack of moderate-sized Beagles the hare has more than a very good sporting chance by the exhibition of her multitude of stratagems to save her "scut", i.e. tail, and no beagler need be stupidly hypersensitive at witnessing such a natural termination to a hare's span of life. It must be recollected that before all things a hare is a creature of the Wild, as also are Beagles.

Bedding.—There are those who hold that a dog requires no bedding, and advance, as their reasons, that in its absence the harbouring of skin parasites is considerably reduced, that there is a great saving of expense and labour, and that dogs are not encouraged to be dirty on their beds. There is truth in these contentions, and yet the man who loves his dog would feel particularly uncomfortable, and even unhappy, to contemplate his dog on a cold night, lying upon a bare floor. Everyone knows how much a dog appreciates warmth and comfort, and there seem no serious or insurmountable reasons why he should not have it. There are several kinds of bedding suitable to dogs, and all of them are comparatively cheap. For one or two dogs of a private owner, there is nothing better than fine wood shavings or wood-wool, a material which is used in the packing of crates of eggs from abroad. Its great advantage is its cleanliness, for the resins in the wood are repellent to fleas and other insect life.

Hay is sometimes used for bedding and is also warm, but tends to become dusty, and contains minute acari (known as forage acari) which can set up a skin irritation not unlike that encountered in true mange.

Oat straw is largely utilized and is probably quite satisfactory for the larger breeds. Wheat straw is not so useful as dog bedding, because its stalks are longer and much stiffer.

Shavings, hay and straw possess the advantage that they can be burnt after use, and their ash is a useful chemical for the garden. Cushions, blankets and other textile materials are not recommended (except for the individual pet kept in a house or flat) as they are costly, unhygienic, and never look clean for long. They can, of course, be washed and disinfected at intervals, and if parasites have invaded them they should be boiled or baked.

Should the supply of bedding fail at any time, a good temporary expedient is to provide the dog with plenty of crumpled-up paper; newspaper is remarkably warm, and can, of course, be burnt daily.

By courtesy of]   AN EARLY CHAMPION.   [E. C. Ash.

One of the most noted of earlier Bedlingtons at the end of the nineteenth century was Ch. "Humbleden Blue Boy". It will be seen that the trimming had not reached the high stage of excellence of the present day. The head shows a "stop": no stop is seen on the present-day head (see opposite).

Bedlington Terrier.—Although the actual origin of the Bedlington Terrier is wrapped in a certain amount of obscurity, he has been known by the name he now bears for over a hundred years: before that he was called the Rothbury or Northumberland Fox Terrier. The earliest mention of the Rothbury Terrier is in the life of the Northumbrian piper James Allan, published some time early in the last century.

The Allans were a branch of the famous Yetholme gipsies, and the piper (who was born in Rothbury forest about 1719 or 1720) was the youngest son of William Allan, who was a tinker by trade, and also was a piper of no little merit,

A YOUTHFUL BEDLINGTON.

Miss H. S. M. Branfoot's "Wild Oats of Bransways" at seven months old, after being dressed.

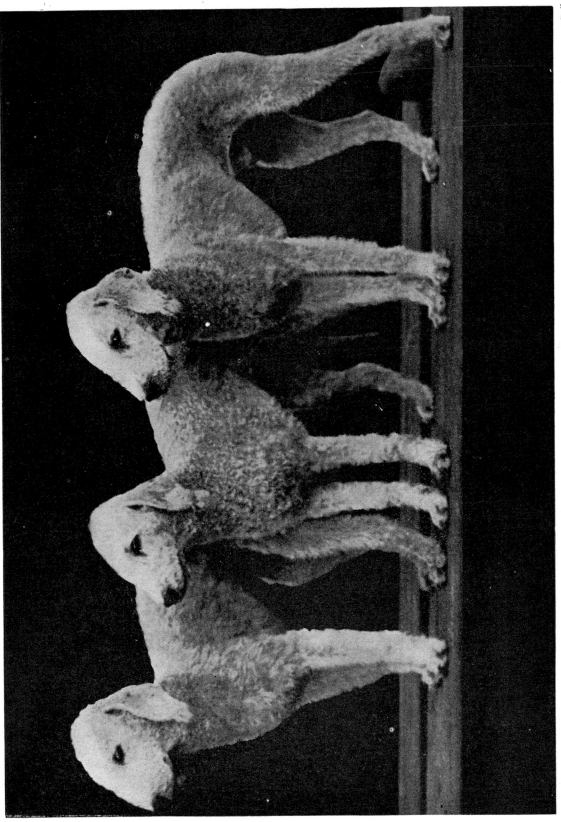

Photo: [*Fall.*

THREE BEAUTIES.

These three Bedlingtons, "Sudston Princess", "Pedlar", and "Paladin", show the wedge-shape head of the breed and the roach back so much desired.

and "the devil for sport". Otter-hunting was his strong point, and he was very popular amongst the gentlemen of the district, as he always kept a number of terriers of the Rothbury type, who could be relied upon to show good sport. "Pincher" and "Peachem" were his favourites, and it is said that once, when very low down in the world, a gentleman offered him fifty guineas for the latter, which he refused. "Peacher" possessed a wonderful nose and was a sure finder. Old Allen used to say. When "Peachem" opened on the trail of an otter he was prepared to sell the skin !

A point that has never been settled, and never can be now —is whether the Dandie was made from the Bedlington or vice versa : it is probable that both were of the same origin, described by old writers as "a small breed, white topped, and game as thunder" ; and as both were famous for their gameness and usefulness as vermin-killers, they divided into two camps, the gentry patronizing the short-legged type immortalized by Sir Walter Scott in *Guy Mannering*, while the more leggy, lathy dog became the indispensable follower and companion of the gipsies and tinkers that in those days infested the Border. Rothbury Forest was a great stronghold of such well-known tribes as the Andersons, Faas, Jeffersons and Make-pieces ; a member of the last-named family— old Nicholas —was a celebrated rat-catcher. The Rothbury Terrier, being unequalled as a ratter, fast enough to catch a rabbit and hard enough to tackle a badger or otter, naturally became a valued adjunct in a gipsy camp.

It was in the year 1825 that the name

Photo]   *[Ernest Fielder.*
IN THE ROUGH.
A Bedlington in the rough is seldom seen, so that it is interesting to compare the above picture, showing Miss E. S. M. Branfoot's "Bailey of Bransways" and his grandson, "Buckwheat of Bransways", with the finished article.

of Bedlington replaced the older one of Rothbury. The breed had been established round Morpeth and Bedlington for a good many years, the latter place being renowned for its dogs, and numbers of these terriers were bred there, and gradually spread all over the country. "Young Piper", owned by Joseph Ainsley, was the first called by the name ; he was whelped about 1820 by Jock Anderson's "Piper", the gamest of the game, a liver-coloured dog, 15 inches at the shoulder, and weighing about 15 lb., out of a blue-black bitch with brindle legs and a tuft of light-coloured hair on her head weighing 14 lb. and measuring 13 inches. She was called "Phoebe", and was descended through her dam "Wash" (A. Riddles), from old "Flint" (whelped 1782), who was owned by Squire Trevelyan, of Neatherwitton. There is no record as to the personal appearance of "Flint", and it is very unlikely that he resembled the Bedlingtons of to-day—or even yesterday ; but, as his name implies, he was pretty certain to have been hard as the nether millstone, for the squire was noted for the gameness of his Terriers, and discarded anything not up to his standard of hardness.

The Bedlington has always been a favourite in the North country, where his indomitable courage and endurance, together with his wonderful nose and general adaptability to take part in sport on land or water, has won for him pride of place in the hearts of the miners and pitmen. During the sixties and seventies the late T. J. Pickett did much to bring the breed into prominence ; he owned and bred a great

By courtesy of]   *[Mrs. Bruce-Low.*
BEDLINGTON PUPPIES.
Mrs. Bruce-Low's Bedlington puppies at the age when all puppies seem to be mostly head and feet. They look a very good lot.

many, the most notable being the famous trio "Tyne", "Tear'em" and "Tyneside". "Tear'em" won first in a class of fifty-two entries at the first show where there was classification for the breed at Bedlington in 1870.

What a wonderful sight it must have been! Fifty-two Bedlingtons, rugged and rough one may be sure, but none the worse for that, and every man-John of them hard as nails, each thirsting to get his steel-trap jaws fast in his neighbour! A somewhat different sight from the shows of to-day, where the majority of the Terriers are so over-trimmed and over-chalked as to resemble woolly lambs —though the heart inside is not the heart of a lamb, however the mighty-have-fallen in appearance through the stupidity of fashion.

It is said that the game-ness of the Bedlington has disappear-ed like the characteristic weather-re-sisting coat; this is not the case, though it must be admitted there are some grounds for the asser-tion. If you get a puppy from a strain that has been kept solely for show for several generations, and has never been allowed to kill a rat, or have a dust-up with others of his kind, and in all probability the only exercise he has had off the lead is in a wired-in paddock or garden, is it astonishing that he does not take kindly to facing stiff cover and all the rough-and-tumble hardship that is the daily meat of a dog kept for work? That, how-ever, only applies to a small section of the breed, and no one who requires a dog as a sporting com-panion will seek for it in a kennel kept only for exhibition purposes.

There has been a danger in the last few years

of an alteration in type, which, if it continued, would be very disastrous. About the time of the Great War there was a vogue for very big dogs, well above the approximate size suggested in the Club standards, though in other respects they retained the characteristics of the breed, namely the correctly shaped body with long muscular neck set on well-made sloping shoulders, and the moderately long back which gives the true Bed-lington arch at the loin—a most important feature. As he stands still in the show ring, the back may look almost flat till he moves, when the beautiful formation of the flexible spine and loins comes into play. When galloping his action is very much like that of a grey-hound. Other characteris-tics are the hare-foot and slightly slop-ing pastern which also aids him in speed.

A few years later a reac-tion in size set in which has not been to the advantage of the breed, for with the small dogs have come the inevitable short backs, straight shoulders, gun-barrel fronts and cat-feet; and with the coming of the short back it is good-bye to the natural roach and typical action; for it is not possible to attain either one or the other in a "blue Fox Terrier", which is what some of the Bedling-tons one sees to-day are like!

The size of the dog is not so important as other points. As long as there have been Bedlingtons there have been "big and little 'uns". Roughly speaking, a dog should be from 15 or 16 inches at shoulder, and bitches an inch or so less; but a quarter of an inch either way is of no importance unless the competition is so close that all other points are equal. Type and conformation is

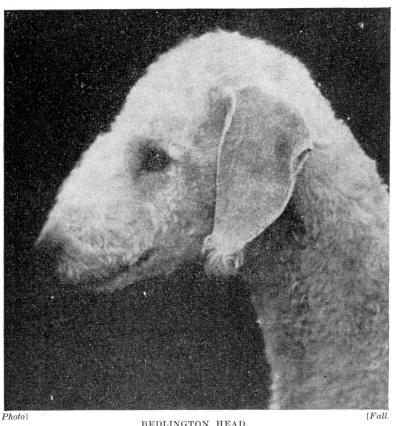

Photo]   BEDLINGTON HEAD.   [*Fall.*

Even the best of modern dogs vary somewhat in their head points, such as size of ear, as the various modern dogs shown in these pages prove. This study offers opportunities of comparison.

THE BEST OF FRIENDS.
A delightful open-air study of Master Horlick with his two favourite Bedlingtons.

Photo]
THE ARRIVAL.
[L.N.A.

Miss Lawis, an owner of a Bedlington Kennel, arriving at Cruft's Show in 1934. The dog on the left won a Challenge Certificate.

all-important—he should be a light-made-up lathy dog, not weedy; hard, strong and muscular, without cloddiness or having the appearance of being too much on the leg; fairly long in the body with naturally arched loin, and with a tail of from 9 to 11 inches according to size of the dog, low set on, and carried in a graceful curve.

The head should be long and narrow, with good length of skull, which should be well domed, thus giving plenty of brain-room; the fore-face long and well filled up under the eyes and slightly tapering toward the nose, which should be large and well angled; teeth large strong and level; the ear, set low and carried close to cheek, fairly long and filbert shaped; the eye small and deeply set, dark brown in the blues and a golden shade in the livers.

The expression, when in repose, is one of extreme boredom, but directly the dog is on his feet it is changed to piercing hardness.

Owing to excessive trimming the old weather-resisting jacket has been nearly lost; breeders do not trouble about the coat when the dogs are shorn within half an inch of their skin. The natural coat is a blend of hard and soft hair, very dense on the body, slightly curly at neck and chest, while the top-knot and ear fringe are silky, silver-white in the blues and creamy in the livers. They are very hardy dogs, highly intelligent and

Photo]   LEVELLING THE HAIR.   *[L.N.A*
"Bet of Bransways'" hair being trimmed by Miss Branfoot. Attention is drawn to the way a Bedlington should be held to ensure the evenness desired.

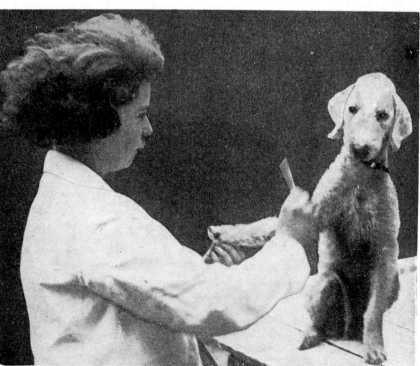

By courtesy of]   FINAL TOUCHES.   *[Miss Goodrick.*
An exhibitor who knows his or her work makes certain up to the very last moment that the dog is looking at its very best. Miss Goodrick is combing out the hair on the legs before taking the dog into the ring.

Photo]   [Ernest Fielder.
MOTHER AND PUPPY.
Miss Branfoot's "Barley of Bransways" with "Wild Oats of Bransways".

very faithful to their owners. The puppies are easy to rear and the bitches are good mothers.

The following is the standard of points as laid down by the National, South and West of England, and Scottish Bedlington Terrier Clubs:

SKULL.—Narrow, but deep and rounded; high at occiputs, and covered with a nice silky tuft or top-knot.

JAW.—Long, tapering, sharp and muscular; as little stop as possible between the eyes, so as to form nearly a line from the nose-end along the jaw of the skull to the occiput. The lips close-fitting and no flew.

EYES.—Should be small and well sunk in head. The Blues should have a dark eye; the Blue-and-tipped with fine silky hair. filbert-shaped.

LEGS.—Of moderate length, not wide apart, straight and square set and with good-sized feet, which are rather long.

TAIL.—Thick at root, tapering to point slightly teathered on lower side, 9 inches to 11 inches long, and scimitar-shaped.

NECK AND SHOULDERS.—Neck long, deep at base, rising well from shoulders. which should be flat.

BODY.—Long and well proportioned, flat ribbed and deep, not wide in chest, slightly arched back, well ribbed up, with light quarters.

COAT.—Hard, with close bottom, and not lying flat to sides.

Tans, ditto, with amber shades; Livers, Sandies, etc., a light-brown eye.

NOSE.—Large, well angled. Blues, and Blue-and-Tans should have black noses; Livers and Sandies flesh coloured.

TEETH.—Level or pincer-jawed.

EARS.—Moderately large, well formed, flat to the cheek, thinly covered and They should be

COLOUR.—DarkBlue, Blue-and-Tan, Liver, Liver-and-Tan, Sandy, Sandy-and-Tan.

HEIGHT.—About 15 or 16 inches.

WEIGHT.—Dogs about 24 lb., Bitches about 22 lb.

GENERAL APPEARANCE. — He is a light-made-up lathy dog, but not shelly.

THE FOLLOWING IS THE VALUE OF POINTS.—Head 20, size,

Photo]   [Fall.
GROWING UP.
The little fellow has left behind his puppyhood and received his first treatment by the hairdresser. Compare his appearance now with the still unshorn puppy on the opposite page.

AN OUTSTANDING PUPPY.

An excellent example of a good puppy at four and a half months old. Miss Branfoot's "Buckwheat of Bransways" in the rough.

The first picture of a Terrier known is seen in an illuminated manu-
script dealing with the seasons of the year of the fifteenth century.
A small Black-and-Tan Rough-haired Terrier appears. It is from
dogs like this that the Black-and-Tan (Smooth) Terrier was evolved.

10 ; teeth, 10 ; colour, 5 ; legs and feet, 10 ; ears, 5 ;
eyes, 5 ; nose. 5 ; body 15 : coat. 10 : tail. 5
Total, 100

Bed Sores.—Bed sores are areas of disintegrated
or ulcerated skin occurring generally on the most
prominent parts of the body.

CAUSE.—The underlying cause in all cases is a
state of debility, brought about by some disease
process, whereby nearly all the tissues of the body
are brought to such a low state of vitality that, in
the case of the skin, any abnormal influence such as
bruising or pressure will bring about a local death
(necrosis) at that point. Thus, sick dogs which have
lain for long periods (through inability to stand) on
one side or the other are very prone indeed to develop
these areas of ulceration known as bed sores. The
direct cause, therefore, seems to be long-continued

pressure, of the undermost side of the body, against
the bed, thereby interfering with the supply of blood
to the parts so pressed.

SYMPTOMS.—The affected area becomes first inflamed and tender ; hairs begin to fall out, and then
the skin surface becomes moist and ulcerative. Very
soon it is an ugly raw sore which resists most
attempts to effect healing. At a later stage a
considerable portion of the sore may slough out.

TREATMENT.—The first point is to eliminate, as
far as possible, the causal factors ; that is to say,
the dog should frequently be turned over and never
allowed to lie for more than one or two hours on one
side of the body. A very soft bed must be provided
so as to reduce the pressure upon the skin, or at least
to distribute it more evenly. Thirdly, the sore must
be dressed with astringents and antiseptics, which
action—together with the removal of black crusts
or gangrenous portions—should be left to the
veterinary surgeon attending the case.

Cleanliness is essential, as also is one's endeavour
rapidly to improve the general health, increase the
circulation, and sustain the patient's strength

Beef Tea. (*See* FOODS AND FEEDING.)

Beefy=over-fleshed.

Belgian Sheepdog. (*See* ALSATIAN.)

Berghund.—The name Berghund means
mountain dog, and although various rough-haired
dogs have been described to be the Berghund.
to-day each variety of these mountain dogs
has some special name by which it is known.
Dogs of the mountain are found all over the
world, wherever hilly country exists. They are

WHEN EARS WERE CROPPED.

At the end of the nineteenth century one of the best Miniature Black-and-Tan Terriers was "Jubilee Wonder", whose
wins included numerous medals, hung on his collar. In
those days Black-and-Tan Terriers' ears were cropped, a
custom ended later by legislation.

mainly used for guarding sheep. The reader is referred to the mountain dogs given in the section devoted to the dogs of each country

Bile.—A secretion of the liver, brown or greenish-brown in colour, bitter in taste, and a very important digestive juice. It aids the action of the pancreatic juice, emulsifies fat, and prevents putrefactive changes in the intestine.

Biliary Fever. (*See* PIROPLASMOSIS.)

Biliousness.—Biliousness, as it is observed in the human species, is fairly prevalent among dogs, although it is difficult to know whether or not a dog experiences a headache.

CAUSES.—Constipation, obstruction of the bowels, dyspepsia, excessive secretion by the liver of bile. errors of diet, etc.

SYMPTOMS.—Malaise, constipation, indigestion, loss of appetite, and vomiting of a yellow or green dis-coloured slimy material. The eating of grass usually causes sickness, and one must not mistake the expulsion of such green-stained dejecta as due to biliousness.

TREATMENT.—The elimination of the cause is of the first importance, and in all cases the administra-tion of a cholagogue or bile-expelling purgative is essential. Reduce the food ration and increase the amount of exercise.

The three Black-and-Tan specimens shown are, at top of page "Dandylion"; below, "Watercan Flyaway"; and on left, "Watercan Swift", three famous dogs, bred by Mrs. Blondin Robiolio of London.

Photos]   [*Fall*.
TYPES OF MINIATURE BLACK-AND-TANS.
In the earlier Black-and-Tan Miniature show days, the ears were often very large, far more so than they are to-day. Breeders, however, by careful selection, managed to reduce the size of the ears, though even now there are two distinct types.

Birth of Puppies. (*See* WHELPING.)

Biscuits. (*See* FOODS AND FEEDING.)

Bismuth.—Several of the salts of this metal are of great value in medicine, and perhaps particularly in canine therapeutics. Bismuth carbonate and subnitrate are well known as gastro-intestinal antiseptics and sedatives when administered in cases of gastritis or enteritis. Their sedative action is probably, in some measure, attributable to their characteristic of adhering to the mucous lining and so affording protection to this inflamed surface.

Bismuth salts, particularly the oxide, are extensively employed as constituents of dry dressings for application to moist sore areas such as are encountered in moist eczema; and for the treatment of wounds. Bismuth is generally not used alone for these purposes, but is mixed with other antiseptics and astringents such as boric acid, zinc oxide, kaolin, and Fuller's earth, etc.

Bites.—(*See also* CAT BITES, DOG BITES, FROSTBITE, SNAKEBITE, *and* WOUNDS.)

OWNERS' RESPONSIBILITY FOR.—The law as to this has not been altered by statute. Human beings and animals which do not come within the statutory definition of cattle or domestic poultry are still governed by the common law. Consequently a person who has been bitten by a dog must prove *scienter re* that the dog is of a disposition to bite mankind and that its owner knew it. Very slight evidence of *scienter* is sufficient, but the Court will not presume it. Where, however, a savage dog is kept, the owner will, it seems, be liable for any injuries that it may inflict even if the animal got loose through the act of a third person—that is, he is bound to keep it secure at his peril (Baker and Snell (1908) 2 K.B. 825). It has been held that a trespasser is not entitled to damages if he is bitten, but this rule cannot be relied on, at least to its full extent, in view of the decision of the House of Lords (Lowery and Waller (1911) A.C. 10) that the owner of land who knows that persons are in the habit of crossing his land and acquiesces in their doing so is not entitled to turn a savage beast (in that case a bull)

Photo]   'WATERCAN JUNIOR.'   [*Fall*

Some of the smartest Black-and-Tan Miniatures (and could anything be smarter?) were bred by Mrs. Robiolio. "Watercan Junior" is a very nearly perfect little dog.

Photo]   "WATERCAN TEDDY TAIL."   [*Fall*.

The smaller Black-and-Tan Miniatures are the greater their value as long as they remain sound in body and limb, and healthy. Mrs. Robiolio's "Watercan Teddy Tail" shows how healthy such a dog can be.

out on the land without giving due notice. The statutory rules for ascertaining who is the owner of a dog do not apply to an action brought under common law for injuries caused by a dog.

Bk. = black.

Black-and-Tan Terrier (Miniature). — (*See also* MANCHESTER TERRIER).—The Black-and-Tan Miniature Terrier is a small edition of the Manchester Terrier proper, from which it has probably evolved. The Miniatures vary in size from very tiny specimens of 3 lb. to dogs of 8 and 10 lb. One cannot breed to scale, litters generally being mixed as to size. Up to as late as 1924 the Kennel Club imposed a weight restriction on dogs on the Show bench, specimens *over* 7 lb. being barred. In January 1925 this rule was rescinded, and nowadays any size dog may be benched, provided it is of Miniature pedigree. To-day the 7 and 8 lb. dogs seem to be the ones most favoured by the judges, provided they are sound on all their points: nevertheless a really good little dog will almost invariably hold its own amongst bigger specimens of equal merit.

This is one of our oldest English breeds and was, in bygone days extensively used for ratting and exterminating other vermin.

THE BLOODHOUND.

(Painted by Maud Earl).

All the strength, nobility and fidelity which characterize this breed are wonderfully portrayed in this expressive painting by Maud Earl, perhaps the greatest of dog artists who ever lived. Besides their aristocratic appearance and old lineage, Bloodhounds have the most delightful disposition to recommend them.

The present-day dog is almost undoubtedly much more gracefully built than in those times, but still retains the plucky terrier characteristics and is game and intelligent to a degree, a good house-guard and staunch friend, with heaps to commend him: clean and obedient, both in coat and habits, easily groomed and suitable either for town or country.

For some years he was rarely seen, but has since returned to popularity.

Ear carriage is a debatable point since cropping was abolished, but in the writer's opinion the erect ears are the smartest giving the dog a sharper appearance.

Photo. *[Fall.*
"GIGOLETIE".
Mrs. Christine Wilkinson, a daughter of the well-known Mr. Krehl, one of the leading "doggie" men at the end of last century, is a noted breeder of Miniature Black-and-Tans, and keeps her dogs in London.

Points and Standard as given by the Black-and-Tan Terrier Club.

HEAD.—Long, flat and narrow, level and wedge-shaped without showing cheek muscles; well filled up under the eyes; with tapering, lightly lipped jaws and level teeth.

EYES. — Very small, sparkling and dark, set fairly close together, and oblong in shape.

NOSE.—Black

EARS.—Small and V-shaped; erect semi-erect or drop.

NECK AND SHOULDERS.—The neck should be fairly long and tapering from the shoulders to the head, with sloping shoulders; the neck being free from throatiness and slightly arched at the occiput.

CHEST. — Narrow, but deep.

BODY.—Moderately short, and curving upwards at the loin: ribs well sprung; back slightly arched at the loin, and falling again at the joining of the tail to the same height as the shoulders.

LEGS.—Must be quite straight set on, well set on under the dog, and of fair length.

FEET.—More inclined to be cat than hare-footed.

TAIL.—Of moderate length and well set on where the arch of the back ends, thick where it joins the body, tapering to a point and not carried higher than the back.

COAT.—Close, smooth, short and glossy.

COLOUR — Jet-black and rich mahogany-tan distributed over the body as follows : On the head the muzzle is tanned to the nose, which, with the nasal bone, is jet-black ; there is also a bright tan spot over each eye, and on each cheek ; the under jaw and throat are tanned and hair inside the ear the same colour. The forelegs tanned up to the knee with black lines (pencil marks) up each toe, and a black mark (thumb mark) above the foot. Inside the hindlegs tanned, but divided with black at the hock joint, and under the tail, also tanned; so is the vent, but

Photo] *[Ralph Robinson.*
ANOTHER CHAMPION.
Ch. "Halfmoon Beau Brummel" is also one of Mrs. Wilkinson's breeding. He weighs between 7 and 8 lb., and by 1934 had won eleven Challenge Certificates, including Cruft's, and a host of First Prizes.

only sufficiently so as to be easily covered by the tail; also slightly tanned on each side of chest. Tan outside the hindlegs, commonly called "breeching", is a serious defect. In all cases the black should not run into the tan, or vice versa; the division between the two colours should be well defined.

General appearance should be that of a terrier, and not of the whippet type.

SCALE OF POINTS

Head, 20; eyes, 10; ears, 5; legs, 10; feet, 10, body, 10; tail, 5; colour and markings, 15; general appearance, including terrier quality, 15. Total, 100.

Black Motions.—The motions are rendered black or nearly so from the presence of blood in the digestive tract, such as may occur in gastro-enteritis, injury caused by swallowed foreign bodies, or when ulcers are present on the mucous membrane of the bowel. The consumption of much meat will make the motions very dark, as also will certain chemicals, of which iron preparations and bismuth are examples. (See FAECES.)

Black Vomit.—When the material vomited is black or very dark brown there is almost certainly a serious lesion of the stomach, the most usual being gastric ulcer, gastric injury, or rupture of blood-vessels as occurs in Stuttgart disease. The dejecta often resembles coffee-grounds, being then so named, and not infrequently such vomit is a precursor of death.

Bladder, Distention of.— Caused by stone in the bladder or urethra; enlarged prostate gland, urethral constriction, paralysis of the bladder; distemper, etc., etc.

SYMPTOMS.—The abdomen seems of increased dimensions, and if manipulated with one's hand the bladder may be felt as a hard ovoid object. The dog shows discomfort and usually strains very frequently to pass water, but evacuates only a few drops with each effort. The urine so passed is highly coloured, or even blood-stained, and may have a strong ammoniacal odour.

TREATMENT.—The malady is one which requires the services of a veterinary surgeon, and should he diagnose cystic calculi (stone) nothing but a surgical operation will give lasting relief. When the bladder is greatly distended the condition is serious, and a catheter must be passed in order to draw off the water and relieve tension. This, again, needs the skill of a surgeon, for great damage can be inflicted by the amateur or quack.

INFLAMMATION OF.—Caused by prolonged distention due to any of the above-mentioned factors; also brought about by blows, undue exposure to wet or cold, bacterial infection, the administration of some aphrodisiacs such as cantharides (Spanish Fly) and

A Miniature Black-and-Tan puppy is a very small creature, as can be realized from this picture showing one of Mrs. Wilkinson's dogs "in hand". Miniature puppies sometimes grow up to be Manchester Terriers.

turpentine, given with the object of improving an animal's breeding qualities; and specific diseases such as, in particular, distemper and Stuttgart disease.

SYMPTOMS.—Pain is evinced upon pressure of the abdominal wall in the vicinity of the bladder. There is straining to pass urine, with, sometimes, indifferent success. A scalding pain is experienced when any urine is voided, and that which is passed may be considerably charged with blood, or even pus. On account of this pain, dogs frequently will avoid micturating, thus causing distention and adding very greatly to the damage already sustained. There is usually a mild fever, with loss of appetite. In acute cases the bladder becomes actually black, its walls greatly thickened, and the patient exhibits signs of collapse, followed quite often by death.

TREATMENT.—Skilled aid should be early sought, especially if the animal is of great sentimental or monetary value. In the absence of such aid, urinary antiseptics may be obtained from a chemist, and be given every four hours. The drinking of water or other fluid should be encouraged in order to flush out the bladder as often as possible. The diet should, for a while, consist only of soups or milk, whilst the drink should be albumen water or barley water in those cases in which a dog has an obstinate aversion to milk. A dose of castor-oil may be given with advantage, but it cannot be too strongly impressed that the condition is serious, for which professional advice is imperative.

Blain.—A condition in which small vesicles may be found along the under-surface of the tongue. It is not very common among dogs, but when it occurs it does so suddenly and gives rise to considerable discomfort and salivation. If not attended to early the small vesicles may coalesce to form larger ones. When the contained fluid has increased in amount, the vesicles then rupture, revealing a red ulcerous-looking area which at first is quite sore. The exact cause is unknown, but a smart purgative generally alleviates the condition, the mouth being simultaneously washed out two or three times daily with glyco-thymolin.

Blaze.—A band or streak of white hairs running along the bridge of the nose and between the eyes.

Bleeding FROM THE BOWELS may be caused by ulceration of the bowels; injury to the intestines by swallowed foreign bodies such as needles, skewers, etc.; inflammation of the bowels; rupture of small vessels; invagination or telescoping of the bowel, etc. When the haemorrhage arises high up, as in the stomach, the motions are black, and the condition is then known as melaena. As the treatment depends upon the cause, a veterinary surgeon should be called in as early as possible, especially if the loss of blood

Specially drawn for this work

FROLICS.

Vivacious studies of a vivacious little creature—the Miniature Black-and-Tan.

by J Nicholson.

is continuous and is accompanied by distressing symptoms of another kind.

BLEEDING FROM THE MOUTH. (*See* HAEMATEMESIS, HAEMOPTYSIS.)

CAUSES.—Gastric ulcer; pulmonary haemorrhage; injury of the stomach, gullet or mouth by foreign bodies; bleeding from the gums; ulceration of mouth; tongue injuries; bleeding from the nose, etc., etc. A small quantity of blood is generally swallowed and does not make any external appearance, but when bright-red blood is seen about a dog's mouth it is usually the result of violence, such as the dog being knocked over by a vehicle, or falling out of a window, etc.

BLEEDING FROM THE NOSE (*Epistaxis*).

CAUSES.—Polypus, infestation of the nasal passages by a worm known as *Pentastoma Taenioides*; rupture of small vessels in the lining mucous membrane due to temporary increase of blood pressure, and due sometimes to excessive exertion, or sneezing, etc., etc.; injuries to the face or lungs, or resulting from crushes such as occur when a dog is run over. If a chemist's shop is available, one can apply for a suitable styptic, which, in proper solution, should be syringed into the nasal passages. A block of ice held on the bridge of the nose might help, and in all cases the head should be elevated well above the level of the body. The dog should be kept very quiet and still, and should receive a purgative such as calomel. The amount of food given daily must be drastically reduced. When tumours or parasites are responsible these must, of course, be sought for and removed. If these measures do not succeed, a surgeon may be required to ascertain the exact cause and apply the appropriate treatment.

BLEEDING FROM WOUNDS.—Alarming haemorrhage not infrequently follows the infliction of wounds, and to the uninitiated might present considerable difficulty in its treatment. Section of a large artery or vein is often a very serious matter, and unless skilled knowledge and help is quickly invoked the victim may bleed to death. Arterial haemorrhage is always more grave than venous haemorrhage, and may be distinguished by the fact that the blood will issue from a cut artery in jets or spurts which correspond to the heart-beats. Arterial blood, also, is of a brighter red than that from the veins.

Nature always attempts, and usually succeeds, in stemming the flow of blood from injured vessels, this result being consequent upon changes in the wall of the artery on the one hand, and in the constitution of the blood upon the other. Every artery is surrounded by a fibrous sheath, and, when cut, the vessel retracts some little distance within its sheath in consequence of the shortening of its muscle fibres, and the cut end contracts, thereby tending to close the hole. When blood comes into contact with air or with any surface other than the smooth lining of blood-vessels, threads of fibrin are formed which develop into a dense network, in the meshes of which the other constituents of blood are held. This newly-formed mass is spoken of as "blood clot", and in the prevention of bleeding this clot formation is essential.

For this reason it is very inadvisable to remove any appliances which have been employed to promote clotting until a considerable number of hours have elapsed, for fear such clot may shift and permit the haemorrhage to start all over again.

TO CONTROL HAEMORRHAGE from a wound, the latter should be packed tightly with wool or tow which has been saturated in some styptic solution. Pressure is then applied over the spot and kept there by

Photo]   [*E.N.A.*
A BLACK-AND-TAN ROYAL FAVOURITE.
The Queen of Norway's favourite dog is a Black-and-Tan of the Miniature type. It is, however, too large to be in such a class or show purposes in this country.

the aid of bandages. It may be possible to apply great pressure over the involved artery at some point above the wound. For instance, a cord, handkerchief or elastic band may be bound round a limb, and twisted to great tightness by the aid of a wooden stick. Very hot or very cold water are also useful to allay bleeding; but if these measures fail, no delay should be countenanced in summoning a veterinary surgeon, who will probably attempt to pick up the cut vessel with artery forceps and affix a ligature upon it.

BLEEDING FROM THE URINARY ORGANS (*Haematuria*).

CAUSES.—Inflammation of the urethra, bladder

or kidneys ; calculus in either of those localities ; tumour formation ; and other urinary diseases.

The amateur can do nothing in such a case, and the matter must be placed entirely in professional hands.

BLEEDING INTERNALLY.

TREATMENT.— The general line of treatment in cases of internal haemorrhage is as follow :

The patient should be induced to lie down and keep quiet, since the heart beats less forcibly then, and the blood pressure is consequently lowered. This also is the reason why all excitement should be avoided. Stimulants must in all cases be withheld, unless and until the heart evinces signs of great weakness. Blood which emanates from the stomach is quite dark as contrasted with the bright-red frothy blood which comes from the lungs, and this is a ready method, in the dog, of distinguishing between haemoptysis and haematemesis. A pint of boiled water containing 1 drachm of common salt should be introduced slowly per rectum, at a temperature of 103° F., to compensate for loss of blood. Various drugs can be administered which have a rapid styptic effect, such as adrenalin, pituitrin, gallic acid (in renal haemorrhage), morphia for its quietening effect, ergot, solution of iron salts, copper sulphate, etc. The purchase, however, by the layman of some of these items is not only difficult or impossible, but their mode of application must be understood, and skilled aid must therefore be sought.

Some of the volatile oils, like turpentine and camphor, which are said to favour

Photo by]   *[Fall.*
CH. "FLYBIRD".
This remarkable little Black-and-Tan, one of Mrs. Blondin Robiolio's champions, shows clearly the healthy, thrifty appearance of the breed, which lives to a great age, and are as healthy as the largest of the canine race.

Photo by]   *[Fall.*
CH. "GLENARTY BOY".
Mr. Whaley's dog Ch. "Glenarty Boy" should be compared with the bitch shown above. Health and activity is depicted in every line. It must be borne in mind that these are Small Toys!

clotting by increasing the white corpuscles of the blood, may be administered when the haemorrhage is from the lungs.

In the haemorrhage which follows *whelping*, vaginal douches of hot water form one of the usual means employed ; or plugs of absorbent cotton wool steeped in a solution of adrenalin are introduced. These, combined with pressure, seldom fail to arrest the bleeding.

Blenheim Spaniel. (*See* KING CHARLES SPANIEL.)

Blindness.— Known also in some cases as amaurosis, though the latter term is limited chiefly to those forms of defect or loss of vision which are caused by diseases not directly involving the eye. An instance of amaurosis is the blindness which follows sometimes as a sequel to nervous distemper. The animal has possibly sustained paralysis of one or more limbs, and has even become deaf and blind. An examination of the eye's exterior reveals little or nothing abnormal to account for loss of sight, and one must assume that the latter is due to paralysis of the optic nerve.

CAUSES.— The causes of blindness, partial or complete, are many and varied, such as injuries to the cornea or glass of the eye, as inflicted by scratches from another animal ; bites or blows in the region of the orbit ; ophthalmia ; some obstruction to the passage of light through parts of the eye which ought to be transparent. The commonest of such obstructions are opacities of the cornea or lens, or cloudiness of the aqueous or vitreous humours. The conditions which

By courtesy of the American Museum of Natural History.]

NATURE'S PERPETUAL WILD DOG SHOW.

Ever since the Azilian phase of the Old Stone Age the dog has been devoted to man   Nature's dog show has been running steadily for millions of years.   The oldest fossil members of the dog family

[Drawing of Fossil Giant Dog by Charles R. Knight.

[continued on p. 133

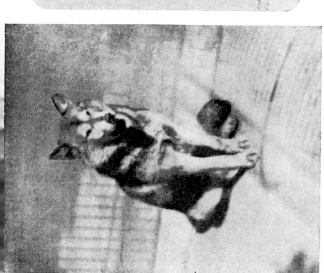

are found in the lower Oligocene of North America, their estimated age about thirty-eight million years. At that remote time the family, according to the late Dr. W. D. Matthew, was already represented in North America by two genera : (1) *Cynodictis*, the common ancestor of all the modern dogs, wolves, foxes, dholes, etc., as well as of the raccoon family, and (2) *Daphoenus*, the common ancestor of the giant dogs (see the drawing above) and the bears. *Cynodictis* was not yet either a dog, a wolf, or a fox, and had something of the long-bodied, slinking habit of the civet. Its predecessors in the Eocene of Wyoming had been still less dog-like. These were arboreal mammals, somewhat like a raccoon, with spreading hands and feet. In fact, the entire skeletal anatomy

[continued on p. 134

of the earliest known true carnivores, as interpreted by Dr. Matthew indicates arboreal, forest-living habits. The fast-running dogs were evolved much later, as the plains replaced the forests in both Western North America and Europe. *Daphoenus*, the contemporary of *Cynodictis*, had a more massive skull, with upper molars of the crushing type. The carnassial, or shear tooth, had a strong blade. The bears, according to Matthew, are only gigantic short-tailed dogs which have become secondarily plantigrade and have greatly increased the size of their crushing molars, while reducing their upper carnassials. In the Miocene epoch (about twenty-odd million years ago) there were many genera and a still greater number of species of dogs, which by this time had become swift-running forms with narrow, compressed feet. All breeds of domestic dog now constitute one single species.

mostly lead to corneal opacities are inflammation and ulceration of the cornea, which in turn may arise from injury or in connection with infectious diseases—particularly distemper.

The condition known as entropion, in which the eye is constantly irritated by inturned eyelashes, is one which may, through neglect, be a cause of blindness. Other causes of loss of sight are disorders of the brain such as tumour formation, meningitis, atrophy or inflammation of the optic nerve ; santonine, quinine, atropine, and some other drugs, when given in excess, may also cause temporary blindness or defective vision.

SYMPTOMS.—In amaurosis proper one notices nothing in the appearance of the dog's eyes suggestive that anything is amiss. The eyes look quite clear

dog's face, there is not a vestige of a flinch. Blindness which is due to true ocular disease such as keratitis, ophthalmia, cataract, choroiditis, etc., will be accompanied by changes which are either patent to the layman's eye, or discoverable by close veterinary examination.

TREATMENT.—This obviously depends upon the cause of the condition, but as a rule it also depends upon attention to the general health. The administration of nerve tonics, such as nux vomica, and a routine feeding and building-up of the nervous system over a period of two or three weeks, may be helpful in re-establishing normal vision.

For further information upon blindness refer to "EYE DISEASES".

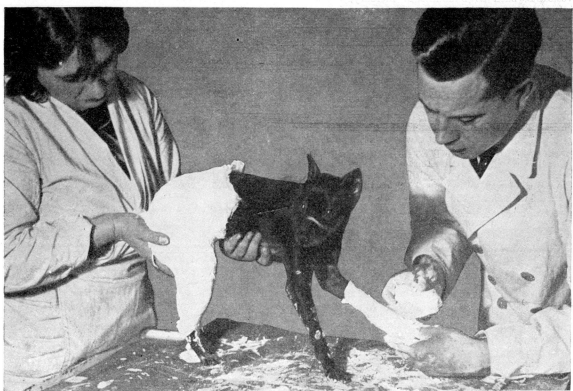

Photo]   [*E.N.A.*

A COMPLICATED CASE.

One way or another dogs frequently break their legs. This poor little fellow had fallen out of a window and broken all four. The whole body had to be put into a plaster of Paris cast. The picture was taken while the cast was being removed.

and transparent, and if their interiors are examined with an ophthalmoscope, possibly no alteration will be discerned. It is, at the same time, obvious that the animal has a blurred or totally deficient vision. Nervous exhaustion, or paralysis of the optic nerve from a blow, or some other obscure condition unconnected primarily with the eye, may be the exciting cause. The pupils of the eyes will probably be widely expanded, and the dog will evince signs of defective sight. These are, uncertainty of gait, such as stepping high and with great caution, whilst brushing against objects, or treading on articles or spaces which otherwise would be avoided. The senses of smell and hearing are, however, often so strong in the dog that usually no grave mistakes are made. But the animal's general bearing leaves no doubt in the observer's mind that vision is poor.

Moreover, when one pretends to aim a blow at the

Blistering.—Blistering an animal is a term used to describe the application of an irritant chemical, usually in the form of an ointment, to the skin for the purpose of producing a counter-irritation. The process is very frequently employed among horses, but is not so popular in canine practice. The substances which may be used are cantharides ointment ; biniodide of mercury ointment ; embrocations containing strong ammonia or turpentine, or both ; tincture of iodine ; pure mustard ; croton oil, and others. Some of these agents are only mild in their action, producing little more than a temporary redness and soreness of the area treated. Others are severe and cause either multiple vesicles or actual pustules with considerable inflammatory reaction.

There are several indications for their use, and among dogs, probably the most common is the relief of sore throat, pleurisy, or pneumonia. In all of these conditions there is an inflammation in progress which, owing to its deep situation, cannot directly be reached from the outside. The principle of blistering them is to relieve such inflammations of their pain and swelling by drawing blood away from them to the superficial areas which have been "blistered". Thus a deeply seated sore throat might be relieved by rubbing in mustard oil, fresh mustard, or turpentine liniment on the outside of the throat. Similarly, a smart application of one of these substances over the ribs (i.e. over the chest wall) would be beneficial in the case of an inflamed pleura (pleurisy), and other instances might be quoted *in extenso*. The more severe blistering agents or vesicants, such as biniodide of mercury, are not infrequently applied, with vigorous massage, into the area of the back which immediately covers the spinal column. Sometimes this is done to relieve congestion of the membranes of the spinal cord, or maybe with a view to reducing thickenings, or collections of fluid, therein. Paralysis of the hind-quarters is often treated in this manner.

Abscesses which are slow in maturing may be hastened by the smart application of a good blister, a means which might well be adopted by those who actually have not the time to devote to frequent hot fomentations. But no matter where the blister may be applied or for what purpose, it is essential that the greatest care should be exercised to ensure that the dog cannot get at the part with his mouth. A close muzzle should therefore be affixed, or the dog might be fitted with an Elizabethan collar. (*See* RESTRAINT.) It is not a custom among veterinary surgeons to apply to dogs either strong ammonia, cantharides, croton oil, or acids for the purposes described, but to rely mainly upon biniodide of mercury ointment, and the various liniments and embrocations, painting with tincture of iodine or rubbing with mustard. Cantharides is very apt to be absorbed through the dog's skin and cause severe poisoning.

Blood.—Blood is an alkaline red fluid which flows throughout every part of the body, and has very definite and vital functions to fulfil. It absorbs oxygen from the lung cells and carries it to all parts of the body, as without oxygen life is impossible. It gathers up carbon dioxide and other waste products of metabolism from the tissues and conveys them to the lungs, bowels, kidneys and skin for elimination from the body. Another important function is the collection of nourishment, elaborated in the alimentary canal, and its distribution throughout the body.

Blood is the active agent in the protection of the body against bacterial invasion, a function which is performed in the following manner : An injury to any tissue is immediately followed by a slight engorgement of the blood-vessels surrounding the injury, and should any foreign body or harmful organism gain entrance, the supply of blood and certain of its constituents becomes very considerably increased. Contained in the blood are mobile cells known as the white corpuscles, some of which have the power of penetrating the vessel walls and so of gaining access to the adjacent areas. Coming into direct contact with minute invading bodies such as germs, they throw out processes in an encircling movement designed to bring the enemy within their own protoplasm. Once the germ has become ingested in this way there is no escape and no chance of multiplication. Provided that an animal can manufacture

sufficient of these leucocytes in time to deal with a heavy invasion, the animal remains immune against the disease, or is, at least, able to recover from it. The process is known as phagocytosis.

Whilst this brief outline serves to indicate in plain words something of the protective mechanism of the body, it is not by any means complete : yet it probably fulfils the purpose of our readers.

Blood consists of a viscous fluid or plasma, suspended in which are three kinds of cells, viz. : (1) the red cells or erythrocytes, (2) the white corpuscles or leucocytes, and (3) blood platelets.

THE RED CORPUSCLES constitute about one third of the total bulk of blood, and are bi-concave circular discs of microscopic size. Each cell offers a certain absorbing surface for oxygen, for which gas they have a special affinity. When these corpuscles are fully charged with it, they impart a bright red colour to the blood (arterial blood) ; but during their journey round the body the oxygen is gradually extracted, thus we find that blood in the great veins returning to the heart has become very much darker in colour. When the red cells die, their haemoglobin is set free and decomposed into an iron-free residue from which, probably, all the pigments of the body are formed, certainly those of the bile. The seat of the manufacture of new red cells is the red marrow of bones.

THE WHITE CORPUSCLES possess a power of amoeboid movement, and one such corpuscle exists in the blood to about every 500 of the red cells, They are able to envelop and digest both liquids and solids, and, as has already been explained, they form the first line of defence for the body. They emanate from lymphatic tissue and from bone marrow. In consequence of their migratory habits, they are found not only in the blood stream, but in lymph, and all tissues of the body.

BLOOD PLATELETS are of round or oval shape, and only one quarter the size of a red cell. Of their function little is known except that it is believed they are intimately concerned with the formation of blood-clot when blood is shed.

It has been estimated by physiologists that the average amount of blood in a normal dog's body is about 9 per cent. of the body-weight, and that its distribution is believed to be as follows : heart, lungs, large vessels, and veins, about one fourth ; liver, about one fourth ; skeletal muscles, about one fourth ; other organs, about one fourth.

In the dog exact observation shows that a haemorrhage of from 2 to 3 per cent. of the body-weight is readily recovered from, whilst a loss of 4·5 per cent., which represents half the blood in the body, is generally fatal. Regeneration of blood is extremely rapid, experiments showing that after slight haemorrhage the normal volume is regained within a few hours, and after severe haemorrhage in from 24 to 48 hours. Healthy blood is sterile or germ-free.

Bloodhounds.—St. Hubert, who died in A.D. 727, was one of the princes of the Church who in early times thought it not unbecoming to his holy office to indulge in the pleasures of the chase. The fame of his hounds—some black and others white— soon spread from the district in the Ardennes where they hunted, and after his death successive abbots preserved the strain zealously, and followed

Drawn by]

A NOBLE HEAD.

[Lionel Edwards

A splendid study of a magnificent head, showing strikingly the sunken eyelid, known as the haw, of the Bloodhound breed—a feature which has been passed on to many other varieties.

PUPPYHOOD.

his example. For nearly eight centuries, from the year 1200 onwards, three couples of the Black - and - tan St. Huberts, as they were called, were sent annually to the King of France. One regrets to say, St. Hubert's hunting so interfered with his religious duties that a super-natural visita-tion was neces-sary to bring him back to the strait and nar-row way. As he was out with his

THEN AND NOW.
Comparing "Nestor" (below) with the Bloodhound of 1800, above shown, we see that the haw so long ago was well developed. The body of the Hound standing up would not be considered the right type to-day, nor are the dog's legs such as are required in the modern specimens.

hounds on a Good Friday he met a stag with a crucifix between its antlers, and St. Hubert was threatened with eternal perdition unless he changed his ways. He is interesting to us, not only as the patron saint of hunting, but because the descend-ants of his hounds came into England at the time of the Norman Conquest, the blacks, or, more correctly, black-and-tans, after-wards being known as Bloodhounds, and the whites as Talbots. The Bloodhounds survive, and it may be that the blood of the Talbots in diluted form was found in our old-fashioned staghounds of the West country.

It is still the custom in France and Belgium to bless hounds on St. Hubert's Day, but the little Chapele of St. Hubert, built in 1610 by Arch-duchess Isabelle on the site of the saint's dwelling-place at Tervueren in Belgium, is no longer used for the purpose. A mass for the

hunting season is held annually in the Church of the Sablon in Brussels. An old dame associated with this church told a friend of the writer once that if he wished his dogs blessed he should take them to the home of Mon-sieur le Curé, who would do them well.

One wonders sometimes if the story of the Bloodhound in England does not really go further back than the Nor-man period, for Gratius, writing before the Christian era, and Strabo at a later date, both referred to the importation of Sleuth-hounds from Britain into Gaul. It was from the south of Gaul that St. Hubert is supposed to have obtained his Hounds. It occurs to one that the "Britain" referred to by the historians mentioned may have been Brittany, and that brings us back to the opening chapter of the *Booke of Hunting* which was Turbervile's translation in Eliza-bethan times of the French author Jacques du Fouilloux. There we learn how "the first race of hounds did come into France".

The author had seen a treatise in Brittany written by John of Monmouth, an English-man, in which it ex-plained that after the fall of Troy, Æneas reached Italy with his son Ascanius, after-wards King of the Latins, and there a

FAMOUS NINETEETH-CENTURY HOUND.
Ch. "Nestor" was a very famous Bloodhound at the end of the nineteenth century and shows the type of head then so much desired. It will be observed that the head possessed less haw than the dog now in favour.

The name of Edward Brough will for ever be linked with Bloodhound history, for he possessed the most noted pack at the end of the nineteenth century and was the greatest breeder. The above is his "Barbarossa".

"Burgundy", also one of Mr. Brough's breeding, is said to be the finest Bloodhound ever bred. Attention is drawn to the remarkable head, to the shape of body and the good legs of this animal.

Ch. "Panther", here shown, was also one of the pillars of the Bloodhound breed. He lived about 1908.

Illustrations by courtesy of]   *[E. C. Ash.*

THREE BLOODHOUNDS OF HISTORY.

son was born to him named Siluius, from whom Brutus descended, "which loved hunting exceedingly" Brutus had the misfortune to kill his father accidentally with an arrow while hunting a stag and the people, thinking that it was done wilfully, forced him to flee the country. Brutus went into Greece, delivered certain Trojans who had been held captive since the destruction of Troy and set sail with them, taking also a great number of hounds and greyhounds.

After passing through the Straits of Gibraltar "they descended in the Isles of Armorie, which at this present time is called Bretagne in France, by reason of his name, which was Brutus". Four years later it was said that Brutus occupied Cornwall.

Fouilloux attached credence to this story because, as far as he could ascertain, most of the great breeds of hounds in France came out of Brittany except the white hounds which were from Barbary. One cannot say which of the hounds described by Turbervile were the progenitors of the St. Huberts, but there is a chapter on the "blacke hounds aunciently come from Sainct Huberts Abbaye in Ardene". We are informed that these are the Hounds which the abbots had always kept in honour and remembrance of the saint who was a hunter with St. Eustace.

By the sixteenth century, when the book was written, the St. Huberts had been a good deal mixed with other Hounds and though commonly black were to be found of all colours. Their legs were shortish and they were not swift, although their scenting powers were exceptionally good. We were told that "the bloodhounds of this colour prove good, especially those that are coal-black" In one or two chapters of Turbervile's we get similar allusions to Bloodhounds, from which one rather infers that the name may have been given to them as hunting the line of wounded animals, though some authorities do not accept this explanation as the origin of the term. It has been suggested that the word Bloodhound was used in the same sense as a blood horse, meaning that they were thoroughbred. One thing is certain—"bloodhound" does not indicate ferocity and a desire for blood, unless the character of the breed has changed entirely, for one seldom meets a Hound that is bad-tempered and untrustworthy. They have the manners of a gentleman, rarely harbouring resentment at any rating that may be necessary in the interests of discipline.

We can imagine how the Normans and Plantagenets, in their passion for hunting, used these Hounds in the chase of the deer. In later centuries, as customs changed and faster Hounds were needed, they or the Talbots were crossed with Greyhounds, and so Foxhounds came into being. Strains of

Photo]

FRIENDS INDEED.

[Sport & General.

Dr. H. G. Tomb's Ch. "Frolic" with ' Fairlight", combining to make a charming picture with their master's daughter, Miss Joan.

A KEEN TEAM.

Occasionally, when the scent is breast-high or the quarry is in view, Hounds lift their heads. This interesting picture
shows a team in a great hurry.

WHEN THE SCENT IS BAD.

In working a Hound it is important for the handler to keep well away, so that his presence may not detract from the dog's attention
to work. This is especially important when scent is bad. Miss Roberts is using Miss E. M. Lowe's "Igraine of Lyonesse".

Bloodhounds were preserved in their purity in certain parts, especially in the New Forest An article written in 1898 stated that at that date each keeper in the New Forest had a couple of Bloodhounds with him on his walk, and that one, named Primer, on the Boldrewood walk, boasted that his were descended from those that had been in his family for upwards of 300 years.

From a couple of these Hounds the late Mr. Thomas Nevill of Chilland, near Winchester, founded a pack about 1840. He called them St. Huberts, and insisted that they traced back to the hounds of William Rufus. The late Mr. Edwin Brough often said how Mr. Nevill hunted anything from fox, hare, and a tame jackal down to water-rats. He also had a tame stag which provided many a run and then trotted home with hounds when he was caught. The jackal lived in the house. After his death, in 1878, *Baily's Magazine* published an article on this eccentric character, in which it mentioned that his Hounds were splendid looking animals, whose deep bay was a grand thing to hear.

Photo]   [*Fall.*
A STURDY CHAMPION.
Ch. "Ledburn Barbarous" is from Mrs. Edmund's noted kennels. He is a well-built Hound and very typical of the breed.

Count le Couteulx, an eminent authority on French Hounds, believed that the Bloodhounds and all the French Hounds came from the St. Huberts, and that the Bloodhound and Talbot were akin except for colour. It cannot be said when the wonderful scenting powers of Bloodhounds were first used in hunting man, but it is evident that they were so employed centuries ago, their ability to keep on the line of the hunted man instead of changing on to a fresher scent making them peculiarly valuable for this purpose. In Barbour's *The Bruce* (1316–95) we read :

A sleuth hund had he thar alsua,
Sa gud that wald chang for nathing.

There is a good deal about a Bloodhound in this poem. Those of us who have read history in its romantic guise

Photo]   [*S. & G.*
A NOTED PRIZE WINNER.
Mrs. Edmund's Ch. "Ledburn Beau Brummell" has an excellent head. He was the winner of many prizes.

are aware that Bloodhounds were kept on the borders of England and Scotland for hunting those marauding robbers known as moss-troopers. One imagines that they were more lightly built in those days, as they were often given a lift on the horses of the pursuers. Sir Walter Scott, a mine of information on ancient customs, once explained that "the pursuit of border marauders was followed by the injured party and his friends with Bloodhounds and bugle horn, and was called the 'hot trod'. He was entitled, if his dog could trace the scent, to follow the invaders into the opposite kingdom ; a privilege which often occasioned bloodshed". Holinshed in his *Chronicles* (1577) may have been the fount of the novelist's information : "There is a law also amongst the borderers in time of peace, that whoso denieth entrance or sute of a Sleuth hound in pursuit made after fellons and stolen goods, shall be holden as accessarie unto the theft."

That Hounds should also have been used in pursuit of sheep-stealers and similar undesirable people is understandable. At times they were made a local charge, being more or less for the benefit of the community. In 1616 an order was made at Carlisle to the purport that "the sheriff, officers, bailiffs and constables

By courtesy of] [*Mrs. Russell Cook.*
A FINE HEAD.
The Bloodhound head is well exemplified here. Notice the shape of the skull, the wrinkles, the ears, and the expression of the face of Mrs. Russell Cook's noted champion, "Ledburn Bas Blue".

within every circuit and compass wherein the Slough-dogs are appointed to be kept, must take care for taxing the inhabitants towards the charge thereof, and collect the same, and for providing the Slough-dogs ; and to inform the Commissioners if any refuse to pay their contribution. so as thereby such as refuse may be committed to the jail till they pay the same".

In the reign of Henry III we read of instructions for the training of Bloodhounds (*De Canibus ad sanguinem adaptandis*), which opened : "Whereas Edward, the King's son, has entrusted to Robert de Chenney, his valet, his dogs, to be accustomed to blood". Not human gore, however, but in the tracking of animals. It would not be profitable to pursue further a branch of the subject that must already be tolerably familiar. Before passing on, however, a quotation, as being little known, may be given from Bellenden's translation of Boece's Latin *History of Scotland* (1527). In describing three Scottish breeds he writes : "The third kind is mair than ony rache ; reid hewitt, or ellis blak, with small sprainges (tints or markings) or spottis ; and ar callit be the peple, Sleuthoundis. This doggis hes sae mervellus wit, that serche thevir and followis on thaim allanerlie be sent of the guddis (goods) that are tane away ; and nocht allanerlie findis the theif, bot invadis him with gret cruelte ; and, thoucht the thevis oftimes cors the watter, quhair they pass, to caus the hound to tine the sent of thaim and the guddis, yet he

Photo] [*Fox.*
POWER AND FREEDOM.
The Bloodhound, in spite of its awesome name, is as docile as any other dog—more so indeed than many varieties.
Miss Mary Wood, kennel-maid at Briarfield, in Herts, is resting during the exercising of her charges.

Photo] THE LARGEST BLOODHOUND IN ENGLAND. [*Fox.*

Mrs. Russell Cook with "Nereholm Falstaff", the largest Bloodhound in England, Watching the Open Trials of the Association of Bloodhound Breeders at Aston Abbots, Aylesbury, where the Earl of Rosebery, M.F.H., was one of the stewards.

serchis heir and thair with sic diligence that, be his fut, he findis baith the trace of the theif and the guddis.   The mervellous nature of thir hounds will have na faith with uncouth people : howbeit, the samin ar richt frequent and rife on the bordouris of Ingland and Scotland ; attour it ih statue, be the lawis of the Bordouris, he that denyis entres to the sleuthound, in time of chace and serching of guddis, sal be haldin participant with the crime and thift committis."

Coming now to more modern times it may be noted that last century Bloodhounds were some-times used in hunting deer.   Mr. Selby Lowndes had a small pack with which he hunted outlying

make a good horse look foolish ; while amongst the enclosures they charge the fences in a line like a squadron of heavy dragoons ; yet for all this fire and metal in chase, they are sad cowards under pressure from a crowd. . . . Only through a thorough knowledge of his favourites, and a patient deference to their prejudices, has Lord Wolverton obtained their confidence, and it is wonderful how his perseverance has been rewarded."

The entire pack, twelve couples in all, were offered at Tattersall's, Rugby, in April 1881.   Two sold at seven guineas each, one at six guineas, and the rest were withdrawn, afterwards being sold in Paris, chiefly to Count le Couteu'x

Photo]   [*Sport & General.*

A GREAT MOMENT.
Mr. W. P. Cowburn is seen with his "Eldwick Meuver" and "Malvo" at the moment of picking up the scent.

deer in Whaddon Chase, and he also occasionally turned them on to sheep-stealers, but the pack that was most talked about was that with which the late Lord Wolverton in the 'seventies hunted carted red deer in Dorset.   Some correspondents latterly have not done justice to this pack.   The late Major Whyte Melville, who was as great an authority on hound work as we have ever had, gave a different picture from actual experience : "Full, sonorous, and musical, it is not extrava-gant to compare these deep-mouthed notes with the peal of an organ in a cathedral.   Yet they run a tremendous pace. . Stride, courage and condition (the last essential requiring constant care) enable them to sustain such speed over the open as will

Some years ago Mrs. Calvert mentioned that her father, when stationed at Christchurch, whipped in to Mr. Frank Lovell, who hunted the deer in the New Forest with Bloodhounds. They were trying to kill down the deer and were out most of the summer.   Her father used to say they worked slowly, but killed the horses, as they never stopped.

The Marquess of Ailesbury, chairman of the Association of Bloodhound Breeders, wrote in 1931 : "I imagine that Bloodhounds were kept here (at Savernake) from very remote times, but the only reference I have ever seen in print about them is a book by the celebrated hunting man, Mr. 'Craven' Smith, who states that to get scenting

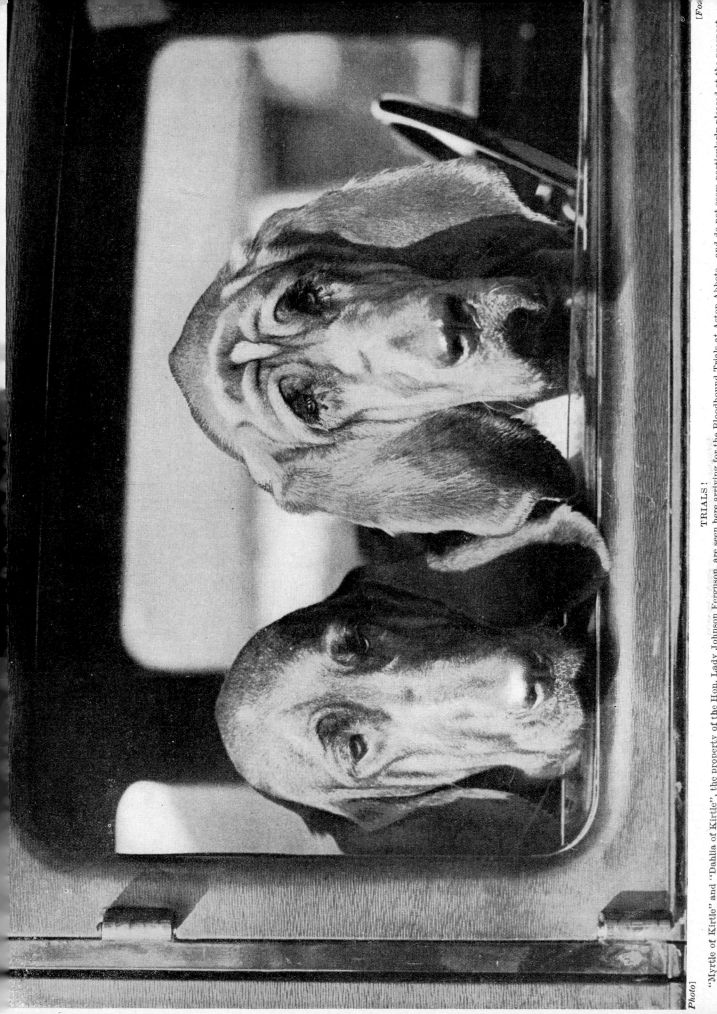

[Fo

TRIALS!

"Myrtle of Kirtle" and "Dahlia of Kirtle", the property of the Hon. Lady Johnson Ferguson, are seen here arriving for the Bloodhound Trials at Aston Abbots—and do not seem particularly pleased at the prospect,

Photo]
[Fox.

A HANDSOME TRIO.

Colonel Sir Edward Johnson Ferguson has a well-known Bloodhound Kennel. Above are shown three extremely typical examples, two of which have exceptionally good heads.
Incidentally, it may be mentioned that often the Hound with the best head makes the worst tracker.

qualities Mr. Warde ot the Craven used Lord Ailesbury's celebrated Bloodhound. But, he adds, the produce inherited the bloodhound independence of character and it did not do. The Bloodhounds here were destroyed by the fourth Marquess in 1887, but the keepers told me they were not pure, having been crossed with foxhounds or buckhounds."

Lord Ailesbury re-started Bloodhounds at Savernake in 1895, keeping them till just after the war, but his daughter, who had charge of the deer-hunting in post-war years, did not like them as well as Kerry Beagles. They used to draw the surrounding country for outlying deer when they had complaints from the farmers. They did not hunt to kill, but of course a certain number of deer did get killed.

As the subject of tracking is being dealt with in another section it is not necessary to say much about it here beyond the fact that the credit of reviving this interesting sport belongs to the Association ot Bloodhound Breeders, which held its first meeting on the moors a few miles north ot Scarborough in 1898. The tests then were of a somewhat elementary character and have since been made more difficult. A few years later the Bloodhound Hunt Club was formed and also organized meetings. It may be said without the slightest fear of contradiction that dog shows were responsible for the preservation of this ancient and noble breed. When shows were started in 1859 the old order, entrenched behind custom and tradition, was changing under the pressure of industrialism and the march of science. The intervention of dog shows was the means of keeping alive breeds that might otherwise have disappeared and introducing many new ones. Classes for Bloodhounds were first put on at the Birmingham Show in 1860. The principal Hounds about that time were two named "Druid", one owned by Colonel A. J. Cowen and the other by Mr. T

Photo   [*Sport & General*.
TRACKING A CRIMINAL.

This picture shows an interesting situation when two Hounds found the scent, whilst a third has not discovered it. They belong to the Chief Constable of Sussex and have tracked many criminals.

A. Jennings, Mr. C. E. Holford's "Regent", "Trimbush", and "Matchless"; Dr. E. Reynolds' "Ray's Peeress" and "Roswell"; Mr. J. Leigh Becker's "Brenda" and Mr. G. Rushton's "Duchess" and "Juno".

It would be waste of space to refer at any length to Hounds that have no practical influence at the present day. One cannot, however, pass over the kennels of one man who did more than any other to establish the breed on its modern lines and also to keep alive the working qualities of the Hounds. That was the late Mr. Edwin Brough who, after retiring from the family silk manufacturing business in Leek, went to live at Wyndyate, near Scarborough, where he led the life of a country gentleman, hunting, riding in points-to-points, and breeding Bloodhounds as well as prize cattle. His first appearance in the show ring was in 1871 and his kennel was at its zenith about 1890, when he produced a succession of magnificent Hounds, characterized by their wonderful legs and feet and their beautiful heads. There is no doubt that he made the head of the Bloodhound what it is, giving it more quality than it ever had before. The heads of his Hounds were longer, narrower and better-balanced than those of their predecessors; the ears were longer and lower set; and the wrinkle had that fine silky texture that is so much esteemed. He was fortunate enough to have two strains running side by side from which he could inter-breed successfully. The one was represented by Ch. "Beckford" and Ch. "Bianca", and the other by Ch. "Bono". From the union of the "Beckford" and "Bono" blood came Ch. "Panther". "Panther" probably had the best head that was ever known, and from his breeding it is not surprising that he was responsible for siring Hounds that afterwards became famous.

Later in the 1890's came Mr. Brough's Ch. "Babbo", who had many duels with the late

By courtesy of]					[E. C. Ash.

A SWISS BLOODHOUND.

In Switzerland a dog with Bloodhound body and limbs and, to some extent the head, was common at the end of the nineteenth century.

Besides their aristocratic appearance and old lineage, Bloodhounds have the most delightful dispositions to recommend them, and anyone who has once kept one will not desire to change. They are prolific breeders, but, as one should not paint a picture without the warts, it may be mentioned that they often get distemper in a severe form. Once over this obstacle they are as hardy as other breeds, and now that preventive measures are possible the dread of losing them young should be removed.

A good deal of attention is required in rearing the puppies in order to get big bone and sound legs and feet. The expectant mother should receive plenty of meat and bone-forming material, and the same regimen is recommended for the puppies. With the knowledge of vitamins now available it is possible to have accessories to the diet that help in the achievement of these objects. It will be seen from what has been said and from a perusal of the standard of points that a long narrow head is required on adults. In choosing a puppy, however, one usually prefers to have a head with plenty of substance, for this is more likely to fine down and give the style that is wanted. The puppy with a fine, narrow head usually becomes snipy. This may seem a contradiction in terms, but in practice it generally works out as stated. A puppy should have an abundance of loose skin of fine texture, possess a sturdy frame, and a lot of bone in the legs. A coarse-skinned

Mr. S. H. Mangin's Ch. "Hordle Hercules". Another Hound that did much winning at that time was Mrs. Oliphant's Ch. "Chatley Blazer", a heavily marked black-and-tan; and two bitches that were conspicuous for their quality were Mrs. Heydon's Ch. "South Carolina" and Mr. Croxton Smith's Ch. "Wandle Welcome". When Mr. Brough retired soon after the opening of this century the succession was taken up by Mrs. Edmunds, of Ledburn Manor, Leighton Buzzard, and Mr. Henry Hylden, of Brighton, both of whom bred some beautiful hounds.

Mrs. Edmunds taught one valuable lesson that had almost been forgotten by those who did not know Mr. Brough's hounds. For a time Bloodhounds had the reputation of being nervous and headstrong in the show ring, where they often failed to do themselves justice by their bad manners. Before Mrs. Edmunds had been long at the game she proved that they were as amenable to discipline as any others, it being merely a question of early schooling. Other breeders of note were Mr. W. N. Unwin, Dr. C. C. Garfit, and Dr. E. E. Semmence. Mrs. Elms's Ch. "Leo of Reynalton" figures among most successful Hounds, being of great size allied with quality, and this lady seems to have achieved the knack of stamping these desirable points upon her young stock. Mrs. Sadleir's Hounds not only win at shows, but distinguish themselves in tracking.

By courtesy of]					[E. C. Ash.

A GERMAN TYPE.

The Bloodhound type is seen in many breeds more or less distinctly, but seldom more than in the Hound of Würtemberg, Germany, at the end of the nineteenth century.

Photo]   *[Fall.*

A LORD OF THE BREED.

Mrs. Elms's Ch. "Leo of Reynalton" shows the desired wrinkle, and the peaked head so typical of the breed is very marked.

[Sport & General.

FULL VIEW OF "LEO OF REYNALTON".

Ch. "Leo of Reynalton", showing side of body and his remarkably head so typically noble, dignified and solemn

Photo]

Photo] *[Sport & General.*

BLOODHOUND HARNESS.

Whilst special harness is not essential, at the same time it eases the neck when at work on the lead. "Sancho", the property of Mr. Theo. M. Crowder, at the Trials at Savernake.

POINTS AND CHARACTERISTICS OF THE BLOODHOUND OR SLEUTH-HOUND.

The following standard was drawn up by the late Mr. Edwin Brough and the late Mr. J. Sidney Turner, and adopted by the Association of Bloodhound Breeders :

GENERAL CHARACTER.—The Bloodhound possesses in a most marked degree every point and characteristic of those dogs which hunt together by scent (*Sagaces*).

He is very powerful, and stands over more ground than is usual with Hounds of other breeds.

The skin is thin to the touch and extremely loose, this being more especially noticeable about the head and neck, where it hangs in deep folds.

Hound looks common, and the ears of such are often flat instead of folding gracefully, and are set on high.

Breeders who have the opportunity and can spare the time should train their young Hounds to hunt man. It is an interesting sport which has its uses, for Bloodhounds, when well trained, can still be helpful to the police. A few of our chief constables, of whom Captain A. S. Williams, of West Sussex, is a notable example, have found them of great value, and in America they are in common use for tracking criminals or disclosing the whereabouts of missing persons.

HEIGHT.—The mean average height of adult dogs is 26 in., and of adult bitches 24 in. Dogs usually vary from 25 in. to 27 in. and bitches from 23 in. to 25 in. ; but, in either case, the greater height is to be preferred, provided that character and quality are also in combination.

Photo' *[Fox.*

A NOTED OWNER AND HER FAMOUS TEAM.

Mrs. Russell Cook, of Ipswich world-famous for her Bloodhounds, is seen being taken along by her team

WEIGHT.—The mean average weight of adult dogs, in fair condition, is 90 lb., and of adult bitches 80 lb. Dogs attain the weight of 110 lb., bitches 100 lb. The greater weights are to be preferred, provided (as in the case of height) that quality and proportion are also combined.

EXPRESSION.—The expression is noble and dignified, and characterized by solemnity, wisdom, and power.

TEMPERAMENT.—In temperament he is extremely affectionate, neither quarrelsome with companions nor with other dogs. His nature is somewhat shy, and equally sensitive to kindness or correction by his master.

HEAD.—The head is narrow in proportion to its length, and long in proportion to the body, tapering but slightly from the temples to the end of the muzzle, thus (when viewed from above and in front) having the appearance of being flattened at the sides and of being nearly equal in width throughout its entire length. In profile the upper outline

By courtesy of] THE BLUE PAUL FIGHTING DOG. *[J. Garrow.*
This variety of the Bull Terrier was bred in Scotland at one time. Mr. James B. Morrison was a leading breeder. The variety is extinct.

of the skull is nearly in the same plane as that of the fore-face. The length from end of nose to stop (midway between the eyes) should be not less than that from stop to back of occipital protuberance (peak). The entire length of head from the posterior part of the occipital protuberance to the end of the muzzle should be 12 in., or more, in dogs, and 11 in., or more, in bitches.

SKULL.—The skull is long and narrow, with the occipital peak very pronounced. The brows are not prominent, although, owing to the deep-set eyes, they may have that appearance.

FORE-FACE.—The fore-face is long, deep, and of even width throughout, with square outline when seen in profile.

EYES.—The eyes are deeply sunk in the orbits, the lids assuming a lozenge or diamond shape, in consequence of the lower lids being dragged down and everted by the heavy flews. The eyes correspond with the general tone of colour of the animal, varying from deep hazel to yellow. The hazel colour is, however, to be preferred, although very seldom seen in red-and-tan Hounds.

EARS.—The ears are thin and soft to the touch, extremely long, set very low and fall in graceful folds, the lower parts curling inwards and backwards.

WRINKLE.—The head is furnished with an amount of loose skin, which, in nearly every position appears superabundant, but more particularly so when the head is carried low; the skin then falls into loose pendulous ridges and folds, especially over the forehead and sides of the face.

NOSTRILS.—The nostrils are large and open.

LIPS, FLEWS AND DEWLAP.—In front the lips fall squarely, making a right angle with the upper line of the fore-face; whilst behind they form deep hanging flews, and being continued into the pendant folds of loose skin about the neck, constitute the dewlap, which is very pronounced. These characters are found, though in a less degree, in the bitch.

NECK, SHOULDERS AND CHEST.—The neck is long; the shoulders muscular and well sloped backwards; the ribs are well sprung; and the chest well let down between the forelegs, forming a deep keel.

LEGS AND FEET.—The forelegs are straight and large in bone, with elbows squarely set; the feet strong and well knuckled up; the thighs and second thighs (gaskins) are very muscular; the hocks well bent and let down and squarely set.

BACK AND LOIN.—The back and loins are strong, the latter deep and slightly arched.

STERN.—The stern is long and tapering and set

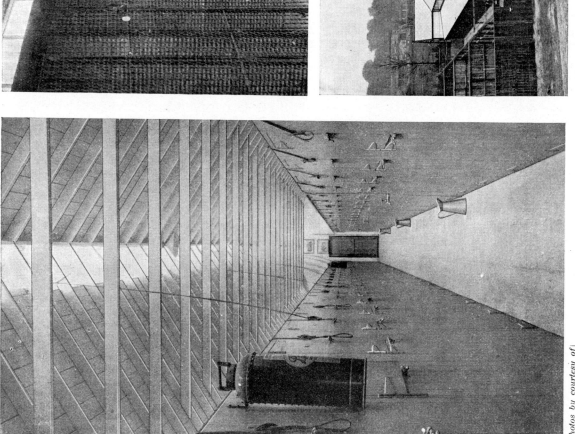

Photos by courtesy of | [*Walter Guiver.*

HOTELS FOR DOGS.

Many much-advertised Boarding Kennels for dogs are disgracefully unhealthy, lacking ventilation and light and riddled with rat-holes. See the place in which you leave your dog and assure yourself that it is airy, lofty, clean and possesses both an isolation hospital and adequate room for exercising. The above photos show interiors and exteriors of what a well-arranged and properly organized "hotel" should be.

on rather high, with a moderate amount of hair underneath.

GAIT.—The gait is elastic, swinging and free, the stern being carried high, but not too much curled over the back.

COLOUR.—The colours are black-and-tan, red-and-tan and tawny; the darker colours being sometimes interspersed with lighter or badger-coloured hair, and sometimes flecked with white. A small amount of white is permissible on chest, feet, and tip of stern.

Blood in Urine. (*See* "BLEEDING FROM THE URINARY ORGANS".)

Blood Poisoning. (*See* POISONS.)

Blotch. (*See* ECZEMA.)

Blue Paul.—The Blue Paul was undoubtedly a Scottish breed of dog, peculiar to the West, where the sport of dog-fighting was carried on. These dogs were really very similar to what was known as the Staffordshire Terrier, the fighting dogs of the Black Country—the chain-makers' dogs of Cradley Heath—only they were heavier. The canine gladiators were all graded as to weight. Many fighting dogs scaled no more than thirteen or fourteen pounds. The Stafford-shires fought usually round about twenty or twenty-two pounds, whilst the Blue Pauls went to sometimes double that weight.

The Staffordshires were, as a rule, all red or all brindle in colour, although an occasional blue one turned up. The Blue Pauls were of an all-blue colour, but they in turn sometimes produced brindles and also reds. The latter were known as Red Smuts in Scotland. No one seemed to have any knowledge as to how they were bred or from whence they originally came. There was a story that Paul Jones, the pirate, brought them from abroad and landed some when he revisited his native town of Kirkcudbright about 1770.

The gipsies around the Kirkintilloch district kept a lot of Blue Pauls, which they fought for their own amusement. They maintained that the breed originally came from the Galloway coast, which lent colour to the Paul Jones legend. In those days the Glasgow contingent were the leaders in the dog-fighting world, and when heavy-weights were in demand they usually put a Blue Paul in the field. These challenges were all advertised in *Bell's Life* and many great fights were brought off in the Burnside district of Rutherglen and the Baillieston district on the banks of the Canal up to the 'eighties. From all the writings on this now extinct variety, all seemed to be agreed that they were a very highly intelli-gent breed of dog, in spite of the somewhat cruel sport they were used in. They were affectionate

and tractable, obedient to a fault when engaged in their work, and mute even under the most trying circumstances. They were game to the death, and could suffer much punishment. They were expert and tricky in their fighting tactics, which made them great favourites with those who indulged in this sport. The nearest approach to them amongst our present-day dogs would be the Bull Mastiff.

Mr. James B. Morrison, of Greenock, the leading authority on all Scottish breeds of dogs in the 'eighties, was the last to exhibit a Blue Paul dog. It was a pleasing blue colour, and it was named Paul, but had no pedigree. It was sup-posed to have been bred in the Kirkintilloch dis-trict. The following is his description of the breed:

"The general appearance of the Blue Paul was that of a smooth-coated, powerfully built cobby dog about forty-five pounds weight and about twenty inches at the shoulder, more after the style of the Bulldog than any other of the present fancy. Head—large, forehead flat; muzzle—short and square; nose black, large and broad, but not receding like that of the Bulldog; jaws and lips even, with no overhanging flews; slight stop between the eyes, which should be dark hazel, and neither sunken nor prominent, with no white or haw seen; ears—small and thin, set on high and invariably cropped; the face not wrinkled, but eyebrows contracted or knit, and, as the dog lowered one side of his head when at attention, this, with the contraction of the eyebrows, gave the dog a peculiarly intelligent but comical look; in fact, there was an expression in the face of the Blue Paul that has never been seen in any other breed, and one can frequently recognize this blood in cross-bred dogs from this peculiarity. Body—round and well ribbed up; back—short, broad and muscular, but not roached; chest very deep and wide; tail set on low, devoid of fringe and rather drooping in carriage, never rising above the back; the dog standing straight and firmly on its legs. Forelegs very stout and muscular, showing no curve, with elbows standing in towards the ribs; hind legs and thighs very thick, strong and well furnished with muscle. The colour was the peculiar shade of dark blue we see occasionally in greyhounds."

Blue Pill.—The active ingredients of blue pill are mercury and liquorice. It is commonly given to dogs as a cholagogue purgative, that is to say, it has a stimulating effect upon the liver and increases the flow of bile.

Boarding Kennels.—A great number of board-ing establishments for dogs are appearing all over the country, and, so far as one can observe, there appears to be no district which is not adequately served in this respect.

Whilst many of these kennels are well laid out and

IN VARYING MOODS.
Delightful attitudes of Border Terriers charmingly illustrated by a skilful pen.

ably managed, there is a considerable number which, unfortunately, fall far short of the standard required for the comfortable and healthy housing of dogs. The proprietors seem to think that almost any kind of shelter is good enough for the temporary lodgment of a dog.

Many places described under dignified and high-sounding titles are disgusting places, and it is highly inadvisable for animals to be boarded in such kennels. They are often draughty, cheerless, sometimes dark or lacking ventilation, riddled with rat-holes, through which rodents regularly appear each night to spread the diseases of which they are such well-known carriers.

Worst of all, in such badly managed or ill-constructed premises there often is absolutely no veterinary superintendence—no qualified person who could go round the kennels each morning in search of disease in any form. It is often only by the very early removal of suspected cases to an isolation ward or hospital that widespread outbreaks of disease may be cut short.

This proviso, again, hinges upon the availability of such isolation or hospital accommodation. Some of the much-advertised boarding kennels offer hopelessly inadequate facilities for exercising the dogs, and it needs no stretch of imagination to visualize what can happen to a dog which is either chained up or otherwise confined to its kennel for $23\frac{1}{2}$ hours out of every 24.

Now let us make a brief survey of the better-class boarding kennels. There is usually a reception-room where newcomers have all particulars entered into the day-book and the dogs are graded as far as possible, so that big dogs cannot possibly exercise with little ones. The whole of the premises should be enclosed with unclimbable fencing, and all fences to exercise runs should be at least six feet high, the top of the fence being made to slope inwards.

The kennels should be lined with asbestos sheets, as this is washable, fireproof, draughtless, and easily replaced if broken. The floor may be of smooth white cement with all corners rounded off. The doors are best made of bar iron, as although their first cost is high, repairs are negligible and they are cheapest in the end. Wooden or wire doors can be chewed through by a determined dog in a single night. The dog's bed should be of wood, raised off the floor quite six inches, and there should be a retaining board along the front edge to prevent straw or other bedding from falling out.

As many windows as possible should be provided in order that light should be almost unlimited. Ventilation, too, is most important, and the staff should avoid having windows open on both sides of the building at once (except in hot summer weather) as dogs are not very resistant to draughts.

A special building or range of kennels should be provided for the reception of any dog which, having come in as supposed healthy, later develops some symptom of illness. Should such an animal develop unmistakable signs of distemper, he is then removed to another special building reserved as a hospital. This must be absolutely isolated, not only as regards its situation, but also as regards the people who are allowed to visit it. A special kennel-maid should be put in charge of the hospital, and she should not be allowed access to any other part of the premises, or to boarders, while she is on that duty.

Every place must be rat-proof and, as far as possible, fly-proof; all buildings should be provided with a slow combustion coke stove for warmth during the winter months. An incinerator is indispensable for the destruction of every kind of refuse. In large establishments these are built of brick, with an iron door on one side, and a chimney.

When a dog is admitted, and before a kennel has even been allotted, his skin should be examined for lice or fleas, and, if any are found, the animal should be bathed at once. Neglect of this precaution, in the summer-time especially, will mean that the kennels will most probably become infested. Fleas are more difficult to eradicate from buildings than are lice, and constant vigilance is required.

The fees chargeable in boarding kennels are somewhat variable, but in the well-conducted establishments where there is no niggardly policy of refusal to spend anything to maintain efficiency, the prices are more or less, per week, as follow: Cats and small puppies, 7s. 6d.; small dogs, such as Cairns, King Charles Spaniels, etc., 10s. 6d.; Terriers, such as Fox and Irish, 12s. 6d.; Chows, Airedales, Setters and similar dogs, 13s. 6d.; Great Danes and other large dogs, 15s.

Some establishments charge less and others more, but care should be exercised in selecting cheap places lest the service and accommodation offered might be very undesirable.

By courtesy of] **THE BOLOGNESE.** [*E. C. Ash.*
Here we have a Toy Dog related to the Maltese, for which the dog on the right might easily be mistaken. Apparently there was also a "short" haired type.

Boarhounds. (*See* GREAT DANE.)

Bob-tailed Sheepdog. (*See* OLD ENGLISH SHEEPDOG.)

Boils.—Boils are really miniature abscesses, and fortunately are not common in dogs.

CAUSES.—They originate as small areas of inflammation in the roots of hair, which become infected with bacteria. Animals which are subjects of diabetes, or kidney disease, are especially liable to boils. Constipation is a common contributory cause, as if there is delay in the elimination of the body's waste products or poisons, via the bowels, these have to be got rid of through some other channel. So far as the dog is concerned the skin is probably the least important of these channels; nevertheless, when the blood becomes thickly charged with effete

THE BORDER TERRIER.

This exceedingly attractive hard-bitten Terrier is used to bolt foxes and for other sports. The head is of Messrs. J. Dodd and
William Carruthers' "Queen o' the Hunt", a great winner.

P

matter, some of the latter finds an exit through the skin.

Boils are especially liable to occur in weakly animals such as those which are just recovering from exhausting diseases. The body's resistance to disease is lowered, and infections and contagions of all kinds are then enabled to become established.

The normal healthy skin always harbours a number of pus-producing microbes which do no harm until the skin becomes broken or chafed, when they are

originate in a position in which the possibility of the skin's expansion is limited (such as in the ear, nose, etc.) then a very great deal of pain is set up.

When several boils arise in very close proximity the condition is known as "carbuncle" and is a much more severe affection. As a rule a boil will rupture and commence to heal on or about the sixth or seventh day. Very bad boils often have a deep - seated greenish-yellow core, which must be removed before any relief can be obtained or

"Winnie of Drysse", a good example of a Border Terrier bitch and a frequent prize winner. The property of Mr. Renwick.

enabled to effect an entrance. Even then, if the defensive mechanism of the blood is not in any way weakened, they are unable to become established or set up areas of suppuration.

SYMPTOMS.—An irritable nodular swelling appears on the skin, having at first a reddened or "pimple" appearance. The summit of the nodule soon becomes yellowish-white and the lesion is said to have "come to a head". The boil is surrounded by an inflamed and very tender area, and should it

"Jedworth Bunty" also belongs to Mr. Renwick. The alertness typical of the breed is well conveyed in the above illustration.

Top: Ch. "Happy Mood", the property of Mr. Renton. Notice the ears and type of coat. A great prize winner.
Lower: Another photograph of "Happy Mood", one of the finest specimens of the breed ever shown.
(Photographs by Fall.)

the boil commence to resolve.

If antiseptic precautions are not taken there is a strong tendency for the escaping pus, by coming in contact with other parts of the skin, to set up new foci of infection resulting in another crop of boils.

Generally, the temperature and appetite of the animal remain unaffected, though its temper may become irritable. Persistently recurring or old-standing boils are very weakening, causing great loss of condition and rendering the animal an easy prey to other and more serious infectious diseases.

TREATMENT.—The ripening of the boil must be expedited by the application of hot fomentations or of hot bread poultices. It may become advisable to have the boil opened surgically and its contents evacuated. The surrounding skin should be cleansed with antiseptic such as Milton or a 1 in 20 solution of carbolic acid. If the boil is large and there is a core, a good plan is to fill the small cavity with one drop of pure carbolic acid in order to kill any remaining bacteria and to ensure a good drainage. The bowels must be relaxed and a course of tonics may be given, the diet meanwhile being generous, nourishing and varied. Ultra violet irradiation appears to abort boils when applied early, and certainly it removes a good deal of their pain.

Bolognese.—It is interesting to note that the Maltese type of Toy Dog has been, and is, a popular Toy Dog in various parts of the world. In 1880 the Toy Dog known as the Bolognese was greatly admired in Central Europe, and as the illustration so clearly shows, it was definitely of Maltese appearance, and may well be said to have been a Maltese Dog. By the side of it, we see standing another of these dogs with a shorter coat.

Bones as Food. (*See* FOODS AND FEEDING.)

Bones, Broken. (*See* FRACTURES.)

Bones, Displaced. (*See* DIS-LOCATIONS.)

Bones, Inflammation of. (*See* OSTITIS.)

Boots for Dogs.—There are occasions when one feels that a properly fitting leather boot could advantageously be applied to a dog's foot. When the pads of the feet have become gravely injured, or very sore, a firm protection is advisable, and not only is further injury prevented, but antiseptic dressings can be retained in position, and the dog itself is prevented from tearing off exposed bandages.

A note of warning should be sounded, however, in the use of these boots, as some people seem to forget to remove them at proper intervals for the cleansing of the foot and the renewal of dressings.

Boracic Acid, or Boric Acid. In canine practice its use is mostly confined to the bathing of inflamed or sore eyes, upon which delicate

By courtesy of]   THE EARLY BORZOI.   *[E. C. Ash.*

"Sokol" was exhibited at Cruft's Show in London, and was one of the Russian team sold after the show. Its period was the early '90's.

organ it exerts no harmful influence; and as a useful constituent of dry dressings employed for dusting wounded or abrased areas of skin.

Border Terrier.—The first mention of a Border Terrier as far as is known appeared in 1882, when a short note was published in a journal of that time as to the Terriers that were to be found in Westmorland and Northumberland.

They were described as small and very active,

By courtesy of]   "OUSLAD".   *[E. C. Ash.*

This was possibly the most important dog bought by the Duchess of Newcastle after her Grace had started her noted Kennel. "Ousland" came from Russia about 1891.

kept entirely for the work of digging out foxes in the rough country, and as exceptionally brave. Their colour was sometimes red and sometimes black grizzle, although the commonest shade was what is known as "pepper-and-salt". They were also said to exist only in a few areas in these two counties, where visitors from England seldom went: so that they were not generally known. Their coats were rough and hard, and to-day the dog generally may be said to be "hard-bitten".

Later, Mr. Rawdon Lee in his book on Terriers mentions this breed, stating that a Mr. Jacob Robson, of Otterburn, had had such dogs in his family for many years, and that all his stock went back to a dog named "Flint".

In recent years this little Terrier was revived by a Northumberland Border Terrier Club, and it was mainly due to Mr. T. Hamilton-Adams and Mr. W. Morris that the breed recovered. In 1920 the Kennel Club recognized the Border Terrier as a pure breed variety.

STANDARD OF THE BORDER TERRIER.

WEIGHT. — Dogs not to exceed 16 lb., bitches not to exceed 14 lb

HEAD.—Otter expression. Skull fairly broad and not too round. Muzzle moderately short and strong. Nose black, but liver not a disqualification.

EYES.—Dark.

EARS.—V-shape, drooping in line with skull.

NECK.—Fair length, not too much arch.

SHOULDER.—Fairly long, sloping and well set back.

BACK.—Not too lengthy, moderately sprung rib.

CHEST.—Fairly deep and to conform with shoulder formation.

FORELEGS.—Straight and good boned.

FEET.—Cat-like.

TAIL.—Otter type, undocked, short and not set too high.

HINDQUARTERS.—Racy.

COAT. — Harsh, with good undercoat essential.

SKIN. — Pelt thick.

COLOUR. — Red-wheaten, grizzle, or blue-and-tan.

Borzoi. — This beautiful dog is, as we all know, a variety of the Greyhound, and certainly one of the most attractive of them all. Whilst it shows its family relationship, it is by no means just a long-haired Greyhound, and a dog that approaches the Greyhound is by no means a good Borzoi.

As a breed the type combines gracefulness and beauty with every suggestion of speed. In the olden days it was said to combine with these virtues strength and size, but the dog of to-day, although by no means a small or delicate one, can hardly be considered as a powerful animal or a very large one.

The build of the finest specimens is symmetrical and well proportioned, and it has been said that every part must be correctly placed and every part correctly distanced and balanced to avoid the dog losing that remarkable beauty which in this breed is so important.

QUEEN ALEXANDRA'S FAVOURITE DOG.
The late Queen Alexandra was presented with this dog, Ch. "Ajax", by the late Czar of Russia. He became her constant companion and was, in fact, a very fine specimen of this beautiful breed.

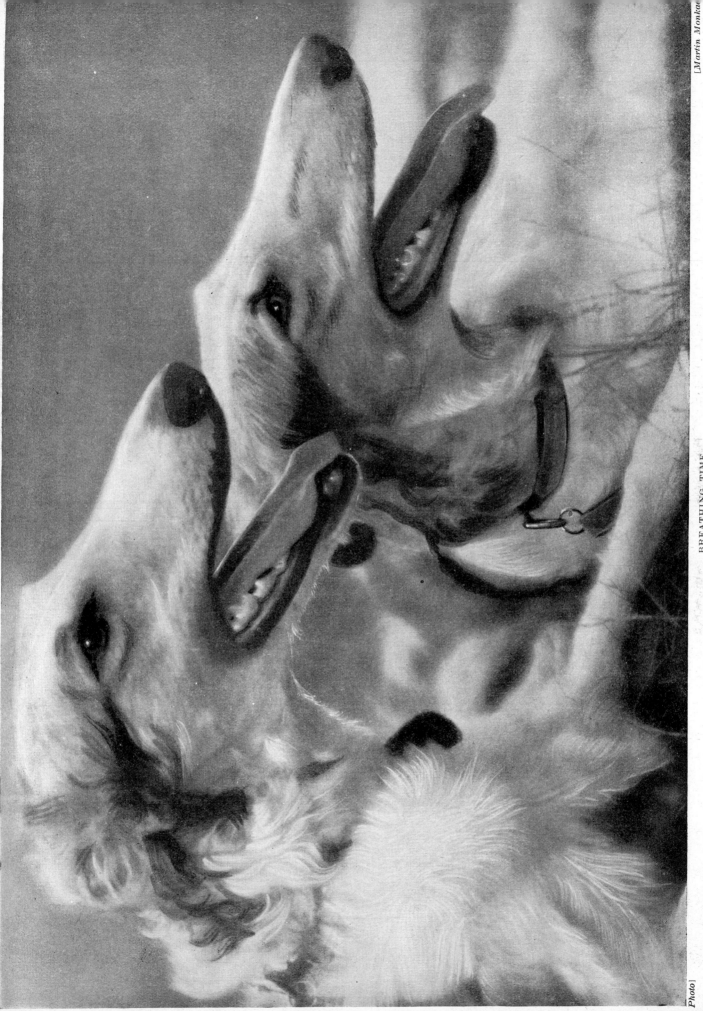

BREATHING TIME.

A remarkable photograph showing two Borzois after a run. They are good exemplifications of the elegance of this fascinating breed.

"QUEEN CATHERINE" AND HER BORZOIS.

Miss Oriel Ross, the "Catherine of Russia" in the 1932 play *Casanova*, exercising the Borzois that appeared on the stage with her.

Photo]
"A TUG-OF-WAR".
[*Ralph Robinson.*

A team of Mrs. Vlasto's puppies are seen pulling at a cord. Attention is drawn to the type of head and the carriage of the tail.

It must be realized that, whilst at one time abroad the variety was kept more or less entirely for its sporting powers in which strength and weight were of far more importance than appearances, in England and in the U.S.A. this has never been so, and the interest of owners has centred on the matter of appearance.

The Borzoi in pre-war days in Russia was famed the world over for its signal prowess in the truly Russian sport of wolf-coursing, a sport of difficulty and danger. In this the Borzois (two being used on one wolf) were trained to chase and seize the wolf behind the ears—both dogs taking a grip at the same moment—and to throw it over. The wolf once down, the two dogs had to hold on to it until the huntsman had time to arrive upon the scene, dismount, and seize the victim, either killing it or gagging and tying it so that it could not escape.

With so strong and savage an animal as a full-grown wolf it was no easy task for the dogs, and unless the tackle and holding were well done they were certain to suffer serious injury, and the wolf was likely to make its escape. If the wolf was held on one side only it would turn that way. It was important therefore that the two dogs should act so well together that the wolf was firmly held at both sides simultaneously.

In Russia, therefore, appearance took second place to coursing intelligence, speed, strength, and fearlessness, but on the arrival of the breed in England no such use could be found for it, and the

by courtesy of]
A GERMAN GROUP, ABOUT 1898.
[*E. C. Ash.*

Large and important kennels of these Hounds were popular in Germany. The type, as will be seen from this picture, has greatly improved since this photograph was taken.

breed became a variety for exhibition and an ornamental breed for the home of elegance.

In earlier times in Russia the Borzoi held a more or less similar position to that of the Greyhound in England, that is to say it was a breed over which the Royal Family and the Court had full control. Thus it was to be found only in the Imperial kennels and in those of the Grand Dukes. Later, however, the stricture on keeping Borzois was removed, and it was taken up by the more important landowners. Wolf-coursing was then considered to be a Russian national sport, and it is

resembled Greyhounds, both in type, size, head, and colouring.

This was naturally displeasing, and it was further said, possibly because of national prejudice against foreign blood, that these Greyhound-improved Borzois, as well as failing in appearance, further failed in working power.

In consequence Russian breeders most assiduously eliminated any of Greyhound type, and so in time to a great extent destroyed it. Huntsmen who had to gag the wolf (a piece of wood was held close to the animal's mouth; it would seize it,

QUEEN OF RUMANIA AND HER HOUNDS.

The Queen of Rumania keeps a kennel of Borzois at her country estate at Sibiu. Her Majesty is obviously happy with her dogs.

therefore not surprising that no expense was spared in developing the pastime.

Visitors to Russia in pre-war days who had the fortune to visit the Borzoi kennels report that these establishments had been built regardless of cost and were in every detail up to date, with good accommodation for the large staff that was employed. Men were on duty both night and day, and the best dogs sold for high prices, and every conceivable plan was tried to improve the dogs for coursing by feeding, breeding, and training.

For this purpose—the fame of the British Greyhound having spread to Russia—at various times Greyhounds had been introduced, so that some of the Borzoi breed began to fail in coat, and some

and the wood was pulled back by cords attached to the sides, the cords being then fastened together behind the wolf's head) were not over-happy to rely on dogs that were not of the purest Borzoi breeding.

Because the two Borzois had to seize the wolf at the same time, it was necessary that dogs working together should approximate each other in running power, so that they should arrive one on each side of the wolf together. It was also important that they should be, as near as possible, equal in strength and courage, for any hesitation or weakness would give the wolf the opportunity of turning the tables upon its enemies. It is therefore comprehensible that speed, strength, and courage were considered important, and that colour, although

THE BORZOI.

(Specially drawn for this work by Geoffrey Williams)

It may be said that of all aristocratic dogs the Borzoi is outstanding as the very embodiment of graceful beauty. He is the most handsome of the "Greyhound" breed. Two distinct types of head are seen to-day, the old style Russian, and the modern, which is the result of the breeder's art. It is a matter of opinion as to which is the more handsome. Mr. Williams depicts a Borzoi after a hard run, showing fine lines and charming expression.

PETS OF A DUCHESS.

The Duchess of Newcastle is one of the many leaders of society who love the graceful Borzois. She is an excellent judge of the breed and is seen here with two fine specimens, "Podar of Notts" and "Vodky of Notts".

A PICTURESQUE GROUP.

A great lover of dogs, Mrs. Arthur Wooley-Hart, seen above with her favourite Borzois, was formerly Vivienne Countess von Bernstorff, daughter-in-law of the former German Ambassador to Washington.   She is dressed here as the Marchioness de Bouchamps, who fought for the Royalist cause in France in 1793.

of interest, would take a very minor place. The Russians, however, had a partiality for white dogs and those with ghostlike marking, the white being considered the most aristocratic, going well with the white leads and white gloves of the huntsmen.

It is an interesting fact that, although the breed was well known in France and illustrated in books of the eighteenth century, British books of that period give no mention of such a breed, nor any suggestion that such a breed might be discovered. This is strange, for these books deal with the rarest of dogs in every corner of the world, and the authors exhibit a marked anxiety to include them all—indeed, to create a few extra breeds to fill the pages !

But in 1812 two Englishmen visited Russia and wrote a book describing, amongst much else, the Russian huntsmen, in their original and attractive clothing, going out wolf-hunting with Greyhounds of great beauty. They described the dogs as not unlike Italian Greyhounds, except that they were much larger and had long silky coats. They called them Fantailed Greyhounds, and went on to say that whilst the Court spent much money on these dogs, they seldom went hunting. Two years later another visitor to Russia mentions dogs known as Siberian Greyhounds.

It was thirty years or so later that great interest was aroused in England by the arrival in London of two of the Russian Fantailed Greyhounds, presented to Her Majesty Queen Victoria. Their beauty was noted, and the "dog expert" of those days hurried along with a tape-measure to report later that they were three feet tall to the top of their heads !

They were described as being very much a kind of Scottish Deerhound, but the authority adds, possibly to show his loyalty to native breeds, that they did not compare with the Scottish breed in courage, for he asserts that these Russian dogs would often run along by the side of the wolf

(By courtesy of "Country Life".)

The heads of "Call Boy" and "Booklaw". These two remarkable Borzois are the property of Mr. E. Herry Guy, the enthusiastic and noted breeder of these Hounds.

for a hundred yards or more before either of them could make up its mind to grapple with him !

This gift to Her Majesty was the start of the breed in England. It became a Society breed. It was never generally kept, for it hardly suited the average person. It became the dog of the fashionable home. The public were, however, greatly interested, and it was only necessary to advertise that a Borzoi was to be seen to collect a crowd. The Czar presented further examples of the breed to the British Royal Family and to some of the nobility. In 1863 the first Borzoi was exhibited at a show held at Birmingham, and immediately became the great attraction. A large number of people visited Birmingham that day with the sole object of seeing "Katae", the Duchess of Manchester's pure-bred Borzoi that had been presented to her from the Czar's Imperial kennels. In 1876 Lady Emily Peel exhibited a dog by the name of "Czar", a son of the Duke of Hamilton's "Moscow", out of "Sandringham", the last-named being the property of that interesting dog enthusiast, the Rev. J. C. Macdona.

Among other Borzois that arrived in England from the Imperial kennels were two sent to the Prince of Wales (later King Edward VII), "Molodetz" and "Owdalzka", the former being exhibited by His Royal Highness at Laycock's Yard, Islington, London.

The Princess (later to be Queen Alexandra) made her Borzoi her constant personal companion, and many pictures are to be seen of her with this very beautiful example of the breed, showing Her Royal Highness standing with "Alex" by her side. "Alex" was much exhibited and became a champion.

In 1885 Lady Innes Ker started her Borzoi kennel, and in 1888 Colonel Wellesley showed "Krilutt", which became the first Borzoi champion in England. He also exhibited a dog named "Damon", noted for the beauty of its head, and it is very possible that this head set the ball rolling that in time nearly brought the Borzoi breed to an end in England. For "Damon's" head roused breeders to attempt to get similar heads and, further, to improve them, and when a thing like that starts it is difficult to stop it.

Perhaps the next milestone in the history of the Borzoi was in 1890,

Photo]　　　A NOTED TRIO.　　　*[Ralph Robinson.*

Mrs. A. A. Vlasto has probably one of the finest kennels of Borzois in the world, and the affix Addlestone suggests good heads. Here we have Ch. "Lookaya of Addlestone" and Ch. "Groom Kaya" and "Ivarin".

when Her Grace the Duchess of Newcastle entered the Borzoi field, and the following year when she purchased from Mr. Blees some of the consignment of Borzois from Russia, including the remarkable dog "Ouslad", one of the best Borzois ever seen. Whilst the interest of well-known people in a breed leads to good times for that particular variety merely because of fashion, the entry of the Duchess of Newcastle, whilst to some extent having that effect, had much more than that attached to it.

The Duchess understood dogs, was an expert and an enthusiast, whose interest was of a distinctly practical kind. The following year the Borzoi Club was formed and the Duchess of Newcastle

was the first president. It was decided to run Borzoi shows, and the first show was, as far as is known, a great success. But the public were getting accustomed to the Borzoi, and later shows met with such bad support that they were given up.

In 1892, as well as the founding of the Borzoi Club, a great impetus was given to the breed and enormous interest aroused in the appearance at the Agricultural Show at Islington of a class of fifty, many of which were direct from Russia, entered from the Imperial kennels by the Grand Duke Nicholas. Further interest was occasioned by the knowledge that after the show these Russian dogs were to be sold by public auction to the highest bidders. Large crowds flocked to Islington to see the wolf-catching dogs from Russia. The sale was an exhilarating experience. "Oudar", weighing 105 pounds and standing $30\frac{1}{2}$ inches at the shoulder, was sold for £200.

Mr. Rawdon Lee gives his opinion that "Oudar",

Photo]　　　　　　　　　　　　　　　　　*[Ralph Robinson.*
BORZOI TYPE.
The graceful build of these dogs is clearly seen in this picture, showing Mrs. A. A. Vlasto's Ch. "Groom Kaya" and Ch. "Lov Kaya of Addlestone".

GRACE AND QUALITY.

A fine group of noted winning Borzois, bred and shown successfully by Ernest Henry Guy, who possesses one of the leading kennels in the country.

A GRACEFUL STUDY.

Ever since Queen Alexandra favoured the Borzoi it has been a favourite with ladies, its graceful bearing and delicate lines appealing to the feminine eye. Miss Peggy O'Neill, seen above, is but one of many famous actresses who keep this type of dog.

"Ouslad", "Krilutt", and "Koratai" were the best Borzois ever seen in England.

The extremely fine head became the main attention of breeders, and in time, by constantly breeding for heads, without considering the other parts of the dog, they obtained remarkable heads on hooped bodies and little more. The breed became distinctly weedy and unsound and rapidly lost ground.

Happily the situation was realized in time, and owners set out to recreate stamina, sound body and

great number of leading champions have been bred or shown from this kennel, amongst others her Ch. "Sparrow Hawk of Addlestone", who at one time had sired more champions in the breed than any other dog.

An important leading kennel with an international reputation was started by Mr. Ernest Henry Guy, whose work has been the building up of sound-bodied stock with good heads and the best of legs and feet, and who has further helped the breed whenever possible by guaranteeing classes at shows.

Photo]   [*"Country Life".*
"MYTHE NOVIKOFF".
The Borzoi at one time, in the eagerness to obtain a yet better head, became weak in body. Breeders of these dogs took the matter in hand and saved the breed by careful selection. This one was bred by Miss E. M. Robinson.

limbs that once had been so characteristic. They have lost nothing by this recovery, for all the increased beauty has been retained. The Russian type as it first was when brought into this country would be considered too clumsy and tall to-day.

In the history of the breed certain kennels were noted for their stock. The Duchess of Newcastle has already been mentioned. In Essex, at Ramsden Heath, some of the finest Borzois were to be found, bred by Major Borman, amongst others the famous show matron "Miss Piostre", unbeatable on the bench and the breeder of remarkable stock. Mrs. Vlasto (affix "Addlestone") is world-famous, and a

Many more kennels deserve mention, many more having been started in the succeeding years.

The Borzoi is not an easy dog to breed; many of the dogs one sees to-day are too much like Greyhounds and fail in the Borzoi character. Borzois too heavy or too light are by no means attractive. The position and carriage of the head make much difference to the dog, for a head pointing too much towards the feet is objectionable. The arch, a characteristic of the breed, must start as close to the shoulder-blades as possible. It will be noticed in many of the best specimens that a line drawn from the hock to the start of the tail is at right angles. Size without coarseness, quality without weakness, are the two things that every breeder of Borzois must keep in mind.

POINTS OF THE BORZOI AS DEFINED AND ADOPTED BY THE BORZOI CLUB.

HEAD.—Long and lean. Skull very slightly domed and narrow, stop not perceptible, inclining to Roman nose. Head so fine that the direction of the bones and principal veins can be clearly seen. Bitches' heads should be finer than the dogs'. Jaws long, deep, and powerful; teeth even, neither pig-jawed nor undershot. Nose large and black, never pink or brown.

EARS.—Small and fine in quality; not too far apart, and when in repose the occiput touching, or nearly so.

EYES.—Dark, intelligent, expressive, set somewhat obliquely, placed well back, but not too far apart; eyelids dark. Eyes should not be light or staring.

NECK.—Clean, slightly arched, continuing the line of back, powerful and well set on, free from throatiness.

SHOULDERS.—Clean, sloping well back, fine at withers, free from lumpiness.

CHEST.—Great depth of brisket, rather narrow.

RIBS.—Nicely sprung, very deep, giving heart room and lung play

Photo]   ["Country Life".

"LONESKA".

It is easy to see in the Borzoi head the Saluki, which many believe was the origin of this breed. Notice the narrow Saluki type of muzzle.

BACK.—Rising in a nice arch, the arch being more marked in the dogs, rather bony and free from any cavity.

LOINS.—Broad and very powerful, with plenty of muscular development.

THIGHS.—Long, well developed, with good second thigh.

FORELEGS.—Lean and straight. Seen from the front, narrow, like blades; from the

Photo]   [Guiver.
CH. "MYTHE MAZEPPA".
Miss Robinson's noted champion, shown here, is said by many to be the best Borzoi seen for many years with the most-desired head.

174

HERE'S LOOKING AT YOU.

The Boston Terrier, of which the above is a typical example, is one of the few breeds which America claims as its own. It is, nevertheless, rather a rare dog even there, so much so that outstanding champions will fetch as much as £2000.

THE BOSTON TERRIER.

Photo] [Fall.
A CHARMING PAIR.

These two Boston Terrier puppies are "Virginia of Canuck" on left and "O.Kay Baby of Canuck", bred by Mrs. McCormick-Goodhart, and now belonging to the Countess of Essex.

side, wide at shoulder, narrowing down to foot; elbows neither turned in nor out, pasterns strong.

HINDLEGS.—Long, muscular, stifles well bent, hocks broad, clean and well let down.

MUSCLES.—Highly developed and well distributed.

FEET.—Rather long, toes close together and well arched, never flat.

COAT.—Long and silky (never woolly), either flat, wavy, or rather curly. Short and smooth on head, ears and front of legs; on neck the frill profuse and rather curly; forelegs and chest well feathered; on hindquarters and tail, feathering long and profuse.

TAIL.—Long, well feathered, carried low, not gaily.

HEIGHT. — At shoulder: Dogs from 29 inches upwards; bitches from 27 inches upwards.

GENERAL APPEARANCE. — Very graceful, aristocratic and elegant, combining courage, muscular power, and great speed.

Points decided on at the Club's General Meeting in 1922: Head complete (eyes and ears included), 15; neck, 10; shoulders and chest, 15; ribs, back and loins, 15; hindquarters, stifles and hocks, 15; legs and feet, 15; coat, tail and feather, 10; general appearance, 5. Total, 100.

The following are the most important dogs and bitches of recent times: Ch. "Felstead"; "Loaningdale"; Ch. "Mythe Mazeppa"; Ch. "Zikovitch of Brunton"; "Trigo"; "Rudolph of Parbold"; Ch. "Mythe Ivanoff"; "Ruski Alexandra Pepita"; "Mythe Oleuka"; "Nitsichin"; Ch. "Sladkaya of Addlestone"; "Ballerina of Bransgore"; Ch. "Mythe Petroushka"; "Princess Sylvia of Vladimar"; "D'Avrille".

Boston Terrier.—This is one of the few breeds that America claims as its own, and though never seen in great numbers there, it is very much sought after and prized, as much as £2,000 being a not unusual price to be paid for a first-class champion.

One is led to believe, nevertheless, that its origins were laid in Britain, for the dog that is really the ancestor of the breed was a cross between the English Bulldog and the Brindle Bull Terrier, imported into the United States in the 'seventies of the nineteenth century.

In those days he was known as the Boston Bull, and was a very much heavier animal than the one we are conversant with in England under the name of Boston Terrier. The Boston Bull weighed about 60 lb., whereas now the smallest variety runs to as low as 15 lb. In America it took some years before the animal was brought to anything like a consistent standard, the chief object being the elimination of the unwanted characteristics of the Bulldog and Bull Terrier, which resulted in a compact animal, very much smaller than the old one.

He has through all his changes retained the attributes of devotion and loyalty that have for so long endeared the Bulldog to the British nation. From his Bull Terrier ancestry he has inherited a definite sporting instinct, and though never in the

Photo] [Fall.
BOSTON TERRIERS.

Here we have two typical British Boston Terriers, both owned by the Countess of Essex. They can be taken as portraying the best type.

"wide open spaces" is he used as a hunter, in a more restricted way he is a terror to all rodents, making him an ideal man's companion as well as an excellent guard-dog. In America he is familiarly known as a "black satin gentleman", and is the only dog that has always remained popular with the American owner.

He is very tractable, will remain without complaint in one room for hours; he does not bark, but he will defend with his life.

It is no easy thing to introduce a foreign variety into Great Britain—for one thing, the quarantine laws demand a six months' detention before admission. Mrs. G. McCormick-Goodhart overcame these difficulties when, in 1927, she brought over a kennel, which she established and developed so much that within five or six years the Boston Terrier had become quite a favourite among English owners, most prominent among them being the Countess of Essex.

The first registered dog in Britain was "Highball Canuck", which, as a six-months'-old puppy, cost £80, but it was not long before the Boston Terrier was on the show bench, and from its first appearance in 1928 at the Kennel Club Show, it gradually increased in popularity until in 1933 it had a class to itself.

The standard of the Boston of to-day shows that there are three weights, 15 lb. and under, 15–20 lb. and 20–25 lb. It is, however, only lightweights that are benched in this country, though many privately prefer the heavier type.

The body should be short and well-knit, giving the impression of strength without clumsiness.

A TERROR TO RODENTS.
The female of the species is slightly smaller than the male, but is just as keen a ratter—which is the beginning and end of its sporting usefulness.

The neck is of fair length and curved to carry the head proudly. This should be short and square and entirely free from wrinkles. The eyes are dark and full and set wide apart. The nose should be short and square, but with a good stop; and the teeth evenly set in a square jaw, never protruding.

The legs are most important. Terrier legs set wide apart on a wide chest and sloping shoulders gives him that Terrier look which counteracts the "bulliness" of the body. The popular colour is seal brindle, i.e. black with gold flecks and white facings. These white facings are essential in the Boston, indeed, white blaze, full white collars and white gloves are the ideal markings for which every Boston breeder aims.

Several kinds of tails are allowed: screw, kink, or straight, but they must be short and not carried "gay".

Ears should be erect, set wide apart, of thin texture and bat-shaped. In America these dogs are cropped, though, as in Britain, some States make this illegal.

The Boston has undergone many changes since he was first introduced—in size, colour, ears, build—but his characteristics remain the same: sporting and affectionate.

BELIES HIS LOOKS.
The American dog is larger than in Britain, and many here prefer him over the usual show weight. His cropped ears tend to give him a semblance of aggressiveness but in reality he is as docile as any breed.

A DISTINGUISHED OWNER.

Among the first to own Boston Terriers in England was the Countess of Essex, and she has been a consistent and successful exhibitor, doing much to make the breed popular. Here she is shown with two of her favourites.

Photo]

PIONEER AMONG BREEDERS.

[*Sport & General.*

Mrs. G. McCormick-Goodhart was the first to introduce the Boston Terrier into Britain. She is seen here with
"Kandy Kid of Canuck", one of her prized possessions. Many of her dogs went to the Countess of Essex's Kennels.

Bouledogue Français. (See French Bulldog.)

Bowel Diseases (a) Inflammation of the Bowels.—Also known as Enteritis when it affects the small intestine, and Colitis when the colon is the seat of the trouble. Proctitis indicates inflammation of the terminal bowel or rectum.

CAUSES.—These are very frequently obscure for, upon post-mortem investigation, nothing whatever can be discovered in some cases to account for the attack. At the same time there are a number of factors which are known definitely to set up enteritis and these are : habitual constipation, stoppage, irritant poison, telescoping of the bowel, chills, injuries, acute worm infestation and the excessive use of worm remedies and purgatives, foreign bodies, coccidiosis, bacterial invasion, and specific diseases such as canine typhus and distemper.

SYMPTOMS.—It is proposed to indicate only the salient features of this frequently fatal and most important disease in order that the novice may be to some extent able to suspect its existence in a sick dog. There is a dullness and listlessness marked, sometimes, by intermittent vomiting. Appetite is usually in abeyance and in some cases there may be acute twinges of pain which cause the dog to cry out suddenly or whine, or look round at its flanks. In other cases the dog may assume the unusual position of lying on its back ; or, failing this, may lie on its side and hold up the uppermost hind leg.

Inflammation of the bowels may be distinguished

Photo]   *[Walter Guiver*

A GOOD HEAD

"Mayfair Imp", owned by Dr. Dunning Sikkenga, is a very good example of what one expects a Boston Terrier to be in Britain with the uncropped ears.

from simple colic by the fact that as a general rule the latter is of more sudden onset and of greater temporary severity. Enteritis is usually more subtle in its incidence and accompanied, more or less, by a rise of temperature. As to the latter point no reliability can be placed upon it, as the writer has met with many cases in which the temperature was elevated but one degree, if at all. It would be correct, however, to expect to find a temperature of about 103 very soon after the first noticeable onset of symptoms. In such a case one would also expect to find the nose hot and dry and the eye perhaps bloodshot.

If one attempts to manipulate the abdomen the dog tenses its abdominal muscles and evinces unmistakable evidence of pain in that vicinity. The back is arched when the dog is in a standing position, and there is a disposition in numerous cases for the affected animal to bring its abdomen into contact with cold places such as stone flags or oil-cloth, in its endeavour to alleviate the pain.

Constipation is apparently present, especially at first, although in many instances the writer, in making a subsequent post-mortem examination, has found absolutely no food in the bowels, and therefore nothing could have been passed. It is often this supposed constipation which induces dog owners to give purgatives and so, too frequently, to sign the dog's death warrant. Blood may sometimes be passed in the stools or these may be very black, indicating its presence.

TREATMENT.—As soon as enteritis is suspected,

Photo]   *[Walter Guiver*

BOSTON PUPPIES.

Even in puppyhood these dogs are very tractable—one of the attributes which has endeared them to the American owner. The above are a trio bred in Britain.

the owner is strongly advised to seek qualified advice because dogs, no less than human beings, may be dead within 12 to 48 hours. Incorrect treatment may expedite this fatal result. As a first-aid measure however, 5 to 25 drops of chlorodyne may be given in water. Failing this, bismuth will be found to exert a mildly astringent and soothing action The two are often combined.

Do not give solid foods, as these only tend to increase the irritability of the bowel lining. Milk, eggs, barley or albumen water; Valentine's or Brand's Extracts, Virolax or Eatan, may all be substituted. Later on, when the condition is not acute, a little boiled fish mashed in milk may be well tolerated.

The patient must be kept warm, dry, and comfortable, and be permitted no exercise. Hot packs to the abdomen help to relieve the pain. (*See also* STUTTGART DISEASE.)

(*b*) FOREIGN BODIES IN THE BOWELS.—CAUSES : Dogs being for the most part voracious feeders, it is dangerous to give them unprepared dishes of chicken, rabbit or fish, as the bones of the two first-named are splinterable and very sharp, and are apt to become stuck in the oesophagus or bowel, with serious results. Stupid or thoughtless puppies may pick up and swallow needles, pins, nails, and stones, etc., from pure playfulness, or possibly in consequence of indigestion. It has been noticed that dogs are apt to swallow unusual articles when suffering from gastric catarrh or dyspepsia, and even as a symptom of rabies.

SYMPTOMS.—The secretions of a dog's stomach are strongly acid, which factor renders the digestion of bones, of all sorts, comparatively easy. But occasions arise when such digestion does not take place, and on other occasions the bowel may be actually perforated by the sharp-pointed spicules of bone, or pins, etc. The symptoms then exhibited are very similar to those seen in enteritis. In fact, it is likely that enteritis soon becomes a complication. One may notice blood being passed from the anus, and this might lead one to suspect an injury. Upon careful examination of the abdomen a foreign body may actually be detected. X-rays must not be forgotten as a most valuable aid to diagnosis.

TREATMENT.—When foreign bodies are known to have been swallowed and are suspected of causing trouble, the common tendency is to give the dog oil with the object of lubricating the bowel and facilitating their exit. It has been found, however, that to feed a dog, forcibly or otherwise, on suet pudding or something stodgy, is to enhance the prospects of clearing the intestines without an operation. It is most unwise to waste valuable time and thus permit the onset of peritonitis, and readers are strongly advised to seek qualified advice at once.

(*c*) STOPPAGE OF THE BOWEL.—CAUSES : Neglected or chronic constipation induced, sometimes by a greatly deficient water supply, or by confining a highly trained dog to a house where it cannot or will not relieve itself. Stoppage may be caused by stricture (temporary or permanent) of one portion of the bowel ; masses of hardened faeces ; foreign bodies ; hernia ; or by the pressure of abscess or tumour formation.

SYMPTOMS.—The dog shows all the symptoms common to constipation plus many of those associated with inflammation of the bowels. Vomiting is frequent, but chiefly noted is the fact that the bowels have not moved for a definite and unusually long time—perhaps even three or four days. Palpation of the abdomen reveals a series of hard lumps in the bowel which, as a rule, cannot be broken down from the exterior. Perhaps only one hard lump may be felt, when one might suspect that a mutton chop bone had become lodged.

TREATMENT.—The position of the impaction should, if possible, be determined, and if within reach of suitable instruments, it might be reduced, or removed. Otherwise, copious and repeated enemata of warm water would be useful, an attempt being made to balloon-out the bowel and thus permit the obstruction to move. Meanwhile, large doses of medicinal paraffin should be given by mouth. It is inadvisable and even dangerous, in some circumstances, to give drastic purgatives, as it is obvious that if some object has become wedged in the bowel, it is unlikely to move by any but mechanical means, and the cure would be worse than the disease. If all simple measures fail to remove the trouble, a canine surgeon would have to consider the advisability of performing an operation.

(*d*) INVAGINATION OF THE BOWEL.—The telescoping of one part into another. Known also as intussusception.

CAUSES.—The actual causes in a given case are frequently most obscure but the condition is known very often to be associated with prolapsed bowel (*see* ANUS, PROLAPSE OF) and sometimes with distemper. Other indirect causes are injury to the abdomen, severe purging, and possibly the consumption of indigestible substances. A theory is now advanced as to the actual mechanism of invagination, and, briefly, it is that a small area of the bowel becomes rigid and immobile by a constricting tonic spasm of its muscular coats. The consequence of this is that the area of bowel, immediately anterior to it, becomes dilated by foods and *flatus*, which is continually arriving through peristaltic action. Colic is set up, and the peristaltic waves become more forceful and eventually overcome the obstruction by carrying the normal bowel wall over it. Once a

By courtesy] [*Mrs. McCormick-Goodhart.*
THE BOSTON TERRIER.
"Highball of Canuck"—a son of the international Ch. "Highball Just It". This was **one** of the first Boston Terriers to be imported into England.

IMPRESSIONS.

G. Ambler, a foremost artist of dog life, here gives a few racy impressions of Boston Terriers, drawn from life. Despite his Bulldog ancestry, this dog is a lively fellow as well as having inherited a fine sense of loyalty and a keen intelligence.

R

THE BOXER OF GERMANY.

This Bulldog of Germany was used for bull-baiting, just as was the British Bulldog in the early days of its history.

patient has become too collapsed to undergo it.

Boxer.—This dog, which appears to derive from the "Dogues" that had been made use of, during past centuries, for animal-baiting, is very little known in Britain. His direct ancestor was the so-called "Bullenbeisser", which means, literally, "Bullbiter"; it was a robust and massive animal, fairly inelegant, utilized in the past in Germany, Holland, France, and Belgium, to follow on the path of bears, boars and deer. His type is that which in France, and principally in the south-west of that country, used to be called *chien de boucher*—butcher's dog. First of all, recourse had been made to crossings with different breeds, particularly with the Bulldog; later on, a selection persevered in had contributed to uniformity of type and in eliminating the aggressive and combative instincts of the primitive type.

It was, thanks to the initiative of Bavarian breeders, that this breed, fairly obscure up till then, began to win the favour of dog-fanciers. Since 1895, when the first Boxer was exhibited at the Munich dog show, the diffusion of this breed became such that, by 1934, about 30,000 entries had been made in the stud-books

portion of bowel has enveloped another part, it is believed that a resumption to the normal never occurs except by surgical interference.

SYMPTOMS.—These are mainly the same as may be noted in stoppage of the bowel or in enteritis, as both conditions may ensue. In addition, however, there is nearly always a blood-stained and jelly-like discharge from the bowel which, in well-established cases, has an extremely unpleasant odour. The dog is gravely ill, exhibits marked tenderness upon manipulation of the abdomen, and may be dead in a very short space of time. A sausage-shaped mass may be discerned by carefully feeling through the abdominal wall.

TREATMENT.—The condition is very fatal and is not one in which any amateurish experiments can be countenanced. It is true that surgeons have claimed success by ballooning the bowel with warm salt water, but in the majority of cases, when invagination has been definitely diagnosed, it is a matter for an urgent operation which cannot be successfully performed when the

A REMARKABLE SPECIMEN.

The resemblance of the Boxer to the French Bulldog, Boston Terrier, and, to some extent, the English Bulldog, can be seen clearly in the above picture

[*Dorien Leigh.*

RESTING.

This way of resting is by no means general, although some few dogs prefer it to any other method.   The reader's attention is drawn to the short docked tail
and the build of the dog which, as will be seen, shows great strength.

of the different specialist clubs furthering the interests of this breed. After the war, the very active Boxer Club of France, for instance, which counts fervent fanciers amongst its members, greatly contributed to popularize this excellent dog in its country.

The Boxer is a dog of medium size, with short and smooth coat, robust and full of muscles, built as an athlete, but elegant and without clumsiness. He measures from about 22 to 24 inches at the shoulder, and weighs about 50 to 60 lb.; the female is somewhat lighter than the male.

The head is characteristic. The judges attach the greatest importance to its shape and to the harmony of its proportions with the rest of the body. The first thing that strikes the eye is that the skin covering the head forms wrinkles on the forehead, on the lips, and on the cheeks. The skull must be arched, but not excessively so, somewhat narrow in its frontal part, and it joins the face in a clearly-defined angle. The distance comprised between the top of the head and that angle must be double the length of the muzzle. The ears are set on very high, cut into a point, of moderate width, and carried vertically. The eyes, of an energetic and intelligent expression, without wickedness, are of medium size and dark-brown in colour.

The well-developed muzzle is almost cubic in shape. It terminates in an always black nose, slightly *retroussé* at its extremity, large, with very wide nostrils, somewhat back from the alignment in relation to the upper lip. The jaws are strong and large at their extremity; the lower one goes beyond the upper one, and bends upwards a little. The teeth are strong, regularly set in; in spite of the slight prognathism of the lower jaw, the teeth must never show. The cheeks are clearly rounded, without being large to excess. The lips are strong and thick, are well united, and not pendulous; the lower lip is such that the line of the chin is about parallel with the upper profile of the nose. The following are a few measurements: the width of the head, between the articulations of the jaws, is equal to two-thirds of its length, and the width of the muzzle, at the root, corresponds to two-thirds of the width of the head. Finally, the vertical distance, comprised between the top of the nose and the sloping part of the chin, is equal to a third of the line from the anterior extremity of the latter to the maxillary articulation.

The neck, rounded, vigorous, but not thick-set, without dewlap, represents a well-propor-

By courtesy]   *[E. C. Ash.*

THE EARLY BOXER.

In the early part of this century the Boxer was far less of a Boston Terrier than to-day's pictures show him to be.

tioned curve from the nape to the shoulder-blade, which latter is well marked. The shoulders are long and sloping, without too much muscle. The chest is deep, descending up to the elbow, with fairly rounded ribs; however, its width is a moderate one, and does not exceed considerably that of the head. The thorax extends itself pretty far backwards. The back is straight, large and full of muscle; the flanks short, tight; the abdomen but little bulky, slightly tucked-up. The crupper is a little sloping and fairly large, especially in females. The tail is set on high, and is always docked at the third vertebra; the stump is straight.

BEAUTY AND THE BOXER.

Dr. Grete Maria Ehrenstein, a noted Viennese beauty, with her pet "Boxer".   Notice the dog's cropped ears.

The general build of the body must be such as to have a square appearance; in other words, the distance from the point of the shoulder to the point of the buttocks is equal to the height at the shoulder; besides, the line from the point of the elbow to the ground is equal to half of the size measured as above. All this does not apply in an absolute manner to the female, which may be a little longer than higher. The forequarters very robust, are strictly vertical, seen from the front and in profile. The elbows are in contact with the thorax, but they should not press too much on the latter. The forearms are long and full of muscle: the knee is fairly low and but little protruding; the pastern is short and almost vertical: the toes are small, cat-like, with very firm pads. The thighs of the hindquarters are large and domed, the hocks are fairly low, open, not "cow-hocked"; the "cannon" (part of dog's leg between the knee and the fetlock or pastern) rather short and slightly sloping backwards; the toes a little longer than those of the front legs. The coat is smooth, short and shiny. With regard to the colour, there are specimens of one colour, and brindle ones. The first-named colour is either yellow or dark fawn. The mask is dark, which is obligatory. In the brindle variety the dark or black stripes must be clearly distinct from the fawn ground colour. Small white patches are allowed. The above very precise standard shows that there are numerous defects that may lead to disqualification at shows. Boxers measuring more than has been indicated above in height are generally admitted if their conformation remains correct and symmetrical; on the contrary, too small specimens are pitilessly eliminated The same applies to dogs too obese, the movement of which is stiff or jerky, or the hindquarters of which swing in movement. Last, and not least, little appreciated are the Boxers with flat skulls and

rectilinear foreheads, with a nose too much *retroussé*, and too protruding a lower jaw (Bulldoghead), the wrinkles too pronouced, the lips badly joined and pendulous, the eye too light, badly carried ears, too much "mask", long back, convex or "saddle-backed", too oblique a crupper. too horizontal a crupper, bad legs and feet.

The Boxer appears to have preserved, from his wild ancestors, only their vigour, energy and courage. At home the Boxer is a quiet, peaceful dog; a gay companion, very little combative.

German fanciers are fond of comparing the Boxer with the English Bulldog, in appearance at least; but one cannot but share their opinion that, while our national dog has now become a "show ornament" pure and simple, the Boxer is not only that, he is also a dog that may be brought to the highest efficiency for guarding, protecting and defence by judicious training. Furthermore, the Boxer is an excellent mover and can jump over very high fences.

AN ATHLETE.
Nowadays the Boxer is a dog of medium size, with short and smooth coat, robust and full of muscles built like an athlete. but elegant and without clumsiness.

Brace.—Term used for two exhibits (either sex or mixed) at a show, belonging to the same exhibitor, and each entered in another class besides brace or team.

Brain, Inflammation of. (ENCEPHALITIS, MENINGITIS.)

CAUSES.—Injuries to the head; extension of disease from contiguous parts such as caries of the bones of the ear; exposure to cold or extreme heat; excessive fatigue; tumours in the brain or cranial cavity; fevers; rheumatism; tuberculosis; distemper.

SYMPTOMS.—There often are premonitory signs such as a fear of observation, or a desire to hide beneath furniture. The dog vomits occasionally and may be restless and nervous, whining continuously, but rarely showing any aggressive spirit. It appears unresponsive and somewhat stupid, but when the attack is acute, maniacal symptoms will make their appearance. Thus the dog, if unrestrained, may rush aimlessly about in a most excited manner, knocking over objects which stand in its way. It stares about with wild eyes; the conjunctivae are infected; the temperature 104 to 106°; great heat

GERMAN BRAQUE.

The Braques are sporting dogs. The above betrays his Pointer ancestry and is of the type common in Germany in the 'eighties.

over the skull; grinding of the teeth; and the animal staggers and may have epileptiform convulsions. There is sometimes a tendency to walk in circles, and always to one side.

Later, paralytic phenomena are manifest, affecting a single muscle or group of muscles. Blindness and deafness may follow, and constipation is usually present.

TREATMENT.—Little of practical value can be offered to the amateur in the way of first aid treatment. The best advice is to handle or frighten the

and has been given to a number of dogs, of a variety of types, which can hardly claim to be, in every case, a distinct variety, for the differences are very slight, and often only such differences as one might expect to find in a single breed.

In some instances the type is so dissimilar as to make us doubt if they should not appear in some other group rather than the Braque, for although a number show distinctly the Pointer head and are

RUSSIAN BRAQUE.

The dog shown here was given in a dog paper published about 1875 as the Russian Pointer, but whether it can truly claim to be a definite breed is doubtful.

animal as little as possible and if the administration of medicines causes undue excitement, do not give them. Sedatives, as aspirin or bromides, are indicated, as also is a purgative, and ice may be frequently applied to the head. But beyond these measures, the case will require the skilled aid of a veterinary surgeon.

Brandy. (*See* ALCOHOL.)

Braques.—The name signifies a Pointer,

in shape Pointer-like, others might well be mistaken for a variety of hound, the Chien Courant, so often illustrated in French sporting journals.

It is highly probable that some of these Braques are indeed Hound crosses, and as it is quite impossible thoroughly to investigate all the claims, we can only show a representative collection of Braques claimed to be of distinct types in the Russian, German, French, and Dutch Press. Of these, the

Russian Braque appears to be in the nature of a caricature rather than a dog as it actually was.

It must be remembered that in France and other countries there has not been so much interest taken in the isolation of varieties, nor have claims been taken so seriously, as they have been in England, so that no offence was given and no ridicule caused by claims that slight variations constituted distinct varieties. Various French Braques, however, will be found separately dealt with in their appropriate places in this Encyclopaedia.

Bread, as Food. (*See* Foods and Feeding.)

Breaking. (*See* Gun Dogs.)

Breast, Inflammation of. (*See* Mammitis.)

Breasts, Diseases of. (*See* Mammary Glands.)

Breath, Bad.—Causes. In nearly every case the cause of bad breath is to be found in the mouth. Loose or bad teeth, tartared teeth, pyorrhoea, ulcerated mouth, bleeding gums, gangrenous pneumonia, constipation, chronic nasal catarrh, and indigestion are all causes of bad breath.

Treatment.—By careful examination and a process of elimination, the cause of the unpleasantness may be ascertained, and obviously no remedy will be of any avail unless it aims at the particular origin of the odour. Attention to the teeth is the first essential, and when one is quite satisfied that no septic process exists in the mouth, a more extensive search must be undertaken. In 95 per cent of cases, however, a clean mouth will mean sweet breath. (*See* Pyorrhoea; Teeth.)

Breath, Loss of.—Breathlessness is seen in old dogs or in those which are the subject of some pathological abnormality. It is induced, in every case, by any factor which can interfere with the adequate oxygenation of the blood.

Heart disease will cause breathlessness because of the inability of that organ to pump sufficient blood through the lungs in a given time. Anaemia, whether quantitative or qualitative, has a similar effect in consequence of the diminution of the total blood in the body, or because of its poorness in red blood corpuscles. Pulmonary diseases, such as pneumonia or emphysema, produce breathlessness as a result of the restricted area of lung available for the passage of air.

It is obvious—if in a state of good health, fifteen respirations to the minute are required in order adequately to oxygenate the tissues—that in the conditions above described an increased

By courtesy]   [*E. C. Ash.*
ITALIAN BRAQUE.
It will be clear to the discerning reader that this variety of sporting dog undoubtedly had Hound prominent in its make, for it closely resembles the Beagle.

number will be essential. What that increase shall be is determined by the severity of the disease responsible for it.

Mechanical obstruction to respiration will obviously result in quickened breathing.

Breeching.—Tan-colour at rear of thighs.

Breeder.—A breeder of an animal is the person who owned its mother at the time she whelped; or the person in whose care the bitch had been placed either by way of hire, loan, or other arrangement.

Breeding—The breeding of dogs is carried on by many thousands of men and women for pleasure

By courtesy]   [*E. C. Ash.*
FRENCH BRAQUE.
About 1880 the French variety of Pointer was very much more of the type found in England.

and profit. To many, the production of puppies having the good points of their parents means everything, and the sensible breeder will study closely any bad points that his bitch might possess so that by judicious mating with a dog showing pronounced superiority in the point or points that the bitch lacks she will eventually be productive of more or less perfect offspring. The experienced breeder knows as a result of his experience at the various Championship Shows what points in a dog are fashionable and are required by the judges. He will take steps to mate his bitches with dogs that will tend to reproduce the points needed. The novice will be well advised to consult an experienced breeder before mating the bitch. Defects which are not obvious to the owner are only too apparent to the expert.

Fashions in attire are always changing, and so in the doggy world fashions in conformation have undergone radical changes from time to time. To get a type of dog absolutely true to the one demanded by fashion, in-breeding has been carried on to an alarming extent.

If one studies the pedigree of any well-bred animal,

OUT OF HAND.

When puppies begin to crawl, the mother's anxious moments come, for her family meander off exploring, and constantly entering into noisy arguments against kennel discipline. Note the expression on the mother's face.

one can soon trace in-breeding to a greater or lesser extent. A certain amount of in-breeding can be very useful in order to attain certain desirable concrete characteristics. The owner that possesses a stud dog that conforms in every way to the existing standard of fashion is a lucky individual, and it behoves that individual to see that his dog is only mated to bitches that promise to perpetuate all the better points of the sire.

In almost every breed there are latent Mendelian characteristics that in-breeding causes to make their appearance. They are often deleterious and undesirable.

Mendelism, a branch of the study of heredity, is concerned with facts and theories centred upon the discoveries made by Gregor Mendel from his experiments on plant-hybridization and announced in 1865. The essence of the Mendelian hypothesis is that certain characteristics in plant and animal remain by themselves (unit characteristics), and will not blend with other unit characteristics. A tall pea bred with a dwarf pea gives a generation of tall peas—there are no dwarf or intermediate individuals—and

Photo]   [Sport & General.

FEEDING TIME.

Seldom has such a photo as this been taken, showing four different breeds—a Gordon Setter, an Irish Setter, an English Pointer and an English Setter—feeding their healthy families.

[*Dorien Leigh.*

Photo]

WHY PUPPIES DO NOT THRIVE.

This shows clearly what so often happens. A puppy, less plucky, than the others, sits by, snarling, fearing to put his head down to feed whilst others eat his share.

Photo] [E.N.A

DOBERMAN MOTHERHOOD

To British readers this picture is of more than usual interest, because it shows the noted German breed, the Doberman (also popular in America) with a family.

in the proportions just stated, 3—1, one pure tall, two impure tall, one pure dwarf. Dwarfness has been latent or implicit even in the first tall (hybrid) generation—it is the *recessive* characteristic.

It is stated by authorities on breeding that if the animal is pure through and through, then in-breeding itself will do no harm. If there are no undesirable characteristics present, then in-breeding will accentuate and fix the desirable. If there are faults, then in-breeding must of necessity be harmful. The wise breeder discards all individuals likely to convey mischievous characteristics, no matter how good they be in themselves. There are well-known strains of Terriers that are physically perfect and yet they are extremely nervous and uncertain in temper. This recessive characteristic can be traced back through generations to a very popular sire of his day.

There are certain characteristics, such as turned-in eyelids (*Entropion*) in Chow-Chows, that are invariably passed on ; and it is held that one should not breed with a Chow even if he has been successfully operated on to relieve this condition, as the defect will invariably be passed on to a large proportion of the offspring.

It is usual to mate bitches at the second oestrum, as they are too young to have puppies by a mating at the first. The flat-nosed varieties, however, are usually mated at their first oestrum, as the passage of puppies before the pelvic bones have "set" makes matters easier for the mother at subsequent whelpings.

It is the custom to mate a bitch twice, with one day's interval between the matings, but this is not necessary and is merely subscribing to an old-fashioned fallacy which has been passed on from father to son. A bitch is "on heat" three weeks, but she will not allow a dog to touch her during the first week. The mating is usually arranged between the tenth and fifteenth day, but any time after this is usually satisfactory. The gestation period of a bitch is from sixty to sixty-three days, but puppies can be born before this period and live, whilst many bitches have been known to carry their puppies five and six days over the time. Many bitches die annually during (or from the result of) parturition—from exhaustion, from protracted labour caused by unusually large puppies, or from big litters where skilled veterinary advice is not called in.

To be a successful breeder it is necessary to see

tallness being apparent is called the dominant character. But when these tall peas are inter-bred, the offspring is not uniform but possess individual characteristics, dwarf and tall in definite ratio ; for every dwarf pea (and this, self-fertilized or inter-bred, remains dwarf through all generations) there are three tall peas, but only one is pure, and when self-fertilized shows pure, tall progeny. The other two are impure, and when inter-bred yield mixed generations of tall and dwarf

Photo] [Dorien Leigh

AFTER THE WOOLLY-BEAR STAGE.

A group of puppies showing the starting of the long hair coat which comes after the wool-like puppy coat

that the bitch is in good health at the time of parturition. A certain amount of special attention is necessary. Three weeks after mating a vermifuge should be given, especially directed against round worms, for it has been shown by German investigators that the mother can infect the puppies *in utero*, and it is desirable that the mother should be free from intestinal parasites of this nature when "carrying".

Daily exercise is necessary, and it is left to the good sense of the owner to know how much to give. The ordinary habits of the bitch should be interfered with as little as possible. She should not be tired, and during the last few weeks she should be allowed to please herself how far she walks or how much exercise she takes.

During the first four or five weeks no special alteration need be made in the diet, but after this period the meals should be smaller and more frequent. Rickety puppies are seldom seen now. This is due to

It is a good plan to wash the stomach and breasts a few days before the bitch is due.

As has been stated before, the bitch carries her puppies from sixty-two to sixty-three days, and as the time draws near an experienced breeder can tell when a bitch is going to commence whelping. A bitch having her first litter will be very uneasy for hours before the actual operation takes place. She will wander about, looking here and there for a nest, scrape up or even tear the blankets that may be in her pen or box, and will be generally uncomfortable. If she can, she will select a quiet spot away from everyone.

As labour approaches she is more restless, pants, and may even cry out. She licks herself and constantly looks round at herself. If everything goes "according to plan" she will strain several times, and the "water bladder" will appear and burst, allowing a quantity of clear fluid to escape. The first puppy should soon follow. If the straining

Photo]   [*Dorien Leigh.*

LITTLE TROUBLES.

Bitches, when feeding their puppies, are extremely conscientious and take a great interest in their family. The picture shows the mother wondering why the last puppy in the row is not feeding, and is probably calling to it.

the increased knowledge of diatetics possessed by the masses. It is a good point to give a mixed diet with plenty of meat and fat, but not too much starchy food. A small quantity of cod-liver oil can be given with benefit, as this oil is rich in vitamin D, so necessary to the body in order that the lime salts in the food may be absorbed from the bowels.

Some breeders also administer soluble salt of lime with good effect, and state that puppies from bitches that have received this addition to their diet always possess good bone. It is necessary to examine the bitch's skin from time to time in order to treat and check any skin disorder such as mange. If a bitch is affected with sarcoptic mange she will pass it on to her puppies, and this will cause such discomfort that the puppies cannot rest, and accordingly do not thrive. This attention is especially necessary with Greyhounds that have been in racing kennels. A bitch may continue to be washed up to the seventh week, but if the animal is clean in its habits and has a bed that is frequently changed, there should be no necessity for an excessive amount of washing.

continues for some time and nothing happens, it means that things are not going as they should. The pelvis, or even vagina may be too small to admit the passage of the puppy. A careful examination of the vagina with the finger (after careful washing and oiling) should be undertaken to find out if the puppy is coming "right and straight".

One hour may be safely given after the first expulsive effort is seen, especially with a bitch having her first litter ; but it is unwise to allow longer, especially if the straining is severe, and skilled veterinary advice should be immediately called in.

Bitches of the larger breeds may take all day over whelping, but as long as the puppies arrive at regular intervals there is no need for alarm. Some of the smaller breeds sometimes do not possess sufficient strength to expel the puppies. In these cases it is necessary to administer some drug to contract the womb, but this should only be given by a skilled person and after examination has failed to reveal any abnormality in the passage or position of the oncoming puppy.

3. A German Wire-haired "Setter" 4. A German Short-haired "Setter", crossed with the
bitch, mother of the dog shown in   Wire-haired bitch shown in Fig. 3.
Fig. 10.

1. A Schnauzer bitch—crossed with an Alsatian—gave 2. An Alsatian dog—crossed with a
the result shown below.   Schnauzer—was father of the dog shown
                                                         in Fig. 9.

10. The second generation : an improved Wire-haired "Setter", produced from crossing the
above pair.

9. The second generation : an Alsatian-Schnauzer bitch, produced from crossing the parents
shown in Figs. 1 and 2.

THE FAMILY TREE OF A NEW BREED OF "BOAR-HOUND"

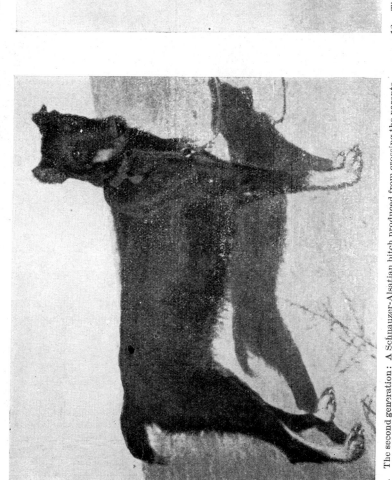

7. A German Short-haired "Setter" bitch, mother of the dog shown below.

8. A German Wire-haired "Setter", crossed with the bitch shown in Fig. 7.

12. The second generation: an improved Wire-haired "Setter", produced from crossing the parents Short-haired "Setter" and Wire-Haired "Setter" shown in Figs. 7 and 8.

PARENTS AND SECOND GENERATIONS.

5. An Alsatian bitch—crossed with a Schnauzer—gave the result shown below.

6. A Schnauzer dog—crossed with an Alsatian bitch—result shown in Fig. 11.

11. The second generation: A Schnauzer-Alsatian bitch produced from crossing the parents shown in Figs. 5 and 6.

13. Third Generation : A "Boar-hound" bitch, produced from the parents shown in Figs. 9 and 10—the female representative of the threefold crossing of Schnauzer, Alsatian, and German "Setter".

14. Third Generation : A "Boar-hound" produced from the parents shown in Figs. 11 and 12—the male representative of the threefold crossing of Schnauzer, Alsatian, and German "Setter".

15. Produced in the fourth generation by crossing the bitch and dog shown in Figs. 13 and 14 ; the new breed of "Boar-hound," combining the good qualities of Schnauzer, Alsatian, and German "Setter", and now breeding true.

THIRD AND FOURTH GENERATIONS—"THE PERFECT DOG".

Cases where there are good labour-pains and yet no puppies appear are usually due to malpresentation of the foetus, and this requires putting right before the puppy can be born. The prompt removal of the "offending" puppy will mean that the remainder will be born alive and well, even if the first one has to be sacrificed ; but to leave the mother hoping that matters will right themselves will only mean that all the puppies will be dead, and there is a good chance of losing the mother as well.

The mother will not usually leave her bed until every puppy has arrived, and one can tell by a manual examination of the abdomen if any puppies are left. After producing, say, six puppies, the bitch should be offered a little warm milk to drink. Providing the parturition has been normal the bitch may be given her ordinary diet ; but in order to produce a plentiful supply of milk, plenty of liquids should be available, especially milk. By degrees the quantity of food may be increased.

For the first ten days or so the mother is very attentive to her offspring and will only leave them for very short intervals. A bitch may rear from five to ten puppies quite easily but the number that she can successfully rear depends upon her type and condition. A very small type of dog will not rear more than four or five, whereas a large dog such as a Bull Mastiff will suckle and bring up ten or more. If the puppies are not getting enough milk they will not be contented, but will be constantly pulling at the mother and uttering plaintive cries. In cases like this it is wise to keep the stronger puppies and destroy the weaker ones or to obtain the services of a foster-mother. Puppies are weaned and taken from their mother by degrees at the sixth or seventh week.

BREEDING, PRINCIPLES OF.—(*See also* "IN-BREED-ING.")

BREEDING, To PREVENT.—Bitches which are "in season" acquire a remarkable ability to escape, and go off—sometimes for miles—in search of a mate. They will go to any length to get away and often stay away all night. Unfortunately, it is frequently only after the lapse of many precious hours that the owner discovers what has occurred. He has no definite knowledge that mating has taken place, although he might well believe it, nor does he generally know the breed of dog responsible.

His anxiety, then, is directed towards adopting some immediate steps to counter the damage, and if he is wise he will waste no time attempting to manage it himself, but will go at once to a veterinary surgeon. The problem is to kill all spermatozoa which have been deposited in the vagina, and whilst they still are in that cavity they can be reached. But it so often happens that considerable time has elapsed since the act of coitus, and then the spermatozoa may already have entered the womb. The uterus must therefore be irrigated, and this is where skill and a strong sense of surgical asepsis are required. To pass an instrument through the mouth of the womb is no easy matter, even for a surgeon, and if the most scrupulous cleanliness is not observed of both instrument and solution, then the results may be very grave. It is not advisable to give directions for the carrying out of this task because it is felt that amateurs should not (in their own interests) attempt it.

Breton Spaniel (*Épagneul Breton*).—The existence of this breed is mentioned in hunting accounts and paintings that go back to the eighteenth

THE BRETON SPANIEL.
This large variety of the Spaniel is the international Ch. "Fanchio de Cornonaille" of Breton.

GOOD POINTERS.
Ch. "Aotrou de Cornonaille" is seen pointing. The breed resembles an English Springer Spaniel of Setter type.

Photos]   *[Emile Bourdon.*
A NOTED WINNER.
This dog is a noted worker, and the winner of numerous prizes.

century. It must be added, however, that the Breton of those days was not the Breton of to-day. If selection has been careful to conserve his moral qualities, his morphology has changed much.

The ancestor was a hunter of from fifty to fifty-five centimetres high, with long white-and-tan or white-black hair, of clean build, highly nervous rather than muscular, with the tail naturally short. This son of a country,

Photo]   CH. "MARS".   *[Emile Bourdon.*

That these dogs are really Setters is proved by their appearance, which closely resembles the English Setter, though the name Épagneul is used in France. The illustration shows the ideal type in 1909.

bristling with thickets and spiny furze, was physically and morally adapted to his habitat. The inseparable companion of the Breton hunter—whose meagre reward he shared—he owed to this his endurance and level-headedness, just as he owed to his native heaths his energetic fearlessness.

The official recognition of the Breton Spaniel goes back to about 1900. He was the sensation of the Paris Dog Show, with his thick coat, his short ears, his pointed muzzle, and his stump of tail held erect as for battle, like a Terrier's. It is easy to believe that there was little of the seductive about him at that time!

But certain dog-lovers interested in his qualities as a hunter formed a commission, presided over by M. de Conink and consisting of MM. Mégnin, Huguet, Flensy, Trenttel, de Cambourg, and Dursand-Gosselin, which in May 1907 drew up the first standard of points; this underwent some modification in 1908.

The Breton of the original stock was a tracker and retriever of the highest order, loving to hunt furred quarry, though it is averred that his nose lacked power and his back firmness.

At the time, numbers of English tourists used to winter in Brittany to hunt woodcock, and, whether by design or accident, their Setters were crossed with the Breton dogs, and the show, which was held in Loudéac in 1908, was a census of the elements of the breed due to this crossing. To judge from what was written at the time, the ninety entrants were very diverse, and conformed little enough with the standard of 1907–8.

But under the impetus of the Committee which was drawn up, and over whose destinies presided

MM. Enand, de Pélé, and Lessard, the breeders, by a splendid effort, undertook to fix a single type, retaining the ancestral qualities.

Little by little, the Breton won an envied place for itself among its Continental relatives, both on the show bench and at the field trials.

As early as 1908, "Mirza", a white-and-tan Breton belonging to M. Trenttel, took part in the Normandy Field Trials and won a first place.

She was followed on this road to triumph by several other Bretons in the following years: "Bombarde", "Arvor", "Ruden", "Leda", "Loustic", etc.

The Great War held up this magnificent progress for five years, but from 1919 onwards the breeding, which had been carried on by certain breeders secure amid the Breton heights from war's devastation, blossomed forth anew at the point where its advancement had ceased; and the diminished numbers rapidly increased.

The appearance of the new Breton at the post-war hunting trials was a veritable revelation. The dog had much improved. Endowed with a powerful nose, galloping at full speed, and tracking with intelligence, he soon out-classed other Continental dogs, and even several English dogs well known for their success in field trials.

In 1925, the special show of the Breton Spaniel Club at Rennes called together a collection of about a hundred entrants of astonishing similarity.

The head of the present-day Breton Spaniel (or Armorican, as it is also called) is less massive, more finely chiselled and attractive to the eye than that of its ancestor.

The silhouette is more harmonious beneath its white-and-orange coat, which colour is preferable to the white-and-tan because it is more visible in the coverts and pleasanter to the eye. The old coat has consequently disappeared, in spite of the efforts of the Club to preserve it.

The official standard adopted by the Breton Spaniel Club is in substance as follow

"Height 40 to 50 centimetres with margin of 2 centimetres for the males; body close to ground, short in the withers; head round with muzzle pointed ; ears rather short and high up ; hair smooth ; coat wavy but never woolly ; nose brown or deep pink ; eyes hazel ; general colour orange-and-white or tan-and-white, with several patches ; outline compact but elegant ; face intelligent ; tail short (naturally or by docking), being of 10 centimetres maximum length."

The short-*grown* tail, which originally had been considered by the Club as an essential character-istic of the breed, is no longer demanded, and since 1933 Spaniels with docked tails have been admis-sible the same as the others, to the highest awards.

In the woods, he excels after the woodcock, hunting sometimes in the open copse with his nose up, then following the scent into a thicket as he outwits the long-beaked bird in her multiple ruses, and finally seizing her and retrieving her to his master.

Among the marshes he shows himself inferior to none, pouncing on the young birds from afar, and not hesitating to take to the water to seize the winged duck which threads among the reeds and water-plants of the creeks and ponds. He adapts himself to every circumstance, and it is to this adaptability that he owes his popularity.

His training, which is neither more difficult nor less so than that of other English and Continental breeds demands, however, a cer-tain dexterity. He requires gentleness that does not pre-clude firmness—one might almost say severity in his earlier days.

His innate love of four-footed game is legendary. Toward 1850, the Reverend Davies men-tioned him in his work on Wolf-Hunting as an "animal perfect for the chase, an excellent retriever, fear-less of thickets, but with an inveterate love

of furred game". The dog of that day lives again in the Breton Spaniel of the present.

Breton Spaniel kennels are numerous and very flourishing, not only in Brittany but all over France. Most of the show-bench champions of the breed prove themselves also prize winners at the field trials, which implies that the Breton breeders have solved the difficult problem of a dog both clever and handsome.

Bright's Disease (*see also* DROPSY) is a term used to signify acute or chronic inflammation of the kidneys. It is common in old dogs, as is proved by the appearance of the kidneys upon post-mortem examinations, no matter from what cause the animals may die. But, strangely enough, dogs do not readily exhibit the classic symptoms of nephritis unless the disease is so extensive and advanced as to affect other organs. It is quite possible that many mild cases have escaped detection in the past, but the present-day veterinary surgeon is much more par-ticular about obtaining specimens of the patient's urine in cases of doubt. If albumen is found upon test, a diagnosis of nephritis is justified so long as the clinical symptoms are consistent. (*See* ALBU-MINURIA.)

CAUSES.—Nephritis is a common complication or sequel of distemper and of Stuttgart disease. It also arises in consequence of exposure to wet and cold ; as a result of some violence ; and following the absorption or ingestion of irritant poisons, such as canthar-ides, etc.

SYMPTOMS.—In acute Bright's disease the urine passed is scantier than usual, whilst in the chronic form its volume is generally in-creased. The dog may have slight vomiting attacks at various times of the day, but quite often these are confined to the early morn-ing. The animal may evince some pain upon pres-sure being exerted over its loins, and it may walk stiffly as though affected with rheumatics.

If urine re-mains very scanty for long, the dog may have convulsions, followed by col-lapse and death. In the chronic type of the

Photo]   [Alfieri.
BRUSHING.
The brushing of a dog is an important every-day matter of hygiene, but the Wire-haired Fox Terrier has to have the hair on its legs brushed up to give it the correct show appearance. On the left a Terrier is being chalked, but this chalk must be entirely removed before the dog is exhibited.

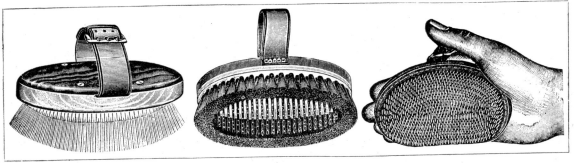

COAT STIMULATING AND CONTROL.

The various brushes and gloves used to control a coat and to stimulate healthy growth and remove dead hair are shown here.

disease, the dog may evince a great thirst and progressively becomes thinner, is very dull, and dainty about its food.

TREATMENT.—If any of these symptoms suggest to the owner that the case might be one of kidney disease he had better obtain advice and a course of treatment, rather than experiment with this or that quack remedy. He is only wasting time and money.

A milk diet should be instituted, and if the dog is very ill, a hot bath should be given whilst professional help is being called.

Bright's Disease is not a complaint which can be treated with success by amateurs, for even in skilled hands therapeutics are very difficult, and it is invariably preceded by careful examination of the heart, urine etc.

Brindled. (*See* COLOUR.)

Brisket is the area over the breast-bone or sternum, and lies between the two forelegs.

Broken Colour.—White patches on an otherwise dark coat.

Broken-haired Terrier.—One of the old names, of which Bingley and Waterside Terriers are other examples, for the Airedale.

The last word in brushes of the curry-comb type.

Broken-up Face.—Type of face such as a Bull dog's, Pug's, Pekingese's, etc.

Bromides.—Bromide salts are commonly employed as sedatives in canine medicine for calming excitable dogs ; inducing sleep in those which suffer from insomnia in consequence, perhaps, of chorea or of painful lesions ; and for subduing sexual excitement. They are not of much value in the prevention of fits, but may be incorporated with stronger sedatives for this purpose. Potassium bromide is the most powerful salt of those used for dogs, but it is also more depressing than the others and exerts a greater tendency to the disturbance of digestion. On these accounts, sodium bromide or ammonium bromide may be prescribed with greater advantage ; or all three may be combined. The dose is three to twenty grains, two or three times daily,

Bronchial Tubes are the small branching divisions of the two bronchi, and as they penetrate deeper into the lung tissue the more they subdivide and the smaller they become. The main air passage—leading from the throat, down the neck, to the chest cavity, and known as the trachea—divides up into two main branches called bronchi. Just as the branches of a tree subdivide over and over again, so do the smaller air passages.

Bronchitis.—Inflammation of the bronchi or windpipes may be caused by exposure, sudden changes of temperature, misdirection of liquid medicine, inhalation of poisonous gases or injurious

The brushes may be either bristles, rubber, whalebone, or wire. The shorter bristled brushes are mainly for smooth coats.
(See page 204).

THE BRITISH BULLDOG.

"Jasperdin of Din," Mrs. M. B. Montgomery's world-famous dog, the winner of a further certificate at Cruft's in 1934 (a body study is given on page 205), shows the points of the head so much desired by Bulldog breeders

CH. "HIS LORDSHIP".

A powerful Bulldog at the end of the nineteenth century.

Broncho-Pneumonia. (*See* BRONCHITIS.)

Bronzed.—Tan-coloured hairs in a black coat.

Broth. (*See* FOODS AND FEEDING.)

Bruises, known also as contusions, may be deep or superficial.

SYMPTOMS.—The part is usually swollen if the impact was severe, and it is hot, painful, and discoloured. The blue or red appearance of the over-lying skin is due to rupture of small blood-vessels in the underlying tissues, with extravasation of blood. A part may be bruised, however, without exhibiting any sign other than tenderness upon pressure; and bruises may be so deep down that their chief effect will be lameness, general stiffness, or a disinclination to move, thus simulating rheumatism to some extent. Bruises are not infrequently the forerunners of serous cysts, abscesses, and perhaps even of malignant tumour.

TREATMENT.—Pain is much relieved by frequent and sustained bathing with hot water. When the necessary time or the water are not available, the part may be gently massaged with ordinary embrocation, soap liniment, or belladonna liniment. Other soothing applications may be employed, such as lead lotion and tincture of arnica.

dust, extension of neighbouring inflammations as tracheitis, laryngitis, etc. It also is frequently secondary to distemper.

SYMPTOMS.—There is usually a cough with bronchitis, although, in dogs, this is not by any means a certain accompaniment. Its nature, at first, is dry, short, and intermittent, and its severity depends, of course, upon the extent of the inflammation. It may become very loud and frequent and, later, probably of a moister character, when a discharge may not only be coughed up into the mouth, but also run from the nostrils. Anatomically, the bronchi become progressively branched and smaller as they descend and ramify into the lung tissue, and when these finer branches become involved the condition is then much more severe. There is, too, a greater difficulty in breathing, the respirations being noticeably more rapid. This is accompanied by an acceleration of the pulse and generally by a marked rise of temperature, say to 104° or 105° F. The case has then become one of broncho-penumonia, a matter of much graver portent.

TREATMENT.—The main essentials are restriction of exercise; avoidance of changes of temperature, cold, damp, and draughts. A fairly warm and dry apartment is therefore needed, and there must be a continuous and good supply of pure air. The dog can be given hot milk, hot soups, and similar foods which are soothing to the throat and chest. Steaming the head from a bronchitis kettle into which has been poured a teaspoonful of eucalyptus to a pint of water will help considerably to relieve distress. Many cases are not amenable to medicinal treatment, and those associated with distemper are particularly obstinate. They usually run their course, so that one's endeavours are directed chiefly towards the maintenance of the best hygienic conditions, and of the patient's strength, and to prevent any circumstance likely to favour complications.

CH. "DOCK LEAF".

This dog, noted curiously enough for its attempt to win a walking race, was the property of Mr. Sam Woodiwiss.

Brushes. (*See also* GROOMING.)—For large dogs or those with heavy coats, perhaps the ordinary dandy brush would be hard to beat. At the same time, special brushes are nowadays obtainable, which are designed to reduce to a minimum the amount of labour necessary to bestow upon a given case. The best brushes possess a band of webbing over the back which facilitates the retention of one's grip of the brush. Some brushes have the bristles set at an angle, and to use this type properly, the bristles should point in the same direction as that in which the brush is moving. For smaller dogs, a very good

Illustrations by courtesy]　　　　　*[E. C. Ash.*
CH. "GUIDO".

At one time "Guido" was considered to possess the soundest of Bulldog bodies ever seen.

INTERNATIONAL CHAMPION "JASPERDIN OF DIN".

One of the most important Bulldogs of 1934 is here depicted. He should be compared with the old-time Champions on the opposite page.

type of brush is that in which the bristles are made of soft metal and are set in a pneumatic base.

Most breeders keep a set of varied brushes, one, at least, of which is exclusively used for removing mud caked upon the legs and underparts.

All brushes require cleansing from time to time, and a good method of carrying this out is as follow: The bristles are first combed of hair (which is at once burnt) and the brush is then stood in warm, soapy, carbolized water, bristles downwards, taking care that the solution does not quite reach the body of the brush. By a rapid up-and-down movement, dirt and grease are gradually loosened and removed. Combing is repeated, the bristles are rubbed with the hand and then dabbed in rinsing water. Brushes are dried by standing them in the open air, bristles downwards, and it will take many hours before the bristles regain their normal stiffness. If the brush is very greasy, a little washing soda may be added to the water; and if the dog has fleas or lice, paraffin oil may be added.

Brussells Griffon. (See GRIFFON BRUXELLOIS.)

Bucket Muzzle.— A closed muzzle, generally made of leather. (See RESTRAINT.)

Bulldogs. —In point of popularity the Bulldog probably attained its zenith in the years which immediately preceded the Great War, when it was not an uncommon thing to see something approaching or even exceeding 200 individual dogs benched at the annual

By courtesy]   [E. C. Ash.
"OAK LEAF".

In the early part of the twentieth century this Bulldog was hailed as one of the best yet seen.

By courtesy]   [E. C. Ash.
CH. "PRESSGANG".
This remarkable dog of about 1903 may be said to be a leading pillar of the breed. It was one of the most noted Bulldogs in history.

championship shows of the Bulldog Club Incorporated and the London Bulldog Society with an entry of 400 or more.

The attractiveness of the breed to-day undoubtedly lies in the difficulty of producing the "perfect Bulldog" and its docile disposition and its faithfulness to and love for its master or mistress.

By some it may be looked upon as a clumsy mass of ugly flesh, but there is not the slightest doubt that a properly proportioned Bulldog, in spite of its clumsy gait, can have great activity, and its power to twist and turn while running at a fast speed is really remarkable.

The dog is frequently depicted as our national emblem of British pluck and endurance and is generally considered to be of purely British origin. Of its great antiquity there cannot be any doubt. It is claimed by some to have been descended from the Pugnaces or war dogs of the early Britons, which were broad-mouthed dogs of a large size and tremendous strength. The Bulldog is stated to be first referred to in literature by W. Wulcher in 1500 as the Bonddogge, because of its fierce nature which necessitated it being chained or tied up for fear it caused injury to man or beast. Dr. Caius, in his

TWO GREAT BULLDOGS.

"Boomerang" and "Katerfelto", Mrs. L. Crabtree's Bulldogs, were born in 1893. Their sire was "King Orry", and so they represent a famous strain noted for their size, long skulls, good turn up of under-jaw, and excellent lay back. This effective painting was specially made for *Hutchinson's Popular and Illustrated Dog Encyclopaedia* by F. T. Daws.

LEADING-ON POINTS!

Lady Vansittart, wife of Sir Robert Vansittart, K.C.B., C.M.G., M.V.O., a great lover of animals, is here seen at Denham Place, Bucks, with two favourite dogs, of which the Bulldog seems to consider himself deserving of premier position—on points perhaps, if not on account of a prepossessing countenance.

"DON BRAE" AND "SMASHER."

"Don Brae", about 1876–1879, was considered to be the best Bulldog under 40 lb. and was the property of Capt. Holdworth.   His measurements are given as follow:
Tip of nose to stop, 1 inch; stop to occiput, 5 inches; neck 17¾ inches (circumference), and height at shoulders 17½ inches.   "Smasher" was 20 inches round the neck and weighed 43 lb.

Treatise of the Dog (1576) refers to the Bulldog as the "Bandogge", a vast, huge, stubborn, ugly and eager dog of a heavy burdensome and body serviceable to bait a bull, and that two dogs at the most were capable of subduing the most untamable bull. About 1631 or 1632 the breed was first mentioned in literature by an approach to the modern spelling when it became known as the "Bulldogg".

The origin of the breed and its antiquity has been the subject of much speculation and dispute ; mastiff breeders claiming that it is descended from the Mastiffs, and Bulldog breeders claiming the reverse. In all probability both breeds are descended from the "Alaunt", a breed which is supposed to have had a short, thick head, short muzzle, short body with great strength in forequarters, noted for its high courage and for its capacity to retain its grip when it got hold. These are all characteristics of our national breed and the Bulldog has for long years been used by artists to depict the true "John Bull" character. A claim has been put forward that the breed originally came from Spain, and this was founded upon the fact that an old bronze plaque was found in Paris by an Englishman, Mr. John Proctor, which portrayed the head of what appears to be that of a cropped Bulldog, with an inscription above the head which reads : "Dogue de Burgos Espaque," and bearing the date 1625.

It must be remembered, however, that Philip II, who became king of Spain in 1556, is supposed to have imported many of the English fighting dogs into Spain and that we had a meeting with the

Photo]　　　　　　　　　　[*F. Lamb, Altrincham.*
CH "DAME'S DOUBLE".
In its day this fine animal was an outstanding pillar of the breed. Owned by the late Mrs. A. G. Sturgeon, it was the winner of twenty-four Certificates.

Spanish Armada in 1588. It is quite possible that some of the British ships might have been manned with members of the national breed in addition to our sailors, and that in hand-to-hand fighting which took place some of our dogs got aboard the few Spanish ships which escaped and were carried back to Spain and founded the breed there. Also, is it not a fact that a letter has been forthcomin , which was written at St. Sebastian in 1631, in which the writer asked that the recipient should procure him two good Bulldogs and send them by the first ship ?

There can be little doubt that the Bulldog was originally bred for the purpose of fighting and baiting and was popular with all classes of society, and the dog in those days was a large one and probably weighed from 80 pounds to exceeding 100 pounds. The fighting dog was treasured by our ancestors, and all over the country, and particularly in London and the Midlands, bear-gardens, bull-rings and dog-pits abounded where the so-called sport was carried on. Bull, bear and boar baiting appear to have been the first of the "sports" enjoyed, and the dogs were supposed to attack or lay the baited animal by the ears. Later, the attack was at the animal's nose and a smaller and more active dog became quite fashionable. As bull and bear baiting declined, the more brutal "sport" of dog fighting became popular, and as a consequence the dog suffered from the degenerate and uneducated minds of the owners, who were generally of the lower

Photo]　　　　　　　　　　　　　[*S. & G.*
CH. "HEFTY MASTER GRUMPY".
This Bulldog, purchased for £225 by Mr. George Cresswell, was unfortunately suffocated in his kennel owing to mail bags being inadvertently thrown over him. His death was a great loss to the fancy.

classes and by whom the "sport" was chiefly practised. Thus Bulldogs were trained to be cruel and dangerous brutes, who would undergo the most brutal treatment and, dog-like, they naturally responded to their owners' repulsive instincts. Anyone wishing to read of the horrible cruelties practised in those times can refer to the late Mr. Edgar Farman's book on the Bulldog published in the early days of the present century. Although dog fighting became illegal by legislation in 1835 (almost 100 years ago) it was continued for a time, and as it was gradually suppressed the Bulldog lost favour, but later it was cultivated as an

dog had cropped ears (presumably to reduce the chance of its opponent getting a hold of them), but this has long been done away with.

It has been suggested that in breeding the fighting dog a cross of the Manchester or some other Terrier was introduced to increase the dog's activity and stamina, and that as the result the black and black-and-tan coloured dogs which are occasionally bred to-day are the outcome of this cross. It is stated in Mr. Farman's book that Ben White, who was a well-known figure in canine circles when the Act referred to was passed, was probably the last member of the "Fancy" in London who

       [of the Proprietors of "Punch".

"MR. PUNCH VISITS A VERY REMARKABLE PLACE".

Mr. Punch's visit to Bill George at "Canine Castle". From a drawing by Leach, published in *Punch* in 1846.

attractive and docile member of the canine race, and became very popular with working-man fanciers.

An idea of the type of the fighting dog can be obtained by reference to a reproduction in Mr. Farman's book of a painting of "Crib and Rosa", by Abraham Cooper, engraved by John Scott, and first published in 1817, which was before dog fighting as a sport became illegal. This dog was higher on the leg and smaller in skull than the present-day dog, also lighter in bone, longer in muzzle and not so wide in front. The earlier show specimen of the breed naturally retained many of the characteristics of its ancestors, and the undesirable ones have only been eliminated by the method of selection in breeding. The fighting

made dog fighting and kindred diversions the main business of their lives, but that his successor, Bill George, who died at the age of 79, in June 1881, conducted a really legitimate business in dogs until his death. It has already been stated that when dog fighting was prohibited the breeding of Bulldogs declined, but Bill George and others took up the breed and specialized in producing a dog more on the modern type, which is clearly shown in the drawing representing "Mr. Punch's visit to a very remarkable place" which appeared in *Punch* published in 1846. When dog shows came into existence during the latter part of Bill George's career his kennel not only produced winners on the show bench but dogs which are to a great extent the foundation of the modern Bulldog. One of his

Photo] CH "NOVO NIVO". [Walter Guiver.

One of the best Bulldogs of 1933, Mrs. Shaw's champion, above, won many high honours. Note the strong legs, massive back and head, jaws and turn up.

Photo] "SIR TRISTRAM". [Fall.

We show this dog to exemplify the roach back and good body, so important in a breed that is expected to be agile as well as strong.

dogs, Bill George's "Dan," is portrayed in Mr. Farman's book, and is stated to have been sold for £100.

Dog shows were inaugurated in about 1859, and the chief entries for Bulldogs were London, Birmingham, and Sheffield, and it is remarkable how the people in these districts have retained their love for the breed and produced the goods. The Manchester district has now for some years also been a hot-bed of the variety. To Birmingham, it is believed, must be given the credit of staging the first classes for the breed in 1860, and Leeds and Manchester followed the following year, as did London a year or so later.

"Old King Dick" would appear to have been the outstanding dog of that time, and a descendant of his in Ch. "Crib" can be traced in the extended pedigrees of many of the great dogs on the show bench of the past and to-day. Chs. "Monarch" and "Gamster", bred by the late Mr. J. W. Berrie, in 1878, were sons of "Crib"

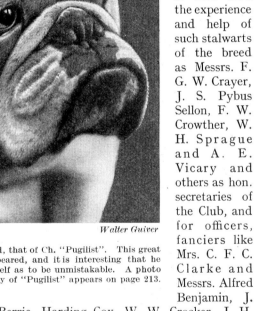

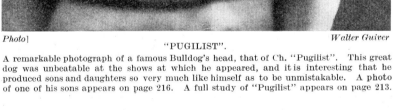

Photo]   "PUGILIST".   *Walter Guiver*

A remarkable photograph of a famous Bulldog's head, that of Ch. "Pugilist". This great dog was unbeatable at the shows at which he appeared, and it is interesting that he produced sons and daughters so very much like himself as to be unmistakable. A photo of one of his sons appears on page 216. A full study of "Pugilist" appears on page 213.

out of the same litter. Ch. "Monarch" sired Ch. "British Monarch," who ultimately passed into the hands of Mr. Sam Woodiwiss, who has been such a pillar of the breed. Mr. Woodiwiss gave £175 for the dog, which was a record price at the time. Ch. "Monarch" also sired Chs. "Britomastris" and "Wheel of Fortune". Ch. "Gamster," through his son "Alaric," was the grandsire of "King Orry" (whelped in 1889), who was sire of the late Mr Luke Crabtree's Chs. "Boomerang" and "Kalerfelto" (whelped in 1893) and Mr. Cassell's Ch. "Facey Romford". "Reevis Crib" was another descendant of "Crib" and he sired Chs. "Queen Mab" and "Forceps". The latter sired Mr. Woodiwiss' great bitch, Ch. "Blackberry," who was

the dam of the remarkable litter bred by him in 1895, which included Chs. "Baron Sedgemere", "Boaz" and "Battledora" and "Barney Barnato". Numbers of other great dogs were descended from Ch. "Crib," including Chs. "Dockleaf" (whelped in 1890), "Ruling Passion" and "Dolores".

The Bulldog Club was founded in 1874, and the following year became the Bulldog Club Incorporated. The late Mr. J. W. Berrie, who was one of its founders and pioneers of the breed, produced several champions besides Chs. "Monarch" and "Gamster", including Chs. "Venom" and "Blackwall Beauty". The Incorporated Club has done much to foster and improve the breed, as is only to be expected when it has had the experience and help of such stalwarts of the breed as Messrs. F. G. W. Crayer, J. S. Pybus Sellon, F. W. Crowther, W. H. Sprague and A. E. Vicary and others as hon. secretaries of the Club, and for officers, fanciers like Mrs. C. F. C. Clarke and Messrs. Alfred Benjamin, J. W. Berrie, Harding Cox, W. W. Crocker, J. H. Ellis, Edgar Farman, E. W. Jacquet, A. C. Jackson, H. Layton, T. J. Mackness, W. J. Pegg, J. W. Ross, G. W. Richards, P. Soundy, W. G. Smartt, F. W. Taylor, R. D. Thomas, and S. Woodiwiss.

In the early days of the showing, separate classes were provided for heavy-weights and light-weights, the latter in some cases being for dogs not exceeding 12 pounds. The first show held for Bulldogs alone was probably that promoted by the Incorporated Club in 1875, and this show became an annual affair and is still continued. As the breed prospered other clubs sprang up in London and other parts of the country, including the London Bulldog Society,

CH. "PUGILIST" AND HIS MODEL.

If any Bulldog might be said to be weighed down with honours it is this famous dog, the winner of thirty Challenge Certificates. He was bred by Mrs. B. J. Walz.
Attention is drawn to his great width and legs and his immense neck.

The British Bulldog Club, The Manchester and Counties Bulldog Club, the West of England Bulldog Club, The Yorkshire Bulldog Club, The Bulldog Club of Scotland, The Leeds and County Bulldog Club, The Leodensian Bulldog Club, The Durham and Northumberland Bulldog Club, The Airedale and Bulldog Club, The North London Bulldog Association, the Oldham and District Bulldog Club, and Junior Bulldog Club. Many of these held annual open shows and many members' shows during the year, and the London Bulldog Society, British Bulldog Club, and Manchester and Counties Club now hold annual championship shows in addition to that held by the Incorporated Club. It is probable that to-day the breed has as many clubs to look after its interests as any other breed, although several of the clubs ceased to exist during and after the War. There is no doubt that the members' shows held by the various clubs have done much to encourage the breed and promote its popularity.

As to the merits of the present-day Bulldog there can be no doubt. It is quiet, docile and not given to barking, whilst its appearance is a sure guarantee to keep undesirables (who are not acquainted with its quiet nature) away from its owner's dwelling. It is a difficult breed to master, as good specimens do not appear too frequently, and in breeding there may be difficulty during labour owing to the abnormally large heads which the puppies have and, in addition, brood bitches seem to have a habit of not breeding. A lot of the trouble in whelping is occasioned by breeding from unsound and unhealthy stock and lack of exercise and improper feeding. Some veterinary surgeons are to-day so clever at performing a successful Cæsarean operation, whereby both whelps

Photo] "PUPPIES ALL". *[Ralph Robinson.*

Bulldog puppies of good build are exceedingly attractive. Here are seven belonging to Mrs. Seymour, including one with the attractive black eye that reminds us of "Bill Sykes."

and dam are saved, that the risk in breeding is not nearly so great as it used to be. It is frequently stated that the bitch should be left alone and undisturbed during labour, but this is very questionable as regards a bull bitch.

The working-man fancier who has stuck to the breed through thick and thin, and is undoubtedly the mainstay of the breed to-day, seems to be more successful than the large kennels in obtaining and rearing litters, and a larger number of the best dogs have been produced by him. This is attributable to the fact that the bitch is kept in the house and lives with the family, and when the time of labour comes she remains there and is carefully watched and, if assistance is required, it is given and the puppies removed as they are born and placed in a basket beside the kitchen fire. In the larger kennel the bitches do not live in the house, and as they are naturally not used to their owner's general presence they may be liable to resent intrusion at the time of whelping. Care and attention is, however, just as necessary, and if it is not possible to have the bitch in the house for some days before labour is expected it is advisable to provide a special kennel for whelping, with room in it for the owner or attendant to be with the bitch, who should be installed and settled in it for some days before the pups are due. In addition, the bitch should be about as much as possible during those days with the one who is to have care of her during her labour. The bitch thrives best on three light meals a day during her period of gestation, after she shows she is in whelp, with frequent doses of a dessertspoonful of liquid paraffin or cod liver oil. Ample exercise is advisable up to the last, but this must not be overdone.

If difficulties arise, or there is protracted labour, there should be no delay in getting veterinary or other help. The Caesarean operation in skilled hands, and before the bitch is exhausted, is the most merciful course to

THE BULLDOG SPIRIT.

Lord Charles Beresford, the famous Admiral, is seen here with the noted team of "Stone" dogs.

HEAD OF "SIRLOIN OF PUGILIST".

As the name suggests, this dog is a son of the noted champion (see page 212) and appears to be very similar to his illustrious sire.

Photo]   [Guiver.

"SIRLOIN OF PUGILIST".

The breadth of chest, the lay back, the heavy upper lip, the good legs and body, and the way this dog stands on his feet, suggest that he is as good as his sire.   He was exported to America by Mrs. Walz.

take if trouble arises, and it is surprising how soon the bitch gets over the operation. In this case a foster-mother is desirable but not essential, as there are cases of bitches rearing the puppies themselves after the operation; but they are better left to recuperate without the pups, and there appears to be no trouble with regard to the milk, which seems to disperse of its own accord.

When the whelping is completed the bitch's box should be cleaned and a clean sack tacked on the bottom, and the use of what is sometimes termed a "pig rail", which consists of a loose rail being placed round the inside of the box some four inches from the sides and the same distance from the floor of the box, is recommended. This will frequently save the life of a puppy by preventing the bitch crushing it up against the side of the box.

The pups, which should be thoroughly warm, may then be returned to the bitch and, if they commence to suckle, all will generally be well, provided a temperature of between sixty and seventy degrees is maintained during at least the first forty-eight hours. Warmth is the most essential part of the bulldog puppy's existence during the first few days of its life; after then it appears to become as hard as any other breed. Some bull bitches have a remarkable penchant for licking their puppies, and if this be the case it is best to procure a foster-mother, as the pups, by frequent licking, get wet and are pushed away from the mother and lose her warmth and then catch cold.

Some Bulldogs are very prone to pant excessively when excited or when exercised. There is no clear reason for this unless it arises from nerves or heart trouble, but as the same thing is frequently reproduced in the offspring, breeding from a bull bitch which is badly subject to this is not to be favoured. The condition may, of course, be caused by the dog being excessively fat and not from any infirmity, when the remark against breeding from such specimens does not apply.

The purchase of a young Bulldog puppy is, generally speaking, a gamble, as the most perfect-looking puppy may turn out an absolute waster, whilst another poor-looking specimen, but without glaring faults, may steadily improve. As, however, good Bulldogs and the promising older puppies are much sought after and invariably command high prices, the person with a limited purse has no alternative on taking up the breed but to purchase a young puppy or a well-bred bitch which is not up to show form. If the latter, the best advice is never to bry a bitch which has not bred. So many Bulldog bitches are non-breeders, and a bitch without show qualifications is not much use except as a pal if she will not breed.

Before purchasing a puppy the prospective purchaser should endeavour to see the dam to be assured that she is a reasonable specimen as regards type and is healthy and has no really bad fault. Select a puppy by a fashionable sire who

Photo]   *[S. & G.*

A GOOD BRACE.

A good run has not damped the keenness of these two excellent dogs. They are "Goedenfast of Bellehatch" and "The Duke of Bellehatch", held in by their owner, Lady Rathcreedan.

Photos]   [Sport & General.

THE "PERFECT" BULLDOG.

To settle all argument, the Powers-that-be decided to fix for all time what they considered the perfect points
of the Bulldog.

is producing winning stock if possible. Assuming that the age of the puppy is six weeks (the usual time for them to leave the dam), the purchaser should select a healthy heavy-boned pup with small ears, short back, great depth of brisket, ample loose skin and a short tapering tail. Many Bulldogs are born with screw tails which look short, and this is not looked upon as a fault ; in fact many fanciers prefer it, as it has a tendency to make the back look short.

It is impossible to give a diet for the rearing of puppies, as so many people vary in their methods of feeding and there are so many admirable puppy foods on the market to-day. Warm quarters, with a dry floor (preferably wood) and free from draughts, are almost essential, and after weaning the puppy should have frequent small meals of varying diet. Milk foods should form the staple food at first ; oatmeal flour porridge and some of the prepared meals and a little finely-minced raw lean meat should be given after the seventh week is over. One or two small doses of cod liver oil daily and a little phosphate of lime are often very beneficial. Five or six meals a day are not too many for the first few weeks, but after the tenth week four meals a day are ample and at sixteen weeks they may be reduced to three daily.

Bulldog puppies seem to be very subject to worms, and during the early part of their lives should be dosed frequently for this complaint. There are several very effective and safe remedies

A bronze was cast showing what was considered to be the absolutely correct animal, and our reproductions
on this page show the figure from four angles.

on the market to-day and the puppies never thrive unless they are free from worms.

Young pups should be encouraged to take exercise, but until they are three months or more old it is not usually necessary to exercise them on the road. When they have reached this

food than the older dogs. The milk of goats is a fine food for young puppies, particularly if fortified with virol. Adult dogs require no more exercise than the larger puppies, and for food good biscuits in the morning and prepared biscuit meal scalded with broth at night are excellent, while some-

Photo] [*Fox.*

BEWARE OF THE DOG!

"Cloverley Barley Boy" does not really mean to look fierce. It is merely his way of expressing pleasurable anticipation—he is awaiting his master's return.

age they should be taught to go on a lead and, when used to it, taken for short walks on the road or hard ground to keep the feet close and the pasterns from giving way.

When six months old the pups can go on to two meals a day, but frequently it pays to continue the cod liver oil up to a year old or more, and the pups should always have more concentrated

raw meat two or three times a week is helpful, particularly if not too lean. Experience has shown that when fat is included in the meat there is little or no chance of the dogs suffering from hysteria. Bulldogs get tired of one kind of food, and a change of diet, if only in the make of biscuits, meal or rusks, is desirable. If a puppy or dog refuses its food take its temperature at once

BULLDOG JUVENILES.

and if found to be above normal (101.4°) keep it warm and on light diet. The lives of many good puppies and dogs would have been and, it is to be hoped, will be saved if this had been or is carefully attended to. In spite of its width of chest, the Bulldog's chest seems to be its weak spot, and many deaths which are put down to distemper are really the result of pneumonia.

One of the great merits of the Bulldog is that it requires no trimming for the show bench, and, as a consequence, the novice stands on a level with the experienced breeder, and there is no need to engage an expert to get the dog up to show form or to handle it. Ring manners are essential, but these can be taught by anyone with patience, and consist of the dog being taught to stand in position in the ring and to move with his owner when required by the judge.

Before dealing with the standard of points for the breed from the show point of view the question of weight might be noticed, which is stated in the standard to be about fifty pounds, or rather less for a bitch. It will be gathered from remarks on the early days of show Bulldogs that variation in weights was recognized from the earliest days, and weight classes have always been and are still recognized to-day.

When the breed was at its zenith from a show point of view in the years immediately preceding the Great War, it was not uncommon to find at the shows classes for dogs of 55 lb. and over, for dogs of 45 lb. and under 55 lb., and for dogs under 45 lb.; whilst there were classes for bitches of 45 lb. and over, and for bitches of 35 lb. and under 45 lb., for bitches not exceeding 40 lb., and even for bitches under 35 lb. This clearly shows that breeders had the greatest difficulty in breeding to the weights fixed, and that the various clubs and shows recognized the fact and provided classes accordingly.

The question as to which are or have been the best dogs must be a matter of opinion, but experts will agree that Ch. "British Monarch" (born in 1884), was undoubtedly a great dog and a great sire, though the first great Bulldog the writer ever

CH. "CRIB".

In the early days of Bulldogs "Crib" was taken to be the ideal type and we can see from this illustration how the type has altered since then. He was owned by Mr. T. Turton. Born in 1871, he was bred by Mr. Lamphier, the owner of "King Dick".

saw was Ch. "Boomerang" (born in 1893), when he was owned by the late Mr. Luke Crabtree, of Manchester, who also owned Ch. "Prince Albert" (born in 1897). Ch. "Rodney Stone" (born in the same year as Ch. "Prince Albert") was looked upon as the greatest dog of his day, and a sensation was caused in the dog fancy when his owner and breeder, Mr. Walter Jeffries, sold him to America for £1,000. Ch. "Broadlea Squire" (born in 1900) was another great little dog, and Ch. "Heywood Duchess" (born in 1902) was one of our finest bitches. Mrs. E. Waterlow's Chs. "Nuthurst Doctor" and "Nuthurst Lad" (father and son born in 1901 and 1908 respectively) were good dogs, and in 1910 and 1911 two wonderful bitches, in Mr. George Woollons' Ch. "Roseville Blaze" and the late Mrs. Sturgeon's Ch. "Oak Nana", were born. A wonderful dog in Mr. S. Crabtree's Ch. "Failsworth White Knight" (born in 1913) appeared in the early days of the Great War and found a home in America, when shows ceased during that period. Ch. "Dunscar Draftsman", owned by Messrs. Naylor Bros., was born in 1922 and, apart from his great achievements on the show bench, will be remembered as the greatest sire of all time, and his name appears in the pedigrees of most of the leading dogs of to-day. A wonderful bitch was Ch. "Carissima", owned by Mrs. J. Berry, of Oldham.

Born in 1924, Ch. "Carissima" became a champion within a few days of being twelve months old, and her early death soon afterwards was a distinct loss to the fancy. Another wonderful bitch which was lost to the fancy before she was two years old was Ch. "Sheesadraftsman", bred in 1929 by Mr. Petty, of Orrell, near Wigan, and afterwards an inmate of Mr. E. Roddy's famous kennel at Basford.

More recently Ch. "Pugilist" (bred in 1926 by Mrs. B. J. Walz, of Shackleford, in Surrey), won thirty Challenge Certificates, whilst in bitches the palm must be given to Ch. "Dames Double" (also bred in 1926 by the late Mrs. R. G. Sturgeon, as the winner of twenty-four Challenge Certificates.

FOUR OF A KIND.

A bright lot of youngsters, belonging to Mrs. F. M. Law. Bulldog puppies have playful ways and, until maturity, do not live up to their doleful and worried looks.

Other good dogs and bitches bred a few years later include Chs. "Son o' Jill", "Anglezarke Sonny Boy", "Basford Revival", "Mountain Lassie", "Mountain Queen", "Basford Victorian Lady", "Anglezarke Sheesa-draftsman", "Noisette", and "Carissima", all sired by the late Ch. "Dunscar Draftsman"; Mrs. Van Raalte's Ch. "Hollycroft Sugar" and Major Rousseau's Ch. "Oakville Supreme". On the whole the quality of dogs was better round about 1932 and 1933 than at any time during the previous forty years, except perhaps for the period during the years 1910 to 1913. They are lower to ground than those of the past and ear carriage has greatly improved, but there is a distinct tendency towards losing the graceful hind-quarters, the tuck-up of loin, and the roach back, which are such features in the perfect Bulldog.

Two standards for the breed are in existence to-day, that of the Bulldog Club Incorporated and one which was drawn up and adopted by the Allied Bulldog Clubs in 1910 This latter standard, which is given below, is the one adopted by The British Bulldog Club, and is believedly favoured by more Clubs to-day than that of the older club.

This standard is set forth in three sections, to each of which is allotted a certain number of points, making up an aggregate of three hundred points, as follow : General appearance, 60 ; head properties, 130 ; body properties, 110. Total, 300.

The number of points so allotted to each section is further apportioned amongst the sub-heads into which that section naturally divides itself. Although judging by points is not recommended, it is nevertheless convenient, for the purpose of instruction and reference, that the value of the numerous properties, to be considered in forming a judgment on any Bulldog, should be appraised in numbers, with the object to deciding the relative value which perfection in one property has to perfection in another.

GENERAL APPEARANCE.—In appraising the merit of any Bulldog

TWO FAVOURITES.

"Sally", seen here, is Miss Helen Trevelyan's favourite dog.   Miss Trevelyan is, of course, the novelist actress.
"Sally" is a healthy agile specimen of the breed.

it is of the first importance to take into account the impression its general symmetry as a whole makes on the mind of the judge, due allowance being made for sex, as the female is seldom so massive or well developed as the male.

In this general survey should be noticed to what extent all properties are in due harmony with, and in proportion to, each other. A perfect show specimen should be of uniform merit throughout, and should not excel in one point more than another, although animals with certain points superexcellent are useful for breeding purposes.

It should also be observed whether or not the animal is totally blind, totally deaf, castrated, spayed, or suffering from an infectious or contagious disease so to wholly disqualify it from receiving a prize (*see* KENNEL CLUB RULES): or whether it is blind, deaf, lame, deformed, mutilated or unsound to such a partial extent that the defect only weighs severely against its chance in competition.

head square and strikingly massive in proportion to the animal's size, as well as, when compared with that of any other animal, well broken up by the clearly defined "stop" and "furrow" and well wrinkled. (30 points over and above the points for perfection of properties in detail)

Its face extremely short : with broad blunt muzzle distinctly inclined upwards.

Its body deep at chest, with well-rounded ribs; limbs stout and muscular; hindquarters higher, and of a slighter build than its more heavily made foreparts; the couplings short.

The back rising from the shoulders to the loins, thence falling away more rapidly to the stern, thus forming the "roach" or "wheel" back, an essential characteristic of the breed. The tail set on low and never carried gaily.

The body of the animal should appear to be what is known as "pear-shaped", i.e. of great breadth and depth graduallytapering off, in width and depth, to

Photo] [*Sport & General.*
THE BULLDOG SPIRIT.
"Blossom Westall", the pet of Miss Dorothy Pearson. Something of the National dog's grit and tenacity was evidently possessed by Miss Pearson, who succeeded in winning the English Ladies' Golf Championship.

Next should be considered the several characteristic properties of the animal, as follow :

DESCRIPTION.

PROPERTIES.—A Bulldog is a smooth-coated, thick-set and compact dog ; enveloped in a loose skin, apparently too large for it, round-footed, low in stature, but conveying the idea of activity, muscularity and immense strength.

FORMATION, SHAPE, MAKE, STYLE, MUSCULARITY, TEMPER, EXPRESSION AND ACTION.—Its

the stern, as much as possible being in view in front of the shoulders. A pear-shaped body as thus described is most desirable, but a pear-shaped front, i.e. a front widening from the top of the shoulder-blades to the elbows and then gradually narrowing to the feet, which, in their turn, almost touch, is a most objectionable deformity which should always be deprecated.

Temper should not be overlooked, a savage dog being undesirable, and equally so an animal with-

AS SEEN BY THE ARTIST
A page of studies of Bulldogs by that fine delineator of animal character, J. Nicholson, specially drawn for this work.

FOUR NOTED WINNERS.

Of the outstanding dogs that were shown in 1934 here are excellent examples. *Top left*: Mr. George Roscoe's "My Lord Bill", notable for his deep face, good lay-back, and neat ears. *Top right*: Mrs. Edwards's bitch, "Ch. Mountain Queen", very sound on her legs. *Lower left*: Mr. Barnard's Ch. "Keysoe Golden Sovereign", a dog with very wide front and sound body ; and *lower right*: "Sir Tristram", a big winner in his time.

out expression or animation, apparently disregarding insult or injury. Considerable weight should be attached to the freedom and activity displayed by the animal in its movement as well as to the typical roll in its gait. By activity is meant not that of a Terrier, but a freedom of movement proportionate to the massiveness of the animal's formation.

SIZE.—The weight most desirable to be encouraged is 50 lb. for a dog and 45 lb. for a bitch, in show form (5 points).

COLOUR.—The colouring should be brilliant and pure, and the colours white, brindled, red, fawn, or fallow, either whole, smut, mixed, or pied. Black and white, or black ticked, are undesirable colours. Black or black-and-tan, or blue or blue-brindled, absolutely disqualify (5 points).

With these exceptions colour is a matter of little importance.

CONDITION, SOUNDNESS.—A Bulldog when shown should be in perfect health and good condition : nose moist, eyes bright, in good coat, well groomed, clean, free from skin eruptions, muscles well strung and not flabby, and perfectly sound in body, limbs, lungs and heart (15 points).

COAT.—The coat should be of fine texture, close and smooth when stroked from head towards tail, and hard, owing to its closeness, but not wiry, when stroked in the reverse direction (5 points).

Total, 60 points for general appearance.

HEAD PROPERTIES.

JAWS.—The jaws should be broad, massive, square and powerful. The lower jaw should project beyond the upper jaw, and have a *distinct sweep or upward curve*, this point being one of the characteristics of the breed. The lips should be black, and the mouth well cut back (15 points).

CHOP.—The upper lip, called the "chop", should be deep and very thick, hanging completely over the lower jaw at the sides, but only joining the lower lip in front, yet quite covering the teeth (5 points).

TEETH.—The canine and molar teeth should be large and strong, the tusks set far apart ; the front teeth between the tusks should be regular and

BORED.

The Bulldog never betrays any ecstatic enthusiasm for life, usually looking ready to give in to a feeling of boredom.

straight, and all the teeth should be sound and perfect (5 points).

A distorted or wry-face, when caused by an irregular or twisted formation of the jaws, is most objectionable and should be severely penalized.

Photos] [J. T. Roberts, Croydon.

WHO CARES ?

And sometimes he does! Even then, however, he maintains his worried expression.

NOSE AND NOSTRILS.—The nose should be laid well back, and the nostrils should be large (i.e. both broad and very deep) and perfectly black.

When viewed in profile, it should appear as if the tip of the nose would just intersect an imaginary straight line drawn from the extremity of the lower lip to the frontal eminence between the brows.

A flesh-coloured, mottled, parti-coloured or "butterfly" nose handicaps the animal, while the liver-coloured nose of a "Dudley" forms an absolute disqualification to any Bulldog being awarded a prize.

Liver-coloured nostrils with their concomitants, liver-coloured lips, yellowish eyelids and a generally jaundiced appearance of the eyes and skin are indicative of a "Dudley".

A well-defined straight line should be visible between the nostrils, but a split septum or a hare-lip disqualifies any specimen in competition. (Nose 5 points, nostrils 10 points.)

SHORTNESS OF FACE.—The nasal bone should be short and incline upwards, the effect, combined with that of the jaw properties, being to give the animal a short, upfaced appearance, which is an important characteristic of the breed (10 points).

MUZZLE.—The muzzle should be broad, square in front and turned upwards, of great depth through the jaws, and the foreface square and well filled up under the eyes (10 points).

SKULL.—The skull, an important characteristic of a Bulldog, cannot be too large if in proportion to the face, and should be of great length from eye to ear as well as from the occiput to the base of the lower jaw, of great circumference but squarely shaped, and it should not be in any degree wedge-shaped, dome-shaped, or peaked, nor wider than it is deep (10 points).

FOREHEAD.—The skull should be flat between the ears, the forehead large and flat, not overhanging the face, and of great breadth (10 points).

CHEEKS. — The cheeks, in an adult specimen, rounded and well defined, extending in some degree laterally beyond the eyes, as this property is characteristic of the breed (5 points).

FURROW. — The brows should be prominent, broad, square and high, separated by a deep and wide furrow extending from the stop up the centre of the forehead, and gradually disappearing as the occiput is reached (5 points).

STOP.—The furrow commences from a deep cavity formed at the junction of the nasal bone with the forehead, which cavity is known as the "stop". This stop should be broad and very deep, as this is a point of the greatest importance (10 points).

WRINKLE.—The existence of this stop and furrow causes the appearance known as "broken up", which should be accompanied by loose skin about the head, well wrinkled (such wrinkle to be close and rather fine, not houndy), together giving the animal a pronounced style and finish (5 points).

EARS.—The ears should be small, thin, but not pendulous, situated at the top edge of the skull, far from the eyes, and set well apart from each other, so as not to restrict the breadth of the skull between

---

A Grand Match at the Westminster Pit,
FOR 100 GUINEAS,
By 2 DOGS of 43-lb. weight each,
THE PROPERTY OF TWO SPORTING NOBLEMEN.
One, that famous
WHITE BITCH OF PADDINGTON,
Whose wonderful performances are so well known to the Fancy
to require no further comment—the other
A BRINDLE DOG OF CAMBRIDGE,
A remarkable and well known favorite, as his fame bears extensive proof —to fight from the scratch,
ON WEDNESDAY, 16th of JUNE, 1819,
at 6 o'clock in the evening precisely.—Doors open at half past 5.

ADVERTISING A DOG FIGHT.
Bulldog fighting was, after the days of Bull-baiting, the pastime of the sporting fraternity. Once again efforts were made to build a dog better able to fight and, since the underside of the body was vulnerable, the desire was to get a dog low to the ground

---

them, yet sufficiently high up on the skull to obviate any appearance of round or "apple headedness."

In shape they should be what is technically known as "rose", i.e. folding at the back, the tip and upper edge lapping in a backward and outward direction, thus exposing some part of the burr or inner folds of the ear.

Ears of any other shape are objectionable and should be discouraged, especially so the Fox-terrier or "button" ear (in which the tip falls forward and hides the inner folds), the bat ear, the pricked ear, and almost as much so the "tulip" ear, but less so the semi-pricked ear like that of a Collie, which in many cases merely betokens an excess of muscle. A dog with only one ear cannot win a prize (15 points).

EYES.—The eyes should be placed low down, but quite in front of the forehead, as far from the ears, from the nose, and from each other as possible, as long as their position leaves the clearly defined outline of the cheek-bumps extending beyond and below them. They should be placed at right angles to the vertical "furrow" running up the centre of the forehead, and very slightly higher than the level of the base of the nasal bone.

The eyes and eyelids must be absolutely free from any of

By courtesy]   *[E. C Ash.*
BULL BAITING.
The "sport" of baiting bulls led to developments in the Bulldog breed for, although this custom started, so it is said, merely as a local pastime, later it was taken seriously and efforts were made to produce a dog that would beat all others and be able to hang on to the bull longer, because of the position of its nostrils

A FINE HEAD.

Ch. "Basford Revivue", Mr. Roddy's noted Bulldog, has a very fine, but not exaggerated, head.

Ch. "Nuthurst Lad."   Ch. "Centaur."   Ch. "Oak Nana"

Ch. "Phul-Nana"   R. "Roseville Blaze"

SIX CHAMPIONS.

A group of Bulldogs of the first class, all champions, at the end of the nineteenth century, painted by R. Ward Binks, one of the leading animal painters of his time.

the indications of a "Dudley", which have been previously described.

The eyes should be round, of moderate size, neither prominent nor sunken and intensely dark, appearing full of life, intelligence and determination, and conveying a sour expression which suggests that the dog will resent any liberties being taken with him.

The deformity known as "wall-eyes", i.e. one eye of a lighter colour than the other, or eyes in which the iris is whitish, very light grey, or eyes in which the whites are distorted, or on one side, is an absolute disqualification. A dog with only one eye cannot win a prize (10 points).

Total, 130 points.

BODY PROPERTIES.

NECK AND DEWLAPS.—The neck should be moderately short, very thick-set, deep and muscular; well arched at the back, furnished with thick loose skin forming a dewlap on each side of the throat for a slight distance downwards from the base of the lower jaw towards the brisket (5 points).

BRISKET.—The brisket should be capacious, of great depth and breadth, and well let down between the arms (10 points).

CHEST AND RIBS.—The chest should be of great width and depth, and with well-rounded ribs, giving the animal a broad and short-legged appearance in front (10 points).

SHOULDERS.—The shoulders should be set on low, the points of the scapulæ, or tops of the shoulder-blades, not touching or even being close

Photo]　　　　　　　　　　　　　[Walter Guiver.
CH. "CLOVERLEY BRIGHT STAR'.
Mr. Palmer's noted champion Bulldog bitch is of a type that differs, as will be seen, from many others.

together. They should be deep, and slope from their narrowest point at the edge of the back to their greatest breadth at the elbows, and should indicate the possession of great muscular power (15 points).

The barrel, formed of well-rounded ribs, cannot be of too great circumference (consistent with proportion) when measured round the chest behind the shoulder-blades, and it should gradually taper off in front of the belly.

The belly should be well tucked up and not pendulous, a small or narrow waist being desirable.

BACK.—The back should be broad, short in the couplings, and while it should not fall away so as to dip and be swamped behind the shoulders, it should rise from its lowest point behind the shoulders in a graceful curve to its highest point over the top of the loins, and thence fall away more suddenly to the stern. This curve is technically known as the "wheel" or "roach" back, and forms one of the essential characteristics of the breed. This property cannot be correct unless the tail is set on low.

In width the back should taper off from its greatest breadth between the shoulder-blades to the loins, where it should be comparatively narrow (10 points).

LOINS.—The loins should be strong, muscular, and indicative of freedom of movement (5 points).

TAIL.—The tail, technically called the "stern", should be set on low behind the rump bone, deflecting almost vertically downwards. It should

Photo]　　　　　　　　　　　　　[Walter Guiver.
CH. "NOVONERO".
This dog, owned by Mrs. Shaw, displays a good broad head, a well-balanced body and stands well on its feet.

be moderately short, round in bone, thick at the root, and tapering towards the end, devoid of "feather", not curved upwards at the end, and the animal should never be able to raise it above the level of its backbone. A screw or twisted tail is undesirable, a dog without a tail cannot win a prize (10 points).

FORELEGS.

BONE.—Any deformity or weakness is highly objectionable in either hind- or fore-legs, and the latter should be of great strength and muscularity and possessed of immense bone.

The animal should have perfect freedom of movement and activity notwithstanding the peculiarly constrained manner of gait natural to the breed caused by the immense development of head, chest and shoulders, and by its hindlegs being higher than its forelegs (10 points).

FOREARMS AND ELBOWS. — A Bulldog in stature should be compact and low to the ground, lower in front than behind, and should not carry its body on its forelegs, but between them. The height of its foreleg from the ground to the elbow should not exceed the distance from the elbow to the centre of the back between the shoulder-blades.

The forelegs should be set wide apart very thick, stout and strong, straight and moderately short.

The elbows should be set on low, and while not standing well away from the ribs should be placed so as to admit of the body swinging between them giving the legs the appearance of being tacked on the side of the body.

The forearms ought to be well covered with muscle, especially on the outside, thus conveying a suggestion of bow-leggedness, which should not however, exist (10 points).

PASTERNS, FEET AND TOES.—The pasterns short stout, upright and strong.

The feet round rather large turning very slightly outwards with toes thick compact and

well-split up to the knuckles, which should be prominent and high. A dog with less than four feet cannot win a prize (5 points).

HINDLEGS.

The hindlegs should be strong and muscular, but of a slighter build than the forelegs, and of moderate length, but distinctly longer than the forelegs, so that the loins may be elevated above the level of the top of the shoulders.

STIFLES AND HOCKS.—The stifles should, by their covering of muscle, appear rounded, and stand slightly away from the body, thus inclining the hocks inward and the hind feet outward, but not so much as to give a cow-hocked appearance, which is highly objectionable. (Points: Stifles 5, hocks 5).

PASTERNS.—The hocks should be strong, well let down, slightly bent, and low, making the pasterns short, but longer than those on the forelegs (5 points).

FEET.—The feet, rather smaller than the forefeet and turned slightly outward, should be round and compact, but not necessarily so much so as the forefeet, the toes, however, being well split up and knuckles prominent (5 points). Total, 110 Points.

Photo]   [Fall.
CH. "ANGLE ZARKE SHEESADRAFTSMAN".
This bitch was exceptionally good in almost all its points and it was unfortunate that she died young.

SUMMARY OF POSITIVE POINTS

GENERAL APPEARANCE.—Formation, shape, make, style, muscularity, temper, expression and action, 30; size and weight, 5; colour, 5; condition and soundness, 15; coat, 5. Total 60.

HEAD PROPERTIES.—Jaws 15, chop 5, teeth 5, 25; nose 5, nostrils 10, 15; shortness of face 10, muzzle 10, 20; skull 10, forehead 10, cheeks 5, 25; furrow 5, stop 10, wrinkle 5, 20, ears, 15; eyes, 10. Total, 130.

BODY PROPERTIES.—Neck and dewlaps 5, brisket 10, 15; chest and ribs 10, shoulders 15, back 10, loins 5, 40, tail, 10; forelegs (bone 10, forearms and elbows 10, pasterns, feet and toes 5), 25; hindlegs (stifles 5, hocks 5, pasterns 5, feet 5). 20 Total 110.

BULLDOG AND TERRIER CROSS.

In olden days attempts were made to make a more active Bulldog, and here are three results of Bulldog-Terrier crosses with cropped ears, which at one time were fashionable.

PENALTY POINTS.

Beyond withholding, where necessary, the points allotted for perfection in any property, a judge should by way of penalty deduct from the aggregate number of positive points obtained the respective number of points shown against each of the undermentioned bad faults.

FAULTS.—Maximum number of negative points : Want of soundness, 25 ; colour, black ticked, 15, or black marked with white, 15 ; wryfacedness, 20 ; ears, button, 15, tulip, prick or bat, 10 ; bad temper, 15 ; bad teeth, 15 ; nose not black (puppies excepted), 10 ; tail raised above level of back 10 ; lack of alertness 10.

THE BULLDOG MINIATURE. Here we have a Miniature Bulldog of 1902. Ch. "Nina de L'Enclos" weighed 15¼ lb.

Bull Mastiff.—This breed was dormant for a great many years, but again grew in favour with those who like a noble animal. In the earlier part of this century these dogs were used by gamekeepers for night work and their keenness made the lot of the poacher a nightmare. In 1900 there was a show devoted to night dogs of the old style Bull Mastiff : this being bred for power and attacking intruders on the game preserves of the large estates. The pillars of the breed in those days were "Thorneywood Terror", owned by Mr. Burton, of Nottingham ; "Thorneywood Lion", same owner ; "Osmaston Viper", "Osmaston Nell" and "Osmaston Daisy", owned by Mr. J. Biggs.

At this period these dogs were a cross between a Bulldog and a Mastiff. Most of these dogs were brindles, which at night could not be seen very easily. By photographs one notes the old breed had tremendous skulls and had the appearance of more Bull than Mastiff, with an immense underjaw: weight about 112 lb. and about 27 by 28 inches at the shoulder. Although so heavy, they were wonderfully quick and could down a man quite easily. The training of these dogs was undoubtedly perfect, as when on duty at night no sound would escape from them until the keeper was ready for them to do what he wanted.

The modern Bull Mastiff is a different type of dog. The old breed was a cross of Bull Mastiff and Bulldog ; the new type is a dog bred from both parents and the three preceding generations, all Bull Mastiffs without the introduction of a Mastiff or Bulldog. This was accepted by the Kennel Club about 1925.

The standard to be attained should be 50–50, viz. Bulldog and Mastiff, and this is set by the British Bull Mastiff League, the premier organization of Bull Mastiff breeders.

Dogs should be 26 inches, weight about 100 to 112 lb. ; bitches 25 to 26 inches, and about 85 to 95 lb.

HEADS should be typical, slightly wrinkled. Muzzle not too long, about 3 inches. Large nostrils, flews fairly level. Jaws should preferably be undershot, not overshot, although some may be seen with quite a level jaw. Eyes dark (light eyes should not be encouraged). In fawn or red dogs the dark mask is preferred. Skull should be very large and broad, with cheeks well developed, and a flat forehead.

NECK.—Arched and rather short, muscular, and equal in circumference to skull.

CHEST.—Wide and deep, and well set between forelegs. Girth should be more than the dog's height. Ribs arched and deep.

BACK.—Short ; muscular shoulders.

FORELEGS.—Well boned and straight.

HINDLEGS.—Muscular and broad, proving strength. Cow-hocks are a great disadvantage, as also are straight hocks.

LOINS.—Wide and muscular.

PASTERNS.—Straight ; feet large ; rounded toes, well arched. Splayed feet are a great fault.

TAIL.—Well set up, thick at root and getting slightly thinner, reaching to the hocks.

COAT.—Short and dense (must not be woolly). Puppies are hardy, but to

By courtesy]   *[the "Field."*

ARTHUR WARDLE'S PICTURE OF MINIATURES. This leading British artist shows two Miniatures (as can be gauged from the size of the cushion), one typical of the British and the other of the French Bulldog type.

Photo]   [*Miss Compton Collier.*

SPORTING HOSTS.

The Bull Mastiff is becoming increasingly popular in country houses.   Here is one, the constant companion of
Sir James and Lady Dunn, who are seen at Dale End, Slindon, Sussex.

Photo   *Fall.*

THE BULL MASTIFF.

With the idea of making a more active Mastiff suitable to accompany the gamekeeper and police the Bull Mastiff was evolved.
Miss Lane's Ch. "Athos" is one of the best type.

Photo)   *Fa'l.*

INTERNATIONAL CH. "FARCROFT FELON FRAJEUR".

Mr. S. E. Moseley, the breeder of this great dog was the originator of the Bull Mastiff breed and breeder of some of the most powerful
and best in the variety.

build up their constitution it is wise to give them a good start. This does not infer weakness in any degree, but common sense tells us it is to their advantage in building up a good frame and good health. It is wise to commence their training early ; gradually but firmly. Owners will be greatly surprised at the intelligence of the breed. If a Bull Mastiff is unruly, it is not the dog's fault. He is faithful, capable of looking after himself if necessary, intelligent, a staunch ally and never quarrelsome.

Bull Terrier.—Those people whose hearts are warmed by the lovable qualities of the Bull Terrier are regarding with satisfaction the marked improvement that is taking place in the fortunes of this thoroughly genuine breed.

There is a good case to be made for the statement that the present popularity of the Bull Terrier, already greater and wider than at any other period of his history, is steadily increasing. The number of Bull Terriers registered annually at the Kennel Club, the increase in Challenge Certificates allotted to the breed, the growing entries at shows—all these facts speak of consistent progress. Indeed, at the Great Joint Terrier Show at Olympia in 1931 Bull Terriers delighted their own friends and dumbfounded the supporters of more fashionable breeds by achieving the largest entry in the show—223. It is no wonder that these dogs are far more frequently encountered in the streets nowadays, and that the Bull Terrier Club has not only in the last few years increased its membership from a problematical eighty to one of over 250, but is, probably, one of the richest dog clubs in the canine world.

Credit for this eminently impressive state of affairs may be equally divided between the improved quality of the dog himself and the self-

Photo]
BULL MASTIFF HEAD.
[Fall.
'Jeanie", the property of the Hon. G. Murray Smith, shows the type of head of the female of the breed.

lessness, resource and energy of the Club's honorary secretary, Dr. G. M. Vevers, and his able assistant, Miss T. E. Salter. Bull Terrier enthusiasts are extremely fortunate in the work done on their behalf by Dr. Vevers, who, by conducting the breed's affairs with wisdom and far-sightedness, won for it the high respect that it at present commands.

If there is one regret more than another amongst those with an accurate knowledge of dogs, it is the atmosphere of suspicion that in the past has clouded the ordinary man's judgment of this fine and wholly British breed.

It used to be a grievance of the ignorant that this dog is quarrelsome, whereas in reality he is a sober-minded animal, slow to anger ; and who shall condemn him if, being roused, he bears himself manfully in the fight ? Surely the ability to defend oneself is a matter of allure rather than alarm. The truth is that the modern Bull Terrier, while retaining all his old unquenchable spirit, is no longer the ugly ferocious Bill Sykes dog that was bred for battling to death in the pits, for breeders have achieved remarkable success in retaining and developing only the best points of this lovable animal's ancestors. In fact, he is a real dog and a man's dog, combining all that is best of the two breeds from which he has been evolved, and displaying the exaggerations of neither.

Equally immoderate is the uninformed accusation of deafness, whereas, in fact, deafness in the breed amounts to no more than two per cent, and is steadily growing less ; and it seems to be forgotten that, owing to lack of pigment, all white animals —white mice, white cats, etc.—display this tendency towards deafness. Dr. Vevers himself has with his customary thoroughness established the responsibility for such occasional deafness that

A FAMILY GROUP.
This excellent young stock is proof of the powerful kennel of Bull Mastiffs
owned by Miss Lane, a noted lady breeder.

occurs, just as he has been adamant in insisting on the proper steps being taken for its suppression. He has no doubt that the lack of hearing associated with Bull Terriers and other animals deficient in pigment is an hereditary defect due to the degeneration or absolute absence of a small passage in the ear known as the cochlear duct. This form of deafness is almost certainly a Mendelian recessive, and he is of opinion that if all deaf specimens are killed as soon as the trouble is established, and if deaf sires and dams are not used for breeding purposes, deafness in Bull Terriers will die a natural death within ten to fifteen years.

This considered opinion has the official support of the Bull Terrier Club, who now require all new members to sign a declaration of honour that they will not exhibit, sell, or breed from deaf specimens ; and it is a fact that every reputable breeder destroys all deaf puppies as soon as possible. There cannot be much doubt that the strong action taken by the Bull Terrier Clubs of England and India in this matter has done much to stamp out one of the most deplorable infirmities from which any dog can suffer.

The original Bull Terrier, or Bull-and-Terrier, as he was then styled, bred for fighting in the pits, bore a far closer resemblance to the Bulldog of that day than to his Terrier forbears ; for there exist scores of old prints as evidence that the old Bulldog, as well as the Bull-and-Terrier, had the unexaggerated (in comparison with the absurd modern standards) Bulldog head, and the legs, straight and longer, of the Terrier. At the same time that the new Bull-and-Terrier made its appearance, the Bulldog fanciers began breeding their animals heavier and lower to ground, so that the Bulldog acquired a new type and the Bull-and-Terrier, roughly speaking, and with the difference that his head was slightly longer, took the old type's place. Moreover, these Bull-and-Terriers, evolved by crossing Bulldogs with Terriers, mainly retained the colouring and markings of the Bulldog.

At the end of the 'fifties, however, a great and vital revolution was effected. Mr. James Hinks, of Birmingham, after years of experiment, burst upon an astonished and frankly sceptical world an entirely new animal —an immaculate white-coated Bull Terrier, from whom the undesirable points of the Bulldog (the roach back, the bent legs, the splay feet, the undershot jaw, etc.) were still further eliminated, and for whom he claimed equal courage and greater activity. The attractive appearance of the new dog in itself gave rise to a certain antagonism—it was considered that Mr. Hinks, in eliminating the Bulldog, had also eliminated its courage, and that the white Bull Terrier was altogether too "pretty" to hold its own in effective combat with the brindled and more pugilistic-looking heroes of so many fights. Mr. Hinks, however, found little difficulty in providing

A DOG OF HISTORY
When, in 1928, the Marquis of Londonderry sent a Bull Mastiff to Cruft's show, it became evident
that the breed was well established and would become a fancy of all dog-lovers.

SOME OF THE BEST.

Mrs. Adlam, owner of a noted kennel of Bull Terriers, which is one of the best in the world, with Ch. "Brendon Gold Standard" and Ch. "Brendon Beryl" with "Boomerang". Notice the ears and heads.

By courtesy]   [E. C. Ash.
"OLD DUTCH'
The property of Mr. Hink, who made the
modern type of Bull Terrier. "Old Dutch"
was the best he ever had.

By courtesy]   [E. C. Ash.
"NELSON".
In 1872 Mr. S. E. Shirley, President of the
Kennel Club, bred Bull Terriers, and his
"Nelson" was considered to be an out-
standing example,

But this difficulty was rapidly and successfully tackled by breeders, and to-day the smart, naturally pricked ear is almost universal.

The introduction of quality into this breed has effected such progress that, both in appearance and characteristics, the Bull Terrier of to-day rightly has more friends than at any previous period in his history. From the point of view of looks, it is difficult to find a dog that satisfies the eye more completely than does the perfectly balanced Bull Terrier, standing as he does, or should, on the tips of his toes, with every steel-like muscle taut, his piercing little eyes and his tight-fitting skin combining with the proud lift of

practical demonstration of the error of these views, and from that day the white Bull Terrier has steadily established and increased his excellence and his popularity.

Only when cropping of the ears was barred about 1895 was the success of the new breed threatened for since the new dog was eminently both gladiator and terrier, alertness of appearance was essential.

his head to intensify a picture of perfect physical fitness.

It is, however, the Bull Terrier's serenity of character and his unexpected gentleness that command respect and provide his greatest charm. Though he is possessed of invincible courage, he is rarely the aggressor in a fight, and to this slowness to anger, this lack of "nerves", is due the fact that he is probably the only terrier never known to snap; indeed, there is no breed of dog to whom the word "treacherous" is less applicable. Though his strength is exceptional, he makes the gentlest use of it. The stronger the dog the gentler and more reliable he seems with all young things, whether they possess two legs or four; and it is probably just because the Bull Terrier has the blood of a thousand fighting ancestors in his veins that he can safely be left alone with a baby and will suffer himself to be killed rather than betray his trust.

A gallant, patient, sweet-dispositioned gentleman is this White Cavalier, and some think that he will eventually establish himself as the most desirable Terrier of all in the eyes of those men and women who desire their dog to be a staunch friend, a true sportsman and an indomitable protector. Nor is he any less human and lovable because he is sentimental; and, being little given to barking, he has silence as well as

By courtesy]   [E. C. Ash.
THREE NOTED BULL TERRIERS OF YESTERDAY.
Mr. W. I. Pegg had a very strong winning kennel of Bull Terriers and was one of the
most successful breeders. Here is his "Sherborne Queen", "Woodcote Teaser" and
"Woodcote Tartar", at the end of the nineteenth century.

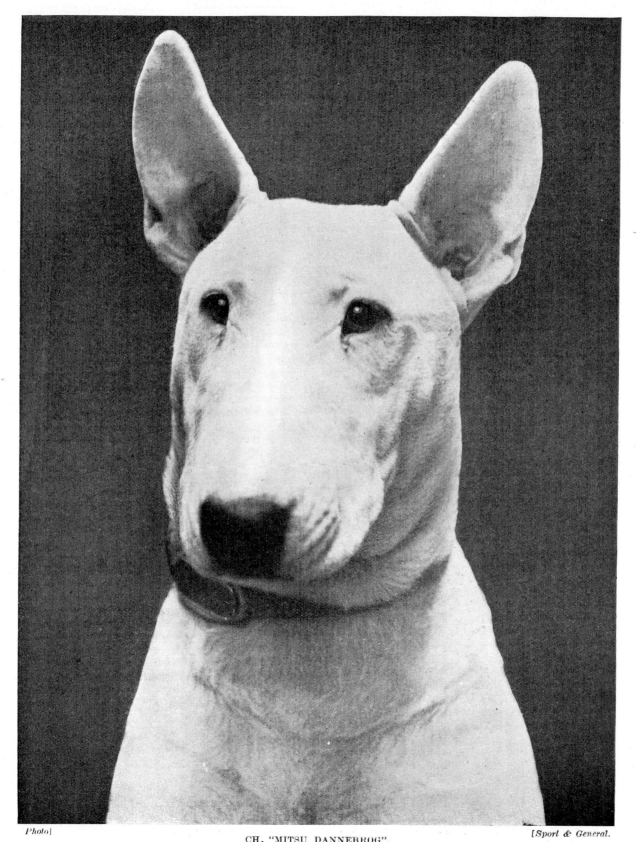

Photo]   CH. "MITSU DANNEBROG".   [*Sport & General.*
Here we have the typical head of the Bull Terrier of 1934.   The dog was bred by Major Mitford Brice.   The reader's attention is
drawn to the head of "Old Dutch" opposite.

strength to commend him. A hardy healthy active lovable old fellow.

As material for future building the breed is fortunate in the continuance of famous strains and the possession of breeders of wide and established experience. No summary of Bull Terrier history would be complete without some reference to

By courtesy]   [E. C. Ash.
BULL TERRIER MINIATURE.
At the end of the nineteenth century Bull Terrier Miniatures were very popular and weighed from 4 to 8lb., and had the characteristics of the larger dog. To-day as the illustrations in this work show, attempts are being made to rebuild the variety.

Her Ch. "Rhoma" became the best Bull Terrier of modern times, whose usefulness to the breed is exemplified by the fact that she gave birth to four champions. For this peerless bitch Mrs. Adlam refused £250.

Other famous breeders are Mr. Carleton Hinks, grandson of the founder of the white Bull Terrier; Mrs. D. H. Robbs,

that fine old gentleman, Mr. Fred North, in whose character unvarying courtesy and utter devotion to the breed are there for all to see. It is not easy to speak, without being fulsome, of a man who showed his first dog in 1884 : who exhibited at St. Stephen's Hall at the first Cruft's show ever held ; who has owned a score of Champions who in 1933, at the age of 75, had a desperate illness, and who on recovery exhibited and handled at every available show ; who through all these years never found it possible to speak an unjust word of any man, and never failed to give encouragement to newcomers. Mr. North has

whose Cylva strain has contributed more towards the introduction of quality than any other factor, and whose judgment is unsurpassed ; Mr. W. J. Tuck of the Gladiator prefix, and through whose hands have passed many of the most famous dogs of olden times ; Dr. G. M. Vevers, of "Regent" renown ; Mr. H. K. McCausland, so quick at spotting promising youngsters ; Colonel and Mrs. Baldrey ; and Mrs. S. G. Yearsley, whose Ch. 'Black Coffee' is, in the opinion of many, the best dog of his period. There are also many others scarcely less renowned : to Miss M. L. Grey is due a real debt of gratitude for her Northumberland-

a fine record, at all times a magnificent loser and a modest winner, and by the strength and charm of his character, commanding respect where others could not.

In Mrs Adlam, of the Brendon Kennels, the breed has been equally fortunate, for her helpfulness has become proverbial and her support of the Bull Terrier invaluable

By courtesy]   [E. C. Ash.
OF MORE THAN ORDINARY EXCELLENCE
Ch. "Green-hill Wonder" was one of Mr. C. P. Lea's winning Bull Terriers at the end of the nineteenth century. She is described by Mr. Rawden Lee to have been of more than ordinary excellence.

bred Howsden dogs, while without Mr. Tom Gannaway the breed would lose half its attraction.

Distinguished dogs are less easy to enumerate if only because the degree of distinction must inevitably be a matter of opinion. But since 1929 the following may be said to have been outstanding amongst dogs : Ch. "Classical Cotton":

Photo]   *[Sport & General.*

GOING UP FOR JUDGMENT.

Whilst in the olden days dogs travelled in boxes, baskets, and even sacks to the various shows and newspaper correspondents went to them in fear and trembling, to-day they go on their way in cars, as do these Bull Terriers, "Jerry" and "Peg of Judington", the property of Mrs. Phillips.

CH. "RHOMA".

Although Bull Terrier fanciers usually prefer a pure white dog, and much colour places it among the Staffordshires, a patch round the eye is allowed, though at one time this created ill-feeling—so much so that one noted dog is reported to have been poisoned by an irritated rival breeder.

Ch. "Regent Juno"; Ch. "Brendon Becky"; Ch. "Mitsu Dannebrog", who at 7½ months won her first Certificate at the Great Joint Terrier Show where Bull Terriers topped the entry with a record of 223; Ch. "Brendon Barbed Wire" and Ch. "Isis 10". Amongst many celebrities whom I must necessarily omit are a number who have achieved fame abroad after exportation, chiefly animals from the kennels of Mrs. Adlam, Mrs. Robbs, and Mr. McCausland.

Miniature Bull Terriers up to 18 lb. have displayed a slight but not very decided improvement, and in the case of these small specimens there still seems to be some difficulty in approximating the real Bull Terrier type. Poor head qualities, and the lack of that fire that is so essential a feature of the breed, appear to stamp this variety; although the brindle miniature "Lone Knight" must be exempted from these two criticisms.

Present events abundantly show that the coloured Bull Terrier is not only achieving a wide popularity but is improving in quality, although it has to be admitted that his quality is at present far from equalling that of the whites; nevertheless, much is being accomplished in that direction. It is to be feared that the coloured dogs are, generally

Ch. "Howsden Bailfire"; Ch. "Beshelson Bayshuck"; Ch. "Num Skull," the possessor of a phenomenal head and the winner of countless certificates; Ch. "Ringfire of Blighty"; Ch. "Black Coffee"; Ch. "Brendon Gold Standard". Of a large number of successful stud dogs, I have only space to quote "Galalaw General", Ch. "Cylva General", "Regent Pluto" and "The Sheik of Chartham".

Outstanding amongst bitches during the same period are the following: Ch. "Silver Belle," a perfect but unusually small specimen; Ch. "Trafgar Winalot"; Ch. "Lady Winifred", the first and so far only coloured champion, although there is no doubt that, had he lived, the magnificent red dog "Hunting Blondi" must have achieved champion status; Ch. "Rhoma", in my opinion the queen of them all; Ch. "Pamela Skellum";

Photo]   *[Fall.*

CH. "BUTTERFLY WHITE BUD".

That the breed has not altered in recent years except to acquire greater quality may be noticed by comparing this champion of past days with dogs illustrated on other pages.

speaking, less reliable in temper than the whites, and the multiplicity of colours offers a problem that will require attention before long. Brindle dogs are acceptable ; red dogs are understandable ; but parti-coloured dogs of black-and-tan-and-white and other variations of the rainbow are as difficult to harness to the imagination as is the rainbow to the earth. Nevertheless, from the show point of view these dogs must be judged as Bull Terriers, and should not be penalized for any eccentricity of colour scheme.

But whether immaculately white or handsomely brindle, to those who desire their dog to be in no sense commonplace ; to those who want him to be a staunch friend, a true sportsman and a courageous defender ; and to those who require that their pet should combine strength with endurance, gentleness with friendship, and protection with loyalty, the Bull Terrier is confidently commended.

POINTS OF THE BULL TERRIER.

TYPE.—The Bull Terrier is the gladiator of the canine race, and should be a strongly built, muscular, active, symmetrical animal, with a keen, determined expression. Full of fire, but of sweet disposition and amenable to discipline.

THE HEAD.—Almost egg-shaped. Fairly long provided strength is not sacrificed to length. Deep, but not too wide or coarse. Cheek muscles not prominent. The profile, without a stop, should be almost an arc from occiput to nose.

The forehead fairly flat and shorter than the foreface. The foreface filled right up to the eyes. The muzzle strong, with deep underjaw and tight lips. Teeth even. The undershot jaw of the Bulldog is anathema. Ears small and erect on top of the skull. Eyes are most important, as giving the character of the breed. These should be small, well sunken, and dark ; and they should be almond-shaped or triangular and placed obliquely and close together, nearer the ears than the nose. The resulting expression should be a piercing, rather wicked glint. A soft expression in a Bull Terrier is as inappropriate as scented hair on a boxer.

THE NECK should be moderately long, tapering from shoulders to head. Muscular, arched, and free from throatiness.

THE SHOULDERS strong and muscular but not heavy. Shoulder blades wide, flat and sloping well back. No dip at withers.

THE CHEST broad viewed from the front and deep from withers to brisket.

THE BODY should have well-sprung ribs ; a short, strong and muscular back ; and only a slight arch at loin.

THE LEGS should be strong boned but not coarse, the front legs not too high and perfectly straight. A Bull Terrier should stand well on his feet and be low to ground. The elbows must not turn outwards and the pasterns must be strong and upright.

A PROMINENT SPORTSMAN.
Sir Harry Preston, a great lover of dogs, always had a special liking for the Bull Terrier and has here posed for his photograph with his favourite dog.

CH. "BRENDON BERYL".

This is one of Mrs. Adlam's noted bitches, and its longer legs and general difference in build will be recognized in comparison with "Num Skull".

THE FEET should be cat's feet, round and compact, with the toes well arched.

THE TAIL is required to be short, tapering, set on low, and carried horizontally.

THE COAT has to be short, flat, rather harsh, but with a fine gloss. A Bull Terrier's skin should fit him tightly.

COLOUR for whites is pure white, with the exception of permissible markings on the head. Markings behind the set-on of head are disqualifications.

FAULTS OF THE BULL TERRIER.

Light bone. Legginess. Soft expression. Badly placed eyes. Light eyes. Domed skull. Butterfly nose. Pronounced cheekiness. Dish-faced. Lippiness. Throatiness. Unevenly meeting teeth. Long and slack back. Long, thick and gay tail. Loose shoulders. Loaded shoulders. Crooked elbows. Weak pasterns. Cow-hocks Big and splay feet. Toes turning either in or out. Soft coat. Long coat. Narrow chest. Flat sides. Ewe neck. Ticked coat.

DISQUALIFICATIONS.

Deafness. Wall-eye. Wholly flesh-coloured nose. Markings behind the set-on of head.

Bull Terrier (Coloured).—The Coloureds are descended from the old breed of Staffordshire Bull Terriers, and from the modern Pure White Bull Terrier. The Staffordshire was bred to fight in the pits in the days when staged dog-fights were a national amusement. They were much smaller and lighter than the modern White Bull Terrier, and entirely different in type, having short heads and thick skulls. They were all colours; every shade of brindle and brindle-and-white, fawn and fawn-and-white, seem to have been the most common.

The Pure White Bull Terrier was standardized many years ago by the late Mr. James Hinks, of Birmingham, and has now been bred to a high state of perfection. It was the blending of these two, the Pure White and the Staffordshire, that produced the modern Coloured Bull Terrier.

The breeder's ideal is a dog as good in type and quality as the best Pure White, but with the Coloured coat of the Staffordshire. To do this, the best Staffordshires available were mated to the finest Pure Whites. The results were an immediate improvement in type. Again, the

CH. "NUM SKULL".

It is difficult in a few words to describe the correct Bull Terrier and just as difficult to point the faults of an excellent specimen. Even champions vary to some extent, as will be seen if we compare Mr. H. L. Summer's "Num Skull" with the picture above.

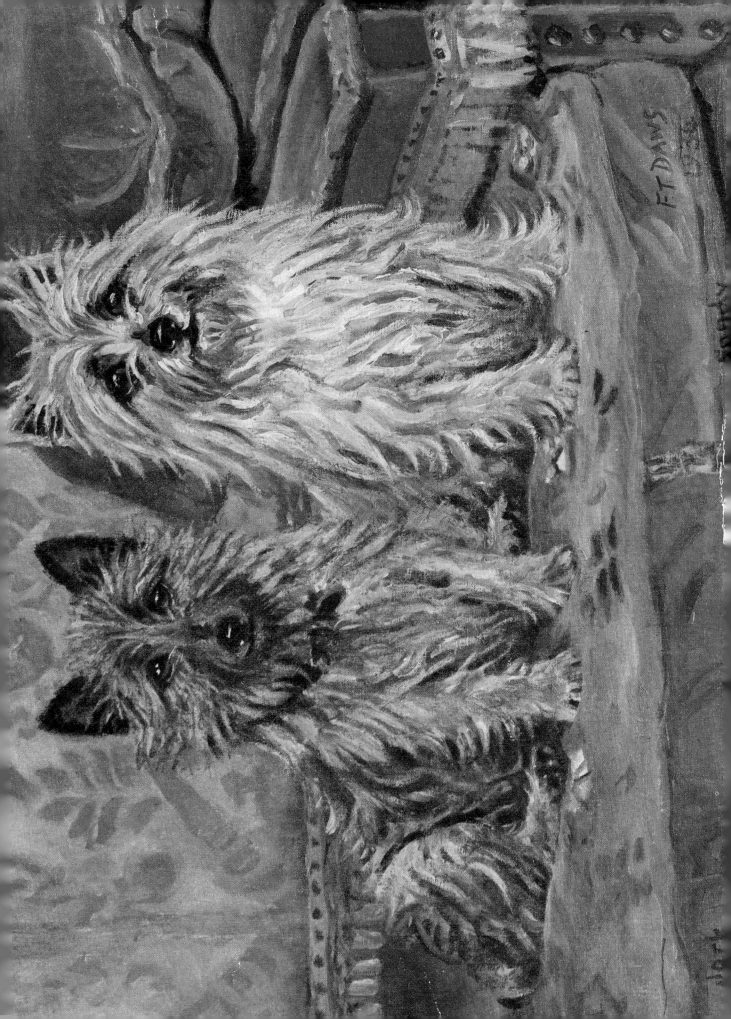

CAIRNS OF DISTINCTION.

(Specially painted for this work by F. T. Daws.)

This well-known animal artist has here caught the alert and friendly expression of two delightful Cairns, both excellent specimens of the breed.

"JOCK" IS THE PROPERTY OF LADY HUTCHINSON, AND "SANDY" BELONGS TO MRS. WALTER HUTCHINSON, WIFE OF THE EDITOR (WHO IS CHAIRMAN OF THE WELL-KNOWN PUBLISHING COMPANY, and its many Associated Printing and Publishing Concerns throughout the Country).

Photo]   [L.N.

A TEAM.

There is nothing very much nicer than to see several dogs of the same variety standing side by side, and it is particularly interesting in a breed such as the Bull Terrier, for it allows comparison. Mrs. Yearsley's Bull Terriers are seen here.

-most typical specimen was selected, and again mated to a quality dog, and so on. But it was not a fast improvement, as breeders had continually to return to the Staffordshire for the desired colour, so losing a little of the type already gained.

The first Coloured dog to win a Kennel Club Challenge Certificate was "Bing Boy", a brindle-and-white, bred by Mr. Sievier. He won his first Certificate under Count V. C. Hollender at the Great Joint Terrier Show in 1919, and a second later on. The next Coloured to make a name on the show bench against the pick of the Whites was Mr. Dockerill's Ch. "Lady Winifred", an outstanding brindle-and-white bitch This was ten years after "Bing Boy". She won her first Certificate in 1929 at the Great Joint Terrier Show under Major Owen Swaffield, her second at the National Terrier Show in 1931, and her third at Cruft's in 1931. She thus became a full champion, and at that time was the only Coloured dog or bitch to have this achievement to her credit. The third outstanding Coloured to be benched, and in the opinion of many the best ever seen, was a brilliant red-and-white dog, "Hunting Blondi", bred by Mrs. Ellis. He won his first Certificate at the National Terrier Championship Show under Count V. C. Hollender, and a second at Taunton under Major Owen Swaffield. He was Reserve for the Certificates at Cruft's, and at the Great Joint Terrier Show in 1931. He would undoubtedly have

By courtesy]   [E. C. Ash.
ONE OF THE BEST.
Breeders are striving for perfection as seen by this specimen.

Photo]   [Sport and General.
BULL TERRIER TYPE.
"Cylvia Bubbles", the property of Mr. F. North shows clearly the Bull Terrier type.

become a full champion but for his death when under two years of age. His early death was a misfortune to the Coloureds as he would have been a valuable sire.

The fourth Coloured dog who deserves special mention is Mr. J. S. Symes' brindle dog, "Nelstan Cotton". This dog won a Certificate at the Metropolitan and Essex Championship Show in 1932, under Count V. C. Hollender, and was Reserve for the honour at Manchester Championship Show in 1933. He holds a very fine show record—shown against the Whites as well as in Coloured classes, he has never, with the exception of one occasion, been unplaced at Championship and Open Shows. He has also done well at stud, Mr. R. H. Glyn's "Tigress of Blighty" (brindle) and Miss P. K. Timins' "Boko's Double" (brindle-and-white) both big winners, owning him as sire.

Other present-day brindle dogs worthy of mention, who have made names for themselves in the show-ring, and who are further proving their worth as successful sires are: Mrs. Horton's "Batchworth Barrister" (brindle-and-white), Mrs. Robbs' "Tiger of Blighty" (brindle), Captain and Mrs. Strettell's "Cheddington Warrior" (brindle-and-white, litter brother to "Nelstan Cotton") and Miss D. Montague Johnstone's "Romany Radium" (brindle-and-white).

At one time it was not easy to get Coloured classes scheduled, even at the major events, and the breeders themselves had to guarantee to pay any losses which might be incurred through lack

Photo]   [Fall.
CH. "BRENDON GOLD STANDARD".
This dog, the property of Mrs. Adlam, is claimed to have been the most typical and up-to-date Bull Terrier in 1933.

of entries. And pay they nearly always did as at that time there were rarely sufficient dogs benched to cover the prize money. It is at this point in the development of the breed that breeders really started to study seriously the question of colour ratios; how to produce the particular colours they wanted without sacrificing type or quality. The breed as a whole had advanced very definitely in type, and quality generally was noticeably improved. Show specimens were still few in number, but the general type was such that there was no question of having to go back to the Staffordshire again. There was plenty of Coloured dogs, Colour-bred—not Staffordshire-bred—available for breeding. Careful study of the law of colour inheritance and the keeping of very accurate records brought the following invaluable facts to light:

On Producing the colour Brindle—Breeders are almost unanimous in agreeing that the brindle colour is the most desirable. The specification of a Coloured Bull Terrier is "Any Colour, other than White," and "White not to Predominate". This means that show Coloureds can be any colour: brindle, brindle-and-white, red, red-and-white, tawn, fawn-and-white, black, black-and-white, providing only that the colours, and not the white markings, shall predominate. Actually, brindle and brindle-and-white are unquestionably

Photo]   [*Fall.*
CH. "BRENDON BERYL".
A head-study of this well-known champion, bred by Mrs. Adlam. Notice the eye expression and shape of head.

the most popular from the show point of view, and are undoubtedly, as will be shown, the most valuable for breeding purposes. The all important fact now put forward with regard to this colour is. That to breed brindles, it is necessary that one of the parents should be brindle. Until this theory was made known, it was considered quite possible to get brindle puppies from two parents, neither of which were brindles themselves, but which were brindle-bred. Example: If the sire used was red, out of brindle parents, and the bitch also red (or fawn or black), but also out of one or two brindle parents, it was considered quite reasonable to expect a proportion of brindle puppies in the resulting litter, especially as it is known that puppies frequently resemble their grandparents considerably more than their sire and

Photo]   [*Fall.*
CH. "BRENDON BARBED WIRE".
On page 253 we give the head of this dog and here is a picture of him showing his remarkable type. His shoulders neck body and chest are particularly fine.

"BRENDON BLONDE VENUS".

Bred by Mrs. Adlam and owned by Captain Goldsmith, "Blonde Venus" in 1934 was considered one of the best Coloured Bull Terrier bitches exhibited.

"BRENDON DRAGON".

Mrs. G. M. Adlam's remarkable brindle dog won the Lady Winifred Challenge Cup for the best Coloured Bull Terrier at Cruft's in 1934.

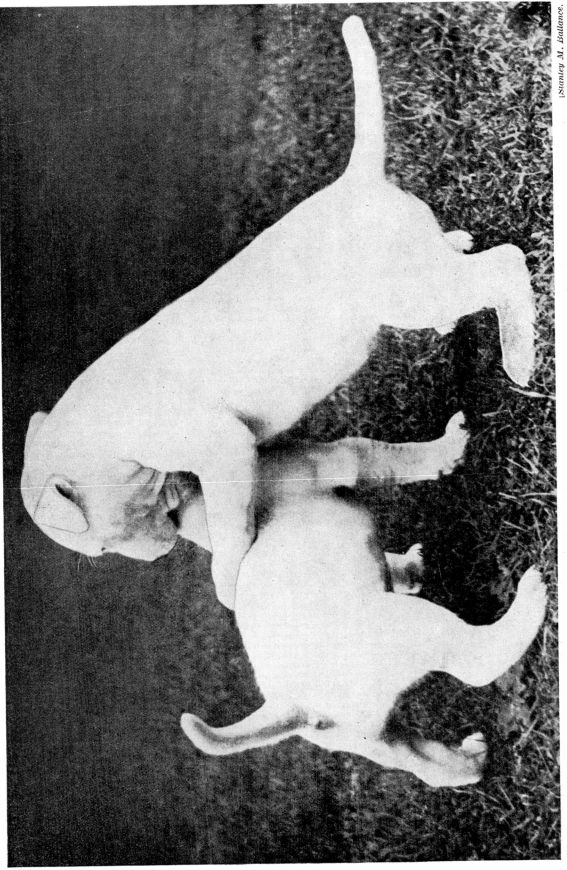

Photo]

[Stanley M. Ballance.

PUPPY DAYS.

Two Bull Terrier puppies, owned by Mr. Dugald McGregor—one showing a good type of head—are playing together and taking it very seriously.

dam. In practice, however, it is not so. Miss Montague Johnstone, who has kept accurate records of all matings, has never yet bred or seen a brindle puppy produced from two non-brindle parents.

Breeders should make it a firm rule to use one brindle parent in all their matings. Not to do so is to ask for disappointment. The fact is stressed here, as novices taking up the breed without this knowledge would become disappointed and discouraged at their inability to breed this most popular and most saleable colour. It is also necessary for the good of the breed, as constant and continual non-brindle matings carried on on a large scale would in time result in the loss of the brindle colour, since it is by far the most elusive.

It has been proved, by a survey of hundreds of litters, that the brindle colour does not appear in equal ratio to the others, but considerably less often. Reds and fawns appear almost exactly as calculated. Black, being the strongest colour of all, appears more often.

Reds, and Red-and-Whites.—This colour comes second in popularity to the brindle. Although not quite so popular in the show-ring, it runs a very close second with the general public. The ideal shade is a bright red, similar to the summer coat

EXPRESSION.
The head of "Cylvia Brigadier", Mr. Robb's Bull Terrier, shows clearly the expression of uncertainty.

on a chestnut horse, and it should look glossy and shining. The almost whole-colour red has nearly always a blackish mask, and is sometimes called a "red-smut". The red-and-white often shows no sign of a darker face colour, but carries instead a white blaze, with white chest and feet. A common fault of the reds is a light amber-coloured eye. This is to be avoided on breeding animals, as it is frequently passed on. It is a thoroughly bad fault, and spoils the typical expression. On the other hand, a brilliant red, with really dark little eye, is most attractive, and has many admirers. The reds are not difficult to breed, as they can be produced from any colour combination : brindle to brindle, brindle to red, black or white ; red to red, or to white, black or fawn ; fawn to any colour, etc., can all produce reds. Care should be taken not to introduce too much white blood, as in this case the red will lose its brightness and become pale and washed-out looking.

Fawns, Fawn-and-Whites, Fawn-Smuts.—These can be produced similarly to the reds, from any combination of colours, and appear in about equal quantities to the reds.

Blacks, Black-and-Whites, Black-Brindles, Tri-Colours. — This class is not so popular as the

THE BLACK EYE.
Black eyes caused no little trouble in olden days but nowadays a black eye is no longer a subject of dispute. Ch. "Brendon Barbed Wire" is one of Mrs. Adlam's famous dogs.

others, but can be very striking in appearance, and has quite a following. The coat should shine like black satin, and a dark eye is absolutely essential. A light eye shows up on this colour more than any other and is an abomination. It is doubtful if there is a completely black dog, though several breeders have been trying to produce an all-black specimen, and very handsome he would be. They are usually either black with white points, or black with white points and brindling on the cheeks and legs (black brindle), or tricolour (black, with white markings and tan points). It is interesting and important to note that the black-brindles can pass the brindle factor to their progeny, when mated to other-than - brindle bitches. The black - brindle should there-fore always be chosen for breeding purposes when breeding from blacks, as they can rank as brindles from the breeding point of view, though they will also undoubtedly produce a large proportion of their own colour. They are the easiest colour of all to breed, and turn up in large quantities in matings of all and every colour combination. Curiously enough, the more Pure White blood introduced, the greater the number of blacks produced. If one of the parents used is a Pure White, and the other parent fifty per cent white-bred, a good proportion of the resulting litter will almost certainly be black. The fact that the Pure White parent has no blacks in his pedigree, and that the other parent has none for generations will not alter the fact. While dealing with this colour, mention must be made of Mrs. E. Mallam's outstanding black-brindle dog, "Isis Nap". He won a Challenge Certificate at Taunton Championship Show in 1933 under Mr. Holgate, and is the first of his colour to win a Certificate. He was Best Coloured Bull Terrier at the Great Joint Terrier Championship Show 1933, under Mr. P B

Grain, and has distinguished himself elsewhere, only once being beaten by another Coloured dog.

Colour - Bred Whites.—"Colour-Bred Whites" is the name given to the white puppies which appear in large or small quantities in many litters produced by Coloured dogs. Every well-bred Coloured is more or less closely related to the Pure Whites, for, as already stated, the Coloured breeders use as much Pure White blood as is possible (without losing the coloured coat) in order to improve the type of their stock. It was thought, quite naturally, that the Colour-bred White, when mated to a Coloured dog, would produce a greater proportion of Coloured puppies in her litters than would a Pure White bitch. Some breeders are still of this opinion, but they cannot be certain. It is stated, by those who have studied the question, that the Colour-bred White breeds true to its coat, and when mated to Pure Whites never produces anything but white puppies. This leads one to imagine that, mated to a Coloured, it would still breed true to its coat, and

Photo]   "WURRICOE".   [*Walter Guiver.*

The Coloured Bull Terrier Miniature seems to be more of the Bull Terrier type than the White Bull Terrier Miniature.

that the Coloured puppies in the litter owed their colour to the other parent. The whole question is still being investigated, and is as yet extremely vague. It is not advisable (in Miss Johnstone's opinion, though some breeders disagree) to keep these white puppies, except, of course, for experimental purposes. They are neither one thing or the other. They are obviously not as valuable as their Coloured litter brothers and sisters to the Coloured breeder, and the breeder of Pure Whites does not want them.

The Value of the Pure Whites in Breeding Show Coloureds, and the Disadvantages of Using them to Excess. — The Pure Whites are at a higher state of perfection as a whole than are the Coloured dogs. We therefore use them to lift the general type of the Coloureds up to their higher

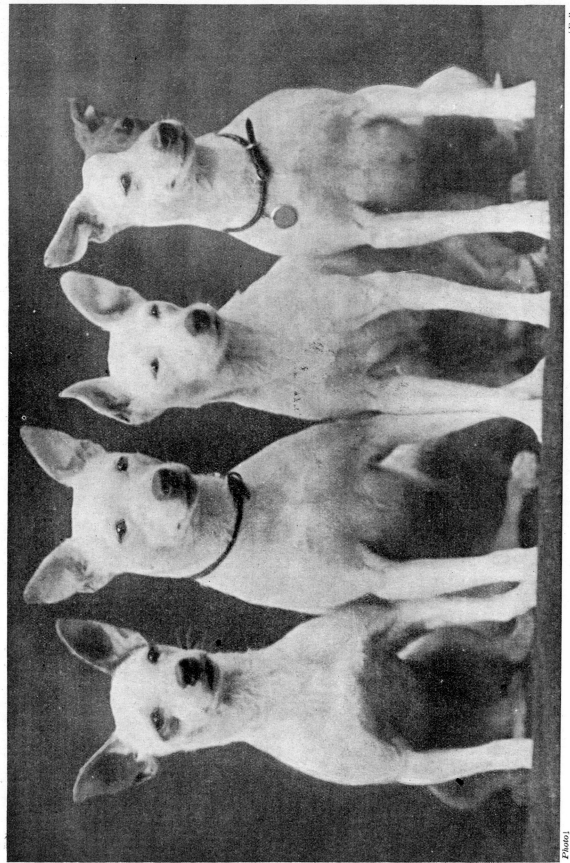

MINIATURE BULL TERRIERS.

Attempts have been made to re-establish the Miniature Bull Terrier, so popular at one time, and here we have some of the breed prominent in 1933.

Photo] "ISIS NAP". [Fall.

This is Mrs. Ernest Mallam's fine coloured Bull Terrier "Isis Nap", a very useful specimen.

Photo] "BETTER LATE THAN NEVER !" [Fall.

The alert expression of the Bull Terrier is here in evidence. Could a dog's face exhibit more expression ?

level. Quality, we know, will be improved, but there are disadvantages if used too often : (1) We get too many Colour-bred Whites. (2) We get a far greater proportion of Blacks than we want. (3) We lose the Brindle colour. (4) The Coloured puppies that we do get will be badly marked, with too much white on them, such as white splashes on the back behind the shoulders, completely white face, etc., so that it can hardly be said of them with truth that white does not predominate. (5) The Reds and Fawns will lose their brightness and become pale and washed out. As soon as the breeder notices any of the above faults in his stock,

he should immediately put his bitches back to the best Coloured dog (preferably brindle) that he can find, and if he can find one to suit his bitch that is Colour-bred on both sides, as well as being Coloured himself, so much the better. He will then get back to properly marked, bright-coloured puppies, but of good type, since they are closely related to Pure Whites. It is better that the sire should be the White parent rather than the dam, when using a Pure White. A Coloured bitch, mated to a White, seems to produce a greater proportion of Coloured puppies, better marked, than vice versa.

Bumpy.—With protuberant cheeks.

Burmese Wild Dog.—This dog closely resembles the Malay Wild Dog, but is more strongly built. It appears to be one of a group of which the Indian Wild Dog and the Malay Wild Dog are part. The Burmese Wild Dog was found in Upper Burma.

Burns and Scalds.—CAUSES : Moist heat, such as boiling water, melted tar or wax, etc. ; dry heat, such as flame, hot cinders or pokers, or contact with hot cooking stoves. Also strong mineral acids, and unslaked lime.

SYMPTOMS.—The severity of the symptoms will depend, naturally, upon the intensity or degree of heat applied ; or in the case of acids, etc., upon the concentration of the acid or the length of time it remains in contact with the tissues.

Slight burns or scalds may produce little worse than redness and some tenderness of the part ; but with burns of greater intensity there is a dermatitis (or inflammation of the skin) set up ; whilst after severe burns blister formation will undoubtedly occur and in most cases the roots of the hairs are

A CONSISTENT WINNER.

"Nightrider's Bronx Cocktail" won many prizes between 1927–1932. Three of his sons were exported to India.

MRS. MONTAGUE STURRIDGE AND HER BULL TERRIER.

Once upon a time the Bull Terrier was a breed debarred from society because it was associated with the gamester, pugilist and dog-fighter; but to-day the Bull Terrier is a member in leading households.

destroyed. These blisters may run together and cover large areas. They eventually rupture, and the escaping fluid dries into scabs which should be allowed to remain in order to protect the raw surface beneath. Sometimes infection takes place, as a result of which a varying degree of suppuration follows.

In many bad cases of burning a considerable amount of shock is sustained and when the area burned or scalded is extensive, death is usual, preceded by vomiting, convulsions and collapse.

Photo   BUTTON-EAR.   Ralph Robinson.

Three of Miss Thelma Evans's Corgis. The Welsh Corgi puppy on the right shows what is known as the Button-Ear, that is to say, the ear drops over in front, covering the inner cavity The ear will turn up later.

to resemble the ears of Fox Terriers or Irish Terriers, it is called a button-ear. It is common to find puppies belonging to breeds (such as Alsatians) which should have erect ears, showing one or both ears dropped. As the months go by, in some cases, without the ears showing the least sign of becoming erect, the matter becomes one of great concern to the owner of an otherwise perfect specimen of its breed. Generally, if a button-ear is ever becoming erect, it will do so by about the ninth month of age.

TREATMENT.—The first aid treatment is to clean the burn, rendering it free from dirt, straw, hair and other extraneous substances. Then, as quickly as possible, to preclude all air from it by dressing it with suitable applications and covering with dry cotton wool and perhaps a loose bandage. The applications most commonly used are carron oil, linseed oil mixed with beaten egg, olive oil, medicinal paraffin, vaseline, powdered starch, flour, boracic acid, etc. Spraying, through an atomizer, with a solution of tannic acid is the newest and best remedy.

For the alleviation of pain, pure turpentine may be dabbed frequently on the lesion ; or possibly an anaesthetic ointment could be obtained from the chemist. When the blisters become broken, the drying powders mentioned above may be employed. In all cases of severe burning, a veterinary surgeon should be sent for, as one never knows whether the result will or will not be fatal. This having been done, and pending his arrival, the owner may treat any sign of collapse or shock with brandy.

Burns by Acid are treated by immediately washing away the acid with a solution of washing soda or some other alkali to neutralize the acid ; then by applying one of the remedies already mentioned. Do not apply oil of any sort until the acid has first been thoroughly washed off with alkali.

Burr.—The inside of the ear.

Butterfly Dog. (*See* PAPILLON.)

Butterfly-Nose.—A term used to indicate a spotted or mottled nose, the black pigment being absent in small areas or spots. It is distinguished from a "Dudley-nose" in that the latter is flesh-coloured all over.

Button-Ear.—When an ear, which normally should stand erect, falls over in a forward direction

The cause of the abnormality is thought to be a weakness of the muscle, cartilage, or nerve supply of the ear, or of all three, and the remedy usually lies in toning up the body generally, or, in other words, improving the general health. This is accompanied by rational feeding, regular exercise, supplying every essential vitamin, exposure to sunlight, and perhaps the administration of a good tonic such as Parrish's Food over two or three weeks. Finally, the ear should be reinforced across the cartilage where the latter bends over, by sticking short strips of adhesive tape to the inner surface of the ear flap. If this is carefully done, the effect will be to make the ear-flap rigid and upright, and in course of time all the tissues concerned will adapt themselves to this new shape. From time to time the supporting strips require warming and gentle removal, as it will be found that, as the few fine hairs grow, they tend to make the tape loose. New pieces must then be applied. It is usual to affix two strips of tape in a horizontal direction, i.e. along the line of the bend in the cartilage, and two other strips converging from the base to the apex of the ear.

Buying a Dog.—The average householder, or novice in doggy matters, is invariably in a quandary as regards where or how to buy a dog, and there is no doubt but that a good deal of thought should be devoted to the matter in order that the purchaser may not be "sold a pup", so to speak.

To purchase a dog from a "Home for Lost Dogs" is invariably to purchase trouble, as it is a practical impossibility for the management of any such concern to keep out infection of any kind. One has in mind, of course, distemper ; but should the dog bought be of middle age, it may already have contracted this disease and have acquired an immunity against a further attack.

Generally, therefore, dogs brought to the home from such institutions, should first undergo a veterinary examination, and secondly a week's isolation from all other canine members of the household.

To purchase a dog from the average dog-shop is a proceeding largely attended with risk, and in every such case the small cost of having a veterinary examination and certificate of health will be abundantly repaid. It is, however, only fair to say that so far as the animal departments of some of the large London stores are concerned, infinite pains are taken to ensure that none but a healthy and saleable dog shall be offered to the public.

In one or two of these large stores, all dogs are examined by the firm's own veterinary surgeon before such are accepted for sale.

At the same time, it should be understood that the veterinary surgeon can only certify in accordance with what he sees at the time of examination, and neither he nor the shop proprietor can justly be held responsible for what may happen some days after purchase. There is a period of incubation in all diseases, and it sometimes happens that a dog changes ownership during such period.

Possibly the last alternative may be the best, that is, to deal direct with the breeder. If this is done, the buyer should visit the seller's premises and endeavour to see all the dogs in the place, in order that he may discover for himself if any one of them is sick. Dealing privately with an individual makes it a simple matter to draw up special terms regarding the return of a dog should it prove in any way unsuitable.

Dogs are always more expensive than bitches, and those which have reached about six months of age are naturally worth more than young puppies. So far as cost is concerned, it must be remembered that a puppy is not

weaned until it is six weeks old, and that during those six weeks special foods have had to be supplied and much care and time have had to be devoted to the bitch and her whelps. Thus, even at two months of age, the most ordinary crossbred has entailed as much expenditure in its upbringing as would have been requisite in the case of a pure-bred specimen. Nobody, therefore, should expect to be able to purchase the veriest mongrel at that age under £2. From the breeder's point of view, however, since it costs no more to feed and house pure-bred stock, it is a far saner plan to leave the common stock alone and demand such prices for his puppies as will give him an adequate profit for his labour. So we find that at two months of age a well-bred puppy will probably sell at about £4 4s., though naturally the price must be governed by the excellence or otherwise of the pedigree.

The price of a puppy is enhanced if the latter has been house-trained, and especially if it has been inoculated against distemper. (*See* CHOOSING A DOG: HEALTH, SIGNS OF.)

But remember that although show points and type are important, and pedigree is also something to study in making your choice, that the most valuable thing to buy is good health, for nothing else can make up for that. All Mopy Dicks ought to be looked upon with much suspicion, for such a dog may indeed be constitutionally unsound and be, in consequence of this, a trouble and expense and very little pleasure. You may say that a puppy can and will indeed grow out of this condition of "dopiness", or that it may be due to worms or other causes that can be eradicated. Although this is so, it is always well to make it a rule to start right, to buy a dog free from troubles, rather than buy one that has already something wrong with it. The jolly puppy and the active one is the type to buy!

Photo]   *[E. O. Hoppé.*

FOR SALE.

The selling of puppies in the street is a sight of London. Here every pocket may contain a puppy or something of doggie interest. The salesmen are often fanciers and are allowed to "tell the tale".

C

Caecum.—A blind pouch of intestine situated at the ileocaecal valve—a point where the small bowel ends and the colon begins. In the dog it is generally not more than about three-quarters of an inch long. Its function, if any, has not been discovered; but it certainly never causes the dog any trouble.

Caesarian Section.—An operation named after Caesar, whose birth was alleged to have been affected by its agency. It consists in the opening of the

from the dam an impossibility. Canine surgeons have found that hysterectomy is attended by less risk to the mother' life.

Cairn Terrier.—When the late Dr. Gordon Stables, R.N., was touring the Highlands of Scotland by caravan, in 1878, keen observer as he was of dogs, he wrote a charming set of verses in dialect in which he referred to the "Terrier o' the North" than whom "Ye'll search frae Tweed to Sussex

By courtesy]   *[James Garrow.*

CAIRNS OF 1835.

Here possibly is the ancestor of both the present Cairn and the Scottish Terrier, seen at work amongst the rocks after an otter which is attempting to escape.

abdomen, into the wound of which the gravid uterus is brought. This in turn is opened and the foetus removed, after which all wounds are sutured. It is a somewhat difficult and intricate operation, especially in the lower animals, and is undertaken, generally, only when it is considered that birth of the foetus would not be possible in the normal way. Its performance is undoubtedly attended by grave risk to the mother, but not to the offspring. As, among the lower animals, there are sometimes instances in which the progeny would be far more valuable than the dam, this risk is in such cases readily accepted. If we are certain that birth cannot occur via the vagina then the only alternative to Caesarian Section is hysterectomy. The latter involves the amputation of the womb, thus rendering any further breeding

Shore but never find his like." He headed his poem *The Scotch Terrier*.

A more fitting title, however, would have been the Highland Terrier, for he saw this variety of terrier in its original state before it had been introduced to the show bench. The genial doctor was actually describing the Cairn Terrier of the present time, which was not recognized as a distinct variety until thirty-odd years later. The Cairn or Highland Terrier was the tap-root from which sprang the present-day Scottish Terrier, West Highland White Terrier, the Skye Terrier and the Clydesdale Terrier—

260

THE PRINCE'S CAIRN.

H.R.H. The Prince of Wales, like many other members of the Royal Family, is a dog-lover and possesses several excellent specimens. among them two Cairns, one being "Jaggers", a delightful sketch of whom is here reproduced.

H.R.H. THE PRINCESS ROYAL'S CAIRN.

Her Royal Highness the Princess Royal has a favourite Cairn, "Peggy", which is frequently seen in her company.

all of which have been so much bred for exhibition purposes and altered that it takes a big stretch of imagination to think that they all came from the one common source.

There is no question that the Cairn Terrier of the present time comes the nearest to the original Highland Terrier, which was essentially an earth dog whose only vocation in life was the bolting and destroying of foxes, otters, badgers and such-like vermin that abounded in the rocky fastnesses of the rugged Highlands. They were solely in the hands of keepers, whose duty it was to keep these destructive animals in check, and it was their sole aim to keep only such terriers that were able to do the work that was expected of them.

When a new breed of dog takes the public fancy at dog exhibitions, the true index of its popularity can be gauged by

FIDELITY.
A lovable pet is the Cairn. faithful and obedient. This is "Mac", which was a constant and admired companion of Mrs. Walter Hutchinson. The loss of him left a gap—which is the best of all testimonials to his memory.

observing the number of individual specimens registered with the Kennel Club. Both the Scottish Terrier and the West Highland White Terrier received recognition long before the Cairn Terrier, so that the latter was distinctly under a handicap for a time. There has not, however, been any other variety of dog that has so completely captivated the public fancy as the Cairn Terrier, and it has maintained its popularity.

It was recognized by the Kennel Club in 1910, and in 1914 the registrations totalled 191 Cairns against 631 West Highland White Terriers, which were very popular about this time, and 600 Scottish Terriers. For the three years 1928, 1929, and 1930 there were no less than 6,521 Cairns registered against 2,104 West Highland White Terriers and 6,112 Scottish Terriers. During 1933 the popularity of the Scottish Terrier reached its zenith, and there were 3,464 registered; but the Cairn Terrier was not so far behind with 2,768 registrations.

There is no disputing the fact that the history of this Highland Terrier dates far back into the hazy and misty past. Many early writers take note of such a terrier. Johannes Cains in his work *English Dogges*, published in 1576, makes reference to these vermin-killing dogs, and John Lesley, Bishop of Ross, in his *Historie of Scotland from 1436 to 1561* (Edinburgh, 1830), makes mention of a dog of low height which, creeping into subterraneous burrows, routs out foxes, badgers, martens and wild cats from their lurking-places and dens. Webb, in his *Book of Dogs*, comes nearer the mark when he describes two varieties of terriers found on Skye—a long and a short-haired variety. He also mentions an extraordinary strain of Skye Terriers now very real—the small white terrier with light yellow-tipped ears.

The late Lady MacDonald, of Armadale Castle in Skye, was famed for this strain. This is the strain of Skye Terriers which were supposed to be descended from a cross of some Spanish white dogs and the island terriers. The Spanish dogs were cast on to the island when the Spanish Armada was wrecked on the western coast. There is no doubt but that the lairds and landowners found it necessary to keep a pack of terriers to keep otters and foxes down, so as to protect their lambs, etc. The tod- or fox-hunter was known as the brocaire, and he never travelled without his pack of terriers. Sometimes a hound or two was kept to trace the quarry by scent, which was usually run to earth in some huge cairn. It was then the terrier's work began, and they seldom waited for the brocaire's signal of "Staigh Sin". They needed no second command, for they went eagerly to ground, to do or die.

Many a game little bit of dogflesh met its death in these underground fights, and many a one carried his scars proudly to his dying day. These western chiefs and lairds were proud of their terriers and sang their praises at every opportune moment. Thus we find, James, the First of England and Sixth of Scotland, writing to Edinburgh to have half a dozen "earth dogges or Terrieres" sent carefully to France as a present, and he specially ordered that they be sent over in two or more ships, in case any harm should befall them on the voyage to the Continent.

The King also directed that they be got from Argyllshire, so that he seemed to have an intimate knowledge of the gameness of these terriers The

By courtesy]   [*James Garrow.*
EXPRESSION.
The Cairn Terrier expression is a mixture of jolliness and wickedness, with that 'varminty" note so much desired.

Roseneath Terriers were descended from the pack owned by the Duke of Argyll.

Captain Mackie, of Port Bannatyne, made many excursions into the Western Highlands in quest of suitable material for the building up of his famous strain of Scottish Terriers. Captain Mackie bred the famous Scottish Terrier, Ch. "Dundee". He was keenly interested in the evolution of the Scottish Terrier, then in the making, and he left much interesting data regarding the terrier on his native heath. They played an important part in the lives of the men who owned and worked them. Man and dog were closely identified, and the intelligence of the canine was greatly developed through this close intercourse.

One old writer gives an interesting description of how the terriers were worked. He says: "In many districts of Scotland foxes did very considerable damage by pillaging and killing lambs. Lambs, sheep and poultry were frequently taken by them in open day, and I have known as many as twenty lambs slaughtered in one night. I can remember being in a certain Kirk, where after the Sermon and before the Blessing was pronounced the precentor [i.e. a leader of the congregation in the Psalmody of the Scottish Churches] rose up and exclaimed: 'Noo lads, min we're gaun to hunt the Tod [fox] of Tuesday. Be a' up at the Laird's hoose in guid time and Johnny Fraser's comin' with a' his dogs.'"

This last was quite a character in his way. He hailed from Glenlivet. He had a few hounds, large, heavy-headed animals, much resembling in appearance the Irish Wolfhound They were

Photo]   [*Walter Guiver.*

A GOOD HEAD STUDY.

Lady Gooch's "Drungewick Jennifer" is a very typical Cairn.   The remarkable coat protects the body from injury by thorns and rough edges of the rock.

not so fast as the present race of Foxhounds, but could stick to a scent a great deal better, not loosing when once on it, and the deep baying they made when following was enough to frighten "Auld Hoofy" himself. In addition to these great dogs Fraser had a few small terriers, perfect demons at work, and which always kept as near to the hounds as possible. Several tods would escape from the coverts and take to the hill cairns, in spite of the old Queen Anne muskets of the farmers.

Photo]   [Fall
CH. "HAMISH OF GESTO".

Mrs. Alastair Campbell, whose terrier this is, was the first breeder of Cairn Terriers. She had one given her, a puppy, in 1875. Here, then. is the true type.

"On went the hounds, followed by old Fraser and his little varmints, with the gunners and beaters following behind, till they came to the place the tod had taken refuge, frequently some huge cairn perhaps a quarter of a mile in circumference. The big dogs and the Queen Annes surrounded the cairn, an outer line was composed of the beaters, while old Fraser advanced on the boulders; and, at the words 'Hie, in, my darlin's!' off they went like so many ferrets into a rabbit warren, and the fox had either to come out and face death or be killed by these game little terriers."

Otters in a like fashion sought shelter in the cairns near the seashore. The terriers used to bolt them, and as they endeavoured to escape to the water they were shot. Many a terrier has been dragged into the water and nearly drowned, for nothing can induce these dogs to release their hold once they get it.

A story is told of

Major Stewart of Ensay, Harris, who was famed for his game terriers. He had a terrier named "Cruadel", renowned for his activity and gameness. Major Stewart was out hunting otter, when the quarry was run to earth in a cairn, near the sea. "Cruadel" was duly entered and the otter bolted with the terrier hanging on. They plunged into the sea, which was about ten feet deep at the place. As they did not come up Major Stewart dived into the water, where on the clear sandy bottom he could see the struggle going on, seized the terrier, still holding on to the otter, and brought them out—the otter dead.

These terriers had sometimes a lot of water-work to face, not to speak of wet dens and peat holes, which necessitated them having water- and weather-resisting coats. Many a weary long walk they had in snow and sleet, so that a warm jacket and stout hide were necessary.

From the above it will be seen the kind of work that was expected from a Cairn Terrier, which of course must have a certain bearing on the make-up and type of the dog himself. These keepers and tod-hunters were much attached to their terriers, and delighted in relating the exploits of their little heroes. They bred them only for gameness, not for type or colour or anything else, which accounts for the very many varying types that can still be bred from one set of parents.

It was also with

Painting by Landseer.]   [Photo by courtesy E. C. Ash
DIGNITY AND IMPUDENCE.

Landseer's world-famous painting of a Bloodhound with a Cairn Terrier (West Highland White being in those days merely a White Cairn) is very true to life

"MICKIE", THE CAIRN.

Those who are so fortunate as to know Miss Joyce Pilkington will also have had the good fortune of meeting "Mickie", her red Cairn.

[Photo]
[Sport and General.

ON THEIR WAY TO THE SHOW.

Baroness Burton is seen taking her Cairns to the Ladies' Kennel Association Dog Show. The two dogs are Ch. "Dockfour Ean" and "Tedworth Twitter".

difficulty that some keepers could be got to part with their favourites, as the following episode will show. A Southerner once tried to purchase a dog from an old Highlander, who still loved a day with his few terriers, but he could not part with any of them. Times were bad, and he could hardly get food for himself, but he remarked that the little rascals did not need much and were so fond of him. Then he went on to say : "See yon ugly deil yonder wi' half a lug. There's no money eneuch in the Bank o' England that could buy him. He's the best terrier that ever stood on four legs in braid Scotland and he fears neither man nor devil. Isn't that so, Roy?" and the little chap winked one of his bleary eyes, wagged his long drawn-out tail, and even endeavoured to prick up the mutilated lug that marred his entire physiognomy. "Eh, Roy, when I pairt wi' you, ye may expect to see a soo sitting on the tap o' a thistle, whistling, 'Ma Nannie's Awa.' No, sir. I need a' my dougs. Ye see, they're friends o' mine, and their bite and sup are never missed."

Later on, when the craze for native-bred dogs was at its height, some crafty Highlanders made quite small fortunes by palming off anything that looked like a terrier on the Sassenachs.

It has been found that the chief owners of the old-time Cairn Terriers were the MacKinnons of Kilbride and Kyle, the MacDonalds of Waternish, and the MacLeods of Drynoch, and their dogs were known as the Waternish Skyes, the MacKinnon or Kilbride Skyes and the Drynoch Skyes on the island. On the mainland they were known by the name of their kennels, such as Roseneath Terriers, Poltalloch Terriers, etc., much in the same way as farmers were only known by the names of their farms.

Coming to the time that the Cairn Terrier made its first appearance on the show bench, its path was certainly not one of roses. The other offshoots of the family, including the long-bodied, long-coated Skye had made their positions secure.

Mrs. Alastair Campbell, who was residing at that time at Ardrishag, Argyllshire was the pioneer of the

ARRIVED.

There is no difficulty in differentiating between the Cairn Terrier and the more recently developed Scottish Terrier. The heads are distinctive.

A VERY GOOD HEAD.
"Dochfour" Cairn Terriers (owned by Baroness Burton) are world-famous Nothing looks better than black points against a light coat.

enjoyed a certain amount of popularity. There was a hue and cry against the new-comer, and the other breeders demanded that the name of Skye should be abandoned. Mrs. Campbell was adamant and insisted on calling them Skyes, as she maintained they were the original terriers of the Island of that name. She exhibited her first short-haired Skye at Inverness Show in 1908.

Controversy raged up until 1910, when the dogs received recognition from the Kennel Club. The ruling authority decreed that they were to be known in future as Cairn Terriers.

This decision was not too well received at first by the enthusiasts, but with the passage of time it looks as if it is the most comprehensive name of the lot, and only goes to prove that it is the original terrier of the Highlands, from which all the others are descended.

Amongst the early pioneers of the breed were Mrs. Alastair Campbell, Lady Mary Hawke, Baroness Burton, Lady Sophie Scott, Miss Lucy Lockwood, Mr. Errington Ross and Mr. Charles F. Thompson. Each and every one were enthusiasts, and were largely responsible for the position that the Cairn Terrier holds in the canine world to-day. Mrs. A. Campbell adopted the very appropriate prefix of Brocaire, and she produced the first champion of the

breed in the show arena. Knowing as she did of their very close association with the Isle of Skye, she very naturally named them the Short-coated Skye, to differentiate from the Long-coated Skye, which had

CH. "DIVOR OF GUNTHORPE".
This Cairn Terrier, bred by Mrs. Dixon, won his championship honour both in England and America. He is the sire of "Dividend". shown on page 272.

breed in Ch. "Gesto". She also owned the famous terriers in the early days, "MacLeod of MacLeod", "Doran Bhan", "Roy Uhor", and "Call Uhor", all Skye-bred Cairns.

Many famous champions have these days emanated from the Brocaire Kennels, and Mrs. Campbell is considered one of the best judges of a Cairn that ever entered a ring. Lady Sophie Scott owned one of the first great bitches in Ch. "Tibbie of Harris", which was bred by Sir Samuel Scott, of Harris, and was of quite a different lineage. Lady Mary Hawke bred the wonderful bitch Ch. "Brocaire Speraig" from her bitch named "Bride", her sire being Ch. "Gesto". This Kennel was founded from the Waternish Skyes. Mrs. Campbell's first Cairn, or Short-haired Skye as she would call it then, came from the kennels of Mr. Martin MacKinnon. Later she bought "Moighan" and the great dam "Callarnchor" from the Nicholsons of Drynoch. Ch. "Gesto" was purchased from Mr. MacKinnon and became one of the earliest pillars of the breed as it is known to-day.

Another pillar, "Firring Fling", was bred by Macdonald of

"MOORLAND HONEY BOY".
Once again we have a picture showing the expression of the Cairn Terrier that has made the breed so popular all over the world. "Honey Boy" is one of Mrs. Pope's dogs.

VERE TEMPLE

Specially drawn]   *[by Vere Temple.*

CAIRN COMPANIONS.

These jolly fellows, hailing from the North, make happy subjects for the artists' pen—and Miss Temple's pen is always skilful.

"DIVIDEND OF GUNTHORPE"
This great winning Cairn Terrier, by the International Ch. "Divor of Gunthorpe", is a most excellent type.

"DANAE OF GUNTHORPE".
This excellent show Cairn Terrier, after winning numerous first prizes, was exported to the United States by Mrs. A Dixon.

Skye and sold to Messrs. Ross and Markland, and he ultimately passed into the hands of Baroness Burton and was the sire of that beautiful bitch Ch. "Rona", who did so much to further the popularity of the breed in its early show days. "Firring Fling" was also the sire of Ch. "Sporran"; and his brother, Ch. "Firring Frolic", was the sire of "Raeburn Conas", a red dog which sired Ch. "Carngowan Ailsaveg", which was the dam of Ch. "Carngowan Canach", sired by Ch. "MacSporran", a son of Ch. "Sporran". All had the blood of Ch. "Gesto" and another famous terrier, Ch. "Skye Crofter". The latter was sired by "Ferracher", which was owned by the Countess of Aberdeen, who was deeply interested in Cairn Terriers as well as droop-eared Skye Terriers.

Another great Cairn at this time was Mr. Charles F. Thompson's, of Inverness, Ch. "Inverness Doran", which was sired by Mr. Simon MacLeod's of Portree, "Will o' the Wisp". Both these gentlemen did much to popularize the Cairn, as did also Mr. Errington Ross, of Inverness, who held pronounced views of what a Cairn Terrier should be. His prefix "Glenmhor" was well known, and in time laid the foundation of Mr. J. E. Kerr's, famous "Harviestoun" strain. His old stud dog, "Harviestoun Raider", was responsible for a long list of champions.

Baroness Burton bred many champions in her

By courtesy]   [Mrs. Pope.

"MOORLAND ROYSTERER".

This charming Cairn study shows expression from one end to the other. "Roysterer" is bred by Mrs. Pope, world-known for her Papillons.

Dochfour Kennels, and did more to popularize the Cairn Terrier in the south than any other breeder. She knew the terrier in his native surroundings, and judged it accordingly. Mrs. N. Fleming, who owns the famous "Out of the West" affix, founded her kennel on the real old Skye blood. She bred Ch. "Froach Gail" and Ch. "Bagpipes", both of which founded the American Cairn fancy. Mrs. Fleming has benched many champion Cairns. Mrs. Stephen, of Bath, founded the famous Hyver Kennel of Cairns, with a bitch by "Roy Mhor", from the Brocaire Kennels. All these kennels have played important parts in Cairn Terrier history.

To-day there are thousands of breeders all striving to produce champions. Such, however, are elusive, and, strange to say, there is still a great diversity of opinions as to what really constitutes our ideal Cairn Terrier.

The breed is a great favourite with lady fanciers, and it has suffered a good deal through young inexperienced judges. Type was often discarded for personal fads, but still the great uncertainty that prevailed was the means of ensuring large entries at the various shows. "In and out" judging may do for a time, but as the knowledge of the breed increases, this type of judging will not be tolerated. Consistency in judging is now much more apparent, thanks to the influence of the various specialist clubs. All judges, however, must bear in mind that gameness must be maintained. They must never forget that the Cairn Terriers' main objects in life are to kill, to suffer punishment unflinchingly, and to remain leal to their owner. Dileas is an ideal name for a Cairn Terrier. To allow them to degenerate into mere ladies' lap or pet dogs is to ruin the breed. The fiercest Cairn can be the most gentle and affectionate dog in the house. The old tod-hunters depended upon them to be kind and to guard their children indoors. The Cairn Terrier has inherited that faculty as well.

Size has long been a stumbling block in the show ring, and the Southerners were inclined to breed their Cairns too small.

Photo]   [Miss Compton Collier.

A DELIGHTFUL GROUP.

The Cairn in the centre of this charming picture, taken at Acklington, Northumberland, is a very good specimen. The boys are the sons of Sir Leonard and Lady Milburn. They are great dog-lovers.

These were very neat and pleasing to look at, but at their work in the Highlands they would have been useless against a 16-lb. fox or a 20-lb. otter. The ideal weight is undoubtedly 14 lb., as laid down by the clubs. Cairns are however, very deceptive in appear-

Photo]   WE ARE CAIRNS!   [Ralph Robinson.
'Tam O'Shanter", "Thane" and "Tread" all of Kildare, and "Hush of Mercia" (seated) are a delightful group.

too short and compact. Such is not ideal for work. Neither the fox, the otter, nor the badger are built on these lines, and it must be remembered that the Cairn Terrier has to face these, so it is desirable that he should be built on similar lines. The very short, con-

ance. Some big-looking dogs will not scale the standard weight, whilst smaller-looking dogs will go over the desired weight. The judges must use their own discretion and must handle the exhibits before jumping to conclusions.

There is too much made of what is known as the Scottie type. It is a poor simile. No Cairn has any resemblance to a present-day Scottish Terrier. What is meant by this is that the muzzle is too heavy and blunt-like in appearance, which kills the real alert, catlike face which is demanded. Great heavy jaws are not wanted. A fox's muzzle is not of this description, yet he possesses great mouth power. This strength, however, comes from the cheek and neck muscles. A small vixen can carry a fair-sized turkey clear of the ground and this is all done by neck and cheek power.

Many of the old Cairns had bowed forelegs which were unsightly; and, although the close, straight Fox Terrier front is not desired, a good straight pair of forelegs improves the appearance of all Cairns. Another point which has caused a lot of controversy is the "compactly built" phrase in the standard. This does not mean an extra short back with deep ribs. The torso can be got

tracted body is not of much use to the dog when he is underground. There must be a certain freedom of spine which will allow full play for the powerful quarters. All judges should insist on good compact feet with strong, well-developed pads.

A good Cairn cannot be of a bad colour, but a good Cairn can be of any attractive colour. Some very beautiful terriers have made their appearance in the show ring during the past few years. The short, well-carried tail is undoubtedly one of the chief characteristics of a good Cairn. It should not be too long and should be carried rather gaily. Many showy Cairns get their tails too far over their backs, which, however, is preferable to one which carries its tail at too low an angle. The style of ear is very essential to a good expression. Round or bat-ears should be heavily penalized. The erect, pointed ears should, however, not be placed too closely together on the head. The eyes should not be prominent and should not be set too closely together. Dark eyes are now essential. The old tod-hunter did not worry about the colour of the eye in his terriers; in fact, some of the old hands preferred the light eye, as they considered they lasted longest and their owners

Photo]   [Fall.
TWO OF THE REAL TYPE.
Here we have two very typical Cairn Terriers, belonging to Mrs. Alastair Campbell, little "varminty" souls that are always on the look-out and so often dream of rat-hunting and foxes No wonder they are popular.

By courtesy]   [Miss Edwards.
MOTHERHOOD.
Perhaps one of the greatest pleasures of breeding puppies is to share the delight of the mother and to watch the antics of the youngsters. Miss Edwards' "Thistle of Jarvisbrook" sits enthroned with her young.

274

"KIM".

"Kim", the favourite of Miss Violet Petrie, daughter of Blanche, Lady Petrie, is here seen with its owner, who is interested in many sports, including beagling, tennis, and golf.

"PRESTBURY CHIEFTAIN".

Miss Gardiner's dog is just the kind we all should like to have. His expression is very typical indeed of that liveliness which is the Cairn's outstanding characteristic.

could see better when underground. From a show point of view the dark eye is very desirable.

The coat of a Cairn Terrier is very important and many judges do not put enough stress on this. All dogs that have to face stormy and inclement weather need two coats. Nature has provided these, so that the wet and cold cannot penetrate the undercoat, whilst the outer coat can throw off the rain or the snow. Some water dogs can come out of the water and, with a shake or two, will be as dry as before they entered same. Exhibitors, in a desire to make their dogs look their best, comb out most of the under coat, leaving the outer coat without any foundation. Dogs put down in this state always look out of coat. Judges should insist on an under coat. The outer coat should be of a wiry texture, whilst the under coat should be soft and close, though not woolly. Fluffy, woolly coats are objectionable. The outer coat should be straight, and yet should present a rather rugged rough appearance. It should not be over-long, and the legs should be quite apparent.

Photo]   STILL IN FINE FETTLE.   [*Guive:*

The age to which a dog will live is always interesting, but more so the age to which they will remain active. The above photograph shows Mrs. A. Dixon's "Lochbuie Argent", still a prizewinner at the age of fifteen years.

There must be, however, no leggy appearance.

There is something both about the general appearance and the expression of a Cairn Terrier that cannot be put down in black-and-white, and yet it is that something that finishes the real Cairn. It appeals at once to the experienced judge, and it to a very great extent governs his awards.

The following standard of points was adopted by the Cairn Terrier Club in 1922 :

GENERAL APPEARANCE.—Active, game, hardy and shaggy in appearance ; strong though compactly built. Should stand well forward on fore-paws. Strong quarters, deep in ribs. Very free in movement. Coat hard enough to resist rain. Head small but in proportion to body. A general

foxy appearance is the chief characteristic of this working terrier.

SKULL.—Broad in proportion ; strong but not too long or heavy jaw. A decided indentation between eyes ; hair should be full on forehead.

MUZZLE.—Powerful but not heavy. Very strong jaw, with large teeth, which should be neither undershot nor overshot.

EYES.—Set wide apart ; medium in size, dark, hazel, rather sunk, with shaggy eyebrows.

EARS.—Small, pointed, well carried and erect, but not too closely set.

TAIL.—Short, well furnished with hair, but not feathery ; carried gaily, but should not turn down towards back.

BODY.—Compact, straight back, well-sprung deep ribs ; strong sinews ; hindquarters very strong. Back medium in length and well coupled.

SHOULDERS, LEGS AND FEET.—A sloping shoulder, and a medium length of leg ; good but not too large bone. Forelegs should not be out at elbow, but forefeet may be slightly turned out. Forefeet larger than hind. Legs must be covered with hard hair. Pads should be thick and strong.

COAT.—Very important. Must be double-coated, with profuse hard but not coarse outer coat, and under coat which resembles fur and is short, soft and close. Open coats are objectionable. Head should be well furnished. Colour : Red, sandy, grey, brindled, or nearly black. Dark points such as ears and muzzle very typical. In order to keep this breed to the best old working type, any resemblance to a Scottish Terrier will be considered objectionable.

FAULTS.—Muzzle.—Undershot or overshot. Eyes.—Too prominent or too light. Ears.—Too large or round at points. They should not be too heavily

CH. "CORRIE-BA OF FAIR CITY".

The Misses D. and M. Bell's champion Cairn is seen much on the alert and very interested in something. Photographs, unfortunately, fail to show the "foxy" appearance, so typical of this breed.

coated with hair. Coat.—Silkiness or curliness objectionable ; a slight wave permissible. Nose.—Flesh or light-coloured most objectionable.

SCALE OF POINTS.—Skull, 5 ; muzzle, 10 ; eyes, 5 ; ears, 5 ; body, 20 ; shoulders, legs and feet, 20 ; tail, 5 ; general appearance (size and coat), 30. Total, 100.

The ideal weight for the Cairn Terrier should be about fourteen pounds.

Calcification.—A term used to indicate the deposition, in a tissue, of calcium salts. The cartilage (or gristle) which is found separating long bones, and forming part of the joints, occasionally becomes calcified as a result of disease or injury. Calcification also takes place wherever bones are fractured, and the ultimate union of broken bones is effected partly by this process, and partly by another phenomenon known as ossification.

Calcium.—A yellow metal, the basic element of lime. Many of the calcium salts are used commercially and medicinally, for both of which purposes they are very valuable.

Calcium oxide, or quicklime, is a cheap and efficacious disinfectant for sprinkling over floors of kennels and in exercise runs. It has a caustic action also, on account of which it should not be allowed to come into close contact with the living body. It is frequently thrown over dead carcases at the time of burial to prevent germ-multiplication and to expedite the disintegration of the flesh. As a solution with water, calcium oxide is employed as "limewash" for whitening walls. (*See* CARBOLIC ACID.)

Lime-water is made from a purified oxide dissolved in distilled water, the finished product being largely used medicinally as an antacid, and for the prevention of rickets, given internally. Externally it is valuable for its astringent properties in the healing of sores and abrasions, etc.

Calcium carbonate or chalk, is used in dyspepsia, colic, diarrhoea ; and locally as a dusting powder.

Calcium sulphate is the well-known plaster of Paris, employed frequently in canine surgery for the setting of broken legs.

Calcium chloride, also known as bleaching powder, is used as a disinfectant and deodorant.

Calculus.—Also known as "Stone", may occur in the bladder, kidneys or urethra. Dogs do not suffer from stone in the gall-bladder, and only rarely do stones form in the bowel. The commonest situation is perhaps in the bladder, but even cystic calculi may originally have been renal (kidney) calculi which had passed through the ureters into the bladder. Similarly, urethral calculi must originally have come from the bladder. X-rays should not be forgotten as a valuable aid to diagnosis.

SYMPTOMS.—The symptoms arising from the presence of a renal or kidney stone are not very diagnostic, but generally there is a tenderness, stiffness, or even acute pain about the loins, whilst the urine will occasionally contain blood. So far as the bladder is concerned, stones in this organ are not often large and singular, but small and multiple ; so that if a small stone is seen to pass out of the body with the urine, there may still be others to be voided. They set up erratic periods of pain and relief, evinced by a desire continuously

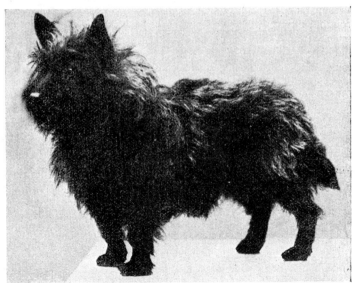

CH. "FIMOR BEN BREAC".

Although the tail ought not to be carried down (as shown here) it must be remembered that a dog, usually with his tail up "according to the book," will occasionally lower it.

A DISTINGUISHED PAIR.

Very good examples of the breed are these two Cairns, "Mousie" and "Victory", which are seen with the Hon. Lady Morrison Bell and her daughter, Miss Shelagh Morrison Bell.

to pass water. The dog strains very frequently but emits only a few drops of urine at each attempt, which may or may not be blood-tinged. Sometimes it is possible to detect a well-developed stone through the abdominal wall, and at nearly all times by radiography.

When a calculus passes into the urethra and becomes lodged therein, there may be a complete stoppage of the flow of water, in which case the bladder will soon become very distended. (See BLADDER, DISTENSION OF.) If left long in this condition inflammation sets up and unless relief is soon afforded the animal may die from pain and exhaustion, uraemic poisoning or rupture of the bladder.

TREATMENT.—When a dog is noticed to have urinary trouble, the owner is advised to waste no time in getting a diagnosis from a qualified man, as to indulge in guessing or trying out various remedies, is not only exceedingly unkind to the dog, but courting disaster. (*See illustrations on page* 284.)

Calomel.—Mercurous chloride. Used as an alterative, and cholagogue purgative. Increases the flow of bile from the liver and, being tasteless, it is easy to administer to dogs. The dose is $\frac{1}{2}$ to 2 grains, which may be dusted on the tongue or mixed with the food.

Camphor.—A white, crystalline, fragrant substance extracted from the wood of a laurel known as *Cinnamomum Camphora*. It is a powerful stimulant, diaphoretic and narcotic, poisonous in overdoses, sedative in small ones. The compound tincture of camphor, better known as paregoric, is largely used in cough mixtures for its sedative and expectorant effects. Camphorated oil is a preparation commonly employed for rubbing the chest wall or the throat when either of these regions is inflamed. Camphor in oil is of great value, too, as a heart stimulant when injected subcutaneously. Incidentally, those male dogs which annoy their owners and others by their excessive sexual excitement will calm down considerably after a short course of camphor—say for two or three days.

Cancer.—Malignant tumours of cancerous origin are rather frequently met with in dogs, particularly in those of middle or advanced age. Their cause is as yet unknown and, so far as our present knowledge is concerned, they are neither infectious nor contagious. They are, however, apparently hereditary ; or, possibly, it may be more correct to say that the offspring of parents which are subjects of cancer are a suitable soil in or upon which malignant tumours are likely to appear.

The formation of these growths is usually in connection with a mucous membrane, but they have occurred on the skin, ears, eyelids, and almost every other tissue in the body.

SYMPTOMS.—They do not appear to give rise, at first, to pain, although as time goes on and they increase in size, the dog commences to lick the part a great deal when the growths are superficially placed. Later, there may be a constant slight oozing or discharge from the part, and there is no tendency whatever for healing to take place.

Whenever persistent discharges (sometimes blood-stained) occur either from the vagina or any other locality, or when slowly forming growths are observed, it is wise at once to have the animal examined, for the great chance of successful treatment lies in very early surgical excision of the new tissue.

Cancers are noted for their power of reducing gradually a dog's bodily condition, until a time may arrive when the animal looks little more than a skeleton. With some types of cancer there is an accompanying and most offensive odour, particularly when the growth is situated in the rectum.

In a small percentage of cases there is no recurrence when an operation is well and early performed ; but unfortunately, in the majority of cases, the tumour returns either in the same or some other place. So far as is known, a cancerous dog is not a danger to human beings with whom it comes in contact.

By courtesy]   [*Mrs. A. Dixon.*
CH. "GEUM WOFFINGTON".
The Cairn should carry its tail gaily but not turned over the back. The body should be compact and well coupled, as this picture of Mrs. A. Dixon's champion shows.

Canine Teeth.—The dog has four canine teeth, one on each corner of each jaw. They are the largest, strongest and most prominent teeth in the mouth, known variously as "eye teeth", tusks, or "dog teeth". The temporary canines commence disrupting at about the fifth month of age, and the permanent ones are usually fully developed at about six and a half months. (See AGE, TO TELL THE.)

Canine Typhus. (See STUTTGART DISEASE.)

Canker of the Ear. (See EAR DISEASES.)

Cantharides.—A brown powder prepared by pulverizing the dried whole bodies of a fly which is native to Spain. Hence the term "Spanish Fly". The irritant properties of this powder are liberated by boiling it in fat or oil, and if the resulting ointment (when cold and set) be rubbed into an animal's skin, a blistering effect is produced. (See BLISTERING.) The skin becomes red, smarts a good deal, and after some hours will be found to have produced small vesicles, or pustules. If applied over a comparatively large area, its active principle —cantharidin—becomes partly absorbed into the blood-stream and sets up severe constitutional disturbance. Since it is eliminated from the body mainly by the urinary system, it exerts inflammatory reactions in the urinary organs, notably inflammation of the kidneys, bladder and urethra.

For this chief reason, cantharides ointment is rarely or never used upon dogs and must be regarded as a dangerous agent, if used upon dogs.

Cape Hunting Dog. (See SOUTH AFRICAN HUNTING DOG.)

Capped Elbow.—As a result of continuous pressure or bruising, arising from dogs habitually

Photo]   *[Fall*

CH. "TADWORTH TWITTER".

The Rt. Hon. Baroness Burton's Ch. "Twitter" is a fine-headed
dog, and has the Cairn Terrier expression.

Photo]   *[J. Garrow.*

BROTHER AND SISTER.

The dark dog is Ch. "Fimor Ben Breac", and the light one
'Fimor Babette'. They are full brother and sister, but not of
the same litter.

"OFFLEY FERROX".

Mr. and Mrs. E. L. Pope's Norfolk-bred Cairn "Ferrox" comes
from the Harviestoun strain, whilst the dogs (see number 5)
are Harviestoun crossed with Brocaire.

Photo]   *[Fall.*

"BOUNCER".

It is no easy matter to get a perfect body, head, good tail-carriage
and expression. Mrs. C. Rudland's "Bouncer" is remarkable
for its legs, head and tail-style.

Photo]   *[Fall.*

THE OLD TYPE.

On the left is "Brocaire Righorn Ruadh", and on the right
Ch. "Brocaire Jurk". They are of the old type, before the
breeders aimed at a heavier jaw.

Photo]   *[Fall.*

CH. "DEMISH GUNTHORPE".

This noted little champion, one of Mrs. A. Dixon's famous kennel,
apart from his other good points, has the small-pointed ears (so
hard to get) well carried.

SOME CANINE NOTABILITIES.

resting upon their elbows, there is an increased secretion of serous fluid in the bursa which covers the point of the elbow. A swelling occurs which may be painful but which is generally chronic in character and giving rise to no lameness. At a later stage the swelling becomes hard or tumefied, and its removal can only be effected by surgical means.

The only way to prevent a recurrence is to apply some protective covering to the elbows. The large breeds, such as Great Danes, etc., are almost exclusively affected with this malady.

Captive or Yard Dog. (*See* CHAINING OF DOG.)

Carbolic Acid.—A product of the distillation of coal, and known also as phenol. It is water-white in the pure state, of somewhat oily appearance, and possesses a characteristic and rather pleasant odour. When immoderately or improperly used it is poisonous to dogs, but applied in correct proportions it is an excellent and clean disinfectant. Used undiluted, as an application, it is ᴜ severely caustic and thus becomes employed sometimes for the burning-off of warts, the latter being just touched by a small drop of the acid. The process may need repeating two or three times.

As a wound lotion it is usually employed in $2\frac{1}{2}$ to 5 per cent. solution with water. For certain diseases of the ear its use is popular as "carbolic oil" when 1 part of the acid

Photo]   OVER THE TOP.   [*Sport and General.*

An innovation of an unusual nature are dog sports, as they are termed, carried out at Kennels owned by Miss J. Trefusis in Surrey. Here is a Cairn taking a hurdle in a race.

is shaken up well with 10 parts of olive or almond oil. Sometimes it is similarly mixed with glycerine for the same purpose. Its action as a disinfectant is, however, less powerful when combined with oil than when dissolved in water. Many other uses are known to surgeons for this disinfectant, but these would hardly interest our readers. It might be borne in mind that when infected kennels are to limewashed, the addition of half a pint of pure carbolic acid to each gallon of wash would very effectually disinfect the walls and kill parasites.

It is strongly condemned for the internal medication of dogs owing to its poisonous nature.

Carbonic Acid Gas.—A product of metabolism formed in the tissues and removed by the blood, which conveys it to the lungs to be exhaled. Res-

pired air, therefore, is charged with this poisonous gas, and our duty in the kennel is to ensure that there is free and full ventilation.

Carbon Tetrachloride.—A remedy for round worms largely used in America. It is given, in capsules, in doses ranging from half to three drachms.

Carcinoma.—A malignant tumour. (*See* CANCER.)

Cardiac Diseases. (*See* HEART, DISEASES OF.)

Care of the Sick Dog. (*See* NURSING.)

Caries.—Death or decay of the teeth. Most textbooks upon canine diseases deny that dental caries ever occurs in dogs, but upon a number of occasions the writer has extracted teeth which have shown a definite and typical picture of caries, and has no doubt that, whilst rare, it does occur. Curiously enough, the dog does not often exhibit any sign of toothache, and it is generally only when advanced pyorrhoea has rendered the tooth so loose in its socket that the necessity for extraction becomes evident. Persistent foul breath should arouse one's suspicions that a diseased tooth is present in the mouth. Although few people will go to the expense or trouble of having a dog's tooth "stopped", this process can, nevertheless, be carried out by a dental surgeon provided a veterinary surgeon will administer a suitable anaesthetic.

Carlin.—Another name for the Pug, being actually the French for it.

Carminative.—A medicine which relieves flatulence and assuages abdominal pain. Most of the volatile and aromatic oils are carminatives, the best known being peppermint, ginger, aniseed, cardamoms, juniper, spearmint and cloves. Purgative pills usually contain one or more of the carminatives in order to prevent any griping effect which might otherwise take place.

Carriage of Dogs. (*See* TRANSPORT.)

Carron Oil.—A mixture, in equal parts, of linseed oil and limewater. This, when well shaken,

JUST A PET.

It is not necessary to be a show dog of great renown to be attractive, and although this Cairn may never win a prize it makes up in personality for what it may lack in show points.

forms an emulsion which is still commonly used as a protective and soothing application for burns and scalds.

Cartilage.—Popularly known as gristle. An elastic, tough and bloodless tissue, commonly found interposed between any two bones which, by contact with each other, form a joint. The presence of articular cartilage in a joint serves to prevent jars and shocks between two bones, and also provides a soft smooth bed in which the articular surfaces of bones may glide. The flap of a dog's ear is mainly composed of cartilage, other examples being found as circular discs between each vertebra of the spinal column.

Castor Oil.—The oil expressed from castor beans which are the fruit of a plant known as *Ricinus communis.* The oil is nearly colourless, very viscid and has a nauseating odour. For generations it has earned popularity as a mild purge for dogs, as it acts without causing colic. But if a dog offers resistance to the administration of medicines, and so many of them do, then readers are strongly advised to select some easier and cleaner agent such as a mercurial powder. (*See* MERCURY.) On the other hand, some dogs will readily lap it up out of a spoon, and appear to relish it. Even so, castor oil has an unfortunate drawback in that it tends to create costiveness after its purging effect has worn off. Advantage is occasionally taken of this characteristic, where a dog, suffering from diarrhoea believed to be due to the ingestion of putrefying material, is in need of a good purging which will then stop. Castor oil is rendered less viscid if it is first warmed before use. The dose varies roughly between ½ oz. and 1½ ozs. according to the size of the dog. In surgical practice, this oil is useful as a soothing lubricant when applied direct to the eyeball. It makes a good protective, too, in cases of burns or scalds. Lastly, it can be used for softening leather articles which have become hard and brittle, such as leads, collars, harness. etc.

Castration.—An operation for the surgical removal of testicles from the male, or of ovaries from the female. It is also known as emasculation, and neutering, and additional terms may be used to signify the operation upon bitches. If the ovaries are diseased, then the term ovariotomy is employed; if they are healthy it is spoken of as oöphorectomy; but the word "spaying" might be used to include either.

It is seldom that male dogs are castrated, but when they are it is usually because their habits in the household have become decidedly objectionable from a sexual point of view. One cannot keep

A large cystic calculus
(*See page 278.*)

such dogs on sedatives for months upon end, and the radical operation is a sure cure. The only possible effects of the operation in either sex are inability to breed, diminution of aggressiveness or bad temper, a tendency to obesity and occasionally the development of a slight lethargy.

If it is possible to make a decision as to the time when the operation shall be performed, this should be under the age of six months. A local anaesthetic may be employed for young animals, but over the age of six months a general anaesthetic is compulsory by law (*See* ANIMALS' ANAESTHETICS ACT.)

Castration of either male or female dog must never be attempted by unqualified persons, as considerable care and skill are essential in each case to avoid profuse haemorrhage and sepsis.

Cataract.—A disease of the eye characterized by the formation of an opacity in the lens.

CAUSES.—Senility is a very constant cause of the condition, both eyes becoming equally affected. In young dogs it may arise as a complication of generalized inflammation of the eye (ophthalmia) resulting from scratches, bites or blows about the orbit or eyeball. Cataract of mild or severe degree has also been known to occur spontaneously without any apparent inducement; at other times in consequence of diabetes; or it may be congenital.

SYMPTOMS.—A milky or whitish spot may be observed in the lens of the eye; or the opacity, instead of being discrete, may be diffuse, thus clearly outlining the whole of the lenticular body. Unless a considerable part of the lens is affected sight is little interfered with, so far as one can judge by watching the dog's movements. But as a cataract becomes gradually diffused over the major portion of the lens, the sense of sight proportionately decreases. There is no pain associated with the lesion once the provocative inflammation (if any) has died down.

TREATMENT.—No amateurish efforts will be of any avail in the treatment of this disease, for if any interference is desirable, the one with the most promise is that of surgical excision under a general anaesthetic. The prognosis (chance of recovery) if this be not done, is not very hopeful, and "So and So's Drops", or "Somebody's Sure Cure" will be absolutely of no avail. Any home treatment attempted should be directed entirely towards the promotion of good general health, and further than this one can only advise that if the dog is worth it, a canine surgeon should be consulted.

Catarrh.—This term means the inflammation of a mucous membrane, with an accompanying discharge. Any mucous surface throughout the

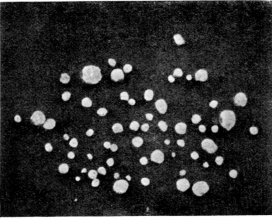

Calculus: A group of small stones from a dog's urethra.
(*See page 278.*)

Photo]   *[Capt. G. Dénes.*

YOURS TO COMMAND.

Though for years the Cairn in England has been little more than a show dog and domestic pet, it has never lost its expression
of eagerness, a legacy from its hard-working ancestors. This jolly fellow seems ready at a call to set out again in pursuit of
the old quarry.

body may be affected, and the condition, which exists in any given case, will be named according to the organ or part implicated. For instance, we recognize nasal catarrh, gastric catarrh, preputial catarrh, etc.

GASTRIC CATARRH. — Also known as acute dyspepsia, gastritis, and inflammation of the stomach. It may arise from the swallowing of irritants or poisons (such as chemicals like carbolic acid, turpentine, etc.) rat and beetle poisons, stones, nails, decaying foodstuffs, hot, frozen, or fermenting materials. Parasites have been blamed, and indigestible matter, such as excess of cabbage, are probably often responsible. The majority of cases of gastric catarrh are, however, most likely the outcome of specific infections such—in particular—as distemper and Stuttgart disease. Simple chills arising from exposure to cold or from getting wet are no doubt sometimes responsible for catarrh of the stomach.

SYMPTOMS.— Probably the first noticeable sign observed is occasional vomiting, especially soon after any food or drink has been swallowed. The dog evinces an increased thirst for cold water, the consumption of which often induces renewed sickness, when all the water is returned.

Photo]   *[Fall.*
"SPINNEL JOAN".
Mrs. Mirrlee's "Spinnel Joan" makes a delightful head study and also shows the Cairn coat, profuse, but not coarse.

Appetite is affected and, later, becomes totally in abeyance. The animal shows a disposition for lying on its abdomen, at full length, upon the coldest place it can find, such as a stone or lino-covered floor. The temperature taken at the rectum is not usually elevated to more than 102° F. (i.e. one degree) ; it may be normal.

TREATMENT.—It is unwise to force food into such a dog, a twenty-four hours' complete rest for the stomach proving very beneficial. Water, in greatly restricted amount, should only occasionally be allowed, and may be substituted by cold barley water or by soda and milk. A purgative, such as $\frac{1}{2}$ to 2 grains calomel, may be indicated in the beginning of an attack, especially if some irritant or bad food is suspected as the cause. Constipation must, in any event, be overcome. Further than this, the dog may be treated on more or less the same lines as would a human being suffering from the same complaint. If the usual home remedies prove ineffectual, then professional advice should be sought, especially as the case may be one of distemper in its early stages.

Reverting once more to questions of food, it will be found that white of egg in water, and whey, are both well tolerated and sustaining. As improvements sets in, a small quantity of boiled fish or raw scraped beef may be offered at intervals during the day.

NASAL CATARRH—Congestion or inflammation of the lining membrane of the nasal passages, is caused, among other reasons, by the continuous inhalation of irritant dust or smoke ; or by exposure to cold or rapidly moving wind as occurs when a dog rides in an open car ; by simple chill arising from any cause ; but mostly as an accompanying symptom of distemper.

SYMPTOMS.—A hot, raw or tender sensation in the nasal passages, which gives rise to snuffing or sneezing, and nearly always to a discharge varying in character according to the severity of the attack. At first the discharge is mucous or watery, the presence of which causes the dog continually to lick its nostrils. At a later stage the nasal discharge becomes muco-purulent, and finally thickly purulent. Some of the latter usually remains about the angles of the nostrils, where it dries and cakes, setting up a cracked and tender condition of these parts.

The temperature is not raised nor the appetite lost unless there exists a concomitant inflammation of some other organ or part.

A CHAMPION CHOW CHOW OF FORMER DAYS.

In this fine painting by Maud Earl, the changes which selective breeding can bring about are admirably marked, for Mrs. Lionel Faudel-Phillips' Ch. ''Papoose'', attractive though he undoubtedly appears, is plainly many generations removed from the Chow Chow of to-day.

TREATMENT.—As a rule, none is needed for all ordinary or mild cases. Nature generally effects a fairly rapid cure unaided. In more obstinate or severe instances, however, comfort may be rendered by bathing the nose and nostrils with warm water. Inhalations of steam medicated with eucalyptus also give relief. Oil of eucalyptus may be smeared on the bridge of the nose so that it may be continuously inhaled; and the cracked and sore condition of the nostrils is countered by frequently applying vaseline, or boracic ointment. The dog should be kept indoors. especially during inclement weather.

PREPUTIAL CATARRH.—A thick yellow bead of discharge is very commonly seen at the end of the dog's penis, evidences of which are far too frequently observed upon the household furniture. It appears not to affect the dog's general health in any way, and is only of annoyance to the owner. It probably arises mostly in consequence of a lowered vitality and may be one of the manifestations of a mild generalized catarrh of the mucous membranes. It is a very usual accompaniment of distemper; but from whatever cause arising it calls for little attention unless very pronounced and loathsome.

TREATMENT is the same as that prescribed for Balanitis (*which see*).

CATARRH OF BOWELS. (*See* DIARRHOEA.)

CATARRH OF EYES. (*See* EYE DISEASES CONJUNCTIVITIS.)

Cat Bites.—Almost without exception, the bites which a cat may inflict upon a dog are of the punctured-wound variety, and need to be carefully searched for and treated. The treatment is simple and consists merely of removal of overlying hair, and the continuous bathing of the part with warm antiseptic solution. A hot poultice may even be indicated. (For treatment. *see* WOUNDS.)

Cat-footed.—A term applied to a dog which has feet like those of a cat, i.e. small and round the dog seeming to stand well on its toes

Cathartics.—Another name for purgatives.

Catheter.—An instrument used for drawing away urine, in cases of inability of animals normally to urinate. Catheterization is an operation which in no circumstances should be attempted by any person who has no veterinary or medical qualification. It is fraught by risk of sepsis, and injury to the urethra, and since catheterization cannot be described as a home-remedy. no details of its accomplishment will be given.

Caustics.—Agents which have a burning or corrosive action when applied to living tissues. Many of the concentrated acids are caustics, such as pure carbolic and nitric acid and, to a less extent, pure acetic acid. Perhaps the most popularly used caustic is nitrate of silver, followed closely by blue stone or sulphate of copper. All of these may be used for the destruction of warts or other small tumours; for the reduction of granulations; and to destroy the lining membranes of cysts and sinuses etc. Sticks of caustic potash are occasionally employed for the same purpose. The tissue to be destroyed is perhaps touched only once, or a daily application may have to be made for several days should the area be extensive or hard and obstinate.

Cautery.—To cauterize a tissue may mean the application to it of a chemical caustic. but frequently

Photo]   *[Fall.*
"PRESTBURY CHIEFTAIN."
This Cairn Terrier is Scottish through and through, for it is bred from Scottish parents on both sides.

one implies the use of a hot iron. In the latter case, the correct term would be *Actual Cautery*. Deepseated inflammations are often treated, in equine surgery, by the method known as "firing", but this has only a very limited application in canine practice. In racing greyhounds, "point firing" has sometimes been adopted for the relief of fibrous thickenings

Photo]   *[Sport & General.*
CH. "DEMIS OF GUNTHORPE".
Mrs. A. Dixon, the breeder of "Demis", won several first prizes and specials with this dog, and, in 1933, the honour of the best Cairn at Cruft's

Photo] [Hay Wrightson.

INTELLIGENCE.
The Cairn's instinctive keenness is well displayed by "Dhoran", seen here with Miss Margaret Warner,
grand-daughter of Lord Borwick.

about the toe joints, for tendon sprains, and inflammations of bone, but only moderate success has attended the method, and veterinary surgeons have not regarded it with much favour. One of the effects of actual cautery is to seal those blood-vessels which are severed by it, and for this reason it is not an uncommon procedure to excise new and vascular growths by its agency. The most modern method is to use an electric cautery in which a platinum blade is rendered from dull-red to white heat by the passage of an electric current. One can hardly expect to arrest haemorrhage from cut arteries, but venous haemorrhage is generally easily controlled by the mere touch of a dull-red applicator. Needless to say, local anaesthesia should be induced in and around the affected area before cauterizing it.

Cemetery for Dogs. (*See* MEMORIALS AND MONUMENTS.)

Cerebellum.—The smaller portion of the brain, situated behind the cerebrum, and consisting of a median and two lateral lobes. It appears to be chiefly concerned with the co-ordination of movement.

Cerebrum.—The main portion of the brain occupying the anterior part of the cranium, and consisting of two equal portions called hemispheres.

Chaining of Dogs.—There are many people foster the erroneous notion that a dog, which is obtained and kept solely for guard purposes, can legitimately be kept on the chain month in and month out. They think that by providing, say, ten feet of chain the dog obtains sufficient exercise by pacing to and fro when strangers approach the premises. It may be pointed out, however, that such an idea is not only wrong, but cruel. A test case was instituted by the National Canine Defence League several years ago in which this Society prosecuted a man for keeping his dog on a chain for sixteen years. The evidence showed that only on two occasions had that poor animal been released for short periods.

The owner contended that as it was liberally fed it was not neglected and had not been cruelly ill-treated. But what of the mental agony of the dog ? Did it not break its heart for freedom, until its spirit was broken and its temper soured ? Here, then, was a dog well treated and well fed, but had been kept on a chain for long periods at a time.

The magistrate took this view and inflicted a fine. The case serves as a warning to others who in perpetrating similar offences, prove that they have failed to realize there is such a thing as mental torture. It is not necessarily incumbent upon a prosecution to prove physical cruelty in order to obtain a conviction

CH. "PRESTBURY SILVERFYORD".
No wonder they consider that these are "varminty" dogs, for whatever other meaning than fearlessness and mishap to rats could be expressed in those eyes and carriage ?

It is an undeniable fact that dogs which are kept much on a chain do become ill-tempered and not altogether to be trusted off the chain; however, these same animals seem docile enough when at exercise and appear to save all their ill graces for the hours of captivity.

It is not infrequently the case that dog owners hesitate or actually refrain from taking out their animals on the plea that, when out, the dog becomes an intolerable nuisance. Its delight is intense and is manifested by galloping madly about, barking, jumping up and soiling its owner's clothing, chasing dogs and cats, and probably escaping a motor's wheels by inches. All this exuberance of spirit, which is often so distasteful to its more sober-minded owner, would be conspicuous by its absence if the dog were more often out ; in other words, if the safety valve were more frequently opened the pressure within the boiler would become negligible.

The moral which one tries to point is, "let the dog have freedom at every possible opportunity", not only for the maintenance of health. but in the interests of humanity.

Challenge Certificate.—Awarded, at a Championship Show, to the dog or bitch which, in the opinion of the judge, is of such outstanding merit as to be worthy of the title of Champion. If the dog wins three Challenge Certificates, under three different judges, it becomes a Champion.

Chesapeake Bay Dog.—This breed is probably more buried in the soil of America than any other. In most characteristics it belongs to the type of Lesser Newfoundland. It was found in the neighbourhood of St. Johns, and there seems little reason to doubt that here really was its origin. It is almost as old as the Constitution of the States, for it is reported to go back at least to the beginning of the nineteenth century.

The Chesapeakes have long proved to be a really useful dog, somewhat on the lines of the English Retrievers. For many years they were bred for use, with little regard to pedigree, though they maintained a certain standard. It is, however, because the dog has been used very much more than shown that he has not gained in refinement.

There are many stories as to how he came to be. Perhaps the one that reads best concerns the ship *Canton* which was sailing in 1807 from Baltimore in Maryland when it fell in with a disabled English brig which was on its way from Newfoundland to Liverpool. In rescuing the brig's crew, two puppies, a dog and a bitch, were taken on board. The dog puppy was called "Sailor", was a dingy red and became the property of a Mr. John Mercer, of West River. The bitch was black, named "Canton" and was given to Dr. James Stuart, of Sparrow Point. Being in the neighbourhood of Baltimore, which was not far from the big ducking shores of Chesapeake Bay, where the dogs flourished and grew in numbers, they were called after the locality

Their retriever qualities made them much sought after by the hunters. So keen were the dogs that heavy seas and even ice did not daunt them from following a wounded duck for miles.

There are other versions of this story of their origin, and one related by General Latrobe, an old Maryland sportsman, may have much truth in it because he was genuinely interested in, and very knowledgeable about, ducking dogs. According to him, many years ago a Newfoundland vessel was stranded on the shores of Chesapeake Bay. On board the ship were two Newfoundland dogs, which were given by the captain to a Mr. George Law, who showed great kindness and hospitality to the shipwrecked crew. The General asserts that these Newfoundlands were crossed with a common yellow-and-tan coloured hound or "Coon" dog, which inhabited that part of the country, and that the Chesapeake Bay Dog was the result. Whatever the actual beginnings were, it is certain that the Carroll Island Club kept the pedigrees of the

Chesapeake Bay Dog for over a hundred years. There is this also that substantiates in a measure General Latrobe's story : the wet sedge colour of the dog suggests that there may be something of the yellow hound in its composition.

There are those who give support to this theory by a half-cynical admission that the nondescript hounds known as the "Coon" dog down South would produce an unfinished type of dog such as the Chesapeake. It certainly does lack finish, but those who bred him were thoroughly aware of the purpose for which they were breeding him. He contains just the qualities necessary to fulfil his job. His broad skull, his wedgy foreface, and his powerful jaw, make him ideal, if not unique, to face heavy seas and broken ice in the pursuit of duck or goose.

There are those, too, who ridicule the high set of the ears, but here again they are fitted for the dog's job. He may not be symmetrical in the shortness of his neck, but there is certainly strength, and that is what is

Photo] A GOOD WORKING TYPE. *[Wide World.*
"Bing", the winner of the Derby Stake, is an excellent example of the modern Chesapeake. He is a fine water and marshland worker.

required in a dog that has to carry a big bird probably through rush and reed, as well as water.

The yellow eye is another "proof" of the "Coon" dog cross, while the Chesapeake also carries a long tail, often criticized by the fancier, but which is most serviceable as a rudder to the dog in the water.

One of the first essentials of the Chesapeake is his coat. He must have a covering that will protect him from the cold, for when out with the guns he will swim in the icy water for hours. Perhaps no other dog has just such a coat; it is very dense, and, despite its coarseness, it is

THE CHESAPEAKE.

The Chesapeake Bay Dog is somewhat like the Labrador Retriever, but the American dog is said to be sturdier and works under harder conditions. Often he will swim for hours in icy-cold water, retrieving duck. Note here in what workmanlike manner he carries the bird, dead in the centre, allowing no wing to flap over his eyes.

reinforced close to the skin by an under-coat that affords a most efficient protection. There are curly-coated dogs that are known as Chesapeakes, but it is the comparatively short-haired dog that is truest to type. The hair should not exceed an inch and a half in length.

For show purposes, a small white spot on the breast is allowed, but no other white ; and it is also permitted that a slight thickening tendency can

Chest.—Extends beneath dog from brisket to belly.

Chiens. (*See* FRENCH BREEDS.)

Chihuahua.—The Chihuahua is one of the few breeds of dogs native to the United States of America. and its name has been derived from a province in Mexico. The Chihuahuas are dogs of small size, notwithstanding which

Photo]   [*Wide World*.
DUCKING.
It is important, more especially when wild fowling, to have a dog so well trained and so accustomed to the business that he will sit quite still at the moment when the duck heave into range.   This Cheaspeake dog knows his job.

appear over the shoulders. As a matter of fact, however, it is not much of a show dog.   In Britain it is unknown, and even in its native country, though often classes are arranged for it, there is a very poor entry.   The numbers, indeed, are so scanty that more often than not the Chesapeakes find themselves consigned to the Setter judge.

But this does not matter to the man who owns a Chesapeake.   In the vast majority of cases the dog is not wanted for looks but for work, and from this angle an owner has seldom a complaint to make.

they are very game, are fond of retrieving and of hunting vermin of small size.   It is said that it is a very old breed of dog.   It is rather popular in the United States, where it is being frequently exhibited, although not in large numbers ; for instance, at the great Westminster Kennel Club's Show in 1934, there were only eighteen of them benched, as against only thirteen in the previous year.   The general type is not altogether uniform, but the efforts of the breeders tend towards the evolution of entire uniformity, in which they are being greatly aided by the

THE CHIHUAHUA.

Among the smallest dogs in the world, the Chihuahua belongs to Mexico.   Here is "King", so tiny that he takes his meals from the eye-dropper of his mistress, Miss Lupe Velez, the film star.

Chihuahua Club of America, which issued a standard of this breed. The dog is a very small one, and there are specimens of it that weigh only about two pounds when full grown. The Chihuahua is extremely intelligent, and takes interest in everything.

The following is the standard of the above American Club, which, by the way, is very precise, and from which the most important points of the breed strike the eye :

HEAD.—Well-rounded ; "apple-dome" ; cheeks and jaw lean ; teeth level. Nose moderately short and black. In chocolates—coffee, seal, brown. and mole, self-coloured.

EARS.—Large and thin ; "rose"- or "tulip"-pointed, held erect. placed well back, flaring slightly to the side.

EYES.—Round and full, prominently placed, set well apart ; black, dark, or luminous.

NECK.—Clean, not throaty, slightly arched, gracefully sloping into shoulders.

SHOULDERS.—Sloping lean. neither too narrow nor too broad.

CHEST.—Neither narrow nor broad, with good depth of brisket.

BACK.—Level. gracefully sloping over hips to the tail

FORELEGS.—Straight well placed under fine

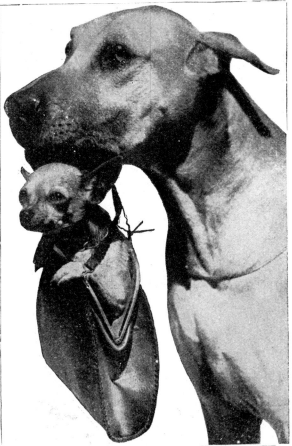

[Photo]　　　　　[Keystone.

THE LARGE AND SMALL OF IT

The Chihuahua dog can comfortably be carried in a lady's handbag. This amusing picture, taken in America, shows a Great Dane carrying a diminutive Chihuahua.

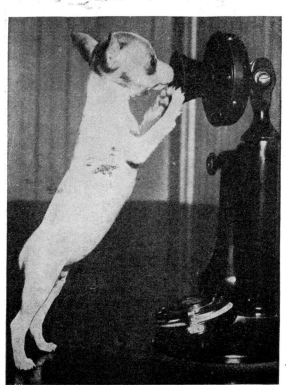

[Photo]　　　　　[Keystone.

THE 'PHONE CALL.

This Chihuahua weighs a mere 15 ozs. He is standing up to the 'phone just to show how very tiny he is.

pasterns, free play at elbows, but not turned out, not leggy and not short, holding the shoulders well up, giving balance and soundness to forequarters.

FEET.—Very small, neither "hare" nor "cat" ; toes well split up, but not spread ; pads well cushioned.

NAILS.—Moderately long.

HINDQUARTERS.—Muscular ; hocks well apart, not out or in, well let down, giving firm and sturdy action.

TAIL.—Moderately long, upper portion meaty, and break or kink is felt midway or near end, below which tail finishes to a "rat"-end, carried cycle- or loop-fashioned. Born bob-tails are common and not disqualifying.

COAT.—Smooth, fine, glossy in dark shades; well placed over body and neck ; more scanty on head and ears, inner portion of legs and under body bare.

COLOUR.—All shades of fawn, gold, red or sand, most popular cream, white, black, silver, mole.

ARMSFUL OF PRIZE WINNERS.

The famous Westminster Kennel Club's 1934 show in New York attracted 2,462 entries, and among them were the above Chihuahuas, the second from the left being Ch. "Juanita", though all in the entire group, in the arms of Miss Florence Clark, were prize winners.

chocolate, and many shades of brown, marked or solid preferred to broken or ticked.

WEIGHT.—Two to six lb. The more diminutive the better desirable.

GENERAL APPEARANCE.—A graceful, alert, swift-moving little dog, with saucy expression, compact and tiny, with terrier qualities.

DISQUALIFICATIONS.— Broken or cropped ears or cropped tail.

SCALE OF POINTS.

Head—Skull should be apple shaped. Ears large, held erect, slightly flaring to side. Eyes—large, luminous, black preferred. Nose—short, moderately pointed, black preferred, 20 ; Body—compact, short-coupled, but slender, well-ribbed, tucked-up in loins ; deep-chested ; terrier-like, 10 ; Tail—moderately long, carried cycle-shape. 10 ; Legs—slender, well-sinewed, feet small and dainty ; nails strong, moderately long, 10 ; Coat—short, soft and smooth, 10 ; Weight—two to six lb., 10 ; Colour —any, preferably solid or marked, not splashed or ticked, 10 ; General Appearance—an alert compact, terrier-like little dog, 20. Total, 100.

Chills.—Notwithstanding the opinions of some authorities whose views command respect, there seems no reason to doubt that dogs can and do contract ordinary chills which are in no way connected with distemper infection. One draws this inference from the fact that dogs are often observed with the symptoms of chill, which run a rapid and mild course and are not transmissible to other dogs ; also from the fact that such animals do not present a typical picture of distemper as the clinician knows it. One is forced, however, to regard all chills with the greatest suspicion, because it can never be known in the beginning whether such attacks are simple or specific in nature, until further developments have taken place.

SYMPTOMS. — Chill is usually ushered in by a marked rise in temperature, notice being first drawn to the patient on

Photo]					[Wide World.
A CANINE MIDGET.
The Chihuahua can be comfortably balanced on the palm of the hand.

account of its refusal to feed. It may become tired or listless, at which stage it is often taken to a veterinary surgeon. The temperature may be 103° F. or even more, and frequently no other symptoms are observable. With proper care at this time the dog may recover normal health without having developed any further abnormality. In other cases we may see discharges from the eyes and nose, and even diarrhoea. Usually there is neither cough nor nervous phenomena, both of which are frequent concomitants of distemper.

A chill may affect almost any part of a dog, and whilst in one case it may settle upon the lungs, in another it may affect the stomach, or the bladder, head, etc., etc.

TREATMENT.—So far as first-aid treatment is concerned, for the case which evinces a rise of temperature with no other symptoms, a simple aspirin tablet given three times a day in conjunction with enforced rest, warmth, and nourishing food, will usually bring about recovery. For the other specialized cases, the reader is referred to paragraphs which deal with the various organs of the body ; and for complicated cases professional help is advisable.

Chinese Crested Dogs.—These remarkable hairless dogs in some instances are crested, and, in consequence, cause no little interest. The explanation of this is dealt with fully under African Sand Dog on page 16. Occasionally one or two of these hairless crested dogs have been kept in England.

Chlorine.—A yellowish-green gas which is the active principal of many proprietary and other disinfectants. It has great germicidal, deodorant and bleaching properties.

Chlorodyne.—A proprietary anodyne mixture containing chloroform, hydrocyanic acid, capsicum, cannabis indica, and morphia. It is a valuable substance to keep in the medicine chest, as it relieves cough, colic, sleeplessness, and diarrhoea. The dose for dogs is 5 to 20 drops in water or milk three or four times daily.

Photo					Wide World.
A SLOW STEED.
This diminutive Chihuahua enjoys occasional rides on a pet turtle.

Choking.—Most dogs are careful in the way they eat bones, but occasionally accidents happen when a chop bone, or a piece of a larger one, becomes lodged in the pharynx or gullet, causing difficult or restricted respiration, a good deal of fright and probably considerable pain.

Greedy feeders are susceptible to choking as well as are those which forage for food in dustbins, etc. Fish, rabbit, and chicken bones are more often the cause of choking than are beef or mutton bones; but other foreign bodies such as pins, nails, bits of wood,

TREATMENT.—If the obstruction can be reached with the finger, an attempt should be made carefully to withdraw it—though preferably with a pair of forceps.

This, however, may lead to severe laceration of the adjacent tissues, and if such is imminent, no further effort should be made, but a surgeon should be called. Unless the foreign body is smooth in structure, it is of little use trying to work it back again into the mouth by outside manipulation (even if it could be located) because in nine cases out of ten it would not move.

By courtesy]　　　　　　　　　　　　　　　　　　　　　　　　　*[E. C. Ash*

THE CHINESE CRESTED DOG.

Of the several examples of hairless dogs in various parts of the world the Chinese Crested is one of the most unusual in appearance. Some fault in pigmentation is the reason for the lack of hair.

rubber balls, etc., are not infrequently implicated.

Tumours, abscesses, and the swellings caused by wasp stings may also impede breathing, if contiguous with the windpipe.

SYMPTOMS.—The dog refuses to feed or even to swallow water although it shows great interest in the dishes; if its hunger forces it to feed, the food is returned as soon as it reaches the obstruction. The head is protruded and lowered in a stiff, peculiar manner, and there are many and oft-repeated swallowing movements. The dog scratches at its face and neck with its forepaws, looks terrified, breathes rapidly, and may show a bluish discoloration of its mucous membranes.

Experience proves that objects, such as bones, are difficult enough to remove, even by experts using suitable instruments. One's best plan is to waste no time and inflict no useless pain upon the animal, but endeavour to get it to a surgery where every instrument, restorative, operating table and other equipment are ready to hand. An immediate operation may be the only way of saving the animal's life.

Cholagogue.—A medicine which increases the flow of bile. The most important examples are aloes, calomel, jalap, podophyllin and rhubarb.

Choosing a Dog. (*See also* BUYING A DOG.)—The following remarks are directed to those who, whilst contemplating the purchase of a dog, are in considerable doubt as to the breed which is likely to suit them best. To the uninitiated, the choice of a dog must undoubtedly present many pitfalls and difficulties, especially when the prospective purchaser entertains the desire to found a kennel and start breeding. The particular breed of dog eventually chosen will depend very materially upon the purpose to which it is to be put, and since this discourse is intended largely for the guidance of the householder requiring a guard-companion, consideration of show specimens or sporting dogs will, for the present, be omitted.

The larger breeds, such as St. Bernards, Mastiffs, etc., whilst undoubtedly handsome and noble creatures of great intelligence and invaluable as protectors, are nevertheless too large and unwieldy for the average house, and far too much of

be relied upon with any certainty. There are people who deride this popular opinion of the Collie, and say it is quite unfounded ; but the writer's experiences with them have taught him to regard them with increasing distrust. Much the same must be said of the Chow (the Chinese dog with the black tongue), and, in fact, of all intractable dogs this breed is the worst. It is a lover of luxury, and needs much attention to its toilet, both of which factors rather negative its usefulness as a house-dog.

It is comparatively only recently that any serious notice has been taken of the Alsatian Wolfhound in this country, and although considerable prejudice still exists against it in some quarters, there is yet much to be said in its favour. These hounds gained great favour with the officers and men of the British Army of Occupation, who brought them to England in good numbers. The Alsatian

Photo]   [Dorien Leigh.

ASTONISHING EARS.

Nature, under certain conditions, may go too far. Some factor of development abnormally developed, or some factor of control handicapped, may bring strange results, such as the abnormal ears depicted here.

a handful for most people to undertake, beside requiring a well-lined purse for their maintenance.

Greyhounds, Wolfhounds, and Deerhounds are eminently unsuitable, as they require much more exercise than usually can be conveniently afforded them, whilst, in addition, sharing the disadvantages of the first-mentioned breeds. Of the Wolfhounds, too, the Russian variety (Borzoi) is, in the writer's experience, not only delicate but none too trustworthy. The Bob-Tailed English Sheepdog has a most lovable disposition and is extremely sagacious, but cannot be recommended as a house-dog on account of his mass of shaggy hair, which, in dirty weather, becomes rapidly corroded with mud, and is a source of annoyance in the house. Much time and attention must be devoted to the Sheepdog's coat if justice is to be done to it, and unless it is, the dog soon gets into an appalling tangled mass. The Collie suffers to the same extent from the same drawback, and, in addition its temper cannot always

commands a high price, and is undoubtedly a sagacious and very handsome creature. It would be eminently suited to a suburban or country house, though on account of its size and long coat, perhaps, would not be recommended for town. Like the Chow, it is a dog which becomes tremendously attached to its owner or keeper, but, as a rule will have no relations with strangers.

The Bulldog, though looked upon by a good many people as an awesome creature, is in reality quite the reverse. Of all breeds, this dog is probably the mildest tempered, although doubtless easily roused ; should he once take hold, nothing can induce him to release his grip. He is, however, lacking in grace and agility, running being his weakest quality, whilst his voice—for the purposes of raising an alarm—is negligible. The Bull Terrier is a more useful house-dog, being well able to bark and run, and, when necessary, to give a good account of himself in a scrum. He is even-tempered, smooth-

Photo]   [Dorien Leigh.

WON'T I DO ?

Probably the best all-round dog for the average home is the Fox Terrier. He is such an appealing, loyal, lovable fellow and fits in to all and any conditions.

BE CAREFUL.

There is much unintentional cruelty to animals and many a puppy is cowed by the over-affectionate child who is inclined to crush its new pet, causing it pain and, occasionally, injury. Children should be taught not to play with puppies, but to allow puppies to play with them   there's a difference.

coated, very powerful, and his tenacity is second only to that of the Bulldog. One of the greatest drawbacks to many members of this breed is a peculiar and apparently inherent deafness, which is a serious disability in a dog required for house protection. Handsomeness is not its strong point, and, being all white, it requires regular and fairly frequent bathing.

The Irish, Fox, and Welsh Terriers are very similar in their various qualities, and all are excellent little dogs in many ways. The Irish Terrier is, perhaps, inclined to be rather quarrelsome and delights in being "top-dog" of his street. The Fox Terrier is thoroughly good all round, being sharp, hard-working, alert, hardy and usually a good ratter. He is a good-tempered little fellow, takes up little room, and has an ever-increasing popularity.

Of the various Scotch dogs, one's choice would probably fall upon the Scottish (or Aberdeen) Terrier, this being a reliable, intelligent, and hardy little dog, and staunch friend—even if not over demonstrative. A close second would be the West Highland, followed by the Cairn Terrier and the Dandy Dinmont. The Cairn, though shaped on similar lines to the Scotch Terrier, is, however, of a finer build, and perhaps not so strong, although undoubtedly a hard worker and an excellent companion. Better than all the breeds so far mentioned for the purpose under consideration is, in the writer's opinion, the Airedale Terrier. He has every attribute desirable in a guard-companion, possessing as he does all the good qualities of the terrier class, unsullied by any of the bad ones. His only possible fault, if it can be considered as such, is his size ; but personally, his size and strength are looked upon as a distinct asset where house or other property is to be protected. A burglar would find in a well-trained Airedale a tough opponent not to be despised. This terrier is very resistant to disease, has a good, hard coat, which does not show dirt, and is as full of exuberant spirit as a puppy ; he is fearless and feared, loving and lovable, and, as the ideal combination, the writer plumps for him every time.

The pet dogs cannot claim to any consideration as *guard*-companions on account of their diminutive size and frailty ; yet undoubtedly they are very useful for raising an alarm, even if they afterwards run away. Many of the Toy breeds are very difficult to rear, and the majority, too, are more or less delicate.

Probably of the small dogs, those showing the greatest utility are the Dachshund and Schipperke. The first-named is blessed with a very sweet and faithful disposition, has a good bark, and (like the Schipperke) is fairly active and hardy. The Pekingese enjoys an immense popularity among those who desire a dog solely as a companion, and their adaptability for this purpose need not, perhaps, be enlarged upon.

But there is one peculiarity pertaining to these dogs (which is nearly equally true of Pugs and other prominent-eyed breeds) and that is the ease with which their eyes may

Photo]   *[Dorien Leigh.*
CAT AND DOG LIFE.
The cat is the dog's natural enemy, and though in domestic circles they form tolerant friendships, the best of dogs will usually strain to tell a strange cat what he thinks about it.

Photo] [Hugh D. Martineau.

GOOD COMPANIONS.

The Dachshund is good company, gentle and faithful, as well as being one of the best "guards" among the smaller dogs.

be induced to leave the orbits. Many instances have been known in which owners struggling for some reason with their dogs—have suddenly been horrified to find an eye lying loose upon the cheek. This is no exaggeration, for it has been repeatedly seen after accidents in the streets, fights with other dogs, or, as above described. Owners of such dogs may therefore take warning to exercise great care in handling them.

It is hoped, and indeed assumed, that the prospective purchaser will have gleaned sufficient data from the above brief survey of the breeds to have enabled him to make his choice. The next question which besets him is that of sex. The large majority of those who buy dogs for purposes other than breeding, choose males, and this for the sole reason that the bitch needs a short bi-annual seclusion. The general health of the bitch is unaffected during oestrum, and no burden will therefore be imposed upon the owner other than the necessity for confining her strictly to the house or grounds. Certainly, from the monetary point

of view, a bitch is preferable, as she is usually much cheaper.

Chop.—Fore-face of Bulldog.

Chorea.—Also known as St. Vitus's Dance. It is a disease of the nervous system which nearly always depends for its origin upon a previous attack of distemper. The latter, moreover, need not be severe, for it has been often observed that a quite mild attack may be followed by one or more of the nervous sequelae, of which chorea is one. Myelitis, or tumours contiguous with the brain or spinal cord, may, however, be predisposing causes.

SYMPTOMS.—Convulsive movements may be seen affecting a single muscle or a group of muscles, the movements or twitchings being fairly constant and regular. There may be a rhythmic shaking or nodding of the head, or twitching of the temporal muscle ; a limb or pair of limbs only may be affected, or the whole body may shake. When the disease is not severe, the contractions generally subside during sleep. Excitement or fright increase symptoms. In bad cases there is much distress and often shrieking, which leads one to believe the condition is accompanied by muscular pain. It is a serious matter when the patient is so severely afflicted that it obtains no rest or sleep whatever.

In fatal cases, the convulsions lead to epileptiform fits, during one of which death may occur owing to spasm of the heart muscles.

TREATMENT.—Most cases have proved incurable, but all seem worthy of some effort until found to be hopeless. Some of the cases appear to be best treated with powerful nerve sedatives, whilst others would be better on tonic medicines. The remedies which have been tried for the relief of this condition are very numerous and varied, but which one should be selected in any given case must depend upon the particular case, and advice in this respect should be obtained in the first instance from a veterinary surgeon.

Photo] [Ralph Robinson.

NOT SUITABLE.

For town dwellers big dogs, such as this Irish Wolfhound, should be avoided. It is not fair to such dogs to keep them closely confined, and the owner never enjoys their natural attributes

Photo]   [E.N.A.

RECORDS.

Those who choose a Peke must remember it is a pet that has to be taken much care of.   It is one of the most popular of breeds
with both sexes of all classes.   Here is Alfred Piccaver, the famous tenor—a "best-seller" of the gramophone—with his Pekingese,
for which he paid £200.

Fresh air, sunlight, liberal and nutritious meat diet with milk and other fatty matter, are essential. There must be an avoidance of fatiguing influences, excitement, and anything likely to reduce the strength, condition, or resistance of the animal. Recovery may eventually occur after one or more months of good treatment and hygiene. The writer knows of at least two cases of racing greyhounds, affected with chorea, which regularly raced and often won.

Chow Chow.—The Chow Chow is the principal indigenous dog of China. The Pekingese is the lap dog of the country and the Chow is the only other dog which can be used for the various purposes for which a dog of average size is required.

In China he is used for hunting, for caravan guards, for guarding sampans and junks in the coastal regions, and, as the Chinese are omniverous feeders in a country which does not produce meat, for food.

The black, or rather dark-blue tongue, is a characteristic shared by no other breed of dogs and by only one other mammal. The Polar bear has a darkish tongue.

In the mists of antiquity, when all living things were in the course of evolution, the Chow Chow may have been derived from some other ancestor than that which produced the Western dogs, a creature somewhat akin perhaps to the bear. Like the bear, the Chow is undoubtedly extremely sure-footed: he will scale high wire-netting by deliberately climbing it, and will occasionally reach perilous places with complete safety and confidence. As an instance, a Chow would get out of the writer's window overlooking a porch and take a two-foot drop on to what was little more than a two-foot ledge. In that somewhat perilous position she would sleep.

The jumping power of a Chow varies to an extraordinary extent. Some can jump a 3 ft. 6 in. fence in a clean flying leap, and, with the utmost neatness and minimum of fuss, leap on to any ordinary table; others seem unwilling to jump even on to a chair.

The Chow is capable of powerful pulling effort, as anyone who has had two excited Chows on a harness and lead can testify, and yet he does not appear to be used in China for haulage purposes.

It is possible that the comparatively rare blue is a "sport" from the mating of reds and blacks. The cream also may have originated from this breeding, and as the Chinese do not regard the dog as the friend of man, but merely as an animal of utility, colour is not bred for, and blues may occur locally where a few "sports" may chance to have been bred.

The real smooth is only occasionally seen in China.

THE SHORT-COATED CHOW
The short-coated Chows were brought into England as a curiosity They were then known as the Edible Dog.

Casual observers might easily mistake the ordinary variety seen very much out of coat for the true smooth. Whether the breed in China has deteriorated in modern times is a matter of conjecture. It may be said emphatically that if any enthusiast went to China expecting to find good breeding stock to bring to this country he would be very disappointed The Chinaman is utilitarian; as long as the dog of the country suits his purpose he does not concern himself with the delicate art of improving the breed. He is not interested.

The Kennel Club has a list of over eighty classified breeds, and one cannot but be struck with the fact that all but about six, which includes the rarely seen Tibetan Mastiff and the Lhassa Terrier, are found in the Occident. The Chinese have for some reason not found it necessary to breed the numerous varieties of the Western world which vary in size from the Deerhound to the diminutive Toy dogs. Most breeds have been bred and modified for particular uses in sport of various kinds. For purposes of sport the Chow has limitations; he has considerable speed for so heavy a dog, but for short sprints only. Two of the writer's Chows hunted and pulled down a deer in one of the Royal Parks. They seemed to understand what they had to do and finally caught the deer on the face

Photo]   [L.N.A.

CHOW EXPRESSION.

This wonderful brace, the property of Miss Joshua, show the expression of the Chow face. It is officially described as a "scowling" look, but perhaps leonine would be more accurate.

Photo]   *[Fall.*

A NOTABILITY.

No one has more staunchly supported the Chow than Lady Faudel-Phillips. Her kennel name of "Amwell" is synonymous with excellence. Here she is shown with one of her noted dogs.

QUEEN ALEXANDRA'S CHOW.
Amongst Her Majesty's pets was, as this photograph shows
a Chow. Attention is drawn to the difference in type of the
dog of those days from the present time.

below the eyes and pulled it down. They will
chase anything that runs, from cats to hares, uttering a peculiar hunting bark which they voice only
on such occasions.

For the general external appearance of the Chow
here is an admirable description given in *The
Popular Chow Chow*, by Messrs. Leighton and
Baer, who are well-known American authorities.
The American ideal is obviously exactly the same
as ours :

"In general contour the Chow Chow is a thick-
set, sturdily built dog, short coupled and cloddy in
outline, with a broad, deep chest ; straight, thick,
rather short legs, and small round feet. The level
back is wide, and the powerful loin is partly
hidden by the heavily-furnished tail, which is
curled over the back. The proudly lifted head is
massive, with small pointed ears carried stiffly
erect and looking forward over the wrinkled,
frowning brows. The dark, almond-shaped eyes
are deep set, and there is very little depression, or
stop, between them in the nasal bone. The muzzle
is broad and blunt, not finely tapering to the nose,
and the black lips meet evenly with no loose overhanging flews.

"Much of the dog's distinction depends upon the
abundance and density of its crisp outstanding
coat and the fullness of feathering in the ruff, yoke
culottes and tail. The action of the Chow is
different from that of any other breed, the walking
stride being short and mincing, owing to the hind
legs being constrained by the straight, inflexible
hock, so that the feet do not extend far backward
for the propelling push. This produces the charac-

teristic stilty gait. Seen at his best, whether the
colour of his coat be red, blue or black, with or
without lighter shadings, the typical Chow is an
arrestingly beautiful animal, giving the impression
of symmetry, balance, power and alertness."

For the detailed points of the breed we reproduce
between inverted commas the points as accepted
by the Chinese Chow Club and published in their
list of rules, and we have added a number of
observations under each heading which will be
of use to those who are studying the breed.

HEAD.—"Skull, flat and broad, with little stop ;
well filled out under the eyes."

On the whole Chows of to-day conform well to
this. An "apple-head" would be a grave fault.

MUZZLE.—"Moderate in length and broad from
the eyes to the point (not pointed at the end like
a fox)."

This broad, blunt muzzle has probably been
bred to in comparatively modern times. The
native Chow, as well as many of the old-time
exhibition Chows, whose photographs can still be
seen, are distinctly more snipy in muzzle than the
exhibition Chow of to-day. The breed has
certainly been improved in this respect.

NOSE.—"Black, large and wide (in cream and
light-coloured specimens a pink nose is allowable)."

This exception may not be in the best interests
of the breed. It is quite possible to breed creams
and fawns (that is if anyone wants the latter) with
the normal black nose. The admission of light-
coloured noses for exhibition purposes only tends
to "breed in" other faulty pigmentation, such as
light eyes, light-coloured and spotty tongues and

WAS IT A CHOW ?
Amongst the finds of ancient Egypt was this curious model dog.
A noted resemblance to the Chow may be detected. Notice
also that the tail is curved over the back.

Photo]　　　HELP, PLEASE.　　　[S. & G.
Dogs make highly successful collectors. How
can one resist giving a copper for a deserving
cause when such a friendly beggar as this
Chow pleads?

pink gums. The unique pigmentation of the tongue is so
important a feature of the
breed that it should be safe-
guarded in every possible way.
In some Chows a certain amount
of smudginess of nose is seasonal.
Puppies' noses may go off colour
when teething, and bitches before
and during season Noses may go
"off colour" occasionally for no
apparent reason, but it would be
better if on these occasions the dogs
in question were not shown.

TONGUE.—"Black".

The colour is really a deep bluish-black; the
darker the better. It is a most interesting and
unique feature entirely confined to this one breed.

GUMS.—The Club "points" list makes no mention of this. They should be black.

EYES.—"Dark and small (in a blue or cream dog
light colour is permissible)."

A light eye is a serious fault, and as there are
many blues and creams with normal dark eyes it
is a pity to make an exception. It is quite reasonably possible to breed good dark eyes. A dark-
eyed sire very seldom sires light-eyed puppies
As to the *shape* of the eye, the phrase "almond-
shaped" is often used. This would seem to imply
an elongated narrow eye. The most esteemed type
of eye would better be described as triangular.
Certainly small and deep set and surmounted by
heavy brow that helps to give the so-called scowl.
Chows' eyes frequently suffer from inversion.
Sometimes one or two, sometimes every puppy,
in a litter will have this defect. which seems in-

herent in the breed. Unless it is so bad as to cause
obvious suffering, operation should be deferred
until five months of age. If done earlier, it may
have to be done again. Every lover of a dog will
see that this operation is performed as soon as
possible.

EARS.—"Small and stiffly erect, they should be
placed well forward over the eyes, which gives the
dog the peculiar characteristic expression of the
breed, viz. a sort of scowl."

The ears, it might be added, should be thick
broad at the base, and not too acutely pointed
The fur which covers the outside should be short
and dense. They should be tilted very slightly
forward and set fairly widely.

SCOWL.—It is difficult to define exactly this peculiar Chow characteristic. Perhaps that is why in the
C.C.C. rules no separate mention of this point
is made. The loose skin on the forehead is
slightly ridged : these ridges are
accentuated by slight differences
in pigmentation on the high lights
The light and shade so produced
give character to the whole face.

TEETH.—"Strong and level."

Many people consider this to
mean that the teeth, when
closed, should be edge to edge
or dead level. It is quite correct
for the upper teeth to overlap
the lower to the extent that the
bevels of the two sets are covered.
a matter perhaps one-thirtieth of an
inch—very much to the extent of
ordinary human front teeth. Chow
puppies before the change of teeth

Photo]　　　[Fall.
HEAD STUDY.
A Chow of distinction with a
good type of head.

Photo]　　　[Fall.
CH. "ROCHOW DIADEM".
Mr. Rotch's "Diadem", the winner of twelve Challenge Certificates, shows the correct proportions and desired squareness
of the modern Chow, as well as the slight forward tilt of the ears.

Photo]   [L.N.A.

MR. LLOYD GEORGE AND HIS "BEST FRIENDS".

Mr. Lloyd George's Chow, a great favourite of the famous statesman, is seen on the right side of him, apparently unwilling to stand still to have its photograph taken.

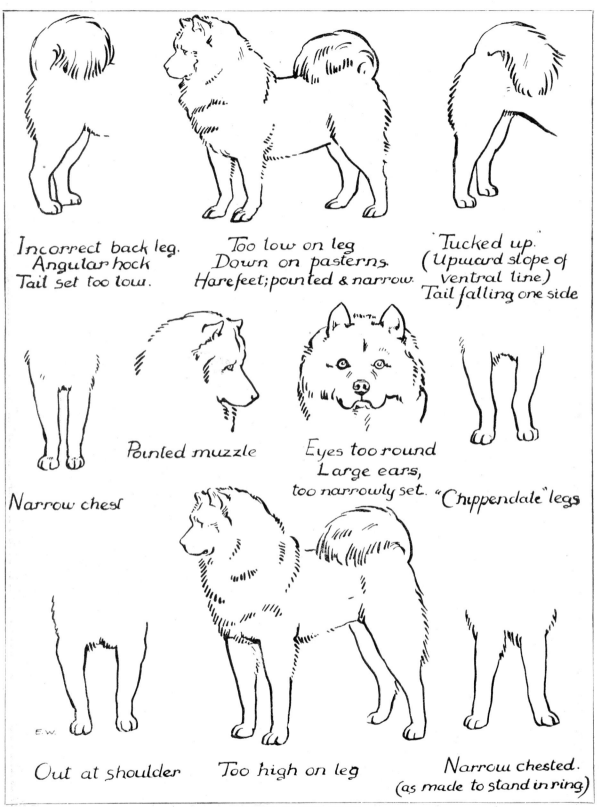

Incorrect back leg.
Angular hock
Tail set too low.

Too low on leg
Down on pasterns.
Hare feet; pointed & narrow.

Tucked up.
(Upward slope of ventral line)
Tail falling one side

Narrow chest

Pointed muzzle

Eyes too round
Large ears,
too narrowly set.

"Chippendale" legs

Out at shoulder

Too high on leg

Narrow chested.
(as made to stand in ring)

E.W.

FAULTS IN THE CHOW.

These diagrams have been specially drawn to show readers the outstanding faults in this beautiful breed. It is true that there is no such thing as the perfect dog, but one can form a good judgment all the better by knowing the more obvious failings, such as those depicted here.

are often slightly overshot. Unless this is very exaggerated the fault usually rectifies itself. An undershot mouth is a much more serious affair, but fortunately it is rare.

NECK.—"Strong, full, set well on the shoulders and slightly arched."

The average Chow is so well covered with hair that the anatomical structure is not easy to see. This part of a Chow is, however, fairly constant

The back legs of a Chow are highly characteristic of the breed. They are totally unlike those of a Terrier, which has marked angulation. The hocks should be very short. Some Chows carry their angulation, or lack of it, to the extent of being what is called "double-jointed". The action of a Chow is a unique feature of this breed. From his stifle downwards a correctly made Chow will walk with a stilt-like action with very little

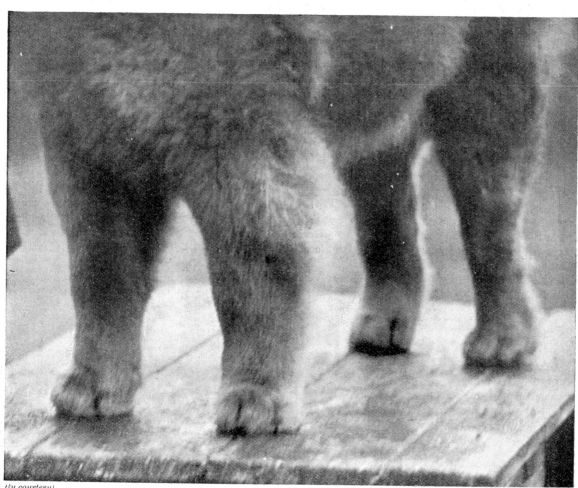

By courtesy] [*C. D. Rotch.*
CHOW LEGS AND FEET.
It is very difficult to describe in words the ideal legs and feet of a Chow; a photograph shows it better. Notice the position of the toes.

and one seldom sees exhibited a Chow with a long thin neck. When standing normally at attention the height of the head should be carried well over the tail level.

SHOULDERS.—"Muscular and sloping."

LOINS.—"Powerful"; i.e. muscular and hard.

BODY.—No special mention is made of this, but as the chest must be deep it must merge gradually into the abdominal line and not show a "greyhoundy" or tucked-up appearance.

HINDLEGS.—"Same as forelegs, muscular and straight with hocks well let down."

flexion of his hocks. This produces a short, mincing stride, totally unlike the free "pedalling action" of most other breeds. Judges should pay very great attention to this feature. It would be deplorable if a tendency arises to disregard this interesting and naturally inherent characteristic.

CHEST.—"Broad and deep"—with some spring of ribs.

FORELEGS.—"Perfectly straight, of moderate length, and with great bone."

The legs must be well spaced, about three inches clear daylight between them. A narrow front is a

Photo]   [Walter Guiver.
CH. "YOUNG CHENG OF AMWELL".
Lady Faudel-Phillips' "Young Cheng of Amwell" shows how
Chow should carry its tail.

most serious fault and one all too commonly seen.

BACK.—"Short, straight and strong"

If anything it may slope a shade downwards from shoulder to tail, but never the reverse.

FEET.—"Small, round and cat-like."

This applies to fore- and hindlegs. The feet must never be pointed.

TAIL.—"Curled tightly over the back"

"Laid tightly to the back" would convey a better meaning. Many perfectly correct Chows have a straight tail, with only a suspicion of a kink at the end. It should not be so long as to fall loosely along the sides. It should not be carried high or proud, and above all it should be carried well forward. If set too low it spoils the outline by making the back appear too long.

COAT.—"Abundant, dense, straight, and rather coarse in texture, with soft woolly undercoat."

Dark-red specimens seldom carry the coat of the "reds with cream shadings", and therefore do not present the same leonine appearance. In the latter type the mane is usually lighter in colour and covers the shoulders like a fur cape.

COLOUR.—"Whole-coloured, black, red, fawn, cream, blue, white, etc., not in patches. (The under part of tail and back of thighs frequently of a lighter colour.) The colour is the point of least importance."

Real creams are very beautiful, but very rare, especially when they have dark eyes and black noses.

The fawn is a most unfortunate addition to the list of colours, for two reasons: firstly, the colour is neither attractive nor typical; and secondly, if fawns are inter-bred with other colours there is a serious danger of spoiling the unique pigmentation of the breed. Pale tongues, pink noses, and light eyes will be the risk of such matings.

A good black is a handsome creature, but must always lose somewhat in comparison with reds because the wrinkles in the face cannot show up.

Blues are much sought after by Continental buyers. Although there are some excellent specimens, notably Ch. "Chilo-Sa" of Hankow, the only blue champion for more than thirty years, they generally lack the sturdy, cobby structure of the reds.

Both blacks and blues in respect of coat are certainly harder to maintain. The assertion that colour is of least importance may occasion some surprise, but it can be said that it is very difficult to draw a hard and fast rule as, for instance, in the amount of cream or very light shadings permissible in a red. As long as a dog is well put down and in first-rate coat does it matter very much if the chest or feet are very light in colour? The question of rusty red shadings in blues and blacks is a far more serious matter. A dog with this ugly admixture of colour is certainly less desirable, and therefore less saleable. Colour, therefore, in blues and blacks should certainly be considered carefully, and for that reason mixed breeding, reds to blacks, for example, is not to be recommended.

GENERAL APPEARANCE.—"A lively, compact, short-coupled dog, well knit in frame and tail curled well over the back."

A male Chow can hardly be too closely coupled; a bitch, however, must necessarily be appreciably longer in the back because of maternal duties. There must always be sufficient room to carry the family without crushing or interference with the normal intestine movements.

Smooth Chows "are governed by the same scale of points, except that the coat is smooth"

Photo]   [E.N.A.
A NOTED TRIO.
Miss Lil Dogover (Mrs. Witt) is well-known in Central Europe, so also are her two Chow dogs: indeed no two dogs are more popular.

Specially drawn for this work]

A FAMILY ALBUM.

[by Vere Temple.

Here is a lively family, grandfather Chow and the children, only a few weeks old, all delightfully subjected to the expressive art of Miss Temple.

A DELIGHTFUL PERSONALITY

A three-months-old puppy from the kennels of that successful breeder, Lady Faudel-Phillips, explains why Chows should be so popular. A real beau

This variety is decidedly rare. A good specimen is an object of real beauty to a Chow specialist, because his structure can be so readily seen Many a defect is hidden by the profuse coat of the ordinary Chow But when all is said and done, one of the chief beauties of a Chow is his beautiful coat

WEIGHT.— Bitches should run between 50 -60 lb., dogs 55--65 lb. The Chow is a slow developer and is probably not his best until he is five years of age. A good big dog is better than a good little one. If it is not leggy and "rangy", a Chow up to 70 or 75 lb. should not be penalized for his size.

Photo] A BASKETFUL OF VANITY. [Sport & General.
Mrs. M. Wickham's five-weeks-old Chow puppies wait impatiently to have their photographs taken.

and leonine appearance, and perhaps it is as well that the smooth is rare, for inter-breeding would not tend to improve the coats of either variety.

"Special attention should be called to the following very serious blemishes

"Drop ears, red or parti-coloured tongue, tail not curled over the back, white spots on coat, and red nose (except in fawn, cream or white specimens) Light eyes in red or black specimens"

The occasional importation of this interesting and beautiful breed into this country has been made for many years. Gilbert White, the naturalist, in a letter written about 1780 writes as follows

". . . about the size of a moderate spaniel, of a pale yellow colour with coarse bristling hair on their backs, sharp upright ears and peaked heads which gives them a very foxlike appearance. Their hind legs were unusually straight without any

Photo] A LITTLE CADGER. [Fox.
Puppies—and babies—often make interesting pictures. Here we see a greedy puppy determined to get a taste of chocolate even if it cannot get any more.

bend at the hock or ham, to such a degree as to give them an awkward gait when they trotted. When in motion their tails were curved high over their backs like those of some hounds. . . . Their eyes were jet-black, small and piercing; the insides of their lips and mouths of the same colour and their tongues blue."

Gilbert White missed very little in his excellent description, much of which holds good for the modern Chow.

Several great dogs have arisen like meteors, and each, as well as winning many honours at shows, has contributed much to the general improvement of the breed. One or two dogs in particular may be mentioned. Ch. "Lenming", whose name will be found in most pedigrees. Ch. "Akbar" is specially noteworthy as being the prototype of the massive bone and symmetrical balance which is so much esteemed. Had this dog enjoyed better health the breed would be still better. His services at stud were limited by his by no means robust health. As a puppy he had distemper so badly that only the devoted attention of Miss Peck, his owner, saved him, and so rendered possible the breeding of his distinguished progeny, Ch. "Choonam Brilliantine"; Ch. "Choonam Brilliantina"; Ch. "Chinnery" and Ch. "Rochow Akbella".

Ch. "Rochow Dragoon" was born in 1928, and, unrelated in recent generations to most of the best bitches of his time, arrived when an out-cross was much wanted. He won his first championship at the age of six and a half months, and was a full champion at eight and a half months. He has won 31 Challenge Certificates at thirty-six championship shows and thereby holds the record in the

history of the breed. So far he has sired four champions: Ch. "Rochow Diadem", Ch. "Rochow Diaphenia", Ch. "Hussar of Chunking", and Ch. "Niklos Marksman". It is not every great winning dog that sires the best progeny. In this case it is doubtful whether any Chow has sired so many winning dogs in the short space of four years. It is to be hoped that another outstanding dog may presently appear of fairly remote parentage to the bitches of his time. When this occurs we shall once more make an advance towards the perfection for which all keen breeders are striving.

One can speak enthusiastically on the altogether admirable characteristics of this breed. The Chow has been described as very "standoffish" to strangers. He is, and quite right too. He adores every member of his household and frankly has no use for strangers. The Chow is a highly strung dog and must never be beaten. He is so sensitive to rebuke that a word is sufficient. He is not a fighter by disposition, but when set on can hold his own easily with any dog of his own size. Two male dogs should not be kept together in the house. Jealousy may occur and inevitably sooner or later a fight will start.

Photo] 　　　　THE BLACK CHOW. 　　*[Hay Wrightson.*
Nowadays a black Chow is rather rare. Here is a good specimen with its owner.

A Chow is a non-barking variety. He will bark like any other dog, but only when there is some good reason for it. As a house dog he is naturally very clean and, as a puppy, very easily trained. He is not a greedy dog and casual scraps given at meals (quite improperly!) are viewed with suspicion. Taken gingerly by the lips, they are dropped on the floor, sniffed at with great caution and sometimes eaten, but by no means always.

A Chow requires a few minutes' brushing every day. It must be done regularly with a suitable

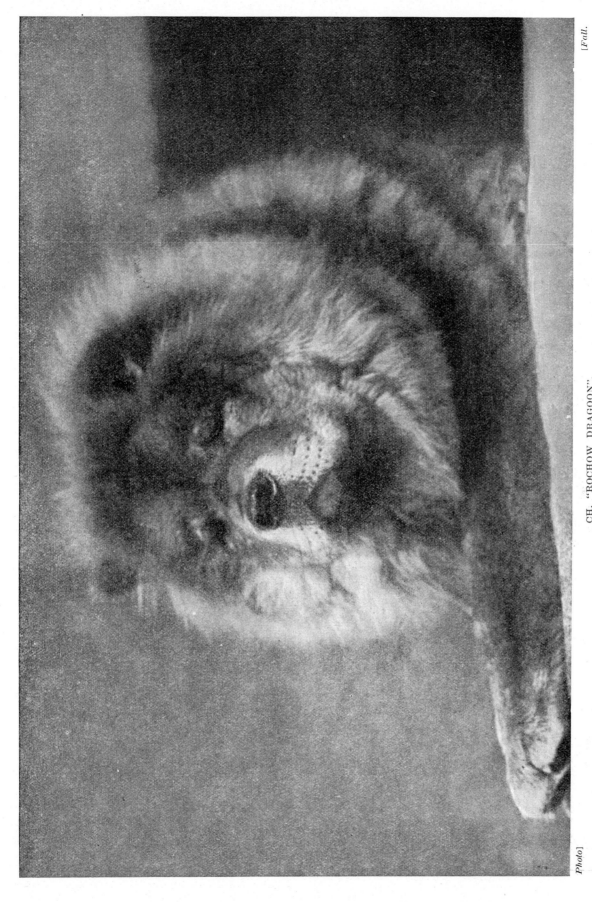

CH. "ROCHOW DRAGOON".

Here is a remarkable head study of a famous Chow champion, the property of Mr. C. D. Rotch. This is the type of head so much desired—the full ruff, the lion-like look, and the so-called "scowling" expression. See also next page.

FULL VIEW OF CH. "ROCHOW DRAGOON".

In 1933 this dog held the record of winning thirty-one Challenge Certificates. Indeed, almost in every point he indicates what a really good Notice the cat-like feet and the bold body. Chow should be.

brush (wire or coarse bristles) and can be maintained with very little trouble. When changing coat the dead undercoat will come away freely. This must on no account be dragged out forcibly; it should be quite lightly brushed or combed out.

A moderate amount of exercise will suffice to keep him healthy, and for that reason, in addition to his quietness, natural cleanliness devotion and freedom from doggy smell, he is an ideal town dog. When kept in the country he must be carefully trained when young not to chase sheep or other animals. The desire to chase anything that runs away is inherent in the breed, and is a fault that must be corrected from puppyhood.

In selecting a puppy in so slow a maturing breed careful allowance must be made for the age. Generally speaking, squareness, balance, straightness of legs, substance, dark eye, small ear, correct tail setting and adequate spacing of front legs are the chief points for consideration. Perfection of head is hard to estimate when the puppies are very young.

The following is a useful guide to weights of puppies, and represents the average of a considerable number of specimens:

By courtesy]   *[C. D. Rotch.*

A THREE-MONTHS-OLD SON.

Here is the three-months-old son of Ch. "Rochow Dragoon". He carries his tail well, and the hindquarters and body are exceptionally good

Three months, 20 lb.; four months, 30 lb.; five months 35 lb.; six months, 42 lb.: twelve months, 49 lb.

Chyle.—The milky fluid taken up by the lacteals from the food in the intestine after digestion. It consists of lymph and emulsified fat, and passes into the veins by the thoracic duct, becoming mixed with the blood.

Cicatrix.—Contracted or scar-tissue which remains, sometimes permanently, after accidental or surgical wounds.

Cirrhosis.—A disease of the liver in which specific portions of the hepatic cells are replaced by fibrous tissue producing, at a later stage, atrophy and degeneration. It results, generally, from inflammation of the liver.

Classes at Kennel Club Shows.—The following are the definitions of certain classes.

1. WHEN COMPETITION IS OPEN TO ALL EXHIBITORS:
Maiden Class.—For dogs which have never won a prize in any class at an Open Show.

Débutant.—For dogs which have never been exhibited, prior to the date of closing of entries, at a show where Challenge Certificates were offered for the breed.

Novice.—For dogs which have not won a Challenge Certificate or a First Prize at an Open Show. Wins in Maiden, Débutant, Puppy, Members', Local or District Classes excepted.

NOTE.—Dogs which have won the title of Champion

Photo]   *[Sport and General.*

A CHOW CLASS.

Chows always show themselves well, for as a breed they are very fearless and do not suffer from "stage fright" as this photograph so clearly shows. Notice the second dog from the right.

under American Kennel Club Rules, are not eligible for entry in Maiden, Débutant, or Novice Classes.

Puppy.—For dogs of six and not exceeding twelve months of age on the first day of the show.

Junior.—For dogs of six and not exceeding eighteen months of age on the first day of the Show.

Undergraduate.—For dogs which have not won a First Prize of the value of £2 in classes confined to the breed. Wins in Maiden, Débutant, Novice, Puppy, Local, Members', District or Selling Classes excepted.

Graduate.—For dogs which have not won more than three First Prizes, confined to the breed. At Open or Limited Shows, wins at Sanction Shows do not count.

Post-Graduate.—For dogs which have not won more than three First Prizes confined to the breed, and each of the value of £2.

Minor Limit.—For dogs which have not won more than two First Prizes in all, in Open, Limit, Mid Limit, and Minor Limit Classes, confined to the breed, at shows where Challenge Certificates were offered for the breed.

Mid Limit.—For dogs which have not won more than four First Prizes in all, in Open, Limit and Mid Limit Classes confined to the breed, at shows where Challenge Certificates were offered for the breed.

Limit.—For dogs which have not won more than six First Prizes in all, in Open and Limit Classes, confined to the breed, at shows where Challenge Certificates were offered for the breed.

Open.—For all dogs. If confined to a breed or variety, for all dogs of that breed or variety.

Photo]　　　　　　　　　　　　　　　　[*Sport & General.*

CH. "AKBAR" AND "CHEEFOO".

Miss A. Peck's two Chows won the Brace Championship at the Kennel Club's show at the Crystal Palace.

Veteran.—For dogs aged five years or upwards on the first day of the show.

Field Trial.—For dogs which have won prizes or Certificates of Merit in actual competition at a recognized Field Trial.

Brace.—For two exhibits (either sex or mixed) of one breed or variety, belonging to the same exhibitor, each exhibit having been entered in some class other than Brace or Team.

Team.—For three or more exhibits (either sex or mixed) of one breed or variety belonging to the same exhibitor, each exhibit having been entered in some class other than Brace or Team.

Litter.—For whelps of one and the same litter (being not less than six weeks and under three months of age on the first day of the show). Not more than one entry can be made for the same litter, and the dam must not be exhibited with the litter.

Foreign Dogs.—For dogs of any breed or variety of foreign extraction not classified on the registration form issued by the Kennel Club.

Sweepstake Class.—Is one in which the entry fees are given as the prize money in such proportion as the Committee of the show may determine.

2. WHEN COMPETITION IS LIMITED TO MEMBERS OF SOCIETIES OR TO EXHIBITORS WITHIN SPECIFIED AREAS, the definitions of classes shall be as above, except that the following definitions shall apply :

Maiden.—For dogs which have never won a prize at any show.

Novice.—For dogs which have never won a First Prize at any show. Wins in Maiden, Débutant, and Puppy excepted.

Photo]　　　　　　　　　　　　　　　　[*Sport and General.*

CH. "CHOONAM MOONBEAM" AND "CHOONAM CHANG LI".

Any dog with the prefix "Choonam" (the property of Mrs. V. A. Manooch) is always likely to excite interest because of the Kennel's remarkable record and high prices.

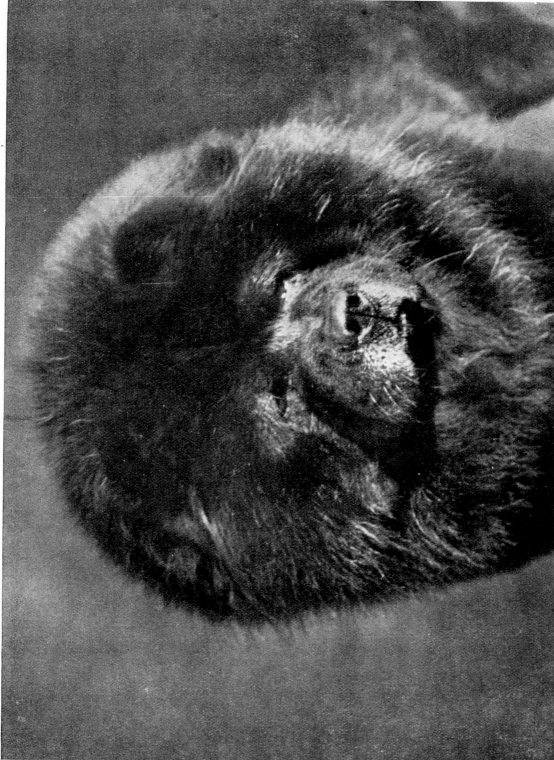

"BLACK SUN OF LI MOON".

Is the Chow a cross between the Eskimo dog and the Mastiff of Thibet? Some think so, and this magnificent head of Lady Faudel-Phillip's dog certainly suggests the Thibetan Mastiff type.

[Paul F

WHAT'S THAT ?

Could any pair of eyes speak more plainly, we wonder, than this ? Look at this fine head with half-closed eyes, and he seems to question you:
"What do you want ? I'm ready."

(*From Hobday's "Surgical Diseases of the Dog and Cat" by courtesy of Baillière, Tindall & Cox.*)

This dog's claws are all out of condition.

3. Subject to the above, and to any regulations, Show Committees may offer such prizes and make such classification and definitions thereof as they think fit, except that—

(*a*) If any be provided other than those defined above, the word "Special" or "Restricted" or both must precede the name of such class.

(*b*) All classes advertised in the schedule of a show must be clearly defined in the schedule, in accordance with the Kennel Club Show Regulations.

(*c*) The words Grand, Champion, or Challenge, must not be used in the

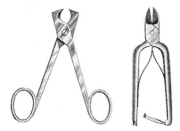

Two good kinds of claw cutters.

designation of any class or prize for which an entrance fee is charged and for which entry has to be made prior to the day of the show.

(*d*) No show may give Sweepstake Classes except for Brace and Team.

Claws, Inflammation of. (*See also* Foot, Diseases of.)

—The claws or nails of dogs are continually becoming damaged as a result either of the toes being trodden upon, run over, caught in doors, entangled in wire-netting, or torn away during the act of digging holes, etc. When the nail is broken, the loose part should be snipped off and, quite likely, a new nail will grow. But not infrequently the break in the claw permits of the entrance of germs, which is followed by redness, swelling and pain about the base of the nail. Sometimes a considerable amount of pus collects and the condition causes the animal exceeding pain, so much, in fact, that he cannot put the foot to the ground. The nail then generally sloughs off but is replaced by a new one in about two months.

Occasionally, the base of the claws becomes swollen and tender when no injury can be discerned as the exciting cause. Some authorities believe that these are due to gout following an excessive and highly nutritious diet in fat, plethoric dogs. Whatever may be the cause, the animal is generally very lame and spends a good deal of its time licking at the affected

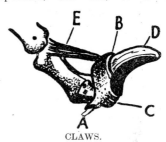

FILE

A

B

C

Filing the nails is to be recommended when the "quick" is too near the terminal point. A shows the file being applied; B shows the effect of such application; and C illustrates how the claw is finally shortened.

[*From "Popular Dogs"*]

toe. One should ensure that too long a nail is reduced, for the longer it is the more likely is it to become caught up or hurt. All broken nail must be excised, and the swollen toe should be bathed very frequently in a hot antiseptic solution. If the water is too hot, the dog will greatly resent a repetition of the process and difficulty will be experienced in future. The temperature of the water should be gradually increased by judicious additions of hotter water. After the bathing, a cotton-wool dressing should be applied and then a special boot (*see* Boots) or a bandage.

In nine cases out of ten the owner will find it more expedient to leave the dog for a few days with a veterinary surgeon. The comparatively small amount of money expended in this way will be amply repaid by immunity from bites, the mess and the trouble, and by getting the job properly done.

It might even be necessary to have the third phalanx (or terminal bone) amputated, and this, of course,

CLAWS.

A. Tubercle of pad. B. Horn groove.
C. Groove of sole. D. Third phalanx.
E. Dorsal Ligaments.

Diagram showing second and third phalanges. The dorsal ligaments (E) pull the claw upwards for its protection when out of use.

requires local anaesthesia and surgical experience.

Overgrowth of.—This is due solely to lack of exercise upon hard ground, and is very commonly observed in very old dogs, or in lapdogs such as King Charles, Pekingese, Pugs, etc., or any dog which is habitually carried about by

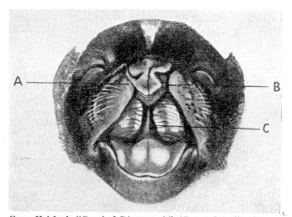

From Hobday's "Surgical Diseases of the Dog and Cat"
[*by courtesy of Baillière, Tindall & Cox.*]

Showing a cleft palate. A and B—Double hair-lip. C—Cleft palate.

its owner. Exercise, which is taken generally upon soft grass, does not tend to reduce the claws to their normal length. Claws of the dog, like the fingernails of human beings, are continuously growing, and unless they are naturally worn down, or clipped, they will grow in a circular direction and eventually pierce the pads of the foot, causing intense pain and lameness. The dewclaws cannot, of course, become worn down, as they do not reach the ground ; but they will, similarly, grow to such length that eventually they pierce the soft contiguous tissues.

How to Shorten Them.—For the cutting of claws no instrument should be employed which has a scissor-like action. The cutting edges, in other words, should not pass each other, but must come directly together in order that the claws may be cleanly cut, instead of being partially crushed or broken off. We illustrate both types of nail-cutter.

Care should be exercised when cutting a dog's nails to ensure that the nervous and vascular area is not involved in the process. White claws show clearly where the vascular area (or quick) ends, but black claws give no such indication, and one must, in the latter case, exercise judgment based upon observation as to where claws are generally cut. It is a good plan, in such instances, to place the cutters in the position one thinks they should be, but before actually snipping off the nail, apply some of the pressure only. If the quick has not been included, the dog will give no indication of pain. If he cries out, however, another position must be found nearer the tip of the nail. It has been observed that the "quicks" come down—in some dogs—very near to the points of the nails, so that although the latter are obviously too long for the dog's comfort, it is almost impossible to reduce their length by cutting. The proper course to adopt, then, is to obtain a fine sharp rasp and file away a small amount each day. The vascular area gradually recedes, until eventually it will be found that considerable reduction in length has been effected without causing bleeding or pain.

Cleft Palate.

—A congenital abnormality of the roof of the mouth, in which the two portions of the palate have never properly united. A decided fissure or gap is present, which may be so wide as to permit of communication between the mouth and the nasal passages. This defect is most usually found in short-nosed breeds such as Pekes, Japanese Spaniels, Bulldogs, etc., and not infrequently it is associated with another condition known as "Hare-lip". It is the young puppy which is affected, and such pups commonly die in consequence of inanition. The fissure in the mouth prevents the pup from forming the necessary vacuum enabling it to suckle its mother. It is possible to operate for this condition, but there are great difficulties and the prognosis is not good.

An electric clipping machine, quick and efficient.

Clinical.

— This word arises frequently throughout this work, and it denotes anything which pertains to the clinic, or to the patient and the practical observation of its condition. In the realm of veterinary science there are pathologists, bacteriologists, anatomists, etc., etc., but the clinician is he who studies the symptoms at the bedside. The type of thermometer used for recording a patient's temperature is described as a clinical thermometer.

A small type electric clipper.

Clipping.

— The clipping of a dog is not very frequently resorted to except for veterinary reasons, and then it is performed in order that, in cases of skin disease, one may be better enabled to bring skin dressings into closer contact with the affected parts. For instance, it is futile to attempt to treat the skin of such dogs as the Chow or the Bob-tailed Sheep Dog unless their masses of hair are first removed. Should a dog be extensively affected with mange, eczema, or even lice, it might be far more practical to clip all over rather than to render the animal an object of derision by denuding it of hair in patches. Moreover, it is a common occurrence to find, upon clipping completely, that far more of the body surface is affected than was formerly supposed.

Infestations with lice or fleas are much more expeditiously dealt with if the dog's coat is clipped off and burnt, for with the hair go all the nits or eggs. Drying after bathing, too, is facilitated. A warning note, however, may be sounded here. Should the weather be cold and a dog have to be clipped, it is wise to compensate the dog by applying an artificial coat of wool or flannel, especially when the animal goes out of the house.

There are instances of dogs being in very bad coat, sometimes due to debility following distemper, sometimes due to anaemia, starvation, nursing a litter, or other causes, the coat then being exceedingly patchy and unkempt. In many of these cases, to completely clip the dog is a far better and more expeditious method of making the animal presentable than any other which can be adopted. Complete removal of the hair stimulates its growth.

Apart from veterinary reasons, many dogs are clipped in the hot summer months for the sake of their comfort, and certainly, observation proves that the freedom from a hot, tangled coat is appreciated.

Certain breeds, such as the French Poodle, need the clippers in order to give them their characteristic appearance. So far as other breeds are concerned, owners are warned to beware of entrusting their dogs (for the purpose of clipping) to those who are inexperienced in that kind of work. The writer has seen many a good specimen entirely (though, of course, temporarily) ruined in consequence of having had the beard, the feather or the brush ruthlessly sheared off.

Some books devoted to the dog advise that scissors may be used for clipping dogs, but we condemn such advice, as no stretch of imagination is needed to conjecture what a dog might look like after numerous scissor-cuts going in all directions around the body. Hand-clippers may be employed, but better than all are the modern electrical clippers. Whatever type of apparatus be used, it is still necessary that he who operates shall be skilled and experienced in clipping, in order that there shall be no tufts or lines of hair, or any appearance which might be described, in popular language, as rat-bitten. The usual charge for clipping a dog is 7s. 6d., though this may be increased if the animal is very large, or in a dreadfully matted and neglected condition.

Clitoris.—A small erectile organ of the female body and situated at the lower angle of the vulva. It is homologous with the penis in the male but appears to have no useful function. In hermaphrodites the clitoris is usually abnormally large.

Clothing. (*See* COATS FOR DOGS.)

Clotting of the Blood.—When blood is released from the vessels containing it, as will occur if any wound is made into a living tissue, it will be found that within a few minutes the spilt blood will have undergone a process of clotting. The hot fluid blood first becomes a jelly and then a firm clot. Later still, this clot contracts and squeezes out a fluid known as serum. As the latter accumulates, the clot sinks to the bottom. If the clot be examined microscopically, it is found to consist of fine fibrils, entangled in which are the blood corpuscles. The physiology of blood-clotting is a very long and complex story, a detailed account of which might weary the reader. It is sufficient, therefore, to outline, quite briefly, what occurs when a blood-vessel is cut. First, the muscular fibres shrink and their cut ends are slightly retracted within the fibrous coat. The result is that there is a considerable reduction in the size of the hole, thus restricting the escape of blood at that point. So soon as blood comes into contact with air, or encounters any surface rougher than the smooth lining of intact blood-vessels, fibrin makes its appearance and a clot commences to form. At the point of injury, therefore, a tiny clot is created which gradually spreads in all available directions, until the lumen of the vessel is occluded and no more blood can escape.

Clumber Spaniel.—There is a theory that these dogs are descended from an Alpine Spaniel and are, therefore, related distantly to the St. Bernard, but the evidence in favour of this argument rests on the somewhat frail foundation of a certain similarity in head, ears, and colouring. We are also told that the Clumber takes us back only to the last quarter of the eighteenth century, when it is related that the Duc de Noailles sent a kennel of Spaniels to the second Duke of Newcastle, who lived at Clumber Park.

The dogs assumed the name of their owner's residence, for this kennel seems to have been the origin of the breed in England. It is a curious fact that, while we can trace its history no further back than that incident, the Clumber itself seems to have been unknown in France, where it was looked upon later as an English breed. We reproduce a picture showing the second Duke of Newcastle with his Clumber Spaniels, not only a very fine painting by Francis Wheatley, R.A., but vastly interesting from a doggie point of view as showing the first draft of these dogs in the country. It was painted in 1788.

One is struck with the fact that the Clumber has changed in type since those days. It has grown longer in body and heavier in build and the head has become more houndlike, often showing the haw.

It was not long after their introduction that the Clumber's popularity began to spread. We find that almost every important country house in the neighbourhood of Clumber Park became possessed of specimens. Among these was Osberton Hall, owned by Mr. Foljambe, and it was through this gentleman's kennel that the most successful strain was produced, especially in regard to the show bench. Nearly all the big winners of the early days of the breed were descended from Mr. Foljambe's dogs, including "Nabob", which was the son of "Beau", and was considered the best dog of its day.

In passing, one ought to allude to another famous pillar of the breed, "John o' Gaunt", which must have been a model of all a Clumber can be, if we are to credit the eulogies written about him some thirty odd years ago. Mr. H. H. Holmes, his owner, certainly possessed some of the best specimens of his time.

In those days the field trials had a great deal to do with the popularity of the breed, for in these the Clumber scored a distinguished success. Owners, then, were not so keen about speed, but nowadays a Clumber is considered a little heavy and slow. He is, of course, far from fast, and one

Photo]　　　　　　　　　　　　　　　　　*[Guiver.*
The scientific clipper being used so that dressings can be applied direct to the skin.

[Guiver.

Photo]

CARNFORTH CLUMBER SPANIELS. The dog on the outside left shows the Hound ancestor used to make the breed. The Clumber is essentially a working Spaniel and here is a team of these dogs, all of excellent type.

can hear people, when looking at him say, "What good would that dog be in a field of roots on a hot day in September?" The Clumber fancier's reply is that there are a good many breeds of dogs not much use in early September, for the simple reason they are not in condition, and that, however hot the weather, at the end of a hard day's work other dogs are down and out while the Clumber is still moving about and ready for more. All he ever required was a good flat coat, and not too much feather.

The Clumber went through a very lean time after the Great War, but during the following decade an upward movement gradually set in and the numbers entered at the principal shows kept on increasing. At Cruft's, in 1934, there was twice the number as in previous years.

The chief pillars of the breed since the War were "Royalist of Wilts" and "Fulmer Prince". In looking through the pedigree of any Clumber to-day it is almost impossible to discover one that does not descend from one of the above-mentioned dogs. The Clumber of to-day, in the opinion of experts, is far superior, although in their day the afore-mentioned dogs were considered the ideal. The present-day dog has lost half his coat, which is undoubtedly a step in the right direction.

His Majesty King George V has always been a keen supporter of the breed, in which respect he followed in the train of King Edward VII, who also was fond of the Clumber and possessed, among many other fine specimens, "Sandringham Lucy", a beautiful bitch which was often out with him shooting over the Sandringham estate. King George entered three Clumbers in the 1934 Show, out of his kennel of fourteen. It was long ago decided that they were the best dogs for working in the bracken at Sandringham, where there are many acres of it, and it is asserted that one dog did the work of three or four beaters.

Dogs that made their name at stud were "Biggin Chum" by "Fulmer Prince" and, secondly, "Carnforth Traveller" by "Royalist of Wilts". The former, which was owned by Mr. Flower, was sold by him, at a very high figure, to one of the Indian rajahs. "Biggin Chum" left some very good youngsters behind, and it was no trouble to sell puppies sired by him.

"Carnforth Traveller", owned by the late Mrs. Cape, was a great success both as a stud dog and on the bench; he was hardly ever beaten, until age caused his retirement. His kennel companion, "Carnforth Beauty", was the best bitch of her period.

More recently, two Clumbers seem to stand out above the others: "Auckwear Ripper" and "Hardon Don", both out of the same litter and bred by Miss Reid, the sire being "Oakerland Repeater".

H.M. THE KING'S "SANDRINGHAM SPARK".
This beautiful specimen of the Clumber Spaniel has won many awards for H.M. King George V,
who has a preference for the breed when shooting over the Sandringham Estate.
King Edward VII also kept a kennel of Clumbers.

H.M. THE KING'S "SANDRINGHAM SPARK".

H.M. King George V is, as was his father, King Edward, a great believer in the Clumber Spaniel, and has a strong working kennel.
Attention is drawn to the charming expression of the head of "Sandringham Spark", which took the 1931 Challenge Certificate
at Cruft's.

"WITLEY ACTING MAJOR".

Many a Clumber bears the imprint of the St. Bernard dog which, history suggests, was partly its origin. Certainly a dog of the above type seems to lend credence to that theory.

THE MODERN SHOW CLUMBER.

"Withybrook Ch. Donovan" is a Clumber of modern times—a powerfully built dog on short legs.

Those who are thinking of taking up the breed and desire to own a show specimen should see that he has plenty of bone and straight on his legs. Above all, he should be a good' mover, because a Clumber that is not a free mover is useless in the field or on the bench. He should also have a good head, with plenty of expression, nicely rounded on top, and a deep muzzle, with well-sprung ribs, not too long in the back, and a dark eye ; also a good, straight, flat coat.

length, broad on top, with a decided occiput ; heavy brows with a deep stop ; heavy freckled muzzle, with well-developed flew.

EYES.—Dark amber ; slightly sunk. A light or prominent eye objectionable.

EARS.—Large, vine-leaf shaped, and well covered with straight hair and hanging slightly forward, the feather not to extend below the leather.

NECK.—Very thick and powerful, and well feathered underneath.

THE ORIGINAL CLUMBER.

Here is a reproduction of the famous painting by Francis Wheatley, in 1788, showing the Second Duke of Newcastle with the original type of Clumber. These dogs were the gift of a French nobleman and took their name from the Duke's seat, Clumber Park, where this picture now hangs.

Anyone who possesses a promising young dog should not part with him until the animal is four years old, for he is not at his best until then. Clumbers are very slow in maturing.

The markings on Clumbers are not so heavy as they were years ago. The dog with very dark markings rarely gets looked at when in the ring. There is another point in favour of this old breed, and that is they are very easily broken to the gun. In their work they are much steadier than most breeds, and whilst certainly not swift, they do their work well.

HEAD.—Large, square and massive, of medium

BODY (including size and symmetry).—Long and heavy, and near the ground. Weight of dogs, about 55 lb. to 65 lb. ; bitches, about 45 lb. to 55 lb.

NOSE.—Square and flesh-coloured.

SHOULDERS AND CHEST.—Wide and deep ; shoulders strong and muscular.

BACK AND LOINS.—Back straight, broad and long ; loins powerful, well down in flank.

HINDQUARTERS.—Very powerful and well-developed.

STERN.—Set low, well feathered, and carried about level with the back.

"LAPIS".

This Clumber was an outstanding dog and one of the first of the breed as it is to-day. He weighed 60 lb. and was bred by Mr. W. Arkwright, one of the leading authorities on gun dogs.

FEET AND LEGS.—Feet large and round, well covered with hair; legs short, thick and strong; hocks low.

COAT.—Long, abundant, soft and straight.

COLOUR.—Plain white, with lemon markings; orange permissible but not desirable; slight head markings with white body preferred.

GENERAL APPEARANCE.—Should be that of a long, low, heavy, very massive dog, with a thoughtful expression.

SCALE OF POINTS:

POSITIVE POINTS.—Head and jaw, 20; eyes, 5; ears, 5; neck, 5; body, 15; forelegs, 5; hindlegs, 5; feet, 5; stern, 5; colour of markings, 10; coat and feather, 10; general appearance and type, 10. Total, 100.

NEGATIVE POINTS.—Curled ears, 10; curled coat, 15; bad carriage and set on of tail, 15; snipy face or faulty jaw, 20; legginess (they should be up on leg a little, not too low), 10; light eye, 10; full eye, 10; straight stifle, 10. Total, 100.

Clydesdale or Paisley Terrier.—This dog was undoubtedly a descendant of the original Highland Terrier, but whether or not it inherited its soft silky coat from the Spanish dogs which were supposed to have been introduced to the island of Skye when some ships of the Spanish Armada went to pieces on the Western Islands it is useless to surmise. The Clydesdale Terrier was one of the last off-shoots to materialize, and it is generally admitted it was a direct descendant of the Lothian type of Skye Terrier, and there is no

disputing the fact that it was the most beautiful of all this family of terriers. Had it made its appearance under happier circumstances, it might have flourished. Controvery marred its existence all along. It was really a Skye Terrier, as now recognized, in everything but quality of coat, and for several years it was exhibited in the same classes as the ordinary Skye Terrier, known as the Silky-Coated Skye.

It was indeed a lovely exhibit, and appealed strongly both to the judges and the general public. This, however, did not suit the breeders of the true Skye. All Skye Terriers occasionally throw a soft woolly-coated puppy, which were immediately destroyed as undesirable—for soft coats were a heinous offence in the Skye Terrier cult.

However, some enthusiast set about perpetuating this silky coat, and by mating these mutations together the purpose was achieved. The true Skye Terrier breeders denied all knowledge of this new variety, and insisted that they were mongrels and should not be entitled to be called Skyes. It was suggested that they were a cross from the Dandie Dinmont Terrier or the Poodle, which of course was not feasible. They carried their point that all Skye Terriers were hard coated, and the silky-coated variety became the Ishmael of the breed.

THE CLUMBER OF THE 'NINETIES.

"Snow", the Clumber Spaniel of the 'nineties, was certainly an exceptionally good specimen for that time and appears to be much heavier than the dogs of to-day.

Had the admirers of these fancy Skyes been content to steer clear of the name of Skye, their favourites would have certainly enjoyed their fair

"ROCKETTER".

Amongst noted breeders at the end of the nineteenth century, when this dog was living, were Mr. R. S. Holford, Mr. Foljambe and Mr. W. Arkwright, the breeder of the noted "Lapis" in 1875.

CH. "OAKERLAND REPEATER".
Miss M. F. Reed's Ch. "Oakerland Repeater" is rather shorter in the body than "Young Donovan".
Notice the typical Clumber head.

CH. "SIR PETER"
Clumbers vary to some extent in length of body and height from ground. Once they were very low down. This was
exaggerated. To-day a more active dog is required.

share of popularity. They, however, insisted on sticking to the name, which only led them into disaster. In the 'seventies a great paper controversy raged, and the breeders of the Paisley Terrier, as they were beginning to be called, lost the day. The leaders were sorely disappointed and the breed was allowed to languish. At this time the breeders nearly all resided in the Valley of the Clyde, and, as they were now debarred from competing in Skye Terrier classes, they decided to found a specialist club to protect and further their interests on the show bench. The inaugural meetings were called in Glasgow in 1884 and the Clydesdale Terrier Club was duly formed. Here again the name proved a stumbling block. The founders considered that the Paisley or Glasgow Terrier was too localized, and decided in favour of the more comprehensive name of the Clydesdale Terrier. The dignity of the Paisley and Rutherglen breeders was hurt and they withheld their support from the Club.

For a time they did not exhibit, but the temptation was too great for them. They did at last come into the fold, but it was too late; the Club, being handicapped from the first, did not make the progress that it might have done.

These constant bickerings ruined the chances of one of the most beautiful varieties of dogs ever benched. Classes were given for Clydesdale Terriers at all the Western shows, and they were also catered for at the Edinburgh and London shows, but owing to the continual internal friction, the classes were never well supported.

It was exhibited at the Glasgow shows as far back as 1864 and 1869, and its short zenith of popularity was reached when Mr. Harry Martin ran his famous Glasgow shows.

They were really excellent dogs, with all the characteristics and disposition of the true Skye and the beauty of the diminutive Yorkshire Terrier. They made intelligent, faithful companions, but their coats were the source of much work and close attention, if they were to be kept presentable and attractive.

The Paisley and Rutherglen breeders were mostly weavers, and they were adepts in benching their Clydesdales in perfect bloom. The dogs lay beside their owners whilst they were at work at the looms, so that any spare moment the owners had they were brushing and keeping their terriers in order. In this way it was impossible for the dogs' coats to become matted or destroyed.

MADAME LOWNDESTONE NORTON.

A fine Gainsborough painting of Madame Lowndestone Norton with a Spaniel. Apart from the beauty of the work it is of peculiar interest, for it shows the type of dog that was known as the Clumber before breeders started improving it.

With the passing of the hand loom, the Clydesdale Terrier also faded into obscurity. The Clydesdale was principally of a light blue or silver colour, although the dark blue was most prized and the most difficult to get : they invariably went too light on the head and ears, which was not considered desirable. The head and ears were the crowning glory of the winning Clydesdales.

Mr. Thomas Erskine, of Glasgow, was a most enthusiastic supporter to the last of the Clydesdale Terrier Club and was the breeder of the wonderful "Blythswood Pearl", and which was considered to be one of the best Clydesdale Terriers ever exhibited. Mr. Erskine bought his mother from a woman in the old Bird Market in the Saltmarket, Glasgow, which was registered as "Blythswood Queen". His father was "Lorne of Doune", owned by a Mr. Cumming, of Paisley. "Blythswood Pearl" was born on September 11, 1891, and was shown very successfully for eleven years. He won just on forty first prizes, and won first prize two years in succession at Cruft's Show, also first in the brace class with his mother at Cruft's. He also won firsts and championships at the Edinburgh Show of the Scottish Kennel Club in 1893 and 1894. His coat was $22\frac{1}{2}$ inches in length ($11\frac{1}{4}$ inches on either side). He had a blue body, with exquisite silvery head, wonderful feathering, and his coat was entirely free from crimpiness. Mr. Erskine used to spend from three to four hours every day grooming him. He was a demon on rats and could kill them with any terrier living. When engaged at this work, his owner used to pin the hair back from his eyes. He was the sire of a great many winners. In his latter days his mouth became ulcerated and his owner had very reluctantly to put him

Photo]   [*Hugh D. Martineau.*

H.M. THE KING'S
"SANDRINGHAM SWIRL'

The Clumber Spaniel is a breed emanating from the Duke of Newcastle's estate at Clumber. It has always been a Royal favourite, and the Sandringham kennel is famous.

Photo]   [*Fall.*

"YOUNG DONOVAN".

This dog, shown resting, draws attention to the similarity between dogs of to-day and the original type in the painting at Clumber Park. (*See page* 329).

down. It is to be regretted that this great dog was not stuffed and preserved, for at his death he was still in perfect bloom. Mr. Erskine bred several famous Clydesdale Terriers and sold that lovely dog, Ch. "Ballochmyle Wee Wattie", to Sir Claude Alexander, Bt., which had a phenomenal show career. There may be, however, one or two odd specimens still to be found in the Rutherglen and Cambuslang districts of Glasgow. (*See page* 336.)

Coal Gas.—An invisible, explosive and poisonous gas prepared from the combustion of coal. Its dangerous component is carbon monoxide which, even when well diluted, may cause death from its inhalation. It is owing to the risk of leakages that we do not recommend gas as an illuminant or source of heat in dog kennels. Occasionally, pipes conveying the gas are so situated on walls that mischievous dogs can gnaw them ; in other cases it is possible sometimes for dogs to interfere with gas taps in such a way that the latter become accidentally turned on. Then, unless the ventilation is very adequate, all that the attendant finds, next morning, is a kennel of dead dogs. Obviously, therefore, if gas must be used, it should be conveyed in iron pipes

Photo]   [*L.N.A.*

"CARNFORTH BEAUTY".

Mr. R. Cope's "Carnforth Beauty" won many honours in 1932

and the jets and taps must be high out of a dog's reach.

It ought to be needless to warn the reader that should he smell gas, upon approaching the kennel, he must refrain from investigating its source with a lighted match. This has, unfortunately, been done upon too many occasions in the past, and with dire results. His first duty, even though it be night and he is compelled to grope about in utter darkness, is to throw open all doors and windows and bring any animals out into the open. The symptoms of poisoning, if any, exhibited by the dogs will depend upon the dose of gas they have inhaled. In the early stages they may appear merely drowsy, or they may be tottery and unable to stand, the respirations being increased in rapidity. Badly affected dogs will be unconscious. Artificial respiration is immediately necessary (qui vide) and, if possible, oxygen should be administered either direct to the nostrils, or through an anaesthesia mask. Massage of the heart region and of the body

Photo]　　　　　　　　　[Ballance.
BATH TIME.
Two of Mr. A. A. Smith's Clumber puppies are finding sitting in a bath a novel occupation.

Photo]　　　　　　　　　[Fall
A CHARMING STUDY.
Here are two of Mr. R. Cope's Clumbers, "Silky of Runnymede" and "Carnforth Commodore". Attention is drawn to the hound type of head of the standing dog.

generally, will help to revive consciousness, and when this has occurred the dog may be given a teaspoonful of whisky or brandy plentifully diluted in water.

Complete recovery may be delayed for several days, depending on the severity of the attack, and to aid it the dog should be afforded plenty of air, rest, mild stimulants and an aperient.

Coats for Dogs.— The average breed of dog has sufficient coat of its own to render any further raiment unnecessary. When dogs are ill, however, the application of a warm coat sometimes becomes essential. Many house-trained dogs insist upon going out-of-doors to relieve themselves, and should they have a temperature, the sudden change from heat to cold might induce a further chill or even pneumonia. Very short-coated dogs, such as Dachshunds, Greyhounds and Manchester Terriers, etc., are prone to feel the cold, and they are accustomed to wear a coat in inclement weather.

By courtesy]　　　　　　　　　[L. B. Hedley.
A LOVABLE LOT.
Here are "Bess" and "Bell", "Laurie" and "Era", "Lex" and "Don Junior", a family any Cocker mother might be proud of. They are more than attractive—they are little aristocrats.

IN THE COUNTRY.

The Clumber suits itself to town or country life. This one was photographed at Grundisburgh Hall, in Suffolk, with its owner,
Miss Camila Gurdon, eldest daughter of Lady Cranworth.

Some very elaborate garments are purchasable nowadays, but a dog-owner can quite easily fashion a useful home-made coat for the cost of a few pence only.

There are breeds of dogs possessing long shaggy coats whose great drawback, from the householder's point of view, is the ease with which the abdominal surface becomes plastered with wet mud on rainy days. There is no reason, however, why little waterproof, washable coats should not be provided for such animals. It only needs a little ingenuity and tailoring knowledge on the part of the owner to prevent not only the soiling of the dog's coat, but also a great deal of dirt in the home.

In the article upon BANDAGING it was mentioned that a good deal of difficulty was generally experienced in bandaging the trunk because of its tapering shape. It was said, also, that the difficulty could be overcome, in instances where a protective covering of some sort was desirable, by making a temporary coat of white linen. A ready way to do this is to lay an oblong of linen, of suitable dimensions, upon the floor, stand the dog upon it and note where the four feet rest. At those points cut out a small hole. As the thigh is thicker than the elbow the rear holes will have to be larger than the front ones. The legs are passed through these holes and the material lifted upwards until it surrounds the body and its lateral edges meet over the spinal column, where they are fastened together with safety pins. The linen should be of sufficient length in front to go around the neck nicely ; and should be shaped, behind, so as to avoid impeding urination, etc. Unless the latter point is carefully regarded, the coat will be continuously wet, and the dog's skin will become excoriated.

A similar but shorter type of coat is known as a "pneumonia jacket". When used for this purpose it is usually stuffed with cotton wool for extra warmth. (*See page* 338).

Cobby.—Well ribbed up ; short and compact in proportion, like a cob horse.

Cocaine.—An alkaloid obtained from the coca plant. It occurs as very fine white crystals which the denizens of the underworld are pleased to refer to as "snow". Its great use in the realm of surgery is as a local anaesthetic, for which purpose it is extremely efficient. For use on dogs, however, it is not devoid of risk since even a slight overdose may produce ‾in them alarming symptoms. Cocaine dissolves readily in water and is generally injected subcutaneously in a strength of from 1 to 3 per cent. Any painful minor operation, and sometimes even major ones, may be rendered absolutely painless by paralysing the nerve supply to the site of operation.

By courtesy]   [J. Garrow.
TWO FINE CLYDESDALES.
Sir Claude Alexander, Bt., of Faygate Wood, Faygate, at one time the leading breeder of Smooth Collies, also had a strong kennel of Clydesdale Terriers. Note the type of the head. For story of this breed *see page* 330.

as can be done by the aid of cocaine. The latter is also extremely useful for allaying sensation in the case of eye injuries, but for such use it is instilled direct on to the eyeball.

Owing to the poisonous nature of cocaine, there has now come into popular use a number of excellent substitutes, notably novocaine, eucaine, stovaine, ether spray and phenol, etc., which, whilst quite rapid and efficacious, are not so dangerous. As it is impossible for unauthorized people to obtain cocaine, no useful purpose will be served in detailing dosage or toxic symptoms. (*See* ANAESTHETICS.)

Coccidiosis.—So far as the lay public is concerned coccidiosis is a comparatively rare disease and yet, often a severe and important one. The modern veterinary practitioner is, however, usually mindful of its possible existence in those cases of chronic and mysterious diarrhoea which have seemed to resist all therapeutic treatment. Coccidiosis means the invasion of the digestive tract by microscopic bodies known as coccidia isospora. These are ovoid bodies which lurk in the interstices of the mucous lining of the bowel, and may be demonstrated under a low-power lens of the microscope, if diluted faeces, from a dog so affected, be smeared upon a glass slide.

SYMPTOMS.—An obstinate diarrhoea, the stools passed being coated with mucus, or perhaps bloodstained. There is usually a marked loss of flesh, and sometimes an abdominal tenderness.

TREATMENT. — Prevention is effected in large measure by disinfection of kennels, runs, and other habitats, and by withholding the entrails of rabbits, fowls, etc., as a food. Few medicinal agents appear to have an effect, but intestinal disinfection is the object to be aimed at.

Cocker Spaniel.—Volumes could be filled with tracing the evolution of the Spaniel, as its antiquity is beyond all doubt. Confirmation is found in extracts from the earliest English literature, mention being made in *The Wif of Bathe's Prologue* (1340-1400), attributed to Chaucer, the famous author of the *Canterbury Tales*, who employs this simile : "for as a Spaynel she would on him lepe". ·

Frequent mention is made of Spaniels in the household records of Henry VIII, one reference being, "Robin, the King's Spaniel Keeper", being paid "for hair, cloth to rub the Spaniels with". Nicholas Cox, writing in 1677 in *The Gentleman's Recreation*, makes mention of the land Spaniel, "nimber rangers of active feet, wanton tails, and

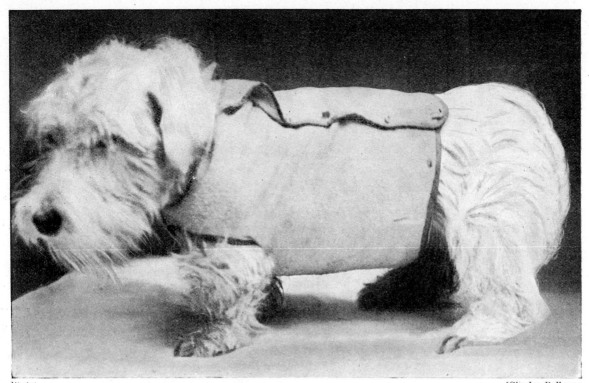

Photo] CHEST PROTECTION. [Stanley Ballance.
After severe chills, pneumonia, and other chest troubles, it is often necessary on a cold, windy day to protect the dog against the cold. Above is a suitable jacket.

Photo] KEEPING THEM DRY. [Dorien Leigh.
Dogs have a great aversion to rain. The owner of these two Dachshunds, in wet weather, dresses his dogs in mackintoshes.

A smart coat for occasional use.

busy nostrils, whose tail was without weariness, their search without changeableness", thus stamping the breed from the earliest records as a recognized aid to man in his sporting pursuits.

Coming down to 1803, *The Sportsman's Cabinet* published at that date graphically describes the breed in these words: "The race of dogs passing under the denomination of Spaniels are of two kinds, one of which is considerably larger than the other . . . the smaller is called the Cocker or Cocking-Spaniel, as being more adapted to covert and woodcock shooting, to which they are more particularly appropriated and by nature seem designed". Further on, having described the larger ones, he returns to the Cocker: " . . . the smallest Spaniels passing under the denomination of Cockers is that peculiar breed in possession and preservation of the Duke of Marlborough and his friends, these are invariably red-and-white with very long ears, short noses and black eyes, they are excellent and indefatigable, being in great estimation with those sportsmen who can become possessed of the breed".

The same authority, to prove his point, draws attention to the paintings of Vandyke which bear out his assertions: "The large springing Spaniel and the diminutive Cocker, although they vary in size, differ but little in their qualifications except that the former does not equal the latter in the rapidity of action, nor do they seem either to catch the scent so suddenly, or to enjoy it

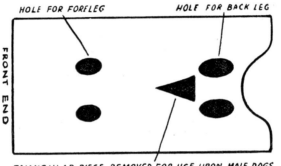

HOLE FOR FORELEG   HOLE FOR BACK LEG

FRONT END

TRIANGULAR PIECE REMOVED FOR USE UPON MALE DOGS

A simple coat in linen or flannel that can be made at home.

This pattern has an extension up the neck for extra warmth.

with the same ecstatic enthusiasm when found".

References have been freely made by historians of the love of the Spaniel by that unfortuate monarch Charles I, writers and painters of that period giving full vent to the theme.

Sufficient has been written to prove both the antiquity and the pride of descent of the Cocker as a separate entity, that it may not be out of place to quote a modern authority. The late Mr. James Farrow (founder of the justly famous "Obo" strain of Cockers), wrote: "The original Blenheim was a sportsman and it is certain the breed was used as a gundog as well as a companion, and what is more, was built on the lines for work."

At Chatsworth, the Derbyshire seat of the Dukes of Devonshire, a painting of Charles II depicting a Spaniel in attendance compares very favourably with the modern Cocker, and although the evidence is not altogether satisfying, it is now generally accepted that the original Cocker and Blenheim were closely allied.

Two points which are of the greatest interest to those who have thoroughly studied the history of the breed are that every writer refers to their "down carriage of tails", and although all

A practical chest protector.

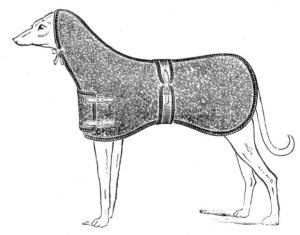

An original type of coat for Greyhounds and Whippets.

METSU'S COCKER.

In 1630–67 Metsu, the noted Dutch artist, painted market scenes in which he portrayed a Cocker Spaniel.   Here is one of them.
The original picture is in the Dresden Gallery.

CH. "OBO".

'CROWN PRINCE".

'RIVINGTON REDCOAT".

"BRAESIDE BUSTLE".

apparently are agreed that the Cocker was originally a hunting dog, no reference of any kind is made of the breed being used to retrieve game.

"Stonehenge" (1687), recognized as the outstanding historian of his period, makes reference to "a musical tongue", which was by the old school of sportsmen considered a desideratum, in order not only to give notice that the dog is on game, but also the particular kind which he is "questing", and "which many good Spaniels enable their masters to distinguish by a variation in their notes". How times change is here typified, as to-day most shooting men look askance at a Spaniel which attempts to "babble", considering that by so doing he is heralding unnecessarily his approach, and clearing the ground of game before the guns can reach it.

The Cocker undoubtedly played a very important part in the early days in helping to establish the Field Spaniel, definite data being found of this in *The Sporting Spaniel* (1906) by Mr. C. A. Phillips, who states: "Last year I took the trouble to trace the pedigrees, as far as I could find reliable records, of three Spaniels which had won championship honours at Cruft's show, viz. the Cocker dog, the black Field Spaniel dog, and the coloured Field Spaniel bitch, and found that every one of them traced his or her descent, either in the male or female line, to two Cockers, Burdett's black-and-tan dog 'Frank', and Mousley's black-and-white bitch 'Venus'."

These Cockers, and others of Burdett's and Boulton's kennels, may be taken as the bedrock on which the modern Cocker was founded. One of the very first to attract attention in the early 1870's was Mr. J. J. Farrow's "Emperor", which won at a show at Manchester in 1873. In 1880 Farrow's Ch. "Obo" made his first public appearance, and it has always been recognized that he was the veritable cornerstone which the whole of the present-day specimens trace back to. His breeding ("Fred" ex "Betty") conveyed little information, but it was generally believed that Burdett's strain was responsible for this line of blood.

The "Obo" family brought the breed into greater prominence than it had ever before known, and to Mr. J. J. Farrow is owed an enormous debt for the knowledgeable manner in which he continued to reproduce Cockers of similar type.

The next step was the production of "Braeside Bustle", described at that time as a "black-and-white flecked", now known as a blue roan. This dog claimed close allegiance to "Obo", boasting at least three direct crosses of his blood, and it

"FAIRHOLME RALLY".

"GALTREES MAY".

"CORN CRAKE".

HISTORY OF THE COCKER.

The story of the Cocker Spaniel is told in the above illustrations by courtesy of Mr. H. S. Lloyd. First we have the noted "Obo" that started the "Obo" family of Mr. Farrow, then "Crown Prince" of 1889 and the noted "Rivington Redcoat", then came the others as shown here, all pillars in the story of the Cocker breed.

is an irrefutable fact that to "Bustle" one can now trace the vast majority of the parti-colours. On this blood, Mr. R. de C. Peele built up his famous "Bowdler" kennel.

Competition at the earlier shows for Spaniels usually comprised classes for "Field Spaniels under 20 lb.", and one for those exceeding this weight. Dogs of the same type competed in both.

for them, the year 1883 marking the official recognition.

Progress was now definitely asserted, and events moved with rapidity. In 1901, on the proposition of Colonel Claude Cane, seconded by Mr. J. J. Farrow, the Spaniel Club abolished the fixed weight limit of 25 lb., The Kennel Club confirming this progressive step.

AT WINDSOR CASTLE.

Charles, Prince of Wales, James, Duke of York, and Princess Mary with their Cocker Spaniels, painted by Van Dyke between 1599–1641. The original is at Windsor Castle.

At The Kennel Club's 1875 show the "Under 20 lb." class was dropped, evidently through lack of support, and classification was not bestowed upon them again till 1880.

The year 1883 is the first on record when the breed was given the courtesy of a separate title. A "Cocker Class" was then scheduled for the first time, but even then a separate place in the Kennel Club Stud Book had not been found

This proved the turning point in the fortunes of the breed, as the very next year the Cocker Spaniel Club was formed, brought about by a guarantee fund contributed to by several of the leading lights of that day, to enable shows to give further consideration without financial liability.

From this humble commencement, the Club has gone on and flourished, having fostered the interest of the Cocker both in the field and on the bench, so that one can look back with the deepest gratitude to those founders whose faith in the breed has been so fully justified.

From this date onwards a decided influx of those taking an interest in the breed occurred, and from the scant material to hand, kennels sprang up which have since splendidly carried on the work of the early pioneers. Mr. C. A. Phillips' "Rivingtons", Mr. R. Lloyd's "Wares", Mr. R. de C. Peele's "Bowdlers", Mr. W. Caless' "Brutons", Mr. T. Harrington's "Trumpingtons", Mr. E. C. Spencer's "Doonys", Mr. W. H. Edwards' "Pinbrooks", Mr. F. C. Dickenson's "Rocklyns", Mrs. R. Fytche's "Fulmers", and Mr. Gordon George's "Fairholmes", amongst others all doing splendid work in building up and establishing the type.

Tracing the outstanding individuals which have stood out in the breed as "pillars of the stud book" from the early 'seventies onwards, mention must be made of "Obo", and his innumerable sons, "Viceroy" (sire of "Braeside Bustle"), "Rio", "Braeside Bustle" himself, and his famous sons "Blue Peter" and Ch. "Ben Bowdler", Ch. "Bob Bowdler" (and his undefeated son Ch. "Dixon Bowdler"), Ch. "Rufus Bowdler" (the first red Champion), "Heir Apparent", a bulwark of the blacks, "Rivington Redcoat", Ch. "Rivington Rogue" (a son of the imported "Hampton Guard"), "Rivington Regent", Ch. "Doony Swell", Ch. "Doony Blackie", "Galtrees Raven", "Hampton Marquis", "Grindon Gerald", etc., all of which had a definite influence on the post-war specimens.

Immediately after the Great War, when the resumption of active breeding was recommenced

By courtesy]   [H. S. Lloyd.
"WHOOPEE OF WARE".
The world's record-holding Cocker Spaniel, bred by Mr. H. S. Lloyd. "Whoopee" won 50 Challenge Certificates and 500 first prizes.

in earnest, two dogs in the coloured variety stood right out, "Corn Crake" and "Fairholme Rally", both blue roans, and both claiming the cleanest possible descent. They had, more than any others of their period, uplifted the breed, and many were the gorgeous children and grandchildren which appeared from the intermixing of this blood.

"Rocklyn Magic", in blacks, had a great sway and was most prepotent in his influence for many generations. Ch. "Pinbrook Scamp", a result of "Galtrees" and "Rivington" strains, was responsible for a forward movement in blacks. His numerous descendants were very much valued, and included many reds.

"Fulmer Ben", probably "Fairholme Rally's" greatest son, carried on the traditions of the strain by reproducing Ch. "L'ile Beau Brummel", and many others.

"Fanfare" and "Broadcaster of Ware", the latter a Canadian importation, rich in latent "Obo" prepotencies, appears to be one of the great foundation stones on which the very fashionable reds or goldens were built in conjunction with "Pinbrook" and Trinder's "Arabian" bred reds, the latter being from "Bruton" and American stock.

Ch. "Invader of Ware", the blue roan, is generally accepted as one of the greatest stud forces. Descended from the "Fairholme", "Ballywalter," "Grindon" and "Rivington" blood lines, he had a far greater influence than any other, and his progeny, which numbered amongst them an enormous amount of prepotent sires and dams, continued the good work. Especial mention must be made of his son Ch. "Churchdene Invader,"

Photo]   [Fall.
CH. "LOVABLE OF WARE".
The Ware strain of Cockers is undoubtedly the most important strain in the world.

which had inherited his sire's influence, and "Falconer's Cowslip", whose championship winning descendants are too numerous to mention.

"Dominorum D'Arcy", a black son of "Corn Crake", the blue roan, had a most desirable effect on present-day blacks.

DESCRIPTIVE PARTICULARS.

HEAD. — A nicely developed square muzzle and jaw; with distinct stop. Skull and forehead should be well developed, with plenty of room for brain power, cleanly chiselled and not cheeky.

EYES.—Full but not prominent, hazel or brown coloured, harmonizing with colour of coat, with a general expression of intelligence and gentleness, decidedly wide-awake, bright and merry.

EARS.—Lobular, set on low, leather fine and not extending beyond the nose, well clothed with long silky hair, which should be straight—no positive curls or ringlets.

NECK.—Long, strong and muscular, and neatly set on to fine sloping shoulders.

BODY. (including size and symmetry).— Compact, and firmly knit together, giving the impression of a concentration of power and untiring

Photo]   [Hedges.
CH. "PINBROOK SCAMP".
A black Cocker of 1917.

Photo]   [Fall.
"INVADER OF WARE".
The wonderful champion at ten years of age.

Type has not varied as much through the ages as at a casual glance one might think. Evolution has made it necessary at many periods of Cocker history to strive for a particular group of points at possibly the temporary sacrifices of others. The shortening up of the back without loss of neck and the retention of good galloping shoulders and action, did for a time lead breeders to get many a trifle bigger than the ideal, but these served their turn, and eventually, through unremitting care and thousands of disappointments, the lovely modern dog has been produced.

In the field Cockers have added year by year to their laurels. The inauguration by the Kennel Club of a separate Field Trial Championship Stake for Cockers in 1925 did much to forward the movement, and in mixed competition with the larger members of the Spaniel family they have held their own.

His delightful nature, handy size, great intelligence and hardy constitution admirably fit the Cocker for any walk of life.

activity; the total weight should be about 25 to 28 lb.

NOSE.—Sufficiently wide and well developed to ensure the exquisite scenting power of this breed.

SHOULDERS AND CHEST.—The former sloping and fine, chest deep and well developed, but not too wide and round to interfere with the free action of the forelegs.

BACK AND LOIN. — Short in back. Immensely strong and compact in proportion to the size and weight of the dog; slightly drooping towards the tail.

Photo]   [Fall.
"BAZEL OTTO".
The desired profile.

THREE WORLD-FAMED COCKERS.

Truly these may be said to be the heads of the breed. Reading from left are Ch. "Irador", Ch. "Lucky Star", and Ch. "Whoopee", all of Ware. These three, of Mr. Lloyd's breeding, won 1,000 first prizes and 108 Challenge Certificates, and on seventy occasions were best of all breeds.

HINDQUARTERS.—Wide, well rounded, and very muscular.

SCALE OF POINTS.

POSITIVE.—Head and jaws, 10 ; eyes, 5 ; ears, 5 ; neck, 10 ; body, 20 ; forelegs, 10 ; hindlegs, 10 ; feet, 10 ; stern, 10 ; coat and feather, 10. Total positive points, 100.

NEGATIVE.—Light eyes, 10 ; light nose, 15 ; hair curled on ears (very undesirable), 15 ; coat (curly, woolly or wiry), 20 ; carriage of stern, 20 ; top knot, 20. Total negative points, 100.

Cod-Liver Oil.—As its name implies, this oil is expressed from the livers of codfish. It contains a comparative abundance of vitamin D and a smaller proportion of vitamin A. The former is particularly efficacious in the prevention or cure of rickets, and the "A" vitamin seems to be essential for the proper development and growth of an animal. Thus we find that cod-liver oil is so very valuable when administered to puppies. Animals recovering from wasting diseases such as distemper are considerably helped by a daily dose of this oil, with or without admixture with malt extract. Other indications for its use are loss of condition, poorness of coat, chronic cough, and debility. A terrier could take a teaspoonful daily, whilst a large dog would need twice that amount. Many animals will readily lick it out of a spoon, but in the case of others which manifest a decided dislike for it, one has to use a little cunning. The method then employed is to teach the dog to eat a sardine every day. The cod-liver oil can then be poured over the fish and the dog will be none the wiser. If this artifice fails, then one must forcibly administer the dose as described under MEDICINE, How TO GIVE. In purchasing cod-liver oil, it appears to be quite unnecessary to insist upon having the

By courtesy]   [R. Langford.

EXPRESSION.

The delightful expression of these eyes, not quite certain if they have done right, shows the almost human intelligence that has endeared the Cocker to so many.

purified variety, as this is made especially for the human palate, and it is thought that in the process of purification a good deal of the vitamin content is lost. That product known as veterinary cod-liver oil is doubtless more valuable and certainly cheaper, although it may retain a decidedly fishy and even nauseous flavour. Occasionally, animals are encountered which appear to be unable to digest the plain oil ; in other words, it often makes them sick. In such cases, the cod-liver oil emulsion should be tried, as this usually exerts no such effect.

Cold Abscess. (*See* ABSCESS.)

Cold Nose.—It is a very popular belief that if a dog's nose is cold and wet, he is definitely in good health ; conversely that a dry or warm nose indicates some kind of illness. Whilst it is true that the normal condition of the noses of dogs in good health is one of coldness and moisture, it does not by any means follow that a departure from this state portends a departure from good health. On countless occasions when supposed healthy dogs have been presented for the purpose of anti-distemper inoculation, it has been discovered that, notwithstanding cold, wet noses, their temperatures have been too high for the injection to be given. In one particular case such a dog was found with a temperature of 105° F., and the animal was bright and looked very well. Similarly, dogs with dry noses have quite commonly no discoverable symptom whatever of any kind of malady.

Colic.—Abdominal pain is generally caused by indigestion, flatulence, constipation, or other derangements of the alimentary canal. Simple colic is unaccompanied by inflammation of any organ and is of a temporary character. On the other hand, colic may be present as a symptom of gastro-enteritis or enteritis, etc.

The dog is uneasy and signifies its discomfort by whining, crying out, shifting

Photo]   [Fall.

"OVERDALE ARROW".

The Golden Cocker is a breed of its own, a development from the other varieties.

from place to place, sitting down and getting up, looking round at its flanks, rolling or lying upon its back, and perhaps scratching at its abdomen.

TREATMENT is directed towards removing the cause if this can be ascertained. If the attack is severe expert advice should be sought. In the majority of cases relief is obtained by getting the bowels to act either by administering a purgative or an enema.

A carminative can be obtained from a chemist, and hot packs should be kept applied to the abdomen.

Colitis.—Inflammation of the colon or large intestine.

CAUSES.—It may arise in consequence of habitual constipation, the presence of foreign bodies, chills, and, in general, from similar causes as detailed under *Inflammation of the Bowels.*

SYMPTOMS.—There is a good deal of pain with colitis, and an obstinate diarrhoea (accompanied by straining) which seems to defy any kind of medication given by the mouth, and the motions are generally more or less gelatinous. A tenderness is evinced if one palpates the bowel through the abdominal wall, and there may be occasional vomiting.

TREATMENT.—Consult a veterinary surgeon.

Collapse.—A state of extreme prostration and depression with failure of the circulation and a loss

Photo]   [*The Daily Bulletin.*
YOUNG THOROUGHBREDS.
What expression indeed! Three really good puppies of the Cocker breed. Note their large ears even at this age, and particular attention is also drawn to the width of head and sturdiness of limb.

of blood pressure. The ears and feet, and even the mouth are usually very cold, the pulse is weak and rapid and the temperature is generally below normal, i.e. about 99° or 100° F. The animal cannot stand and is too exhausted and "collapsed" even to lift its head.

CAUSES.—This may be severe shock as a result of fright or injury from an accident ; extreme pain ; long-standing debilitating disease ; starvation ; exhaustion ; internal or external haemorrhage, etc.

TREATMENT.—As collapse is nearly always associated with cold extremities and subnormal temperature, the first procedure is to raise internal and external heat by every means at one's disposal. The following precautions should be taken. Rubber or glass hot-water bottles should be placed beneath the dog's bed so that the warmth percolates through to the patient without actually coming into uncomfortable contact. Others may be placed around the sides of the dog, and the glow of a radiant heat lamp may be directed downwards on to it ; or, as an alternative, several thicknesses of blanket should be laid over the dog. A teaspoonful of brandy in water can now be given, and a veterinary surgeon should be called to give subcutaneous injections, either of digitalin, pituitrin, or normal saline solution, with the object of sustaining the heart's action. The practitioner will make it his business to endeavour

Photo]   [*Daily Herald.*
NEARLY GROW'D UP.
Here are some puppies growing up. Notice the heads, legs, feet, and ears. Black is a favourite colour.

346

ANXIOUS TO PLEASE.

Few artists can better interpret the soul of a dog than Nicholson, who has drawn here a glorious Cocker, instinct with beauty and with loyalty, and eagerness to obey.

IN PROFILE.

Photo]   [Sport & General.

A FIELD TRIAL CHAMPION.
Mr. H. S. Lloyd's "Tokened of Ware" is seen retrieving the shot, holding
the game well in the mouth, as a Spaniel should carry game.

Photo]   [Fox.

"TORMENT OF WARE".
A Cocker Spaniel retrieving in snow, no pleasant or easy matter for the dog.

country is obvious. There is no doubt
that these dogs were bred with great care
by the farmers and shepherds simply with
the object of aiding them in their work
of tending sheep.

Having to exist in high lands, where
the climate is cold for a great part of the
year, it follows that the shepherd's dog
developed a long, dense, weather-resisting
coat. Then Nature, too, endowed this dog
with an active and graceful outline to fit
him for a pastoral occupation. Nature has
also provided the dog with ears specially
adapted to catch distant sounds. When
the dog is on the alert the ears are
brought forward and carried semi-erect,
with tip slightly drooping in attitude of
listening. This formation acts as a "sound
trap" to pick up far-away sounds, such as
calls from its master. Then the eye is
exceedingly keen and alert and is provided
to catch sight of the shepherd, who may be
a long distance off. This explains why
critics look for good eyes and ears when
judging a Collie.

The common sheep in Scotland in early
days were known as "Colleys", from the
Anglo-Saxon word "Col", meaning black.
This, together with the fact that the dogs
used for the herding of these sheep were
themselves mostly black in colour, led
to their being called "Colley Dogs", and

to discover the cause of the
collapse, and having satisfied
himself as to this, his line
of treatment will be clear
and appropriate.

Collars.—Ordinary and
Elizabethan. (*See* RES-
TRAINT.)

Collie.—The Collie is a
dog whose natural home
was in the Highlands of
Scotland, where he has
been used for hundreds
of years, probably since
earliest times, as the
Shepherd Dog, to assist
his master in the work of
guarding and herding
sheep in the extremely
difficult country among
the hills and mountains.

The need for a good
sheep-dog to a people who
depend upon pastoral
pursuits in a mountainous

Photo]   [Sport & General.

BRINGING TO HAND.
The Cocker should bring the game straight to the gun, and not hesitate as some do.
Miss J. Wykenham-Musgrave's "Poddle Crunch" makes no mistake.

COCKER FIELD TRIALS.

[*Sport & General.*

The Cocker is essentially a working dog, and the photograph shows the competitors with their owners and handlers at Kintbury, near Newbury, Berks.

Photo]

later simply Collies. This breed of sheep-dogs was fostered as such during the sixteenth, seventeenth and eighteenth centuries, so that specimens of the breed were to be found throughout the whole of Scotland. Specimens, too, were to be found in the Highlands of Wales and the North of England.

Up to 1860, this dog was simply used as a working sheep-dog, and was only seen in the company of a shepherd. In this year Queen Victoria, during one of her visits to Scotland, became attracted to the shepherd's dog because of its intelligence, sagacity, beauty and devotion, and she became the owner of a beautiful specimen. So the sheep-dog now became housed in the Royal Kennels, together with aristocratic dogs of other breeds. This action called public attention to the breed, and the Collie rapidly grew in public favour. In time, great numbers of Collie breeders sprang up throughout the country. Strenuous and successful efforts were made to improve the breed, especially from the point of view of beauty.

The Collie became one of the most popular dogs in the country, and it might almost claim to have set the pace in canine fashion for many years. During the Great War, however, its breeding was restricted, but soon again this essentially British dog attracted more and more attention.

In the early days of Collie history type was not by any means fixed and pedigrees were not recorded. Tricolours (black, tan and white) were the most common colours. Blue merles, too, were rather numerous. In fact, the first sable-and-white of which we have record was "Old Cockie", which lived in 1872) Sable-and-whites were very uncommon and scarce. In time the latter colour became very popular. So much so, that in the early days many breeders destroyed their tricolour and merle puppies. Later, tricolours became less common and merles were almost completely wiped out. Then, at the end of the nineteenth century, when merles were very rare, several breeders devoted much attention to this colour, and formed societies to foster the love of them. At the beginning they had to resort to dogs which were merle in colour but whose type was common compared with the sable-and-whites, which were much improved in type because of careful and scientific breeding. To-day the blue merles compare favourably with the best quality Collies of any colour, but this has been done by careful crossing with tricolours and sable-and-whites. As a matter of fact, it is necessary to mate tricolour to merle, for if merle is bred to merle continuously, the tendency is to produce Collies which are almost wholly white, and the nearer to white we breed the more likely are we to produce specimens with very small eyes, which are often

A HAPPY POSE.

"Peter", posing to have its photograph taken with his mistress, Mrs. Granville Soames, cousin of Lord Torphichen, strikingly displays the faithful expression so characteristic of Spaniels generally.

Photo]   [*L.N*

A CRUFT'S CUP-WINNER.

A fine head has "Lucky Star", one of the famous Cockers belonging to Mr. H. S. Lloyd.   In 1931 it won the Challenge Cup for the best dog in the show at Cru

both blind. Deafness often results from mating merle to merle.

Though the original home of the Collie was in Scotland, many of the early breeders lived in England, particularly in the Birmingham district, the centre which produced the best dogs in the early history of the breed. The first show at which Collies were exhibited was at Birmingham in 1861, but at this time the breed was known as "Scotch Sheep Dogs". The Birmingham Dog Show Society retained "Sheepdogs" as their class title until 1895, when the section was classified as "Collie".

In 1860, when the breed was provided with one class at Birmingham Dog Show, the entry was very small, but it is from this date that the history of the show Collie begins. In 1863 there were six entries in the one class provided at this show, but after that date there was notable progress both in breeding and exhibiting. In 1871 seventeen Collies were entered in the one class provided. Two of the exhibits at that year's show became famous and appear in the pedigrees of all present-day Collies. The first prize winner was "Old Mec", and the second winner was "Old Cockie".

"Old Cockie" was undoubtedly the better dog of the two, though he was placed second in the awards at his first show. Later he was best Collie at Birmingham for two or three years. He was a "sable-and-white" and was the first Collie of this colour of which we have any record. He has earned remarkable distinction as being the "fountain head" from which the popular and beautiful sable-and-white Collies first sprang.

In colour, "Old Cockie" was a rich sable with a white neck and frill, and white on his legs and tip of tail. He was a medium-sized dog, sturdy in build, and his well-proportioned body was set upon legs and feet that were strong in bone. He had a plentiful supply of a correct class of coat, to the density of which a full undercoat contributed. The coat was very full on neck and shoulders, forming a handsome cape and mane.

No photos of "Old Cockie" are in existence except some taken after he had reached the age of ten years. The picture illustrated here shows him to be a quite typical Collie. Nothing is known of "Old Cockie's" antecedents, but his name can be traced in the pedigree of every modern Collie. In 1875 he was offered for sale at the Midland Horse Repository, Birmingham. On his collar were fixed twenty-one plates, on which were engraved the names of shows where he had been victorious. He was purchased by Mr. G. Dean Tomlinson, of Birmingham, who retired him from the show ring. With his new owner, he lived a life of retirement until his death in 1882.

Breeding now developed rapidly. It commanded the attention of a great number of breeders.

Photo]   *[Gaber.*

ON SHOW POINTS ONLY.

A scene at a Club Show. Whilst, as we have said, Cockers are mainly working dogs, yet they are naturally exhibited for purely show points.

To those who love the Collie, names of fanciers like Mr. J. Bissell, Rev. Hans Hamilton, Mr. C. H. Wheeler, and Mr. A. H. Megson will always be remembered, for in the early days they laid the foundations of the breed as we know it to-day.

It was about 1882 when Mr. Megson first became interested in and attracted by the breed. He owned the best specimens of their day, and the prices he paid for some of his stock is almost staggering. A few of his numerous purchases are "Rutland", £250; "Metchley Wonder", £530; "Caractacus", £350; "Edgbaston Floss", £250; "Southport Perfection," £1000; "Edgbaston Marvel", £500; culminating in the purchase of Ch. "Ormskirk Emerald" from Mr. T. H. Stretch for £1500.

What has already been stated will convince the reader that Collie breeding at this time was a

Photo] [*Ralph Robinson.*
"EVERGREEN OF DOWNSWOLD".
This dog, the property of Mr. W. A. Peeks, is a good example of the Cocker of a favourite colour.

Photo] [*Miss Compton Collier.*
A SAFE COMPANION.
The Cocker is of course not alone in being perfectly safe with children, but no dog is a more reliable pet, and the youngest child can be left in its care.

Photo] [*Ralph Robinson.*
"BILLY BOY OF DOWNSWOLD".
Mrs. W. A. Reeves' noted Cocker Spaniel. The breed is world-famous, both as a working dog and as a companion.

very profitable business. All the same, hundreds, and perhaps thousands, of Collies were bred which were simply ordinary, but none the less beautiful, specimens which commanded a ready sale as companions.

It was not until the late 'nineties that we could claim to have established strains which became prepotent in type. From this time great breeders introduced us to specimens which stamped their type on the Collies bred. In 1898 Mr. R. Tait brought out Ch. "Wishaw Clinker", which proved himself a great sire. In 1899 Mr. Hugo Ainscough brought out Ch. "Parbold Piccolo", a most beautiful sable-and-white, with great wealth of coat. He stood on good legs and feet, and possessed a nicely moulded head and particularly well-carried ears. This dog undoubtedly proved the greatest sire of the day and sired Ch. "Anfield Model" in

"WOODMANSTERNE DEREK".

This beautiful dog, painted by Lilian Cheviot, was bred by the Rev. Hans F. Hamilton, the noted breeder of Collies. The dog is by "Squire of Tytton", a golden sable, sold for £1,250 to the United States of America.

1901. He was of fine quality, of only medium size, but carried a good coat, and he had a wonderful pair of ears. In fact, this dog's head was photographed and the photo became the model which all breeders aimed to reproduce. The year 1903 introduced us to Mr. R. Tait's Ch. "Wishaw Leader", a lovely tricolour (black, tan and white), with a most profuse coat and frill. He had a typical head and a neat pair of ears. In 1904 Mr. W. T. Hurry produced Ch. "Squire of Tytton", a high quality sable-and-white, with a lovely head.

These dogs are mentioned individually because they show that fanciers were by this time beginning to learn something about the laws governing breeding and reproduction. They appear prominently in the pedigrees of the Collie of to-day. Speaking generally, it should be stated that the blood of Ch. "Parbold Piccolo" and his son Ch. "Anfield Model" appear most prominently in the modern Collie.

Mention has been made of the high prices that have been paid for Collies. It should be borne in mind that the breed is not only popular in this country but particularly so in the United States of America, which purchased the best Collies from this country for a large number of years. The Americans have drawn on Britain's best for very many years, and at times there have been more high-class exhibition specimens in America than in Britain. These dogs, more often than not, beat the best that America has produced.

There is only one correct type of Collie, and the novice is urged not only to read the description that appears here but to study and compare the best specimens exhibited at shows so as to train his eyes to find out what is meant by quality in a dog. It must not be supposed that even experts will agree as to which is the best of a set of excellent first-rate specimens, for, if so, dog shows would be unnecessary if all judges unanimously agreed in placing the same dog first. When the same dog is placed first by a number of judges, it follows that this dog must be a first-rate specimen, provided, of course, we are discussing competition at our really good Collie shows. To become a "champion" a dog must be the best of his sex at three championship shows, judged by three different judges. It must be borne in mind, too, that only certain shows carry championship status. So, if a dog wins the Championship Certificate at three different championship shows, and thus become a "champion". he is, as a general rule, a first-class specimen.

By courtesy]　　　　　[E. C. Ash.
18TH CENTURY COLLIES.
At the end of the 18th century a book showing dogs was published, including the two pictures shown above, the upper one undoubtedly a rough Collie and the lower a smooth-coated Collie.

At a conference of the various Collie Clubs held at the Crystal Palace, London, the following description of the Collie was compiled

THE SKULL.—Should be flat, moderately wide between the ears, and gradually tapering towards the eyes. There should be only a slight depression at the stop. The width of skull necessarily depends upon the combined length of skull and muzzle, and the whole must be considered in connection with the size of the dog. The cheek should not be full or prominent.

THE MUZZLE.—Should be of fair length, tapering to the nose, and must not show weakness or be snipy or lippy. Whatever the colour of the dog may be, the nose must be black.

THE TEETH.—Should be of good size, sound and level; very slight unevenness is permissible.

THE JAWS.—Should be clean-cut and powerful.

THE EYES.—Are a very important feature and give expression to the dog; they should be of medium size, set somewhat obliquely, of almond shape, and of brown colour, except in the case of merles, when the eyes are frequently (one or both)

By courtesy]　　　　　[E. C. Ash.
IN 1653.
In 1653 a book on dogs gave some crude woodcut illustrations, including this dog, which the owner believes is intended to be a Collie dog.

blue-and-white or china ; expression full of intelligence, with a quick, alert look when listening.

THE BRUSH.—Should be moderately long, carried low when the dog is quiet, with a slight upward "swirl" at the end and may be gaily carried when the dog is excited, and not over the back. *Faults.*— Short tail or tail carried over the back or twisted to one side.

above the hocks profusely so ; but below the hocks fairly smooth, although all heavily coated Collies are liable to grow a slight feathering. Hair on the brush very profuse. *Faults.*—A soft, silky, or wavy coat, or insufficient undercoat.

COLOUR AND MARKING.—Are immaterial, but other points being equal, a nice showily marked dog is preferred. All white or red setter colour is most objectionable.

GENERAL CHARACTER. — To enable the Collie to fulfil his

COLLIES, ROUGH AND SMOOTH.

In 1800 some very typical Collies were portrayed. The picture is of exceptional interest to us, for it not only shows the rough Collies of the time, but the curtailed dog with "wall-eyes". The lower dog may well be the ancestor of the present Bobtail.

THE COAT.—Should be very dense, the outer coat harsh to the touch, the inner- or undercoat soft, furry, and very close, so close as to almost hide the skin. The mane and frill should be very abundant, the mask or face smooth, as also the ears at the tips, but they should carry more hair towards the base ; the forelegs well feathered, the hindlegs

natural bent for sheep-dog work, he should be built on lines of strength, activity and grace, with a shapely body and sound legs and feet. He should be lithe and active in his movements, and entirely free from cloddiness and coarseness in any part of his conformation ; and lastly, he must be gifted with true expression. Expression is obtained by the perfect combination of head and muzzle, size. shape, colour and placement of eye, and correct position and carriage of ears, which gives the dog that sweet, dreamy, semi-cunning yet alert outlook that makes the perfect Collie the most beautiful of the canine race.

SIZE AND WEIGHT.—Dogs, 22 to 24 ins. at the shoulder ; bitches, 20 to 22 ins. Dogs, 45 to 65 lb. ; bitches, 40 to 55 lb.

FAULTS.—Length of head apparently out of proportion to the body and of the Borzoi type are to be strongly condemned. Weak, snipy muzzle, overshot mouth, heavy or gooseberry coloured, also glassy or staring eyes, are very objectionable. Domed skull, high-peaked occiput, prominent cheek, dish-faced, or Roman-nosed.

THE NECK.—Should be muscular, powerful, and of fair length and somewhat arched.

THE BODY.—Should be rather long, with well-sprung ribs, chest deep, fairly broad behind the shoulders, which should be sloped : loins slightly arched and powerful. The legs should be straight in front. *Faults.*—Flat-sided, short or cobby

THE FORELEGS.—Should be straight and muscular, neither in nor out at elbows, with a fair amount of bone ; the forearm somewhat fleshy, with pasterns showing flexibility without weakness. *Faults.* — Weak long pasterns, out at elbows crooked forearms

THE HINDLEGS.—Should be muscular at the thighs, clean and sinewy below hocks, with well-bent stifles. *Faults.*—Cow-, or straight-hocks.

THE FEET.—Should be oval in shape soles

"ORMSKIRK AMAZEMENT".

This famous Collie was exported to Australia during the great Collie boom. He was a son of a noted matron, "Sweet Lassie", which was sold for £250.

well-padded and the toes arched and close together. The hind feet arched, the hocks well let down and powerful. *Faults.*—Large, open, flat, for hare feet ; feet turned outwards or inwards.

SCALE OF POINTS.

Head and expression, 15 ; ears, 10 ; neck and shoulders, 10 ; legs and feet, 15 ; hindquarters, 10 ; back and loins, 10 ; brush, 5 ; coat and frill, 20 ; size, 5. Total, 100.

Collie (Bearded). — The Highland or Scottish Bearded Collie is a distinct breed with many characteristics peculiarly his own. It has been known by a number of names. The late D. J. Thomson Gray dubbed him the Hairy Mou'ed Collie. He has also been called the Scottish Mountain Collie.

He was at one time very popular with the Border shepherds, and was known as the Border Collie.

Hogg, the Ettrick shepherd, had always a Border Collie as his favourite helper, and as he lived in 1771–1835, this is evidence of his long pedigree, which would go much further back than Hogg's time. These Border Collies were supposed to be of a different strain from the Highland Collie. The former were of a slate-coloured hue, whilst the latter were supposed to be of a reddish colour, were slightly smaller and did not carry such a profuse coat, which, however, was inclined to curl. At the present time the red-coloured specimens have the same characteristics. Again, the old breeders insisted that the dogs should be like the Highland Collie and the Scottish Deerhound, viz. self-coloured. They were of the opinion that the old Highland Collie had some deerhound blood which was quite in keeping with the texture and the colour of his coat. The original Scottish Deerhound was

All illustrations by courtesy] [*E. C. Ash.*

CH. "CHARLEMAGNE".

A grandson of "Cockie", the property of Mr. Bissell, "Charlemagne" was a famous sable-and-white. He was first shown in 1879.

CH. "KILMENY JESS".

A Collie bitch, well-known at the end of the nineteenth century showing the type so much desired then.

THE MODERN COLLIE.

Although so much has been said as to the type of Collie of the boom period, there is little doubt that the dogs of 1934 are as good as the most famous dogs of the past. Mrs. R. E. James has a powerful kennel. On the left we have a head study of her "Mariemeau Brilliantine", a son of Ch. "Laund Lindrum", which has what is known as "Collie expression". *Below*, "Knight of Monastir" (*Photo, Guiver*). On the *top right*, "Mariemeau Mary Rose", an outstanding daughter of "Lindrum"; *centre*, "Mariemeau Fan Tail", a sable-and-white son of "Lindrum"; and *lastly*, the famous Ch. "Laund Lindrum". "Knight of Monastir" was bred by Mrs. P. Carter, and all the others are owned by Mrs. R. E. James.

IF

THE WORKING COLLIE.

also either of a blue-grey or red-sandy colour. Broken colours were supposed to be a sure sign of alien blood and were not countenanced. In later years, however, quite a number of broken-coloured dogs made their appearance in the lowlands of Scotland, where no doubt crossing was freely indulged in.

Photo]　　　　　　　　　　　　　　　　　　　[Compton Collier.
A COUNTESS'S TRIO.
Taken in the charming grounds of Bleddyn, Monmouthshire, this picture shows the Countess of Essex (formerly Mrs. Scott-Brown) with her three favourite dogs. which include a fine Collie.

certainly have become extinct except for the enthusiasm of one or two fanciers.

The Highland or Mountain Collie is far-famed for his intelligence. This, no doubt, was bred into them through their long and close association with their masters. The old cattle drovers who

The British Collie is known all over the world, but the Highland Collie is a much older variety. It may even have existed at the time of the Roman invasion, when the Britons reared their famous fighting dogs which the Romans took back with them to Italy to fight wild beasts in the arena. In these early days the Sheepdog was either tail-less or had only a half tail, and there are still some strains of Hill Collies bred to-day that have naturally abbreviated caudal appendages. This no-tail fashion can be seen clearly demonstrated in the Old English Bobtailed Sheepdog. This variety is akin to the Highland or Bearded Collie, but to-day have very little in common, the Bobtail being kept largely for exhibition purposes, whilst the Bearded Collie is as good at his work as ever he was. The variety in its pure state has become somewhat scarce, and would

used to bring their cattle great distances to the annual sales by road, practically lived and slept with their dogs, and they depended much on their Collies to assist them on their long and wearisome journeys. Through long acquaintance even the cattle and sheep used to know their own dogs, and even looked upon them as their guides and protectors. It is certainly a fact that the dogs knew the members of their own herds and flocks by scent. There is a story told of a Scottish breeder who once bought some sheep in Edinburgh and on the way home lost two of them. This was not only a misfortune, but it cast a slur upon his dog. Several days after, John heard that a farmer who lived near the highway had found a pair of sheep and went with the dog to see if they were his. The farmer, with proper caution, asked him how they were marked. As John had bought sheep

Photo]　　　　　　　　　　　　　　　　　　　　　　　[Guiver.
A FOURSOME.
The Collies of Mrs. J. K. George, of Chelsea, London, are seen at all important shows. On the left is one of the much desired blue merles.

"BEULAH NIGHTSHADE".
A head study of one of Mrs. George's Collies.

from several sellers and had hurried out of town, he could not inform the farmer, who said, "Very well then, it is only right I should keep the sheep." "It's a fact," said John, "that I cannot tell the sheep, but if my dog can, will you let me have them ?" The farmer thought hard, was honest, and having little fear of the ordeal, had all the sheep upon his farm turned on to a large park. John's dog also was turned into the field and immediately singled out first one and then the other of the strays.

A Bearded Collie can be kept in good condition with only occasional grooming. Too much grooming and brushing would bring out too much of the undercoat and give the dog a half-coated and unfinished appearance. Its coat is entirely different from that of the Bobtail, being of a much harsher texture ; and should be perfectly free from curling. The outer is perhaps the most important of his two coats, for without it, the under coat would soon become soaked and sodden, and the dog would suffer from colds, etc., causing all kinds of complications. These Bearded Collies work and sleep out on the hills in mist and rain, and yet the elements never reach the soft warm coat. Even when it has to take to the water, once it shakes itself the bulk of the moisture is gone.

The following is a description of the breed which was published some thirty years ago or more :

HEAD.—Large, square, plenty of space for the brain.

EARS.—Medium size, drooping, covered with hair.

EYES.—To match coat in colour ; the typical wall-eye (otherwise called china or marble), either single or double, suiting the merle coat. The eyes should be rather widely apart, big, soft and affectionate, but not protruding.

EYEBROWS. Slightly elevated, covered with shaggy hair.

COAT.—A Bearded Collie should have a thick skin with two coats, the under one furry and the outer one hard, strong, shaggy, unkempt. The legs covered right down to the feet, not bare as in the better-known Collie.

COLOUR.—Immaterial, but preference given to slate or reddish-fawn ; if the coat be varied by a white collar or white on the legs, that is no defect.

NOSE.—Large, square and black, with little hair so as to afford contrast to the shaggy "beard" running from each side of the nose.

TEETH.—Large and white ; never overshot or undershot.

TAIL.—Moderately long ; must be carried low while walking and extended when at high speed.

MEASUREMENT.—Dogs 20 to 24 inches at shoulder. Bitches rather less.

GENERAL APPEARANCE.—An active dog with none of the stumpiness of the Bobtail and which, though strongly made, does not look too heavy. The face should have a sharp inquiring expression.

FAULTS.—Thick rounded ribs ; too rotund in body ; too short in length ; meagre short tail ; narrow skulls, bare legs ; too long nose.

A NOTED BLUE MERLE.
Ch. "Eden Blue Blossom", bred by Mr. F. Robson, the winner of five first prizes and Championship Certificates, was exported to New York.

CH. "ASHTEAD APPLAUSE".

A fine study of this noted champion Collie, the property of Mr. Roberts. A body study appears on page 365.

A REMARKABLE TEAM.

It is very seldom that one is able to see so fine a kennel of Collies as here depicted, the property of Mr. R. H. Roberts. Note the type of head, free from any suggestion of the Borzoi.

"ASHTEAD BLUE ENSIGN".
This blue merle is one of Mr. Roberts's kennel. Attention is drawn to the head, front, and limbs of this dog.

colour, or it fails to attract even the notice of the judge. When one considers that there are over seventy well-known breeds of dog, and that almost every breed has its own peculiar colour or mixture of colours, it will be realized that to go into detail regarding every one would entail the writing of a very voluminous chapter. The reader who is interested in any particular breed, and who would know more about its correct colours and markings, is recommended to peruse the authoritative articles appearing each week throughout this work.

It is curious how the very mention of a certain colour will suggest at once, to the experienced dog enthusiast, which breed is being referred to. For instance, "Sable" is associated with Pekingese Spaniels, "Wheaten" with Cairn Terriers, "Harlequin" with Great Danes, "Red" with Chows, "Fawn" with Greyhounds, and so on indefinitely.

WHEATEN. — Indicates a pale yellowish colour.

HARLEQUIN.—Is a term applied to mottled, pied, or patchy dogs such as are frequently encountered among Great Danes.

BRINDLED. — Dark streaks or spots on grey or tawny ground.

TRICOLOUR.—A mixture of black, tan and white.

PARTICOLOUR.—Red and white, as frequently applied to Pekes.

MERLE.—A bluish-grey with black intermingled.

ROAN.—Roans are either red roans or blue roans. In the former variety the basic colour is a dark-red flecked with white hairs; blue roans have a basic colour of blue or blue-grey flecked with white hairs. Mrs. Phyllis Robson once wrote, and with great truth: "One of the results of breeding pedigree dogs to the fancy points exacted by judges is that general preference for a certain

Very little has been written about this breed, and consequently it suffered in popularity.

Yet the Beardie has a marvellous temperament, is gentle and affectionate and very easily controlled, even very young puppies readily obeying commands.

Collie (Smooth Coated).—Only differs from the rough in its coat, which should be hard, dense and quite smooth

CH. "ASHTEAD VIOLETTA".
This beautiful tricolour Collie (and what a demand there was at one time for tricolours), is owned by Mr. Roberts, and is one of the most charming specimens of the breed.

Collunarium. — A nose-wash. Treatment by this means is rarely undertaken in dogs, mostly on account of the great exception they take to it, but partly because it is a little dangerous. Any benefit likely to be derived from a collunarium can usually be as easily conferred by inhalations of medicated steam, and this line of treatment is the one advocated.

Collutorium.—A mouth-wash. Very popular is glyco-thymolin, being non-poisonous and not unpleasant in flavour. The strength for use is one part to three of water. A solution of ordinary salt is, however, very efficacious as a mouth-wash and may be used several times daily.

Collyrium.—An eyewash. The safest of all is probably the well-tried boracic lotion made in the strength of one teaspoonful of boracic acid to one pint of distilled water.

Colour.—Colouring in dogs is a matter of great importance, at least, so far as exhibition dogs are concerned. Any individual of a breed "put down" at a show must be absolutely correct as regards its

CH. "ASHTEAD APPLAUSE".
Sable-and-white, made famous by Dr. Gordon Stables, R.N., is always an attractive colour. This great winning Collie is the property of Mr. Roberts.

colour in the coat has, in many instances, led to a limited uniformity which makes it difficult for the uninitiated to distinguish one individual specimen from another in a group of the same breed. The hounds in a hunting pack rarely differ in essential complexion. A whole black, a pure white, or an entirely red Foxhound would be a ridiculous incongruity. It can never be said of dogs, as of racehorses, that a good one may be of any colour. There are many canine breeds in which the unvarying colour, or combination of colours, is accepted as an indubitable index of purity, a credential of true descent.''

Nobody would ever expect an Irish Terrier to be of any colour than wholly red, or an Airedale to deviate from black - and - tan. It is essential for the flat-coated Retriever to be black ; the Bull Terrier to be pure white ; and similar instances could be quoted at great length.

There may be manifested, in some individuals of a breed, a generalized or localized lack of pigmentation known as albinism.

ALBINISM signifies the deficiency of pigment in an animal's skin, hair or other tissues. An albino is distinguished by having a pink skin, a preponderance of white hairs, and a white iris to the eye. The dog's iris is that muscular ring of brown colour which surrounds the pupil. When brown pigment is absent the iris comes into greater prominence on account of its very light or nearly white or pale blue hue. Such a condition in horses is known as "wall-eye". Albinism appears to be an hereditary character, for if an albino sire and dam are mated, their progeny will also be albinos.

Coma.—A condition of complete unconsciousness which quite frequently precedes death at the termination of severe illnesses. It is a state of profound stupor from which the patient cannot be aroused, nor can any reflex responses be induced by the application of stimuli. It is caused by a number of con-

ditions, such as brain diseases or injuries ; narcotic, uraemic or other poisoning ; excessive fever ; diabetes, and occurs (as previously mentioned) when life is at such a low ebb that it is nearly extinct. Very energetic measures must be adopted to arouse the patient and instil into it some vitality. Alcoholic stimulants and vigorous massage would be helpful; and if the body is cold, hot-water bottles should be packed around it. Then send for a veterinary surgeon.

Communicable Diseases (Dog to Man).—

The possibility of disease dissemination from animals to man is a question which not only merits, but receives, the closest attention. Many charges are laid at the door of the dog by people who are more or less ignorant of animal pathology and, usually, they succeed only in scaring the nervous folk or the mothers and guardians of children.

The dog suffers from very few diseases indeed which are infectious or contagious to man. Only two specific diseases of the canine tribe have any significance for the human being, and these are rabies and tuberculosis. There are skin complaints which may sometimes be readily conveyed from a dog to its owner, ringworm and mange being here referred

Photo]   *["Daily Mirror."*
CH. "MOUNT SHANNON BLUE SPLENDOUR".
Famous as this dog was, perhaps its owner was yet more famous, for everybody in the Collie world knew the Rev. Tom Salter, who brought this dog to the fore.

to. External and internal parasites are also occasionally transferred, but in few cases indeed does the resulting disability amount to any importance or severity.

DISTEMPER.—This universal canine plague often gives rise to fear and doubt in the minds of the laity as to whether it can be a menace to the health of man. Briefly, the answer is "No".

Although this disease has been likened to measles, influenza and smallpox of man, it has, in reality, no connection with any of them. The writer has heard of no case in practice in which any pathological condition has been communicated to man from animals suffering with distemper. However, some years ago Dr. M'Gowan (who conducted extensive investigations

"FASHION SUPERIOR"

NINA SCOTT-ANLEY.

        A FRENCH ACTRESS AND HER FAVOURITE.
Mme. Hugette Ex-Duflos, here seen, is well known to Parisians as an "ornament of the French stage". Moreover, wherever she
decides to be ornamental, she takes her pet Collie along to be ornamental too.

into the cause of distemper) published a report in which he referred to the incidence of an obstinate nasal catarrh among his laboratory workers. Only in one case was he able to detect the presence of the identical organism which M'Gowan considered was the germ responsible for distemper in dogs. This man was said to have suffered from a most intractable chronic nasal catarrh ; but no other symptom was ever manifest, the condition produced thus falling far short of that which we recognize as distemper. It has since been established, too, that no visible germ is responsible for distemper, the latter being caused by an ultra-visible virus. Excepting M'Gowan's assertion, the writer has never before heard it suggested that distemper could be transmitted

Fortunately, rabies is one of those diseases which have become extinct in this country, thanks to our rigid system of quarantining all dogs arriving from abroad. So we Britishers have nothing to fear in our country from this fatal malady, provided that we strictly observe the law. It was only through the gross thoughtlessness, or criminal wilfulness of some person who, in 1918, smuggled a dog into this country, the dog by great misfortune being in the incubative stage of rabies, that there was an outbreak in which some 180 people in the vicinity were bitten by supposed mad animals ; of this number, indeed, 46 were later proved to be rabid. All human cases received treatment at Pasteur Institutes and no deaths were recorded.

Photo]   [Ralph Robinson.

THE COLLIE BODY.

Here is Miss Fincham's "Wisbang Sunlight", which exemplifies the alert and speedy readiness of the Collie.

to man, and under natural conditions he feels convinced it never is.

RABIES.—There is no doubt whatever of the transmissibility of rabies to the human being. This disease, however, is contagious and not infectious. By this is meant that the virus can be conveyed only by direct contact, and is not air-borne. The saliva of a rabid dog is most poisonous. It gains entrance to the system of the victim, generally through a wound caused by the animal's teeth. Nevertheless, it is not essential that a person should be bitten by a rabid dog in order to contract hydrophobia (the analogous condition in man), for should such a dog merely lick a person's hand, the greatest danger arises if that hand should bear a scratch or abrasion through which the virus can gain entrance.

A particularly interesting case was reported (*Journal of the American Veterinary Medical Association* for August 1922) in which an apparently healthy dog bit a child rather badly about the face. The child's father reported the matter to the police, who caught the dog and placed it in veterinary charge for a period of observation. Five days later the dog developed clinical symptoms of rabies and was destroyed. Immediately this diagnosis was confirmed the child received Pasteur's anti-rabic inoculations, which saved its life. At the time the child was bitten, a young man also received a bite on the lip, of which little or no notice was taken. A month later he showed signs of hydrophobia and very soon died, having received no Pasteur treatment. This authentic incident alone proves the value and necessity of anti-rabic vaccine,

Photo]   [*Sport & General.*

A PRIZE WINNER.

Gracefulness, combined with fidelity, are characteristics of the Collie, whether Rough or Smooth. This is Mrs. C. N. Baxter's
"Heatherbourne Sheila"

Photo]   CH. "LAUND LYNNE".   *[Fall.*

Smooth Collies are by no means as numerous as the Rough in regard to pedigree dogs. Here is Mr. Stansfield's champion, a very fine example of the breed.

and the folly of treating such matters lightly, especially in America (where this happened) and on the Continent, where rabies is rife.

TUBERCULOSIS.—Unfortunately, the canine species is not immune from tuberculosis, the domestic dog being affected to the extent of about two or three per cent. The disease gathers importance from its communicability to the human race, little children being especially endangered from their habit of cuddling and kissing their pet animals.

Tubercle attacks mostly the adult dog, but it is not unknown among young puppies. "Whilst it is well known that tuberculosis of man and of some of the domestic animals (such as cattle) is very common, it is rather rare in dogs. These animals seem to possess considerable power of resistance and are able to throw off the disease. Certain experiments by inoculation and inhalation have demonstrated the fact that only one-third of the cases develop the disease, the remainder escaping, and that the feeding of tubercular matter in the food invariably produces negative results". (Muller and Glass.)

An ever-present and insidious source of tuberculosis in man and the cat, is the drinking of milk from infected cows. But since dogs are not easily infected by ingestion of the contagium, one must assume that cows' milk plays little part in the causation of tuberculosis in these animals. Furthermore, it would appear that, so far as the dog is concerned, inhalation is the chief method by which it becomes affected. The assumption, therefore, is that any dog found suffering from tubercle has at some time or other been in close contact with a person who was in an advanced stage of consumption. Many specific in-

stances have been known in which dogs, cats, parrots, and other forms of life, have contracted the disease from their consumptive owners.

It has been shown how man may infect his dog; but how does *he* become a prey to infection? Man is naturally susceptible to the disease, although, fortunately, many are able to offer a stubborn resistance; yet he contracts it by all known methods, i.e. ingestion, inhalation and inoculation. Dogs affected with the pulmonary form of tuberculosis sometimes sneeze, the material so ejected being charged with tubercle bacilli. Thus it is not wise to allow children to kiss their animals' heads or pet them too closely. It is not uncommon for cats and dogs to sleep with their owners, and where this is permitted, the latter run a certain amount of risk of contracting several complaints.

There is every reason to believe that there is a danger of infection to both man and animals from the bite of a dog afflicted with intestinal tuberculosis. So it would appear, at first glance, that the dog is a somewhat dangerous animal in so far as tuberculosis is concerned; yet we should bear in mind that only two or three per cent, at the outside, of dogs are affected, and that none of them emulate the dangerous and objectionable human habit of expectorating, and therefore usually have very little opportunity of spreading the disease.

MANGE.—It can safely be said that only upon rare occasions does a human being contract this disease from an animal. When one thinks of the millions of dogs and cats which reside in these islands, and of the hundreds of cases of sarcoptic mange occurring among them annually, one has only to realize how exceedingly rarely one encounters, or even hears of, a person who is able to state definitely that his or her skin complaint can be directly traceable to an animal.

Veterinary surgeons are handling such cases daily, yet they seem

Photo]   THREE CHAMPIONS.   *[Planet News.*

At a Paris dog show these three excellent specimens of the Collie breed were much admired. The Collie is popular not only in Great Britain, but all over the world.

Photo] "FULKE OF NASHILL". [*Ralph Robinson.*

A splendid type of Smooth Collie, belonging to Miss A. E. B. Nunneley.   The Greyhound strain is clearly seen.

Photo] CH. "LAUND LAWSON". [*Sport & General.*

In 1932 this beautiful dog took first prize and championship and cup for the best Collie, Rough or Smooth, at the Manchester Show.

practically immune from such affections. Nevertheless, concrete cases are known to have arisen from time to time, in which mange in the dog or cat has been followed by an itchiness in its owner, microscopical investigation having proved that the parasite taken from the lesions in each case were identical.

Mange is, of course, a parasitic disease, the acarus being practically invisible to the unaided human eye. All animals have their special variety of parasite, and it only needs a certain length of time in contact with the skin of man for the acarus to change its residence.

The canine sarcopt, if left untreated, may live on the human subject for five or six weeks, but when suspected, diagnosed and treated, it is easily eradicated. In conformation, these mites are very like those which abound in ripe Cheshire cheese, each animal's individual parasite possessing a characteristic size and shape ; so that once the creature is found, there is no mistaking its source of origin.

Scabies, which is contracted from a dog or cat is, however, a much more benign malady than the true *human* scabies. The earliest manifestation in either man or animal is an unusual irritation, which later becomes intense, although an initial examination of the skin may reveal little or nothing to the naked eye. In the human being this intensity is always greatest when in the warmth of a bed, or when sitting before the fire. A subsequent and more careful scrutiny of the skin may disclose the presence of very small reddish elevations ; the skin of the dog becomes scurfy, the hair falls out, and it is at this stage that one's doubts should be confirmed or negatived by submitting the suspected animal to veterinary examination.

There is another type of skin disease known as follicular mange, the cause of which is a totally different parasite. Curiously enough, when this occurs in a dog, it is often regarded as incurable and eventually fatal. Cats, on the other hand, rarely, if ever, suffer from it, and man is known frequently to harbour the parasite upon his skin without it ever occasioning the slightest inconvenience.

RINGWORM.—This fungoid affection of the skin is comparatively common in domestic dogs and cats, on account, no doubt, of its great prevalence among rodents. Rats and mice are affected principally with a type of ringworm known as Favus, and it follows that this type will be most prevalent in the cat ; in dogs Favus is more rare, other varieties pre-

dominating. All the ringworms are contagious to man, and whilst ringworm is not by any means a serious disease, it sometimes proves very troublesome to eradicate. Animals are also able to contract the disease from man.

The ringworm which is conveyed from dog to man usually attacks the body and limbs only, whilst that conveyed from man to man most often affects the head. The former type may often be cured in from three to seven days, thus differing from the scalp or human variety, which usually requires several weeks, and is frequently amenable only to X-ray treatment.

Here again, we should bear in mind that practically every mansion, cottage, farm, or workshop throughout the country, harbours its dog or cat, and their numbers aggregate to a colossal total. Yet how often do we find a case of ringworm among them ? Comparatively seldom ; And if one *is* found, it is suitably dealt with and kept under control. Nevertheless, it is feared that many readers who have animals at home will begin to feel alarm and wonder whether they are in any danger. But if they take ordinary precautions and refrain from amateurish dabbling with empirical remedies, their fears may be allayed, and what has been stated above is merely what possibly *could* happen, and not what probably *would*.

WORMS.—Of all the many types of worm to which the dog is susceptible, only one offers any real danger to man. That is a tapeworm known as the *Taenia Echinococcus*. It is the smallest

THE BEARDED COLLIE.
The Bearded Collie can quite easily be mistaken for the Old English Sheep-dog. This is "Balmaeneil Rork", a great prize winner, the property of Mrs. Cameron Miller.

known tapeworm, measuring something under half an inch, and never exceeding four segments. As showing how man may become infected with the cystic form of this worm, a dog which is harbouring this parasite in its bowel, may void a number of the worm's eggs on the grass of a garden or field. It is not uncommon for people in the country to pluck stalks of grass and put them in their mouths, thereby infecting themselves.

When the egg gains access to the human system, it soon becomes a cyst, which may be attached to almost any of the internal organs. Usually, the sites of their location are the liver and peritoneum, and they grow to such an enormous size that they not uncommonly cause death.

Fortunately, the incidence of *Taenia Echinococcus* in dogs is very rare ; and so far as other worms are concerned, there is little or nothing to fear.

"BALMAENEIL SCOTT."

This is a good example of the Highland Collie, winner at the Scottish Kennel Club and Ladies' Kennel Association Shows, owned by Mrs. Cameron Miller. Observe the remarkable coat.

KNOCK-KNEES AND SPLASH FEET.

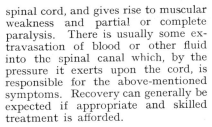

CORRECT FORE LIMBS.

Compress. — An application of moist heat or cold to the body for the relief of pain, to soften hard tissue, to strengthen parts which have become bruised or sprained, and to expedite the ripening of abscesses. Compresses may be cold or hot according to the purpose for which they are used. If continued cold is required, as in the case of localized inflammations and sprains, it is necessary constantly to renew the applications. For this reason cold compresses are not very practical. Hot ones retain their heat longer than cold compresses remain cold. Any absorbent material, such as thick pads of wool or flannel should be steeped in water and then wrung out. It is applied to the injured part and kept moist by covering it with oiled silk or rubber sheeting. (*See also* FOMENTATIONS.)

Conception.—Means that the ovum or egg of the female has been fertilized by a spermatozoon of the male, following the act of coitus. Bitches may be mated with dogs but it does not follow that they will conceive, and if for any reason they do not, then there will be no pregnancy and no puppies. When semen is injected into the female genitalia, it is not known how long a time elapses before the spermatozoa have migrated far enough along the walls of the uterus to meet with the ripe ova descending from the ovary.

Non-conception may be dependent upon a variety of circumstances, such as cystic ovaries, inflammation of the womb, fallopian tubes or vagina, etc., etc. But fuller and further discussion of this subject will be found under "STERILITY".

Concussion.—A violent jar or shock, or a condition which results from it. When the brain is implicated, there has been some severe blow to the head such as may be inflicted by a dog falling out of a window, being run over, or being struck by a hard missile.

SYMPTOMS.—As a result of fracture of the skull bones, or of a portion of bone pressing upon the brain, unconsciousness is generally produced, which may be transient or may persist until death supervenes. The breathing is shallow and slow, there is giddiness, nausea, and a weak pulse, and there may be haemorrhages from the ears and nose. The exact effects of concussion of the brain will depend largely upon the situation of the blow or bruise, because different areas of the brain-substance control certain and specified parts of the body. Thus, while consciousness may not have been disturbed, we may find a complete loss of balance, or even a paralysis of one part or another.

TREATMENT. — Handle the dog as little as possible, provide it with a soft bed, and see that it is kept quiet and at rest. Sal volatile held to the nostrils will help recovery from the first shock, and a veterinary surgeon should be summoned to examine the skull, as an immediate operation may be necessary.

CONCUSSION OF THE SPINE results from shocks or blows affecting the spinal cord, and gives rise to muscular weakness and partial or complete paralysis. There is usually some extravasation of blood or other fluid into the spinal canal which, by the pressure it exerts upon the cord, is responsible for the above-mentioned symptoms. Recovery can generally be expected if appropriate and skilled treatment is afforded.

BOW-LEGS.

CORRECT HIND LIMBS.

Condition.—To the average layman the term "condition", as applied to animals, conveys little or nothing. It is vague. Many people believe that a packet of so-called "condition powders" will produce in their dogs a tip-top state of good health. Unhappily, this assumption is very far from the truth, for the matter is not by any means so simple. Good condition, as a veterinary surgeon or a trainer know it, is that state of perfect health and ability for endurance which is brought about by regular and systematic exercise and a correct diet. It may be defined as follows : A firmness of muscle and the fullest development of the powers of heart, lungs and flesh to sustain the animal during long-continued exertion. It is brought about by a system of training which has become a fine art. Many a novice, however, has been heard to remark, when handling a grossly fat dog, "What fine condition he is in !" Obesity is *not* a sign of good condition ; it is the reverse. A dog which is sleek of coat, hard as nails, bright and alert, is in the sort of condition which the man desires who keeps Greyhounds, Sheep-dogs or other fast-moving breeds, but it is not necessarily what is known as "show condition".

It is very doubtful whether those dogs which spend their lives going from show to show have half the vitality or vim in them which is possessed by the ordinary common cur. To get a dog into show condition other things have to be considered besides exercise, though the latter is still highly important. It is one thing to possess a beautiful animal with a faultless pedigree, exhibiting every point typical of its breed, but quite another matter to bring it up to "show condition". Most novices have, at one time or another, experienced the difficulty, and they only begin to learn the art after many months, or even years of weary experimentation and practice.

Most people who continually show dogs will agree that such animals really lead a very artificial and forced sort of existence. They are always at concert pitch and their exhibitors must, of necessity, become specialists in the art of show preparation. Many of the little pleasures that the ordinary dog enjoys are, for various reasons, denied his more showy and aristocratic relative, as even a romp, just prior to a show, may tend to spoil the coat and jeopardize the chance of winning a prize. One can only begin to know how a particular breed of dog should look, in the show-ring, by constantly visiting such places and noting all the points sought by the discriminating judge such, perhaps, as length of nose, body, or legs, texture of coat,

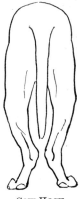

COW-HOCK.

weight or size of the dog, etc. To become really proficient in this knowledge one should join a specialist club dealing with the breed in which one is interested ; go to all the big shows, exchange views with other breeders, and get a fixed impression of what should constitute a typical specimen of the breed, and what is meant by "show condition". The surest way to learn is by placing one's own dogs in competition with others, taking care to profit by the mistakes made, eventually eliminating these errors.

Returning, however, to the question of fit condition, it may be reiterated that the only way to get a

Condy's Fluid.—A proprietary disinfectant consisting of a concentrated solution of permanganate of sodium. It is an excellent deodorant and antiseptic, but is not so potent a germicide as are many of the other well-known disinfectants—such, for instance, as perchloride of mercury. Condy's Fluid is used by adding so much of it to water as will render the latter of a deep-pink colour. It is non-poisonous to animals ; in fact, it may be given internally as an intestinal antiseptic.

Conformation.—This term refers, in general, to the shape of the body, whether that be normal or

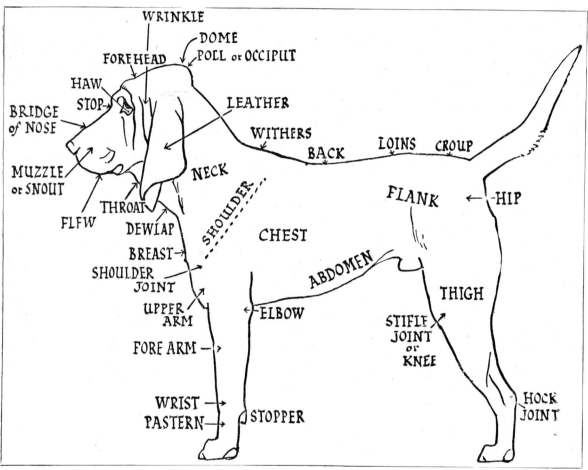

THE POINTS OF A DOG.

dog into "condition" is to provide him with a *sufficiency* of regular non-fatiguing exercise, the best and plainest of food in correct amount and kind, and a dry, well-ventilated kennel. Hygiene is most important. A dog which is badly infested with worms, or with fleas or lice, cannot possibly look well. An overfed, bloated, unexercised dog will not be healthy ; and a starved, tangle-coated or dirt-begrimed animal will be a living testimony to the neglect or stupidity of its owner. No one matter is alone concerned in the production and maintenance of good hard condition ; it is a process which entails the close observance of a combination of all questions connected with the general management of the kennel. Finally, then, exercise is of paramount importance, followed very closely by foods and feeding.

abnormal. So far as horses are concerned (in which weight-carrying or pulling render those animals so valuable) a correct conformation is absolutely essential in order to obtain the best results. Experience has taught stock-owners that whilst the majority of members of a species of animal possess a certain shape and characteristics, any departure from the rule constitutes a malformation or perhaps even a deformity. With malformed or badly shaped animals experience also has taught that the same amount of work or speed cannot be performed as one commonly expects from those of normal conformation. For instance, a narrow-chested horse would not be considered capable of sustaining long-continued or rapid movement so well as a horse with good width and depth of chest, other points being equal; and scores of similar comparisons could be made.

But here we are dealing with the dog, and since we do not in this country expect dogs to carry weight or pull carts (*see* DRAUGHT DOGS), we do not seek in them quite the same points as the horseman requires in horses. Nevertheless, there are very stringent standards laid down for the many breeds of dogs, any departure from which would jeopardize the individual in a show-ring. Some dogs must have broad chests and large, round, massive heads as, for instance, the bulldog; some, to be correct, must have very short legs (Sealyham, Dachshund); others should have long legs, as in Greyhounds; and so one could go on *ad infinitum*. We illustrate, however, a few of the types of bad conformation which look wrong in any dog. Perhaps the faults which are mostly noticed by the general public are bandy-legs, knock-knees, cow-hocks, over- or under-shot jaws, prick-ears which should be button-ears and vice versa, and long backs which should be short.

The reader will be able to decide what is good or bad conformation in any breed only by referring to the official standards laid down.

Congenital.—Any condition which is present at birth or which, although not appearing until a little later in life, has been transmitted from one or both of the parents, is called a congenital condition. For instance, such abnormalities in a puppy as a cleft palate, or six toes instead of five, would be congenital.

Congestion. — Excessive or abnormal accumulation of blood in any organ or tissue. For instance, there may be congestion of the liver, the lungs, kidneys, or brain, and, in fact, of any part which has a blood supply. Congestion is not necessarily a pathological condition, as there are times when an increased supply of blood to a part is a normal process, as during digestion. When food has been swallowed and is awaiting digestion, there must of necessity be an enhanced blood supply to the bowels to aid in the natural function. This is known as functional congestion. If a dog is unable to stand, through sickness or accident, it follows that one or other of the lungs must be undermost. Should the circulation be at the same time enfeebled, as it generally is, then the lowermost lung becomes congested. The term applied to this type of congestion is "hypostatic". Instances occur in which there is an obstruction to the outflow of blood from a part, resulting, of course, in "passive" congestion. Finally, congestion may be the forerunner of an attack of inflammation.

Congo Terrier.—This is one of the breeds indigenous to Africa, where it is both distinctive

and common. It is a lightly built dog with a longish head, dark, alert eyes and very upstanding ears. In height it varies considerably, indeed, as much as from 12 to 24 inches. The casual visitor to Congo villages should not confuse the many mongrels he will see in the streets with the true native Terrier. The former have a certain resemblance to the original breed, but have degenerated into pariahs.

The genuine Congo Terrier—specimens of which have been acclimatized in European zoos—has definite points. The legs are straight as a Scottie's. The feet are small. The tail is inclined to curl and has a suggestion of bushiness about it. One noticeable feature is a ridge of longer hair that runs along the spine, while for the remainder the coat is short. Mouse-grey and red, with white patches, are the predominant colours. The natives north of the Zambesi use these dogs for terrier work.

English people have had an opportunity of seeing the breed, for on one occasion a couple were shown at Cruft's, though they were entered as Lagos Bush Dogs. They died of distemper soon afterwards. As in the case of several Central African dogs, they could not properly bark.

By courtesy]   *[Miss Thelma Evans.*
A FAMILY GROUP OF WELSH CORGIS.
"Rozavel Lady Supreme" and two of her puppies. She is an offspring of the famous Ch. "Crymmych President".

Conjunctiva.—The mucous membrane which lines the eyelids and extends thence to the eyeball. When this membrane is inflamed and reddened the condition is conjunctivitis. (*See* EYE, DISEASES OF).

Conjunctivitis. (*See* EYE, DISEASES OF.)

Constipation.—A term applied to the condition in which defaecation is considerably slowed down as regards the number of times it occurs in twenty-four hours. It is also applied to difficult defaecation, provided that the latter is not caused by mechanical obstruction. In other words, constipation is not the same thing as stoppage.

CAUSES.—Lack of exercise; overfeeding; unsuitable food such as an excess of potato, pastry, bread, beans, cornflour, or too much bone; old age; feverishness; catarrhal jaundice; deficiency of drinking water; weakened nervous impulse, etc.

SYMPTOMS.—Faeces are dry and impacted, and they pass out with difficulty or not at all. The dog strains a good deal, his breath is offensive, appetite in abeyance and the animal is listless and miserable. Many other symptoms may ensue,

PET OF A PRINCESS.

[*Keystone*.

...use the Welsh Corgi is so lovable and safe the Duke of York purchased one for his daughter.   Here Princess Elizabeth is seen with her pet descending
the steps of the railway station near her mother's home, Glamis Castle.

THE BLUE MERLE CORGI.
Very rare is the Blue Merle Corgi, and "Geler Coressa", a very frequent prize winner, is one of the best types of the
Cardiganshire variety.

Photo] [Fall.

"CLARION OF CWMRHAIDR".
The Welsh Corgi is a coming breed. The males have a head reminiscent of the Alsatian.

ground over which the diseased animal had passed, to have come into indirect contact with it, and to have exposed itself to contagion. (*See* DISEASE, SPREAD OF; INFECTION.)

Contagious Disease. — A contagious disease is one which may be propagated by contagion; i.e. transmitted from one animal or person to another. Also known as a specific disease in that it is caused by a specific or single kind of micro-organism.

Contagium.—Any virus or living organism, animal or vegetable, which is or may become the cause of a communicable disease.

Contusion. (*See* BRUISE.)

Convulsions.—A convulsion consists of a series of rapid muscular spasms (i.e. contractions and relaxations) accompanied generally by loss of consciousness. Such a convulsion may be termed a "fit". There is, however, a milder type of convulsion, as when an animal is shaken by muscular spasms but does not lose its consciousness.

CAUSES.—Epilepsy; worms; distemper; fright; excessive physical exertion; high fever; cocaine, strychnine or other poisoning; eclampsia; blows; cerebral abscesses; inflammation of the brain or its coverings; hysteria; irritations of the ear; etc.

SYMPTOMS.—There is generally an intense excitability at first, gnashing of the teeth, rapid muscular spasms, and staring of the eyes. The dog rushes about blindly, champs its jaws up and down very rapidly and so churns its saliva into froth; hence the "frothing at the mouth". The dog may fall to the ground, with or without loss of consciousness, and

in consequence of the absorption of poisons which follows their non-evacuation from the body.

TREATMENT.—Ascertain, if possible, and eliminate the cause. A good home remedy is a warm soap and water enema by means of which the colon is emptied. Then castor oil or grey powder may be given, and attention should be paid to the amount of exercise the dog is permitted. The diet, too, should be overhauled, and nothing but a rational fare provided. (*See* FOODS AND FEEDING.)

Raw beef and underdone liver have a laxative effect; and for dogs which habitually suffer from constipation, it is a safe and good plan to administer a teaspoonful of medicinal paraffin daily. If this appears to ooze out of the anus, after it has been taken for some days, then the dose or the number of times it is given should be decreased.

Consumption. — Another name for tuberculosis (*which see*). It is not a common disease of dogs.

Contagion.—The spread of disease by contact. The contact need not necessarily be actual or direct, as germs can quite easily be conveyed by indirect contact. A dog must come into actual touch with another dog to effect direct contact; but it need only feed out of another dog's food-dish, smell its bedding or the

Photo] [Ralph Robinson.

CH. "CRYMMYCH PRESIDENT".
One of the most famous members of the Welsh Corgi family. This dog was a great prize winner.

its legs continue to move as though running. In true epilepsy, there is a loss of consciousness with every convulsion. Those attacks which are not due to true epilepsy are spoken of as "epileptiform" convulsions.

TREATMENT.—The malady is so complex and may arise from so many causes that professional advice should be sought as soon as possible in order to ascertain the nature of the convulsion, and to obtain an appropriate treatment.

As first-aid treatment, however, the attendant should take steps to prevent the animal from injuring itself, and should throw cold water over the poll of the head and back of the neck. No attempt should be made to pour any liquid into the dog's mouth whilst it is too excited or in a state of unconsciousness.

dog of which there is any record in Wales, but it was also the only dog of any kind known in some parts of Wales until the latter half of the nineteenth century,

The origin of the breed is obscure, but old Welsh farmers assert that the breed has been known in their families for hundreds of years, and that these little foxy dogs have tended the herds from time immemorial.

The occasional deviations from type that still recur in certain strains have caused some people to doubt the breed's antiquity, but it would be strange if some throwbacks did not occur now and

Photo]   [Ralph Robinson·
THE WORKER.
The Corgi is essentially a working dog, especially trained to handle cattle. One dog will easily do the work of half a dozen men in rounding-up.

When such a mistake is made, the liquid invariably finds its way into the trachea and perhaps into the lungs, causing either choking or pneumonia.

Keep the dog very quiet, in a half-darkened room; do not allow children to play with it or make any noise; give a purgative, and then await the veterinary surgeon.

Corgi.—The Welsh Corgi, although only in comparatively recent years has it become widely known outside of Wales, traces back its history as far as A.D. 920. At that time reference to the cattle dog was made in some ancient Welsh laws and statutes, and not only was it the only cattle

then to the crosses that were bound to have been introduced when the dog was bred for work alone, and when his appearance was of no object.

The breed has made remarkable progress since it was first entered in the Kennel Club's Register in 1928.

Classes are scheduled at most of the principal shows in the London district, and in Wales itself, while Corgis are also largely represented at important fixtures in other parts of England.

There is a steady demand for well-bred young stock, and typical puppies up to eight weeks old

By courtesy]

[Mrs. O'Shaughnessy.

THE PEMBROKESHIRE TYPE.

"Bowhit Belle" and her family. This dog was an unbeaten champion and can be taken as a good example of what the Pembrokeshire Corgi ought to be.

Ralph Robinson.

WE ARE SIX. A jolly group of Corgis owned by Miss Thelma Evans.

A bunch of the best.

Photo]

fetch from three to ten guineas, according to their merits and the reputation of the parents. The bitches are excellent mothers, and usually have five strong puppies in a litter, although six or seven are not uncommon numbers to expect, and nine has been known. Corgis whelp easily and rear their puppies without any trouble, requiring little attention other than that usually afforded to a bitch at such a time.

Longevity is a feature of the breed, the average attaining a ripe old age. Not long ago a Corgi died at the age of eighteen, but this must naturally be regarded as unusual.

Lively, willing and affectionate, their hard-working cattle-driving ancestry have endowed the Corgis with their full share of brains, and it is usually simple to train them in almost any capacity. As keen guards and alert watch-dogs it would be hard to find their superiors. A one-man dog, the Corgi maintains a loving and rational attitude to the rest of the family, and to his owner's friends, but his master or mistress alone can command him, while his fidelity and devotion are the subject of a hundred fireside narratives in Wales and out of it.

Where there is a young family it would be difficult to find a better dog, and it was this, coupled with the attractive and foxy appearance, that prompted H.R.H. the Duke of York to purchase a Pembroke-shire type Corgi for Princess Elizabeth and her little sister, Princess Margaret. The Corgi makes a delightful companion for either town or country. It is strong and hardy, far less prone to the usual doggy ailments than many other breeds, easy to feed and simple to exercise.

Its high spirits keep it continually on the move, and it thrives equally well in a town flat, with a daily run in the park or square, as it does in the country, where it can follow a horse for fifteen or twenty miles with ease.

Endurance must be considered in the breeding of these dogs, and although they must not be too large, on account of the risk of being kicked while working, they must not be too small, lest they tire too easily.

The Corgi's natural work is the driving and rounding up of mountain ponies, which it does by barking at the animal's heels, ducking down and jumping with great agility out of the way of the kicks which usually follow.

Pembrokeshire Type.—There are two distinct types of Corgi, one peculiar to Pembroke-shire and the other hailing from Cardiganshire, and although the general outline is somewhat similar, the two kinds differ in a variety of important points.

The Pembrokeshire Corgi is a firm, compact little dog, weighing between 20 and 22 lb. and not

exceeding 12 inches at the shoulder. He has a dry, muscular body of medium length, very short legs, which should be as straight as possible, and round and cat-like feet.

The coat is dense, thick and short, and slightly harsh to the touch, without being in the least wiry. In texture it probably resembles the hair of the Alsatian more than that of any other breed, but it is shorter and somewhat harder.

However, it is the head that commands attention, for it is exactly like that of a fox.

The medium-sized ears are carried pricked, and

bred tailless puppies to a long-tailed dog of another breed altogether. Some strains are more dominant in this respect than others, and it is not unusual to find a long-tailed specimen in a litter of bob-tailed puppies, and although it detracts very much from the dog's appearance, it should not make any difference to its show career or its breeding possibilities.

It was formerly the custom to dock all long-tailed specimens of this type, but the Kennel Club have prohibited the practice, and dogs that came into the world with something to wag must be left as Nature made them.

Photo]   [L.N.A·

FOUR OF A KIND.

Four members of the Rozavel Kennels : "Godfrey", "Lady Supreme", "Red Dragon", and "Gwenda", each exhibiting the bright-eyed alertness which so endears the breed.

the tapering muzzle, broad skull and bright eyes all add to the effect.

The colours most favoured are red and sable-red, but black-and-tan, or any of these colours marked with white, are popular. The white markings appear on the chest and legs, and sometimes as a collar round the neck, but too much white is objectionable and pure white constitutes a disqualification.

The Pembrokeshire type are usually born tailless, or with a very short stump. This characteristic would appear to be a proof of pure lineage, for the lack of tail recurs with extraordinary persistence in breeding, and cases have frequently been recorded where a Pembrokeshire bitch has

The rule has led to considerable confusion, for the sight of a number of dogs with tails of odd lengths, yet of the same breed, is one that may puzzle anyone, and it is especially misleading to judges, who have difficulty in telling whether the long-tailed dog before them is a good Pembrokeshire or a bad Cardiganshire.

As a type, the Pembrokeshires are smaller and more compact than their Cardiganshire brothers, while the fact that the majority possess the fascinating fox-red colour is no doubt a great factor in making them the most popular of the two types.

Judging from the entries at shows, and the demand for stock, the general public seem of the opinion that a long tail looks somewhat incongruous on a dog of the size and build of the Corgi, and that the short stump, or entire absence of tail, adds greatly to the smart appearance.

THE STANDARD OF POINTS AS ADOPTED BY THE WELSH CORGI CLUB.

HEAD.—Like a fox, and wide between the ears.

JAW.—Medium, inclined to be snipy.

NOSE.—Black.

TEETH.—Level and square, large for the size of the dog.

EYES. — Well set, round, of medium size and of hazel colour.

EARS. — Pricked, medium size.

NECK.—Fairly long.

CHEST.—Broad and deep, well let down between the forelegs.

BODY.—Of medium length.

TAIL.—Natural, preferably short.

RIBS. — Well sprung.

HINDQUARTERS. — Strong and flexible.

LEGS AND FEET.— The legs short and as straight as possible. Feet like a Collie.

COAT.—Of medium length. Dense.

COLOUR. — Any other than pure white.

WEIGHT. — Dog, preferably 20 to 24 lb; bitch, preferably 18 to 22 lb.

HEIGHT.—Not exceeding 12 inches at the shoulder.

Cardiganshire Type.—The Cardiganshire Corgi is an altogether larger and heavier dog than the Pembrokeshire.

Photo] [*B.I.P.*
MRS. BRUCE FLETCHER'S CORGI.
There is a foxy look about the female of the Corgi breed and "Sal-O'r-Bryn", Mrs. Bruce Fletcher's bitch, an excellent example, shows this characteristic.

Its body is thicker-set and longer, and while the legs must also be short, they may be slightly bowed, which is believed to be of assistance in ducking down in the course of its work.

The coat is shorter and harsher, resembling that of the Bull Terrier in texture, although it is denser and less wiry. The most usual colours are white, heavily marked with black or brindle, and sometimes marked with fawn or sable-red. All-black,

or all-brindle, with white legs, chest, and tail-tip are often seen, and sometimes fawn or light-red with white marks, although these latter are more unusual.

The rich fox-red colour so predominant in the Pembrokeshire Corgi is uncommon in this type.

Blue merles, though somewhat rare, are also popular, and they generally have one or both eyes silver. This is usually referred to as a "wall-eye", as in Sheep-dogs.

The Cardiganshire Corgis always have long tails, which are supposed to be carried hanging down, and not waved in the air or curled over the back.

The question of tail carriage is one that most perplexes breeders, as the majority seem to carry their tails very high, especially in movement.

The head is different from the Pembrokeshire dog, being longer, with a strong muzzle and broad, but slightly domed skull. The ears are very large, set out more to the side of the head, and are carried erect.

Although a generally foxy appearance is aimed at, the differences in head and colour makes it less apparent among dogs of this type, in spite of the long tail.

Both types seem equally intelligent and manageable, and have similar characteristics, and it is really only outwardly that they differ so greatly from each other.

THE STANDARD OF POINTS AS ADOPTED BY THE WELSH CORGI ASSOCIATION.

HEAD.—The skull should be wide between the ears and almost flat, tapering towards the eyes, above which it should be slightly domed.

MUZZLE.—The muzzle should measure about

CORGIS.

No breed is more friendly than the Corgi, docile, jolly, companionable. Here Ambler, the well-known animal artist, has caught the dog in happy and frolicsome mood. He drew these studies specially for this work.

THE LADY'S DOG.

The endearing traits of the Welsh Corgi have caused it to become a great favourite with ladies. Here is Lady Jackson with her "Rozavel Golliwog".

3 inches in length or in proportion to skull as 3 is to 5. It should be powerful and taper gradually towards the nose, which should be neither blunt nor excessively pointed, but should slope back slightly to the mouth.

TEETH. — Strong, level and sound.

NOSE.—Black in colour, nostrils of moderate size, slightly projecting.

JAWS.—Clean cut and strong, of moderate width and depth.

EARS.—Large for the size of the dog, slightly rounded at tip, moderately wide at base, carried erect, set fairly high and well back (so that they can be laid flat along neck). When erect, they should tend to slope forward a little.

EYES. — They should be of medium size, well-rounded, wide-set, and corners clearly defined,

By courtesy]　　[Mrs. O'Shaughnessy.
A FOX-RED CORGI.
A commendable example of the Pembroke Corgi, with good head and body a son of Ch. "Crymmych President".

full but not too prominent, preferably dark in colour but clear, possessing plenty of depth so as to convey the impression of a keen and lively intelligence. Silver eyes are permissible in blue merles.

NECK.—Muscular, well-developed, strong, and in proportion to the dog's build.

SHOULDERS.—Strong, muscular, with neat, sloping shoulder-blades.

CHEST. — Moderately broad viewed from the front, deep and well let down between the forelegs, with prominent breast-bone.

BODY.—Long and strong, with deep brisket, well-sprung ribs, clearly defined waist, and no slackness of loin.

FORELEGS. — Short, slightly bowed, with strong bone, elbows should lie close to ribs.

HINDQUARTERS —Strong, with well-turned stifles, very muscular

Photo]　　　　　　　　　　　　　　　　　　　　　　*[L.N.A .*
A REPRESENTATIVE TRIO.
The Corgi has but recently become a favourite, but his keenness and friendly manners have at last given him the popularity he deserves
The above photograph shows what jolly and bright friends Corgis can be.

thighs, sound hocks well let down, bone to heel short and straight.

FEET.—Rather large, round, compact and well-padded, dew claws removed.

TAIL.—Moderately long, set on in line with the body, resembling as much as possible that of the fox.

COAT.—Fairly short, dense, and of hard, weather-resisting texture.

COLOUR AND MARKING.—Any colour except pure white.

GENERAL APPEARANCE.—In general appearance the Welsh Corgi (Cardiganshire type) is a long, low dog of moderate size, with rounded forehead, large erect ears, sharp watchful eyes, a powerful but tapering muzzle of fair length, a slightly bowed front, ample bone, a long, strong and powerful body, with a slight arching of the back above the waist, strong hind-quarters, a long tail and a weather-resisting coat of hard texture; and a characteristic dancing gait to his canter as may be seen in no other breed. His body-length causes him to sit on one hip rather than squarely on his haunches. He may aptly be described as a "big" little dog, with plenty of lung space and depth of body, yet to enable the Corgi to fulfil his natural bent for cattle working he must be built on lines of strength and activity, and should be lithe and vividly alive in all his movements. Lastly, he must be gifted with true expression, reflecting his unique depth of character and wide capacity for devotion and affection. Unmistakable expression is obtained by the perfect combination of head and muzzle, size, shape, placement, and light of eye, correct position and carriage of ears, which all combine to give the dog that alert, intelligent outlook that makes the perfect Corgi one of the most satisfying and fascinating members of the canine race.

APRPOXIMATE MEASURES AND WEIGHTS.

HEIGHT.—As near as possible to 12 ins.

WEIGHT.—Bitches, 18 to 25 lb.; 2 lb. more allowed for dogs.

APPROXIMATE MEASUREMENTS.—The dog should

Photo]　　　　　　　　　　　　　　　　　[Fall.
"CLARION OF CWYRHAIDR".
This dog, belonging to Capt. G. Checkland Williams
has won many prizes.

measure from point of nose to tip of tail a Welsh yard, which is slightly longer than an English yard; from point of nose to stop, 3 ins.; stop to occipital peak, 5 ins.; from occipital to butt of tail, 21 ins.; length of tail, 9 ins.; totalling 38 ins. A dog should measure about 4 ins. between the ears, and a bitch $3\frac{3}{4}$ ins.

Cornea.—The colourless, transparent, convex structure which covers the front of the eyeball. It is popularly referred to as the "glass of the eye". It is devoid of blood-vessels, although in inflammatory conditions, adventitious vessels soon creep over its surface and may be seen by the aid of an ophthalmoscope.

Corns.—Corns are not generally regarded as a disease of the dog, and yet they undoubtedly do sometimes occur. The exciting cause is usually penetration of the horny sole of the pad by a thorn or some other similar foreign body. An area of inflammation is set up immediately beneath the horny layer, the latter becomes thickened at that point and progression causes the dog to go lame. Corns have been observed by the writer more often in Greyhounds than in other breeds. Pressure with the finger-nail over the hard and thickened area, although the latter may not measure a greater size than that of a split pea, will cause the animal to flinch.

The remedy lies in continuous soaking with hot water, or the application of ordinary or chemical poultices, until the horny sole is softened. A corn cure may then be painted on or it may become necessary for a surgeon to shave the epithelium with a razor. Should a foreign body be still embedded in the tissue, this must be removed with the aid of local anaesthesia.

Corpuscles. (See BLOOD.)

Corrosive.—A substance which corrodes, breaks down or destroys any living tissue with which it comes in contact. All the concentrated mineral acids, such as nitric, sulphuric and hydrochloric, have a corrosive action. Similarly, silver nitrate, caustic potash and soda, zinc chloride, pure carbolic acid, and a number of other chemicals may be described as corrosive poisons.

Coryza indicates a catarrh of the head, characterized by a mucous or muco-purulent discharge from the eyes and nose. (See CHILLS, CATARRH, EYE, DISEASES OF.) It is not as a rule accompanied by elevated temperature and is not contagious from one

A BATCH OF JUNIORS.
Three studies of young Corgis in varying moods and attitudes.   The top pictures show some of Mrs. O'Shaughnessy's puppies.

dog to another. Steaming the head with medicated steam (i.e. steam emanating from a bronchitis kettle containing water in which a small quantity of eucalyptus oil, friar's balsam, turpentine or creosote has been added) is very efficacious in soothing the mucous membranes and ridding the nostrils more readily of their discharges. Discharging eyes must be bathed with warm antiseptic solutions appropriate to such delicate organs. (*See* EYES DISEASES OF.)

Cotton Wool may be obtained in two varieties viz. absorbent and non-absorbent. The former is slightly more expensive than the latter and is used almost exclusively in the surgery on account of its greater purity and of its ability to soak up discharges, blood and other moistures. The non absorbent wool is so named because it is impregnated with the natural oil of the cotton seed plant and will not absorb liquids. For this reason and on account of its cheapness it is used mostly for stuffing inside pneumonia jackets, etc., to keep the dog warm. The cost of cotton wool varies from 1s. to about 1s. 9d. per lb.

Cough. (*See also* BRONCHITIS, LARYNGITIS, PHARYNGITIS.)
CAUSES.—Inflammation of the larynx or pharynx; bronchitis; pneumonia; worms; chills and exposure to wet and cold; distemper; tuberculosis; etc.
SYMPTOMS.— The cough may be of a husky, short nature, causing the patient, apparently, to attempt to remove some object from the throat. Such coughing often ends in retching, and perhaps with the ejection of a frothy mucus. The owner will often believe that the dog has been sick and may, in that way, mislead the veterinary surgeon. In simple cases of chill with cough, there is frequently no rise of temperature, and the dog may even retain its usual liveliness and continue to feed well.
TREATMENT.—The dog must be kept warm, dry, and without fatiguing exercise; warm milk or soups to drink are very soothing, and should the cough become very troublesome, the inhalation of medicated steam is of great service. The veterinary surgeon attending the case will decide whether any cough mixture would be beneficial, and if so, whether it should be of an expectorant or sedative nature. He will also advise as to the desirability or otherwise of applying any kind of counter-irritant to the chest.

Counter-Irritants.—Substances used for external application to induce an inflammatory reaction in one part in order to relieve congestion in some other inflamed part. (*See* BLISTERING, CANTHARIDES.)

Couple.—The correct term to use when referring to a pair of Hounds, though a pair of any other breed is a "brace".

Couplings.—A dog may be alluded to as long or short in the couplings, the term being used to denote the length of the dog's body.

Cow-hocked.—When the hind limbs of a dog approximate each other at the hock joints, that dog is said to be cow-hocked, or to have an appearance common to cows when viewed from the rear.

Crab Eating Dog.—This dog is very similar in appearance to the Azara's Dog shown on page 77 of the Encyclopaedia, and is found in an area roughly described from Guano to La Plata, but it is seldom found on the pampas. In colour it is often a light reddish grey with reddish legs, whilst the back is black and the end of the tail is always black. The ears have black tips. It lives in the jungle, feeding on small reptiles, and natives say that a cross between their domestic dog and a Crab Eating Dog is of special value. Whether these actual crosses take place it is difficult to say.

(From Hobday's "Surgical Diseases of the Dog and Cat". By courtesy of Messrs. Baillière, Tindall & Cox.)
CROPPING.
The left hand photo shows the ears carried naturally; whilst that on the right shows how they appear after "cropping" has been performed.

Cramp.— Involuntary and sustained contraction of one or more muscles, giving rise to pain and preventing movement of the affected part until the muscle relaxes. Occasionally the cramp is only mild in severity and may occur in one or more limbs, thus causing the animal to move in a stiff, stilty fashion.
CAUSES.—In some cases it is a functional disorder of the nervous system not dependent on any discoverable lesion; but in the majority of instances it arises as a result of defective heart action. It is quite commonly encountered among racing greyhounds. Affected dogs are apparently quite normal before starting in the race, but about halfway through they are noticed to fall behind the others, and upon arrival, at the conclusion, are found walking only with difficulty, the hindlegs being stiff and possibly even lame. After a little massage and rest, recovery is complete. A course of cardiac tonics is indicated.

Creosote.—The purest creosote is an oily, transparent, yellowish and poisonous distillate of wood-tar. It has powerful properties as a local anaesthetic, disinfectant and parasiticide, but on account of its poisonous effect upon dogs it is little used in canine practice. For dogs which are suffering from ozaena, accompanied by a stinking, purulent, nasal discharge, the inhalation of steam, medicated with a few drops of creosote, would be beneficial.
Crude black creosote is largely used as a wood-preservative and stain for dog-kennels and wooden buildings generally. It kills all kinds of insect life in the wood, is an efficient germicide, and protects the wood against damp and rot.

Photo]   *[L.N.A.*

CAN I COMPETE ?

Cruft's is the biggest dog show in the world. A happy and amusing snap of a small dog-owner wondering whether she—
and her pet—could be entered.

Crest. — A term used to signify the upper arch of a dog's neck.

Criminal Law Relating to Dogs.

— (*a*) *Stealing.* — By the Larceny Act 1861, *s.* 18, stealing a dog is made a summary offence, with imprisonment up to six months with hard labour, or payment of the value of the dog and a fine up to £20. For offences after a first conviction the offender is triable on indictment before a jury, and the penalty may involve imprisonment with hard labour up to eighteen months under the Larceny Act 1916, *s.* 5.

(*b*) *Unlawful possession.* — Knowingly being in possession of a stolen dog or of its skin is also a summary offence under the Larceny Act 1861, *s.* 19 (maximum fine £20). Subsequent offences are triable, as in stealing after a previous conviction.

(*c*) *Reward for recovering a dog.* — Corruptly taking a reward for recovering a dog is punishable under the Larceny Act 1861, *s.* 22, as for stealing after a previous conviction.

Photo]   A DISTINGUISHED VISITOR.   [*Sport and General.*
Here is Ch. "Thet Tetrarach" in his stall at Cruft's waiting for the verdict.
He has won over one hundred first prizes and four championships.

1921 and 1927. It is a summary offence (penalty, £25 fine with or without imprisonment with hard labour for six months) for any person to : (1) Cruelly beat, kick, ill-treat, torture, infuriate or terrify any dog, or do, or omit to do, anything which will cause a dog unnecessary suffering. (2) Convey or carry any dog in such a manner or position as to cause it unnecessary suffering. (3) Take any part in the fighting or baiting of any animal (but this does not include coursing, beagling, fox-hunting, etc.). (4) Wilfully administer to any dog any poison or injurious substance or cause it to take such poison or substance. (5) Subject a dog to any operation which is performed without due care and humanity. It is equally an offence if a person causes or procures another person to do any of the forbidden acts. The owner is also punishable if he merely fails to exercise due care and supervision over an animal, which is so treated, but

The Court has power to make a restitution order, i.e. order that the dog or its skin shall be handed to the owner.

In any of the above crimes the offender, charged with a first offence, may elect to be tried by a jury ; if he is convicted summarily and sentenced to over one month's imprisonment or fined over £5, he may appeal to Quarter Sessions.

(*d*) *Advertising for return of a dog.* — It must be noted that advertising for the return of a dog with any words implying that no questions will be asked or no prosecution will follow (e.g. no questions will be asked), is a penal offence under the Larceny Act 1861, *s.* 102, for which a common informer may obtain £50 in an action (which is only quasi-criminal). The section has been held to apply to dogs. If the action is brought against a newspaper, the consent of the Attorney-General is necessary and the action must be brought within six months. (Larceny (Advertisements) Act 1870, *s.* 3.)

(*e*) *Cruelty.* — Cruelty to dogs is now punished under the Protection of Animals Acts 1911, 1912,

in that case he can only be fined and not imprisoned. When a conviction is recorded, the Court can also order the animal to be destroyed, but, unless the owner consents, the Court can only make the order upon the evidence of a veterinary surgeon that it would be cruel to keep the dog alive. The owner is bound to pay the cost. If the person convicted is the owner, the Court may deprive him of the ownership. If the offender is not the owner he may be ordered to pay compensation up to £10. (6) Selling or giving or offering grain or seed which has been rendered poisonous (other than for *bona fide* agricultural purposes), or placing in or upon any land or building any poison or any fluid or edible matter (not being sown seed or grain) which has been rendered poisonous. The penalty is a fine up to £10. The sale, etc., of grain for *bona fide* use in agriculture is not an offence, nor is the placing of poison or poisoned substances for the purpose of destroying rats, mice, or small vermin, provided the person doing so proves that he took all reasonable precautions to prevent dogs and other domestic animals having access to it. (7) Using a dog or causing any dog to be used for draught purposes on any highway. For the first offence, a fine up to £2 ; subsequent offences up to £5. (8) The Dogs Act 1906, *s.* 6, as amended by the Dogs (Amendment) Act 1928, *s.* 3, imposes a penalty not exceeding 40s., recoverable by summary conviction on any person who knowingly and without reasonable excuse permits the carcase of any head of cattle belonging to him to remain unburied in any place to which dogs can gain access. (*See also* VIVISECTION.)

Cropping. A useless practice of amputating portions of a dog's ears in order to make them supposedly more shapely, pointed and erect. It is still somewhat common on the Continent, but fell into disrepute in this country about the year 1900.

Croton Oil.—A vegetable-oil possessing very irritant and purgative properties. It is rarely, if ever, used upon the dog, but when so employed, the dose is one or two drops only. The best excuse which can be offered for administering this drastic remedy to a dog is that an almost immediate evacuation of the bowels is essential. One would probably be better advised, in such a case, to give a strong dose of salts and a warm soapy enema.

Cruelty to Animals.—By statutes passed from 1849 to 1911 any form of cruelty to animals is prohibited under severe penalties. Veterinary surgeons were among the first to support the movement, which began early in the nineteenth century, for preventing cruelty to animals ; and their profession requires and develops a sympathetic attitude to, and understanding of, all domestic animals. Their duties often involve the performance of operations to relieve pain, to repair an injury, or to effect a cure, but they are careful to provide that no operation of a painful nature is performed except under scientific precautions to prevent suffering. Their training gives them the knowledge and ability to operate upon animals for the relief of disease or the repair of injury without the infliction of pain, an advantage which is not possessed by unqualified persons.

The Cruelty to Animals Acts, 1849-1909, are incorporated in the Protection of Animals Act, 1911, and the Protection of Animals (Scotland) Act, 1912. These provide that if any person :

(*a*) Shall cruelly beat, kick, ill-treat, torture, infuriate or terrify any animal, or shall cause or procure or, being the owner, permit any animal to be so used ; or shall, by wantonly or unreasonably doing or omitting to do any act, cause any unnecessary suffering ; or, being the owner, permit any unnecessary suffering to be so caused to any animal ; or

(*b*) Shall convey or carry, or cause, procure or

Photo]　　　　　　　　　　　　　　　　　　　　　　　[*Sport and General.*

IN THE RING.

A typical scene at Cruft's, the great show. Borzois are here seen in the judging ring.

permit to be conveyed or carried, any animal in such manner or position as to cause that animal any unnecessary suffering ; or

(*c*) Shall cause, procure or assist at the fighting or baiting of any animal ; or shall keep, use, manage, or act, or assist in the management of, any premises or place for the purpose of fighting or baiting any animal, or shall permit any premises or place to be so kept, managed, or used ; or shall receive, or cause or procure any person to receive money for the admission of any person to such premises or place ; or

(*d*) Shall wilfully administer or cause or procure or, being the owner, permit, such administration of any poisonous or injurious drug or substance to any animal, or shall wilfully cause any such substance to be taken by any animal ; or

(*e*) Shall subject or cause or procure or permit to be subjected any animal to any operation which is performed without due care and humanity ; such person shall be guilty of an offence of cruelty within the meaning of the Act, and shall be liable upon summary conviction to a fine not exceeding £25 or, alternatively, or in addition thereto, to be imprisoned, with or without hard labour, for any term not exceeding six months.

It is to be noted that the *omission* to do anything, in consequence of which suffering results, is equally an offence as is the commission of any act. The

Photo] [*Planet News.*

THE PENALTY OF GREATNESS.

Like a favourite actress, a dog which has won honours at Cruft's has to run the gauntlet of the camera.

following provisions are of importance as setting out the special duties and responsibilities of veterinary surgeons : Where the owner of an animal is convicted of an offence of cruelty within the meaning of this Act, it shall be lawful for the Court, if the Court is satisfied that it would be cruel to keep the animal alive, to direct that the animal be destroyed, and to assign the animal to any suitable person for that purpose ; and the person to whom such animal is so assigned shall, as soon as possible, destroy such animal, or cause or procure such animal to be destroyed, in his presence, without unnecessary suffering. Any reasonable expenses incurred in destroying the animal may be ordered by the Court to be paid by the owner, and thereupon shall be recoverable summarily as a civil debt.

Provided that, unless the owner assent, no order

shall be made under this section except upon the evidence of a duly registered veterinary surgeon.

If a police constable finds any animal so diseased or so severely injured or in such a physical condition that, in his opinion, having regard to the means available for removing the animal, there is no possibility of removing it without cruelty, he shall, if the owner is absent or refuses to consent to the destruction of the animal, at once summon a duly registered veterinary surgeon, and if it appears by the certificate of such veterinary surgeon that the animal is mortally injured or so severely injured or so diseased or in such a physical condition, that it is cruel to keep it alive, it shall be lawful for the police constable, without the consent of the owner, to have the animal slaughtered so as to inflict as little suffering as possible.

If any veterinary surgeon summoned under this section certifies that the injured animal can without cruelty be removed, it shall be the duty of the person in charge of the animal to cause it forthwith to be removed with as little suffering as possible and, if that person fail so to do, the police constable may, without the consent of that person, cause the animal forthwith to be so removed.

A police constable may apprehend without warrant any person whom he has reason to believe is guilty of an offence under this Act, which is punishable by imprisonment without the option of a fine, whether upon his own view thereof or upon the complaint and information of any other person who shall declare his name and place of abode to such constable.

It would appear that these special provisions do not apply to dogs or cats that may be found injured, but in London, by special arrangement with the police and the R.S.P.C.A., veterinary surgeons are called also to these small animals.

The Cruelty to Animals Act, 1876, amends the law by extending it to the cases of animals which, for medical, physiological or other scientific purposes are subjected, when alive, to experiments which would cause pain if the animal were not anaesthetised. The Act provides (*Sec.* 2) that a person shall not perform on a living animal any experiment calculated

UP FOR JUDGMENT.

A typical scene at Cruft's during the great two-day business of judging the world's best dogs. Here Mr. S. Grubb is seen pronouncing his verdict on the Great Danes.

to give pain, except subject to the restrictions imposed by the Act, under a penalty not exceeding £50 for the first offence and not exceeding £100 or imprisonment for a period not exceeding three months for a second or any subsequent offence. The person who performs the experiment must hold a special licence, and no experiment may be performed unless it is with a view to the advancement of knowledge useful for saving or prolonging life or alleviating suffering. The animal must be under the influence of an anaesthetic of sufficient power to prevent the feeling of pain, and must, if the pain is likely to continue after the effect of the anaesthetic has ceased, or if serious injury has been inflicted, be killed before it recovers consciousness.

The experiments may only be performed on premises licensed for the purpose. Proper returns of all experiments must be made, and the premises, and all the animals kept therein, are subject to regular periodical inspection by a Home Office inspector.—(*Bullock's Handbook for Veterinary Surgeons*.)

Cruft's Show.—Promoted by Mr. Charles Cruft in 1886, this show has for very many years held a world-wide reputation as the greatest dog show the world over. Cruft's not only draws entries from the very best Kennels in the British Isles, but it also attracts visitors from every country in the world; and each succeeding year sees a greater and more representative gathering of foreign visitors and buyers.

Cruft's first show was confined to Terriers. There was an entry of 570, quite modest when we consider recent totals. This grew as the years progressed, and in 1914 the entry totalled 4200. This was considered by the knowledgable Canine Press, and by dog-lovers generally, to be the peak to which a show of this class could hope to attain, but this figure falls into insignificance when compared with the following list of entries over ten years : 1924, 6818 ; 1925, 8188 ; 1926, 9157 ; 1927, 9816 ; 1928, 9466 ; 1929, 9682 ; 1930, 9565 ; 1931, 9389 ; 1932, 9206 ; 1933, 8564 ; 1934, 9363.

Charles Cruft, the promoter, is without doubt a great personality. He has been given all sorts of titles at various times, but probably the most apt is that of the Barnum and Bailey of Dogdom, for he is without question the greatest showman we have ever had in canine circles, and had he been a publicity seeker he might have been one of the best-known men in the country. He has always, however, kept himself in the background, and his constant remark to journalists who have desired information about him has been, "Don't worry about me, it's the show that matters."

The actual start of this great showman is a romance, for Charles Cruft's first job was that of office-boy to the late James Spratt, the founder of the firm of dog biscuit and appliance manufacturers.

Mr. Cruft's progress with Spratts was such that from office-boy he rapidly moved along to more important positions, and later visited owners of shootings, head gamekeepers and others for his firm, and here he no doubt built up the strong and valuable connection he has always had amongst sporting dog-owners, for the sporting dog has always been remarkably well catered for at his show.

Do not let there be any suggestion, however, that Gun-dogs have better treatment than that afforded other breeds, for this is not so ; Mr. Charles Cruft has always paid great attention to the question of the judges, and none but the very best are ever extended an invitation to officiate at his shows. Neither does he haggle over expense to get the best. We have seen there the most prominent of the Continental judges, as also others from the United States and Canada.

Coming to exhibitors, here again Mr. Cruft has been well honoured, for he has received the entries of kings, queens and princes at his shows, and in old catalogues we find entries from Queen Victoria, the late King Edward and Queen Alexandra, whilst H.M. King George V has shown his Labradors and Clumber Spaniels, and the Prince of Wales his Alsatian.

Cryptorchid.—A male animal in which either one or both of the testicles have failed to descend into the scrotum at the proper time. Cryptorchidism is a somewhat rare condition in dogs, but should it occur among pedigree animals which are required for stud purposes, the question arises as to whether they will be of any value as sires.

A retained testicle usually atrophies and plays no part in the production and supply of spermatozoa. But as a rule, in such cases of monorchism, the testicle which *has* descended will have been found to be fully developed and functioning normally. A dog with one testicle is undoubtedly well able to prove himself as a sire ; but should both be retained the reverse would be true. Surgical operation, or recovery of the testicles, would be of no practical value (so far as dogs are concerned) as a means of rendering the male fertile. There is evidence in support of the belief that cryptorchidism is hereditary.

By courtesy]   *[E. C. Ash.*
CUBAN MASTIFF.
Rather like the old type of British Mastiff this dog was used for bull-fights.

Cuban Mastiff.—A pair of these dogs were presented to the Zoological Society of London about 1832. They were not unlike the old type of British Mastiff as portrayed in the sixteenth century, and were between the size of a Bulldog and a Mastiff. Strong and well covered with muscle, they were used for bull-fights. The head was broad, and the muzzle short. The lips were heavily developed. The ears were drop-ears, and the coat was short and close.

Culotte.—The feathery hair on the thighs of Pomeranians.

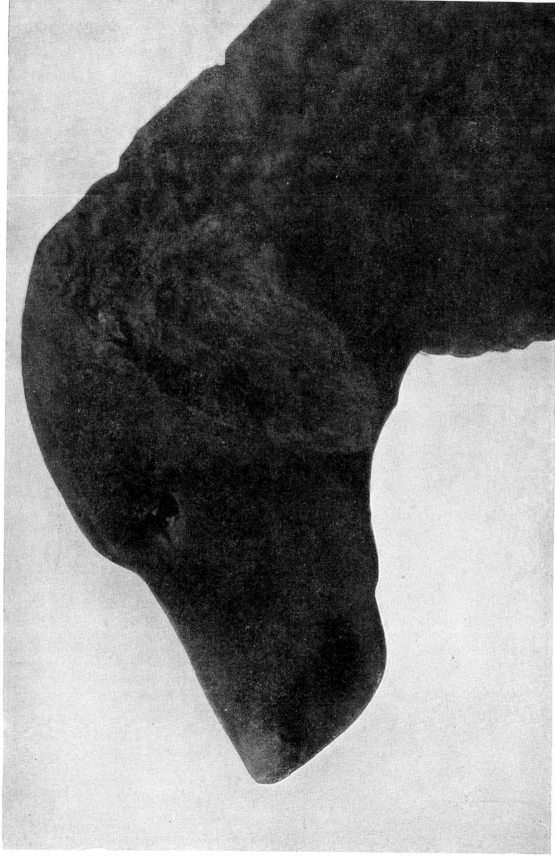

CURLY-COATED RETRIEVER.

A very excellent example of the rather rare Curly-coated Retriever—Mr. H. Stacey's "Coombehurst Ella". The breed is gaining in popularity.

A GOOD TYPE.
Brigadier-General F. F. Lance's Curly-coated Retriever 'Penworthan Protector''.

A CANINE NOTABILITY.
"Hoover" is an outstanding member of the breed, considered by some to be rather on the heavy side.

Curly Retriever.—This probably was the first breed of dog used seriously as a Retriever in England. We can safely say that it is now definitely established that the small Newfoundland was used on one side of the cross in producing the original Curly Coated Retriever, but opinion is divided as to whether the English or the Irish Water Spaniel was used on the other side ; probably the former, or possibly the old Water Dog, which is described in the *Sportsmen's Cabinet* published in 1803 : "These dogs are exceedingly singular in appearance, and most probably derived their origin from the Greenland Dog, blended with some particular race of our own." It goes on to say that : "The hair on these dogs must be adhering to the body in natural elastic curls, not loose, long, or shaggy ; the former being considered indicative of constitutional strength, the latter of bodily weakness, or hereditary debility." *The Museum of Animated Nature*, a very old book, states : "The Rough Water Dog is a most intelligent animal, is robustly made, and covered in deep, curly hair ; it exceeds the Water Spaniel in size and strength, but has the same aquatic habits and docility ; it is much used as a retriever by the shooters of water fowl."

"King Koffie". The last-named dog became well known through his progeny, being the sire of "Chicory", Cocoanut", and "Garnet" ; all famous show bench winners at that time. Another interesting dog was "True", owned by Dr. Morris. It is said that "True" was bred by a well-known poacher, and had been shot at several times by keepers before Dr. Morris acquired him ; it is also stated that he was very tender-mouthed and sensible. He was most successful on the bench and sired many of the best dogs of his day. A well-known bitch then was "Duchess". She secured six or more first prizes, and her owner, Mrs. Arkwright, was one of the pillars of the breed. Later came such well-known dogs as Ch. "Devronside Kaffir", Ch. "Rolyat Startler", Ch. "Preston Sultan" "Penwortham Brown Boy", Ch. "Bellevue Surprise", and Ch. "Hoover", all famous names in the Curly Retriever world.

A well-known Curly Coat owner and breeder, from the 'seventies onwards, was Mr. Samuel Darbey, who owned the famous Tiverton kennel. He had one particularly high-class dog, Ch. "Tiverton Victor". His dogs won many prizes all over the country, and were sometimes judged

By courtesy   "CALGORY GRIZZLY".   [*C. A. Monson.*
A first prize winner at Cruft's in 1934, it was a distinguished competitor
at field trials.

If there had been a cross with the Irish Water Spaniel, there would surely be more evidence of the top knot (which is peculiar to that breed) being reproduced. Some authorities suggest that a cross with the Poodle was attempted ; of course, it is well known that Poodles are excellent retrievers, and have been used extensively in France for this purpose ; therefore the cross should have improved the retrieving qualities, although it is possible that it may have been detrimental to his coat.

Separate classes were given for Curly Retrievers at Islington International Show and at Birmingham in 1864. Mr. Gorse's "Jet" and his son "Jet II", between them won the first prizes for Curlies for four years in succession. Other famous winning dogs of that period were Mrs. Arkwright's "Sweep", Mrs. Large's "Sam", and Mr. Salter's

as the "Best sporting dog in the show".

This breed should weigh from 70 to 80 lb., be strong, deep-chested, compact, well ribbed up, with powerful loins. The head long and wedge-shaped, with strong jaws, free from lippiness. Eyes dark, and intelligent. The ears should be small and set close to the head. The tail should be carried straight. Feet ought to be round, with arched toes. The colour of these Retrievers is jet-black or liver, though the latter are thought to be slightly inferior. The coat should be a mass of close, crisp curls (too much attention cannot be paid to this point) from the occiput bone to the tip of a tapering tail. It should resemble Astrachan, and must on no account be woolly. A good tight curl is essential to give that waterproof and thorn-resisting quality which is an outstanding feature of this breed. Curlies are as much at home in the water

A dog's paw showing two distended cysts. (*Hobday's "Surgical Diseases of the Dog and Cat." By courtesy Baillière, Tindall & Cox.*

as they are on land; they will dive continuously after wounded duck, and will also tackle the thickest of briars and hedges. These dogs have excellent noses especially on runners, with great sagacity and are always fresh and keen at the end of a hard day when other breeds are flagging. They are fast workers, and retrieve game quickly to hand. One of the outstanding characteristics of this grand old-fashioned Retriever is his ability to mark down and memorize the fall of a bird; this is especially useful in shooting over rough marshes.

Entries of Curlies at shows have been on the increase, and some of them have recently been successful in Field Trials. Public interest in these dogs has been reviving; visitors to shows are very pleased with their "come back", and talk quite wistfully of the Curlies they used to own, and many say that the finest and best dog they ever owned was one of these.

Curlies make excellent guards. They do not bark unnecessarily, but let you know immediately anything is wrong. They are wonderful companions, and are very affectionate and faithful. They have splendid memories, and are quick to learn; in fact, they can be trained to do almost anything.

Cyanosis.—When the blood is not sufficiently oxygenated its normal bright-red colour gives place to a purplish-blue. Observation of the mucous membranes of an animal (such as the conjunctiva, the gums and lips, etc.) will serve to show the approximate condition of the blood. When these parts are seen to be more blue than pink, the animal is said to be cyanosed.

The condition may be brought about by weakness of the heart with consequential inability to pump the blood around the body quickly enough; or it may be due to interference with the air supply,

such as might be produced by strangulation, pneumonia, or other causes.

It is a serious condition, and no time should be lost in removing the causes if they can be found; or in calling professional aid if they cannot.

Cysts.—A cyst is a bladder or cavity containing fluid or semi-fluid material. There is a great number and variety of cysts, appearing in all parts of the body, for some of which we know the cause. There are others, however, whose origin is quite unknown. The cysts most commonly encountered in dogs are: haematomata or blood cysts of the ear; inter-digital cysts (between the toes); salivary cysts; and ovarian cysts; less common are sebaceous cysts on the skin, and dermoid cysts.

INTERDIGITAL CYSTS.—Cysts or abscesses which form on the lateral surfaces of the toes, and always between one toe and another, that is to say, they never appear on the outer surface of the corner toes. At the present day the bulk of veterinary opinion seems to favour, as the cause, the penetration of the solar surface of the foot by thorns, gravel, tar, and other foreign bodies, which, having become lodged or packed in between the toes, work their way through the skin to an interior position. Fluid is thrown out, or perhaps pus is formed, and we find later a shiny, red, tense swelling which gives rise to a good deal of pain and lameness.

These cysts will eventually rupture if nothing is done for them, but the process is long and painful, and one is really guilty of some degree of cruelty if no step is taken to give the dog relief. Hot water bathing expedites ripening, but when the cyst at last breaks it heals almost at once, and more fluid is secreted. Thus there is an unfortunate repetition just when the owner thinks the trouble has abated. The best advice one can offer readers is to have these cysts surgically and completely excised by a surgeon, as it is unusual for a cyst to recur in the same situation after this has been done.

Many preventives and remedies have been tried by veterinarians, including autogenous vaccines, but nothing as yet has been discovered to be of any value. When research workers have established the real cause of the condition—beyond any doubt—

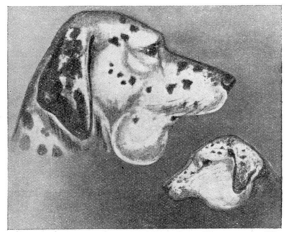

Dalmatian with mucoid cyst in the submaxillary space. The small picture portrays a similar dog suffering from an abscess. Note the difference in appearance.

Hobday's "Surgical Diseases of the Dog and Cat". By courtesy of Messrs. Baillière Tindall & Cox.)

THE SMOOTH DACHSHUND.

This breed has gradually become more and more popular in Britain.   The above are typical specimens, showing their remarkable ears and shortness of leg.

THE BADGER-DOG AT WORK.

"Dachshund" means literally "badger-dog", since it was for digging badgers that he was first bred. The above picture shows him in the early days at various stages of his task.

the clinician will probably be able to evolve a method of prevention or cure, or both.

In any case, however, in which a dog is a martyr to these cysts one might recommend the owner to try the effect of applying two specially made leather-soled boots. (*See* BOOTS.) It is just possible that if foreign substances can be prevented from entering the solar surface of the feet, no further recurrence of cysts may be noted so long as protectives are worn.

SALIVARY CYSTS.—A well-known type of salivary cyst is that which appears beneath the tongue. It is called a ranula and may be of any size between that of a pea and of a hen's egg. It is an ovoid swelling filled with saliva, and arises through blockage of one of the salivary ducts leading from the base of the tongue into the cavity of the mouth. It gives rise to considerable discomfort, if not pain, and causes a continuous dribbling. Treatment is entirely surgical, and must be done by an expert.

SEROUS CYSTS.—The commonest serous cyst in dogs is that occurring on the inner side of the ear-flap, positioned actually between the skin and the cartilage. It is an ovoid swelling filled, as a rule to capacity, with serum and blood. There is often so much blood that the condition is known also as a haematoma. It is caused by blows or other injuries which, quite frequently, are self-inflicted on account of some irritation inside the ear. The dog, in its efforts to allay the itching, spends all its time continuously scratching at its ear and rubbing the latter along the ground. Eventually, the ear-flap becomes so bruised and inflamed that a serous cyst begins to develop. The dog then holds its head characteristically on one side, the injured ear being lowermost. A great deal of pain is occasioned, and the ear and its surrounding area will be quite hot to the touch. Nothing can afford any relief but the surgeon's knife, and once the cyst has been opened, the intensity of the pain is immediately dispelled.

A word of warning, however, is necessary here. There is a type of man in this world who imagines he is an expert at any other man's craft. Such a person, reading

this article, will say to himself, "The cyst merely wants opening," and he will probably consider he is able to do this without seeking the services of anyone else. Of all the minor operations, however, which fall to the lot of the veterinary practitioner, there is not one which offers more difficulties or disappointments. The primary operation is, of course, not difficult, though even that must be performed with a maximum of celerity and a minimum of pain. It is in the after-treatment where the amateur would fail ; and should this not be scientifically correct, the dog will have a disfigurement for the rest of its life in the shape of a shrivelled or crinkled ear.

OVARIAN CYSTS.—Occasionally the female ovary becomes the seat of cystic formations which may be the cause of barrenness, and not uncommonly give rise to nymphomania (*which see*) or viciousness. On the other hand, it is not infrequent to discover small cysts on the ovaries whilst operating for some other condition, and they are found, of course, upon post-mortem examination. As no symptoms had been manifested in many of such cases, it is obvious that ovarian cysts can be apparently harmless.

SEBACEOUS CYSTS.—These cysts are rare in the canine species. Tumour-like elevations are found upon the skin in almost any part of the body, but mostly upon the trunk. They rarely exceed the size of a walnut. When pressed upon, a thin, cheesy material exudes from a small orifice at the apex, which is the inspissated product of a sebaceous gland. The body surface is normally provided with multitudes of these glands whose ducts open on to the surface of the skin supplying it with an oily secretion designed, presumably, to render both skin and hair impervious to the effect of water. Should these minute ducts become blocked up, the glands continue to secrete and the occluded ducts become cysts. The treatment also here is surgical excision.

Cystic Calculus. (*See* BLADDER, DISTENSION OF : CALCULUS.)

Cystitis.—Inflammation of the bladder. (*See* BLADDER.)

DACHSHUNDS OF YORE.

Another quaint old print, valuable chiefly for showing the great likeness between the Dachshund of three centuries ago and his modern descendant.

OF HISTORICAL INTEREST.

Some of the old stamp of Dachshund were much more of Terrier type than those of to-day, and many resembled the Basset Hound.

A FINE TYPE OF DACHSHUND OF SOME YEARS AGO

D = Dog (male), as opposed to B (bitch), female.

Dachsbrack.—The Dachsbrack is a Dachshund with longer legs and was at one time very well-known amongst sporting men in Germany. These dogs were straighter-legged and larger than the Dachshund, and whilst the name suggests a pointer cross, that is, Brack, they show nothing of this trait, having the typical Dachshund head and sufficient of the body shape to leave no doubt as to their being Dachshunds.

Dachshund (*Smooth*).—Although very few people realize it, there are no fewer than six varieties of Dachshund: The Smooth, the original variety from which all the others have been made; colour: black-and-tan, red, chocolate or dappled. The Wire-haired, probably made by a cross with a Scottie; colour: black-and-tan, reddish and brindle. The Long-haired variety, probably a cross with some Spaniel breed. These are said to be excellent for all kinds of hunting. The coats are smooth on the back, with beautiful feathering under the body, legs and tail. Colour: usually black-and-tan or red. The Miniature Smooth-coated, which should exactly resemble their big brethren. Weight, in this country, under 10 lb.; in Germany somewhat less. The Miniature Long-haired, which should exactly resemble the ordinary ones, except in size, which is as in the Smooths; and the Rabbit Dog.

The history of the Dachshund is a very long one and they seem to be descended from a short-legged, long-backed race of dogs which existed in Egypt at a very early date. There is a statue of one of the early kings seated with three dogs round him. The one between his feet is a long dog, bearing the name "Tekal", which looks as if the German name of "Teckel" (by which they are usually known there), had come from it.

All down the ages there are occasional references in European history to small hounds, which were undoubtedly the family from which the Dachshund evolved. The Goblin tapestries show a very dachshund-like dog at work.

Although the Dachshund is the national dog of Germany and they were but sparsely represented here, Britain had a specialist club for the breed many years before they had one in the former country. Queen Victoria owned one or two Dachshunds, and such names as Mudie and Millais are among those of the earliest breeders in England. Mr. John Sayer, one of our most respected judges, was for many years the breeder and importer of many good dogs. Next come such men as Mr. Woodhead and Mr. Lever, who jointly imported a number of dogs, the most notable of these, perhaps, being 'Brandesburton Filius', a great little dog, who did so much towards improving the breed, bringing back the vigour and grace of the Terrier.

THREE NOTED DOGS.
"Festus" Waldman", and "Schlupferle" were three important dogs at the end of the nineteenth century.

Photo] "MR. WEBSTER" AND THE COUNTESS. [*Hay Wrightson.*
A great lover of animals, the Countess of Northesk is here seen with her favourite Dachshund, "Mr. Webster".

One can only mention here a few of the great names of history, and "Brandesburton Filius" stands right out as a landmark. It was a funny little dog, not really beautiful to look at, but its owner saw that it was what was needed here. This dog did not become a champion, but its work will carry its name down to posterity as no title could ever do.

The wonder dog Ch. "Honeystone", a son of his, was the sire of so many champions that one loses count of them. The curious fact is that it

dog, the friend replied, "That is a Dachshund, not a dog". They are very clever too. Not only do they quickly learn the ordinary dog tricks: they are dogs who really think. If a Dachshund is shut up it will spend hours trying patiently to find a way out. There was a Dachshund once which taught itself to open all the patent fasteners on the kennel gates and, having let itself out, would then go across to the pen where the bitches lived and open their gate, which had quite a different fastening.

Photo]　　　　　　　　　　　　　　　　　　　　　　　　　　　　[E.N.A.
FROM AUSTRIA.
There is something very intriguing about the young Dachshund, as will be seen by this photo from Vienna of a typical mother and her family.

sired far more bitch champions than dogs. Then comes the reign of "Remegan Max", the wonderful red dog imported by Mr. Dunlop, who did much for the breed by importing many good dogs, including Ch. "Faust v. Forstenberg". Most of the great German families have sent members here from time to time. Luitpoldesheim, Asbecks, Forstenberg, Weidmannsfreud, Berkenschloss, Neumarkt Webber, are among the number.

In character the Dachshund is most lovable and intelligent. His qualities are so highly placed by the German race that once, it is said, when a man spoke to his friend about his Dachshund as a

They are marvellous diggers, and it is next to impossible to keep them in runs, such as are used for Terriers ; one has to sink the wire below the ground because they tunnel under ordinary fences. A dog has been known to tunnel right under a four-foot kennel to get out.

The type of the Dachshund has altered considerably as, following on the German lines, they have become very much lighter, though something has been sacrificed in the way of bone strength. When first the Dachshund came to this country it was a very clumsy and inelegant dog, owning huge floppy ears and weighing anything up to

TWO CHAMPIONS.

The famous spotted dog—plum-pudding dog—the Dalmatian, was once upon a time the dog of all smart stables. To-day it is a great favourite with motorists. Miss E. V. Barnes, a leading breeder and authority, has many champions. This plate shows two of them: Ch. "Lucky James" and Ch. "Venus of the Wells."

Photo]   *Fall.*

ARISTOCRATS.

Two handsome Dachshunds belonging to Mrs. Basil Huggins.

30 lb., whereas now the popular weight is round about 17 lb.

The standard in this country varies very little from that accepted in Germany; in fact, our list of points is practically copied from theirs. Most judges here prefer stronger hindquarters than the German judges, who lay rather more stress on immense length of body, but in all essentials we strive for the same thing—a real working dog.

Although, unfortunately, Dachshunds are not much worked in England, all the chief breeders keep work in mind when breeding, with the result that our dogs are nearly all of a type which could and would work, given the chance.

All Dachshunds will hunt a rabbit or any small quarry on scent and, when trained, will follow a trail laid for miles. The clever bitch Ch. "Foxhope" was splendid at this work—a rabbit-skin being used to lay the trail. A Colonel in India owned a bitch which went to ground with a civet cat, remaining so long underground that she was given up for dead; but she returned after thirty-six hours, bringing the cat with her, dead. Another man recounts that he was out after wild boar with his Dachshund, which got badly mauled and had to be nursed for a long while before it recovered. When it was well again it went back with its master to the same place and helped to get a boar, possibly the same one.

Dachshunds are not aggressive dogs, but once their temper is roused they will fight to the death,

disregarding pain. They are perhaps the most exclusive "one man" dog of all breeds and will, at about a year old, make up their minds once and for all who is to be master or mistress. Thenceforward they will follow that person to the end of the earth.

In Germany there are not a great many very large kennels for Dachshunds, as they are so often bred by foresters (keepers as we should call them), and when they are bred purely for show purposes they are usually bred in small numbers, having the run of the house, with a barrel and a small run in the yard.

They are quite hardy dogs but, like all other breeds, they can be made delicate by excessive pampering, overheating, and indulgence. Greedy they are, so that it is easy to spoil them; the horrible fat lazy ones, which used to be seen about so often in towns, were the result of over-indulgence with pampering. The true Dachshund is a dog who loves nothing better than to be racing about all day.

One great attraction of the breed is that they do well in any climate—even in the Plains of India. They revel in heat; by reason of their short, smooth coats they do not seem to feel it.

During the war there were only about six breeders who kept the Dachshund going, one of whom was the Secretary of the club, Major Hayward, O.B.E., who had his wonderful dog Ch. "Honeystone" with him in garrison for some time.

In this breed, family features are very clearly marked, and it is interesting to watch the judging at a big show and see if one can trace the family from which each exhibit came.

One of the reasons why many people think them nervous is simply because they hate to be handled by strangers; this adds to their value as guard-dogs, as does also their large bark, which is

Photo]   *[Fall.*

A NOTED CHAMPION.

Ch. "Fir Tinkergirl", one of Mrs. Huggins' famous kennel, is a well-known winner.

often more the bay of the hound than the bark of a terrier.

The Long-haired variety are, many of them, splendid water dogs and learn quickly to retrieve in water.

Some people say that they are not good whelpers, but this is untrue, and if proper care is taken of them at these times they are no more trouble than any other valuable dogs.

They usually have litters of five or six, and make splendid mothers, being very devoted to their puppies. More than once bitches have brought up puppies of other breeds very successfully.

Photo] TIMIDITY. [Fall.

Dachshund puppies, if confronted with a stranger and a camera, prefer, like most other puppies, to seek safety in flight.

The puppies are the merriest and most attractive little things, and make delightful pets for children. They are usually late developers, often not coming to their prime until two or even three years old, but many have been known to live to a great age. Mrs. Saunders, the well-known breeder, had a dog who lived for eighteen years. Ch. "Honeystake", too, lived to a good old age. They are not delicate, and need very little fussing. Many breeders use unheated kennels for them all the year round.

As house dogs they are good, because they do not bring dirt into the house, and once trained they are amusingly conservative in their habits, insisting on retiring to bed and having their meals at the same time every day.

OFFICAL STANDARD OF POINTS:

GENERAL APPEARANCE.—The form is compact, short-legged and long-backed, but sinewy and well muscled, with bold and defiant head carriage, and intelligent expression. The body should be neither too plump nor too slender. Height at shoulder should be half the length of the body measured from the breast-bone to the set-on of the tail, and the girth of the chest double the height at the shoulder. The length from the tip of the nose to the eyes should be equal to the length from the eyes to the base of the skull.

HEAD.—Long and conical when seen from above, in profile sharp and finely modelled. Skull neither too broad nor too narrow, only slightly arched, without prominent stop. Fore-face long and narrow, finely modelled.

LIPS.—Tightly drawn, well covering the lower jaw, neither too heavy nor too sharply cut away; the corners of the mouth slightly marked.

MOUTH.—Wide, extending back to behind the eyes, furnished with strong teeth which should fit into one another exactly, the inner side of the upper incisors closing on the outer side of the under ones.

EYES.—Medium in size, oval, set obliquely, clear, expressive and dark in colour.

EARS.—Broad and placed relatively well back, high and well set on, lying close to the cheeks, broad, long, and very mobile.

NECK.—Sufficiently long, muscular, showing no dewlap, slightly arched at the nape, running gracefully into the shoulders, carried well up and forward.

Photo] A STUDY IN EXPRESSION. [Fall.

Here are shown some charming heads of Mrs. Barr's Dachshunds. Looking at this picture there is small wonder that the Dachshunds are becoming more and more popular.

A CHARMING PICTURE.

Viscountess Harcourt, with her two babies, and a Smooth-haired Dachshund, their constant companion.
Dachshunds make admirable pets for children, because they are so even-tempered, kind, and reliable.

FOREQUARTERS.—Muscular, with deep chest. Shoulders long and broad, set obliquely, lying firmly on well-developed ribs. Muscles hard and plastic. Breast-bone prominent, extending so far forward as to show depressions on both sides. Upper arm the same length as the shoulder-blade, jointed at right angles to the shoulder, well boned and muscled, set on close to the ribs but moving freely as far as the shoulder-blade. Lower arm comparatively short, inclined slightly inwards, solid and well muscled.

well muscled. Hocks set wide apart, strongly bent and, seen from behind, the legs should be straight.

FEET.—Broad and large, straight or turned slightly outwards : the hind feet smaller and narrower than the fore. Toes close together and with a distinct arch to each toe. Nails strong. The dog must stand equally on all parts of the foot.

TAIL.—Set on fairly high, not too long, tapering and without too marked a curve. Not carried too high.

Photo]   [*Dorien Leigh.*

AN INTERLUDE.

The serious business of learning seems to be endangered by the accidental meeting of a schoolboy and a Dachshund puppy
Young Dachshunds are such playful little fellows.

BODY (Trunk).—Long and well muscled, the back showing oblique shoulders and short and strong pelvic region. Ribs very oval, deep between the forelegs and extending far back. Loins short, strong, and broad. The line of the back slightly depressed over the shoulders and slightly arched over the loins, with the outline of the belly moderately tucked up.

HINDQUARTERS.—Rump round, full, broad, with muscles well modelled and plastic. Pelvis bone not too short, broad, strongly developed and set obliquely. Thigh bone strong, of good length and jointed to the pelvis at right angles. Second thigh short, set at right angles to the upper thigh,

COAT.—Soft, smooth, and glossy.

COLOUR. — Black - and - tan, dark - brown with lighter shadings, dark-red, light-red, dappled, tiger-marked or brindled.

NOSE AND NAILS.—In black-and-tan, red and dappled dogs these should be black ; in chocolates they are often brown.

WEIGHT AND SIZE.—The same as Long-haired Dachshund (*which see*).

Dachshund (*Long-haired*).—This is an old fixed sub-variety of the "Teckel", though his origin is by no means clear. Some say he used to do the groundwork for the Salukis in Abyssinia,

WHAT CAN IT BE?

Two youthful Smooth Dachshunds, the property of Mrs. Huggins, are here seen displaying an alert interest in something "off-stage".
The keen expression is very typical.

A CHAMPION AND HIS FRIEND.

A charming study of a dog and bitch belonging to Miss D. Spurrier. They are "Saucy Sue" and Ch. "Dicker von Kornerpark'
an attractive pair, and representative of the breed.

while others profess to trace the breed to Egypt. A further opinion has been expressed that the breed is directly descended from the Basset Hound of La Vendée.

There is some doubt as to whether the breed is original or something developed. According to Dr. Fritz Engelmann, who wrote his well-known book on the Dachshund in 1925, every breed has more or less the blood of some other breed in it, and the Dachshund, in his opinion, has a large strain of Spaniel blood.

In 1812, mention is made of the Long-haired variety in Germany, and in 1820 the Long-haired

Photo]   [*B.I.P.*

KEEPING OUT OF THE COLD.

In April 1934 a Dachshund Show was held at Tattersall's. Our picture shows Mrs. D. W. Elliott, the well-known breeder, keeping her three entries warmly covered with a rug.

village and which, after a short search, successfully located the wounded roebuck. Captain von Bunau acquired the dog and subsequently bought a bitch and bred from them. He found them very good both at picking up scent and in groundwork, and equal to the smartest Water Spaniels in duck-hunting, owing to their assiduous and indefatigable searching and retrieving.

Persons not aware of the sporting properties of this breed, but who exercise their so-called sense of humour by referring to the Dachshund as a good family dog —because all the members of the family can

Dachshund is referred to by Dietrich aus dem Winkell; and Dr. Reichenbach in 1836 enumerated all the varieties, and this is especially interesting, as some of them are still in vogue at the present time.

The popularisation of the Long-haired Dachshund is due to some extent to Captain von Bunau of Bernberg, who wrote a book in 1882 entitled, *Dog*. He referred in that book to the hunting qualities of this breed, and gives as an instance of this an account of what happened in the course of an Archducal hunt in or about 1874. On this occasion a roebuck was badly wounded and took refuge in an impenetrable thicket, which even normally strong dogs could scarcely penetrate. After holding a council of war, the hunters put their last hope in "Manne", a Long-haired Dachshund, which was brought from a neighbouring

stroke it at the same time, a sausage-dog, or as "the dog that is sold by the yard"—do not know that this comparatively small dog engages in a fierce fight with an animal as vicious as the badger, and in its lair too. Dachshund means "badger dog", and this title has been well earned in Germany. Furthermore, its terrier qualities would make it useful in assisting the Otter Hounds. It combines in its small person the characteristics both of hound and terrier. Its long ears and abnormal powers of scent, and, for its size, enormous bone, prove its descent from the dog that hunts by scent. Its small size, iron courage, and anxiety to go down a hole in the ground illustrate the terrier qualities.

The characteristics of the breed demand that a Dachshund of the right size should have the maximum strength, skill, endurance, hardihood and zeal. It is these qualities, together with sureness of scent and determination and a certain obstinacy, which form the basis of the Dachshund character.

The most characteristic quality of the Dachshund is an inborn hatred of all that preys—a hatred that will not rest until the adversary has been annihilated either by its own strength or with the help of the huntsman. This will-to-kill is the father of endurance and sharpness. It is doubtless owing to the greatest curse which rests on the Dachshund, viz. their being bred in kennels and in large numbers through many generations that this "will" has been already greatly weakened.

There are more Dachshunds bred than can possibly be worked. It is a biological fact that organs which are not used grow weaker, so that the hunting impulse is growing weaker and there is an ever-increasing number of non-hunters amongst them.

The following is the official standard of points adopted by the Long-haired Dachshund Club:

GENERAL APPEARANCE.—Form, colour, size and character similar in all respects to those of the Smooth Dachshund, except for the long, soft hair. The form is compact, short-legged and long, but sinewy and well muscled, with bold and defiant head carriage and intelligent expression. In spite of the shortness of the legs the body should be

neither too plump, nor so slender as to have a weasel-like appearance. Height at shoulder should be half the length of the body measured from the breast-bone to the set-on of the tail and the girth of the chest double the height at the shoulder. The length from the tip of the nose to the eyes should be equal to the length from the eyes to the base of the skull. The tail should not touch the ground when at rest, neither should the ears (i.e. the leather) extend beyond the nose when pulled to the front.

HEAD.—Long and conical when seen from above, and in profile sharp and finely modelled. Skull neither too broad nor too narrow, only slightly arched, without prominent stop. Fore-face long and narrow, finely modelled.

LIPS.—Tightly drawn, well covering the lower jaw, neither too heavy nor too sharply cut away; the corners of the mouth slightly marked.

MOUTH.—Wide, extending back to behind the eyes, furnished with strong teeth which should fit into one another exactly, the inner side of the upper incisors closing on the outer side of the under ones.

EYES.—To be medium in size, oval, set obliquely, clear, expressive and dark in colour.

EARS.—Broad and placed relatively well back, high and well set on, lying close to the cheeks, broad and long, nicely feathered and very mobile.

NECK.—Sufficiently long, muscular, showing no dewlap, slightly arched at the nape, running gracefully

Photo] [E.N.A.
FROM STYRIA.
Styria is the Dachshund's native land. Here is a Styrian lad, in national costume with his Smooth and Long-haired "Dackrels".

into the shoulders, carried well up and forward.

FOREQUARTERS.—Muscular, with deep chest. Shoulders long and broad, set obliquely, lying firmly on well-developed ribs. Muscles hard and plastic. Breast-bone prominent, extending so far forward as to show depressions on both sides. Upper arm the same length as the shoulder-blade, jointed at right angles to the shoulder, well boned and muscled, set on close to the ribs, but moving freely as far as the shoulder-blade. Lower arm comparatively short, inclined slightly inwards, solid and well muscled.

BODY (Trunk).—Long and well muscled, the back showing oblique shoulders and short and strong pelvic region. Ribs very oval, deep between the fore-legs and extending far back. Loins short, strong and broad. The line of the back slightly depressed over the shoulders and slightly arched over the loins, with the outline of the belly moderately tucked up.

HINDQUARTERS. —Rump round, full, broad, with muscles well modelled and plastic. Pelvis bone not too short, broad, strongly developed and set obliquely. Thigh-bone strong, of good length and jointed to the pelvis at right angles. Second thigh short, set at right angles to the upper thigh, well muscled. Hocks set wide apart, strongly bent and, seen from behind, the legs should be straight.

FEET.—Broad and large, straight or turned slightly outwards ; the hind feet smaller and narrower than the fore. Toes close together and with a distinct arch to each toe. Nails strong. The dog must stand equally on all parts of the foot.

TAIL.—Set on fairly high, not too long, tapering and without too marked a curve. Not carried too high. Fully feathered.

COAT.—Soft and straight or slightly waved, of shining colour. Longer under the neck, the underparts of the body and particularly on the ears,

Photo]　　　　　　　　**A GOOD COMPANION.**　　　　　　　*[Fall.*
Head study of "Cato of Carlisle", Mrs. Hayne's prize-winning Smooth Dachshund

behind the legs, where it should develop into abundant feathering, and reach its greatest length on the tail, where it should form a flag. The feathering should extend to the under sides of the ears, where short hair is not desired. Too heavy a coat gives an appearance of undue plumpness and hides the outline. The coat should resemble that of an Irish Setter, giving the dog an appearance of elegance. Too much hair on the feet is ugly and useless.

COLOUR. — Black-and-tan, dark-brown with lighter shadings, dark-red, light-red, dappled, tiger-marked or brindled.

NOSE AND NAILS.—In black-and-tan, red and dappled dogs these should be black ; in chocolates they are often brown.

WEIGHT AND SIZE.—As a rule Long-haired Dachshunds are classified as follow : Lightweight up to 10 lb. for bitches and 11 lb. for dogs. Middleweight up to 17 lb. for bitches and 18 lb. for dogs. Heavyweight over 17 lb. for bitches and over 18 lb. for dogs. The lightweights are best suited to rabbit hunting ; the middleweights for badger and fox drawing ; and the heavyweights for tracking, hunting larger animals and for water work. The last-named are also very useful for retrieving rabbits and waterfowl.

BREEDING.—The Long-haired Dachshund is more difficult to breed than the Smooth, as the perfect coat is more perplexing to produce. The crossing of Long-haired with Smooth or Wire-coated Dachshunds should be discouraged, since such crosses render it impossible to fix in heredity the correct type of coat. Crosses of this kind frequently result in faulty specimens or intermediate forms which are undesirable. Chance bred Long-haired Dachshunds, that is, long-haired dogs bred from smooth parents, are not uncommon and are throwbacks to long-hair blood in the pedigree. Such dogs should be used in breeding provided they conform to type and have correct coats, but only

"GOLDEN PATCH".

This attractive Long-haired Dachshund is the property of Lt.-Col. Sir Beauchamp St. John and Mrs. Smith-Rewse. It won a Challenge Certificate at the Kennel Club Show in 1933. The breed's graceful lines are well depicted, and attention is drawn to the Dachshund type of head.

Photo]   *[Ralph Robinson.*

A CHARMING SPECIMEN.

A portrait showing Col. E. L. Harrison's Long-haired Dachshund "Strop". It is one of the most delightful examples of a breed that is steadily gaining popularity in this country. When in good coat few dogs are more attractive than are the Long-haired Dachshunds.

Photo]   *[Fall.*

"CINDERELLA OF ARMADALE".

This Long-haired Dachshund bitch, the property of Mrs. Hugh Rycroft, of Cirencester, may be taken as a good female example of the breed. Note the length of the body and shortness of the legs and the coat she carries. The breed, in coat, resembles the Cocker Spaniel.

Photo]   *[S. & G.*

PIONEERS OF THE BREED.
This is the first known picture of Wire-haired and Long-haired Dachshunds.
It appeared in a book published about 1876.

in conjunction with mates which are known to be pure bred for generations; in this way new blood may be introduced.

VALUE OF POINTS.—General appearance, 15; head and skull, 10; eyes, 5; ears, 5; jaws and teeth, 10; neck, 5; forequarters, 15; forelegs, 5; trunk, 10; feet, 10; hindquarters, 15; tail, 5; coat. 10. Total, 120.

The Kaninchen-teckel Club has also a standard which was laid down by a resolution of the Club at a meeting in Stuttgart in 1925. It may be said that the British and German standards are very much alike, although, if anything, the German standard, so far as some of the faults are concerned, is slightly stricter.

Colonel Harrison, who first became interested in the breed in 1921, had several well-known dogs in his kennels in Somerset, including Ch. "Jesko von der Humboldshohe", and a bitch he imported from Germany, "Vossa von Bergwald" which won a Challenge Certificate at Cruft's Show the first time she was shown in this country.

Colonel W. G. Bedford was one of the first in this country to own a Long-haired Dachshund, as in 1924 he purchased "Hengist of Armadale". He then imported "Elfe von Fells", which, before leaving Germany,

had been mated to "Stropp von der Windburg", and she produced in this litter Ch. "Rufus of Armadale", a winner of several Challenge Certificates and prizes and a well-known sire; and Ch. "Rose of Armadale", a successful show bitch.

Mrs. L. S. Bellamy also established a successful kennel from which many winners have sprung. One was Ch. "Chloe of Armadale", a beautiful brindle, one of whose litters secured close on one hundred prizes. Ch. "Michael von Walder", a very beautiful red dog, the property of Mr. H. Hartley Russell, was also bred by her and was one of the litter referred to.

One should also mention Mrs. Raymond Reade in Suffolk, whose kennel includes Ch. "Captain of Armadale", a dark-red brindle; and Mrs Violet Ryecroft, who had many successes with the offspring of "Cinderella of Armadale", which came from Colonel Bedford's kennel, including "Bartonbury Vesta", the winner of many prizes and two Challenge Certificates; Mrs. Smith Rewse of the Primrose Patch kennels, in conjunction with her brother, Sir Beauchamp St. John, K.C.I.E., C.B.E.; Miss Ursula Still, owner of "Diana von Walder", a notable red brindle bitch, winner of several prizes and a Challenge Certificate, and "Hugo von Walder", a brother; Mrs. Midwood, owner of "Daffodil of Dilworth", a winner of Challenge Certificates; Miss Allison; Miss Sturt; the Dowager Countess of Cranbrook; and the Hon. Mrs. Parsons.

GOOD-NATURED.
The charming disposition of the Dachshund is well expressed in the eyes of "Ferdinand," above which is of Austrian origin. Note the "feathery" effect of the ears.

Dachshund (*Miniature*).—The German dwarf or Rabbit Teckel, commonly known in this country as the Miniature Dachshund, is a comparatively recent importation, and until a very few years ago it was practically unknown in England. The breed was started in Germany about the year 1900 with the object of producing a Dachshund of the smallest possible proportions, to enable it to get into the narrowest rabbit burrows ; hence the name Rabbit Teckel.

It was uphill work at first ; Dwarf Pinschers and Black-and-tan Terriers were used type and character being sacrificed to the main object, viz. small size. Having achieved the desired size, it was then necessary to secure a dog that would go to ground, and one that displayed true Dachshund type and character.

The dog which in those days had most influence on the breed was called "Zwerg v. Barrach," of the Staffelstein Kennel. The Kaninchen-teckel Club was formed in 1905, with thirty-four members, and the dogs were used instead of ferrets, and also to put rabbits up out of thick undergrowth. In many instances they were used successfully against foxes, and some have been known to tackle a badger.

Black-and-tans were favoured, as were also the reds, who were much less distinguishable from the ground in autumn, and more liable to be confused with rabbits. All these three coats are bred in Germany, but the original Smooths seem the most popular.

The Kaninchen-teckel Club only registers dogs measuring a fraction over 11 ins. or less round the chest. They also register Dwarf Teckels, whose minimum chest measurement is 13 ins. and maximum weight 8 lb.

The best-known kennels in Germany were originally the v. Sonnenstein, v. Hexentanzplatz, Harras, and Hainichen. They were quickly followed by the Fleesensee, v. d. Jeetzel, v. Hoehlenkampf, v. Eulengebirge, Fehmarn, and

FAITHFULNESS.
A head study of a curly Dachshund. Note the kindness and faithfulness expressed in his calm brown eyes.

others. The Miniature type is now firmly established, and there is little fear of throw-backs to large size, but there is still room for improvement in general type and soundness.

With a view to popularizing this breed in England Miss F. E. Dixon, Mrs. Howard and Major Maitland Reynell brought over a batch of these little dogs about the year 1929, and the two latter have imported others since then. Several other Dachshund breeders have also taken up this fascinating variety.

Up to date the Kennel Club do not recognize the Miniatures as a separate variety. There is no Club, or standard of points other than the official Smooth- or Long-haired standard. Classes confined to Miniatures, generally for all types of coats, have been put on at the principal shows, with weights restricted to 10 lb.

The German custom of measuring the chest circumference has not been adopted here.

As will have been noted, slightly heavier dogs are allowed in England than in Germany, but the desired object is, by careful selective breeding, to produce perfect replicas of the best specimens of the breed. A 10 lb. dog is not too big to go to ground, and it has been observed that the smallest specimens in each litter are more leggy and less typical in head than their larger brethren.

Major Maitland Reynell has the best-known kennel of Miniature Long-hairs in this country, and his "Hallodri v. Fleesensee" is a well-nigh perfect little model of a Long-hair. Another celebrity in this kennel is "Zwergin Ariel v. Himmel", whose chief claim to fame is that it was born in the aeroplane coming over from Germany, when its mother was only six weeks gone in whelp. Its adult weight is only just over 5 lb.

It is doubtful if there are any Miniature Wirehairs in this country, and judging from those seen in Germany in 1933, it will be some time yet before breeders will be able to produce a dog which resembles the genuine article.

Undoubtedly the best-known Miniature Smooth sire in England is Mrs. Howard's "Kleinkurio". Born in quarantine in 1929, and bred by Miss Dixon, it was sired by "Fips-Harras", out of "Mara Harras". Its weight at first was 6¼ lb. His daughter, "Mignonne of Seale," out of Mrs. Howard's imported bitch, "Hexe v. Duesternsee," is recognized to be the best Miniature in this country, having beaten every Miniature she has met in the show ring, with the one exception of its mother, at the time of writing. In addition, it has also won in Variety class at Championship and Open Shows. Its weight is 9½ lb. and chest measurement 15½ ins.

The demand for typical, well-bred stock is already far in excess of the supply, and all that is required to help these fascinating little dogs—which combine intensely sporting characteristics with small size and attractive appearance—to become more widely known is a recognized club and separate registration.

Photo] [S. & G.
THREE MONTHS OLD.
An interesting litter of prize-winning pups belonging to Miss P. Seton-Buckley. These puppies are the Wire-haired Dachshund variety.

Dachshund (*Wire-haired*). — Wire-Haired Dachshunds were originally bred in Germany, and one of the first shows at which one appeared was the Berlin Show in 1888. They were first obtained by mating a Smooth-haired Dachshund and a Rough-haired Pinscher, but although this gave the rough coat the head was rather short and small. Later it was discovered that the Dandie Dinmont had an excellent Dachshund pose, so that they were used for mating with the Smooth-haired Dachshund and a much better result was obtained. The Dandie can still be traced in some of the Wire-haired Dachshunds, especially about the head when the coat is long and silky.

In Germany they are bred for hunting badgers, stags and wild boar. They are keen, courageous sportsmen, with very good noses, deep voices, and are quite untiring. Their quick intelligence, strong bodies and short limbs, make them most suitable for field hunting, and in England they are used for rabbiting, ratting, etc., with great success.

Photo] [*Sport and General.*
FATHER AND SON.
"Hannes von der Abtshecke" was a double grand champion of Germany, and "Kadett of How" has also won prizes. The dogs belong to Mrs. W. Buisfield and Mr. H. A. Fischer.

Photo]

A CANINE HELPER.

[L.N.A.

"Astra", a Miniature Long-haired Dachshund, entered for Tattersall's Dachshund Dog Show, is assisting a juvenile programme seller.

They are very much a "one-man" dog, and having attached themselves to one person, as far as they are concerned no one else exists. They are extremely clean little animals, very easy to house train, excellent house dogs, very sensitive to rebuke or unkindness, but at the same time extremely determined and liking, if possible, to get their own way. Their short coats make them easy to keep clean and they have one great advantage that, when wet, or indeed at any time, their coats never smell.

The Wire-haired Dachshund was little known in this country until about 1927. In that year the Wire-haired Dachshund Club was started, some of the chief originators being Lady Kitty Ritson, Mrs. Schuster, Mrs. Howard, and Air Vice-Marshal Sir Charles Lambe, and two classes were guaranteed, viz. : Open Dog and Open Bitch at the Veterinary College Show. From that time to the present the Wire-haired Dachshund has made

Photo]   [E.N.A.

A BEVY OF BEAUTIES.

Fräulein Maria Paudler, particularly well known as the star of the German Talkie version of "Waltzes from Vienna", is a great dog-lover. The dog on the left is a Long-haired Dachshund.

tremendous strides in England both in numbers and in the breeding.

The Wire-haired Club started an Open Show at Tattersall's in 1932, and in 1933 was joined by the Southern Smooths and Long-haired Clubs. Major Ilgner, one of the oldest and most experienced German judges, judged the Wires and he was delighted with them.

The first dog to become a champion in England was Ch. "Fritzle von Paulinenberg", born 1925, an imported dog owned by the late Mrs. Rattee and afterwards by Mrs. Allan. Another imported dog to become a champion was "Dictator Ditmarsia", born 1928, and owned by Mrs. Mitchell.

The first English-bred dog to become a champion was "Achsel", born 1929 and owned by Miss Theo Watts. Ch. "Achsel" was awarded best Wire-haired dog or bitch by Major Ilgner at the Open Joint Show at Tattersall's, 1933, also by "Myrhea Fokker" at Cruft's, 1933. He sired Ch. "Amelia", owned by Mrs. Blandy, born 1931. Ch. "Anneta", born 1929, bred and owned by Mrs. Blandy, was the first Wire-haired bitch bred in England to become a champion. Ch. "Brita of Tavistone", born

Photo]   [Sport and General.

IN THE HANDS OF THE JUDGE.

The picture of the Countess Reventlow (of Denmark) judging Wire-haired Dachshunds at a Kennel Club Show. Notice the dappled colouring of the dog furthest from the camera.

Photo]   *[Sport & General.*

A CHARMING LOT.

Miss Pamela Howard, with her mother's extremely attractive Miniature Dachshunds, at the Club's Jubilee Show at Tattersall's, London, in 1933.

1925, was an imported bitch owned by the late Mrs. Rattee. There was one other English-bred bitch, Ch. "Diana of Tavistone", owned by Mmes. Howard and Schuster, but she died when only two and a half years old and was a great loss to the breed.

The chief features as adopted by the Wire-haired Dachshund Club in the main are similar to those of the Smooth-haired variety already given, with the exception, of course, of the coat.

Apart from jaw, eyebrows, and ears, the whole body is covered with a completely even, short, thick, rough coat, but with finer, shorter hairs everywhere distributed between the coarser hairs, which resembles that of the German spiky-haired Pointer. There should be a beard on the chin. The eyebrows are bushy. On the ears the hair is shorter than on the body; quite smooth, but nevertheless in conformity with the rest of the coat. It is a fault if the texture of the hair is soft, if too short or too long anywhere, if it sticks out irregularly in all directions, or if curling or wavy. All colours are admissible. White patches on the chest, though allowable, are not desirable. The colour of the nose and nails should be black.

Photo, Ralph Robinson.

"KLEINKURIO"
Said to be the smallest toy Dachshund in the world.

Dalmatian.—The origin of the Dalmatian is very uncertain; but there is one fact which stands out clearly. The breed has been known in England for over two hundred years at least. At the second recognized dog show held in this country, in 1860, only five breeds were scheduled. One of these was the Dalmatian. This is their first authentic appearance as a show dog.

As far back as 1790, however, Dalmatians were mentioned in contemporary literature, and they also figured in early heraldry. One

Photo]   [Ralph Robinson.
"MIGNONNE OF SEALE".
An adult example of the Dachshund in miniature. It is the property of Major Howard.

theory suggests that they originated in Dalmatia and were imported into this country during the eighteenth and nineteenth centuries by the gentlemen of the period who were making the "Grand Tour". They found them useful as guards as well as being ornamental. If this is their true origin, it is curious that no trace of them remains in Italy. Another suggestion is that they were used as gun-dogs in Spain, but there seems little corroboration of this theory. Models of a spotted dog have been found in ancient Greek excavations and on friezes, and E. C. Ash, in his *Dogs and Their History*, refers to one shown on a tablet, of *Antelaa II*, date about 2000 B.C. Anyway, there appears to be no doubt that Dalmatians are a breed known to the Ancients, though they have passed through many evolutions in type during the centuries.

Ever since they have been known in this country there have been variations. At one time it was considered correct for them to have spots in assorted colours. There was even a tricolor, with black, liver and blue spots. Lemon spotting is quite common, but useless from a show or breeding point of view. The perfection of "spotting," which is fast being attained, was certainly absent in the middle of last century, as the old prints show a far more blotchy marking.

Mr. Fred Kemp, president of the British Dalmatian Club, having kept the breed for fifty-five years, stated that his forbears did so before him for two generations. He was certainly one of the very few who kept the breed in existence from 1914 to 1918. It is doubtful if there is a pedigree which does not contain dogs from his kennel.

Ch. "Panworth", Ch. "Tess of Coldharbour", Ch. "Silverden", "King of Coldharbour", and the "Mogger" family are always in evidence. In the old days, when farmers' wives took their produce to market in panniers on pack ponies, they used

Photo]   [Ralph Robinson.
DACHSHUNDS IN MINIATURE.
Mrs. M. Howard has a noted kennel of Miniature Dachshunds; here a bitch is seen with her puppies.

THREE GOOD TYPES.

It is not often that such fine specimens of the Wire-haired variety are seen, as those shown above. That in the centre is "Diana of Tavistone", the property of Mrs. M. Howard. That below shows "Kingswalden Flute". The Wire-haired Dachshund is often quite different from the Smooth type, sometimes giving the impression of being a distinct variety.

"spotted dogs" to guard their goods. These dogs were called "Pack dogs" or "Talbots". Mr. Kemp remembers seeing an inn in the West Country with the sign "Packhorse and Talbot". The latter name was used in heraldry. Mrs. Beal, a well-known breeder and judge, is the authority for asserting that the "Talbot" shared with the Greyhound the most frequent place on coats of arms, referring, of course, to dogs only. Mrs. Beal also owned a Rockingham china group depicting a pack of Dalmatians in full cry after a stag. It seems to prove that they were used for hunting, and supports the theory that they are really the descendants of Old English hounds.

They are classified now as non-sporting and connected in everyone's mind with horses. They were known as carriage dogs, generally lived in the stables, and were used to run under the axle of the carriage.

The increase in their numbers since the Great War has been amazing. In 1918 two were registered at the Kennel Club; in 1925, 185; and in 1933, 889. At the first Cruft's show after the War two were exhibited and in 1934, 199 entries filled fifteen classes. This all goes to demonstrate the increasing demand for the breed, which is due to their delightful character and adaptability, as well as their striking appearance.

Two predominant characteristics are, faithfulness and wonderful memories. The writer had a bitch

By courtesy]   THE BENGAL HARRIER.   *[E. C. Ash.*
Did the Dalmatian originate in India ? This eighteenth century depiction of a dog known as the Bengal Harrier shows much of the Dalmatian type.

which had left her kennel for two and a half years. She did not see the animal for a year, and then went to stay with her new owners. It took the dog thirty seconds to realize who was the visitor, but after that the animal attached herself absolutely to her previous owner and ignored her own people. Many similar examples of a Dalmatian's retentive memory could be quoted. On one occasion a well-known breeder was judging, and one of the exhibits suddenly behaved like a mad dog, jumping and fawning on him. The judge had sold him as an eight months' puppy quite eighteen months previously.

Another strong point is that they train instinctively as guards. This trait can be usefully adapted to the guarding of a motor-car. A woman, with a Dalmatian as company, can walk anywhere and need have no fear of molestation. Nowadays, when motors are such a danger, and the roads are so congested, a dog with "road sense" is essential. In a Dalmatian this is highly developed. It has a natural instinct for keeping to heel, and let it have a horse to follow and no dog is happier. It loves to run ten miles per hour with a motor if a private road makes the practice safe, but two miles is quite a sufficient course for it.

It has many more attributes, and is not pugnacious, but goes peacefully on its way unless attacked, and it is devoted to children.

Dalmatians have a knack of fitting into their own niche in the household. They are

Photo]   A WELL-KNOWN CHAMPION.   *[Hedges.*
Ch. "Golden Dawn of Coelan", the property of Miss Stephenson, is a very beautifully bred and well marked bitch.

DINNER TIME.

The reason for the nickname "Plum pudding dogs" is well evidenced in this picture of half-grown Dalmatians helping themselves greedily from the bowl.

ALL AGOG!

This handsome and alert Dalmatian seems to be quite as interested in a passing aeroplane as is its young master.

exceptionally easy to house-train, and quickly accustom themselves to their own bed. Once this habit is learnt, they are singularly peaceful, and do not fidget incessantly, and expect to be taken out if anyone appears with a hat on. They rarely bark. Unless some stranger at the door rouses their suspicions, or they hear an unusual noise at night, they are absolutely quiet. They do, however, talk! The writer knows of no other breed with such a facility for "conversation", carried on with a most expressive intonation.

Critics of the breed assert that they are very nervous, and are not at all intelligent. Of course, one does get a nervous specimen at times, as in all breeds. They undoubtedly are sensitive and react badly to rough treatment. Their training should be carried on firmly, but quietly. Also, it is essential to take them out in the road, when still young puppies, so as to accustom them to the noises and traffic. A purchaser often buys a puppy which has never been out of the kennels. The poor little youngster is packed off by train and arrives a nervous wreck, and it probably never recovers.

As for intelligence, it is predominant in most

Photo] THE FIRST SPOTS. [*S. M. Ballance.*
Miss L. B. Clay, of Ayot St. Lawrence, is a well-known exhibitor of Dalmatians at Cruft's. Here is one of her puppies, at an age when the spots just begin to appear.

Dalmatians. An old man, who had been coachman to a family resident in London with a country house at Southborough, tells of one in the days before the advent of the motor-car. It was their custom to drive up to town with a carriage and pair and a Dalmatian underneath. On one occasion the dog was left behind, much against its will. About an hour after the carriage arrived in town, the dog turned up at the mews, having travelled the thirty-five miles on its own, and the route included the Old Kent Road, which was a crowded thoroughfare even in those days. On one occasion the writer arrived at a large rambling hotel after a long motor run and, placing her bag in her room, went straight out with her dog for a run without paying attention to the room number. Upon returning, it was the owner who couldn't find the room. She realized this, but on reaching the corridor said to the dog: "Go on to your bed." It went unhesitatingly to the correct room. Examples like this could be multiplied indefinitely.

Of course, the "one-man dog" develops more intelligence, because it is in constant contact with its master, and grows to understand every movement.

Photo] A DELIGHTFUL GROUP. [*Ralph Robinson.*
Here is a group of Dalmatian puppies at their most attractive age, plump and good-natured.

[Planet News.

SIX OF A KIND.

Here are some noted dogs belonging to Mrs. D. K. Hackney, of Essex, who owns one of the leading kennels in England. "Snow Leopard" the second dog from the left is world-famous.

[Photo]

It is incorrect to say that Dalmatians are stupid. The big majority certainly are not. They can be easily trained to do the work of a retriever, as they have naturally soft mouths. In some cases they definitely "point" at game, but if they put anything up, they use sight as well as scent to hunt it.

A Dalmatian should be built for endurance and moderate speed. Anyone who can pick the winner of a "hunter" class could detect a properly built Dalmatian. Their points are very similar.

The dog should have straight forelegs, with good bone, elbows close to the body, and round, cat-like feet. The hindlegs should be muscular, with hocks well let down. The body compact, well ribbed up, with a deep chest, allowing heart room, but not overladen on the shoulders. The back strong and the loins nicely arched. The head should be stylish and not coarse, with a fair length of foreface, a flat skull and a medium stop. There should be no wrinkle, and the lips should set close. The ears should be of fine texture, set rather high and carried close to the head. They ought to be spotted, but more often are blotched and sometimes black. The last is not considered desirable. Eyes are an important point, as expression depends largely on them. They should be set rather wide apart, and be bright and sparkling and, if possible, dark in colour. Above all, they should be set in black rims. This is most important, as fleshy rims really spoil the dog's appearance. A "wall" or blue eye is not technically a fault, but it is undoubtedly a handicap. The nose must always be black ; a flesh one is very detrimental and spoils the whole character of the head.

Another strong point is a nicely-set-on head. The neck should be arched, elegant and free from throatiness, and should rise from clean muscular shoulders. The two ends of a Dalmatian are equally important, if it is desired to attain the quality, outline and finish which is so essential. The tail must consequently be considered. It should be a "whip" one, and carried on a slightly upward curve. Spots should be there, but in a large percentage of specimens they are absent.

Markings are of great importance, as they count thirty per cent in judging. The coat should be hard, close and satiny,

CH. "MIDSTONE EBONY".

This outstanding Dalmatian bitch, the property of Mrs. L. W. Bonney, of Flushing, New York, was bred by Mrs. M. E. Walford in England and exported to America.   Attention is drawn to the shape and carriage of the head.

"GOWORTH VICTOR".

Miss E. V. Barnes' sturdy dog, "Goworth Victor", was a great winner of prizes, including five firsts at Cruft's in 1934.
The Dalmatian may be either black- or liver-spotted, both of which are most attractive colourings.

DALMATIANS IN TRAINING.

and the markings distinct and of a dense black, clearly defined. Runs, ticky spots, greyish spots and patches are all blemishes, and the last named is a definite fault. It may be advisable to warn novices that puppies are born white. Any black mark visible at birth becomes a patch.

There are, of course, liver-spotted Dalmatians. In their case the eyes are golden and the rims and nose and lips liver colour. They are not necessarily bred from liver parents, but crop up in a litter sometimes from black ancestry. Their markings have not reached the high standard of the blacks as yet.

The height of a Dalmatian dog should be 22 ins. at the shoulder and the bitch may be rather less, and they should weigh respectively 56 and 50 lb.

Their type of action is most important. They should have a free, easy stride, springy and untiring, and should move straight, with no throwing out of feet or shoulders and, above all, they should not be at all cow-hocked. When they followed a trotting horse it was considered very incorrect for them to break into a canter.

Among famous winning Dalmatians, mention should be made of Ch. "Silverden King of Coldharbour", bred by Miss Kemp and owned by Miss Shirley Mallion. He was a consistent winner in Breed and Variety Classes, and a wonderful stud dog. Another wonderful dog, Ch. "Snow Leopard", was bred and owned by Mrs. Hackney. He made history as a show dog, winning the Challenge Certificate at every show where one was offered for the breed. A beautifully made dog and a great mover. Ch. "Bookham Swell", another favourite, owned by Mrs. Walker Smith, had to fight for his championship, but fortune came his way at last. Rather on the small side, he must, nevertheless, be described as very typical.

No list would be representative without mention of Mr. Fred Wardell's Ch. "Best of Cards", a very stylish dog and wonderful showman ; and Ch. "Winning Trick", an attractive dog, rather more cobby than some. Miss Clay's Ch. "Lucky James" lived up to his name, as he became a champion before he was eighteen months old. 'He was a big, quality dog, a shade long in the back, but with the best of legs and feet and a delightful expression. He and his kennel companion, Ch. "Venus of the Wells", won the International Brace Class at Cruft's in 1934.

Photo] *[Fox.*

FAMILY LIFE.

A mother Dalmatian and her family posing gracefully for the camera. Most puppies when placed thus are only too anxious to run away, but these obviously knew how to behave.

The late Mr. Proctor's Ch. "Hannah of the Highway" took a lot of beating. She was full of quality, a nice mover and well decorated, though perhaps rather heavily for present-day fashion.

The winner at Cruft's in 1934 was Mr. Sorby Straw's Ch. "Manor Mischief". She attained her title there. She looked very attractive, with lovely markings, and possessed a good head and expression.

Some mention must be made of "livers". The

the latter can withstand a fair amount of hardship or cold, it readily falls sick if subject to draughts or damp. Bacteria of all sorts multiply with greater facility in damp conditions, especially if there is an absence of sunlight. Dogs, being susceptible to rheumatism, will often exhibit symptoms of that aggravating malady if housed in damp quarters; or even sometimes if they get wet in the rain, notwithstanding a good rub down with a towel. All kennels, whether permanent or transportable, should be built well above the ground so that a current of air can pass beneath the floor. Should the latter be of

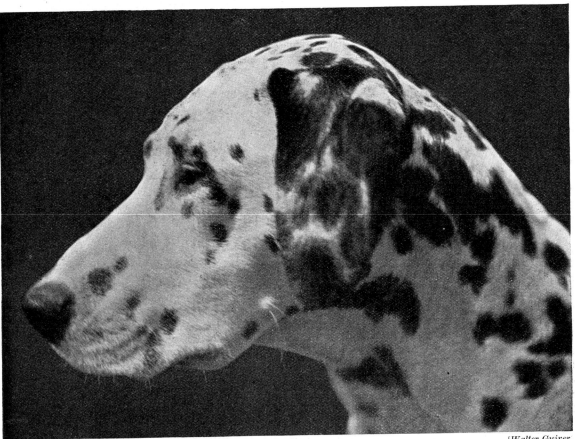

Photo]   [*Walter Guiver.*
"WESTELLA VENTURE".
Miss Barnes' well-known winning bitch, "Westella Venture", shows the beautiful head of the Dalmatian.

best of the 1933 exhibits were Miss Smither's Ch. "Bruno of Brow", a grand dog with wonderful outline and perfect tail carriage. His markings were exceptionally distinct for a "liver". Miss Stephens' Ch. "Golden Dawn of Coelan" was one of the most elegant of bitches. She had style all through, and a most lovely colour.

Dam.—A dam is the mother of a puppy; also known as a bitch. Reference has been made to the care of the dam under "Breeding"

Damages for Injuries by Dogs. (*See* Ownership.)

Dampness.—Damp kennels, or damp bedding therein, are great enemies of the dog, and whilst

cement, then the foundations should consist of four or five inches of ashes, three inches of concrete and one inch of smooth white cement. No dampness will penetrate that, once it has thoroughly dried out and set hard. Even so, a dog should not be allowed to sleep actually on the cement, but should have a wooden dais or shelf provided, which is raised at least six inches above the floor.

The newest material for floor construction in kennel buildings is a flat, hollow brick. These are laid in the ordinary way and then are faced on top with a thin layer of cement to render them impervious. Floors so built are absolutely dry and very warm. Adequate ventilation, without draught, helps considerably to dispel any tendency to dampness.

Where the walls of a kennel are built of ordinary bricks, it is essential to have a damp-proof course

FRIENDS.

Miss Griselda Hervey with her two Dalmatian friends. The Dalmatian has become a popular breed, and deservedly so.

PEN-AND-INK PORTRAIT.
Head study of a Dandie Dinmont Terrier, specially drawn for this work by Ernest G. Chapman.

of slate or some other impervious material, just above the level of the ground surface, to prevent moisture from rising up the wall.

Dandie Dinmont.—This dog owes its name to Sir Walter Scott's novel, *Guy Mannering*, and is the only breed in existence whose name springs from a literary source.

Dandie Dinmont was not a man who actually lived, but Scott gives that name to typify the farmers of the Border, and it was among these gentry that there was bred a hard-bitten, courageous Terrier. It was these that Scott described as Dandie Dinmont's dogs. That was in 1814, but these rough-haired, short-legged Terriers of the Border counties had led an un-named existence long befor that. The actual origin of the Dandie is not known. PossiblyRough-haired Terriers were crossed with the Dachshund, or, maybe, the Otter Hound, though there is quite a body of opinion that believes the dog gradually evolved itself to its present standard untouched by outside influences.

There is some relationship between the Dandie and the Bedlington. In both there is the same pendulous ear and similar top-knots, the

Photo]　　　　　　　　　　　　　　　*[J. Garrow.*
A MAN OF MARK.
The late Paul Scott of Tedburgh, one of the pioneers of the Dandie Dinmont Fancy.

chief difference being that the Dandie is low to the ground, with a long body, and the Bedlington is long-legged and short-bodied. There is a case on record, indeed, in which two animals from the same litter were shown and won prizes, one as a Dandie and the other as a Bedlington.

The original Dandie Dinmont is said to have been James Davidson, of Hyndlea, who certainly had a pack of these Terriers, though we have no record where he obtained them. They may have been near to the Rough-haired Skye Terrier. We

come across the name in 1754 in the story given by Dr. Brown of a tinker sportsman named Piper Allan. It was assumed that his dogs were of the Dandie type. They were intelligent and delightful enough, at all events, to attract the covetousness of the Duke of Northumberland, who took a great fancy to one of the dogs named "Hitchem". His Lordship endeavoured to buy the dog, and even went so far as to offer Piper Allan a farm rent free on his estate in order to get possession of the dog. But Piper Allan wouldn't part. "Na, na, ma Lord," he replied, "keep yer ferum. What would a Piper do wi' a ferum?" Allan's sayings about his dogs appear to have become famous. Another offer, made for a second dog named "Charlie", met with the same refusal, the Piper declaring that His Lordship's whole estate couldn't buy the animal.

The Piper's son carried on the Terrier strain, and he, in his turn, had a son who possessed a dog which was the descendant of "Hitchem", named "Old Pepper", and thus is established the relationship between Piper Allan and the Dandie Dinmont of to-day.

All these dogs of the Border were either mustard or pepper, but it was some years before they became established as a recognized breed. In 1867 the judges of the Birmingham show did not consider that any Dandie exhibited was worth a prize, and it was not until 1875, when the first club was started for Dandies, at Selkirk, that they began to come into their own. Before considering the show point, it should be pointed out that the Dandie is essentially a working Terrier. In considering modern efforts to reduce the length of leg, it must be remembered

[Sport and General.

ARRIVING AT TATTERSALL'S BY COACH.

In 1930, the Southern Dandie Dinmont Terrier Club held an Open Show at Tattersall's. Here are seen some of the Hon. Mrs. S. McDonnell's eighteen entries arriving in up-to-date style.

Photo]

that the dog should be active enough to follow its master all day over rugged country, to fight fox or badger, and follow those instinctive enemies into their underground lairs.

A Dandie, too, is an excellent guard. For so small a dog it has an amazingly deep, authoritative voice ; its courage is tremendous, and though it has an aptitude to fight cats and other animals, becomes an affectionate and reliable companion if trained from puppyhood. It is not wise to keep two in one kennel ; there is sure to be a fight, and unless interfered with such fights usually go on to the death.

It is a curious circumstance that Dandie Dinmont pups are born smooth-haired ; the peppers are black-and-tan in colour, while in the colouring of the mustards there is a good deal of black.

The Dandie has improved during the years since Scott labelled him. There is a painting of Dandies by Emms towards the end of last century, and from that we find the breed had then taken on roughly the shape which we now know. And certainly, whatever differences have developed under the breeders' care, there has been no change in the grit and courage of the dog since the days of James Davidson.

STANDARD OF POINTS OF THE DANDIE DINMONT TERRIER.

HEAD.—Strongly made and large, not out of proportion to the dog's size, the muscles showing extraordinary development, more especially the maxillary.

SKULL.—Broad between the ears, getting gradually less towards the eye, and measuring about the same from the inner corner of the eye to back of skull as it does from ear to ear. The forehead well domed. The head is covered with very soft, silky hair, which should not be confined to a mere topknot, and the lighter in colour and silkier it is the better.

CHEEKS.—Starting from the ears proportionately with the skull, they have a gradual taper towards the muzzle, which is deep and strongly made, and measures about three inches in length, or in proportion to skull as three is to five.

MUZZLE.—The muzzle is covered with hair of a little darker shade than the topknot, and of the same texture as the feather of the forelegs. The top of the muzzle is generally bare for about an inch from the back part of the nose, the bareness coming to a point towards the eye, and being about one inch broad at the nose. The nose and inside of mouth black or dark coloured.

TEETH.—Very strong, especially the canine, which are of extraordinary size for such a small dog. The canines fit well into each other, so as to give the greatest available holding and punishing power, and the teeth are level in front, the upper ones very slightly overlapping the under ones. (Many of the finest

"DARRENTH REMMY".

The Hon. Mrs. Angus MacDonnell's Dandie Dinmont is well-known on the show bench and has won several prizes.

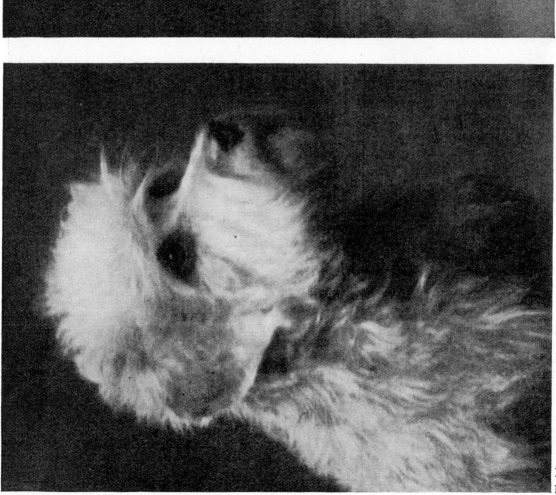

CH. "HOWCAPLE JOANNA".

Mrs. Gordon's noted champion Dandie Dinmont has the typical Dandie expression. Mrs. Gordon is a leading breeder.

specimens have a "swine mouth", which is very objectionable, but it is not so great an objection as the protrusion of the under jaw.)

EYES.—Set wide apart, large, full, round, bright, expressive of great determination, intelligence, and dignity ; set low and prominent in front of the head ; colour, a rich dark hazel.

EARS.—Pendulous, set well back, wide apart, and low on the skull, hanging close to the cheek, with a very slight projection at the base, broad at the junction of the head and tapering almost to a point, the fore part of the ear tapering very little—the

shown. The cartilage and skin of the ear should not be thick, but rather thin. Length of ear, from three to four inches.

NECK.—Very muscular, well developed, and strong, showing great power of resistance, being well set into the shoulders.

BODY.—Long, strong, and flexible ; ribs well sprung and round, chest well developed and let well down between the forelegs ; the back rather low at the shoulder, having a slight downward curve and a corresponding arch over the loins, with a very slight, gradual drop from top of loin

WE ARE THREE.
"Salisbury May Queen", "Solomon" and "Milord" show three different Dandie Dinmont expressions.

tapering being mostly on the back part, the fore part of the ear coming almost straight down from its junction with the head, to the tip. They should harmonize in colour with the body colour. In the case of a pepper dog they are covered with a soft, straight, brownish hair (in some cases almost black). In the case of a mustard dog the hair should be mustard in colour, a shade darker than the body, but not black. All should have a thin feather of light hair starting about two inches from the tip, and of nearly the same colour and texture as the topknot, which gives the ear the appearance of a distinct point. The animal is often one or two years old before the feather is

to root of tail ; both sides of backbone well supplied with muscle.

TAIL.—Rather short, say from eight to ten inches, and covered on the upper side with wiry hair of darker colour than that of the body, the hair on the under side being lighter in colour, and not so wiry, with a nice feather about two inches long, getting shorter as it nears the tip ; rather thick at the root, getting thicker for about four inches, then tapering off to a point. It should not be twisted or curled in any way, but should come up with a curve like a scimitar, the tip, when excited, being in a perpendicular line with the root of the tail. It should neither be set on too high nor too low. When not excited it is carried gaily, and a little above the level of the body.

LEGS.—The forelegs short, with immense muscular development and bone, set wide apart, and chest coming well down between them. The feet well formed and not flat, with very strong brown or dark-coloured claws. Bandy-legs and flat feet are objectionable. The hair on the forelegs and feet of a pepper dog should be tan, varying according to the body colour from a rich tan to a pale fawn; in a mustard dog they are of a darker shade than its head, which is a creamy-white. In both colours there is a nice feather about two inches long, rather lighter in colour than the hair on the fore part of the leg. The hindlegs are a little longer than the fore ones, and are set rather wide apart, but not spread out in an unnatural manner, while the feet are much smaller and the hair of the same colour and texture as the fore ones, but having no feather or dew-claws; the whole claws should be dark, but the claws of all vary in shade according to the colour of the dog's body. The thighs should be well developed.

COAT.—This is a very important point. The

HEADS.
The Dandie Dinmonts always appear to be mainly head, for they are large-domed, and the top-knot makes much difference to their appearance.

hair should be about two inches long; that from the skull to root of tail a mixture of hardish and short hair, which gives a sort of crisp feel to the hand. The hair should not be wiry; the coat is what is termed pily or pencilled. The hair on the under part of the body is lighter in colour and softer than that on the top. The skin on the belly accords with the colour of the dog.

COLOUR.—The colour is pepper or mustard. The pepper ranges from a dark bluish-black to a light silvery-grey, the intermediate shades being preferred, the body colour coming well down the shoulder and hips, gradually merging into the leg colour. The mustards vary from a reddish-brown to a pale fawn, the head being a creamy-white, the legs and feet of a shade darker than the head. The claws are dark as in other colours. (Nearly all Dandie Dinmont Terriers have some white on the chest, and some have white claws.)

SIZE.—The height should be from eight to eleven inches at the top of the shoulder. Length from top of shoulder to root of tail should not be more than twice the dog's height, but, preferably, one or two inches less.

WEIGHT.—From 14 lb. to 24 lb.; the best weight as near 18 lb. as possible. These weights are for dogs in good working order.

The relative values of several

Photo]
THE GREAT JOINT TERRIER SHOW.
[Sport and General.
A nice bed of Dandie Dinmont Terriers, all prize winners. Mrs. M. C. Stubbs' and Miss C. A. Miles' "Bellmead Saffron", "Bellmead Defender" and "Bellmead Seraph", shown at Olympia in 1933.

points in the standard are apportioned as follow :
Head, 10 ; eyes, 10 ; ears, 10 ; neck, 5 ; body, 20 ;
tail, 5 ; legs and feet, 10 ; coat, 15 ; colour, 5 ; size
and weight, 5 ; general appearance, 5. Total, 100.

Dandruff.—A scurfy condition
of the skin due to abnormal
dryness in consequence of
failure of the sebaceous
glands to secrete a
sufficiency of lubri-
cating material. It
may also arise
from functional
or other disorder
of the thyroid
gland. It is a
condition often
difficult to cure,
but it may be
considerably im-
proved by regu-

Photo] 　　　　　　　　　　　　　　　　　　[Fall.
AT EARLY AGE.
Dandie Dinmont puppies at this age are most attractive, and this photograph
suggests a show future for both of these, the property of Mrs. Simpson Shaw.

larly and energetically grooming the dog once or twice
daily. The friction applied stimulates the circulatory
and nerve supply of the skin, and thereby improves
general health. The dryness may be overcome, in the
first instance, by carefully anointing the affected areas
with a mixture of lanoline and vaseline in equal parts ;
or with coconut oil. Only a thin film is necessary, and
the hair should be parted in order to get the medicament in close contact with the skin. If carelessly
done and the coat is clogged up with grease, the dog
will become a source of great annoyance to the
household. Internally, the dog should receive
alteratives and tonics, the latter being preferably a
combination of iron and arsenic.

Dangerous Drugs Act (1920 and 1928).—
Controls the importation, manufacture and distribution
of "dangerous" drugs, and imposes a penalty not
exceeding £200 (or imprisonment, with or without
hard labour, for six months) for any offence against
the regulations made under the Act. The
dangerous drugs referred to in this Act are not
so called because of their poisonous nature, but
because of the danger to human health and
happiness, and perhaps life,
which ensues when man
acquires the "drug habit".
The drugs particularly
referred to in the Act are
cocaine and morphine, or
any preparation contain-
ing more than one-tenth

and one-fifth per cent,
respectively, of them.
Many a person, addicted
to the taking of drugs,
might seek to obtain his
supply from a veterinary
surgeon on the pretence,
perhaps, that his dog
was in pain and needed
a sleeping draught.
The D.D.A., how-
ever, provides that
should a prescrip-
tion be given,
which included a
"dangerous" drug,
the prescription
must be in writing,
must be dated and
signed by the
veterinary surgeon
with his full name
and address, and
must specify the person to whom it is supplied, and
the total amount of the drug to be supplied in the
prescription. The latter must be marked "For
Animal Treatment only" and "Not to be repeated".
Fortunately, dogs have no opportunity of acquiring
a mania for drugs ; and very happily they have
not been deprived of the inestimable benefits which
(in suitable cases) these alkaloids can confer. (*See also*
Cocaine, Drugs, Morphine.)

Darwinism.—The theory of evolution propounded
by Chas. R. Darwin, English naturalist, 1809–1882,
according to which higher organisms have been
developed from lower ones through the influence of
natural selection.

The late Sir Fredk. Smith wrote : "As no living
thing arises spontaneously, but is built up from a
pair of other living things (with certain exceptions in
the simpler forms of life), it is
probable that so long as man
has been able to reason he has
regarded the offspring of a given
union as consisting of a mixture
of its parents. As knowledge
became extended, more especially
since the origin of species has been
traced almost step by step from the

Photo] 　　　　　　　　　　　　　　　　　　　　[Ralph Robinson.
PUPPIES.
Dandie Dinmont juniors of good type, belonging to Mrs. Wolseley. Note the head of the centre puppy.

"BELLMEAD DEFENDER".

The Dandie Dinmont is one of the most attractive Terriers, and is a real worker as well as being a popular show dog.

lowest to the highest forms of life, and all life shown to be the outcome of a common primitive form, the facts underlying these extraordinary changes have been the subject of enquiry, in order to determine the natural laws by which they are governed. In his *Origin of Species* Darwin held that, in the struggle for existence, only those individuals survived which were naturally selected by their environment, and this selection took place through the medium of impalpable differences and through the course of a long period of time. In other words, owing to the removal of the least fit, selection took place through the most fit, i.e. most fit for the conditions in which the organism existed. There is evidence that both parents contribute in an equal degree to the construction of the offspring, and there is not much difficulty in conceiving that not only the parents concerned, but their ancestors, are represented, though in ever-diminishing degrees. An

perhaps as the result of a severe blow on the head ; or possibly as a sequel to distemper. White animals are singularly subject to deafness, an outstanding example of which is the Bull-terrier. Many members of this breed, and particularly those with pink (or Dudley) noses, white eyelashes, and other signs of deficient pigmentation, are stone deaf.

SYMPTOMS.—A dog with a defective sense of hearing appears to be strange in its manner, in that it seems sometimes to have lost interest in its master, is quite unresponsive to the voice, pays no attention to the front-door bell or to cat-calls, or other noises which previously would have caused it to prick up its ears or commence barking.

TREATMENT.—The treatment of hereditary or of chronic deafness usually is of little avail, particularly if the cause is some injury involving shrinkage or paralysis of the nerves or centres associated with hearing. Deafness arising from canker, growths, or dirty conditions of the ear, may eventually be cured if these and

Photo]   CH. "POLFORD HIGHLANDER".   *[Fall.*
One of the best Dandie Dinmonts, the property of Mrs. Foster Rawlins. Note the type of head and shape of body.

animal or plant is therefore a mixture of its ancestors, and the question whether in this complex the individual characteristics remain distinct, or whether they are blended, is one which, during the last few years, has received the closest attention."

Dead Animal Disposal. (*See* DISPOSAL OF CARCASES.)

Deafness.—Temporary deafness is often caused by accumulations of wax, discharges, or dirt, or all three. Occasionally one finds new or adventitious tissue in ears which have been treated *too much* or treated with irritant dressings such as pure peroxide of hydrogen. Indeed, it is not uncommon to find the meatus of the external ear practically occluded from this cause. New growths in the ear are usually polypi or warts, but mostly the latter. Deafness may be due to paralysis of the auditory nerve,

other predisposing conditions can be eliminated. Constriction or occlusion of the auditory meatus by swellings or growths may in some cases be successfully dealt with by the surgeon. Each individual case must be examined and prescribed for on its merits.

Death, Signs of.—Death is assumed to have taken place when respiration and the heart's action have both stopped. If either one is still functioning, then it is frequently quite possible to induce the other to recommence normal activity. In other words, if the heart is perceived to be still beating but breathing has ceased, then artificial respiration must at once be proceeded with. If no pulse or heart-beat can be felt, but the animal still breathes, vigorous massage over the region of the heart, plus stimulants, will often cause the heart to resuscitate. Stimulants injected subcutaneously or intravenously would, of course, have a much quicker and safer

Photo]

CH. "DARENTH PENNY".

[Ralph Robinson.

A remarkable study of this noted champion, showing its roach back, top-knot and good head.

By courtesy]

THE DANDIE.

[James Garrow .

These hard-bitten working Terriers will always be identified with Sir Walter Scott's famous novel, *Guy Mannering*, where they are first named.   Here we show one owned by Mr. Archibald Steel, of Kelso.

action than anything one attempts to give by the mouth.

Respiration may be so slow and so shallow that the inexpert observer might conclude it had stopped altogether. By holding a small mirror or piece of glass close to the nostrils, one could see whether any condensation of breath appeared upon it.

Provided help is quickly at hand, in any given case, it is always wise to make an attempt to revive an apparently dead animal.

DEATH, SUDDEN.—Probably the large majority of dogs die either as a result of severe illness or accident, or are "put to sleep" for one reason or another ; but death from senile decay is not uncommon among them. Natural death is regarded as commencing either at the heart, lungs, brain, or blood. Those sudden deaths which occur during apparent good

Debility.—This condition may, perhaps, best be described as a localized or generalized lowered vitality or loss of strength. The blood circulation and nerve supply are usually both implicated, and the patient is weak, listless, without appetite, losing weight, and very largely or entirely lacking energy.

CAUSES.—It is generally brought about by high or continued fever, wasting diseases such as distemper, typhus, and tuberculosis, by totally improper feeding, or by grossly unhygienic conditions of life. Improper feeding includes not only insufficient food, but food which is innutritious, indigestible, or lacking in essential vitamins.

Severe debility is frequently a forerunner of death, and it must be tackled early and thoroughly. In many instances its onset is quite inexplicable, and these are the cases which usually derive so much

CH. "MAY QUEEN".
Mrs. Salisbury's Dandie Dinmont champion bitch has the top-knot of the breed well developed.

health are almost invariably attributed to failure of the heart's action (syncope). From what is known of the physiology of the heart, respiration and blood, it is very difficult to separate them in discussing the causes of death, as one is so largely dependent upon another.

Should the heart cease to beat, even temporarily, there is a consequent cerebral anaemia, followed at once by fainting or swooning, pallor of the gums and unconsciousness. Unless circulation is immediately restored, this condition known as syncope, becomes one of death.

In some cases, particularly after accidents, severe brain injuries or the rupture of an internal blood vessel will produce rapid death.

Death is not always somatic or general, as it may only be local, in which only a part of the body dies. (See GANGRENE NECROSIS, SHOCK.)

benefit from a vitamin-rich diet such as is afforded by raw milk, raw eggs, raw beef, and cod-liver oil, with a small quantity of baker's yeast daily. Sunlight, cleanliness, and good air are also essentials. During or after attacks of distemper one expects to encounter debility, and if the dog can but retain its appetite and can receive the articles of food above indicated, it should derive considerable help in overcoming this serious and distressing symptom.

A course of nerve or of heart tonics, administered over a period of two or three weeks, would no doubt expedite a recovery.

Deerhounds.—The special attraction of the Scottish Deerhound may best be described as one of "atmosphere", for there is a glamour about him that seems to be peculiarly his own.

[Photo]

[Ralph Robinson.

A NOTED KENNEL.

A charming study of Miss M. Richmond's Deerhounds. The resemblance to Irish Wolfhounds can here be seen. Of course, the Deerhound is much less powerful in build.

Photo] [*E.N.A.*
THE AUSTRIAN DEERHOUND.
Whilst the Deerhound in English-speaking countries means a Wire-haired large Greyhound, in Central Europe various types are known as Deerhounds, as the above Austrian dog suggests.

The worthy descendant of a noble ancestry, no other dog awakes a vision of armoured knights and ancient tapestried halls as does the Deerhound, whose characteristic far-away expression seems to recall the days of chivalry. His rugged, yet graceful exterior, his air of breeding, and his size, create an impression of beauty which accords well with his romantic history, and many artists have delighted to immortalize him in settings well suited to his picturesque appearance.

A long-established and thriving breed is known to have existed in Scotland—as elsewhere—prior to A.D. 1526. It refuses flatly, however, to emerge from the mists of obscurity prior to this date.

That the Deerhound is the Rough-coated Greyhound common to the British Isles from a very early age, we know, and Greyhounds, both Rough and Smooth, are mentioned by Arrian and others among the earliest authorities. Doctor Caius, in his book of *Englische Dogges*, A.D. 1576, speaking of Greyhounds, says: "Some are of a greater sorte and some of a lesser. Some are smoothe skynned and some are curled, the bigger therefor are appointed to hunt the bigger

beastes," and he specifies these "beastes" as "the buck, the harte, and the doe". Holinshed (A.D. 1577) corroborates this description, but uses "Shagg haired" instead of "curled", which presents a more comforting picture to the mind of the Deerhound-lover of to-day.

Endless instances occur about this date of the use of Rough Greyhounds, and it is perhaps interesting to note that the term "Greyhound" itself has long been a bone of contention among etymologists. Caius held that colour was not indicated by a derivation from "gre" or "grie", but a distinction, denoting the high rank these hounds occupied among their fellows. He says: "The Greyhound has his name of this word 'gre', which word soundeth 'gradus' in Latin, in Englishe 'degree', because among all dogges these are the most principall. . . ." This opinion is borne out by other writers, and is a tenable theory. Gesner (A.D. 1560) uses the name Grewhound, and up to forty years ago Greyhounds in the south of Scotland were commonly called Grews. It is here worthy of note that the actual word Deerhound does not appear in old writings, and upon the one instance where "deirhoundis" is introduced (*Pitscottie's History of Scotland*, first published about A.D. 1600) proof exists that this was not in accord with the original edition.

The chief names used to describe the breed were Rough Highland Greyhound, Highland Greyhound, Wolfdog, and later, Staghound. Indeed, the variety of terms is astonishing, but the most important is the word "Irisch" in this connection. Before the terms Celtic and Highland were known, the

By courtesy] [*E. C. Ash.*
"THE DRUNKARD".
A well-known popular sentimental picture, by Hancock, depicting the unshakeable faithfulness of the Scottish Deerhound.

STUDY OF A DEERHOUND HEAD

description Irisch applied equally to Ireland and Scotland, the former country being the better known of the two. Thus in Pitscottie's work we find a description of the inhabitants of Scotland : "They be cloathed with ane mantle, with ane schirt faschioned after the Irisch manner, going bare legged to the knee. All speak Irisch". Holinshed and other writers agree with this evidence, which is significant, because descriptions of Irish Greyhounds about this date (such as occur in Taylor's *Pennilesse Pilgrim*, A.D. 1618) refer without doubt to Highland Greyhounds and not to the great Irish Wolfdog, as has erroneously been supposed. The latter breed had already become so scarce in Ireland in A.D. 1623 that we find the Duke of Buckingham asking for a couple of brace as gifts for princes. At the same period the Earl of Mar could muster, for his deer-drives in Scotland, a couple of hundred "Irish Greyhounds". The Duke of Buckingham would be quite familiar with the Rough Greyhounds used for this purpose, and it is highly unlikely that he would confound them with the all but unique specimens he had caused a search for in Ireland.

Ash, in his great modern work on the Dog, gives an illustration from a book on animals dated A.D. 1583, showing a group containing large Rough Greyhounds, all possessed of such excellence in turn of quarter as to lead one to believe that the picture was made for the express purpose of

Photo] *[Fielder.*
FILIAL RESPECT.
A charming study of two of Miss Bransfoot's Deerhounds, "Rupert" and his son "Bracken of Bransways".

arousing envy in the hearts of all subsequent Deerhound owners. A veritable illustrated counsel of perfection !

There is a record that, at Cowdray Park, Queen Elizabeth saw "sixteen bucks pulled down in a laund", and it is generally supposed that the hounds used were Rough Greyhounds, but just at what point these hounds became peculiarly the pride and possession of Scotland we do not know. All that can be claimed with certainty is that they were long established there before A.D. 1526, and if a graph of Deerhound popularity were made, it would disclose a sustainedly high level for many generations prior to this date, with a sharp decline towards the eighteenth century. Pennant, in 1769, says : "We saw in Gordon Castle a true Highland Greyhound which has become very scarce. It was of large size, strong, deep chested, and covered with very long, rough hair. This kind was in great vogue and used in vast numbers at the magnificent stag chases by powerful chieftains". These chieftains preserved and prized their hounds with a fanatical

CH. "WULPHILDA".
This Deerhound, once the property of Major C. E. Davis, was a fine blue brindle and one of the best of its day.

I O

fervour, and Stewart in his *Buik of Chronicles* recounts the theft by Picts of a dog, romantically described as excelling all others, "so far as into licht the moon does, neara star". This work was a metrical version of Hector Boece's History, A.D. 1526, and continues: "The pictis houndis were nocht of sic speed as scottis houndis, nor yet so gude at need, nor in sic game they were not half so gude, nor of sicpleasures, nor sic pulchritude".

"Scottis" honour was not avenged upon this

harsh, wiry, reddish hair mixed with white". He mentions particularly that they were "formerly used" for deer-hunting.

Between this date and the revival of the breed, around 1830, it became extremely scarce. Several writers went so far as to pronounce Deerhounds extinct as a separate species, because many old strongholds were drawn blank, or, at best, displayed cross-bred, inferior specimens, and the difficulty of communication prevented proper investigation.

Photo]　　　　　　　　　　　　　　"MOINA OF ROTHERWOOD".　　　　　　　　　　　　[*Ralph Robinson.*

Miss Hartley's Deerhound makes a very fine picture and shows the wire coat that protects the dog in the rough country.

occasion until a hundred Picts and sixty of their comrades lay slain upon the field. One of the dogs illustrated in Gesner's *History of Quadrupeds*, A.D. 1560, is a Deerhound, and the drawing is supplied by Henry St. Clair, Dean of Glasgow, whose family is expressly stated to have kept and bred these hounds for many years prior to that date. Bewick (A.D. 1792) indicates the wane of deer-driving in many parts of Scotland, with its inevitable bearing upon the dogs used. He says: "One of these dogs which we saw some years ago, was a large, powerful, fierce-looking animal. Its ears were pendulous and its eyes half hid in hair, its body was strong and muscular, and covered with

The breed lived, however, and had its fastidious supporters as engrossed in pedigree and points as many who had gone before, or were yet to adopt its cause.

Rawdon Lee, Cupples, and other well-informed writers, give lists of districts where good and pure-bred hounds still flourished.

Mr. Menzies, of Chesthill, claimed one strain in his family since 1750. Badenoch and Lochaber possessed "adequate supplies", and numerous historians acknowledge a debt of gratitude to the farmers and to some of the clergy along the West coast, and in the islands, for their efforts in preserving the best stock. Dalzell's *Book of the Dog*

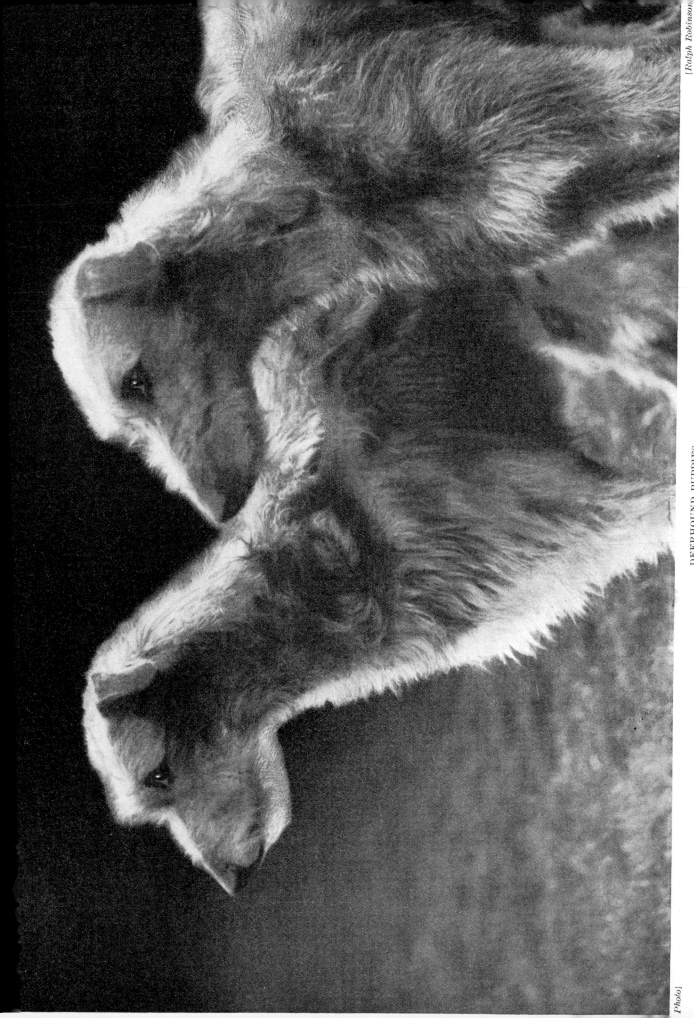

[Ralph Robinson

DEERHOUND PUPPIES.

Two of Miss M. M. Richmond's Deerhounds before they reached the age of discretion and prior to their days of shows. Pictures of some of her dogs on the moors are shown on other pages.

ON EXMOOR.

Miss M. Richmond is here seen with some of the good specimens from her kennel on one of the finest moors in England, which provide ideal surroundings for these noble dogs.

mentions Captain Basil Hall's hounds of the Glenmoriston breed, and Mr. Grant had this line at Invermoriston since 1815. He states that his first dog came from Captain Macdonald, of Moray, in the Braes of Lochaber, and the first bitch hailed from that pillar of the breed, Mr. Mackenzie, of Applecross. She was "celebrated for her great courage and lasting power". This list could be still further augmented, and it seems strange, in face of incontrovertible proof to the contrary, that Mr. Scrope, in his contemporary work on deer-stalking, should pronounce the Deerhound almost extinct. Cupples, in *Deerhounds and their Masters*, explains this, however, by the jealousy with which the

more modern history of Deerhounds, when several great kennels have taken little or no part in the continuation of the breed, one at least being completely lost in consequence.

This great wave of renewed interest dated from the rescinding of the Act (1831) whereby the shooting of game had hitherto been reserved for certain ranks and estates. Enthusiasm was instantaneous, and spread rapidly through the Highlands. Deer-driving, as distinguished from stalking, was no longer practised, but from that date onwards the records of the great stalkers of the latter part of the last century give ample evidence of the quality to which the breed was again raised. Fore-

Photo]   ALL IN A ROW.   *[Fall.*

Five of Miss Hartley's kennel. Like all the Greyhound family (for Deerhounds are Rough-haired and large Greyhounds really), they carry their tails in the usual fashion.

breed was now regarded. Rivalry ran high and, history repeating itself, shows instances after 1830 where the purloining of a Deerhound aroused wrath that, if it were not so vengeful, ranked in heat with the fury of ancient "Scottis" days! We are told, too, that many a Parliamentary vote could be assured by the promise of a single pup!

One kennel is reputed to have resorted to outside stock only three times in a hundred years, and it was the rule with the Earl de Folcoville that no puppy might be preserved beyond the needs of his own forest, excepting as a very rare favour to some stalker in his immediate circle. Cupples likens this attitude to "the man who wished to reserve the enjoyment of Horace for himself and a few friends", and it is a strange coincidence that examples of similar miserliness recur even in the

most in the movement ranks the Colonsay family, whose indefatigable efforts produced splendid results. Of the six sons, the eldest—later Lord Colonsay—and his brother, Mr. Archibald McNeill, took the chief part. They spared no expense, bred extensively, and kept only the best. Lord Henry Bentinck, Mr. Menzies, of Chesthill, and Cameron of Lochiel maintained magnificent strains up to the 'seventies, as did the Duke of Leeds and many others. Crossing was resorted to; in some instances a single introduction, in others a wider range of experiment prevailed. The controversy which raged around this subject makes interesting reading to-day, when it can be reviewed impartially and examined in the light of ultimate results. But none can fail to respect the purists, who so deeply resented the foreign blood

"MAGNETIC OF ROSS".
The Misses Loughrey's "Magnetic of Ross" the winner of the Challenge Certificate
at the Birmingham Show, 1933.

blood completely, and the appearance of the Deerhound suffered nothing in the long run. Indeed, the verdict of authority has long gone forth proclaiming the outcome a general benefit. In many instances, however, these infusions were a failure, and were not persevered with beyond the initial stage. McNeill himself tells us that the Russian Wolfhound and other big dogs which he imported were never used at all, as he did not find them the equal in fire and courage of the strains he had thought then might improve. The question of crossing, however, and the name of Glengarry, have ever been coupled in Deerhound circles, for he experimented more freely than any other kennel of his day. A slur has rested against the record of this great stalker on this account, which should long since have been dispelled. That Glengarry introduced the Cuban Bloodhound, and, in his efforts to produce a race of trackers, "came near to inventing a new variety", everyone knows, but few remember that he was as fastidious of the true stock as the most conservative among his fellows. Again and again occurs testimony to the fact that "Glengarry possessed the best strains", and, as an instance, Mr. Peter Robertson of the Black Mount Forest, describes his brace, "Glen" and "Garry", thus: "The former nearly 33 inches, the bitch 30 inches, both rough, lightish-grey, and they were perfectly pure, would not track a deer, but ran by sight only, and we thought much of them, as would be supposed".

introduced into many strongholds of the breed. It should, however, be borne in mind that these infusions were resorted to for the improvement of working ability only, and never to alter the characteristics of the race. First crosses are invariably hideous, but four generations will absorb the fresh efforts to produce a race of trackers, "came near to inventing a new variety", everyone knows, but few remember that he was as fastidious of the true stock as the most conservative among his fellows. Again and again occurs testimony to the fact that "Glengarry possessed the best strains", and, as an instance, Mr. Peter Robertson of the Black Mount Forest, describes his brace, "Glen" and "Garry", thus: "The former nearly 33 inches, the bitch 30 inches, both rough, lightish-grey, and they were perfectly pure, would not track a deer, but ran by sight only, and we thought much of them, as would be supposed".

Writing of the day upon which Glengarry met his death in the tragedy of Loch Linnhe, his old head-keeper said: "There was a leash of his best along with him in the steamer at the time, 'Truelais', and she was as good a tracker as ever ran, and 'Comstrie', who was thoroughbred, the best that ever I saw of any kind, and I am eighty-six years of age and the most part of that time with Glengarry". (Letter, 1876-77).

The introduction of the express rifle, the division of the great forests into numerous smaller ranges,

CH. "DRAMATIC OF ROSS"
This dog, a champion of the Deerhound family, was well-known at all shows.
The words "Of Ross" explain the breeding.

[by Ernest G. Chapman.

THE DEERHOUND.

The harsh strength of the coat, the gentleness of the dark brown eye, the reposeful ear and the fine long lines of the muzzle—prominent features of the Deerhound—are here well portrayed.

and other causes led to the final disuse of the Deerhound in its native land. Time works many changes, and it is a far cry from the great drives of the sixteenth century to the humble Collie on a string that is all the stalker of to-day requires for his sport, when the avoidance of anything likely to disturb the forest is a point of first importance. The advent of dog shows in 1861 was therefore a fortunate occurrence for Deerhounds, and many of the great sportsmen sent their cracks to these exhibitions. In the list of winning owners for a number of years, one reads a sequence of names which recall the great days that were then drawing to a close. The Duke of Sutherland, Lord Henry Bentinck, Sir St. George Gore, Cameron of Lochiel, Mr. Menzies, of Chesthill, Sir John McNeil—all of whom bred for perfection both in work and appearance, and sent entries straight from the hill to Curzon Hall. From this stock is descended all the hounds existing at the present day. Colonel Inge, of Thorpe, had the honour of winning the first prize at the first show (in Birmingham, 1861), with a dog called "Valiant". This dog's pedigree was given as by Lord Saltoun's famous "Bran", out of "Seaforth's Vengeance". "Bran" was entered to his first stag at nine months old, and killed his last at nine years. His greatest exploit in a marvellous career was the killing of two unwounded stags single-handed in three-quarters of an hour. He was at his best about 1844-45.

The great dog of the 'sixties was Mr. Gillespie's "Torrom", described as "a steel-grey, not very

Photo] 　　　　　　　　　　　　　　*[Fielder.*
A DEERHOUND PUPPY.
This daughter of "Rupert" is "Coronach of Bransways", at the age of four and a half months. Notice the type of head. She was bred by Miss Branfoot.

high but remarkably well formed". Captain Graham mentions (1881) that "all dogs of any note at the present time could trace their descent from this exceedingly grand specimen". From a dog called "Grumach", of the strain belonging to Mr. Campbell, of Monzie, "Lochiel's Pirate" was bred. This dog, together with his litter brother, Ch. "Old Torrom", was pupped in 1866, the former a remarkably fine specimen. The latter, an extraordinarily heavy dog of medium brownish colour, had little to recommend him, and is not to be confounded with his famous grandsire, "Gillespie's Torrom". Of a different

Photo] 　　　　　　　　　　　　　　*[Compton Collier.*
FRIENDS.
There is no more docile breed than the Deerhound, and here we have a youngster with its little mistress. Though good pets, this breed needs plenty of exercise.

Photo]　　　　　　　　　　　　　　　　　　　　　　　　[Ralph Robinson.

THE DEATH.

In the present century all Greyhound breeds have been tried at coursing. Deerhounds, although really too large for coursing hares are, nevertheless, occasionally used quite successfully.

strain, going direct back to McNeill's dogs, stands "Hector", the property of Mr. Dadley, head-keeper to the Marquis of Bristol, one which was considered a truly splendid specimen. Of a good rough coat, darkish brindle in colour, by "Giaour" out of "Hylda", he stood 31 inches, girthed 35 inches, and weighed 105 lb. This dog was a grandson of "Keildar", bred by Mr. Cole, head-keeper at Windsor Park, and at whose death he was acquired by Captain Graham. According to authorities, "Keildar" was one of the most elegant and aristocratic dogs ever seen. He stood "full 30 inches, girthed 33½, and weighed 95 lb."

On the death of General Ross, of Glenmordart, his hounds passed to Major Robertson, and from "Oscar" and "Hilda" he bred "Morni", perhaps the greatest name in the history of the breed. This dog came into the hands of Mr. Hickman, and is confidently described as combining all the graces. He passed on his good points, and Cameron of Lochiel describes his grandson, "Lord of the Isles", as "beyond criticism". The only litter got by this dog contained Ch. "Fingal II" (bred by Mr. Hickman), which was acquired by Mr. Walter Evans. Another great dog, born the same year (1884), was Mr. Morse Goulter's Ch. "Atholl II". These two dominant sires form the tap-roots of the modern breed. The former bred Ch. "Earl II", the latter Ch. "Swift".

Another great kennel about this era sponsored a heavier type of hound, and with stock gathered from Fort Augustus and elsewhere, Mrs. Grew made tremendous inroads on the prize-money for many years. The two schools of thought were definitely opposed, but many of her best hounds are spoken of by the apostles of grace and symmetry in terms of high praise. Ch. "Ayrshire", Ch. "Forester", Ch. "Kelso", three of her great stars, are now incorporated with the lines of "Fingal" and "Atholl", and have in turn produced some notable stock. To mention but a few more of the most remarkable inmates of important kennels, Mr. Hood Wright's celebrity, Ch. "Selwood Morven", sold to Mr. Harry Rawson, held a great position

Photo] "PADDY PROMIS OF BRANSWAYS". *[Fielder.*
One of the best young dogs ever seen, with excellent head, neck, and hindquarters. Bred by Miss E. S. M. Branfoot.

in the 'nineties. This owner's Ch. "St. Ronan's Ranger" (bred by Mr. W. Martin) proved to be one of the most successful sires some years later, and Ch. "St. Ronan's Rhyme" (the result of chance mating at nine months old) holds the record of the greatest show career of any bitch in the breed. Mrs. Armstrong's Ch. "Rob Roy of Abbotsford", another much used and successful sire, produced a large percentage of winners before the war. No record of the breed, however, could be complete without mention of the service rendered by Sir Henry MacLaughlin, whose enthusiasm in Ireland resulted in a nucleus of well-bred dogs there which have since resulted in the salvation of the breed.

Like all other big breeds, the period immediately following the Armistice proved a hazardous one for Deerhounds. However, "Duich of Springfort", an Irish-bred hound, born in the restricted era, was found near Dublin, and proved an immediate success at stud. Himself the sire of three champions, his son, Ch. "Tragic of Ross", may be said to have restored the breed to its pre-war eminence.

STANDARD OF THE DEERHOUND.

HEAD. — The head should be broadest at the ears, tapering slightly to the eyes, with the muzzle tapering more decidedly to the nose. The muzzle should be pointed, but the teeth and lips level. The head should be long ; the skull flat, rather than round, with a very slight rise over the eyes, but with nothing approaching a stop. The skull should be coated with moderately long hair, which is softer than the rest of the coat. The nose should be black (though in some blue-fawns the colour is blue) and slightly aquiline. In the lighter-coloured dogs a black muzzle is preferred. There should be a good moustache of rather silky hair, and a fair beard.

EARS.—The ears should be set on high and, in repose, folded back like the Greyhounds, though raised above the head in excitement without losing the fold, and even in some cases semi-erect. A prick ear is bad. A big, thick ear, hanging flat to the head or heavily coated with long hair, is the worst of faults. The ear should be

[Sport and General.

ON THE ALERT.

Photo]

The Misses Loughrey's "Idric of Ross" and Ch. "Phorp of the Foothills" at Cruft's International Show in 1934. The latter won first pr ze and was the best Deerhound in the show.

soft, glossy, and like a mouse's coat to the touch ; the smaller it is the better. It should have no long coat or long fringe, but there is often a silky, silvery coat on the body of the ear and the tip. Whatever the general colour, the ears should be black or dark-coloured.

NECK AND SHOULDERS.—The neck should be long —that is, of the length that befits the Greyhound character of the dog. An over-long neck is not necessary nor desirable, for the dog is not required to stoop to his work like a Greyhound, and it must be remembered that the mane, which every good specimen should have, detracts from the apparent length of neck. Moreover, a Deerhound requires a very strong neck to hold a stag. The nape of the neck should be very prominent where the head is set on, and the throat should be clean cut at the angle, and prominent. The shoulder should be well sloped, the blades well back and not too much width between them. Loaded and straight shoulders are very bad faults.

TAIL.—Should be tolerably long, tapering, and reaching to within about $1\frac{1}{2}$ inches off the ground. When the dog is still, dropped perfectly straight down, or curved. When in motion, it should be curved when excited, but in no case to be lifted out of the line of the back. It should be well covered with hair on the inside, thick and wiry, underside longer, and towards the end a slight fringe not objectionable. A curl or ring tail is very undesirable.

EYES.—The eyes should be dark ; generally speaking, they are dark-brown or hazel. A very light eye is not liked. The eye is moderately full, with a soft look in repose, but a keen, far-away look when the dog is roused. The rims of the eyelids should be black.

BODY.—The body and general formation is that of a Greyhound of larger size and bone. Chest, deep rather than broad, but not too narrow and flat-sided. The loins well arched, and drooping to the tail. A straight back is not desirable, this formation being unsuitable for going up-hill, and very unsightly.

LEGS AND FEET.—The legs should be broad and flat, and good broad forearm and elbow being desirable. Forelegs, of course, as straight as

possible. Feet close and compact, with well-arranged toes. The hindquarters drooping and as broad and powerful as possible, the hips being set wide apart. The hindlegs should be well bent at the stifle, with great length from the hip to the hock, which should be broad and flat. Cow-hocks, weak pasterns, straight stifles and splay feet are very bad faults.

COAT.—The hair on the body, neck, and quarters should be harsh and wiry and about three or four inches long ; that on the head, breast and belly is much softer. There should be a slight hairy fringe on the inside of the fore- and hindlegs, but nothing approaching the "feather" of the Collie. The Deerhound should be a shaggy dog, but not over-coated. A woolly coat is bad. Some good strains have a mixture of silky coat with the hard, which is preferable to a woolly coat ; but the proper coat is a thick, close-lying, ragged coat, harsh or crisp to the touch.

Photo] "REVIS OF ROTHERWOOD". *[Fall.*
A nicely bred Deerhound, one of Miss Hartley's kennel, standing well at attention.

COLOUR.—Colour is much a matter of fancy. But there is no manner of doubt that the dark blue-grey is the most preferred. Next comes the darker and lighter greys or brindles (the darkest being generally preferred), yellow and sandy-red or red-fawn, especially with black points, i.e. ears and muzzles are also in equal estimation, this being the colour of the oldest known strains— the McNeill and Chesthill Menzies. White is condemned by all the old authorities, but a white chest and white toes, occurring as they do in a great many of the darkest-coloured dogs, are not so greatly objected to, but the less the better, as the Deerhound is a self-coloured dog. A white blaze on the head or a white collar should entirely disqualify. In other cases, though passable, yet an attempt should be made to get rid of white markings. The less white the better, but a slight white tip to the stern occurs in the best strains.

HEIGHT of dogs should be not less than 30 inches, or even more if there be symmetry without coarseness. Height of bitches, 28 inches upwards. There can be no objection to a bitch being large, unless too coarse, as even at her greatest height

Photo] CH. "AETHETIC OF ROSS". [*Fall.*

The Misses M. F. and H. M. Loughrey, of Ireland, are two leading owners of Deerhounds.   Ch. "Aethetic of Ross" is a very good type.

Photo] CH. "PADRAIC OF ROSS". [*Fall.*

A good picture of this well-built Deerhound, showing clearly the desired type.   He is one of the Misses Loughrey's kennel.

she does not approach that of the dog, and, therefore, could not have been too big for work, as over-big dogs are. Besides, a big bitch is good for breeding and keeping up the size.

WEIGHT.—From 80 to 105 lb.

Defaecation.—The natural evacuation of the contents of the bowels. (*See* CONSTIPATION, DIARRHOEA, AND DIGESTION, MECHANISM OF.)

Degeneration.—Deterioration, or change from a higher to a lower form, especially change of tissue to a lower or less functionally active form. The widespread degenerative changes that occur in old age are known as senile degeneration. In fatty degeneration there is an abnormal deposit of fat globules in a tissue which, by their presence, materially weaken the functional activity of the tissue cells.

There are many other types of degenerative change, but their description would hardly appear to be appropriate to this work. The causes are varied and not always patent, but heredity, senility, injury, disease, poisons, and starvation are among the well-known causes.

Delirium.—A mental disturbance marked by cerebral excitement and physical restlessness, accompanied probably by howling or barking. The animal seems quite unconscious of its surroundings, pays no attention to people it knows nor to their spoken word. It dashes about, apparently unseeing, and frequently injures itself very severely. Delirium occurs as a result of high fever, disease or injury. Beyond intimating that potent nerve sedatives should be prescribed, treatment must be left to a practitioner. (*See* HYSTERIA.)

Demodectic Mange. (*See* SKIN DISEASES.)

Demulcent.—A soothing and bland, mucilaginous or oily substance, for internal or external application, which allays the irritation of inflamed or abraded surfaces. The principal demulcents are glycerin, gum arabic, gum tragacanth, linseed, Irish moss, Iceland moss, licorice, sassafras, slippery elm, starch paste, arrowroot, olive oil, isinglass, and barley gruel. They are often given internally to counteract the irritating effects of corrosive poisons, acids, etc.; and externally as soothing protectives after burns or other injuries.

Dentine. (*See* TEETH.)

Dentition.—A term indicating the kind, number, and arrangement of the teeth, as well as the study of the manner and time of eruption of the deciduous and permanent teeth. By eruption is meant the first appearance of teeth through the gums. From one to about four months of age only temporary or milk teeth are present in the mouth. The characteristics of these teeth are their watery-milk colour, their sharp-pointedness and slender structure. The corner or "canine" teeth are particularly curved. Then between four and five-and-a-half months the permanent teeth commence to push through, incisors being first to appear. It may be at the sixth or seventh month of age before all milk teeth have entirely disappeared. The permanent teeth quite commonly grow alongside the temporary ones, and dog-owners are frequently perturbed because the milk teeth do not drop out and make room for the secondary teeth. In nearly every case, however, Nature takes its ordinary and correct course, and there is no occasion for operative interference.

One peculiar characteristic of the dog's teeth is the shape of the incisors, especially when they are newly erupted, this having been likened to a *fleur-de-lys*. At about twelve months of age, however, the middle cusp of the *fleur-de-lys* has usually become worn down a bit, so far as the two centre teeth are concerned. At the expiration of a further year, the middle cusps will probably have departed from all the incisor teeth. Thus a dog's age may be approximately ascertained up to about two years of age, after which one must judge age by the degree of wear and of discoloration. Experience only can afford any sort of idea of the dog's age thereafter, except by observation of other signs associated with advancing years. (*See also* AGE, HOW TO TELL IT; *and* ANATOMY.)

Deodorants.—Chemicals or other substances which destroy or lessen odours, or replace objectionable ones by those of a more powerful or pleasant nature. They effect this, on the one hand, by killing, or preventing the multiplication of, germs which are responsible for generating nauseous gases; on the other hand, by oxidizing fermenting material. In distemper hospitals, where the inmates are continually giving off noxious odours, a deodorant is very essential, and one has a great choice. The dusting about the floor of chloride of lime; the use of "Sanitas" sawdust; or the sprinkling of Sanitas fluid or of Izal or Jeyes' Fluid; or the heating of creosote in a shallow pan, are various methods of deodorizing a kennel. Fresh air is always the best deodorant, but in sick wards its entry must be very carefully regulated.

Depilatory.—A substance which has the power to remove hair. The chief depilatories are arsenic, calcium sulphate, and quicklime. Depilation occurs in dogs, however, by the scalding action of tears when they are continuously flowing, as occurs in cases of conjunctivitis and entropion, etc. Discharges from any part will exert a similar effect when they run over the skin. Boiling water, acids, and other agents very rapidly remove hair when they come into contact with the skin, and in some cases the hair never grows again, as its roots have been killed.

Depraved Appetite.—It is of frequent occurrence for veterinary surgeons to be asked why dogs persist in consuming all kinds of filth. The CAUSES of this phenomenon are many and various. For instance, teething, hunger, indigestion, and worms are all believed to be implicated, though perhaps a lack of essential salts in the food may play an important part. Perfectly healthy puppies, however, do not evince the least compunction in eating the dung of almost any animal, apparently as a result of an inborn filthy depravity. They will, on the other hand, consume bits of wood, rags, needles and cotton, coal (especially coke) and grass. When the cause is indigestion, the effect of eating such objects is to aggravate the condition.

TREATMENT.—Like most other abnormalities, it is best treated by prevention, so that if the causes can be ascertained, their elimination is essential and no other steps need be taken. Certainly it will be wise to purge the bowel of its effete matter, treat for

[*Ralph Robinson.*

THE FAMILY.

A very unusual picture indeed, showing a Deerhound mother with two of her puppies, the property of Miss Richmond. The parent seems to be very proud indeed of her family.

Photo]   [Fall.

"RUPERT OF TROTTISCLIFFE".

Miss E. S. M. Branfoot, of Bransways, the well-known breeder of Bedlingtons, also specializes in Deerhounds.
Here is a distinguished member of her kennel.

suspected worms, and examine the droppings for signs of indigestion. When such signs are apparent, treat for that condition.

Young animals require a great deal of food, and can hardly tolerate being rationed to so many ounces. They seem to need their little stomachs comfortably full of good food to prevent them from filling them with injurious and extraneous substances.

The addition of common salt to the food may be all that is required, or one may need to add lime water, or even bicarbonate of soda. It is to-day thought that a lack of certain vitamins may play an important part in the causation of depraved appetite, and if this view is accepted it appears necessary to overhaul the ingredients of the animal's daily food.

An abundance of employment and exercise are essential; but as important as any, perhaps, is a watchful eye upon the slightest tendency to indulge in the vice, followed, upon detection, by chastisement. If horse droppings can be dusted with powdered aloes and the depraved puppy allowed to indulge as usual in its filthy habit, it will experience so disagreeable a taste that very few such experiences will suffice to make it a wiser dog.

Muzzling a dog when it is at liberty will mechanically prevent the habit.

Dermatitis. (*See* SKIN DISEASES.)

Destruction of Dogs.—Numerous people who consider themselves the very embodiment of humanity where animals are concerned, and far above suspicion of perpetrating a cruel act upon a dog, are nevertheless often the very ones who aid and abet such cruelty when the time arrives for the destruction of a pet. To save a few shillings they will entrust their dog to a "cat's meat man" or to a chemist for the performance of so-called painless destruction.

Some of these agents do not care, but the majority do not know the best manner in which to put a dog to sleep. Chemists have been known to administer strychnine for this purpose; and Heaven knows how the coarser and more ignorant type of man might perform the task. The burden of these remarks, therefore, is to urge the reader to employ the qualified canine surgeon when the unfortunate time at last arrives for him to part with his old pal.

There are several methods in which dogs may be painlessly destroyed, and perhaps the most popular one is that in which morphia is administered, followed about half- to three-quarters of an hour afterwards by the inhalation of chloroform. Chloroform may be given without preliminary morphia, but there is usually a great deal of resistance put up by the victim, and very frequently it takes a long time before the dog is unconscious, and much longer before life is extinct.

The oral administration of prussic acid is

exceedingly rapid in its effect, for a dog may be quite dead within twenty-five seconds. If this poison is injected into the chest the animal drops practically at once and is dead in about fifteen seconds. The only objection to this method of destruction appears to be the writhing and shrieking which sometimes occur in those few seconds ; but nobody seems, as yet, to have been able to decide whether such cries are due to pain or otherwise. It seems quite probable that pain is absent, and that the phenomena are caused by spasmodic contraction and tetany of the voluntary and respiratory muscles.

If prussic acid is administered half an hour after an injection of morphia, the animal passes away absolutely peacefully and almost instantly.

Shooting is undoubtedly the most rapid and painless method of all, but one's aim must be accurate. A special captive-bolt pistol has recently been introduced for use on small animals ; yet it is feared the method will never be a popular one.

A new electrocution device has also been fashioned and installed at one or two centres, and reports received of its efficiency for the small animals are very encouraging.

Lethal chambers are much esteemed in the popular mind because of the universal belief that destruction by their aid is absolutely painless. Physical pain, doubtless, is quite eliminated, but the writer considers that there is, for many nervous dogs, a dreadful period of anxiety and fright coupled with strenuous efforts to become free from the close confines of a box filled with strange and noxious fumes.

A word should be said against the levity with which many poor dogs are condemned to death in consequence of some ailment which is, too frequently, *believed* to be incurable. Veterinary science has made wonderful advances during the past few years and many diseases which, a short time ago, might have been gravely regarded, are now dealt with quite successfully. It is feared that in many cases, too, some callous owners prefer the easier course of destruction to the one which entails some little trouble to themselves. In other cases, suffering animals get into the hands of quacks who, from a deplorable ignorance of veterinary medicine, are quite unable to diagnose the complaint and recommend destruction rather than admit their failure or risk the the loss of a fee.

Numbers of people have been met too, who, because a dog may be temporarily suffering pain, can think of no other way out than to destroy it. It would be hard upon the human being if, because he was in pain, he should be condemned to eternity.

What is good treatment for man is also good for his dog, and even a dog will cling to life.

Detergent.—A cleansing agent such as soap, spirit, ether, or any substance capable of removing dirt.

Photo]   "EUAM OF BRIDGE SOLLERS".   [*Fall.*
Miss E. M. R. Reoch is a breeder of Deerhounds, the old breed from which the Irish Wolfhounds were developed.
463

IP

Dewclaws.—The dewclaw is on the fifth or rudimentary toe, which is situated on the inner surface of either the fore- or hindlegs, just above the foot. It is the counterpart of the thumb in man, but has no such useful function; in fact, it is generally more of a nuisance than of utility. So far as pet dogs are concerned, the dewclaws become caught up in lace, or other articles of human clothing, and are very often made to bleed in consequence of becoming broken or torn. Racing Greyhounds quite frequently injure them severely during races. It is more common to find dewclaws on the fore-feet than on the hind; but in some cases they appear on all four legs. Their removal is recommended preferably when the puppy is about a week old. Should the operation be deferred or overlooked until the dog has become adult, then it must be performed under local anaesthesia. In many instances the dewclaw has a bony attachment necessitating, in fully grown dogs, a certain amount of delicate dissection. In other cases, the appendage is held only by a fold of skin, rendering removal much easier, but still needing the use of a local anaesthetic. In all cases (except in the suckling-puppy stage) a veterinary surgeon should perform the operation, particularly because a large blood-vessel passes very close to the root of the dewclaw.

Dewlap.—The loose, pendulous skin under a dog's chin.

Diabetes.—A disease, the essential character of which is the passage of an abnormal quantity of urine. Dogs are quite commonly affected, and the prognosis is not by any means good. There are two kinds of diabetes, viz.: *Diabetes Mellitus* and *D. Insipidus*, and it is very important that a correct differential diagnosis should be made.

D. Mellitus, also known as Glycosuria, on account of its salient feature being the presence of grape sugar in the urine.

CAUSES.—Research, in comparatively recent years, has established that this type of diabetes is due to disease of the pancreatic gland, the internal secretion,

or hormone, of which has the power (in simple words) of preventing the escape of sugar from the body. Apparently, certain cells of the pancreas pour out a secretion into the blood-stream which has been named *Insulin*, but should its presence fail, diabetes is the result.

"In diabetes the sugar in the blood, instead of being 0.1 per cent, as it normally is, may rise to 0.4 or even as high as 0.7 or 1 per cent. In consequence of the tissues being unable to consume the dextrose brought to them, the sugar passes off by the urine, and the body is starved of its source of heat and energy. As the disease advances, not only sugar, but products of deranged protein and fat metabolism, appear in the urine, such as acetone, etc. These acids, by combining with the alkali of the blood, produce the condition known as acidosis, and reduce the carbon-dioxide-carrying capacity of the fluid; in consequence, the carbon dioxide accumulates in the tissues, and diabetic coma results."—(Smith.)

Temporary Glycosuria occasionally arises from brain injury or from the administration of certain drugs, as chloroform, ether, etc.

SYMPTOMS.—A greatly increased thirst and output of urine. The latter, when chemically tested, reveals the presence of sugar which normally should not be excreted by the kidneys. There may be an excessive appetite too; but in spite of the fact that every desire for food or drink is gratified, the patient becomes progressively wasted and eventually emaciated. The course of the disease is long and slow, during which the animal becomes perceptibly weaker and more easily fatigued. Sometimes cataract, or inflammation of the cornea of the eye, may occur as complications.

TREATMENT.—The diet should consist almost solely of meat. Eggs, bran-bread and occasional green vegetable may also be allowed; but the patient should not have milk, sweets, sugar, cereals, dog biscuits, potatoes, white bread or any starchy food. The only medicinal treatment of any use whatsoever is a daily injection of insulin for the rest of the dog's life, and this must be prescribed, regulated, and

Photo] A WINNING TEAM. *[Fall.*
The three Deerhounds shown here are Ch. "Bran of Bridge Sollers", with "Hector" and "Solomon", all of the famous Bridge Sollers breed.

Photo]

DEERHOUND HEADS.

[Fall.

The Rough-haired Greyhound of the North goes well with the scenery of its native home.   Here is a head study of two of
Miss Lynton's kennel.

Photo]

CH. "PHORP OF THE FOOTHILLS".

[Fall

A head study of this well-known champion, the property of the Misses Loughrey.

administered by a qualified man in order that he may watch the reactions—if any—which might occur. The writer has tried the feeding daily with raw pancreatic gland, but owing always to the dog-owner's decision, sooner or later, to have the animal put to sleep, he is still left in doubt as to the efficacy of such a procedure.

D. Insipidus.—Also known as Polyuria. In this case there is also an excessive thirst and excretion of urine, but the latter is devoid of sugar. The cause is not well recognized, but has been thought to be the ingestion of certain moulds or fungi. Animals so affected may also lose weight, although feeding very well; but emaciation is not a constant symptom. Quite recently a Scottish Terrier was encountered with

discern in their actions and objective signs. It is true, however, that our patients tell us no lies, and we cannot be misled by any endeavour on their part to put us "off the scent". Nevertheless, it is easy to imagine how very hard indeed it sometimes becomes to determine with any certainty what ails the sick dog which is presented for treatment. The dog, although dumb, is sometimes far more eloquent than its owner, for the latter is often quite unable to describe any symptoms, or relate any history of the case which is calculated to be of the slightest value in forming an opinion.

Some clients really believe that a diagnosis should be given in a few minutes, but actually the diagnosis which is of greatest value is that which is based upon

Photo]   [*Ralph Robinson.*

ON GUARD.

Two handsome representatives of Miss Richmond's Deerhound Kennel are seen in the wild country of the moors, very similar to certain parts of Scotland.

this disease, and he was in very good bodily condition, although he had been affected for six weeks. Very soon afterwards, however, an obstinate diarrhoea, with occasional vomiting, set in, and as all kinds of treatment appeared to have no salutary effect, the owner decided (as usual) to have the dog destroyed.

Diagnosis.—The art of distinguishing one disease from another, or of recognizing the disease from which a given patient is suffering. In the practice of medicine and surgery, diagnosis presents the most difficult problem with which the practitioner is confronted, and usually is the one great primary hurdle over which the charlatan and quack can never jump. The diagnosis of disease among animals is even more difficult than it is among human beings, because our dumb patients impart no information to us except that which, by years of training, we are enabled to

some amount of observation of the patient during twenty-four or more hours, combined, of course, with the performance of all forms of clinical enquiry. Many of the canine, agricultural, and society journals have their veterinary advice columns, to which readers are invited to submit their queries for reply. These columns were, however, never intended to be used for the supposed diagnosis of disease; and frankly, it cannot be done.

Great advances have been made in recent years by the veterinary profession in the matter of diagnosis, and to-day there obtains a much finer appreciation of the significance of symptoms, and a disposition to seek far deeper for their origin. It is not customary to accept the surface or obvious signs, as indicating any particular condition, without deeper investigation or, in other words, without exercising a greater precision in diagnosis. Two examples of

CHARACTERISTICS.

Miss B. Branfoot is not only a well-known breeder of Deerhounds, but also a clever artist. She has made these drawings specially for this Encyclopaedia. They depict these fascinating Hounds in all sorts of characteristic moods and attitudes.

what is meant readily come to one's mind, for in the one case a dog which continuously vomits might erroneously be thought—by the untutored or inexperienced—to be suffering from gastritis ; whereas by exercising more modern methods, an examination of the urine might reveal that the dog was actually affected by kidney disease. In the second example, skin eruptions and irritations might be ascribed to simple eczema when, in fact, a microscopical examination would reveal mange or other parasites. The many and varied methods of diagnosing disease are taken full advantage of, so far as is possible, with the lower animals.

The thermometer is, of course, invaluable and in everyday use for ascertaining fluctuations in temperature ; the microscope is freely employed for the examination of skin scrapings, blood samples, urinary deposits, pus and other discharges, and faeces. The last named is searched usually for the microscopic eggs of worms in order to determine whether worms exist.

Stethoscopes for the sounding of the lungs and heart ; electrically illuminated ophthalmoscopes for the examination of the interior of the eye ; electrical specula for inspection of the ear, mouth, rectum and other cavities, are but a few examples of the diagnostic instruments available for the use of the modern veterinary surgeon. The chemical tests of urine for sugar or for albumen, have been simplified and improved, and are extremely important. The presence of poisons in the intestinal contents, or saliva, etc., is, however, still a specialist undertaking relegated to the analyst.

Tuberculosis may be detected in an animal by certain biological tests, which will be referred to more fully under TUBERCULOSIS. Similarly, a more lengthy exposition of the value of radiography will be given under the heading of X-RAYS. It is sufficient for the moment to indicate how exceedingly useful X-ray photography has become in the elucidation of obscure and undetectable conditions. Even ultraviolet rays are being increasingly employed as a ready means of diagnosing ringworm. Further reference will be made under the heading of SKIN DISEASES (RINGWORM).

As a means of ascertaining the seat of pain in a limb, the injection of local anaesthetics over nerves supplying certain areas, is often invaluable. For instance, should one of the digits be suspected of causing lameness, one can completely numb that digit, when all lameness should disappear and one's suspicions would be confirmed.

No mention has been made of the many laboratory or biological tests which can be performed in aid of diagnosis, as these are usually no concern of the clinician. But sufficient of the practical and routine methods of diagnosis will probably have been mentioned to convince the dog-owner that the study of canine disease is marching forward abreast of all other branches of medicine and surgery.

Diaphragm.—A broad, flat muscle which forms the partition between the thorax (or chest) and the abdominal cavity. Its circumference is composed of contractile muscular fibres whilst its centre is tendinous. On its anterior surface are the lungs and on its posterior surface the liver. It plays an important rôle in the respiratory process. Spasm of this muscle causes the well-known symptom—hiccup.

Diarrhoea.—This term signifies the abnormally frequent opening of the bowels, and the passage of softened or fluid faeces.

CAUSES.—The causes are very many, and in some cases are quite obscure. All of the following may produce the symptom of diarrhoea : Worms ; coccidiosis ; indigestible foods, such as an excess of fibrous green vegetable ; wet or sloppy foods ; chills (intestinal catarrh) ; consumption of garbage and decomposing foodstuffs ; poisons ; frights ; distemper ; tuberculosis ; chronic enteritis ; colitis ; and the presence of foreign bodies in the bowel, etc. etc.

SYMPTOMS.—The frequent passage of very liquid and usually offensive motions. There is often a good deal of straining at each defaecation which, in the case of young puppies, not infrequently leads to eversion of the rectum. The bowels and anus feel raw and sore, causing a good deal of dejection in the patient. When the condition has existed some little time the animal begins to lose flesh and becomes distinctly debilitated, which is manifested by its revulsion for food, lack of interest in its surroundings, and increasing weakness. As the two most frequent causes of diarrhoea are worms and distemper, it behoves the owner of a dog so affected to obtain a diagnosis as soon as possible. Distemper is quite frequently ushered in by uncomplicated diarrhoea, and since it is contagious, the animal should be isolated and carefully watched.

TREATMENT.—Diet is very important in this condition, and if the dog has been on a sloppy diet, this should be changed for dry food. Meat is credited with having a relaxing effect upon the bowel, but in many instances it has been found to suit affected dogs far better than milk and milky foods. Milk has, in fact, proved somewhat irritating in certain cases, especially when the stools are acid and have a sour odour. Charcoal biscuits are excellent fare, as also are well-cooked arrowroot or cornflour and blanc-mange. The diet should, in short, be digestible, bland and unirritating. If there is no appetite, and milk is given, one may add to it from one to two tablespoonfuls of lime water to each half-pint, or the milk may be peptonized.

Rather than offer plain tap-water to drink, give the dog barley-water, made without lemon or other flavouring ; or the whites of two eggs may be added to a small bowl of barley-water, stirring only gently. The dog will lap this up in his own time. At the same time, it would be wise to restrict the amount of water consumed, and if the animal is easily managed, white of egg in a little water may be given forcibly at intervals.

It is very necessary to curtail outdoor exercise, in fact, it is advised that the patient be not taken for any walks whatever. He should be kept warm, dry, and at rest. Hot packs to the abdomen are very useful. So far as medicinal remedies are concerned, it is highly desirable at the outset to ask a veterinary surgeon to ascertain the cause of the condition, for upon this will depend the remedy. A preliminary dose of castor-oil may be wise if the condition is due to the eating of some dead bird, rat, or other filth ; on the other hand, it might be very unwise if the diarrhoea is due to an inflamed and very irritable bowel. Should the cause be apparently a simple chill, then the usual astringents (such as chalk, bismuth, etc.) would be prescribed ; or if a bacterial infection is suspected, then intestinal disinfectants would be indicated. Possibly a vermifuge might cut the attack short, but the veterinary surgeon in attendance would be able to ascertain the presence of worms by microscopical examination of the faeces for worm eggs. In the same way he would detect coccidia.

AFTER CHEVY CHASE.

Here is the old Deerhound in company with its Bloodhound companion, evincing that fidelity which is a glowing characteristic of both dogs. They have found their dead master after the famous battle, and who can call these dumb animals when eyes are so expressive ? This fine painting is by H. Dicksee, and hangs in Bentley Manor, Worcester.

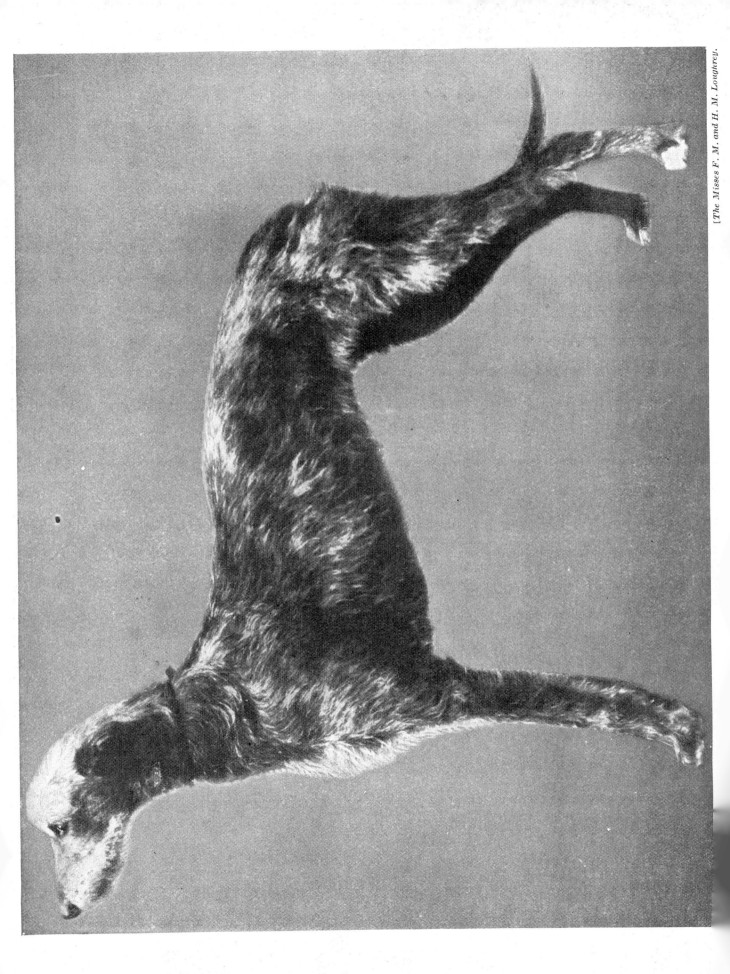

Thus, the reader may begin to realize that even so apparently simple a condition as diarrhoea may prove to be complicated, and that no rule-of-thumb measure exists for its treatment. Each case must be prescribed for on its merits. It has been the writer's experience, in a large number of cases, that diarrhoea is a serious and very refractory condition.

Diathermy.—The application to the body of electrical currents of low tension and high amperage, which produce great warmth of the deeper tissues and thereby relieve pain. On account of the extremely high frequency of the diathermy current, nothing in the nature of a shock, or even discomfort, is felt by the patient. It is a comparatively new method of treatment, having particular value against all rheumatic conditions, and is rapidly being perfected and cheapened for use among the lower animals.

For surgical diathermy a slightly modified apparatus is required, and by its use the most vascular organs or growths can be removed absolutely bloodlessly. When the delicate platinum knife is applied to a tissue, it is remarkable to see the solid flesh fall away on either side, just as though one was cutting a block of butter with a red-hot blade. Undoubtedly there is a big future for this curative electrical treatment.

Dietary. (*See* FOODS AND FEEDING.)

Digestion, Mechanism of.

—Very briefly stated, the function of the alimentary canal is to receive and prepare the food (i.e. in the mouth) and break it down into a fluid state by subjecting it to various digestive juices. The nutritive and valuable portions are then absorbed into the blood and lymphatic systems, and the indigestible residue is passed on to the anus, where it is evacuated. The passage of food during the process of digestion is accomplished by what is known as "peristalsis", or waves of muscular contraction which commence from the pharyngeal end of the gullet (throat) and travel backwards to the anus—thus driving the alimentary contents slowly along. This explains why man or dog can still swallow solids or liquids even though hanging head downwards, and the food having thus to rise vertically.

Food given to a dog is first masticated, or broken up into smaller particles, by the teeth. In the case of meat, fish, or other flesh, most dogs do not attempt mastication, but just bolt it whole.

Their jaws have very little lateral movement, which precludes any possibility of their grinding their food (as herbivorous animals do) even had their teeth

flat grinding surfaces. Therefore the first process of digestion, namely, the thorough mixing of food with saliva, is nearly absent in the dog. Salivary secretion, however, does take place, and the saliva gives the food a slimy coating, serving to lubricate its passage to the stomach. When the food has reached the stomach, an opportunity is afforded to the salivary juice to exert its digestive action upon starches, converting them into maltose and dextrin.

Food remains in the stomach of the dog for several hours, up to a maximum of about twelve hours.

The pyloric sphincter (or valve controlling the exit of food) remains closed until the food has been acted upon for a sufficiency of time by the peptic or gastric juices. If meat is fed to a dog in large pieces, gastric digestion is much slower than when the meat has been cut up for, obviously, the smaller pieces offer a greater area of surface upon which digestive juices can exert an influence. Fat does not undergo much change in the stomach, as it has not yet come in contact with the juices which have a special action upon it. The gastric juice of the dog is strongly acid in reaction (hydrochloric acid) to which fact its antiseptic properties are attributed. Pepsin is one of the constituents of gastric juice and exerts an action, almost wholly if not entirely, upon the protein constituents of food.

Milk is digested but slowly, and the second enzyme of gastric juice, viz., rennin, is the secretion which clots milk into curds, and a fluid known as whey.

THE EMPTY CHAIR.
A typical old-fashioned Deerhound grieving at the loss of its master : an appealing picture by A. Scott Rankin, which attracted much notice at the Royal Academy some years ago.

Food passes out of the stomach in small quantities, and very slowly, into the first part of the small intestines, namely, the duodenum. It is gradually impelled along by peristaltic waves or muscular contractions, being added to *en route* by the bile and pancreatic fluids. It passes through the jejunum into the third portion, or ileum, at the end of which is another valve controlling its admittance into the large bowel or colon.

Digestion is mainly carried on in the small bowel, all solid particles becoming emulsified and nutritive portions being absorbed into the lacteal and circulatory systems. The first action of bile is to neutralize the acid gastric juice and to precipitate the albumoses and peptones. Bile has a solvent and emulsifying effect on fats, being materially assisted in this action by the pancreatic juice. An abnormal decrease in the amount of bile permits rapid putrefaction to occur in the bowels, resulting in constipation, pale clay-like faeces, and extreme foetor of the intestinal contents. This is partly due to the fact that peristalsis slows down when bile is absent, and partly to the fact that fats have not been acted upon and have undergone rapid putrefaction. The liver regulates the supply of sugar to the system and stores up as glycogen what is not required. It guards the system against the formation of nitrogenous poisons, such as ammonia, by transforming them into urea; and it is noteworthy that many metallic poisons are also arrested in the liver, e.g. mercury and arsenic.

The pancreatic juice has a digestive action upon the three classes of foodstuffs, viz., proteins, fats and carbohydrates. Under the heading DIABETES, a description will be found of the manner in which the pancreatic gland controls the output of sugar from the liver.

Practically no digestion occurs in the large intestine, but a good deal of absorption of fluid takes place, thereby causing the undigested fibrous residue to take solid shape. These solids or faeces eventually arrive at the rectum, denuded of every particle of value, and are finally expelled through the anus by the muscular contractions of the rectal walls.

Photo]   [*H. Bastin.*

YOUNGSTERS.

Three youthful Dingos about six months old, enjoying rest and sunshine on a comfortable box.

Digestive Canal.—Also known as the alimentary canal. As is signified by its name, this canal is concerned with aliment or food, and it consists of mouth, throat, gullet, stomach, small intestine, large intestine (or colon) and rectum, in this order from head to tail. Most of it is contained in the abdominal cavity, only a portion of the oesophagus or gullet, the pharynx, and the mouth, being excluded therefrom. As compared with the herbivorous animals, the dog's alimentary canal is short. The portion having the greatest length is the intestines, and these do not usually exceed about 5 yards. The stomach, on the other hand, is comparatively large and has a capacity of from $1\frac{1}{4}$ pints to $1\frac{3}{4}$ gallons, with an average of $2\frac{1}{2}$ quarts. It is manifestly impossible to give any but very approximate figures in view of the tremendous variation in the sizes of dogs.

Contiguous with the alimentary canal, and forming part of the digestive apparatus, are the liver, pancreas, and salivary glands. The size of the liver may be assessed generally at about 5 per cent of the dog's body weight. The ducts leading from the liver and pancreas, and which convey the secretions of these glands, open separately into the duodenum within a very short distance of one another.

Digitalis.—When we see the graceful wild foxgloves growing along the countryside, we either do not know or are apt to forget what a wonderfully useful drug they yield, for it is from foxgloves that the alkaloid known as Digitalin is extracted. When given to the living animal, either by mouth or injection, it exerts a specific action upon involuntary muscle fibres—and particularly those of the heart and the arteries. When the force of the heart-beat (i.e. its muscular contractions) has, for any reason, become enfeebled, digitalis gives additional force and transforms a faint or flickering pulse into one of vigour. At the same time, should the heart be irritable and its contractions rapid, the drug slows it down by causing a longer interval between the beats. It therefore is invaluable in cases of debility or convalescence following severe illnesses. Chronic coughs in old dogs, which so frequently arise in consequence of defective heart action, are often much improved by a short course of tonics containing digitalis. Another distinct attribute is the increased elimination of urine, thereby decreasing abnormal collections of fluid in the tissues or in the two great cavities of the body. Abdominal dropsy and pleurisy with effusion are two conditions which would be benefited by administration of digitalis.

The drug is very bitter, and when the tincture is given in water it is best sweetened with glycerine or some other disguising agent. It can, of course, be given in pill form, but tinctures always seem to retain their full strength for a longer time, and also are absorbed quicker. Digitalis is poisonous, and the medicinal dose must not be exceeded, nor should the drug be administered over too long a period.

Dingo.—The Dingo is a dog of mystery, for no one is certain whether it is an actual wild dog or not; many believing it to be a feral dog, that is to say, one that has returned to the wild from a

Photo]   [*H. Bastin.*

TAILS UP.

Dingos seem to have no set fashions as regards tail-carriage. This one, an authentic specimen, carries its tail proudly curled over the back, and not in the recognised wolf manner.

VERY MUCH AT HOME.

This particular Dingo is evidently tame and harmless, explaining why some specimens of the breed have achieved a considerable degree of domesticity.

A TRUNKFUL OF MISCHIEF.

Five of a litter of seven Dingo puppies, born at the London Zoo, in April 1932. It is interesting to learn that, like wolves, they lift their noses in the air to howl, which is a matter of habit and not of melancholy.

condition of domestication. The first time this dog was seen was, so Ash tells us, in 1688, when William Dampier, landing, was met by "two or three beasts like hungry wolves, so lean as to be as many skeletons, being nothing more than so much skin and bones". Interesting, indeed, showing that Dampier knew that they were not wolves but dogs. They were smaller than the wolf and nothing like so strong in build ; they had not the appearance of the wolf or its savagery, and their legs were longer. Later explorers reported more of such doglike creatures, and when man with his flocks arrived, then the Dingo no longer starved.

This breed stood about 24 inches at the shoulder, the same average height as an Alsatian dog. The tail was bushy, and the long coat was yellow, although some were black. The undercoat was grey and close. A remarkable thing · was noticed — that the Dingo frequently had white feet and a spot of white at the very end of its tail. This probably accounts for the suggestion that the breed was not a wild dog ; except that, in generations of freedom, it lost its knowledge of mankind.

Photo]   WHAT'S UP ?   *[W. S. Berridge.*
These two Dingo puppies are rather suspicious of the camera man's activities. Note the expression and attitude of the one on the left. The eyes give away their feelings.

Found in the wooded areas of Australia it was very numerous during early settler days ; indeed, it was a great nuisance to them, always destroying their stock ; so that a war was waged until the Dingo was seldom seen. But the settlers soon discovered that the Dingo was doglike, even to its remarkable fidelity. The same author tells us how a Mr. Oxley killed a Dingo and threw the body on a small bush. Returning that way a week later, he found that the carcase of the dead Dingo was gone, but discovered it lying a few yards farther on. Against it lay a female in a dying state, weakened from want of food and water. She had stayed by the dog the entire week, and no doubt had pulled him down from the bush and was attempting to take him along with her.

People seldom saw this breed, except in traps, for they hid away in the woods all day, coming out only at night to hunt, when parties of five or six, that is to say, a family of mother and her puppies, might be met pursuing their work of devastation. Often families would unite to form packs or troops to as many as a hundred head.

It is said that the Dingo in New Holland was domesticated by the natives. These dogs, although they lived quite happily with the savages, did not bark, nor were they able to growl or howl, but, if offended, would raise their hair nearly upright and assume a very ferocious appearance. The puppies were easily taken ; for the bitches usually had their families in a hollow tree. Later, after the natives introduced the white man's dog, the tame Dingo learned to bark! In 1889, on the Herbert River, the natives valued the Dingo and were always looking for litters of puppies, which they then carried to their huts and reared with their own children and with great kindness. They let them sleep in the huts and fed them well, giving them both flesh and fish. All was well until the breeding season, when the tame Dingos would slip away from the camp, back to the wild. Often that was the last seen of them. They had very keen scent, and were used for hunting ; the man picking up the Dingo as soon as it was tired and carrying it upon his shoulder. Like the dogs of Europe, they knew their own masters and would follow no one else. There is an interesting note as to the way they carried their tails—always horizontally and never curled. When watching and becoming intent they would carry them low, as do some of our domesticated dogs.

With the coming of civilized man, the Dingo met its brother, the white man's dog, and interbred with it. It is stated by Mivart that fossils of these dogs are to be found in the river gravels and in the cavern deposits of Australia, with and without human remains, and often associated with bones of extinct forms of life ; so it may be that the domestic dog came from Australia and that the Dingo is the last remnant of the wild ancestral dog. To back this up, we have the statement of Dr. Nehring (who has meticulously examined the skeleton of the Dingo), that it is not a domesticated dog returned to the wilds, but of an absolutely wild race.

Dingos have been brought to Europe and exhibited at shows and have, of course, been kept in the London Zoo. A litter of Dingo-puppies were very handsome and very playful, but, in the instance given, were by no means as docile as those of the ordinary dog. They would dig holes and try to burrow into the ground and would invariably attack poultry as soon as they saw any, persistently refusing to be broken of the habit.

Diphtheria.—This disease would not find a place in a work connected exclusively with dogs, were it not for the fact that there are some people who still believe that dogs suffer from diphtheria. This is a fallacy, and dog-owners need harbour no fear of diphtheritic contagion from their sick dogs. Scaremongers have often sought to prove that the domestic cat is a subject of this disease, but there again scientists have disproved the assertion, and have definitely established the fact that the "Klebs-Loeffler", or true bacillus of diphtheria, is never found naturally in the cat's throat.

Disease and its Causes.—By the term disease, is meant a departure, in some form or other, from the normal state of health. It is immaterial whether the animal is lame, has a wound, a growth, or a cold, or how insignificant the new condition may be ; if it is a state which is not common to the huge majority, then it is a disease. A disease may be contagious, that is to say, it may be spread from one individual to another through direct contact ; or indirectly through the healthy dog having access to food

Photo]　　　　　[W. S. Berridge.
TIMIDITY.
Wild creatures, when facing man, often show signs of timorousness in the expression of their eyes, as in the case of this Dingo.

dishes, kennels, blankets or other articles which the diseased dog had previously infected. Distemper and sarcoptic mange are good examples of a contagious disease. It differs thus from an infectious disease, the spread of which is not necessarily dependent upon contact with a sick patient or its discharges. The contagium of an infectious disease is as readily borne by the air as it is by any other means, and we have a good example in tuberculosis. Some diseases are both infectious and contagious, distemper coming under this category.

The symptoms evinced in bad health are so very numerous and diverse that it would be futile to make any attempt to enumerate them. Under the heading of HEALTHY DOGS will be found a fairly detailed description of what a dog should be when enjoying good health. Any departure from the picture outlined there should cause the owner immediately to investigate the matter.

CAUSES.—By far the greater number of diseased conditions are due to invasions of the body by pathogenic bacteria. Whilst it is perfectly true that these harmful germs are everywhere, and in daily contact with the living human and animal body, apparently without doing any damage, it has also to be realized that only a small contributory factor is necessary to enable them to gain an entrance and commence multiplication. For instance, the body may sustain a severe bruise or a cut, thereby breaking down or opening the tissues. In this way injuries may be looked upon as a direct cause of disease, for is it not well known to-day how a blow may be the forerunner of a cancerous growth ? Other and more immediate results of bites, scratches, cuts, burns and other mechanical violence are fractured bones (possibly followed by gangrene) ; abscesses ; tetanus or lockjaw ; septicaemia or blood poisoning ; shock ; and even death.

Starvation is a ready cause of disease, whether the body be deprived of food or water. All reserve supplies of fat become used up, there is no material available for the repair of tissue waste, nor even for the ordinary maintenance of body-heat and energy. Resistance to germs is much reduced, and the animal falls a ready prey to bronchitis, pneumonia, or any disease which happens to come along.

GOOD BUILD.
The shape of a Dingo, when well fleshed, is remarkable for its symmetrical proportions.

Gross over-exertion, too long continued, leads to exhaustion of the body generally, but particularly of the heart, and may be followed by a ruptured blood vessel or syncope.

Unhygienic conditions of life are very conducive to a breakdown in health. Nothing favours the growth of germs so well as darkness, damp, dirt and lack of ventilation ; and there would never seem to be any possible excuse for subjecting an animal to such faulty hygiene, however poor the owner may be. Rickets is a disease notoriously associated with such conditions, especially absence of sunlight ; and tuberculosis is easily induced by living continuously in a close, ill-ventilated atmosphere.

Disease may be hereditary (see HEREDITY), although it appears that the contagious or infectious diseases are not present in the offspring at the time of birth. The newly-born are, however, a suitable soil for the growth and multiplication of pathological organisms similar to those which have consistently attacked the forebears. The opportunity for becoming infected only too soon presents itself, especially if the dam is suffering from the disease at the time of whelping, for the puppy may not only inhale the germs but may ingest them in the mother's milk.

The non-contagious diseases may also be handed down by heredity, for, among other conditions, we find cleft-palate and hare-lip present in the whelps at birth. Cancer is hereditary but not contagious, and appears only later in life.

Internal parasites, such as the various worms, and flukes, are often the cause of serious illness, especially when they are present in large numbers. Fits, diarrhoea, inflammation and even impaction of the bowels are not infrequent sequels to worm infestation. Then the numerous external parasites constitute a formidable array of disease agents. Fleas and lice not only cause considerable discomfort and irritation, but frequently set up severe dermatitis and unthriftiness. Some of the biting flies and ticks are capable of transmitting very serious blood infections through the skin. (See PIROPLASMOSIS.) The fungus of ringworm, and the mites responsible for the two kinds of mange, nearly complete the long list of agents which may be blamed for a breakdown in the health of an animal. It will therefore be appreciated, probably, how essential it is—in face of all this evidence—to maintain perfect hygienic conditions, provide adequate and good food, and to guard the animal against the many deleterious influences which so soon conduce to illness.

How IT IS SPREAD.—Under the heading of

Photo]   *[W. S. Berridge.*
VERY YOUNG.
This photograph shows a Dingo junior barely three weeks old.
At this age the puppies are very small and soft and woolly.

"BACTERIA", a brief description of bacterial life was given, yet in view of their importance it is excusable to reiterate the ubiquity and extreme minuteness of germs, and to emphasize the subtle and insidious manner in which they gain entrance to the body and destroy its health. As a general rule, it requires a magnification of about 1000 in order to render germs visible under the microscope. Thus it will be appreciated that even in a tiny drop of sputum there may be present many thousands of organisms. Given conditions suitable to their growth, they multiply with extreme rapidity. Milk is an excellent medium for the purpose, and everyone knows how—in the hot, humid summer weather —milk will rapidly go bad. This is due entirely to the extraordinary multiplication of its contained bacteria, though all of the latter are not necessarily harmful to health. The law permits milk to be sold as fit for human consumption if the number of microbes in each cubic centimetre does not exceed 100,000.

However, that is by the way. What one wishes to impress is that the spread of the direst disease may be due to an ignorance of the above facts, or due to a failure to take effective measures when they *are* known. The contagious diseases are probably not so easily spread as the infectious ones ; in fact, it is well known in scientific circles that no disease is so rapidly spread as those infections which are caused by the ultra visible viruses. Foot-and-mouth disease of cattle, distemper of dogs, and measles of man, are highly infectious maladies which require no contact for their perpetuation.

Let us review for a moment the many small factors which, in practice, lead to the spread of disease. Suppose one has a small number of healthy dogs ; a new dog is bought one day, or a brood bitch comes in to "stud", and all exercise, feed and live together. The newcomer may appear to be in the best of health, but actually may be passing through the period of incubation of some infectious disease. One day its nose shows a slight watery discharge, or it evinces an occasional cough, or possibly diarrhoea. These discharges, faeces, or coughed-up spray contain harmful germs. They find their way into food and water dishes, on to one's boots, clothing, hands (especially beneath the finger-nails), and may at once be transmitted to any of the other dogs which are susceptible.

Contagium can be conveyed by people bringing the germs in from the street on their shoes ; or by washing an infected dish in the same water in which clean dishes are washed. All infective matter

Photo] DUTIFUL. [W. S. Berridge.

A Dingo mother feeding some of her litter of twelve days' old puppies. She is keenly on the watch to make sure that no enemy shall pounce upon her family.

Photo] A HANDSOME SPECIMEN. [W. S. Berridge.

This photograph of an Australian Dingo illustrates the likeness existing between this breed and the familiar Alsatian Dog.

falling on the ground eventually becomes dried, and later is disseminated by the wind in the general dust of the atmosphere. Since dogs, by nature, have their noses ever to the ground, here again is a ready means of contracting, not only germs, but the eggs of worms and other parasites. How common it is to see ladies, when out shopping with their dogs on leads, congregated around shop windows, quite unconscious of the fact that the dogs are sniffing each other and possibly contracting some ailment. It is not uncommon to see judges in the show-ring at dog shows opening one dog's mouth after another without any attempt at disinfection of their hands. It is assumed, we know, that the exhibits are healthy, but who can tell what an apparently healthy dog may be incubating ?

The herding together of numbers of animals, birds, or humans, is very conducive to the spread of disease, especially if the ventilation is inadequate; and when buildings are erected for the permanent housing of animals, one must ensure that no less than the minimum cubic air space for each animal is afforded.

The house-fly is a potent carrier of disease, and no one will deny that he works hard at it, for does he not from morning till night (and even all night) spend his time first on manure, putrefying material, dropped excretions, and filth of all kinds, and then on milk, meat, and clean aliment intended for consumption ? Think of the number of micro-organisms which could adhere to the foot of a fly—and he has six feet !

Mosquitos are responsible for the prevalence of malaria and yellow fever in man ; and in India the spread of plague is ascribed to the rat flea.

Mention of the rat flea reminds one of the disease-carrying propensity of the rat itself. These pests are subject to numerous diseases which also are pathogenic to dogs and humans, and it has been proved beyond all doubt that they readily spread them. Rats are particularly responsible for the dissemination of lepto-spiral jaundice among dogs.

PREVENTION OF.—If the reader has perused the preceding paragraphs dealing with the causes and spread of disease, then the methods of prevention will probably be self-evident to him. Briefly, however, they consist in the housing of the animal under the best hygienic conditions, which means adequate

Photo]   DINGO AT WHIPSNADE.   [*W. S. Berridge.*

Is there a difference between the domestic dog and the Dingo in appearance ? This picture answers the question. The reader will at once notice the suggestion of wildness.

sunlight, fresh air, cubic space, and absence of dirt and damp. It also entails a sufficiency of daily exercise, good food of the correct kind and amount, and the prevention of contact with sick animals. When symptoms of disease have been detected in a dog, the surest way of preventing its farther spread is to isolate the animal. Now, isolation to be effective must be absolutely thorough. It is insufficient to put the sick dog in another part of the house, or in a separated kennel, whilst the same person continues to feed well and unwell alike. The person who attends to the wants of the isolated dog should in no circumstances have access to any healthy dog or any premises where they exist. Infected dogs should not traverse ground upon which healthy ones will be exercised, and the isolated kennel should be self-contained so far as is possible ; that is to say, all food supplies should be kept and prepared on the spot. In addition, attendants should not have to fetch straw, sawdust, coal or water from a common store, but these should be especially provided for and stored in the isolation kennel. Grooming kit, collars, leads, harness, coats, dishes, etc., must be rigidly separated, and must be disinfected before they return to the common kennels.

Most extraordinary precautions are taken, at scientific experimental stations, to ensure that their healthy inmates cannot possibly become infected with any kind of disease germ. During the distemper investigations at Mill Hill, nobody can enter the compound without first stripping, bathing and emerging through another door into a compartment where a sterilized suit is provided for wear. Every window and doorway is flyproof, and the galvanized iron fencing, which surrounds the premises, is let into the ground three feet to prevent rats from getting in.

In a kennel of dogs, should one inmate be detected as suffering from a contagious disease, not only should that dog be isolated from the others, but all dogs which are known to have been in contact must be segregated until sufficient time has elapsed to prove whether or not they are going to develop the disease. Segregation means the housing of one or more dogs together in one kennel or compound, but apart and isolated from the healthy dogs.

It is realized that the ideal conditions cannot

always be complied with, and that in some cases no person can be spared whose duties shall consist only of attending to, perhaps, one dog. In such cases, the next best method is to supply the attendant with a long washable overall and gum-boots. These should be hung up outside the sick kennel and be put on before entering. Upon leaving, they are washed with disinfectant, and left in the same place for future use.

Lastly, in the prevention of disease, we have disinfection, and this is described fully under that heading. Disinfectants are cheaper than outbreaks of illness, and they should consistently be used in order to destroy the cause of disease at its source.

Diseases of Animals Acts.

—Several Acts of Parliament came into being between 1894 and 1910, designed to control the movement of animals affected with notifiable contagious diseases. Only one disease in the list really affects the dog, and that is rabies. How that is dealt with will be fully described under the heading RABIES. Briefly, however, under the Diseases of Animals Act the owner of an animal, the person in charge of it or the occupier of the premises where it is kept, or the veterinary surgeon attending the animal, must notify an inspector of the local authority, or a police constable, immediately he

Photo| *[W. S. Berridge.*

BROTHERS AND SISTER.
Three of a family. Although so closely related, yet their shading is quite different in each case.

suspects the presence of a notifiable disease. Fortunately, thanks to the veterinary department of the Ministry of Agriculture, and its quarantine regulations, rabies has been eradicated from the British Isles, and nobody needs to apprehend meeting with it among dogs in this country which have their liberty.

Dish-faced.

—Showing a depression in the nasal region; the nose higher at the tip than at the stop. The same as Monkey-faced.

Disinfectant.

—Any agent, physical or chemical, which is capable of destroying pathogenic germs, or of rendering ferments inactive. Chief among the physical agents are sunlight and heat, the former owing its germicidal properties to the ultra-violet and the infra-red rays contained in it. It is common knowledge to-day that sunshine is inimical to the growth and life of germs, and it behoves everybody, having such knowledge, to take full advantage of Nature's disinfectant, supplied gratis.

Heat, whether dry or moist, is also exceedingly valuable; the temperatures which prove lethal to all types of microbe are perfectly well known, and if contaminated articles can be subjected to a sufficiently high temperature, it is certain that they will be rendered sterile and harmless. Establishments exist, in plenty, to which clothing and all kinds of articles

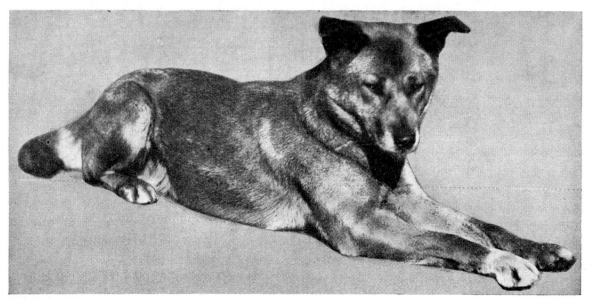

Photo]   *[F. W. Bond.*

DOG LIKE.
Dingos, in time, lose all their fear of the wild, which is only reborn in emergencies. This picture is of peculiar interest, the lay of the coat showing stripes when viewed at a certain angle.

may be sent for "baking"; but sterilization by heat is a process seldom resorted to by those who devote their time and energy to the care of sick dogs, as so many of the appurtenances pertaining to dogs—such as leather leads, collars, muzzles, etc.—are unsuitable for boiling or baking and can better be sterilized by washing or soaking in strong disinfecting solutions.

A very ready and cheap method of applying dry heat to buildings is by means of a blowlamp, and few agents are such effectual germicides or parasiticides as the blue flame from such a lamp.

Of chemical disinfectants one has a huge choice, and whilst it would be futile to tabulate a long list of all their names, it can at least be said that they are divided up into a few main groups according to the manner in which they exert their bactericidal effects. For instance, some are germicidal by oxidation, e.g. chlorinated lime, ozone, permanganate of potash and sodium, hydrogen peroxide, etc.; some disinfect by coagulation, such as silver nitrate, corrosive sublimate, etc.; whilst others do it by protoplasmic poisoning, examples being carbolic acid and its various derivatives.

Some of the best disinfectants are also very toxic to animals, the dog being peculiarly susceptible to certain varieties such as carbolic and tar preparations and the various mercuric germicides. When these substances are employed in kennels, therefore, it behoves one to use every care lest the canine inmates might accidentally partake of a poisonous dose. A number of the proprietary disinfecting fluids on the market are of very doubtful value, especially the cheap ones, and it is extremely important that only the *best* shall be used. Very obviously, to leave articles or premises in just as bad a state of infection as they were before treatment with the so-called germicide, is pure waste of money and time, besides giving one a false sense of security.

Apparatus for spraying walls with disinfectant solution.

When the health and lives of valuable dogs depend upon thorough disinfection, it behoves the purchaser of a disinfectant to ascertain something about its qualities, as in a number of ways it might be quite unsuitable. For instance, the powerful perchloride of mercury is not only highly poisonous but destructive to metalwork, and ineffective when it comes into contact with albumen.

Carbolic acid is less efficient than many other chemical agents, owing largely to the fact that it does not readily mix with water. It may seem to do so, but a magnifying glass would show that it splits into comparatively large globules in water. It is also very caustic and poisonous. Chlorine gas and all water-white chlorine compounds such as Dakin's Solution, etc., damage metals, woodwork, paint and fabrics. Formalin is intensely irritating to the mucous membranes of the eyes and nose, and, in addition, has a very deleterious effect on leather. Permanganate of potash, too, is merely an oxidizing agent, capable of sweetening foul odours, but proving nearly powerless to destroy the germs of infection.

Any disinfectant chosen must, when used, be safe both to the animal and its attendant. It must mix readily with water of any kind, whether it be tap, well, or ditch-water, urine, or sea-water. It must be non-corrosive; must not destroy metals, leather,

paint or fabrics; and, lastly, it must be a powerful and quick germicide.

Do not judge the potency of a disinfectant by its strong or nice odour. Many germs which cause decay and decomposition are easily killed, as compared with the more dangerous disease germs found in association with them. So that a deodorant may not be a disinfectant at all, though the reverse is true. The founder of the modern science of disinfection was Lord Lister, and the germicide he employed was carbolic acid. In his day this was considered a very efficient germicide, but modern research has produced numerous others of far higher efficiency. It is usual now to compare the strength of a disinfectant with the purest carbolic acid; the number of times which a disinfectant is stronger than carbolic acid is known as its "coefficient". When buying disinfectant, therefore, ascertain its coefficient, as established by chemical test, and be sure it is guaranteed.

Disinfecting a Kennel.—Whether a kennel is a
single portable structure, or a building containing numerous compartments for dogs, there is a routine method of disinfection which might, with advantage, be followed. All cobwebs, dust, and dried loose whitewash should first be brushed down. This debris, together with every particle of litter and sawdust, should then be swept up and burned. All removable parts such as the sleeping bench or box, the drinking troughs, dishes, etc., should be scraped and scrubbed with strong disinfectant and soap; then, if possible, they should be placed out in the sun and air.

Floors, walls, and the inner sides of the kennel doors should then be scraped with a wire brush and washed with strong disinfectant. Whilst all is wet one can, at this stage, fumigate the kennel in the manner already described. Leave the germicidal fluid in contact with all surfaces until it dries naturally, that is to say, do not swill down with clean water or wipe away any surplus.

Finally, limewashing may be carried out if desired, but particular care must be taken to ensure that it is not painted over any dried and caked dirt. Limewash is better than whitewash, but both are improved by the addition of half a pint of pure carbolic acid to the gallon.

In kennels which have been contaminated with mange, the blow-lamp is very effectual as a parasiticide. It was much used in the Army during the Great War for the cleansing of stables, etc., but it had to be intelligently applied. If large areas had to be blow-lamped, it was usual to mark out the surface in squares, then giving attention to one at a time. In this way no part was missed.

As to the disinfecting fluids which one may employ either for internal or external work, there is a wide choice. The following are recommended: Corrosive sublimate, strength 1 in 1,000 of water; Kresophen, 5 per cent solution; Izal, ½ per cent solution; Creolin (Jeyes Fluid), 5 to 10 per cent solution; Phenol (carbolic acid), 3 to 5 per cent solution.

Among other agents are: Fecto, Sanitas, permanganate of potash, formaldehyde, and chlorinated lime.

It must be borne in mind that the weaker the solution the longer will be the exposure required of

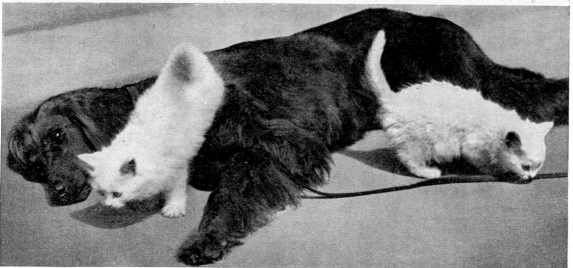

WHY NOT BE FRIENDS ?

Richard Jeffries, the great naturalist, wrote a prose poem in which a five-year-old boy, Boris, makes peace forever and a day among all the animals. In the above charming "friendship" pictures we see that old trust being kept. At the top is a Cocker taking charge of young rabbits ; in the centre is shown a doggie foster-mother of a family of lion cubs ; while below, the kittens and the Afghan Hound show that the traditional enmity of cat and dog can be forgotten.

Photo] FILM STARS. [*S. H. Benson.*

Here is a curiously assorted pair, and the Peke sometimes permits "Budgie" to feed out of its dish. It is only when the pigeon, alighting on the dog's back, pecks playfully at a hair that the dog is not sure about the bird's good intentions.   When this snap was taken these two friends were being rehearsed for a film.

Photo] QUEER PALS. [*J. T. Roberts, W. Croydon.*

It would seem that if the owl is a pet of the master's, the Collie must be friendly too. So also says the owl! An unusual comradeship.

contaminated articles or surfaces in order that disease germs may be killed. Conversely, if one considerably increases the strength of solution above that which is termed "standard", one would be enabled to destroy germs in correspondingly shorter spaces of time.

All occupied kennels should be thoroughly disinfected about once a week and, periodically, buildings should be swept free of cobwebs, dust and other debris prior to the disinfection of every accessible corner. Should the exercise runs be of ordinary earth, a liberal sprinkling of quicklime should be applied immediately before turning the soil over with a fork. This will help very much to destroy the eggs of worms. If the runs are cemented, then one of the above mentioned solutions can be brushed over their surface.

Finally, all iron bars or wire-netting of doors must receive particular attention, as the door is calculated to be in closer and more constant contact with the inmate's nose than any other part of the kennels.

Disinfection.

Disinfection.—Disinfection (or the extermination of disease germs), when thoroughly carried out, gives one a sense of security obtained in no other way. In order to realize what is meant by thoroughness, it is important always to bear in mind how exceedingly minute are the microbes we wish to kill. It must be remembered that thousands of them can repose comfortably on the head of a pin. The man who cannot appreciate this fact will probably find it difficult to realize the real necessity for attention to detail in the process of disinfection. Thus, should one wish to destroy the germs in a fluid, it would be futile to

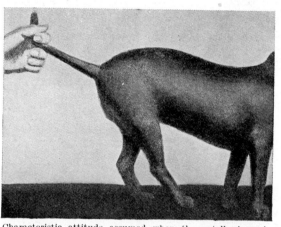

Characteristic attitude assumed when the patella bone is dislocated. In this illustration the right hindleg is implicated.

add so little of the disinfectant that the resulting solution was of too weak a concentration. Again, it would obviously be useless to disinfect one part and leave another undone. The slipshod person will often disinfect a floor but leave the walls and other surfaces untouched. Similarly, to scrub a floor and not go into corners and cracks, or to fail to remove dried faeces or other dirt in order to wash beneath, could hardly be described by the dignified title of "disinfection". Every fraction of an inch must be treated with the germicide, and anything which prevents the ingress of sunlight and fresh air should be removed.

For the eradication of infectious disease our strongest weapon is disinfection, and by employing suitable and reliable chemical agents which carry a guarantee of bactericidal efficiency, we may feel positively certain that all harmful excretions of the sick are rendered innocuous.

In the interests of economy, no less than in those of efficiency, the correct strength of disinfectant, when prepared ready for use, must be ascertained and adopted. We may be wishing to destroy parasites and their eggs, or microbes and their spores, and, according to which it is, will depend the strength of our germicide. A much stronger solution will be required for the destruction of eggs or spores, but as so many germs are non-sporulating, one does not need to waste material in making extra-concentrated solutions when weaker ones would suffice. So far as the proprietary disinfectants are concerned, full directions are supplied with them, and these should be followed to the letter. The haphazard method of pouring a few drops of fluid into a bucket of water is foredoomed to failure. Equally haphazard is the way in which some people seek to disinfect a floor merely by sprinkling a disinfecting fluid over it, leaving some spots dry and untouched. Floors, walls, and other surfaces to be cleaned, should first be prepared by thorough scrubbing, or scraping, to remove caked dirt or old crusted limewash. Cracks of floorboards, inaccessible corners, and other hidden spots must be cleared of dust and grime, and removable fixtures temporarily shifted.

Germs are not destroyed instantaneously by contact with germicides. Sufficient time must be allowed for the latter to do their work, which means that the microbes must be in contact with the wet disinfectant for from five to twenty minutes, according to the agent employed, and its concentration.

Disinfection is not by any means confined to the use of chemicals, as it may be carried out by a variety of means, such as fumigating with gases, spraying, baking, boiling and sunlight.

FUMIGATION. — This method is sometimes resorted to for the disinfection of the interiors of buildings. It is quite practicable—provided that certain rules are observed—and it certainly saves a great deal of labour. All ventilators, doors, windows, fireplaces, etc., must be carefully sealed in order to prevent the premature escape of the lethal gas. As a general rule, the room or building is fumigated for twenty-four hours.

Probably the most efficient fumigator is formalin. One can purchase, from retail chemists, formalin tablets which are placed in the lid of a tin beneath which is a small methylated spirit lamp. Formalin candles may be burnt, or one may make one's own gas by mixing together 10 ozs. of formaldehyde solution and half a pound of potassium permanganate. This amount of material will effectually fumigate 500 cubic feet of space.

The amount of gas generated, however, must be governed by the cubic space of the room, and the chemist will advise any purchaser as to the amount required, provided the dimensions of the room are stated.

Formalin gas is very much more effective in the presence of moisture, and one is advised to spray the walls, etc., with an ordinary atomizer before liberating the fumes.

Sulphurous acid gas is occasionally used for fumigation purposes, but it is not so potent a germicide as formalin. It has a deleterious effect upon metals and paintwork too, for which reason it generally cannot be recommended. It is easily produced, as all one

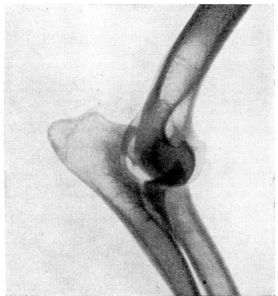

By courtesy]   [Major Hamilton Kirk.

X-RAY PHOTOGRAPHS OF ALSATIAN'S DISLOCATED ELBOW.

Note the lower or articular end of the humerus, which has been driven forward out of contact with the articular surface at the top of the radius and ulna bones.

has to do is to make a sheet of iron red-hot and then heap sulphur on to it. Another way is to light a small gas-ring, upon which an old saucepan (containing sulphur) is stood. Instead of the gas-ring, methylated spirit may be poured over the sulphur and ignited. To fumigate 1,000 cubic feet of space, 5 lb. of sulphur must be burned.

Chlorine gas is an effectual disinfectant, and sufficient for 1,000 cubic feet could be generated by adding 6 ozs. of pure sulphuric acid to 2 lb. of chlorinated lime.

SPRAYING.—The application of germicidal fluids in a very fine state of division, i.e. from an atomizer, is an exceedingly practical and useful method of keeping disease under control. By means of long-handled sprayers it is a matter of great facility to bring the disinfectant in contact with every square millimetre of area, whether it be the ceiling, rafters or walls, in a very short space of time and with a minimum of labour.

Armed with suitable apparatus, it is a matter of ease to spray the whole place throughout once in every week. Flies, spiders, and insect life of all kinds are eradicated. Perchloride of mercury is a cheap and efficient agent for spraying purposes, as 1 oz. dissolved in 1,000 ozs. of water is sufficient to disinfect 3,000 square feet of surface. Here again, formalin can be used if preferred. In the case of distemper kennels, in which the odours are generally very foul, it is of distinct advantage to deodorize the place occasionally in this way, but using, of course, solutions which are not poisonous, such as Sanitas, euthymol or eucalyptus, etc.

BAKING.—Clothing, rugs, and many other articles pertaining to the hospital may be sterilized by baking; but the average householder, or even canine infirmary, is not equipped with the necessary apparatus for the proper performance of this method. Articles to be baked are therefore generally sent away to special cleansing stations.

BOILING.—Any article may be sterilized by boiling, provided it would not be ruined in the process. Enamelled food-dishes and water-vessels can be quite well treated in this way.

SUNLIGHT.—Exposure of contaminated articles to sunlight will render them free of infection, provided sufficient time is allowed to elapse, and that no part is hidden from the sun's rays. Generally, however, nobody has time to wait for Nature's way, so that the precise, quick, and certain chemical process is the one most favoured.

Dislocation.—Dislocation, or luxation of joints, is rather frequent among dogs, and it means that one of the two bones forming a joint has become forcibly displaced. Such displacement is common at the shoulder, elbow, stifle, and hip-joints, but dislocation of the toe- and tail-joints is less frequent. Most forms of violence can account for the condition, such as falls or jumps from high chairs, being trodden upon, run over, or jammed in a doorway. The small bone in front of the stifle or knee-joint, known as the patella, is not infrequently dislocated without any violence. It slips out of, and into, its normal position with no more encouragement than is afforded by ordinary progression. The cause in this condition is quite often a congenital one, and the cure is very difficult, even if possible. Dislocation does not involve only bones or joints, but refers equally to any other part or organ which happens to become displaced. Luxation of an eyeball, for instance, is an example of dislocation, and in this case the eyeball has left its normal position in the orbital cavity.

SYMPTOMS.—When a limb is affected there is severe lameness, the affected leg appearing shorter than the others. The displacement is usually followed by moderate swelling about the joint, which hinders, in some degree, one's ability to feel the exact position of the bones. There is no crackling or crepitus upon manipulation, as is present in fractures; and when the displacement is only slight it is often a difficult matter to decide whether a dislocation really exists, or, if so, whether or not it is accompanied by partial fracture. In all doubtful cases it is highly desirable that the limb should be X-rayed in two positions—one from front to back, and the other from side to side.

TREATMENT.— Reduction of dislocations is sometimes very easy and at others extremely difficult. The joint which seems to offer the greatest

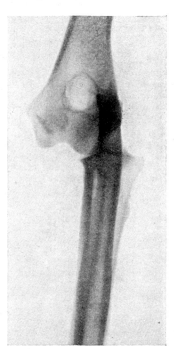

Antero-posterior view, by X-rays, of Alsatian's dislocated elbow. This photo shows that not only was the lower end of the humerus pushed forward but also outwards.

MILL HILL LABORATORY.

A corner in one of the Farm Laboratories of the National Institute for Medical Research (Medical Research Council), where, aided by a voluntary fund administered by the "Field" Distemper Council, much good work is done to alleviate that mysterious disease.

difficulty in dogs is the hip. Radiographs very materially help the surgeon in his efforts at reduction by showing him in which direction the parts are displaced ; and in some cases resort must be had to general anaesthesia.

Should the accident occur in a locality where no veterinarian is available, the guardian or owner of the injured dog might attempt something himself, especially if the dislocation is very obvious. He need not, however, feel unduly worried if his own efforts fail and if many hours have to pass before professional aid can be obtained. Several cases of dislocated hip have recently been encountered in which quacks or amateurs have been entrusted with the diagnosis, and in which they had failed to detect the real trouble. In some of these cases as long as three or four weeks had elapsed before veterinary surgeons were shown the animals and discovered the true nature of the lameness. Even then, however, reductions were possible and recoveries complete.

Reduction of a dislocation is generally a painful affair, and indicates general anaesthesia ; but it is realized that readers of this Encyclopaedia may live far from professional aid or anaesthetics. Briefly, these people should proceed thus : One person takes hold of the part, immediately above the dislocation, whilst the operator grips the part beneath and employs steady traction in whichever direction seems expedient. This he does with one hand, using the other simultaneously to guide the movements and feel for the true adjustment to occur. In some cases rotation is also very useful.

In dislocation of the hip, for instance, the round head of the femur, or thigh bone, is thrust out of its socket in an upward and either backward or forward direction, causing an obvious protuberance, no counterpart of which can be formed on the opposite side of the body. To reduce such a dislocation, one person must firmly hold the dog whilst another pulls the limb downwards and rotates it until the head of the femur is felt to slip back into its socket. This is not easy to describe and still less easy to accomplish, unless he who tries is experienced. Once reduction of a hip is effected, it does not luxate again and no after-treatment is necessary. This is not true, however, of a dislocated patella (kneecap), and very elaborate measures have to be taken to keep this small bone in position. It is replaced easily enough by straightening the leg (distending it) and pushing the patella from its abnormal position back into its central groove. It may stay there without further trouble.

Dislocation of the lower jaw may occur in consequence of the dog's attempt to open its mouth too wide for the purpose perhaps, of carrying some large

object, and may be bilateral or unilateral. If the former, the lower jaw projects beyond the upper, giving an undershot appearance ; but if dislocation is only on one side, then the chin will be out of the normal line and the dog will be unable to close its mouth.

Dislocation of the neck or back are usually hopeless, so far as a remedy is concerned. Paralysis results invariably ; but the diagnosis in many cases could not be relied upon without an X-ray examination.

Disposal of Dead Carcases.—The most sanitary method of disposal is undoubtedly cremation. This process, however, requires a good incinerator, or a fairly fierce fire, if annoyance to neighbours is to be avoided. (*See* INCINERATOR.)

Burial is the next best method, and where rats abound, the depth of the hole should be not less than two feet for a small dog and three feet for a large one. The covering soil must be well trodden down in order to prevent all scent which might attract rodents. Where there are definitely no rats, then one foot of soil above the animal's body is found to be quite sufficient for all practical purposes. In all cases of burial, it is advisable to cover the body with a liberal sprinkling of unslaked lime before filling in with soil.

Many town dwellers experience the greatest difficulty in disposing of dead dogs, first, because they have no garden ; secondly, because burning of the body is out of the question in thickly populated districts ; and thirdly, because the dustmen employed by city and town councils are instructed to refuse to remove dead animals.

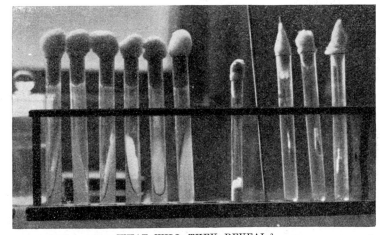

WHAT WILL THEY REVEAL ?
A row of tubes containing cultures of various organisms found in dogs suffering from distemper.

It may be possible, however, to prevail upon the gardeners working in squares and parks to bury small animals for a consideration.

The ideal method for those who can afford it, and who regard their departed pets with sufficient sentiment, is to have a neat wooden box made for the dog and then convey it to one of the Dog Cemeteries which have lately come into being. The charge for a small plot of ground, including burial, ranges from about one to two guineas. The graves are kept tidy thereafter, and sometimes the owner cares to have a small stone erected bearing some inscription. (*See* MEMORIALS).

Distemper.—May be defined as a specific, contagious, and infectious catarrhal fever affecting all mucous membranes, but primarily those of the respiratory tract. Distemper is a most mysterious and complex disease, because one can never foresee what the termination of an attack might be, nor does one know how long it will last. The mildest cases often turn out to be far worse than those which are

ELKHOUNDS

A study of two sturdy Elkhounds, reproduced from one of Nina Scott-Langley's most delightful paintings, specially executed for HUTCHINSON's DOG ENCYCLOPAEDIA. The Elkhound is a sporting dog of Nordic type and descent, and is becoming increasingly popular in England, not only for sport, but also as a pet.

 [Nat. Inst. Med. Research.

ISOLATION COMPOUND.

The top picture shows the Compound as a whole, with the kennel-maids' bungalow in the foreground and entrance to kennels at rear. The second photograph shows kennel-maids receiving sterilized food for the dogs through the hatchway of the "kitchen"; and the third photograph illustrates the entrance to the isolation kennels.

IR

ON DUTY.
The senior attendant in charge of infected animals—shown in rubber clothing at the entrance of the hospital, which is a fly-proof building.

to witness, and usually the most fatal in their termination. Some unfortunate dogs are stricken with all these horrors in one illness, and it is but a robust constitution and a devoted nurse that can hope to effect a cure.

One can never forecast what serious complication may arise in a more or less mild attack, or what dreaded sequels may ensue even months after.

CAUSE.—Innumerable germs have, from time to time, been isolated from distemper victims since the year 1809, when the bacteriological aspect of the question seems first to have received attention. One of the foremost to write intelligently, at any length, on the subject of distemper, was the immortal Jenner, who, while recognizing the true infectious nature of the disease, was the first to differentiate between distemper and rabies, and also the first to show that it was not communicable to man. Most of the microbes discovered by subsequent investigators showed some cultural or morphological characteristic which seemed sufficient to distinguish each from the other; and, after many tests, each was considered by its protagonist to be the causal organism of distemper. From every one, in turn, vaccines were prepared; but in spite of all eulogistic claims, all gave indifferent results. This state of ignorance went on until the year 1923 when a fund was organized to finance a thorough scientific investigation of the disease. The work was carried out by Messrs. Laidlaw and Dunkin (medical and veterinary scientists working in collaboration), under the auspices of the Medical Research Council at its Mill Hill Laboratories.

By the good grace of animal lovers in Great

primarily severe; whilst, in other instances, a dog so critically ill that one despairs of its life, will frequently make an unexpected and uninterrupted recovery. The disease is complex, too, because it has such varied manifestations. There are four different types of distemper, an attack of which may be characterized by the symptoms of any one type, or by an unfortunate mixture of all types. Thus one dog may show mainly respiratory symptoms in which nasal catarrh, bronchitis, or pneumonia are prominent. Another may suffer mostly from alimentary troubles, such as gastro-enteritis or dysentery, with vomiting and severe diarrhoea. Other cases may be remarkable for the nervous disturbance occasioned, such as epileptiform convulsions, St. Vitus' Dance, meningitis, and partial or complete paralysis. These are the most terrible

THE STERILIZING ROOM.
The sterilizer in which all clothing, dog's food, etc., are treated before being allowed into the isolation compound.

Britain, America, and other countries, some £50,000 were raised and were expended in the search for the cause and methods of prevention of distemper during the ensuing seven years. These investigations established, beyond any manner of doubt, the fact that canine distemper is caused by an ultra-visible virus. This conclusion has been accepted by scientists all over the world.

SYMPTOMS.—A very lengthy chapter would be required to explain in detail the numerous symptoms which can arise in one attack of distemper, and it seems sufficient, for the purpose of this work, to give a brief outline of the appearance of a dog stricken with distemper at its early inception. The first thing that occurs is a rise in temperature, of which the owner of the dog is, of course, ignorant. Possibly the first thing he is aware of is that the animal is dull, shivery, creeps up close to the fire, evinces no desire to go out, and perhaps fails in its appetite. This is the stage at which observation, followed by restrictive measures, might save the dog from a long and serious illness. Otherwise, the dog continues to be subjected to draughts, cold, rain, or fatigue, and, soon after, becomes obviously ill. Its temperature now is anything from 102° to 104°, or even more, normal being, of course, 101° F.

The owner may then notice a collection of mucus in the inner corners of the eyes, especially in the early morning. The nose may be hot and dry, and the nostrils may even emit a watery discharge, which, as time goes on, becomes thick and tenacious. A slight cough may arise, and the dog may act as though there was some obstruction in the throat. He attempts to remove this imaginary body by a series of expulsive efforts which sound like a mixture of coughing and retching. Finally, he ejects a small amount of frothy mucus, which leads many people to believe he has been sick. All this, however, has no connection with sickness, and arises merely from irritation (that is, catarrh) of the larynx or pharynx. On the other hand, there may be genuine gastric disturbance manifested by the occasional or even frequent vomiting of gastric frothy mucus. This sort of thing may go on all day and night and, when bad, it reduces the dog to a state of semi-exhaustion.

Sooner or later, a more or less relaxed condition of the bowels will be apparent, and this group of symptoms, taken together, constitutes a very typical picture of distemper in the early stages. In mild cases nothing further arises, and the dog may recover in from one to three weeks. In other cases, the lungs become seriously implicated and the cough goes on intensely, perhaps for weeks. Every precaution must, of course, be taken to guard against pneumonia.

Very frequently it is the bowels which are chiefly affected, and the diarrhoea (often blood-stained) is excessive, and the combination of symptoms produce a great degree of depression and debility. No description of the symptoms will suit all cases, as there are bound to be variations, not only in their nature, but in their intensity.

The disease is contagious and infectious, so that upon the first suspicion of its presence, the sick dog should be isolated from all others. Such isolation must be real and thorough. (*See* DISEASE, PREVENTION OF.)

COMMUNICABILITY.—Man is not susceptible to the disease, but all members of the tribe of *Canidae* are highly susceptible. It is known that the small animals to which dog distemper can be experimentally communicated are the ferret, stoat, and weasel, and that rats, cats, guinea pigs, and rabbits have

By courtesy]   THE DOBERMANN-PINSCHER.   *["De Bond".*
There is something very unusual in the build of the Dobermann-Pinscher, suggesting quickness, intelligence and activity.

all proved to be non-susceptible. The realization of this fact was of inestimable value to the investigators at Mill Hill, as they found themselves able to carry on their research by the aid of very small and inexpensive animals. It is known with what consternation "anti-vivisectionist" readers may view this announcement, but it is asserted with great confidence that the huge majority of dog-owners, and of the general public, will not fail to agree that the results of the research have more than justified the means.

PREVENTIVE INOCULATION.—There may be readers of this work who, until now, had never heard of the extraordinary service which has been rendered to the canine race. They may not know that it is now absolutely possible to render puppies immune against the infection of distemper; that by so doing, countless cases of prolonged and dreadful suffering will be avoided.

The immunization consists of two injections, the

second of which is made about two weeks after the first. The first injection is of a vaccine which confers a temporary immunity, thus permitting of the later introduction of living virus. Without the initial protection the live virus would, of course, set up an attack of distemper; but following—as it does—the protective vaccine, it most usually provokes no reaction whatever. Should it do so, the symptoms are generally of no more severity than a mild lassitude, with temporary loss of appetite, and, possibly, a low fever, which last no longer than two or three days.

The introduction of a live virus into a living body sets in motion all the mechanism necessary for the natural production of a resistance to the disease.

It cannot be too strongly impressed upon the reader, however, that these injections are not merely a matter of introducing a hypodermic needle. There is much more in it than that; and it has been very largely in consequence of non-observance of the rules governing the process, that some failures have been recorded in the past. Many thousands of doses of the prophylactic have been used by veterinary surgeons all over the country, and reports received seem to indicate that the method is effective in about 98 per cent of cases, if we exclude accidents, the causes of which were known.

SAFETY OF THE METHOD.—Veterinary practitioners are constantly being asked whether the inoculations against distemper are likely to cause illness or even

Photo]　　　　　　　　　　　　　　　　　　　　　　　　　　　　　　　　　　[E.N.A.

GOOD TYPES.

Two fine examples of the Dobermann-Pinscher are seen here. These dogs have been trained for police work and were shown at the Police Dogs Show in Moscow.

How this is accomplished would be very difficult of explanation to the lay public, and need not be entered into. Suffice it to say that such a mechanism *does* exist and *can* be stimulated into action. The net result of this method of immunization is to render a dog so completely protected that it can afterwards be placed among badly affected dogs without becoming in the least ill. An alternative method of immunizing a dog is to use a simultaneous injection of serum and virus.

PROTECTION AT DOG SHOWS.—It will be a comfort to thousands of dog-owners to know that an injection of anti-distemper vaccine, given about ten days before a dog is exhibited at a dog show, will protect that dog from any infection which might be picked up there. Another method is to introduce a dose of hyper-immune, anti-distemper serum, the day before the show.

death. The reply can truthfully be "No". In the early days the standardization of both vaccine and virus had not been effected, or at any rate had not been brought to that perfection which obtains to-day. Sometimes the vaccine was too weak, and sometimes the virus was too potent, thus giving only a weak primary protection against a virulent dose of infection. At other times, the fault lay with the death of the virus before it was administered. One of the early difficulties was to maintain the strength of the virus, and it was only comparatively late in the investigation that means were found for attaining this end.

The final safeguard is that the inoculations must be carried out by qualified men who have a knowledge of what they are using, how it should be used, and how to interpret a reaction—if any. At the same time, they have to contend with many unforseen

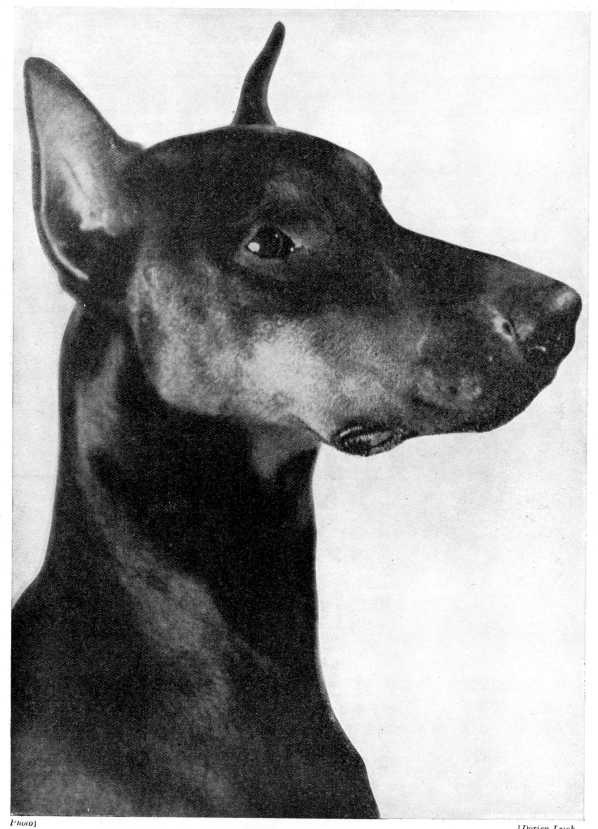

DOBERMANN-PINSCHER.
This breed, although a very important one in Germany, is seldom seen in England.

circumstances, such as the possibility of the patient having been in contact with the disease some time before injection. Such a dog would be in the incubative stage of the disease, and disaster would follow if immunization were attempted in those circumstances. It was with the object of guarding against such a contingency that Laidlaw and Dunkin recommended the bi-daily recording of temperatures for a few days before the administration of the dose. After administration, the dog must be kept dry, warm, and more or less at rest ; and certainly should not be allowed to come in contact with strange dogs in the streets.

These few precautions are well worth while in view of the immense reward which follows their observance.

DOES DISTEMPER RECUR ?—It has been a view strongly held by many veterinary surgeons, masters of foxhounds, dog breeders and others, that a dog

distinguishable from true distemper ; and if this be true, it will be readily realized by all how difficult is the position of the veterinary surgeon who might be called in to deal with the outbreak.

Therefore, although a dog may have been immunized against true distemper, such immunization would not necessarily protect against *bronchisepticus* infection. It would, however, go far towards such an end, since it would ward off the possibility of the dog's resistance becoming lowered sufficiently to permit the *B. Bronchisepticus* to obtain a firm hold of the animal.

A vaccine, prepared from pure cultures of this organism, has been on the market for many years. In addition to this, the dead bodies or extracts of a number of secondary organisms have been incorporated. It is well known that many complications and sequelae of this canine scourge are set up by

Photo]   *[Mondiale.*

A GOOD EFFORT.

In Germany Dobermanns are frequently used for Police work. Here is one going through a phase of its training for this purpose.

could suffer from distemper more than once. To-day we are told authoritatively that there are two diseases of dogs which, although manifesting very similar clinical pictures, are nevertheless of a different aetiology or causation. The exciting cause of true canine distemper is definitely known to be an ultra-visible virus, but that in some outbreaks of distemper many of the symptoms presented, and deaths among the affected dogs, were due to the action of organisms which play a secondary rôle in that they invade the already weakened tissues.

In other words, the Mill Hill authorities state that simple uncomplicated distemper is a mild disease, *per se*, which would not give rise to the horrible symptoms so well known were it not for the presence of secondary invaders. Of the latter, the most important is the *Bacillus Bronchisepticus*, which generally can be isolated from a goodly percentage of dogs suffering apparently from distemper. It is thought now that an invasion of the body by this bacillus can produce a condition which is hardly

recognized secondary invaders. Thus, if we can immunize an animal against these microbes alone, we are undoubtedly doing good work ; and here, then, lies the probable value of at least one popular vaccine.

SUSCEPTIBLE AGE.—The puppy is *most* susceptible to attack, and the disease has been observed in a suckling pup only six days old. A dog is probably most vulnerable between the ages of two months and one year, but the latter is not the limit of susceptibility. Distemper can and does affect dogs of any age up to at least six years.

MORTALITY.—It is estimated that the average mortality from distemper is about 25 per cent of those which contract the disease. It is a huge mortality, and is the source of a tremendous amount of pecuniary loss annually to the dog-owning public. But there is, in addition, a sentimental loss which can never be estimated in terms of cash, nor compensated for. In the light of our present-day knowledge on immunization, this mortality could be

Photo]   [*E.N.A.*

OFF THE "SET".

When Clive Brook is off duty there is nothing he likes better than a stroll in his beautiful garden, a pipe, and the company
of his best canine pal, a Dobermann-Pinscher.

reduced to five per cent or less, if owners would make use of the means at their disposal.

SPREAD OF INFECTION.—The most fruitful source of infection is *direct contact* with a living animal suffering from distemper ; almost as potent, however, is mediate or *indirect* contact, accomplished through the agency of contaminated kennels, baskets, rugs, clothing, brushes, leads and collars, sponges, feeding vessels, spoons, thermometers, human attendants and their clothes. In fact, any article whatsoever which, having been in the immediate proximity of a distempered dog, becomes a source of great danger to the healthy. It is the discharges, both ocular and nasal, but particularly from the nose, and the coughed-up sputum which are so infective. Especially is this the case in the early stages of the disease, and when they become smeared in even the most minute quantity upon the ground or on such objects as are mentioned above, they are likely to be conveyed over wide areas. It follows that the possibility is very real of a person being able to take distemper into his home on his boots, for he can hardly know into what he has trodden.

If all dog-owners would isolate a dog immediately it manifested the slightest symptom, many a serious outbreak would be avoided.

DURATION OF INFECTION AFTER CONVALESCENCE.—Infectivity still exists for a time during convalescence, and in estimating the time which must elapse, after an attack, before a dog can be stated to be free from infection, we must take into consideration the date upon which the very last symptom whatever was observed—such as cough, discharges, diarrhoea, or temperature—at which time the dog might be pronounced as completely restored to health. Then a week should be allowed to pass to guard against the possibility of relapse, and if still well and bright, the patient might receive a disinfectant bath with due precautions, thereafter being safely assumed as germ-free.

SUPPRESSED DISTEMPER. — There is a type of case, quite frequently encountered, in which the subject exhibits an unaccountable emaciation, lack of interest in food, unwillingness to play, and intermittent attacks of diarrhoea, with occasional emesis. There is nothing very definite about such a case, but when the writer meets one he always suspects distemper. It may be several weeks before more definite or characteristic symptoms set in. That is a peculiar feature about distemper—the way it will sometimes hang about for weeks—partially suppressed, the symptoms disappearing from time to time and then returning with renewed intensity. Often, when a dog has been mysteriously out of sorts and then apparently recovers, it is only necessary to give the animal a bath, or take it for a very long walk, to bring about a rapid return of its old trouble and induce the onset of typical symptoms of distemper.

PERIOD OF INCUBATION.—In the official report of the ''Field Distemper Council'', the incubation period was definitely fixed at four days. The observation does not completely coincide with clinical experience, as in practice very varying periods are known to elapse between the infection and the first appearance of symptoms. The minimum and maximum periods have been computed by practitioners at three days and three weeks, respectively. Very much often depends upon this question, such as the difficulties which might arise in connection with the purchase of dogs ; and should a valuable dog exhibit evidence of the disease soon after purchase, the legal position must, to a large extent, hinge upon the period of incubation. In practice, the average period seems to lie between five and seven days, but cases have been known in which the date of known contact between a healthy and a distempered dog was some twenty-one days before symptoms developed in the healthy dog.

TREATMENT.—There are few—if any—diseases of the canine race which so imperatively need the services of a qualified practitioner as distemper, if only, in the first instance, to assure oneself that distemper really exists. The symptoms are so varied and may be so severe that a trained eye is essential for the diagnosis of any complicating conditions such as pneumonia, chorea, enteritis, ophthalmia, etc., etc. It may be said at once that there is no specific cure for distemper, and all efforts must be directed

Photo]   A TYPICAL FEMALE.   *[A. Daner.*
The carriage of the breed shows alert expectation and physical energy. It might be said to resemble a giant specimen of the Manchester Terrier.

towards alleviating the outstanding symptoms. Go direct for scientific advice and let the first expense be the last. Symptoms can only be treated as they arise, and in view of the great variability of types of distemper, it follows, therefore, that a drug which might be of considerable service in one case, would possibly prove useless—if not harmful—in another.

No *one* mixture can be regarded as valuable for *all* types of case. Each one must be judged on its merits. It is quite certain that if the only medicines forced down the poor dog's throat are those chosen from an amazing list of quack remedies, by people entirely without knowledge, and irrespective of their suitability, then one has no hesitation in saying that the administration of medicine is deleterious to the patient.

Restricted movement of the patient is most important. The dog must be kept warm, dry, and comfortable, and be given the best of nourishing food.

Not least important is the observance of hygienic principles, which embrace efficient ventilation, adequate light, cleanliness of the body, etc., etc. Particularly one must remove frequently the discharges from both nose and eyes, for if these are allowed to remain for long they set up great soreness, caking and cracking in the case of the nostrils, and inflammation or ulceration of the eyes. The veterinary surgeon attending the case will advise upon the details of the treatment to be carried out, and the reader is strongly advised to follow his instructions implicitly.

FALLACIES CONCERNING DISTEMPER.—The general public have some wonderful notions concerning distemper in dogs, many of them grotesque and absolutely unfounded. Time after time it is said, in all seriousness, that dogs should not be fed on meat or milk, as to do so would be courting an attack of distemper. This is perhaps the most ridiculous idea of all, for in reality the very reverse is the fact. A dog is essentially carnivorous, and to withhold his *natural* food in favour of artificial and starchy foodstuffs, is likely to stunt his growth and weaken his constitution and resistance to infection.

The majority of people believe that a dog is bound to have distemper sooner or later, but such is again

Photo]   *[E.N.A.*

WITH THE FORESTER.

In Eastern Switzerland the foresters take with them a Dobermann-Pinscher as a guard and companion. In addition, a Dobermann is capable of doing quite a lot of useful work.

not the case. This disease is not hereditary, and can only be contracted by airborne infection or by direct or indirect contagion. Some credulous people believe that if a dog can smell tar at all times it will not fall a prey to distemper. To effect this they daub tar about the muzzle or hang tarred string around the neck. Quite a number of people think that feeding leeks to a dog protects him against distemper, but the idea is about as grotesque as the tar theory.

Diuretics.—Medicinal agents which increase the flow of urine. They act in several ways, some by increasing the blood pressure (digitalis, squills, etc.), some by causing a dilatation of the renal vessels (nitrate of potash, alcohol, etc.) and others by irritating the kidney tissue, such as turpentine, cantharides, etc. The drinking of copious amounts of water or milk will be followed by the increased passage of urine.

Diuretics are indicated in all dropsical conditions, except those which are directly due to disease and inactivity of the kidneys themselves. Since a large proportion of the toxins, elaborated in the body, is eliminated via the kidneys, it is a very salutary treatment to give a dog a course of diuretic medicine when it is fevered, debilitated, off its food, or generally out of sorts. (*See also* ALTERATIVES.)

Dobermann-Pinscher.—There are a few, a very few, Dobermann-Pinschers in this country, and those born here are, of course, uncropped, whereby they naturally lose their distinctive character ; they do not look like Dobermann-Pinschers, but rather like overgrown Manchester Terriers. In Germany, this breed is one of the most popular, and at the shows there it occupies, in numbers, very often the third place, after the Alsatians and the Dachshunds ; it sometimes even beats the latter. The breed is also popular in Holland and France.

The type of the Dobermann-Pinscher is now very definitely fixed, and one would wish that its history were as definitely known. As a matter of fact, opinions greatly differ as to the "constituent bodies" that have gone to the making of this very interesting breed of dogs, which was entirely unknown until the year 1865. What we do know is that the birth-place of this breed is the town of Apolda, in Thuringia (Germany), and that it was Herr Dobermann who was the "father" of it. In his efforts he had had the help of two of his friends—one a grave-digger and the other a church bell-ringer. The purpose of these three "producers" was to evolve a sharp, fearless dog, hardy and suitable for police purposes, but, at the same time, suitable also for the house. The first "manufactured articles" were deplorable, not from Herr Dobermann's point of view, though, for the dogs were ferocious in the extreme. They sold, however, like the proverbial hot cakes, especially as the prices asked "defied every competition".

And so it came about that a breed was "produced" which

"EMIL".
A Dobermann-Pinscher, the property of Mr. G. A. Evers, of Hillsgerberg, Holland.

received the name of "Dobermann's dogs", the word "Pinscher" having been added later on. At the end of the nineteenth century, when Herr Dobermann and his two "assistants" were dead and buried, the breed was on the point of becoming one for guarding and protecting, pure and simple, when there stepped in that famous breeder of Dobermann-Pinschers—to give the breed its present-day name—Herr Otto Goeller, also of Apolda, who was instrumental in giving us the Dobermann-Pinscher of to-day, a dog good for both service and show purposes.

Reverting to the "constituent parts" that have gone to making of this breed, there are several

versions of them : some say that they comprised the Alsatian, the old German Pinscher and the Manchester Terrier ; and it may, perhaps, be admitted that the Pinscher has played an important part in the composition of the Dobermann, as, otherwise, the latter would not have received the adjunct-name of "Pinscher". That the Manchester Terrier probably played a part in this evolution is evidenced by the fact that the Dobermann-Pinscher is very much like the Manchester Terrier in appearance and in colour, especially the latter. There are those also who assert that the blue Dobermann had been produced owing to a cross with the blue Great Dane having been introduced into its blood, but there is some doubt about this. Last, but not least, it is said that one or the other of the German gun-dogs also participated in the "manufacture" of the already so much "manufactured" Dobermann-Pinscher, but no one can say definitely.

The writer of these lines thinks that the time will come when the Dobermann-Pinscher will become popular in this country. In view of this it is important that the standard of this breed should be brought before the notice of the public, the standard to adopt being that of the Dobermann-Pinscher Club in Germany. It is considered one of the most precise standards in existence in any breed of dogs, especially as it makes mention of the faults after enumerating each part of the dog's anatomy.

GENERAL APPEARANCE.—It is that of a dog of good middle size, with an elegant, square and strong body. The dog is compactly built, full of muscle and strength, exhibiting endurance and speed.

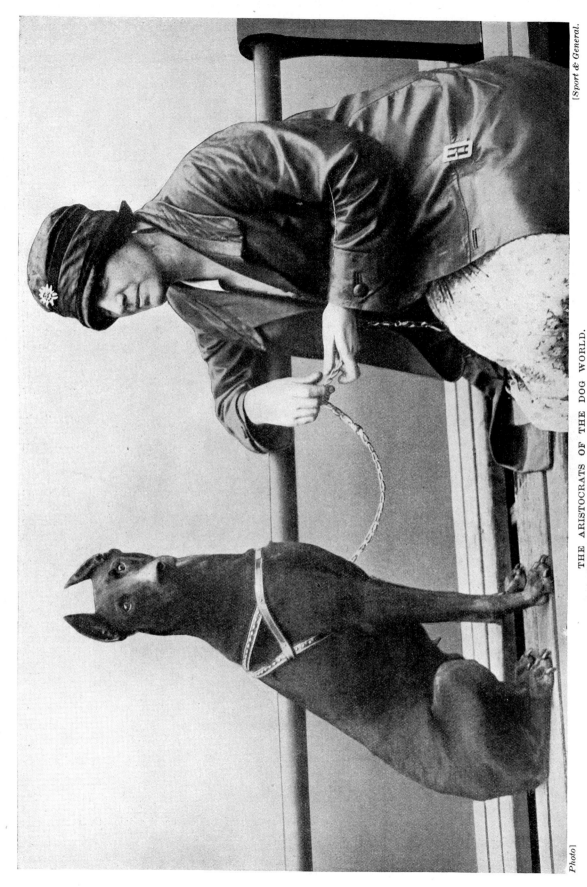

Photo]

[Sport & General.

THE ARISTOCRATS OF THE DOG WORLD.

Exhibits from foreign countries, as well as from all parts of England, arrived for the big show for Sporting and other dogs, organized by the Kennel Club and held at the Crystal Palace, London, in October 1933. The only German dog in the show was a "Dobermann-Pinscher", here shown with Mrs. A. E. Mann, better known as Elizabeth Craig, the well-known writer.

Running gear must be light and free. Temperament lively and ardent, the eye expressing intelligence and resolution. *Faults* : Clumsy, heavy, or Greyhoundy build.

HEAD.—The dimensions must be properly proportioned to the body. The head must be long and dry, and, when viewed in front or in profile, its shape should remind one of a blunt wedge. The top of the head as flat as possible. The line of the forehead should extend, with a slight depression, to the ridge of the nose. The cheeks flat. The ridge of the nose straight and slightly curved. The jaws full and powerful. The lips close to the jaw. *Faults* : Strong ram's head, frontal arch too strongly projecting, occipital bone too plainly visible, too much offset of the forehead, nasal ridge pointing upwards, heavy cheeks, head too short, too pointed, Greyhound-like, jaws not sunken in front of the eyes.

EYES.—Well-closed, dark, of medium size, with clever, energetic expression. *Faults* : Eyes too large, too small, prominent, light.

EARS.—Well set-on, of medium length, clipped to a point. *Faults* : Ears set-on too low or badly carried.

TEETH.—Strongly developed, the incisors of the lower jaw must touch the inner surface of the upper incisors. *Faults* : Undershot or overshot, incisors out of line, poor or black-brown.

NECK.—Pretty long and "dry", well-fitted into the shoulders, slightly arched, nape well-muscled. *Faults* : Short, thick, or like that of the Great Dane ; dew-lap.

BODY.—The back short and firm, the withers clearly defined, the crupper slightly rounded, the brisket full, but not too wide ; the chest arched and reaching deep to the elbow ; the belly drawn well up and forming a beautifully-curved line with the chest ; the tail docked short. *Faults* : Long back, arched or depressed and diagonally sloping crupper ; chest flat or barrel-shaped.

FOREQUARTERS.—Legs straight to the pastern ; upper-arms forming as nearly as possible a right angle with the shoulder-blades ; shoulders powerful, with well-defined muscles, lying close up to the body. *Faults* : Stiff or loose shoulders, feet turning in or out, weak pasterns.

HINDQUARTERS.—Broad and with good angle in the upper section, powerfully defined muscles ; neither let down nor too straight on hocks ; seen from behind, placed straight, turning neither in nor out. *Faults* : Slender or lightly-muscled hindlegs, stiffness or stiltiness in hindquarters.

FEET.—Short, well-arched, compact, dew-claws to be removed at the time of the docking of the tail. *Faults* : Long feet, flat or not compact feet.

HEIGHT AT SHOULDER.—Dogs, 58–65 centimetres ; bitches, 55–60 centimetres. *Faults* : Too large or too small, too heavy or massive, too Greyhoundy in general appearance.

COAT.—Short, hard, close-lying ; grey under-coat allowed, but must not be visible through the outer-coat. *Faults* : Coat soft or wavy, feather on legs.

COLOUR.—Black, brown, blue, with tan, sharply-defined markings, a little white on the chest is allowed. *Faults* : Straw-yellow, dirty, markings lacking in sharp outline, too much white on chest or white on toes.

Photo] HEAD STUDY. *[Dorien Leigh.*
Here is seen an elderly Dobermann-Pinscher. Judging by the expression, it must have seen many saddening things in the course of its life.

QUALITIES.—Pleasant in manner and character, faithful, fearless, attentive, and reliable as watchdog, sure defender of the master, mistrustful of strangers, intelligent, very capable of training, and ideal house-dog and companion.

STANDARD OF POINTS.—General appearance, 20 ; head (including teeth, eyes, ears), 15 ; body (including neck, chest, quarters, tail, etc.), 40 ; size, 5 ; coat (including colour, markings), 10 ; condition, 10. Total, 100.

Docking.—The ancient custom of removing a portion of a dog's tail, presumably with the main object of giving the animal a smarter appearance.

Fortunately the custom has not extended to more than comparatively few selected breeds, among the better known being the Airedale, Irish and Fox Terriers, and the Cocker Spaniel. We are probably so accustomed to see the Terriers with docked tails that when we behold a specimen which has not been so treated, we are perhaps apt to disparage the individual. At the same time, it is the writer's opinion that docking (like cropping of the ears) is really entirely unnecessary and, possibly, cruel when improperly done. In perpetuating the custom we are really only following the dictates of fashion.

At one time a good deal more of the tail was removed than obtains to-day and, usually, about one-third only is amputated. The operation should be performed during the first week of the puppy's life, as at that age there is no troublesome haemorrhage and apparently little pain inflicted. A surgeon can, of course, dock a dog at any age, but the operation requires a good deal more care when the coccygeal vertebrae have become fully developed and bony, and the caudal artery has attained full size and importance. Anaesthesia, then, is essential.

No attempt will be made to describe the operation or its little pitfalls, as the writer holds the firm view that amateurs have no right to meddle in surgical matters of which they have little or no knowledge or experience. They may, to save a few shillings, decide to dock their own puppies, and doubtless would succeed in removing what they had planned should come off ; but one is forced to the conclusion that there is a right and a wrong way, as in everything, and that the latter must entail more suffering than would be the case when it was properly performed.

Dog Act (1906). (*See* OWNERSHIP, RIGHTS AND LIABILITIES.)

Dog Bites.—If a dog is bitten, it is generally by another dog, the consequences sometimes being very serious. For instance, when a Pekingese is attacked by a larger or stronger dog, it is quite common to find that one of the Peke's eyes has been laid upon its cheek. The eyes of Pekingese Spaniels are so prominent that almost any bite about the face will probably terminate as just described. When large dogs bite others, the wounds inflicted are generally contused wounds because they are accompanied by bruising. They often may be described, further, as lacerated wounds on account of the tearing which

Photo]　　　　　　　　　　　　[*Dorien Leigh.*
EYE APPEAL.
There is something very appealing in the Dobermann's look. As a breed they are known for faithfulness and reliability.

Photo]　[*Mondiale.*
AFTER A RUN.
Dobermanns are energetic workers. Here is one which has just returned from a run.

takes place. (*See* WOUNDS.) But the worst of all wounds, from an infective point of view, is undoubtedly that which is known as the punctured wound. In this case, the teeth merely penetrate the victim's flesh, making one or more small punctures, into the depth of which germs or dirt are deposited.

Being only a small hole, it is frequently not observed owing to the hair around it, and in consequence it is neglected. It tends rapidly to close at the skin surface, and the infection placed within is imprisoned. In a short time the animal is found in pain, which becomes increasingly acute, and soon it may develop a temperature owing to abscess formation, or worse still, in consequence of blood-poisoning. These small punctured wounds, therefore, must be seriously regarded, and so soon as a severe complication is apprehended, it is wise to procure the services of a veterinary surgeon in order that the wounds may be freely opened up.

Dog Catchers. (*See* RESTRAINT.)

Dog Fights.—There is nothing more unpleasant than two or more dogs fighting, and although some such battles end in no serious injury, in some instances serious damage is done ; a dog may be so blinded or badly bitten that it has to be destroyed.

It is a fact that people wishing to prevent a dog from fighting, or attempting to stop a fight, invariably do the wrong thing, either making a fight start or causing the dogs to fight more savagely. It must be understood that when two male dogs, strangers, see each other, the instinct is to be pugilistic, one more so if either dog has something it is valuing, such as a piece of meat, a bone, or even friendship for another dog or puppy close by it. Dogs often will fight to defend, as they imagine, their owner from some other dog.

Puppies only play at fighting, although they may in play forget themselves and start a struggle. The older a dog is, the more garrulous it becomes, and the more ready to teach the younger members of its community a lesson. Some old dogs will not even allow young dogs to fight amongst themselves, but interfere at once ; and if any fighting is to be done,

DRAGHOUND TRIALS.

At top, the Tring and District Farmers Draghounds are seen holding a Trial open to all recognized packs of hounds. The Hounds are seen taking the first obstacle. The second photograph depicts a scene at the Trials held at Leighton Buzzard, showing the Draghounds coming in at the end of the run. *(See page 506.)*

suggest by their behaviour that it will be they who do it !

Dogs which normally never fight may attack another dog with great fury in the presence of a female, and this is often the effect upon even the most cordial comradeship of males in a kennel when an attractive female is introduced. The same applies to a male standing at stud when placed later amongst its brothers. Even if a male has been taken away from its playmates for some hours, his return may start a fracas.

Most fighting in streets and parks is the result of jealousy and the desire to protect owners, or, as the dog imagines, its own rights. It looks upon the other dog as a poacher on its preserves. Then things will depend on how the other dog behaves. Somebody must be master. Who ? So the first dog goes slowly towards the stranger ! On this the owner, rather foolishly, hurries after it and (humanwise) threatens the other dog with his stick, exactly as he should not do, for the aggressor, now feeling that his master and he are attacking together, goes hard for its enemy.

Far better is it to walk away, taking not the slightest notice of the dog except to tell it to come along, and when at some distance, to whistle to it. The dog then gives up the idea of fighting, fearing its master may get too far away, and prefers to go after him.

If a dog is on the lead and is trying to get at another dog, it is foolish to strike either with a stick, because the blows rouse its courage, make it more savage, and are mistaken to be part of the battle. If a blow must be struck it should be on the muzzle, for the dog then draws back.

It is far better not to hit the dog, but to shout at it in a voice that carries annoyance : "Stop fighting, *will you* !" Many a dog on hearing that, taught to obey, will indeed hesitate as to continuing.

To try to drag dogs apart when they have a hold is likely to cause torn flesh, apart from the risk of yourself being bitten. A certain way to stop the fight, if it is available, is white pepper well sprinkled over the dogs' noses ! The result is that they start sneezing violently, and it takes a very clever dog to fight then.

A less successful way is to throw with much vigour a bucket of water over their heads. This causes the two dogs to hesitate, giving time for the respective owners to get hold of their dog's collars or necks or tails and drag them away from each other ; for, surprised by the water, they quickly let go their holds.

Although males seldom fight with bitches, the gentler sex will occasionally, more especially at feeding times, or if a male is bothering her, attack him, forgetting that the opponent is of the opposite sex. The male may also, in his anger, forget that by the rules of nature he should not fight with females.

To avoid fights in the kennel, dogs which are pugilistically inclined should not be kennelled together or allowed to meet each other. Where wire-netting divides one from the other, the dog-minded kennelman or owner will see at once what is likely to occur if the dogs should meet. Dogs that are not friendly, watch each other intently, and go towards the dividing wire with a distinct threat in their carriage. At feeding times the arrangements should be so made that each dog has its own feeding tin well away from any other.

Dogs taken out for walks, if under proper control, will not attempt to fight unless they have been itching for a meeting for some time, or have been made jealous

Photo]   *[Fox.*

REMARKABLE DRAGHOUNDS.

Really well-fed and well-bred Hounds are very remarkable, and here are shown some of the finest Draghounds in England ; they belong to the Aldershot Command Pack.

Photo] [E.N.A.

PROTECTION.
Draught dogs in Belgium are well protected by the law. Here is seen
an inspector interrogating a milk vendor.

ot each other. If dogs are at all uncertain with each
other, it is unwise to throw a ball amongst them,
though where they are really good friends they will
play together.

It is always wise, however, when taking a dog
amongst other dogs to which it is not accustomed, to
take it on a lead and carry a thin switch, which a dog
fears much more than a heavy stick, and which, if
used, will do it no injury. Owners of ill-tempered
dogs ought to look after their charges and keep
strange dogs from approaching too closely. To allow
a keen fighter full liberty in public places where other
dogs are to be found is wrong.
Through lack of this common-
sense action many a valuable dog
has been destroyed.

It should be added that
certain dogs have their peculiar
hates. A terrier may be unable
to resist attacking a Chow, and
a Greyhound a Pekingese. Most
short-coated dogs take a dislike
to woolly dogs and Alsatians,
and are in turn often hated by
smaller fry. Dogs, however, have
no little common sense, and very
few small dogs will attack one
out of all proportion to themselves, although this does happen
occasionally.

Dogue de Bordeaux. (*See*
French Breeds.)

Domed Skull.—The skull
round instead of flat on
top. Similar to Apple-headed
(which see for illustration on
page 68).

Dosage of Medicines.—In consequence
of the great variety of breeds of dog, some
large and some very small, it is a little difficult
to state a definite dose of any drug for this
species of animal, as one could do for man or
the horse, etc. Many factors influence the
amount of medicine which may be given
to an individual dog, such as its age, sex,
weight, condition of health, and the channel by
which the dose is administered. One also has
to consider whether only one dose is to be
given, or whether the medicine is to be
repeated two or three times daily for a week
or two. Again, dosage is modified according
to whether the medicament is to be given with
meals or when the animal is fasting. Finally,
it is a curious fact that the same drug may
exert entirely different effects according to
the amount prescribed. Well-known examples
of this are to be found in ipecacuanha and
prussic acid, the former being an emetic
when given in a large dose (such as 1 to 2
teaspoonsful), but having no such property
in doses of 10 minims. In this small dose,
however, it is a valuable expectorant in cases
of bronchitis, etc.

Prussic acid is commonly added to gastric
mixtures to allay vomiting; it is also a very
powerful respiratory stimulant in doses of 1 or
2 drops, yet a dose of 20 or 30 drops will not
only cause paralysis of the respiratory apparatus, but a certain and very rapid death.

Smaller doses of medicines are prescribed for very
old and very young dogs, and some authorities have
attempted to tabulate percentage-doses according to
the age. For instance, Banham's *Posology* states
that where the dose of a medicament, suitable for a
dog of 6 months of age and over, might be 1 part, then
the proportions for other ages should be: 3 to 6
months, ½ part; 6 to 12 weeks, ¼ part; 20 to 42 days,
⅛ part; 10 to 20 days, $\frac{1}{16}$ part.

At the same time it must be remembered that
whilst one Airedale of six months might weigh well
over 45 lb., another specimen of the same age might

Photo] [E.N.A.

AN EVERY-DAY SIGHT.
Belgian milk-sellers, with dog-drawn cart, pausing for a friendly chat.

Photo]

AN UNUSUAL EXPERIENCE.

[L.N.A.

Lady Dalrymple-Champneys, whilst on holiday in Belgium, tries the comfort (or otherwise) of a Belgian Dog-cart, not usually considered a fashionable carriage and pair.

By courtesy] [*G. Horowitz.*

THE LARGE SWISS FARM DOG.

These very excellent dogs are found on the farms all over Switzerland pulling the carts and helping the farmer with his stock.

not top even 30 lb., and therefore dosage must be graduated accordingly. Indeed, it is probably true that weight is of far greater importance than age in estimating the dosage of drugs.

In the tables which follow, minimum and maximum doses will be indicated of the medicinal agents more commonly used in canine practice. If we consider that the minimum dose is indicated for a 15 lb. dog, then (according to Banham) the variations in dosage, dependent upon body weight, may be estimated as under :

For a $2\frac{1}{2}$ lb. dog ..	$\frac{1}{6}$ the dose
,, ,, 5 lb. ,, ..	$\frac{1}{3}$,, ,,
,, ,, 10 lb. ,, ..	$\frac{2}{3}$,, ,,
,, ,, 15 lb. ,, ..	the minimum dose given in the tables
,, ,, 20 lb. ,, ..	$1\frac{1}{3}$ times the dose
,, ,, 25 lb. ,, ..	$1\frac{2}{3}$,, ,, ,,
,, ,, 30 lb. ,, ..	2 ,, ,, ,,

and so on in similar proportion.

Bitches usually take slightly smaller doses than dogs, one of the reasons for this being that they are generally lighter in weight. Reductions must be made, too, in the case of old, decrepit, debilitated or very sick dogs. They have not the strength to resist the effects of drugs, and this is well exemplified in the comparatively small amount of chloroform required to put a feeble dog "to sleep".

In computing a table of dosage, it is to be understood that such doses refer to medicines given by the mouth unless otherwise stated. A dog can tolerate double the dose when it is administered per rectum, but only one-tenth if given subcutaneously, and one-twenty-fifth or even less if introduced direct into a vein.

In the table of dosage which follows, "m." refers to minims, "grs." to grains, "drs." to drachms, and "oz." to ounces. (For measurement tables of liquids and solids *see under* WEIGHTS AND MEASURES) :

Acid, Salicylic	5–15 grs.
,, Tannic	2–10 grs.
Aconite, B.P. Tincture of ..	$\frac{1}{2}$– 5 m.
Aloes	5–40 grs.
Apomorphine (hypodermically as emetic)	$\frac{1}{40}$– $\frac{1}{8}$ gr.
Areca nut	10–60 grs.
Arsenicalis liquor	1–10 m.
Aspirin	3–10 grs.
Belladonna, Extract of ..	$\frac{1}{8}$– 2 grs.
,, Tincture of ..	$\frac{1}{2}$–10 m.
Bismuth carbonate	3–20 grs.
,, subnitrate	1–10 grs.
Blue pill	2– 7 grs.
Bromide of potash or soda ..	3–20 grs.
Buckthorn, Syrup of	$\frac{1}{2}$– 2 oz.
Caffeine (by injection)	$\frac{1}{2}$– 2 grs.
Calomel	1– 4 grs.
Calcium lactate	5–20 grs.
Camphor	1–10 grs.
,, Compound tincture of	2–30 m.
Cascara, Liquid extract of ..	15–60 m.
Castor oil	$\frac{1}{2}$– 2 oz.
Chalk	15–60 grs.
Charcoal	15–60 grs.
Chenopodium oil	1–15 m.
Chloral hydrate	5–30 grs.
,, Syrup of	10–60 m.
Chlorodyne	3–15 m.
Chloroform (by inhalation) ..	2– 6 drs.
Cocaine (by injection)	$\frac{1}{8}$–$1\frac{1}{2}$ grs.
Cod-liver oil	1– 4 drs.
Croton oil	$\frac{1}{4}$– 2 m.
Digitalis, Tincture of	2–10 m.

By courtesy *G. Horowitz*

"ARNO VON FRYBERG".

Here is a famous dog of the Swiss Draught and Farm Hound breed, known as "Grosse Schweizer Sennenhunde". Note the muscular strength of its body.

Dover's powder	5–15 grs.
Epsom's salt	1– 4 drs.
Ergot, Tincture of	10–30 m.
Ether, Spirits of nitrous ..	10–60 m.
Eucalyptus oil	1– 4 m.
Formalin	2– 5 m.
Ferri preparations (*see* Iron) ..	— —
Gentian, Tincture of	$\frac{1}{2}$–$1\frac{1}{2}$ drs.
Glucose	$\frac{1}{2}$– 3 drs.
Glycerine	$\frac{1}{2}$– 2 drs.
Gregory's powder	20–60 grs.
Hexamine	3–10 grs.
Hydrarg c. creta	1– 4 grs.
Iodine, Strong tincture of ..	5–20 m.
Iron, Carbonate of	2–10 grs.
,, Iodide of (syrup) ..	10–30 m.
,, Phosphate of	3–10 grs.
,, Sulphate of	1– 3 grs.
Ipecacuanha powder (as expectorant)	1– 5 grs.
Ipecacuanha powder (as emetic)	10–30 grs.
Ipecacuanha wine (expectorant)	10–30 m.
Ipecacuanha wine (emetic) ..	2– 5 drs.

Jalap powder	20–90 grs.
Licorice, Liquid extract of ..	15–60 m.
Magnesium, Carbonate ..	5–30 grs.
,, Sulphate ..	1– 4 drs.
Mercury with chalk	1– 4 grs.
,, Biniodide of (red) ..	$\frac{1}{16}$– $\frac{1}{4}$ gr.
,, subchloride (calomel)	1– 4 grs.
Morphine hydrochlor (injection)	$\frac{1}{4}$– 2 grs.
,, liquor	2–15 m.
Myrrh, Tincture of	15–60 m.
Nux Vomica powder	$\frac{1}{4}$– 2 grs.
,, ,, Tincture of	2–10 m.
Olive oil	$\frac{1}{4}$– 2 oz.
Opium powder	1– 5 grs.
,, Tincture of ..	3–20 m.
Paraffinum liquidum ..	$\frac{1}{2}$– 4 drs.
Peppermint, Oil of	1– 3 m.
Pepsin	2– 6 grs.
Pituitrin (as injection).. ..	5–15 m.
Podophyllin resin	$\frac{1}{8}$– 2 grs.
Potash, Bicarbonate of ..	10–40 grs.
,, Bromide of ..	3–20 grs.
,, Iodide of ..	2–15 grs.

AN EXCELLENT TYPE.
The Belgo-Dutch Draught-Dog, known as the "Matin Belge", is built for work. Note the way the limbs are put together and the muscular development.

Potash, Nitrate of (as febri- fuge)	2–10 grs.
,, Nitrate of (as diuretic)	4–20 grs.
,, Permanganate of ..	1– 3 grs.
Quinine, Sulphate of	$\frac{1}{2}$– 5 grs.
,, Ammoniated tincture of	10–60 m.
Salol	2–20 grs.
Santonin	$\frac{1}{2}$– 5 grs.
Senna, Infusion of	$\frac{1}{2}$– 2 drs.
Sodium, Bicarbonate of ..	5–40 grs.
.. Carbonate of (or washing soda, as emetic)	10–30 grs.
Salicylate of ..	5–20 grs.
Sulphate of (Glau- ber's Salt) ..	10–60 grs.
Spirits of Aether (nitrosi) ..	10–60 m.
,, ,, aromatic ammonia ..	5–30 m.
Squills, Syrup of	$\frac{1}{2}$– 2 drs.
Sulphur, Flowers of	10–60 grs.
Tannoform	10–40 grs.
Turpentine, Oil of (anthelmin- tic)	5–30 m.
Yohimbine (aphrodisiac) ..	$\frac{1}{400}$–$\frac{1}{250}$ gr.

Douche.—A jet of hot or cold water directed against a part, or cavity, of the body. An enema is also a douche, although for some unknown reason the term enema seems popularly to be used to signify an irrigation of the bowels. Similarly, the general public are usually referring to a vaginal or uterine wash-out when the word "douche" is employed. Actually the terms douche, enema, and irrigation are synonymous. (*See* ENEMA.)

Large wound cavities or sinuses may be irrigated or douched with solutions of eusol, liquor sodii chlor., permanganate of potash, Izal, carbolic acid, sodium chloride, etc., for the purpose of removing hairs, dirt, pus and other debris, this method of treatment being particularly useful if the wound is deep and tortuous, its depths being neither visible nor accessible. A stream of antiseptic solution directed into a sinus with force will assuredly reach the furthest limits of the wound and wash out all deleterious matter. In cases of pyo-metra (suppurating womb) a douche would be very valuable if it were properly performed, and care taken to regain all the fluid which was passed in. Great quantities of pus are sometimes collected in the uterus, and it is of great importance to effect its early escape. At the same time, one must not allow quantities of water to remain in the womb after douching, and to help in avoiding such an occurrence, a two-way tube is generally employed. The cleansing fluid thus enters by one hole, and is discharged through the other, without causing the slightest intra-uterine distension. Douching of the womb, however, may sound easy, yet in practice it is often extremely difficult, perhaps on account of the mouth of the uterus (os uteri) being firmly closed. The whole matter is one which should be dealt with only by a qualified man, for dire results may and do follow ignorant interference.

Dover's Powder.—Also known as compound ipecacuanha powder. It consists of powdered ipecacuanha, opium, and sulphate of potash. As a medicinal agent for dogs it is very valuable, particularly in the treatment of distemper, when respiratory catarrh and diarrhoea are outstanding symptoms. The dose for dogs ranges between about 5 to 15 grains.

Down-Faced or Hog-Faced.—With the nasal region inclining downward toward the point of the nose.

By courtesy]   A STURDY TEAM.   [G. Horowitz.
These two law-abiding Swiss Farm Hounds work at the Penal Settlement of Schachen, in Switzerland.

DR. =Drawn. (A coursing term.)

Draft.—Hounds picked out from the pack.

Draghounds.—Draghound Packs are run by various mounted units, such as the Royal Artillery, and other military commands. There are also private and public subscription packs. As the name explains, the Hounds hunt not living quarry but a drag is laid for them by a mounted man, who rides the course some time ahead. Draghounds usually run mute and fast, so that following a Draghound Pack means riding in the nature of a steeplechase. What the Field must face will depend on what the quarry has made for them. Good riding and good horses are essential.

Draghound Packs were at one time composed of mainly draft Foxhounds and Staghounds, and so were often uneven. Whilst some of the private Draghound Packs are still of this nature, the sport is now well established and packs usually consist of well-built, powerful dogs, comparing very favourably with the best Foxhounds.

Drag-hunting takes place during the autumn and winter, and ends in April. (*See* FOXHOUNDS, STAGHOUNDS, ETC.)

Draught-Dogs.—It cannot be said that there exist dogs more or less capable of being used as draught-dogs. However, there existed, since many years, a club in Belgium for "the improvement of the draught-dog", and Professor Reul, one of its founders, had, right from the beginning of its inception, addressed a very sensible appeal to all the amateurs of this kind of dog, of which the following are some translated extracts :

"The dog in harness renders such precious services to the people, to small traders and to the small industrials (agriculturists included) in Belgium that never will any public authority dare to suppress its current use. A disastrous economic revolution would be the consequence. Penury and poverty would enter thousands of homes where a relative affluence is apparent now. The purpose of the Club for the improvement and the protection of the draught-dog in Belgium is to further the breeding of dogs that are most suitable ; to see that these dogs are better harnessed, better led, and that they are put to better-balanced and better-moving vehicles ; to offer disinterested advice to drivers, relating to the doing away with the flaws that present their vehicles ; also to encourage the deserving ones by according them prizes in cash, in medals, in diplomas, and also in public congratulations."

It is certainly a very curious spectacle for a foreigner who arrives in Belgium for the first time to see, in the morning, numerous small vehicles, loaded with fruit and vegetables, which arrive at the markets, drawn by dogs, the gay barking of which denotes that they suffer no pain, but, on the contrary, that they are really overjoyed. Besides, it is not only market-gardeners and peasants who have recourse to this kind of "locomotion" for their goods ; bakers, butchers, coalmen and milkmen all serve their customers in like manner.

IN BELGIUM.
A picturesque Flemish milk-seller on her daily round.

As a rule, there is only one dog harnessed to each vehicle, but one can often see two or more dogs so harnessed. And that beautiful painting of Hermann Léon, representing a *Relais de Chiens* (Relay of Dogs), and which figured in the Salon of Paintings some years ago, shows us a vehicle drawn by five dogs.

The dog which in Belgium, and elsewhere more or less, is used as a draught-dog represents what is called in France a *mâtin* (literally : mastiff, cur), very strong and powerful, stronger than a Great Dane, of different colours—mostly black

A FLEMISH MILK-SELLER.

On the Continent the use of the dog as a draught animal is a matter of considerable economic importance, for it is undoubtedly the cheapest form of transport.

or fawn, with large white patches. In Belgium, at least, those that have recourse to draught-dogs as a means of transport of their goods, are not at all particular about the type or appearance of their "canine horses", provided the latter be powerful and full of energy. In Brussels and Antwerp good specimens of draught-dogs could be bought as cheaply as £4 each. During their hours of service, these draught-dogs are fed on bread and horse-flesh—the usual diet of dogs—and it seems to agree with them. What is interesting to note is that the dead-weight drawn by these dogs is about 300 lb. on an average, but, naturally, bigger dogs are capable of drawing more. It is curious that for these draught-dogs the drawing of vehicles is just as pleasant as the working in the field for gun-dogs. Owners frequently arrange "coursings" for their animals against each other on the open highway for a distance of two or three miles, and as these "trials" are open to the public, the latter derives great enjoyment therefrom. The following is the procedure : The competitors form themselves in a line ; and the impatience of the dogs is a sight worthy to be seen. At last there comes the signal, and the dogs set off very rapidly, barking joyously all the time. It often happens that the dogs and their drivers fall *en route*, but they are quickly up and off once more, and those dogs and drivers that fall more frequently are not always those that are the vanquished.

The Belgians are of the opinion that a good draught-dog is capable of performing the same amount of work as a donkey, and that the former costs much less to keep.

There are draught-dogs also in Holland and Switzerland, though seldom elsewhere in Europe. There is nothing of cruelty to the dog when the latter is well kept and well nourished, and draws a light vehicle. On the contrary, it does the dog's health good.

In countries where draught-dogs are allowed, municipal councils regulate their use. It is forbidden in Belgium, for instance, to harness

By courtesy]　　　　　　　　　　　　　[G. Horowitz.

SWISS FARM DOG.

A long-haired Farm Dog that bears no little resemblance to the English Collie Dog as it was before the days of pedigrees. They are used greatly for draught purposes.

dogs measuring less than about 24 inches at shoulder ; to use dogs that are too old and ailing ; dogs too young ; bitches in whelp or bitches still suckling their little ones ; to harness a dog together with an animal of another species ; to confide the dogs and the vehicle to children under fourteen years of age ; to take a seat in such vehicles or to let other people do this ; to leave the dogs harnessed to the vehicle in the sun during the hot weather ; to use vehicles, harness, etc., that might wound the dogs. The dogs must be harnessed by means of traces fixed to the collar or to the breast-collar, the latter being at least two inches wide, and going round the animal's chest at the right height. Often the traces must be one yard long as a minimum ; and the collar and the parts of the harness which are in contact with the dog must be padded. Vehicles not provided with four wheels must be supplied with a support or have the ends of the shafts sufficiently curved downwards and outwards, so as to hinder the load from weighing on the animals when the latter are lying down. The vehicles must be provided with a third shaft fixed on the left, at the height of a man's hand, so that the driver, in holding it, may prevent the load from pressing on the neck of the dog ; the vehicle must be on springs and provided with brakes ; the axletrees must always be well-greased ; the load, including the weight of the vehicle, must not exceed, even on flat ground, the weight of 300 lb. for a single dog and 400 lb. for two or several dogs. Any vehicle, with dogs, left on the public road is sent to the pound at the owner's expense. In winter, or during the rainy season, the drivers must, during stops of over ten minutes, shelter their dogs from dampness by covering them with a blanket of good thickness. In bad weather the dogs must be preserved from cold or snow by means of a waterproof tarpaulin.

There exists also a law in Holland regarding the use of draught-dogs, but it would appear that it is not so rigidly obeyed. The consequence is that many people in the Netherlands

Photo]　　　　　　　　　　　　　　　　　　　　　　　　　　　　　　　　　[Harold Bastin.

SEEN IN FRANCE.

Although badly crippled this man gets about pretty comfortably in his canine outfit. The cart was specially constructed for his needs and the dogs were specially trained to take him about.

would wish the draught-dogs to be done away with.

It is quite different in Switzerland, for, were it not so, the question of draught-dogs there would not have been so thoroughly referred to by the *doyen* of the dog-fancy in that country, Professor Dr. Albert Heim, in such an excellent manner, in the book published by the "Schweizer Kynologische Gesellschaft", the canine governing body of Switzerland, on the occasion of the fiftieth jubilee (1883–1933) of the latter. Professor Heim is in favour of the dog doing its work. He says that "the work ennobles one", and that "the workless dog constitutes a misfortune, just as a workless man". There used to be more draught-

dogs at the beginning of the last century in Switzerland than there are nowadays, the retrograde movement having begun towards the middle of that century.

Switzerland had found its best draught-dogs in the "Grosse Schweizer Sennenhunde", which formerly were called "Metzgerhunde" (Butcher's dogs). Their close relatives, the somewhat smaller, long-coated "Berner Sennenhunde" ("Duerrbaechler") are also used. These two breeds, native to Switzerland, had been, during many centuries, considered as almost the only draught-dogs of that country, and constant training had contributed to endowing them with the proper instinct for doing their duties, so that nowadays it requires

Photo]　　　　　　　　　　　　　　　　　　　　　　　　　　　　　　　　　[L. P. V. Veale.

A KINDLY THOUGHT.

This Flemish baker has devised a special harness which permits the dog to lie down and rest while its master is delivering the goods. At the same time it offers the dog a better chance to deal with thieves.

only a few minutes of "inspanning" for a Swiss dog to become a good draught-dog.

Professor Heim is of the opinion that the "Grosse Schweizer Sennenhund", as a draught-dog, is the best in the world.

Drinking Water.—It is a most important matter that a dog shall not be deprived of an adequate amount of drinking water. Actually, the more water an animal or man drinks, the better. Poisons which, in the normal course of metabolism are generated within the body, are thereby diluted and the quicker eliminated because of the stimulating effect upon the kidneys. Therefore it should be a general rule in all kennels that a dish of water is available at all times, and particularly in hot summer weather. Dogs do not perspire, but they get rid of a tremendous quantity of moisture in their breath, and this loss *must* be compensated if good health is to continue. Many kindly people provide dishes of water outside their premises, i.e. in the public highways, and whilst there is doubtless often necessity for such action, yet the writer regards the practice with mixed feelings because of the great facility thus afforded for the spread of distemper.

It should be recollected by dog-owners that if the dog's food is mostly dry—such as biscuits—then a larger proportion of water is indicated than need be afforded if the food is generally moist. Owners often

Photo]   [E.N.A.

FROM CANADA.

An interesting picture showing dogs doing service as farm labourers at Great Slave Lake, in the North-West Territories.

ask whether milk is harmful to dogs. There can be no two opinions upon this point, and the answer is definitely "No"! In fact, it is a splendid plan to teach dogs to like milk so that when they are ill, and have no appetite, they will at least drink milk and thereby receive nourishment. It is curious that one should talk of having to train a dog to drink milk, in view of the fact that they take nothing else during their first six weeks of life. Yet such is the case! Many a dog will not touch a drop of it, and, of course, are quite ignorant of what they are missing. Milk is a good food for dog or man, and where it can be afforded it need not be stinted. It should be unnecessary to remind readers that water vessels need cleansing as much as do food vessels, or a green, slimy scum will soon appear and render the water unpalatable. The dishes should be non-spillable (see illustrations on page 512), as these cannot be kicked over and a dog has much difficulty in turning them over, although some clever dogs habitually persist in doing this. An insufficient supply of drinking water is a potent cause of loss of condition, and it may, if continued over a number of weeks, lead even to emaciation.

Drop-Ear. — Similar to Button-Ear (see illustration on page 258) but with ears hanging closer to cheeks.

Dropsy. — This term signifies an abnormal accumulation of serous fluid in the cellular tissues of the body, or in one of its cavities. Generalized dropsy is manifested by a swelling or puffiness of the limbs and sometimes even of the whole body. Such a state is known as anasarca. If the dropsy is mainly beneath the skin,

Photo]   [E.N.A.

FROM NEWFOUNDLAND.

Dog-drawn vehicles are by no means confined to the Continent. Here is one seen on the coast road of Newfoundland.

DOG-POWER.

These two powerfully built dogs, which earn their living on a Flemish farm, are said to take a great interest in their daily work.

Shallow enamelled iron non-spillable drinking vessel.

the condition is oedema; if it affects the head it is hydrocephalus, and if the chest cavity—hydrothorax. One other dropsical condition, namely, ascites, or that which affects the abdominal cavity, is second to oedema only in its frequency of incidence, though it is generally much more serious.

CAUSES.—Oedema, like the other forms of dropsy, is but a symptom of some other disease or abnormality, and is not a disease *per se*. Often it may be caused by some local interference of the circulation, but more generally it arises through weak heart action. In other instances it is due to faulty activity of the kidneys, or sluggish action of the liver.

SYMPTOMS.—The infiltration of the tissues with fluid gives the body, or limbs, a puffy appearance, and when the swollen parts are pressed upon with the fingers, pits or impressions may be made such as might be produced in a mass of dough or putty. The condition may be only a temporary one, in which case it would not be regarded as serious, for it is not uncommonly encountered in dogs which are afforded inadequate exercise, or in those which are debilitated as a result of having undergone some serious illness. On the other hand, it might be alarmingly recurrent and significant then of advancing age and failing heart action. The swellings are painless and devoid of heat, and the temperature of the animal is not elevated; it may, however, be somewhat subnormal.

TREATMENT.—For these localized dropsical conditions, vigorous hand massage and increased exercise would be very beneficial. A purge should be administered, followed by a course of diuretics combined with heart tonics. If such home-treatment produces no tangible effect, it will be necessary to ascertain the exact cause of the condition, so that appropriate measures may be prescribed.

Ascites or Abdominal Dropsy.—In this malady the abdominal or peritoneal cavity becomes partially or completely filled with serous fluid. Its origin is often mysterious, but there are several conditions which are known frequently to be followed by ascites, such as abdominal tuberculosis, chronic peritonitis, and diseases of the heart, liver and kidneys, etc. It is not at all uncommon in old dogs.

SYMPTOMS.—The abdomen becomes gradually distended, and bitches might be thought to be in whelp. There is no pain, but discomfort might ensue from the impedence of respiration, due to pressure upon the lungs when the disease is well advanced. The animal becomes lazy, pants a good

By courtesy]   [Baillière, Tindall & Cox.

Dog with ascites, or abdominal dropsy, arising sometimes from peritonitis. Reproduced from *Diseases of the Dog*, by Muller and Glass.

deal, may go off its food, evinces signs of indigestion and constipation, and usually appears hollow in the flank.

TREATMENT.—Little advice in the way of treatment can be offered to amateurs, for the surest and most rapid method of effecting relief is a surgical one, which none but a skilled and qualified man should undertake. Other therapeutic measures consist in the withholding to some extent the supplies of drinking water, in ensuring that the bowels are regularly moved, and in the administration of diuretics (in some cases) to increase the amount of urine passed per day. The heart's action may have to be sustained if the pulse becomes weak, and the patient should be rested and fed on a nourishing and unbulky diet.

More intricate methods of treatment are the province of the veterinary practitioner, whose aid cannot in this case be dispensed with. Moreover, as the condition is serious, no delay should be countenanced in ascertaining the cause, for its removal is a matter of prime importance. (See DIGITALIS, DIURETICS.)

Drowning.—Death by drowning is directly due to asphyxia; air in the lungs and bronchi is replaced by water, and the animal's blood cannot be re-oxygenated. A dog is naturally able to swim almost as soon as it is weaned, and will continue to do so for a considerable time if it falls into deep water. But it does not reason the situation nor do anything to conserve its powers; instead, it gets more and more panicky, kicks out more frequently, and quickly uses up its reserves of strength, finally sinking through exhaustion.

If a dog is discovered in a drowning condition, although it may appear inert and apparently dead, it is generally well worth while to attempt resuscitation. This consists of holding the dog by the hind legs, head downwards, in order that the water may escape from the lungs and windpipe. The dog should then be laid on its side, with the head a little lower than the tail, and for a few moments endeavour might be made to squeeze water out of the lungs. When no more can be extracted in this way, artificial respiration must at once be induced and persisted with for about twenty minutes. This is done by regularly pressing air out of the lungs, then releasing the pressure so that new air may enter again; the two actions being alternated at the rate of about twenty-five times a minute (in the case of a large dog), to fifty times a minute in the case

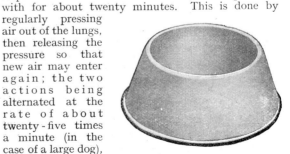

Deep unspillable enamelled iron water vessel.

NOT IN BELGIUM—BUT

This natty little outfit was photographed, quite recently, in a main street of Brno (Brünn), in Czechoslovakia. The dog, a sturdy animal, seems to be more interested in the camera than in the business transaction that is taking place behind it.

of a small one. (A more detailed description of artificial respiration will appear under the general heading of RESPIRATION, *which see*.)

If it were possible to obtain a cylinder of oxygen, or of oxygen and carbon dioxide mixed, it would greatly increase the dog's chance of recovery if this gas could be directed against the nostrils ; so that each time pressure was removed from the chest wall, some gas would enter the lungs.

It is of some importance to infuse warmth into the body. The dog might be laid on hot blankets or over hot (rubber) water bottles, or might be put in front of a fire. Whilst one person is applying artificial respiration, another should be employed mopping the body with cloths or cotton-wool to remove surplus moisture, and should be attending to the heating arrangements, and then, if possible, vigorously rub the legs and trunk to induce circulation. Massage over the region of the heart is very valuable.

Meanwhile, it is assumed that a veterinary surgeon will have been sent for, and that he would have been informed as to the nature of the case. This is important, for in the absence of such knowledge, he might travel perhaps a considerable distance and then arrive without the drugs, gases, or other appliances requisite for dealing with this kind of accident. It is very inadvisable to attempt to pour anything into the dog's mouth until one is quite sure the animal is able to swallow. When the dog is conscious, a teaspoonful of brandy or whisky may be administered in an equal quantity of water, and then only very slowly. Stimulants may be injected hypodermically, too, as soon as the veterinary surgeon arrives.

There is a great danger of pneumonia setting in, and the closest care must be taken of the patient until that danger is past (i.e. about the third day) by applying thick warm rugs, supplying artificial heat, and protecting from chill or movement.

A GERM.
A huge enlargement of the mite that causes canker in the ear.

Drugs.—
A drug is any animal, vegetable or mineral substance which enters into the composition of medicines or chemical preparations. Although this definition is substantially that which is given by medical and other dictionaries, there are numerous people who regard a drug as a chemical substance which, when administered to the living animal, exerts a specific action. There is also a popular belief that if an animal is "drugged" it is narcotized. This is not, of course, strictly correct, for if we adhere to the standard definition of a drug we will see that the administration of any medicinal substance would be an act of drugging.

By courtesy] [Baillière, Tindall & Cox.
Leather cap designed for training faulty ears to lie in the right position.

BEFORE AND AFTER.
The head on the left shows a faulty ear, one being pricked up, the other carried properly. The head on the right shows the same dog after treatment.

Dry Cleaning. —
Dry cleaning a dog can be fairly easily carried out, although it is not pretended that dirt is so effectively removed by this means as it is when soap and hot water are employed. Numerous "dry" shampoos are purchasable nowadays, the use of which is generally confined to *localized* cleansing of the coat when, for any reason, it is very undesirable to immerse the dog in water. These shampoos are made with spirit, and are rubbed into and around the soiled part of the skin until all dirt has been loosened ; and then with a clean dry cloth the surplus is rubbed off, friction being continued until all spirit has evaporated.

Dry cleaning is also accomplished by means of powders, the one in most general use being carbonate of magnesia. This method is mainly adopted among the Fox Terriers, particularly if these are show specimens. The powder is well rubbed in and then brushed out. Even if all dirt is not thereby removed, it has at least received a white coating, and the dog *looks* clean. In addition, a wiry "feel" is imparted to the hair, which, of course, is an attribute sought for in Wire-haired Terriers. Carbonate of magnesia is prepared for use also in block form, which affords a convenient mode of applying the cleanser to the coat.

Dry Dressing.—
A dry dressing is a powder, or mixture of powders, in a fine state of division, and designed—according to its constituents—for the alleviation of local cutaneous irritation or inflammation, or for the drying-up of moist areas and wounds about the skin. The ugly, moist sores so commonly encountered in eczema are admirably suited to treatment by dry dressings, because ointments cannot be applied to wet surfaces, and lotions

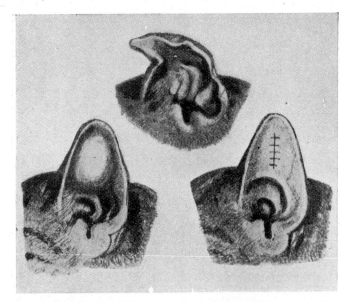

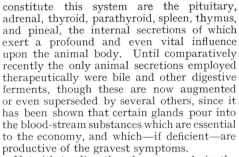

EAR HAEMATOMA.

The first illustration shows a serous swelling on the inner surface of the ear flap. The next shows the same ear after the cyst has been opened and five sutures inserted, while at the top is depicted the shrinkage and deformity which sometimes follows this kind of growth.

are not quite so convenient as are powders for this particular purpose. Many wounds, too, will heal far quicker under the influence of well chosen dry dressings than when continually wetted and covered by wool or bandages.

Abrasions and chafes of the skin are easily soothed by dusting them with good dry dressings. The latter may consist of boracic acid, Fuller's Earth, powdered starch, and others, alone or in combination. A useful dry dressing is composed of 10 parts each of boracic acid, finely powdered starch, and 5 parts of oxide of zinc. To this mixture may be added ¼ part of iodoform in certain cases, particularly if one is very desirous of keeping flies away from the wound.

Another good dusting powder for wounds consists of subnitrate of bismuth 12 parts, tannic acid 6 parts, iodoform 1 part, and wood charcoal powder 25 parts. The easiest way of applying dry dressing is to sprinkle it from a dredger having a finely perforated lid like that of a pepper-box, but a further lid should screw on to the perforated one in order to keep the box air- and dust-tight.

Ductless Glands.—The ductless glands of the body are so called because they possess no discoverable duct or channel capable of conducting away their secretions. The liver has its bile duct; the pancreas, the salivary, and other glands have also well-defined ducts, but no member of the endocrine system is so equipped. The glands which collectively

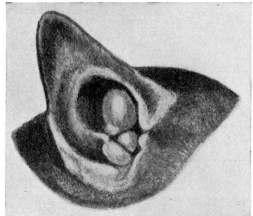

GROWTHS.

Three white tumours can be seen occupying the entrance to the auditory canal.

constitute this system are the pituitary, adrenal, thyroid, parathyroid, spleen, thymus, and pineal, the internal secretions of which exert a profound and even vital influence upon the animal body. Until comparatively recently the only animal secretions employed therapeutically were bile and other digestive ferments, though these are now augmented or even superseded by several others, since it has been shown that certain glands pour into the blood-stream substances which are essential to the economy, and which—if deficient—are productive of the gravest symptoms.

Notwithstanding the advances made in the study of internal secretions, the subject is still really in its infancy, for there are many questions which have not as yet received a satisfactory solution. The chief objects of treating disease with animal extracts are to compensate for a deficiency of the normal secretion, or to stimulate an organ to greater effort; and the brilliant results obtained by the use of thyroid extract, adrenalin, and pituitrin, encourage one to anticipate even greater results from continued research. The control of metabolism is one of the important functions of the endocrine system, taken as a whole, and is, indeed, the main purpose of some of the individual glands. It is not surprising, then, to find that increase in weight, and in amount of adipose tissue, is a symptom of certain glandular disturbances. Obesity in animals, of endocrine origin, is more than frequently associated with aberrations in the pituitary, the gonads (sex glands) and the thyroid.

TREATMENT.

How to hold and mop out a dog's ear correctly.

(All illustrations by courtesy of Baillière, Tindall & Cox.)

THE PITUITARY GLAND, situated at the base of the brain, comprises an anterior and a posterior lobe. Deficient secretion of the former lobe has been observed to produce the following train of symptoms : Retarded growth and development, adiposity, sexual undevelopment, and atrophy of the sex gland. Posterior lobe deficiency is commonly attended with low blood pressure, lethargy, subnormal temperature, and sluggish metabolism. Extracts of the posterior lobe are of distinct service in combating *shock or collapse* following severe injuries or major operations, in controlling *internal haemorrhage*, and in overcoming *uterine inertia* in cases of delayed parturition.

THE SUPRARENAL GLANDS are very minute bodies situated one in front of, and close to, each kidney. For use in veterinary medicine, adrenalin is extracted from the medulla of the suprarenals of oxen, but the yield is so small that the glands of three animals are required to obtain a single grain of it.

Adrenalin is the most powerful haemostatic and constringent known, for which purpose it is mostly employed. Like pituitrin, it constricts the blood vessels and raises arterial blood pressure. It accelerates and increases the efficiency of the heart, for all of which effects it is best administered intramuscularly. Its great practical value lies in its ability, almost immediately, to arrest capillary haemorrhage when applied locally. (*See also* ADRENALS.)

THE THYROID GLANDS are situated in the neck one on either side of the windpipe. Hypertrophy of these glands constitutes a condition known as goitre. Thyroid extract is universally acknowledged to have an extreme value in human and veterinary medicine, and the conditions for which it may be prescribed are many and varied. The thyroid gland is very intimately concerned with the nutrition of the body, and much benefit may follow the administration of its active principle to grossly-fat dogs, especially those whose skins are dry and scurfy and which are losing their hair.

Surgical removal of the thyroids has led, in many cases, to death of the patient ; but in those which survived, the effects of such removal were obesity, mental sluggishness, skin disease, and a lowered resistance to toxic infections. In young animals, too, such an operation leads to arrest of, or interference with, physical and sexual development. In the human species such

EGYPTIAN HAIRLESS DOG.
A front view of the Hairless Dog showing the marking on the skin.

sufferers are termed "cretins". Sometimes the thyroid glands are over-active (hyperthyroidism), the manifestations of which are nervous irritability, trembling, and palpitation of the heart. These symptoms may also be produced by giving a normal dog over-doses of thyroid extract. Where the condition is not artificially induced, however, it may be overcome by the administration of medicinal doses of iodine. (*See* GOITRE.)

PARATHYROID GLANDS.—These minute bodies are embedded in the substance of the thyroid glands, from which they may be distinguished by their paler colour and softer texture. Complete experimental removal of these bodies causes death in a few weeks, preceded by clonic or tonic convulsions. It is said that the injection into the animal of parathyroid extract, or even of calcium preparations, overcomes the tetanic muscular contractions, and averts a fatal issue so long as it is regularly administered. It seems clear, therefore, that the secretion from these glands regulates the calcium metabolism of the body.

In consequence of this discovery it is, nowadays, not uncommon for clinicians to prescribe parathyroid extract in the treatment of chorea, epilepsy, eclampsia, and other diseases of the nervous system, the results, in many cases, being very gratifying.

So little is known of the functions of the PINEAL and THYMUS glands that their discussion will hardly prove profitable. It is known, however, that the thymus gland (situated at the entrance to the chest cavity) disappears very early in life, no trace of it being found in adults. Its normal atrophy, or experimental removal, has been observed to be associated with a rapid growth of the testicles. This fact is one of the links of evidence which proves that there is a very definite co-relation between the various ductless glands.

Smith, in his *Veterinary Physiology*, provides an

EGYPTIAN HAIRLESS DOG.
This Hairless Dog (see notes on Chinese Crested Dog, etc.) was at one time at the London Zoological Society's Gardens.

Photo]

"MERKEL OF THE HOLLOW".

[*L.N.A.*

This Elkhound is the proud winner of the 1934 Championship at Cruft's. Note the well-proportioned, wedge-shaped head, but without any hint at "foxiness"; the moderately small eyes, rather deep-set and slightly oblique; and the upstanding ears, carried slightly forward.

"INGERID".

In 1897 Mr. Leonard Beddome, of Bromley, imported the Elkhound "Ingerid" from Holland, exhibiting her at various dog shows.

interesting contribution to the evidence when he states that : "There is considered to be some connection between the adrenals and the sex glands. During the breeding season, in some animals the glands enlarge ; and in rabbits the cortex of the gland (adrenal) becomes twice the normal thickness during pregnancy. Under the influence of emotion, great muscular effort, fright or anger, the medulla of the adrenals pours out an excessive secretion as a result of impulses received from the brain. This secretion may be regarded in the light of a defensive mechanism against the nervous explosion ; the muscles are "tuned up" for an extra effort, an increased quantity of glycogen is rendered available for their use, the general blood pressure is raised by the pituitary and adrenals, and the thyroid co-operates by furnishing a substance intended to restore the exhausted nerve cells. Whether the storm results in fight, as is common in the case of dogs, or flight, as in the case of horses, probably depends almost entirely on the testicular secretion. In the absence of these glands, it is easy to understand the castrated animal taking no risks, and deciding to get away as early as possible from the source of danger. The female, in the defence of her progeny, will put up a fight under the influence of the internal secretion of the ovary ; and this applies to all animals—from the elephant to the barn-door fowl."

Whilst the foregoing has a general reference to all animals, it applies equally to the dog, and constitutes only a minute portion of the mass of evidence which could be written in support of the view that none of the ductless glands work entirely independently. That view is so universally held to-day that it is a common practice for human and veterinary physicians to prescribe a combination of especially selected hormones to patients in whom the endocrine balance seems deranged, or in which there appears to be a hormone deficiency. Careful selection of the preparations is, however, absolutely essential, as some of them are absolutely antagonistic whilst others are synergistic.

The ductless glands are not the only bodies which produce an internal secretion, for we find that the liver, pancreas, testicles, ovaries, and prostate produce, in addition to their well known and evident secretion, an internal secretion which finds its way into the circulation by the lymphatic system or blood vessels. The spleen is the largest ductless gland in the body, yet it evolves neither an internal nor an external secretion. It can, moreover, be entirely excised from the body without giving rise either to illness or death.

Dudley Nose.—A flesh-coloured nose.

Duodenum.—A name given to the anterior or first portion of the small intestine. It is a part of the bowel which, more than any other, occasionally becomes ulcerated, the lesion being spoken of as duodenal ulcer. It communicates anteriorly with the stomach, and posteriorly with the jejunum or second portion of the small bowel. The ducts of the hepatic and pancreatic glands enter the duodenum, and the latter lies almost wholly on the right side of the abdominal cavity. It then crosses over to the left, where it becomes the jejunum

Dusting Powder. (*See* DRY DRESSING.)

Dysentery.—This term denotes the expulsion of blood from the bowels, whether the former be intimately mixed with the faeces or not. Diarrhoea may, and usually does, accompany dysentery, such a condition being notable in Stuttgart disease. In the last-named malady there is a very free loss of blood from, sometimes, the entire length of the intestines ; and not only may the liquid faeces be highly charged with blood, but the latter may be passed in considerable quantity without the simultaneous passage of a motion.

In such dysenteric conditions, the motions are rendered very foul and may be black, dark red, or flecked with bright red areas. Dysentery is not an infrequent complication of distemper. (For treatment, *see* BLEEDING. DISTEMPER. STUTTGART DISEASE.)

Dyspepsia. (*See* INDIGESTION.)

"FIORD".

A son of "Ingerid", bred by Mr. Beddome. It was one of the first Elkhounds exhibited in this country

ON THE ALERT.

Three very typical Elkhounds, the property of Miss Freeman Taylor.   Note the broad chests, and the short, straight, sturdy build
of the forequarters.   The capacious heads, with up-standing ears, bright eyes, and medium muzzle, are good traits of the breed.

E

Ear, Anatomy of.— The ear consists of three parts, viz.: external, middle, and internal ear, and in comparing the many species of animals it is only in the external ear that any appreciable differences are found. The structure of the middle and internal ears is more or less the same in all animals.

External Ear.—This part (the concha) of the ear consists of a freely movable, more or less funnel-shaped piece of cartilage covered closely by thin skin. The aperture of this so-called funnel is provided with long hairs for obstructing the entrance of flies and foreign bodies. Very deep down, hair-roots are replaced by the wax-secreting glands.

Instead of having to deal with a standard type and size of ear, we are faced with almost as great a variety of auditory organs as abound in the whole animal kingdom. Some dogs are able to express their feelings or emotions, to a large extent, by movement of the ears. An example of such is the Alsatian.

The cartilaginous concha, already referred to, gradually narrows down as the skull is reached, until it takes the shape of a comparatively narrow tube known as the external auditory meatus. This canal is curved, and across its lowest extremity is stretched a membrane known popularly as the *drum* or tympanum.

This membrane is the dividing line between the external ear and the

Middle Ear.—This middle or second portion of the ear is a cavity situated in the petrous-temporal bone, and it is bridged across by a chain of very small bones or ossicles placed end to end. The first

By courtesy]   *[Miss Joyce Esdaile.*

"FOURWENTS SIGRID."

A daughter of Ch. "Garrowby Haakon" and the mother of "Dyfrin" (*See page 535*).

small ossicle is the malleus, which is attached at one end to the drum, and articulates at the other with the next bone—the incus; the latter, in turn, is attached to the third bone or stapes. This ossicle completes the bridge, or communication between the drum and the internal ear, by having an attachment to the membrane covering the fenestra ovalis—which is an opening between the middle and the internal ear.

Internal Ear, also known as the labyrinth, is situated within the temporal bone, and it consists of the semi-circular canals, the vestibule, and the cochlea. All parts of the labyrinth communicate, and all are filled with a fluid lymph. The nerve-endings of the auditory nerve terminate in the cochlea, and it is here that the sound impulses are received.

Mechanism of Hearing.—The sound-waves are collected by the funnel-shaped external ear, and their impact upon the drum causes this to vibrate in the same way as the diaphragm of a gramophone soundbox vibrates when sound-waves strike it. The drum, therefore, moves in and out, causing simultaneous motion in the ossicles. This chain of minute bones transmits the vibratory movements to the membrane which forms part of the boundary of the internal ear, and as the latter is filled with lymph, it follows that agitation is transmitted throughout this fluid and so eventually reaches the auditory nerve-endings of the brain. (*See* DEAFNESS.)

Ear, Diseases of.—Readers who have perused the description of the anatomy of the ear will appreciate that the latter is a delicate and somewhat

Photo]   *[Ralph Robinson.*

Mrs. Hamilton's Elkhound puppies are seen waiting anxiously to be called. Note the tail carriage and the well-marked coats.

difficult organ to deal with.

Auricular disease is more common in long-eared dogs such as Cocker Spaniels, etc., than it is in breeds which have open, short and upstanding ears ; and the signs which might lead one to suspect some ear trouble are : the shaking of the head ; rubbing one or both ears along the ground; deafness; scratching at the ears accompanied, generally, by whimpering or whining ; a moist sucking noise when the ear is compressed between finger and thumb; a discharge, or a foul odour emanating from the aural orifice.

One or more of these signs will doubtless lead the owner to make a preliminary examination of the affected ear. To do this, endeavour should be made to avoid rough handling or attempting to hold the ear in an unnatural position such as stretching or turning back the ear-flap over the top of the head. By the latter procedure one impedes rather than facilitates a view of the interior. The flap (concha) should be held erect between first and second finger and thumb of the left hand, whilst the dog's head is steadied with the right hand.

It must always be remembered that stretching with dilators, or the application of any hard or cold object, will invariably be resented, especially when the ear is already tender ; and if the dog is once hurt, any future attempts at treatment will prove difficult.

Syringing the ear sounds as though it might be

By courtesy]   *[Miss F. Joyce Esdaile.*
"FOURWENTS BRIGHDE".
This Elkhound bitch, the property of Miss F. Joyce Esdaile, is the winner of nearly thirty first prizes.

a very simple operation, but in practice it does not prove to be, and it is a procedure generally best left to the veterinary surgeon.

Inflammation of the Ear.—Also known as otitis. This is an aggravating and often painful condition in which the lining of the external ear becomes inflamed in consequence of blows, accumulations of wax, dirt and other foreign substances, ear mites, dry eczema, soapy water, or general neglect of the ears. It may be unilateral or bilateral.

SYMPTOMS.—The dog evinces obvious discomfort by shaking its head or by holding the head to one side (the diseased ear being lowermost) and by rubbing the ear along the ground. In addition, the dog continually scratches the inflamed ear, thereby increasing the inflammation, causing wounds and drawing blood. Manipulation of the diseased organ, in the early stages, affords the animal a certain amount of gratification and pleasure ; but later, when the condition is more acute, even to touch the ears causes intense pain and resentment, and the dog may readily bite. The ear feels hot, the lining is reddened, and the animal may manifest some degree of deafness.

From this stage the condition may advance into that known as otorrhoea or CANKER, in which a discharge is secreted. Canker may, of course, arise from similar causes to those of otitis, or may be an extension of the last-named condition, after invasion by germs.

Photo]   *[B.I.P.*
A FINE LOT.
A very good lot of six months old Elkhound puppies, bred by Mr. F. W. Holmes, of Hampton Wick.

Ear mites were dealt with under the heading of ACARI, and they may set up otitis or even otorrhoea when their presence is neglected.

The symptoms of canker are very similar to those evinced in otitis, and are usually more severe and extensive. For instance, the whole of the external ear is generally considerably swollen, tense, and painful, and the more it hurts the more the dog injures it by scratching and rubbing. There is not infrequently an exudation of blood, and in very neglected and severe cases the pus may penetrate inwardly, causing ulceration and even perforation of the drum, with nervous phenomena as a sequel.

TREATMENT.—Any line of treatment must be very gently and patiently applied. Cleanliness should be the first consideration, by which is meant that all scabs, discharges, matted hair, etc., should be removed without delay. Such removal is not by any means always easy of accomplishment, for quite often a considerable amount of bathing with warm solutions of borax is necessary before the sticky mess softens and comes away.

A veterinary surgeon should, whenever possible, be allowed to undertake this task, because dogs greatly resent any interference with inflamed ears; and, in addition, they frequently become much alarmed at the crackling noises set up by the frothing of the peroxide. When a veterinary surgeon's services cannot readily be obtained, however, the owner might be content with pouring in a few drops of warm olive oil. After any kind of syringing or washing it is essential that the ear be then dried with soft cotton wool. Apart from curative treatment, the owner can render good service by protecting the organ from self-inflicted violence. He should apply a specially made cap of linen, or string-net, or he may affix an Elizabethan collar. (See RESTRAINT.) Chamois leather socks may also be applied to the hind feet to prevent injurious scratching of the ears.

The veterinary practitioner will be better able to diagnose the condition after this preliminary clear-up, and can decide upon an appropriate remedy.

The owner should be warned not to attempt to

probe a painful or ulcerated ear, as he might do much more harm than good. Particularly he should never use any kind of pointed instrument without being perfectly sure that the point is protected. Lastly, only very small wads of wool should be used.

Ear, Growths in.—It is not uncommon for new growths to appear in the external meatus, and they may increase to such an extent in size and number as to completely occlude the canal.

Pain is not a necessary accompaniment, though one must assume that an affected dog suffers some discomfort, which he will proceed to manifest as the ear becomes more and more blocked up. When this happens, the growths, from opposite sides of the canal, begin to touch each other. At the points of contact, ulceration ensues and a discharge exudes.

Treatment of any kind other than surgical excision is useless. General anaesthesia is essential for this operation, and a complete cure takes two or three weeks.

Ear, Haematoma of.—Also known as blood-blister, serous cyst, and serous abscess of the ear.

CAUSES.—Any injury to the ear-flap, such as bites, bruises or scratches; and it may arise indirectly as a result of self-inflicted injury due to irritation caused by parasites. The latter may be lice on the outside of the concha, or may be mange mites inhabiting the inside of the ear. In consequence of their presence, the dog is continuously scratching and shaking his head, with the result that in long-eared dogs the ear-flap strikes hard upon the top of the poll and becomes bruised.

SYMPTOMS.—A fluctuating swelling appears on the inner side of the ear-flap, sometimes occupying the entire surface, and at others being confined to one end or the other, or to the mid-line. The ear looks very thick and hangs lower than the opposite ear. It is exceedingly tender and hot, and the swelling contains serum and blood.

TREATMENT.—No kind of treatment can replace a surgical operation, and the latter must be well performed if permanent deformity is to be avoided.

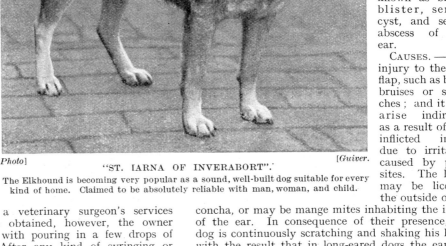

Photo]　　　　　　　　　　"ST. IARNA OF INVERABORT".　　　　　　　　　*[Guiver.*

The Elkhound is becoming very popular as a sound, well-built dog suitable for every kind of home. Claimed to be absolutely reliable with man, woman, and child.

ALL ON A SUMMER'S DAY.

A delightful study, taken in the gardens of Taxal Lodge, Whaley Bridge, Cheshire, of the three daughters of Lieut.-Colonel Henry and Mrs. Ramsden-Jodrell. Their canine companions, from left to right, are an Elkhound, a Cocker Spaniel and a Scottish Terrier.

CH. "GRETEL OF BACOT".

Lady Violet Henderson's noted champion bitch shows all the sturdy strength of this breed. The well-rounded ribs and muscular loins are well defined.

However well done, there are occasions when this lamentable sequel will ensue. A bold incision must be made down the length of the cyst to allow the contents to escape. It is the after-treatment, however, which is so important, because there is a tendency for the whole aperture to refill with fluid. There are several surgical methods of attempting to prevent such recurrence, but they must be left to the practitioner to put into effect. During after-treatment the dog should be made to wear either a linen or a string-net cap, properly fitted and applied. This provision is to prevent the ear from being again shaken and bruised and the wound reopened.

Ear, Odour from.—Quite often dogs' ears smell rather badly, although they may not be diseased in any way. Generally, all that is necessary to eradicate the odour is to mop the interior free from wax and dirt by means of small pledgets of cotton-wool on an orange stick or fine forceps. A good cleansing medium, in which the wool might be dipped, consists of methylated spirit in equal proportion with water. All trace of this liquid must be removed after the cleaning process is complete.

In some cases the odour is due to a stinking purulent discharge. The ear should be bathed with cottonwool, dipped in a disinfectant solution.

Ears, Carriage of. (*See* BUTTON EAR, and also information contained in the articles on the various breeds.)

Ear, Wounds on.—Wounds along the edges of the concha are very troublesome indeed, and they bleed profusely as a general rule.

No treatment will be of any avail in getting the wound to heal unless the string-net is applied. The ear may be wrapped in a piece of lint which has been previously dipped in antiseptic solution; or dry dressing may be used. The string-net keeps all in position and permits the wound to heal up.

East Java Dogs.—The dogs of East Java belong to the category of so-called "pariah-dogs".

Richard Strebel, in his work, *Die Deutschen Hunde*, published by Kern & Birner, of Frankfort-on-the-Main, says that, although the pariah-dogs do not appear to have anything to do with our thoroughbreds, they are of great importance to us, showing the dog in its wild and semi-wild state.

According to Professor Studer, "The skull of these dogs is narrow, the cranium elongated, but arched in the parietal part, tied up in the temporal part; the forehead is narrow, low and very contracted between the eyes. The face is narrow, gradually tapering frontwards, with but little stop, the line of profile at the root of nose more or less concave, the bridge of the nose sinks gradually towards the point of the muzzle. At the basis of the cheekbone the jaws are narrow. The sides of the upper jaw fall very steeply down from the narrow bridge of the nose. The cheekbones are strong, but not wide; as a rule, the brain part is longer or as long as the part of the face; the forehead is low."

These dogs are nowadays to be found only in the mountains of Java. The hair is very thick, light-brown, with a reddish tinge and black-brown stripes, of which one runs from the tip of the nose to the tip of the tail, and the others over the shoulder downwards. The limbs are light-brown, the under-part dirty-white with a brownish tinge.

Eating Deleterious Matter. (*See* DEPRAVED APPETITE.)

Eczema. (*See* SKIN DISEASES.)

Egyptian Hairless Dog.—One of these dogs was in the Zoological collection in London about 1832. On its death in 1833 a careful examination was made, and it was found to be normal in every

Photo]   *[Ralph Robinson.*

CH. "LION".

Major W. H. Melborn's Elkhound champion "Lion", showing the typical head of the breed. Brain power is denoted by the breadth between the ears.

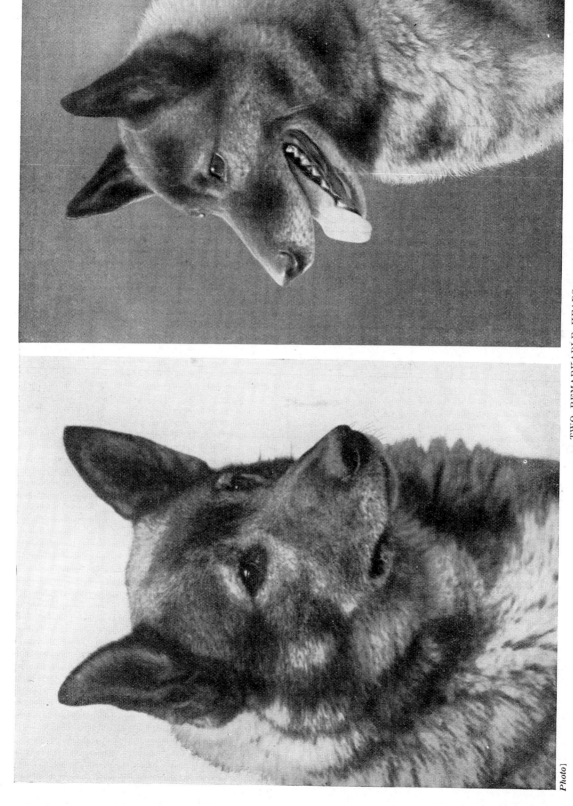

[Photo]

[Fall.

TWO REMARKABLE HEADS. The head capacity is one of the Elkhound's outstanding features, as typified by the above studies. On the left is "Skoll of Dogsthorpe", a challenge certificate winner, belonging to Mr. W. Stuart-Thompson. On the right is the famous International Ch. "Piek II au Glitre", bred by Mr. Holmes, of Hampton Wick.

way except for its teeth. It had no canine teeth nor any incisors in either jaw. (*See* page 516).

Elizabethan Collar. (*See* RESTRAINT.)

Elkhound.—The Elkhound, or, as it would have been better named, Elk Dog, can claim to be one of the oldest inhabitants of Scandinavia. A few years ago, some bones of animals being found in Norway in a stratum belonging to the Stone Age, were submitted to a famous expert, who pronounced four skeletons to be those of dogs practially identical with the Elkhound of to-day. The purity of its race is evidenced by its prepotency; the offspring of any mesalliance

Highlands, and another rounds up ducks and chickens nightly on a farm. It is also a good water-dog.

"Like man, like dog", is an old saying, and all the qualities that tradition gives to the old Norsemen and Vikings, belong to his dog. Strong, fearless and hardy, it is a faithful friend and a delightful companion, is fond of children, clean in its habits, makes a good house-dog, and is an excellent guard. It is sensitive to praise and blame, but is most independent and resents unkindness.

To quote Mr. Bayard Boyesen in the *American Kennel Gazette*:

Photo]　　　　　　　　　　　　　　　　"FOURWENTS".　　　　　　　　　　　　　　　[*Sport and General.*

Miss Joyce Esdaile's team of "Fourwents" Elkhounds are particularly well known in Surrey. The attitude of the dog on the right affords an excellent example of the desirable wide forehead.

invariably inheriting a very large proportion of the breed characteristics.

In its native country, as its name implies, the Elkhound's chief mission in life is to hunt the elk, but it is also used for bears and for retrieving birds. Possessed of extraordinary scenting powers, it can wind an elk at three miles. It is then let loose and will hold the stag at bay till its master arrives. If necessary, it will pretend fear, executing successive strategic retreats to draw the elk nearer its master.

In Britain the Elkhound has to content itself with minor game, such as rats, moles, and stoats, but it has been known to kill both fox and otter. It is very adaptable and is used with some success with the gun, while one specimen known to the writer is working with the Scotch Collies in the

"For dauntless courage coupled with absolute reliability with man, woman, or child, second to no dog on earth; for soundness, stamina, and beauty, for a combination of the rugged and the refined, unexcelled; for prowess in the rough and tumble of big game hunting and for scenting ability (he has been known to scent bear at three miles), unquestionably peerless; as a canine comrade, keenly intelligent, loyal, sensitive, and tenacious in his affections, exquisitely responsive to his master's moods and wishes, and withal of most interesting individuality, unsurpassed."

Types in Norway and Sweden vary somewhat, the one that has been adopted in Britain and U.S.A. being the "Graa Dyrehund" or Grey Elk Dog.

The late Mr. Theo Marples aptly described this dog as the "most rationally built of all foreign

ENGLISH SPRINGER SPANIEL.

Maud Earl's delightful study of this now most popular breed is an impression of an English **Springer** at the end of the nineteenth century.   It is one of her most interesting paintings.

Photo]

GONE AWAY.

Whilst exercising Elkhounds, Mr. Stuart Thompson came across the trail of an otter. Note the way the second dog from the right is lifting its coat.

[Turrall.

AN EXCITING MOMENT.

Mr. W. Stuart Thompson introduces a rat to his excited Elkhounds. The dog on the left is in a very characteristic attitude. The carriage of their tails suggests the excitement of the moment. In the background can be seen Longthorpe Old Manor.

breeds", and there certainly are reasons for the whole of its make-up, which may truly be said to be the survival of the fittest.

Its capacious head shows the Elkhound's brainpower. It should be broad between the ears, wedge-shaped, viewed either way; the muzzle of medium length, with a definite stop.

The eyes and ears reflect its character. The former, brown in colour, should be full, bright and sparkling, and should convey alertness and intelligence, friendliness and honesty, and boldness without ferocity.

The ears, of medium length, are normally carried erect, but are extremely mobile and combine with the eyes and tail in the expression of all its moods. They are turned forwards when excited, dropped when depressed, and laid right back for affection.

His great strength and endurance is apparent at first sight. The body is short and straight as possible, consistent with mobility, with a broad chest, well-rounded ribs and muscular loins. The legs, of length proportionate with the body, should be firm and of good bone; the forelegs set back at the elbow and the hindlegs straight when viewed from behind. Any angulation of the hindlegs or tendency to cow-hocks should be avoided, as it detracts from the appearance of stability and compactness so desirable.

The feet should be oval, toes closed and well padded for service on long treks and rough country.

The story of countless generations of light-hearted travellers in the snow is illustrated by its thick weather-resisting coat, forming a ruff on chest and neck and a triumphant tail, furnished with abundant fur. The tail should be tightly curled and carried centrally well over the back (Scandinavian Standard "set on high"). A low set or limp tail detracts from its victorious air and a lop-sided one from general symmetry.

The colour is grey of various shades, soft gradations being desirable. Blotches or sudden splashes of black and white are objectionable, and dark markings below the knees are "faults". The under-colour should be light, inclining to silver white. A brown or dirty under-colour detracts considerably from the purity and sparkle of the grey, and gives an appearance of vulgarity to an otherwise good specimen.

Bitches make good mothers and seldom require assistance.

The Elkhound's history in Great Britain is comparatively recent, and may well be divided into pre-war and post-war periods. Sundry specimens have been brought over for many years from time to time by sportsmen on fishing expeditions, but among the earliest recorded were some

[Miss Joyce Esdaile.

JUST SIX WEEKS OLD.

This litter of alert and delightful Elkhound puppies, the property of Miss Esdaile, seems to be greatly interested in the "new world" into which they had only so recently arrived.

By courtesy]

brought by Sir Alfred Strutt, when attending King Edward VII in 1878 on his visit to Norway.

Though specimens were continually benched at Cruft's each year, no attempt was made to popularize them and the possession of Elkhounds was confined to a few families, who jealously guarded the breed.

Among the pre-war dogs, one especially stands out : Lady Cathcart's "Jäger", imported in 1896 from Swedish Lapland. From him, through his famous son, Ch. "King", and "Wulfram" may be said to descend what is known as the English strain ; the line being continued mainly through "Woden's" sister "Gerda", "Jansen", "Jarl", "Droma", and "Graftonia Kogi".

Other notabilities amongst his descendants include Ch. "Woden", Ch. "Thorvah", Ch. "Beltsa", "Musti" (who accompanied H.E. Lady Irwin to India), and "Odin Woodbythii".

In 1923 Lady Dorothy Wood (later Lady Halifax), with Lieut.-Colonel G. J. S. Scovell and a small band of enthusiasts, formed the British Elkhound Society, and from then onwards the cult grew slowly and surely, there being very few championship shows without forty to sixty dogs benched.

With the advent of the Society there commenced a fresh era of importation ; initiated by Colonel Scovell, Lady Irwin and Mrs. G. Powell, Mrs. Lombe, Mrs. Cameron Head, and Mr. W. F. Holmes. The winning dogs of Norway and Sweden were gradually transferred to England. Of these Ch. "Gaupa au Glitre", Ch. "Rugg au Glitre", Int. Ch. "Peik au Glitre" and Ch. "Kraus" from Norway, with Ch. "Ialla" and Ch. "Carros" from Sweden, have all left their mark on the breed and have considerably influenced the winning types of to-day. The crossing of these new dogs with the "old English strain" has, of course, prevented any deterioration in stamina and bone, to which all breeds are liable when selection is limited ; but, like Terriers in England, the Elkhound in Scandinavia has its local variations in different parts, and as the new importations were drawn from both Norway and Sweden and varied considerably among them-

Photo]

CH. "WODEN".

[Fall.

A very fine type of Elkhound, owned by Mrs. Powell. Attention is drawn to the coat, and the kindly expression is also worth noting.

selves, the first results were rather confusing and puzzled judges, exhibitors and breeders. The later generations show more uniformity, and it has been admitted by the Norwegian and Swedish judges, and American critics who have come over, that there are no better specimens anywhere than here.

Some of the more successful of the results of amalgamation have been :

"Delhi of the Clyde", Ch. "Lion", Ch. "Wythall", Ch. "Darwejh", "Karl of the Holm", "Finspang", "Major", "Shag", "Van of Dogsthorpe", Ch. "Kit", "Fourwents Dyfrin", "Oline", "Guri", "Bella", Ch. "Gunhilde", Ch. "Vanda of Happy Valley", Ch. "Brenda of Pannal", "Hennie", Ch. "Träe of Inveraillort", Ch. "Rosa of the Holm", Ch. "Stjarma of Inveraillort", Ch. "Elsa of the Holm", "Sköll of Dogsthorpe", "Sküld of Kinburn", Ch. "Mirkel of the Hollow", "Otto", "Fourwents Sigrid", "Tora of the Hollow", Ch. "Ulla of the Holm", "Ulva", "Bunty", "Fourwents Sonja".

As the welding of the various strains continues, it is hoped that while the short back and good bone which have resulted from the importations will be maintained, care will be taken to avoid breeding in to the bad under-colour and bad tails which are now far too prevalent, and both of which detract from the beauty of the dog.

The following is the "Standard of points" as adopted by the British Elkhound Society :

GENERAL DESCRIPTION.—The Elkhound is a hardy sporting dog of Nordic type with good scenting power. It has a compact and proportionately short body, a coat thick and abundant but not bristling, and prick ears ; tail tightly curled over back. It is grey in colour, and of a bold and virile nature.

HEAD.—Broad between the ears ; the forehead and back of the head are slightly arched with a clearly-marked but not large stop. Muzzle moderately long, broader at the base and gradually tapering—whether seen from above or from the side—but not pointed ; bridge of the nose straight, jaw strong with lips tightly closed.

EARS.—Set high, firm and upstanding, height

CH. "STRYX AU GLITRE".

"Stryx" is a notability of considerable importance in the canine world. He is a strongly built dog and comes from Mr. Holmes's famous kennels.

INT. CH. "PEIK II AU GLITRE".

Here is another leading figure in the canine social world. Note the beautiful effect of light on the coat.

[B.I.P.

TAKING NOTICE.

Here are seen "Marko", "Marka" and "Lyn", all of "Holme", watching with keen interest an aeroplane passing overhead.

Photo]

Elkhounds are remarkably intelligent, and also observant.

slightly greater than their width at the base, pointed and very mobile.

EYES.—Not prominent, in colour brown and as dark as possible, giving a frank, fearless and friendly expression.

NECK.—Of medium length, firm, muscular and well set up.

BODY.—Short in the couplings ; back, wide and straight from neck to stern ; chest, wide and deep with well-rounded ribs ; loins, muscular ; stomach, very little drawn up.

LEGS.—Firm, straight and powerful with good bone ; elbows closely set on ; hindlegs, straight at the hock and when viewed from behind.

FEET.—Compact, oval in shape and not turned outwards ; toes, tightly closed ; toe-nails, firm and strong. There should be no dew-claws on the hindlegs.

TAIL.—Set high, tightly curled over the back but not carried on either side ; hair, thick and close.

COAT.—Thick, abundant, coarse and weather resisting ; short on the head and on the front of the legs ; longest on the chest, neck, buttocks and behind the forelegs, as well as on the underside of the tail. It is composed of a longish and coarse top-coat, dark at the tips with a light-coloured, soft and woolly under-coat. About the neck and front part of the chest the longer coat forms a sort of ruff, which with the ears pricked, the energetic eyes and the curled tail, gives the animal its unique and alert appearance.

COLOUR.—Grey, of various shades with black tips to the long outer-coat ; lighter on the chest, stomach, legs and the underside of the tail. Any distinctive variation from the grey colour is most undesirable, and too dark or too light colourings ought to be avoided. Pronounced markings on legs and paws are also not desirable.

DISPOSITION.—Friendly and intelligent, with great energy and independence of character, and without any sign of undue nervousness.

HEIGHT AND WEIGHT.—For dogs, the height at the shoulder is about 20½ ins., and for bitches, about 18½ ins. For such animals their weights in normal

Photo]   *[Fall.*
HEAD OF CH. "RUGG AU GLITRE".
The eyes of an Elkhound should be, as seen here, frank and fearless. They are brown in colour. For full length portrait *see page 534.*

circumstances would approximate to 50 lb. and 43 lb. respectively.

No scale of values has been adopted in Britain, but the scale published by the Norwegian Kennel Club in 1908 may be some guide. It is as follow :

Head, 15 ; tail, 15 ; tout ensemble, 15 ; muzzle, 15 ; ears, 15 ; body, legs and feet, 10 ; coat, 5 ; colour, 5 ; eyes, 5. Total, 100.

Elkhounds should be shown in hard condition, as any excess of flesh is accentuated by their thick coat and short back, and detracts from the desirable appearance of mobility.

Emaciation.—A lean or wasted condition of the body. In normal health the living body stores up quantities of fat in reserve so that when illness occurs, or when an extra drain is imposed upon the animal, there will be a stock of food to draw upon. When these reserve supplies have been used up, the animal becomes lean or emaciated, sometimes to an intense degree. Everybody who has seen a dog suffering from severe and protracted distemper will know what it looks like so far as its bodily condition is concerned. There are many causes of emaciation and, maybe, the most obvious one should be mentioned first— namely, starvation. It follows naturally that if a dog takes no food, all energy and heat must be provided by the fat already stored in the body, and if the starvation is continued there is nothing to replace the reserves or maintain the body in normal condition.

Bitches nursing large litters are often unable to keep pace with the continuous drain upon their systems, and this is why such animals must be exceedingly well fed with the most nutritious foods. Sometimes it is not a question of withholding food, but an inability to digest what is eaten, which causes emaciation. It is quite obvious that if food is passed out almost in the same state as it was in when consumed, the animal has derived no benefit from it. Many dogs, owned by people who are hopelessly ignorant of their requirements, are very slowly but surely starved, and when they have reached an advanced stage of emaciation, the owners bring them for a diagnosis of the "disease". In these cases a little judicious questioning will elicit the fact that the dog has consistently been underfed ; or, if abundantly fed, has been given foods with little nutritive value such as lights, liver, bones, etc.

Occasionally, starvation is found to be due to an intense infestation with worms, but there must be many worms present to make an appreciable alteration in the body state. Mange, or even lice and fleas, will not infrequently induce a degree of emaciation, not only on account of the continuous irritation and lack of rest occasioned, but also in consequence

Photo]　　　　　　　　　　　　　　　　　　　[Fall.

CH. "KRAUS AU GLITRE".

A short coupled dog with good head, the property of Mr. Holmes. Note the breadth between the ears.

of the blood-sucking which takes place.

Malignant tumours, such as carcinomata and sarcomata, are almost certain causes of emaciation ; indeed, where the latter occurs without any ascertainable cause, one inevitably comes to suspect the presence of a malignant growth. Diarrhoea is a ready cause of loss of condition, as also is over work (in draught or Sheepdogs) and, as previously stated under the heading of DRINKING WATER, an insufficient supply of liquid is surprisingly accountable for advanced emaciation.

Diabetes is, of course, a well-known cause, for although the animal may eat and drink voraciously, it has lost the power of storing up any surplus food in the form of sugar or fat. The draining away of sugar in the urine is a characteristic feature of the disease, and eventually an animal so affected becomes little more than a skeleton.

Tuberculosis is not very common among dogs, but it is able very much to reduce them unless they are only slightly affected. High fevers, and any disease of which a symptom is pyrexia, are potential causes of emaciation—especially if their duration is protracted. Stuttgart disease and distemper are invariably associated with the condition, and it is really surprising how rapidly a dog can fall away in the former case.

The treatment, naturally, must be preceded by an investigation into the cause and its removal. An adequate ration of nourishing food must then be afforded (see FOODS), plus some fattening agent such as cod-liver oil, and the enforcement of longer periods of rest, with increased artificial warmth.

Embolism.—The plugging of an artery or vein by a clot or obstruction which has been brought to its place by the circulating blood. The plug is generally a small clot of blood which has emanated from some other part of the body and been carried away to lodge elsewhere. Dependant upon where it settles are the symptoms or sequelae it causes, for if it is caught up in the brain, paralysis or even death may ensue. Occasionally the embolus is a minute portion of a malignant tumour, and wherever such a particle lodges, another tumour will commence growth. In other cases the embolus consists of masses of bacteria, and the place of lodgment then becomes the seat of an abscess. Unless the operation of administering medicaments into veins (intravenous injection) is properly carried out, there is a risk of air entering the vessel, and the embolus then is an air bubble. Such a plug is just as serious as any other kind and is frequently the cause of sudden death. In any case, if an embolism is the means of cutting off all blood supply to any particular part of the body, that part dies.

Embrocation.—Also known as liniment, is a liquid medicament (generally of an oily nature) for application to the external surface of the body. It consists usually of a mixture of oil of turpentine, ammonia, and perhaps acetic acid, in a base of soap emulsion. These ingredients have a counter-irritant effect when well rubbed into the skin, and part of their virtue lies in the vigorous massage which is essential for their proper application. The use of embrocation is as a stimulant to sprained muscles, tendons or ligaments, or to expedite the clearing up of bruises in consequence of the enhanced local circulation which they occasion.

Some liniments, instead of being of a stimulating nature, are actually anodyne (or soothing) in effect, this type being rubbed into parts which are painful—perhaps as a result of rheumatism, arthritis, etc. (*See also* LINIMENTS.)

Embryo.—A name given to the foetus in its earliest stage of existence. EMBRYOLOGY is the name given to the study of the development of the embryo within the female body. An endeavour will be made to give, as briefly and as simply as possible, an account of the creation and development of the embryo in the bitch.

Maturation of the Egg.—When a bitch is born, her ovaries contain several thousand very imperfect cells destined to become matured ova. They are only completed as required, however, and it takes some months (generally nine) before the first few ova have become matured or perfect.

Ovulation. — At each period of oestrum or "heat" the Graafian follicles of the ovary rupture and ova are ejected, and, later, find their way into the uterus via the Fallopian tubes. It has been established, however, that oestrum may occur without ovulation, and *vice versa*, which explains why some matings are devoid of results. There must be a number of eggs ovulated at each period of heat because each foetus represents one egg, and it is safe to assume that some of the ova fail to be impregnated.

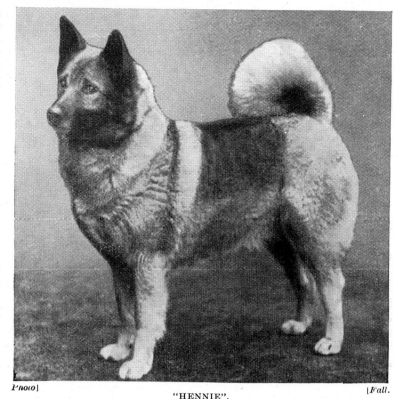

Photo] "HENNIE". *[Fall.*
Mr. Lewis's "Hennie", a remarkably fine female, showing the high set of tail and general good quality, as well as substance.

By courtesy] "FOURWENTS DYFRIN". *[Miss Joyce Esdaile·*
A very good example of the Elkhound, showing body symmetry, a slight arch of the forehead, shortness of body and the desired muscular neck.

A REMARKABLE STUDY.
Ch. "Finne Gutten" and "Elsa of the Holme", a fine pair from a famous kennel.

ing occurs at its posterior third, which is grasped by contraction of the sphincter muscle of the vagina. This serves to tie the two animals together and incidentally prevents the accidental escape of seminal fluid. Furthermore, since dogs are often tied for as long as twenty minutes or more, it ensures that adequate time has been allowed for some of the spermatozoa to advance forwards and enter the os uteri, before there is any chance of their escape. The friction of the male organ leads to ejaculation, a process confined to the male. The glands of the vaginal canal do, however, pour out a secretion.

Artificial Insemination. —Artificial insemination means the introduction, by artificial means, of living semen directly into the womb of the female. For various reasons bitches are sometimes barren, and it has been

Erection in the Male is produced by engorgement of the erectile tissue of the penis with blood. It is a nervous phenomenon which occurs reflexly through an erection centre in the spinal cord, which in turn is directly influenced by higher centres in the brain. A long, narrow bone lies embedded in the penis and facilitates the entry of the latter into the female vagina. Just before ejaculation of semen is about to take place, and when the penis is wholly within the vagina, an enormous bulbous swell-

"RULLE".
The dog, in this forward attitude, shows the desired thick abundant coat and great strength of neck.

ENGLISH SETTERS.

Mr. and Mrs. Eadington, of Prestbury, own one of the finest kennels of English Setters in the world. Here is Mrs. Eadington with some of her dogs.

A NOTED LAVERACK.
The famous Setter "Monk of Furness", one of Mr. Edward Laverack's noted dogs.

found that a few of such bitches can be successfully impregnated by this method. Briefly described, the operation consists in collecting the semen from the vagina immediately after coitus has taken place. The instrument employed for this purpose is called an inseminator. Precautions are taken to keep the seminal fluid warm and free of contamination, and it is passed, as rapidly as possible, through the os uteri, or cervix, into the body of the uterus.

Fertilization.—The male seed, or spermatozoon, having found the entrance to the uterus, swims along in the moisture of its walls until it reaches the Fallopian tube and encounters an ovum, which has descended from the ovary. It is said that a spermatozoon will have reached the upper end of the Fallopian tube in from nine to about twenty-four hours.

The Russian scientist Ivanov stated that a single seminal evacuation of a dog contains as many as 840 millions of spermatozoa. He comments that since only one spermatozoon is required to fertilize one egg, there is an enormous wastage of fertilizing material.

It is believed that the sperm cell meets with the ovum in the Fallopian tube, and that it at once proceeds to penetrate the wall of the germ cell, and, having gained entrance, it sheds its tail. The wall of the egg meanwhile becomes impervious to further attack. Within the ovum there are now two nuclei which meet and fuse, and the process of cell division immediately begins. Each parent is represented in each division of the cell, and in all subsequent subdivisions. When segmentation of the ovum is completed, a sphere is formed which contains an area known as the germinal area, and in this the embryo develops. Soon the embryo possesses within it two tubes—one dorsal (the neural canal) and the other ventral (the alimentary canal). The latter opens in front and communicates with the yolk sac, the earliest source of nourishment to the embryo.

Development of the Ovum.—The fertilized ovum at the end of about one week descends the Fallopian tube and arrives in the uterine horn, where it becomes lodged in a fold of the mucous membrane lining that organ, but it does not become adherent to the

uterus until the twentieth day. The next step is the formation of the *placenta*, a vascular tissue in which the interchange of blood between the mother and foetus occurs. As the placental circulation becomes more firmly established, the yolk sac commences to shrink and become functionless. A membranous envelope, known as the *Amnion*, is now formed, which completely surrounds the foetus. It contains fluid, the function of which is to act as a water-bed and prevent concussion or jar. Another membrane, which grows out from the body of the embryo and completely envelops the amnion, is called the *Allantois*. The space which this sac encloses is connected, via the foetal umbilicus, with the urinary bladder, and it contains a fluid derived mainly from the foetal urine. The allantois is a very vascular membrane, and has been referred to as the organ of foetal respiration, because it is able to bring the blood of the foetus near enough to that of the maternal uterus to permit of the exchange of gases.

The outer covering of the foetus—the *Chorion*—is an elongated sac which envelops the other two sacs previously mentioned. Through the umbilical cord the chorion affords a vascular connection between the foetus and the mother. The *umbilical cord* is, for the purpose of description, a tube or canal through which blood passes between the mother and the foetus. It contains two arteries, a vein, part of the yolk sac, and the connecting channel between the foetal bladder and the allantoic sac (the urachus).

At parturition this cord becomes severed, and the spot where the withered stump recedes is afterwards called the navel.

Pregnancy.—The duration of pregnancy or the period of gestation in dogs is from 60 to 66 days; it is generally agreed that the average is 63 days or 9 weeks. Pups born even a week earlier or later than 63 days have, on plenty of occasions, been perfectly well-formed, quite normal, and have grown into good specimens of their breed.

At the end of the ninth week the foetus is ready to lead a separate existence and parturition takes place. (*See* WHELPING.)

In close connection with this subject are the articles entitled SEX, DETERMINATION OF; SUPERFECUNDATION; SUPERFOETATION; *qui vide.*

CH. "QUEEN ELSIE".
At the end of the nineteenth century this Spaniel bitch was one of the best Setters. She was owned by Mr. M. G. Potter, of Carlisle.

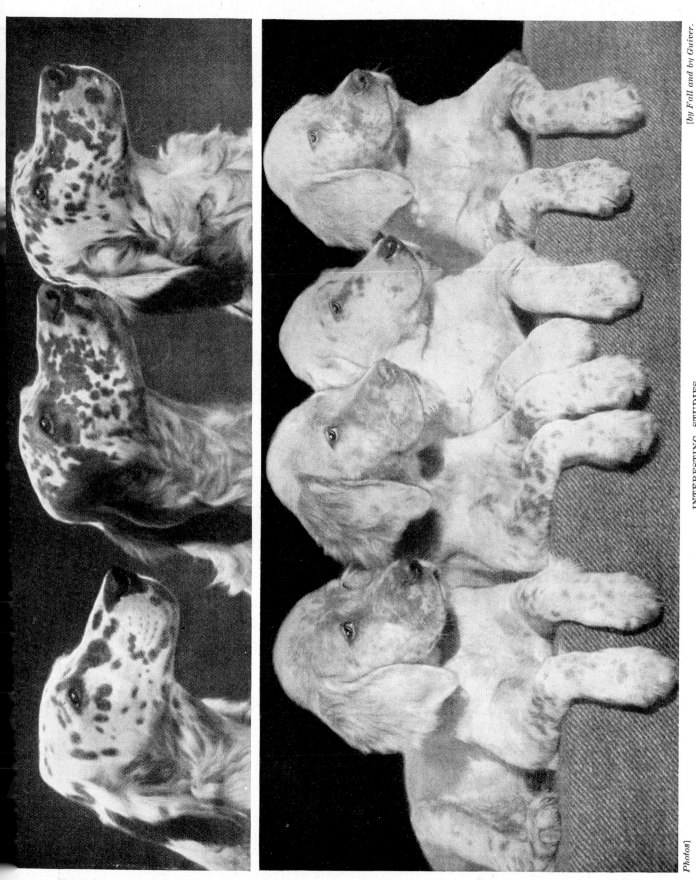

[by Fall and by Guiver.

INTERESTING STUDIES.

Above are seen three excellent Setter heads.   The dogs are from the kennels of Mr. and Mrs. A. W. Rhodes, of Baildon, Yorks, and are just seven months old.
The photograph below depicts a delightful litter of Miss Lewis's English Setter puppies.

[Photos]

"BAILDON BARRA".

A remarkable Setter, showing the feather, or flag. It has won five first prizes, and is the property of Mrs. A. W. Rhodes.

"WITHINLEE GROWSE".

This fine English Setter was best in show on thirty-six occasions. It belongs to Mr. and Mrs. Eadington.

Emesis.—The act of expelling the stomach contents through the mouth. When a dog vomits, it must not be regarded as obvious proof that the dog is ill, for he has the power of voluntary emesis, and uses it only too frequently. Dogs are, by nature, great foragers, and it seems to be fairly well established that if they consider they have eaten anything likely to be harmful they can with great ease return it via the mouth. Object lessons of this are afforded day by day, for if a sugar-coated or otherwise tasteless pill be given to some sensitive dogs, they will at once vomit it. The more cunning may even retain their pill for some time, until nobody is observing, and then reject it. This, incidentally, explains why some medicines are at times discredited by those who purchase them. It is believed, too, that dogs

(3) stimulation resulting from irritation of the larynx, oesophagus or lungs, or following severe coughing; (4) diseases or irritation of the brain and ears; (5) the presence in the blood of urea (uraemia), bile (biliousness), or toxins absorbed from the bowel in constipation, and other conditions.

Dogs are often much upset by journeys in motorcars or trains, especially if they are unaccustomed to the subtle motions of these vehicles. The exciting cause then is an upset of balance which is closely associated with movements of the fluids within the internal ear.

One can plainly see, therefore, that vomiting in the dog is very easily occasioned, and that failure, at first, to ascertain its cause might be reasonably excused. The reader is in a position, too, to

Photo]   Wall.

AN EXCELLENT HEAD.

This picture presents "Stainton Sultan", the property of Mr. T. H. Moorby, who owns a powerful kennel of Setters and Pointers.

instinctively know when their stomachs require emptying, as evidenced by their selection and consumption of certain grasses which make them sick. Some people consider that if a dog has worms in its stomach, it consumes grass in order that the latter may coil about the worms and expel them when the act of vomition takes place—as it inevitably does.

The act of vomiting is rather complex, as it entails closure of the pylorus (or exit of the stomach), dilation of the oesophagus (or gullet), and contraction of the diaphragm, abdominal muscles, thoracic muscles, and of the stomach walls, and closure of the glottis.

Emesis may be caused by: (1) Irritation of the gastric mucous membrane by the presence of too much food, of a foreign body, an irritant poison, or of an emetic; (2) reflex irritation arising from some distant organ such as inflammation of the kidneys, uterus, bowels, or of the peritoneum, etc.;

appreciate that the diagnosis of "gastritis", so glibly and frequently advanced by unqualified people whenever a vomiting dog is presented, is one which should be regarded usually with some doubt or, at least, reservation.

When a dog goes through all the contortions associated with vomiting, but rejects nothing, the act is known as "retching".

Vomited material may take on various colours in different circumstances; thus it may be red as a result of admixture with blood; it may be green from the consumption of grass or copper sulphate; violet from the presence of certain drugs; yellow or greenish-yellow from admixture with bile; or black in consequence of the presence of stale blood emanating possibly from the duodenum; and lastly it may be colourless, when only gastric slimy-mucus is voided.

Bright-red vomit may indicate injury by a sharp

foreign body or by corrosive poisoning, or be a symptom of Stuttgart disease.

When a dog is suffering from impaction of the bowel, especially if of long standing, it may vomit faecal material. It is as well always to ascertain the odour of vomited matter, as occasionally a clue can be obtained regarding the cause. This is notably true in the case of phosphorus, carbolic and iodoform.

Emetic.—A substance which is capable, in one way or another, of causing emesis. There is a great variety of such substances, and by their mode of action they may be split into two groups : (1) Direct or mechanical emetics which act directly upon the nerves of the stomach. Examples: sulphates of zinc, copper and mercury ; alum, mustard and washing soda. (2) Indirect or systemic emetics which act upon the vomiting centre of the brain through the blood. Examples : ipecacuanha, tartar emetic, apomorphine, tobacco, etc.

Emphysema. — A condition in which there is a swelling or inflation due to the presence of air in the interstices of the connective tissues. Emphysema may also occur in the lungs (pulmonary emphysema) when there has been an escape of air from the alveoli or air-cells into the interlobular tissues. Still another form arises when the alveoli themselves are abnormally distended with air. The first-mentioned type is due generally to wounds through which air has been permitted to gain access to the subcutaneous tissues. Both acute and chronic forms of pulmonary emphysema are commonly observed in dogs, and whilst the first-named may arise in association with pneumonia or bronchitis, the chronic form (also termed broken-wind) is usually a result of the acute form, or arises late in life. Thus it is most commonly seen in old, fat, and lazy dogs, and causes them to be very wheezy, easily fatigued, and liable to attacks of coughing on exertion. This chronic condition is sometimes erroneously regarded as asthma, though it would probably require the services of a pathologist to draw a definite distinction.

There is no actual cure, as the walls of the alveoli or air cells have atrophied, thus throwing one compartment into communication with another, and so reducing very considerably the superficial area

Photo]   *[Fall.*
AT TWO MONTHS.
Setter puppies, as Spaniel puppies, are most fascinating. It must be hard for breeders having to part with them. Here are "Withinlee Wondergirl" and "Wonderlass", the property of Mr. and Mrs. Eadington.

available for the interchange of gases between the air and the blood, and vice versa. Treatment of the heart, however. by tonics, is usually beneficial ; and in general the animal should be well nursed, i.e. not fatigued, not overfed, nor exposed to sudden changes of temperature. Adequate food must, of course, be given, but what is meant by "not overfeeding" is that bulky meals should be avoided, and the day's total ration should be divided into small parts and given more frequently.

Encephalitis.—Inflammation of the brain or its membranes ; also known as brain-fever. (See BRAIN, INFLAMMATION OF.) There is another form known as Encephalitis Lethargica (Sleepy Sickness), but this has only rarely been observed in the dog, and little or nothing is known about it.

Endocarditis. — (See under HEART DISEASES.)

Endocrine System. — (See DUCTLESS GLANDS.)

Enema.—A liquid thrown or to be thrown into the rectum. Also known as a clyster or injection.

USES.—Enemata are given for various purposes and usually with great benefit, as when properly injected they invariably achieve the desired result and are free of danger or ill-effects. The commonest use for an enema is to relieve impaction of the colon or rectum, which they do by "ballooning-out" the lower bowel, so permitting of the escape of accumulated dried faecal masses. It is a very common occurrence to find dogs unable to pass a motion, although the lower bowel is full, the contributory causes being fever, debility, or obstruction. The latter may, in turn, be due to a foreign body inside the bowel, or to caking of the hair into a mass outside the anus. In the latter case, the cure generally consists only of removing the mass with scissors, afterwards washing the anus thoroughly with warm water. In other cases, digital examination of the rectum will reveal hard masses of faecal matter ready for expulsion but which require helping out.

If, for any reason, the passage of a motion causes a dog pain, he will often purposely refrain from attempting it, with the result that the longer the faeces remain in the colon or rectum, the more water

THE BIRDS RISE.

Joel McCrea is a famous American radio star, but ranching is his hobby and the gun his favourite sport. An English Setter works for him on his shooting expeditions.

IN THE U.S.A.

Some of the dogs are very heavily marked, according to English standards.

[Photo]

[E.

is abstracted. In due course the erstwhile moist motion becomes dry, and its eventual passage is rendered even more difficult in consequence.

A purgative administered by mouth has not, in such cases, such value or efficacy as local treatment by means of an enema. To relieve the condition, therefore, one obtains a bowl of warm, soapy water and a Higginson's (or ordinary enema) syringe, and, having expelled all air from the latter, the nozzle of the syringe is lubricated with soap and passed gently into the anus, as far as it will go. If difficulty is experienced in inducing the nozzle to enter, give a preliminary bathing with hot water. The dog's tail is held firmly and raised by the left hand, and the bulb of the syringe is worked by the right hand. Ensure that the intake end is kept beneath the surface of the water throughout, or air will enter and the dog may be caused considerable pain in consequence.

As much as a pint of solution may be slowly injected in this way, and then the nozzle is removed to allow the passage of faecal matter. After some has come away, repeat the process, and then permit the dog to run about for awhile. Be in no hurry to inject the water, as it takes a minute or two for the bowel to dilate and the dog to become accustomed to the process.

Occasionally, instead of using soapy water one injects warm olive-oil, castor-oil, or glycerine; but water usually answers quite well and is far cheaper.

Purgative enemas may be repeated daily should they be indicated.

Medicinal enemata are sometimes prescribed, not for the purpose of inducing defaecation, but in order to treat some other condition which is not conveniently treated via the mouth. For instance, sedatives can be introduced for allaying colic, narcotics for quietening nervous excitability, astringents for the cure of obstinate diarrhoea, and vermifuges for the expulsion of worms.

TOGETHER.

Four charming English setters owned by the late Mr. R. E. Potter. The three on the right are particularly good specimens of the breed.

A salt-water enema has often been found of great use for reducing anal irritation to which all dogs are so subject; and the diarrhoea arising from colitis is effectively dealt with by high injection of sedatives and astringents combined.

When an operation is to be performed about the head, thus rendering an anaesthesia mask obstructive, a dog may nowadays be rendered profoundly unconscious by the rectal injection of Avertin. (*See* ANAESTHETICS.)

Finally, nutrient clysters may be employed in cases of severe prostration and sickness, when any food given by the mouth is immediately returned. Such nutrient enemas may consist of eggs, and wheat-flour boiled in twenty per cent grape-sugar solution; peptone, cod-liver oil and sugar; meat juices, etc. Before administration, however, the bowel should be washed out, and the food should be delivered very slowly indeed in order not to induce its expulsion.

English Setter.—The English Setter is undoubtedly one of the most beautiful and elegant of the canine race, the varied colours are most attractive, and they are fast becoming a fashionable and favourite breed. This is largely due to the activities of the English and Gordon Setter Association, the Setter and Pointer Club, and the English Setter Club.

There are varied opinions as to the exact origin of the English Setter, but none of these are convincing or conclusive. It is believed that many centuries ago it was referred to as a Spaniel. In the year 1555, Robert, Duke of Northumberland, is said to have trained a Setter to set partridges in conjunction with the net, and it is quite possible that the dog of that period is the foundation of the English Setter of the present day. It appears that the first

Photo]   IN ITALY.   [E.N.A.

Signor Mussolini owns this attractive team of English Setters and exhibited them recently at a show held by the Kennel Club of Rome.

authentic record of the English Setter, as we know it to-day, occurred in the time of the late Mr. Edward Laverack, who died in 1877, reputed to be the greatest authority on Setters of all times. He bred some magnificent dogs, and doubtless all our present-day Setters trace their origin to this strain.

The late Mr. Purcell Llewellin also did much for the breed, and was probably one of the greatest breeders we have had. He was most successful on the bench and was practically invincible in the field. It makes interesting reading to follow the number of wins at field trials of the Llewellin Setters in the early numbers of the Kennel Club stud books.

In the middle 'eighties Mr. George Potter, late Secretary of the English Setter Club, had many beautiful dogs, and his prefix "Wetherill" is found in many of the pedigrees to-day. Mr. F. C. Lowe's

Photo]   *[Fall.*
"MAESYDD MAYFLY".
Mr. Edward Laverack agreed that the Setter was but an improved Spaniel. Mr. P. Llewellin bought his noted "Countess". He further improved the breed.

was also a name to be conjured with in the Setter world, and his dogs were most successful on the bench and in the field. Mention should be made of Mr. Elias Bishop, who was always well to the fore with his dogs, and of his nephew, Mr. Arch. Bishop, secretary of the English Setter Club.

One likes to think backwards over the—as one might call them—pillars of the breed. Of course, in the very early stages of the pure-bred "Blue Beltons" come Mr. Laverack's "Dash", Mr. Garth's "Daisy", Mr. Purcell Llewellin's "Countess", and Mr. Dickson's "Bella". The pedigree of Mr. Laverack's "Dash" makes history in a way. His sixty G-g-g-g-grandparents consist of four dogs only, which he used solely to perpetuate his strain. They were "Ponto", "Old Moll", "Dash 1st", and

Photo]   *[Fall.*
"BAILDON BRACKEN".
Mr. A. W. Rhodes' dog shows the typical flecking of the Setter breed (note the front legs) which adds so much to their beauty. Notice, also, how the tail is set on, almost in line with the back.

Photo] [*E.N.A.*

TWO PETS.

English Setters are not only good gun-dogs, but make also excellent companions. Of gentle disposition, they are ideal as pets for children. Jackie Cooper, the world-famous boy film star, is here seen with his canine pal.

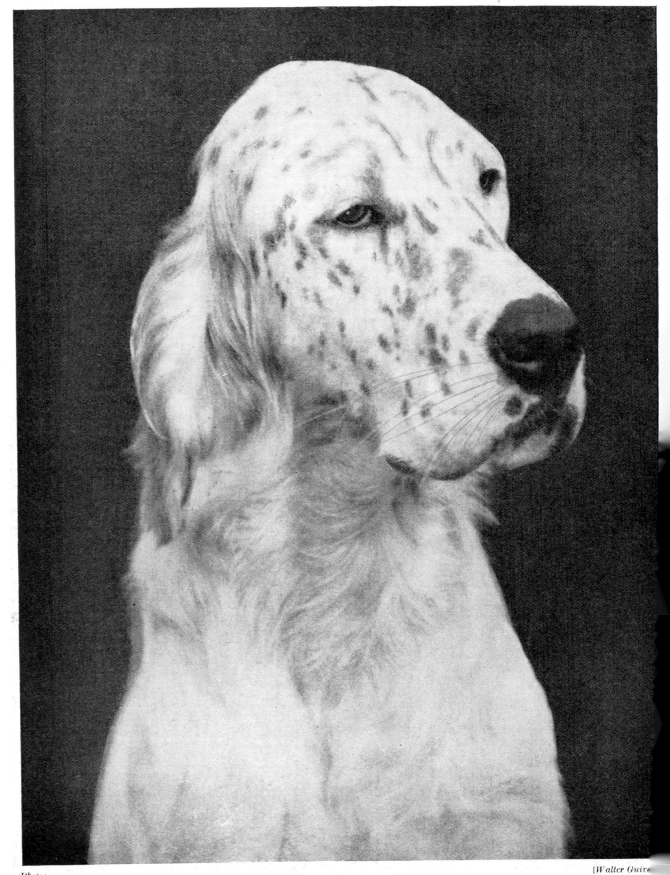

IN SERIOUS MOOD.

This English Setter, "Punch of Fermanar", the property of Miss K. Lewis, is the proud winner of two Champion Certificates and four reserve
Note how long and lean the head is, and how well defined the stop.

"Bella 1st". Later on one comes to the famous Llewellin dogs, the Wind'em's, of which a few survive to this day; in fact, the writer has a great-grand-daughter of "Nick Wind'em". Then comes the world-famous Mallwydd Kennel, owned by Mr. Tom Steadman. Although now retired from the show ring as an exhibitor, Mr. Steadman officiates as a judge at some of the championship shows. That grand bitch, Ch. "Mallwydd Sarah", and that great sire, Ch. "Mallwydd Albert", to mention only two, have left their mark in English Setter pedigrees. Mr. David Steadman is following his father's footsteps, and his prefix "Maesydd" is almost a household word in gun-dog circles.

Among the Setters of recent years that have set their stamp on the breed must be mentioned the late Professor T. Price's "O by Jingo", "Nan of Crombie", "Glaisnook Kate", and "Alice of Crombie"; Mr. C. Atkinson's Ch. "Crossfell"; Mr. D. Steadman's "Maesydd Minnie" and "Maesydd Mariner"; Mr. and Mrs. Smerdon's "Petersham Blue Knight"; and the writer's Ch. "Maesydd Mustard", "Withinlee Albert", and "Withinlee Fay", all of whose names figure largely in the pedigrees of the present-day English Setter.

Photo]   [*Fall.*

AT FIVE MONTHS.
A hamper-load of lively English Setter puppies sired by "Withinlee Albert".

In the field trial world Mr. Isaac Sharpe's Stylish Kennel, Capt. Blaine's West Down Kennels, and Mr. Mitchell's Lingfield Kennels are generally predominant.

The popularity of the English Setter has, within recent years, grown very rapidly, and the registrations are steadily increasing. The reason for this is plain to see. The animal's beauty is beyond question; grace and elegance give it distinction; it is an ideal companion, and possesses a most amiable disposition. It has been proved over and over again that as a gun-dog it is equal to any. As a show dog it is always popular, attracts attention, and is seldom shy. Nowadays there are few show secretaries who do not cater for this breed: a good English Setter is outstanding, and it is not uncommon to see it winning "best in show". The English Setter is less excitable than its Irish cousin; is most intelligent, and easy to train, and is a real, true, affectionate pal, devoid of vice and never ferocious. Those who have once owned one, either as a companion, show dog, or for the gun, seldom take kindly to any other breed.

One often hears from the field trial habitués that the present show type is of little or no use as a worker. It is a pity that more English Setters

Photo]   [*Fall.*

IN THE YOUNGER SET.
Four youngsters from Mr. and Mrs. W. R. Eadington's kennels. Note the nice flecking of the three on the right. It is surprising that the English Setter is not more often kept as a pet, for a better-tempered dog it would be difficult to find.

are not more consistently worked, not necessarily at field trials, but for ordinary shooting. Given the opportunity, the show Setter would hold its own with any. The future of the breed demands attention to the working side if one looks at it from a commercial standpoint alone : at the present time the demand far exceeds the supply.

Undoubtedly one of the principal requirements in Setters is style of movement, which should be quick, easy and true ; a dog with a rheumatic style of movement is most objectionable and is little use as a field trial or show dog. There is a tendency however, to-day, to exaggerate the head qualities at the expense of the rest of the body. This is to be greatly deplored, in spite of the fact that a well-known judge once made the remark that the head was the first and last thing seen when examining a dog. A Setter, to be an object of beauty, must be symmetrical and should have no exaggerated points ; let the dog as a whole be so constructed on sound lines that there is no jarring element to the eye, and one that is capable of doing a good day's work.

The demand from abroad for this now popular breed is rapidly increasing. It is a variety with prospects of a bright and popular future. The writer's conception of a perfect English Setter is as follow : A dog of medium size, neither too large nor too small ; lightly ticked by blue, blue-and-tan, or lemon ; free from heavy dark patches or solid

"CARSWELL MIMORU".

This head study of Miss P. M. Butler's dog well illustrates the occipital protuberance that is so marked in the Setter

colouring. A head that is long, without exaggeration, beautifully chiselled, and with that wonderful expression only to be found in an English Setter, namely, a combination of sadness, intelligence, and dignity ; and a clean, long, muscular neck set on to fine sloping shoulders. The shoulders should be just slightly higher in outline than the hind-quarters ; the front sound and not too narrow ; the brisket deep ; and the ribs well sprung ; a shortish back ; well-developed hind-quarters ; thighs long, short hocks ; the tail well set on, and not too long. Add to this, silky feathering on tail, chest and forelegs, and the result is one of the most beautiful dogs in existence. To appreciate the beauty of an English Setter one should see it ranging a moor in September, when the heather is out, and the sight of a light blue belton-and-tan setting at grouse is a delight.

CH. "MAESYDD MUSTARD".

This very beautiful dog won his championship. Champions are rare in the world of sporting dogs, for they must excel in the field : they must be workers as well as good to look at.

"WITHINLEE TANGO".

This fine Setter, the winner of numerous prizes, is owned by Mr. and Mrs. W. R. Eadington.

CH. "PENNINE PATRON".

A well-built Setter, the property of Mr. H. E. Whitwell, showing most excellent body shape.

ENGLISH SETTER FAULTS.

GENERAL IMPRESSION.—Unintelligent appearance The Bloodhound type, with heavy and big head and ears and clumsy body ; as well as the Collie type, with its pointed muzzle and curved tail.

HEAD.—Pointed, snipy, dropping or upturned muzzle, coarse heads, and short foreface.

EYES.—Too light in colour, too deep-set, or too prominent.

EARS.—Set too high, or unusually broad or heavy.

NECK.—Thick and short ; throatiness.

defined stop. The skull oval from ear to ear, showing plenty of brain room, and with a well-defined occipital protuberance. The muzzle moderately deep and fairly square ; from the stop to the point of the nose should be long, the nostrils wide, and the jaws of nearly equal length, flews not to be pendulous ; the colour of the nose should be black, or dark, or light liver, according to the colour of the coat. The eyes should be bright, mild and intelligent, and of a dark hazel colour, harmonizing with the colour of the coat. The ears of moderate length, set on low, and hanging in neat folds close to the

Photo]   [Fall

"WITHINLEE WONDER".

Another Setter, the property of Mr. and Mrs. Fadington, a dog with plenty of heart room and good head. The breed at one time was taught to go down, but to-day they point in the same manner as the Pointer.

SHOULDERS AND BACK.—Irregularly formed, back too long.

CHEST.—Too broad.

LEGS AND FEET.—Crooked legs ; out-turned elbows ; the toes scattered ; flat-footed ; short, stumpy legs ; stiff or stilted hind action.

TAIL.—Too long, badly carried, or hooked at the end.

COAT.—Very broken or curly, with dry, lustreless appearance.

COLOUR.—Heavy patches of colour on the body very undesirable.

DESCRIPTION AS ADOPTED BY THE ENGLISH AND GORDON SETTER ASSOCIATION.

HEAD.—Should be long and lean, with a well-

cheek ; the tip should be velvety, the upper part clothed with fine silky hair. As a guide, the length of head for dogs about 10 inches, and about 9 inches for bitches.

NECK.—Should be rather long, muscular, and lean, slightly arched at the crest, and clean-cut where it joins the head ; towards the shoulder it should be larger, and very muscular, not throaty ; nor should there be any pendulosity below the throat, but elegant and blood-like appearance.

BODY.—Should be of moderate length, with shoulders well set back or oblique ; shoulders should be slightly higher than the loin ; loins wide, slightly arched, strong, and muscular. Chest deep in the brisket with good. round, widely

Photo "REX OF CROMBIE". [*Fall.*

The feather of a Setter is an outstanding feature of the breed, and Mr. A. B. Nicholson's dog, "Rex", presents a good example.
The English Setter was already popular at the commencement of the nineteenth century.

Photo] "BAYLDOME THATCHER'. [*Fall.*

Truly a Setter is a magnificent dog. The one shown immediately above belongs to Mr. A. W. Rhodes and is lightly flecked all over.

sprung ribs, deep in the back ribs—that is, well ribbed up.

LEGS AND FEET.—Stifles well bent and ragged ; thighs long from hip to hock. The forearm big and very muscular, the elbow well let down. Pasterns short, muscular, and straight. The feet very close and compact, and well protected with hair between the toes.

TAIL.—The tail should be set on almost in line with the back ; medium length, not curly or ropy ; to be slightly curved or scimitar-shaped, but with no tendency to turn upwards ; the flag or feather hanging in long pendant flakes. The feather should not commence at the root, but slightly below, and increase in length to the middle, then gradually taper off towards the end ; and the hair long, bright, soft and silky, wavy but not curly.

COAT AND FEATHERING. — The coat from the back of the head in a line with the ears ought to be slightly wavy, long and silky, which should be the case with the coat generally ; the breeches and forelegs, nearly down to the feet, should be well feathered.

COLOUR AND MARKINGS.—The colour may be either blue-and-white, lemon-and-white, liver-and-white, or tricolour—that is, blue, white, and tan ; the lighter the better ; heavy patches of colour very undesirable.

SIZE.—As a guide to size : shoulder height for dogs, 24 to 25½ inches ; for bitches, 22 to 24 inches.

English Springer Spaniel.—Of all the different kinds of gun-dog, the Spaniel is the oldest. It is not known to what year it dates back, but Dr. Caius gives a description of the Spaniel in his *Treatise of Englishe Dogges* in the year 1576.

Photo]   [Fall
AT ATTENTION.
Mr. H. E. Whitwell's "Fantail" in an attitude that seems to indicate it is waiting for the next order. Note the tense and expectant expression in the eyes.

As regards the origin of the English Springer, nothing definitely reliable can be traced. There are several theories and unfounded suggestions, but we cannot be certain of any of them. The most likely conclusion is, that it gradually appeared through years of scientific breeding and was not originated by any specific person. It takes years of judicious breeding to standardize any particular breed, and we cannot arrive at the goal in a day.

The English Springer Spaniel, together with several other varieties of the breed, have descended from the original Spaniel, but it was only in the first year or two of the present century that the Kennel Club recognized the English Springer as a distinct breed of its own. There is one theory that they originated from the Norfolk Spaniel. This Spaniel was not necessarily a denizen of the county bearing that name, but was produced by one of the Dukes of Norfolk (who, it is stated, was also keenly interested in the breeding of King Charles Spaniels). This Duke, jealous of his strain of Spaniel, could very rarely be persuaded to part with any of them. If he did, it was only on the express condition that it should not be used for breeding purposes, or, at any rate, only to one of a direct line of the strain. Some say, however, that the only kind of gun-dog in which the Duke of Norfolk was interested, was a kennel of Sussex Spaniels. This sounds feasible, as the Dukes lived in Sussex, and the breed originated in that county. It would appear, therefore, that we are in some doubt as to the origin of the English Springer Spaniel.

As its name implies, the Springer Spaniel, or

Photo] [*L.N.A.*

THE ENGLISH SPRINGER SPANIEL.

Mrs. T. Ford-Lowe's Ch. "Worthing Suspense" was exhibited at Cruft's Show in 1934.   The head well illustrates the clearly defined stop.

"Springing Spaniel", was used for springing at game in order to make it "get up" or run, as apart from the "Setting Spaniel", which set game and did not flush it.

These two Spaniels were very much the same in conformation, but, as previously stated, were used for a different purpose. The Springer, in the early days, was most likely used for flushing game into a net, or for pushing it out of covert to be coursed by Greyhounds.

In old records it is stated that the English Springer resembles the Setter, particularly in the head and general outline, except that the former is shorter in the leg, and its head is larger in proportion to its size than the Setter. It is also stated that the Setter originated from the "Setting" or "Sitting Spaniel".

The Springer is larger in size and longer in leg than the Cocker Spaniel, which has a small round head and larger and longer ears. The Springer

Photo] **QUALITY.** *[Hedges*

Mr. J. A. Wenger's "Rufton Repeater" is a fine example of the English Springer Spaniel.

can be practically any colour or combination of colours, but perhaps the most common are liver-and-white and black-and-white.

The type of Springer to-day is more refined than that of a quarter of a century ago. It is much more racily built, and owns a more refined head, with a narrower skull and good stop.

In the field it is a marvellous asset to any shooting man. Possessing the pluck of a thousand, it will go into the thickest of coverts ; is fast, easy to handle (much easier than most breeds of Spaniel), is big enough to retrieve a pheasant at the gallop, and by no means too small to retrieve a good nine- or ten-pound hare.

Several years ago, some so-called "shooting sportsmen" thought the Springer too fast for them in the field, and in order to satisfy their wants, tried to breed a slower dog by crossing it with a strong-headed, low-legged type of hound. Thus they produced a short-legged type of so-called English

Photo] *[Sport and General.*

KEEN ON HIS JOB.

An English Springer Spaniel hard at work. Note the speed and eagerness with which it carries the booty

Photo]   *[Sport & General*

GOOD DOG !

"Bob of Avondale", the property of the Duke of Hamilton, is a great worker. It is here seen handing over a rabbit which it has just retrieved at a Scottish Field Trials Association meeting.

A NICE TRIO.

Here are seen "Blendworth Trout", "Blendworth Roach", and "Blendworth Jest" at the Gun-dog League Spaniel Trials near Horsham. They belong to the Rev. E. J. Nelson.

Springer that would work more slowly for them. But all this was to the detriment of the breed, as it lost a great deal of its Spaniel character, was not easy to control, was inclined to be hard-mouthed, and had not that long, dense coat which protects it from thorns and prickles in thick coverts. Fortunately, the mistake was soon found out, and, thanks to the Sporting Spaniel Society, the Springer was soon once again the perfect gentleman of before.

Perhaps one of the first English Springers to make a name for itself, since the Kennel Club classified the breed in the Stud Book, was Mr. Eversfield's "Velox Powder". In his pedigree he owned "Mop" and "Frisk", two excellent working dogs from the kennel of Sir Thomas Boughey, in Shropshire. Other notable dogs before and round about this time, which can be said to have had a hand in the building up of the present-day English Springer, were "Shirley", "Tissington Bounce", "Ark", "Beechgrove Will", "Tissington Flush", "Tissington Fan", "Fansome", and "Tring". The last-named was particularly noted for its exceptional ability in the field ; in fact, it was the first Spaniel to lower the colours of the well-known Clumber Spaniel, Ch. "Beechgrove Bee", which hitherto had an unbeaten record.

Round about, and directly after the time the English Springer breed was officially recognized, the principal breeders and owners were as follow : Messrs. Arkwright, Harry Jones, Eversfield, Winton Smith, Sir Hugo Fitzherbert, and, later, Messrs. Phillips Llewellin, Williams Carlton

CH. "BANCHORY BOY".

The Countess of Howe, famous for her Labrador Retrievers, has also a powerful kennel of Springer Spaniels, of which the above is a good example.

Prewitt, Cameron, Marriot, MacDonald, and Lorna, Countess Howe. Other names can be coupled with them. The numbers of kennels housing the English Springer are too numerous to mention, but the names of the following owners are too well known to omit : Messrs. Warner Hill, Garratt, Kelland, MacNab, Chassels, Grierson Traherne, Nelson, Carrell, Cornthwait, Clark, S. C. Jones, Edwards, Dalton, and Kennedy.

The popularity of the Springer has increased enormously in the last few years. There is a good classification for them at most shows, and competition is strong. At the 1934 Cruft's Show there were 179 entries, so it will be seen that the popularity of the Springer compares favourably with most of the well-known breeds

It can be guessed how much progress the English Springer has made in the last few years, if one realizes that they often command a high position in

SPRINGER SPANIEL FIELD TRIALS.

As with all gun-dogs, none can be a champion without having earned working honours. The picture shows the English Springer Spaniel Club at a Field Trial at Wootton, near Bedford.

[W. H. White.

NICE TO BE YOUNG.

A bunch of English Springer Spaniels. This breed is a larger Spaniel than the Cocker.

Photo]

Variety Classes at shows. In the year 1931 or 1932 the dog, Ch. "Beauchief Benefactor", owned by Mr. Warner Hill, was judged best exhibit of all breeds at a Championship Show —no mean performance for any dog, breed, or owner. There are also one or two other Springers which have attained this high position, but, unfortunately, they are no longer in this country.

With the help of judicious breeding and the course of time, the English Springer has undoubtedly improved in appearance. By that is meant he is more of a type and standard; this is mainly due to the Spaniel Clubs. Nowadays nearly all, if not all, Spaniel Clubs, besides the Specialist Clubs, cater for the Springer. The types as set up in these clubs, differ very slightly, and then only in some small detail, so it appears that the Springer cannot alter very much in appearance.

The chief characteristics are: Height about 19 ins., weight about 40 lb., although these statistics need not be rigidly adhered to as long as the dog is well balanced all through, and not too large or too small. Its appearance should be that of a worker which can stay a long day in the field, but at the same time it should be a nicely-moulded animal, pleasing to the eye. The head should be long in proportion to its body, with a well-developed skull and a good stop; a long foreface with square muzzle, and powerful jaws. The eyes should be of moderate size, dark in colour, with a nice tender expression. The ears should be fairly long and wide, and like a Setter's as regards position and feathering. The neck should be slightly arched and long, giving the appearance of strength and muscle. The shoulders sloping, and the front straight. Moderately long forelegs, well boned

A CANINE BEAUTY.

A beautiful head study of Mr. R. Bowden's "Foxfield Alpha", incorporating all the typical features of the Springer Spaniel.
This dog has won many prizes, including Challenge Certificates in 1932 and 1933.

and strong. The chest should be deep, giving plenty of heart room, but not too round and wide. The feet should be fairly large, strong, round, and muscular. The body should be well balanced all through, not too short a back, a good set on, and carried on a level with, or below the level of the back ; the quarters should be wide, strong and powerful. It should be nicely feathered, but it must be realized that too much feathering is detrimental to its work in thorny coverts. In fact, the English Springer should be beautiful to look upon, with a nice tender expression, powerful, strongly built, and giving the impression of durability.

No man can be without this dog on a rough shoot, and it is well known that the English Springer is the best type of gun-dog to answer this purpose. It will be noticed, on looking through the records of Spaniel Field Trials, that the English Springer is usually the one to obtain the highest awards.

In concluding, it must be said that the English Springer is a dog which undoubtedly is an asset that cannot be passed over by any shooting man ; in fact, as an all-rounder, it cannot be beaten for show, shooting, or disposition.

POINTS OF THE ENGLISH SPRINGER SPANIEL.

HEAD.—The skull is well developed and the stop is clearly defined. The muzzle is long, lean and square, and the jaw is powerful. It must be neither undershot nor overshot, and the face should be nicely chiselled below the eyes.

Photo]   [Fall.
"STEPSWATER RECOMPENSE".
Miss Napier's English Springer Spaniel affords a remarkable head study.

EYES.—The eyes should be neither too full nor too small, and the colour a dark hazel, dark brown or nearly black.

EARS.—The ears are set low, moderately long and wide, and sufficiently clad with nice Setter-like feather.

NECK.—The neck should be long, strong and muscular.

BODY.—The body (including size and symmetry) should be medium length, well-ribbed up to a good strong loin, straight or slightly arched, never slack, and the whole appearance of the dog should be well-balanced. Excessive length and lowness, however, should be penalized as interfering with the dog's activity.

SHOULDERS AND CHEST. —The former should be sloping and free ; the latter should be deep and well-developed, but not too round and wide.

HINDQUARTERS.—Should be powerful and muscular, wide and fully developed.

Photo]   [Fall.
WELL DONE !
Miss Morland Hooper's "Regalia" retrieves a moorhen. Note how lightly the dog holds the bird and how intent on the work it is doing.

LONELY.

This photograph of "Sidbrook Ranger", owned by Mr. Hebstrip, was taken at Cruft's Show. It appears to be looking round to see if there are any friends or human admirers about.

[L. P. V. Veale.

Photo]

A HAPPY FAMILY.

A mother Springer Spaniel, "Bristles Pet", daughter of the noted champion "Boghurst Bristle", is proud of her family of seven, some of which are shown above. She belongs to Mr. W. Escott.

STERN—Should be well set on and carried low, nicely fringed with wavy feather of silky texture.

FEET.—The feet should not be too small, and have good strong pads.

LEGS.—The legs should be straight and strong, nicely feathered ; over-much feathering is objectionable.

COAT.—The coat should be flat or slightly waved and never curly. It should be sufficiently dense to resist the weather and not too short, silky in texture and glossy and refined in nature.

English Terrier.

English Terrier.—The English Terrier was really a white Terrier, in shape, similar to the Black-and-Tan, and was often bred from the same litters as Black-and-Tans. It has been stated that they had Italian Greyhound blood in their veins.

A Mr. White, of Clapham, was responsible for their first appearance, which was then taken up by leading dog breeders, including Mr. S. E. Shirley. Some of the breed were deaf.

Mr. James Roocroft was the most important breeder and showed the best stock at the time.

Photo]   [E.N.A.

AN AMERICAN EXAMPLE.

The English Springer Spaniel is a great favourite in the United States. It is interesting to note that across the Atlantic this dog has more of a Setter head than is usually seen here.

COLOURS.—Various, black-and-tan ; liver-and-tan ; black, liver, tan-and-white ; liver-and-white ; liver, tan-and-white ; lemon-and-white ; roans, etc.

GENERAL APPEARANCE.—A combination of beauty and utility. Weight about 40 lb.

POINTS.—Head and jaw, 15 ; eyes, 5 ; ears, 5 ; neck, 5 ; body, 10 ; forelegs, 10 ; hindlegs, 10 ; feet, 10 ; stern, 10 ; coat and feather, 10 ; general appearance, 10. Total, 100.

DEDUCTIONS.—Light eyes, 20 ; light nose, 15 ; curled ears, 10 ; curled coat, 15 ; bad carriage of tail, 10 ; top-knot, 15 : crooked forelegs, 10.

The white puppies often had brown or red spots, which disqualified them. One of the leading dogs of the time weighed between 18 and 19 lb. Efforts have been made to revive the breed, but nothing has come of it.

English Water Spaniel.—The name was given at the end of the eighteenth century to a Collie-like dog which had possibly been bred from a Spaniel or Setter crossed with Poodle. Later, at the beginning of the nineteenth century, it is depicted as a strongly made active Spaniel with curly coat.

As a breed, however, it vanished completely—any Spaniel with a curly coat was at once named English Water Spaniel. Later attempts were made to re-establish the variety, but each attempt failed.

One such attempt was made in 1866–1873. In 1887 another attempt was made. Up to 1912 the best seen were the property of Mr. Winton Smith, Mr. H. Jones, and Mr. J. H. Stansfield.

Enteritis.—Inflammation of the small intestines. (*See* BOWEL, INFLAMMATION OF.)

which it may be administered in doses of from 1 to 4 drachms. If this salt is to be given over a long period—say for a fortnight—the dose should be from about 5 to 15 grains twice daily, which can be added to the drinking water, or made up into a capsule or tablet. It is rather apt to cause vomiting in dogs if given in too large a dose or in too concentrated a form.

Ergot.—A parasite which grows on Rye. Medicinally it is an ecbolic, having the property of causing muscular contractions of the uterus in cases of difficult parturition. It is a poisonous drug, however, and is not very popular among veterinarians

By courtesy]   [E. C. *Ash*.

THE GREENLAND DOG.

In the olden days the Eskimo's dog was named the Greenland Dog. This beautiful picture was drawn at the end of the eighteenth century.

Enterotomy.—An operation performed for the removal, usually, of a foreign body from the bowel. The essential character of the operation is that an incision is made into the intestine, which is afterwards sutured. In the operation of enterotomy a portion of the bowel itself is removed.

Entropion. (*See* EYE DISEASES.)

Enucleation.—The removal of a tumour, an eye, or other body or organ in such a way that it comes out clean and whole like a nut from its shell.

Epistaxis. (*See* BLEEDING FROM THE NOSE.

Epsom Salt, technically known as sulphate of magnesium, is a useful saline laxative for dogs, for

for the purpose just described. It probably has a greater value in the checking of haemorrhage after parturition, and in inducing the uterus to resume more speedily its normal state. (*See* DOSAGE OF MEDICINES.)

Eskimo Dog.—The largest member of the Spitz group, and strongest, toughest and most important work dog, is the Eskimo dog of the Arctic regions. A product of the survival of the fittest over a period covering certainly twenty centuries, it is likewise one of the oldest and most beautiful of pure types. Indispensable to its owner, as no other breed has ever been, it

ESKIMO DOGS.

This colour plate, specially executed for HUTCHINSON'S DOG ENCYCLOPAEDIA, by G. S. Dixon, depicts a team of Eskimo dogs after an arduous run across Arctic regions. These dogs are probably the hardest workers in the canine world. They will run at amazing speed, drawing considerable loads, until they, literally, drop in their tracks, as this picture shows.

RESTING TIME.

In the summer the hard-worked Eskimo dogs often spend much of their time resting (unless needed for trekking or river work), thus making up for the winter months, when they have to work so hard.

Photo]   [Douthwaite.

POLICE TEAMS.

The police in the North-West Territory possess efficient and fleet dog teams with which they travel from outpost to outpost.

is also responsible for the remarkable strides made in Arctic and Antarctic exploration since its first use by white men. With its able assistance Peary discovered the North Pole, and Amundsen the South Pole.

Without it the Eskimo race would have been in a very sorry plight, for no other animal can quite fill its place ; the reindeer, for instance, being entirely unsuitable. It draws their komatics (sledges) in winter, carries large loads as a pack-dog in summer, aids greatly in securing their game by hunting, tracks (draws) their umiaks (large skin boats) along the shore, and in times of starvation its body furnishes food for its master. Its fur is used in clothing and its carcass in certain burial and sacrificial rites.

Originating in Siberia, it has since been taken over thousands of miles of Arctic coasts in many countries. According to Dr. Edward Moffat Weyer, junior, one of the foremost living students of the race, the first migration of the Eskimos took place at least 2,000 years ago, and perhaps more, when they crossed Bering Strait to Alaska. Their dogs, of course, went with them.

The Eskimo dog is a very close relative to the other Siberian breeds—Samoyed and Siberian Husky—and considerable evidence points to all three being, at some distant date, one and the same breed. Certainly all of them bear strikingly similar resemblance and have many characteristics in common even to-day.

Perhaps its next closest relatives are the Chow Chow and Norwegian Elkhound. The superficial resemblance here is also apparent. Certain types of Eskimo dogs—notably in Greenland—still resemble rather closely both breeds. The writer is in thorough accord with those authorities who believe that the Eskimo dog played a very important part in the ancestry of the two.

Probably no other breed has such a wide natural distribution as the Eskimo dog. From East Cape, Siberia, across Alaska, Arctic Canada, Baffin Land, Labrador to Greenland—a distance of some 3,400 miles—is its domain. Whether it be known by its right name, Malemute or Husky, it is one and the same dog, or at least was the same dog. It is the original Husky dog, a name derived from the

Photo]   [E.N.A

PULL UP

Evidently the sledge is getting too much for some of the dogs, for they have ceased pulling and are allowing the others to do their work.

fact that the Eskimos were nicknamed "huskies" by early explorers. The term has since degenerated, caninely, until it now means practically any kind of dog used for sled purposes, a single exception being the Siberian Husky, which is recognized

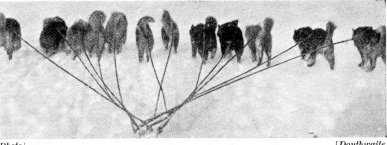

Photo]   [Douthwaite.

A FINE TEAM.

The way the teams are harnessed is, to some extent, a matter of locality, although the police have harness of various kinds. The above method of harnessing allows the dogs to fan out. They belong to police teams.

Photo]   IN NEW YORK STATE.   [E. L. Gockeler.

Felix Leser's team on its way in the Adirondack mountains. A fine team indeed ! The driver rides on long rear runners to balance the sleigh over rough going, and also to be near the foot brakes.

by the American Kennel Club. "Malemute" undoubtedly was given by the miners during the gold rush in Alaska. A large majority of them were located on the Seward Peninsula, where dwells the Eskimo group known as Malemute.

Similar to any other animal scattered over a wide territory, Eskimo dogs vary considerably in type, though fundamentally the same. In many sections nowadays the breed has been so

100 lb., though some, especially well brought up males, will occasionally reach 135 lb. Males are far larger than bitches, this disparity in size being greater, it is believed, than in any other dog. Explorers usually favour a medium-sized animal—neither too large nor too small. An excerpt from a communication by Lieut.-Commander Donald B. MacMillan, the famed Arctic explorer who was with Peary, may shed some light on this subject :

Photo] [Dorien Leigh.

THE PUPPY.

This Eskimo puppy shows clearly the ancestral type, whatever it may grow up to be. Note how nearly it approaches the Samoyed.

cross-bred with "civilized" dogs that they are hardly recognizable. This cross-breeding has proved a great detriment, which is especially apparent in feet. No living dog has such toughness of pads as has the pure bred Eskimo. As an example, the writer drove a team of ten bitches for three winters nearly 3,000 miles, and during the entire time only a single bleeding foot was discovered. It is an old saying among dog drivers "that a dog is only as good as his feet", and, with this in mind, an Eskimo dog is very near perfection.

The breed ranges in size generally from 40 to

"We have repeatedly found out that for long hard trips the 100-pound dog is a bit too heavy for strenuous work. The dogs which came through with tight traces and tightly curled tails [writer's note : a very tired dog carries his brush straight and down] weigh about 85 pounds and are about four years old. The first dog to give out on our North Pole trip was one weighing 125 pounds. We sent him back to the ship early in the game. The 32 dogs which finished the 1,000 miles of travel over the ice of the Polar sea, all weighed between 70 and 80 pounds."

TREKKING.

In the summer the Eskimo sled dog is used as a pack animal.   Felix Angus Leser, 6 feet 4 inches tall, rather dwarfs the dog,
which is capable of carrying 20 lb.

Photo]   *[E. M. Joyce.*

THE KENNELS.

A most unusual picture of kennels amongst snow and ice on the Ross Sea. The snow against the kennel sides protects the dogs
from the icy wind.

Photo]   *[E.N.A.*

TO THE RESCUE.

Some of the dog teams on their way to the rescue of the survivors of the *Tscheljuskin*, the crushed Soviet ship.
This photograph was taken on the mainland at Wellen.

Eskimo dogs come in practically every known dog coloration, though perhaps the majority follow fairly closely the many patterns of the wolf. Blacks and whites, and a combination of the two, are quite common. One of the most beautiful teams ever seen in the United States was composed of white-bodied dogs with coal-black heads. These were bred and trained by Edward P. Clark, secretary of the

generally larger than Eskimo dogs, often weighing 150 lb. or more. They carry a "down" brush, while their canine neighbours carry a plume boldly curled over the back. Then, too, the Arctic wolf is the only animal an Eskimo dog is afraid to attack.

After a rather extensive research, the writer has come to the conclusion that Eskimo dogs, though they may originally have

Eskimo Dog Club of America, and were descended from some dogs brought back by Lieut.-Commander MacMillan from Baffin Land. It is interesting to note that this colour bred true. Unfortunately, a distemper

sprung from wolves, as many authorities believe, have only occasionally since been cross-bred with them. It might be well to point out that breeding wolves and dogs together in the wild state is an entirely different and far more

Photo]   *[E.N.A.*

WITH SHACKLETON.

Some of the team of Eskimo dogs, attached to the Antarctic Expedition, which lived for six months on an ice-floe, hoping to drift 550 miles to Elephant Island.

epidemic, which is very disastrous to the breed, wiped out the entire strain.

The wolf coloration mentioned above may seem to bear out the general impression that Eskimo dogs are frequently wolf-crossed. If such were so, most dogs would be all white, for that is the usual hue of the Arctic wolf found most frequently in their range. Arctic wolves, it may be said, are

difficult matter from when both animals have been brought up together in captivity. However, there are several authenticated cases where such matings between Eskimo dogs and wolves have taken place. Vilhjalmur Stefansson, the famous explorer, wrote that he personally knew of one instance, and that these cross-bred animals were extremely gentle.

[*John F. Collins, F.R.P.S.*

Photo]

FULL SPEED AHEAD.

A team such as this can travel at twenty-two miles an hour with a load. Control is entirely by verbal commands given in the Eskimo language. The dogs understand "Start", "Stop", "Left", "Right", "Faster", and "Lie Down". This team covers 1,000 miles each winter, and is here seen pulling a sixteen-foot-long sleigh.

On the other hand, Dr. Weyer remarks: "It seems altogether likely that the dogs of the Eskimos have crossed to some extent with wolves. The skeletal similarity points to a relationship. . . . I have never heard of an authentic case of dogs and wolves interbreeding under natural conditions, but it seems quite likely."

It might be of interest here to state that pure-bred wolves have been trained and used to a very limited extent as sled animals. In the main, they have proved unsatisfactory, failing to display the ordinary endurance of good sled-dogs.

Eskimo dogs come in two coats—regular and long-haired. The former, greatly in the majority, resemble somewhat a very heavy-coated German Shepherd dog (Alsatian), while the latter has the very long and profuse coat and gorgeous "plume" of the best fancier-bred Samoyeds. Both, of course, have wonderfully dense "woolly" undercoats, which permit their sleeping without shelter in the severest weather, no temperature being too extreme for them once they have reached a month of age.

In Labrador, where the long-haired variety is most commonly seen, it is not infrequent to find puppies of both coats in the same litter. Either coat, however, will breed true if bred pure for several generations. This happening of two different coats in the same litter is not unknown to fanciers of other breeds—particularly Fox Terriers.

Through continued cross-breeding, as mentioned previously, Eskimo dogs are gradually becoming rarer in their native lands, and already over great stretches—notably Alaska and Arctic Canada—it is with difficulty that pure-breds are found. Perhaps the best specimens are confined to certain sections of Baffin Land, Labrador, and Greenland. In connection with this it might be of interest again to quote from Lieut.-Commander MacMillan's letter.

"The dogs which we drove in 1908-1909 [writer's note: 250 in number] on the North Pole trip, and also the 400 which I had from 1913 to 1917, and the fifty or sixty which I had with me on my 1923-24 trip, were excellent dogs, and I thought at the time the best in the world, but since my year in Northern Labrador in 1927-28, I have come to the conclusion that the dog found in the vicinity of Hopedale, Nain, and Okak, Labrador, are superior in almost every way. Possibly they could not endure long days of travel without food as well as the North Greenland dog, but they are a better-looking dog, and much larger and stronger than what I found in the Smith Sound region."

When used as draught animals, Eskimo dogs are able to pull very heavy loads on the komatiks and at considerable speed. For fast travelling, the load is usually limited to approximately the combined weight of all the dogs in the team; for ordinary going, one and a half times the team's weight; and for heavy hauling, double the weight. The speed they can make depends on several factors—condition of the dogs, amount of load, and, above all, snow surfaces. When the going is fine and the load light, a good team will average between six and eight miles an hour.

On down grades they will occasionally reach twenty or more miles per hour, though uphill they are correspondingly slow. The usual gait is a fast, steady trot, which they keep up hour after hour. Some dogs will frequently shift from this trot to a pace, evidently as a measure of rest. Occasionally, too, they will gallop, probably for the same reason. The longest authentic distance covered by a team in one run is one hundred miles, in slightly less than eighteen hours. Lieut.-Commander MacMillan was the driver upon this occasion. The writer has several times driven his team forty miles in less than six hours, and has also pushed them a measured ten miles over a "hilly" route in one hour and five minutes. In both instances the dogs were pulling loads of approximately their body weight. These speeds should not be confused with the rather remarkable time made by some of the best teams of racing sled-dogs—notably Siberian Huskies—for here only a skeleton sleigh is used and the driver runs most grades. It must also be understood that the Eskimo dog is primarily a work dog and not a racing animal.

The original hitch of the Eskimos, still used to a considerable extent in the Far North and Siberia, is the "fan" hitch. In this, each animal is hooked to the komatik by a long, separate trace. This has been superseded by what is known as the Alaskan "gang" hitch. In this, the dogs are hooked in pairs to a central gang or towline. This last is far more practicable and permits utilizing the utmost of dog power.

The original komatiks of the Eskimos were rather cumbersome affairs, made of solid driftwood sides and lashed together with sealskin. Vehicles made almost entirely of animal bone were also used. In emergencies, komatiks were even improvised out of frozen walrus skin. This was first soaked in water, then folded into the general outlines of a sledge, and, after being allowed to freeze, was as strong as any. Another of their ingenious ideas is that of applying an ice-coating to the komatik runners. This makes hauling comparatively easy at very low temperatures when the consistency of the snow is similar to sand. With this condition both steel and bone runners will drag perceptibly, while the ice-covered runners will run smoothly along. The length of the komatik varies from five to thirty feet, with the most common about ten or twelve.

A team consists of from four to twenty dogs, with the average one between seven and ten. In each there is a leader, or king-dog, which is trained to obey the various commands. These are usually six in number—to go, to stop, turn left, turn right, to go faster, and to lie down. There is little truth in the oft-repeated statement that the leader or king-dog bosses his mates with an iron paw. In reality, the lead-dog is usually picked for his great intelligence and speed, and rarely does this combination include physical superiority.

Once trained, the dogs never forget their commands. They seem to have a special aptitude for harness work, and the puppies, usually started at six months of age, are far easier to train than any of the non-sled-dog breeds. It does require, however, several years to "make" a really good leader. No reins are ever used, and all control of the team is verbal.

Dog teams must be better trained in civilized communities where vehicular traffic is encountered. The writer has frequently "tooled" a fifty-foot long team through quite heavy traffic in medium-sized towns. Unlike the Eskimos, most white

[*E. L. Gockeler.*

"DOWN!"

Leser's delightful team of pedigree Eskimo dogs, wearing red horsehair plumes and white saddle trappings. All dogs must lie down on the word of command.

Photo]

men's sleighs are equipped with strong steel brakes. These greatly facilitate control in difficult situations.

A whip is necessary when training a green team —not so much as a weapon of punishment, as for a handy means of guidance. However, the use of a whip by a white dog-driver, except under exceptional circumstances, for any purpose other than breaking up fights or training, is positive evidence of a very poor driver.

Kindness pays a big dividend. Usually, the

case, regular little canvas pack-saddles, with breast straps, girths, and frequently panniers, are used.

As a hunting assistant the Eskimo dog rates among the best. Its nose is as keen as any hound—Bloodhound excepted—and it will trail and unhesitatingly attack quarry as large and formidable as the Polar bear. Wolves, as has been stated, are the only exception. It will chase them, but will not generally approach, and is of inestimable value to the Eskimos in the securing of

Photo]   [Keystone.
THE SURVIVOR.
This dog (note how strongly the wolf-ancestor is denoted) was the only Eskimo dog left of an Alaskan team of seven. It escaped and travelled seventy-five miles on its own, to the nearest trapper's cabin. The other six dogs died of starvation at the camp

more fond sled-dogs are of their driver the harder they will work for him. The majority of natives, however, use whips ranging from ten to thirty feet in length, many of them becoming so expert that they can hit any desired dog when the team is in full flight. It is also said that some of the more proficient ones can snap the heads off ptarmigan (Arctic grouse) with this implement.

In overland travelling in summer, the Eskimo dog greatly assists its owner by carrying a pack securely tied to its back. Generally speaking, a dog is able to carry one-third its weight, and this it can do day after day. White men utilize it in the same way to a considerable extent. In this

seal during certain seasons of the year. In this case it is employed to ferret out the used breathing holes through the ice. These are covered with snow, and it would be impossible to find them without the dog's keen scent. Once located, the hunter waits patiently for the seal to appear, and then harpoons it.

A herd of musk oxen, once sighted by an Eskimo dog, is as good as in the hunter's larder, for it will round them up and hold them at bay until its master arrives and dispatches them.

Probably no sport is quite so exciting as coursing Polar bear by dog-team. When game is sighted the dogs dash madly in pursuit over the ice, with the hunter holding on, as best he can, to the madly careening komatik. Nearing the quarry, if possible traces are cut and the dogs race to the attack. Sometimes, in the confusion, this is either neglected or impossible, and on more than one occasion hunters have been joined by a most unwelcome passenger as the bear was scooped aboard the komatik.

For a breed of dog, so well known by name at least, it is surprising that the Eskimo has not been taken up more extensively by fanciers and breeders in other countries. If British explorers had used him, many feel that he would have been adopted by their countrymen and then sent to the four corners of the earth. As it happened, most of them came into contact with an inferior breed of sled-dog, and hence damned all of them for use in the Arctic and Antarctic. If gallant Captain Scott had only listened to Admiral Peary, who begged him to take along Eskimo dogs before his ill-fated expedition left England, an entirely different result might have been obtained. As poor Scott and his brave companions were struggling to their death after reaching the South Pole, Amundsen was riding back in comparative comfort with his team of eleven Greenland Eskimo dogs.

Due to its extensive use by Canadian and American explorers, the Eskimo dog has gained much popularity in both countries, though in neither is it yet very common in the pure-bred state. It was fortunate for the breed that Edward P. Clark, of North Woodstock, New Hampshire, U.S.A., became interested. Mr. Clark, who was in the fur trade in Labrador, brought back a number

By courtesy]　　　　　　　　*[Canadian Government.*
ONE OF SEVERAL VARIETIES.
Here is a head study of a type of Eskimo dog as found in Greenland.

of the best specimens upon his return. His stock has since been added to by the gifts of explorers until he built up one of the finest kennels of the breed in existence. A number of others becoming interested, including W. Dustin White, prominent writer of outdoor pastimes, the Eskimo Dog Club of America was formed several years ago, and the breed was admitted to registration in the stud books of the American Kennel Club.

Unlike most pure breeds, the Eskimo dogs are rarely seen on the show bench. Their owners, almost to a man, use them for what they were originally intended—driving. The sport of dog-driving is quite one of the most fascinating in the realm of winter. It has taken firm hold in the United States, Alaska and Canada, and a conservative estimate of the number of teams of all varieties of dog would be well up in the thousands. Sled-dog races are now one of the established events at all the better winter resorts, and in the 1932 Winter Olympia at Lake Placid, N.Y., a most successful race was held, with teams competing from the United States, Canada, and Alaska.

Women, too, are taking an interest, and several have already become prominent. Dog-driving, though, is not to

By courtesy]　　　　　　　　*[Canadian Government.*
WOLF-TYPE DOG.
The Eskimo dog of this type is taken to represent the wolf-dog. It is undoubtedly true that they have a strong wolf strain, as their appearance suggests.

By courtesy]   PLODDING ALONG.   *[C. R. R. Douthwaite.*

Sled dogs have an inherent liking for work and enjoy being driven. Indeed, at the mere sight of a harness they are likely to raise a howl of delight. In this instance the word "howl" is used in the literal sense, for, it is said, Eskimo dogs do not bark as other canines.

American Kennel Club, or import them direct from the Arctic. This advice is necessary owing to the number of unscrupulous dealers in the United States who have been selling small white Spitz-like dogs as real Eskimos. Many breeders of the genuine dog are now calling their breed Eskimo Sled dogs, to differentiate them from the counterfeit.

Eskimo dogs, though having many qualities in common with "civilized" breeds, also have several characteristics peculiar to themselves. Perhaps the most unusual of these is their general inability to bark. Instead, most of their vocal effort is in the form of howling, similar to wolves. To those who are fond of the North Country and the great out-of-doors, a good Eskimo dog chorus on a sub-zero night is indeed lovely music. But to non-dog-lovers it is apt to make the evening hideous. It must be said, however, to the credit of the

be recommended indiscriminately to the fair sex, for it requires, besides a great deal of skill, considerable muscular activity.

Some drivers prolong the season by using a training wagon, equipped with a good brake and pneumatic tyres. It is not possible to use sled-dogs in very warm weather, but in

By courtesy]   TWO FRIENDS.   *[C. R. R. Douthwaite.*

Constable Douthwaite, of the R.C.M.P., with "Snowball", a good Eskimo specimen of the pure white variety, on duty in the Yukon Territory. He finds this dog a great asset in his particular work.

spring and autumn they go rather nicely to this rig. It might be well here to state that handling a spirited and powerful team is not for the novice fancier, neither for an ill-tempered individual, no matter how experienced he may be in the training of ordinary dogs.

Breeders of Eskimo dogs in the United States and Canada make use of them as pack animals for summer camping and hiking trips. With two or three dogs loaded, and a pack on his own back, a man can carry sufficient food and shelter to last some time in the bush.

Prospective purchasers are strongly advised to buy only dogs eligible for registration with the

By courtesy]   A SNOWY TRAIL.   *[C. R. R. Douthwaite.*

Along the snowy roads these Eskimo dogs go in single file, this time wearing a different harness than seen in other pictures. Various types of harness are kept for various purposes. This kind is claimed to give maximum dog-power.

By courtesy]

[*Universal Pictures.*]

A TRAGIC MOMENT.

Four men and a dog—the survivors of the ill-starred party—on an ice-floe. The dog which has escaped death over and over again, happily, survives. Here its fate is once again in the balance, but indifferent to want of food it sits faithfully by the side of its masters. (The scene is from the film "S O S Iceberg".)

MAROONED.

A scene from the remarkable film, "S O S Iceberg", showing one of the Eskimo dogs cut off from the party on a floating block of ice. The dog, who is well acquainted with Arctic conditions, is seen wisely waiting for the ice-floe to approach closer to the main ice before attempting to swim.

By courtesy]

dogs that, if properly fed, kennelled and trained, they rarely ever give vent to this weird sound. The writer's dogs have never once howled in their home kennels at night. The only times they indulged was on camping trips into the bush, when each was chained to a tree for the night with a bed of evergreen boughs to sleep upon.

Usually, one dog starts howling and then the others, often one at a time, join in until the whole team is in full "song". This lasts for a minute or two and, as though some pre-arranged signal had been given, ceases abruptly without any tapering off whatsoever. They are never "yappers". Either they are noisy for a minute or two, when being fed, released from kennels or harnessed, or else they are perfectly mute. They are not watch-dogs in so far as barking is concerned, for they rarely make a sound when strangers approach. Everything taken into consideration, when properly handled the Eskimo dogs are an extremely quiet breed and make good pets.

Living as they do in a wild, barren land, often underfed, overworked and otherwise abused, it is surprising that they have one of the best dispositions found in the canine race. Affectionate to a marked degree with their owners, if treated properly, they are also very friendly in a reserved sort of way with strangers. They are never "snappy". Even a very ill-used dog will permit considerable liberties

to be taken before actually attacking. A vicious dog, by the way, is almost invariably caused by an equally vicious owner.

These dogs are, however, incorrigible fighters with their kind, and it is unsafe to leave them together unattended. They are killers also of other animals, but these traits could be readily modified by selective breeding and proper training. The bitches are equally bad in these respects as the males. Both fight running as a rule, slashing their adversaries as they go. This is the opposite method, of course, to the Bull Terrier, who usually hangs on.

The dogs have really remarkable memories—particularly for routes they have once been over. Then, too, they are happy dogs, with smiling faces, and love nothing better than to go for a drive. The mere appearance of their harness causes a gleeful uproar of delighted howls. They are, perhaps, the most highly suspicious of all breeds of strange things. This, of course, is still another manifestation of their closeness to the wild.

DESPERATION.

Here we see the villain of the piece in "S O S Iceberg" with the last of the dog team. Later, maddened by hunger, he decided to kill the dog, but fortunately, just at the critical moment he is sighted, and the dog is rescued. Thus was obviated what is a painful moment to all dog-lovers.

In their Arctic home they are never kennelled. Generally, each dog is staked out on the snow and ice when not needed, though at times, during warm weather, they are left to shift for themselves. So remarkably efficient is their coat that they sleep in apparent comfort, through the worst blizzards and most intense cold, without shelter of any sort. They do not generally dig a hole for themselves into

Photo]　　　　　　　　　　　　[*W. S. Berridge, F.Z.S.*
BLACK AND WHITE.
This remarkable head study of an Eskimo dog looks very canine
when compared with the wolf-type (see illustration on page 577).

the snow, as is commonly thought. Their coat is also wonderfully water-proof, and is impregnable to rains.

They are fed the leavings from their master's menu, which is mainly meat of some sort. Seal and walrus seem to be the best foods, particularly the former, which is approximately half fat.

When kept in civilization, it has been found best to have each two dogs that agree in a separate kennel yard, at least twenty feet square. Two sleeping boxes will be necessary, as very seldom will two dogs sleep together. These need be about three feet square and watertight. A wooden platform for sunning purposes will be greatly appreciated, as will also plenty of shade over part of the yard. Eskimo dogs shed their coats each spring, and are able to stand hot summers exceedingly well, if proper shade is present and fresh water convenient at all times.

In warm weather the dogs will dig earths sometimes eight or ten feet into the ground, where they like to lie during the heat of the day. This practice the writer has always encouraged, for he has found that not only do they appear more contented, but the close contact with damp earth seems to benefit their coats.

If the small yards can open into a large paddock — fenced in, of course—so much the better. Dogs that agree fairly well could be let out for a romp once or twice daily.

It must be understood, however, that the attendant *must* be present at *all* times when this gallop takes place. Further, he should always have a stout whip handy in case of a fight.

The feeding of Eskimo dogs in temperate climes presents no great difficulty. Good sound commercial dog foods and plenty of raw, fatty beef will keep them in excellent condition. When working, however, no prepared foods have so far been discovered that will equal raw, fatty beef fed almost exclusively. In this case, the fat and beef should be nearly in equal parts. The addition of cod-liver oil is particularly beneficial during the winter season.

Eskimo dogs make nice pets when raised from puppyhood by considerate and intelligent persons, though they are rarely cured altogether of their love of fighting. Like Samoyeds and Siberian Huskies, they have none of the usual doggy odour found in most other breeds. It is needless, perhaps, to add that a pet Eskimo dog should not be given unrestricted liberty, without proper supervision.

DESCRIPTION.

WEIGHT.—Females 50 to 80 lb. ; males 65 to 100 lb. Everything considered, the larger the dog the better.

HEAD.—Well proportioned, broad and wedge-shaped. Strong, flat skull and powerful jaws. Muzzle, broad and of medium length, with no appearance of "foxiness". Large black or brown

Photo]　　　　　　　　　　　　[*W. S. Berridge, F.Z.S*
IN A STRANGE LAND.
What a change it must be "To be in England . . ." Here is one of the first Eskimo
dogs, recently arrived, and to be seen at the Zoological Gardens of London.

nose. Lips, black or brown. Bitches' heads are far more refined than males.

EYES.—Moderately small, deep set and oblique, giving an Oriental expression.

EARS.—Short and wide, equilaterally triangular, set fairly low on skull, with considerable breadth between, carried erect always and turned forward. Slightly rounded tips and with "leather" of firm consistency. Well covered with hair inside and out. Bitches' ears are liable to be longer in proportion and set a bit higher on skull.

EXPRESSION.—Wolf-like, always alert, and very keen, piercing eyes. Sometimes quite supercilious, particularly when "laughing".

NECK. — This should be short, heavy and very muscular.

FOREQUARTERS. — Broad, big boned and muscular. Forelegs straight and not too long. Slight spring in pasterns.

CHEST.—Deep, broad and muscular.

HINDQUARTERS. — Should be of medium length, heavy and very muscular. Stifles moderately bent. Enormous development of both thighs and second thighs.

FEET.—Large, long and "flattish" (not to be confused with splay feet), with thick pads well protected with hair between the toes. The nails should also be strong. (Note: A well-knuckled short foot is a distinct disadvantage on snow surfaces.)

BODY.—Back slightly long and straight, ribs well

Photo]   WHAT A LIFE!   [E. M. Joyce.
The dog shown above seems tired of pulling. It has probably arrived at the end of a long and arduous journey. Note how comfortably the harness is attached.

sprung, fairly deep brisket and slightly "tucked up".

COAT.—Regular coated: Heavy covering of master hair varying from two to six inches in length. Long-haired variety: Long shaggy coat of master hair from five to eight inches in length. Both varieties have a dense, woolly undercoat.

COLOUR.—Immaterial.

TAIL.—Large and bushy, carried curled over the back.

Ether.—A colourless, volatile, inflammable liquid which has a boiling point at a temperature lower than that of the body. It is a solvent of fat and oil, for which purpose it is frequently employed to clean up the skin prior perhaps to operation or exposure to ultra-violet rays. Owing to its low boiling point it very rapidly evaporates, which property makes it admirable as a method of freezing local areas of skin. For this purpose it is projected on to the skin by means of a fine atomizer, and in a very few minutes the parts so sprayed become frozen. Thus, it is a local anaesthetic, and minor operations can be performed by its aid without inflicting any more discomfort than is occasioned by the cooling of the tissues.

By inhalation, it is a general anaesthetic and is looked upon as rather less toxic than chloroform. On this account, chloroform is sometimes mixed with ether and alcohol to form what is known as A.C.E. mixture, the proportions being 1, 2 and 3 respectively. This anaesthetic might be administered to old, plethoric dogs with somewhat greater safety than would be the case with chloroform alone.

Eucalyptus.—An oil which is extracted chiefly from the gum which exudes from a tree known as

Small enclosure for very young puppies.

the Eucalyptus Globulus. There are many species of eucalyptus tree, however, and the products of some are more pleasant than those of others. The commonly known oil of eucalyptus has astringent, tonic, antiseptic and deodorant properties ; but it is for the two last-named effects that its popularity depends. In canine practice it is very useful as an inhalation in cases of nasal catarrh, or bronchitis, for which purpose it may be applied directly to the dog's coat, or may be added to water in a steam kettle. It is unwise to sprinkle the oil over the dog's bed, because the usual result is that the animal refuses to sleep in the bed, and accordingly remains, perhaps all night, on the cold floor. This would defeat one's object if the latter were directed towards the treatment of respiratory catarrh. It is better, therefore, to apply a few drops of the oil directly upon the dog's breast so that he can neither lick it off nor escape its odour.

If eucalyptus is to be diffused into the atmosphere in medicated steam, about one teaspoonful may be added to a quart of water, and this should be heated until boiling, when a low gas-jet will maintain a steady jet of steam for an hour or two.

A few drops applied to the bridge of the nose certainly exert a soothing and antiseptic effect in cases of respiratory catarrh ; and the oil is in popular demand also as an ingredient of ointments for use upon inflamed areas of skin.

Various kinds of chain leads ; that in the centre is for leading two dogs.

Eustachian Tube.—Readers, who studied the article on the Ear and its structure, will have noted that the drum or tympanum of that organ was in direct contact with the atmosphere. As the latter exerts a uniform pressure of 15 lb. to the square inch, it is obvious that unless a similar pressure was exerted upon the internal surface of the drum, the latter would at once burst. This balance of atmospheric pressure between the external and the middle ear, is effected by means of the Eustachian tubes which lead from the throat—one on each side—to their respective ears.

Exercise.—Reasonable exercise not only increases muscular strength, but it also ensures symmetrical and properly balanced development, conduces to good nutrition and health, and greatly augments functional activities. As air is to the lungs and food to the stomach, so is exercise to the due development of all the systems of the body of the dog. Insufficient exercise tends to impair both constitution and useful breeding capacity. The degree and character of the exercise vary considerably with the breed, age, sex, and environ-

ment, but extremes in either direction should be avoided.

Growing dogs, as a rule, require more regular exercise than those that have reached maturity, while more care is also necessary in the exercising of young puppies. For adult animals, exercise should be guided to some extent by the purpose for which they are required.

If dogs are to be used for fast work or that which conduces to muscular fatigue, as is the case with Greyhounds and sporting dogs, a hard condition of muscles must first be ensured, as the power of the lungs to sustain violent and long exertion is very much a matter of habit, and this can soon be acquired in a dog whose physical powers are fully developed and bodily condition good.

The power of doing work and sustaining fatigue is cumulative, and, provided the dog is kept in good condition, it increases from day to day until from age its powers begin to fail.

Stud dogs and brood bitches require liberty for ample exercise if they are to produce healthy puppies, although overtaxing the energy of breeding stock may weaken future litters, and even cause temporary sterility.

The general condition of a dog is a fair guide as to whether the exercise is sufficient and proper for it. If it loses weight, in spite of liberal feeding, it may be taken that the exercise is excessive, while if it continues to gain in weight, the reverse is probably the case. Any change in the form or amount of exercise should be gradual, but it should at all times be regular, as the whole machine then becomes accommodated to the regular demands made upon it, and the body becomes active and well-conditioned. Dogs are naturally active animals, requiring considerable open-air exercise all the year round, but the larger and heavier breeds require more enforced exercise than the smaller.

Many toy dogs are kept practically caged up the most part of their lives, though close confinement is always prison for a dog, even if the surroundings are beautiful. To be their real selves, the toys require liberty for open-air exercise as much as the larger breeds. The confined life that these so often have to lead partly explains the warped and snappy dispositions found in these small pets, and when owners come to realize that they are built upon the same physiological plan, and out of the same materials, as ordinary dogs, requiring much the same treatment for their health and reproduction as ordinary dogs, then little dogs with irritable, peevish dispositions will become the exception rather than the rule.

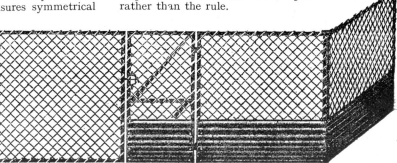

A substantial type of wire fencing for the construction of exercise runs for dogs.

[Dorien Leigh.

ON THEIR WAY.

Photo]

Owners have their personal likes and dislikes as to colour and marking of their Eskimo dog teams. Some prefer white, others wolf colour, while this owner has chosen black-and-white.

No dog should be allowed to become too exacting or be spoiled by being taken out always by the same person, otherwise it will become a nuisance and be miserable when that person cannot exercise it.

Exercise may be given at any time of the day, with the proviso that it is better to let a dog rest after its chief meal, while in the summer the hottest part of the day is better avoided. It may be given in a variety of ways, but accompanying one on a walk is the commonest and most useful. For the larger breeds, a run behind a horse

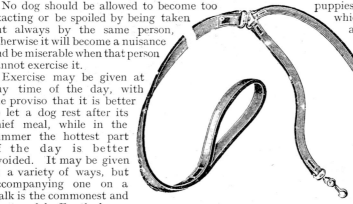

Special leather lead for leading two dogs at once.

or bicycle, ridden at a moderate pace, is excellent exercise, and fully enjoyed by the dog, while for Curly Retrievers and Water Spaniels, swimming in fresh or sea water has the added advantage of improving the coat. When the amount of exercise is necessarily restricted owing to the smallness of the run or business of the owner, jumping makes it a little more vigorous, either over a low wall or artificial fence.

In towns and cities exercise must, necessarily for the dog's safety, be given on a lead, unless it be very well trained to keep close at heel, or never to leave the path, as an uncontrolled dog bounding about a busy thoroughfare has not only its own, but human lives, in peril. To compensate for this restraint of the town-dog, parks, meadows and downs offer splendid facilities for it to have a free run and play with a stick or ball or other dogs once or twice a week. Even for a large dog, if it retrieves well, ample exercise is afforded by throwing a ball and keeping it running for half an hour in this way. A friendly game of one's pet with other dogs, while ideal from the point of view of exercise alone, should not be allowed without first considering the disadvantages that may attend it, and should be prohibited a puppy that has not had, nor been inoculated against, distemper. Parasitic skin diseases might also be contracted in this way.

Where a dog cannot be properly exercised, good grooming can be of great assistance by stimulating the circulation and massaging and toning up the skin and underlying muscles, but, of course, both ample exercise and good grooming are to be preferred.

EXERCISING PUPPIES.— Puppies should, wherever possible, have absolute freedom to play as they like, and when it is necessary to confine them the pen must be dry, and so constructed that they can look through its sides without spending too much time on their hindlegs. Natural play is certainly the best form of exercise for young

Scissor hook shown open.

Three kinds of double hooks.

Scissor hook shown closed.

Ordinary spring hook.

puppies. Given playmates, and ample space in which to play, they are almost constantly active, and in this way are freely and naturally exercised by performing over and over again every movement of which they are capable, resulting in graceful growth and vigorous health.

With good grass-runs and a shed for shelter, puppies may be kept up to eight or nine months in this way, with occasional walks on the road to become accustomed to following or being led, and to traffic. A nervous puppy is a nuisance as a pet, and hard to show.

Accidents from their frolics are very rare when puppies are left to play together all day long, and the advantages are so great as fully to outweigh any disadvantages from accident, but when kennelled singly, or in pairs, too many should not be let out at one time, nor puppies that vary greatly in size, lest the play be too strenuous and accidents result. There is no risk of a healthy, well-fed puppy overtaxing its strength in voluntary play, since when it is temporarily exhausted it will curl up and rest, and be unattractive to a puppy that wishes to play; but the enforced exercise of a young puppy needs to be carefully regulated. The fact that a puppy wants, or is willing, to follow a horse or bicycle, does not mean that it is good for it to do so.

At weaning time, if the puppy is taken from the rest of the litter, and has no companion, in addition to its freedom of house and garden, it should be encouraged to follow one or taken on a lead for two or three hundred yards two or three times a day. This should gradually be increased according to the breed, condition, and development of the puppy, so that the larger breeds get a half to one mile daily at three months old, which should be increased to four or five miles at six to eight months old, and so on until twelve months they are capable of doing up to fifteen or twenty miles comfortably. For an adult of the larger breeds, four miles a day should be considered the minimum, and for Spaniels and Setters a fair amount of exercise is necessary on a hard surface to wear down the feathering between the toes and so prevent "mats", and consequent lameness.

Terriers at weaning time require no extra exercise to their play, but should spend a fair amount of time each day out of doors. At three months old they should be given short walks two or three times a day, which may be increased gradually as for the larger breeds. An adult of this class should get a minimum of two miles a day.

Exercise does not play so prominent a part in connection with toy dogs as in most other breeds. Still, a

Harness, as an alternative to collar. The bridle goes under the chest; the link is at top.

[*Canadian Government*

IN THE ROCKY MOUNTAINS.

Touring in the Rockies—or indeed any snow-clad mountains—in a dog-drawn sleigh, is great fun.   This photograph was taken at Banff, Alberta, and the members of the party are obviously enjoying the glorious scenery around them

certain amount is essential to keep them healthy, and at six months old, Poms, Pugs and other toys can, with benefit to themselves, do as much as a small Terrier. At the same time, excessive exercise among toys should be avoided—a little and often is the best.

Photo]　　　　　　　　IN THE ARMY.　　　　　　　*[E.N.A.*

The sledge dog serves many purposes. In the Russian Army it makes itself helpful by drawing machine-guns. This photograph was taken in the neighbourhood of Archangel.

If a puppy is inclined to get splay feet, it should be exercised for two or three hours a day in a hard-floored run which has been well sprinkled with fine gravel. If this is not available it should be made to go at a slow trot for about two minutes twice a day on a rough road or cinder track. This causes it to tighten up its toes.

BREEDING-STOCK.—The stud dog requires no special treatment, and the brood bitch wants no change in her usual exercise for the first five or six weeks of pregnancy, but for the last few weeks her exercise should not be strenuous, such as jumping. Regular walking exercise right up to the time of whelping is desirable and necessary.

REGULARITY.—Regularity is essential for the best results, and moderate exercise each day is better than heavy exercise in fits and starts, while sudden changes in form are not desirable, as a dog used to covering four to six miles at walking-pace, may overtax itself if made to run the same distance. If through neglect or illness the dog gets out of condition from lack of exercise, it must be gradually brought into condition by regularly increasing exercise and good feeding, until its strength is recovered.

Winter exercise, especially in wet or foggy weather, is that most likely to be neglected, but neither wet nor cold weather harms dogs provided they are not exposed to cold winds while wet after exercise. Given good quarters, even without being rubbed down after a run in the rain, no ill will result.

CHAINING.—No dog should be chained for more than a few hours at a time, and if this is the only method of keeping it safely at home, a ring on a wire, fixed between its kennel and a wall or post, if only a few yards away, is much more desirable than chaining to a fixed point, since it gives some freedom of movement and slight exercise.

SICK DOGS.—As a general rule, the first sign of ill-health should be a signal to curtail all enforced exercise until the exact nature of the condition has been ascertained, when the amount of exercise to be allowed must be one part of the treatment to be decided upon. Even skin diseases, by their irritation, can keep a dog so exercised by scratching and cause loss of sleep that the usual amount of exercise would be prohibitive. It would be extremely foolish to use any energy needed to overcome disease by enforced exercise. Here, again, a dog's willingness or even keenness to go for a walk when obviously unwell, does not mean that it should be allowed to do so. Non-observance of this simple point has caused many possibly minor ailments to become complicated and serious, and what might have been mild and simple cases of distemper have ended fatally.

Expectorant.—A drug which increases the respiratory secretions and assists in their removal. Ipecacuanha, for instance, is a drug used against inflammatory conditions of the respiratory passages, as it increases the secretion of the bronchial mucous membrane and tends to render it more fluid so that the mucus can be coughed up more easily. When the secretion of the bronchi is already excessive, the cough is to be encouraged, but an expectorant would not be indicated. (*See* DOVER'S POWDER.) Among other expectorants are the following : eucalyptus oil, potass. iodide, turpentine, Friar's balsam, syrup of squills, medicated steam inhalations, creosote inhalations, ammonium carbonate, etc., etc.

By courtesy]　　　　　　　　　　　　　　　　　*[Dept. Interior. Ottawa.*

A DIFFERENT TYPE.

A group of Baffin Island Huskies, differing considerably in appearance from many other Eskimo dogs. In some of the heads the wolf-like appearance is distinctly evident.

The use of expectorants is particularly valuable where the respirations are abnormally rapid, the cough is weak, and the elimination of sputum is almost nil.

Eye, Anatomy of.—In considering the dog's eye we are concerned with the eyeball itself, the muscles which move it, the eyelids which protect it, the lachrymal glands which supply it with moisture and lubrication, and the orbital cavity in which it is enclosed. The cavity is lined by a layer of what is known as '*peri-orbital' fat*, which serves to prevent concussion or shock to the eyeball, and to afford a soft fatty bed facilitating the free and smooth movement of the eyeball.

Incidentally, when one notices that a dog's eyes are "sunken in", that is to say, have receded into the orbital cavities, it is because the peri-orbital fat has, to a more or less extent, become absorbed, or reduced in quantity.

The dog has three eyelids, one above, one below, and the third situated in the corner of the eye. The third eyelid is known also as the *Haw* or *Membrana Nictitans*, and consists of a more or less triangular-shaped membrane which can be retracted downwards and inwards practically out of sight. This nictitating membrane affords additional protection to the eyeball, and undoubtedly such added protection is highly desirable when one comes to think how fearlessly dogs will push through thick undergrowth in woods and hedges. The upper and lower eyelids bear eyelashes, but it is the upper eyelid which has the greatest power of movement, the lower one being only feebly motile. The main eyelids are lined on their inner surfaces by a mucous membrane known as the *conjunctiva*, which is, of course, continually coming into close contact with the "glass" or cornea of the eye, from the surface of which it removes any small particle of grit, dust or other foreign matter which might accidentally obtain ingress.

The moisture or tears, secreted by the *lachrymal glands*, is designed to prevent the front of the eyeball from becoming dry, and thus to facilitate the movement of the eyelids over its surface. This fluid is continually drained away through two very minute ducts—the *lachrymal ducts*—to the nasal cavity. Any excess of tears which cannot quickly enough find exit through these ducts, overflows and runs down the cheeks. On the inner surface of the third eyelid is situated the *Harderian gland*, which is a rudimentary lachrymal gland.

This gland occasionally becomes enlarged and tumefied, when it has to be surgically removed.

The eyeball of the dog is almost spherical, and consists of a circular transparent or glassy convexity known as the *Cornea*, which appears to be continuous at its periphery with a white, fibrous, opaque layer called the *Sclerotic*. In reality, however, the white fibres of the sclerotic are showing through the transparent cornea which superimposes it.

The *Anterior Chamber* of the eyeball is a cavity bounded anteriorly by the corneal layer and posteriorly by the lens. This chamber contains a watery fluid known as the *Aqueous Humour*. By far the larger space in the eyeball is that which lies behind the lens. It is known as the *Posterior Chamber*, and is dark, and filled with a viscid humour called the *Vitreous*. This vitreous humour is contained in a very fine membrane—the hyaloid—and accommodates itself exactly to the shape of the posterior

[E.N.A.]

Photo]

IN THE SUMMER.

The Eskimo dogs, and by that term are included the various types of the breed, are used often in summer to pull the boats along the waterways. This picture was taken by the Snake River, near Nome, in Alaska, U.S.A., and proves what untiring workers these sturdy dogs are. Summer or winter, they are always busy.

chamber, serving to maintain intra-ocular pressure and keep the delicate retina in position.

When one looks into the transparent cornea of an eye, one sees inside a coloured tissue composed of muscular fibres. This is the *iris*, and it has the power of contracting or dilating, through the influence of light upon the retina, thus closing or opening the circular hole in its centre, which is called the *pupil*. The iris is generally brown in dogs, though it may be of very varied hues in man and in the different breeds of cat. Its sensitiveness to light is exceedingly valuable, for if brilliant light strikes the eye, the closure of the pupil prevents its penetration to the delicate retina within. Conversely, when the available light is very dim, the pupil dilates widely and permits the maximum of light to enter. The pupil dilates under the influence of atropine and cocaine (these drugs being described as mydriatics), and it contracts under the effect of morphine and eserine, these and other similarly acting drugs being known as myotics. Violent exercise, sudden death, or impending death also cause wide dilation, which lasts for a few hours after death.

Light which enters the pupillary opening has then to penetrate the *Lens*. This is a bi-convex, elastic, glass-like body suspended immediately behind the iris by a ligament. It is enclosed in a capsule, tension upon which will cause its convex faces to flatten somewhat. Relaxation of the capsule tension permits an increase in convexity, and this mechanism is very intimately concerned with *Accommodation*.

The latter may be defined as the means whereby the eye is adjusted or focused for varying distances. The nearer an object is to the eye the greater the focusing required. This focusing is brought about by alteration in the convexity of the front surface of the lens. The greater the convexity, the shorter is its focus, and in this way images of near objects are correctly focused on the retina and distinctly seen. This explains why the human being, advancing in age, has to wear spectacles in order to be able to read at a convenient nearness. He, in fact, adds another lens, and the greater the failure of his "mechanism of accommodation", the more convex must be the lenses of his spectacles.

The *Retina* is the innermost tunic and perceptive structure of the eye, formed by an expansion of the optic nerve all around the point at which this nerve enters the posterior chamber. Though the retina perceives the picture it cannot see it, this being effected by a special centre of the brain. The retina is exceedingly delicate and composite, consisting of very many minute nerve fibres (derived from the optic nerve), blood vessels and coloured or pigmented cells. As viewed through an opthalmoscope, the retina is a beautiful structure. In blind animals, the retina may be in normal and healthy condition, the loss of sight being due entirely to degeneration of, or damage to, the specific area of brain which permits an animal to know what it is looking at.

It is interesting to relate that disease of one eye, in the dog, does not necessarily cause a sympathetic disease in the opposite eye, as is so commonly the case in the human being. In man, sympathetic ophthalmia undoubtedly does occur, and is due to the inflammatory process extending along the nerve fibres from the affected eye to the healthy one.

Eye, Diseases of.—It is perhaps hardly necessary to remind readers how exceedingly delicate and vulnerable an organ is the eye. It follows, then, that damage or disease must occur with great ease. Moreover, several canine ailments, while not of themselves eye diseases, are easily reflected in the eyes, and we have, as examples, distemper and diabetes. It is unwise for the amateur to attempt diagnosis or treatment of ocular diseases, as he may do great damage involving, perhaps, the loss of the animal's sight.

The tests for vision which are applied to man cannot be applied to dogs, and we have to rely almost entirely upon the palpebral and pupillary reflexes. In the palpebral test, if the retina is still sensitive, a pretended blow aimed at the face will induce a reflex protective mechanism to come into action, i.e. the closure of the eyelids. Each eye should be tested separately, and the one not under test should be covered by the palm of the hand. No noise or draught must be created in this operation, or a false result will be obtained. The pupillary reflex also depends upon the normal functioning of the retina, and is accomplished by placing a light before the suspected eye and watching whether the pupil contracts before its influence and dilates upon diminution of the light. A fixed pupil denotes an insensitive retina. (*See also* BLINDNESS.)

Ingrowing Eyelashes.—A condition known technically as trichiasis. It refers to ingrowing hairs or eyelashes from the upper eyelid. The writer has not seen its occurrence in the lower eyelid. The eyelashes, although growing in normal eyelids, take an abnormal direction downward and backward so as to impinge upon the eyeball. This frequently causes profuse lachrimation (or watering) and semi-closure of the eye through fear of light, inflammation, ulceration and pain. But these symptoms are not necessarily co-existent, as quite often the only symptom is what may be termed a weak, watery eye. When such a condition is not amenable to any treatment, the dog should be taken to a veterinary surgeon in order that a minute examination may be made. If trichiasis is found to exist, he must pluck out the offending hairs, or he may perform a similar operation to that which is usual for the relief of entropion (*which see*).

Watery Eyes seem characteristic in some breeds, e.g. some of the toy Spaniels. The condition then is a constitutional weakness and certainly hereditary. But in all cases search should be made for a cause, and any of the following conditions may be responsible : grit or other foreign body in the eye ; slight scratch or other injury from a cat or thorn bush, etc. ;

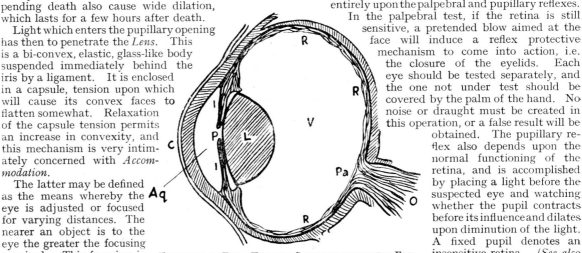

STRUCTURE OF EYE : VERTICAL SECTION THROUGH THE EYE-BALL.

Aq., Aqueous humour. C., Cornea. P., Pupil. I., Iris. L., Lens. V., Vitreous humour. Pa., Papilla. R., Retina. O., Optic nerve.

PLEASANT AND SAFE TRANSPORT.

[E.N.A.

...en women can safely undertake dog-sledge journeys.   The ladies here shown are enjoying an exhilarating drive close to Lake Arrowhead, in California.

conjunctivitis ; pimple on inside of eyelids ; inturned eyelashes ; inturned eyelids (entropion) ; loose, hanging eyelids (ectropion) ; distemper, and blockage of the lachrymal duct. Foreign bodies should immediately be removed by the aid of a very fine pair of forceps, or by wiping the mucous membrane with the point of a piece of cotton-wool which has been twisted into an elongated shape. Possibly a solution of cocaine might have to be applied prior to the attempt at removal, especially if the dog is of a very nervous disposition.

For scratches and other small injuries, the application of a suitable eyewash is generally all that is required.

Blue Film over the glass of the eye is very common in dogs and owes its origin to a large number of conditions, including all those enumerated under "Watery Eyes". It is merely a sign that the cornea is inflamed, the condition being known as keratitis or corneitis. It is a common precursor and accompaniment of distemper, but is not of very great importance. When the case is uncomplicated, the blue haze may clear away within a week, though generally it remains for three or four weeks. Extensive opacities may, indeed, linger for two or three months. Those which result from wounds of the cornea or from loss of corneal tissue, may be succeeded by permanent cicatrices or scars.

Keratitis.—It is a rather remarkable fact that, although the cornea is not vascular, it is freely susceptible to inflammation ; and in some types of the disease adventitious blood-vessels are soon perceived ramifying in all directions over the cornea. In such cases they are derived from the conjunctival vessels, are situated beneath the epithelial layer and are bright-red in colour. Keratitis may be superficial or non-suppurative, and ulcerative or suppurative.

THE CAUSE of the superficial variety may be injuries, foreign bodies, dust, cold draughts of air, irritant gases, inverted eyelashes or eyelids, and may be secondary to distemper. It would probably also occur in tuberculosis of the deeper structures of the eye.

SYMPTOMS.—There is some degree of loss of transparency of the cornea, which is followed by more or less opacity of either local or diffuse disposition. Sight is not much interfered with unless such opacity becomes dense and is situated in the direct path of vision. The formation of corneal opacity is said to depend upon a migration of leucocytes (*see* BLOOD) from the nearest blood-vessels. In unfavourable cases these bodies, instead of dispersing, become organized, and eventually cicatricial tissue is produced which constitutes a permanent opacity. The early stage of keratitis is denoted by a flow of tears increasing with the severity of the inflammation, and then accompanied by avoidance of light, semi-closure of the eyelids, some tenderness, and a desire continually to rub the part along the floor.

Very often this completes the picture, and after a few days have elapsed, the mucous discharge lessens, the milky opacity decreases and resolution becomes complete. Sometimes there is a quiescent period in which neither progression nor retrogression is observed. This may last for weeks. The most unfavourable termination is ulcerative or suppurative keratitis. In this case, when the leucocytes infiltrate the layers of the cornea, they may continue to crowd in and become so tightly packed that the pressure exerted upon the epithelial cells brings about the destruction

of the latter. One or more layers of the cornea having become destroyed, there is created a point of entry for suppurative organisms, and corneal abscess is the result. An ulcer on the cornea looks like a shallow depression having a grey or yellowish-grey colour. Resolution may occur at this stage, or destruction may go on until there is complete perforation of the cornea. The contents of the anterior chamber are lost, thus allowing the iris and lens to bulge forward and block the exit. There may be very much more serious sequelae to this condition, and an expert only can deal with it. No attempt will be made to guide the amateur in the treatment except to say that no metallic salt such as lead, silver, or zinc, should be used in such a condition, as some only aggravate it, whilst others would become deposited in the ulcer and cause permanent opacity. Shade the eye from wind, light and dust, and bathe frequently with warm boracic solution until expert assistance arrives.

Staphyloma.—A condition which is somewhat common in dogs and brought about by perforation of the cornea. This permits the iris to protrude through the hole, and this protrusion is known as iridial staphyloma. When the new body is large in extent it may impede the closure of the eyelids. It is a serious condition, and must receive immediate and proper attention. Many weeks will elapse before healing is complete, and much care and patience must be exercised by both owner and veterinary attendant to attain this happy end. Even then a lifelong blemish may remain, with more or less loss of sight, though the latter will depend upon what complication has arisen, such as organization of the herniated portion.

Precautions must be adopted to prevent the patient from injuring its eye during treatment, for which purpose a bandage, or, better still, a wire eye-guard may have to be applied.

Dislocation of the Eye.—A common occurrence in all large-eyed dogs such as Pekes, King Charles Spaniels, etc., and generally due to bites and other rough usage. Even in attempting to give a Pekingese a dose of medicine, if it struggles and has to be held, it is quite an easy matter to make an eye protrude so far that the eyelids slip behind the eyeball instead of remaining in front of it. It is not by any means an easy matter to induce the eyelids to resume their normal position. When an eyeball has departed from its orbital cavity, it very soon becomes congested and much swollen. Reduction must be accomplished soon, therefore, or with increasing size in the eyeball comes an increasing difficulty in getting the organ to resume its ordinary place.

Where the ball has sustained some injury such as a cut or scratch, the chances of success are considerably lessened, for these injuries are rapidly followed by oedema of the membranous and muscular attachments, and very soon increase the volume of the eye to such an extent that replacement seems almost hopeless.

It is strongly urged that nobody but a surgeon should attempt to replace a luxated eyeball unless he be so geographically situated that such services are unobtainable. For such a man only, the following brief directions are given. The first step in the process will be the careful disinfection of the ball with pure warm water and chinosol (1–1000) or with boracic solution. It is then lubricated with castor-oil, and pressure brought to bear upon it through an oiled wad of cotton-wool, at the same time endeavouring to lift the upper eyelid and

Photos] [*Douthwaite.*

WORKING IN LONELY PLAINS AND MOUNTAINS.

The top picture shows a couple of dog-drawn sleighs wending their way through a lonely plain. Who knows what their errand may be ? Perhaps they are laden with goods to sell or exchange ; or with foodstuffs and clothing to take home. In the lower picture a team of Eskimo dogs is seen resting in the clean, white snow after a long and arduous pull uphill.

By courtesy]   [Müller & Glass
Gray cataract of both eyes.

Foreign Bodies in the Eye. (*See* "Watery Eyes" p. 590.)

Cataract of the Eye.—Denotes an opacity of the lens which may be in a localized spot or diffused all over the lens. Sight will be affected in accordance with the position of the lesion. It is exceedingly commonly seen in dogs' eyes as a result of senile decay, appearing from about the age of six years, sometimes earlier and at others later. It can, however, occur at any age as the result of injury, or, secondarily, to some other disease of the eye. It is feared that there is no treatment of the slightest value, and even the operation which is performed upon human beings with cataract is practically useless in animals.

Ophthalmia.—By this term is meant an inflammation of all the tissues of the eye, though it is observed that some authors reserve the word to indicate a purulent inflammation of the eye. It has been seen during distemper, after severe concussion of the eye, or may arise from wounds or perforating ulcers of the cornea. It is usually a very grave condition, running a rapid course and ending in total loss of the eye.

SYMPTOMS.—In some instances this disease originates in the interior of the eyeball, without any exciting external lesion ; in this case visible symptoms may not at first be displayed. In the later stages, when the disturbance has progressed forward to the anterior chamber, symptoms will then be observed which very soon will assume a character similar to those which arise in consequence of external violence. These are . closure of the eyelids, great pain, fear of light, inflammation and swelling of the conjunctiva, opacity and vascularity of the cornea, pus in the anterior chamber. The humours of both chambers are invaded by sero-purulent and haemorrhagic fluid, and there is great tenseness of the eyeball. Later, a perforation of either the cornea or sclerotic occurs, through which a suppurating mass—including the lens and the humours—escapes. This is at once overcome the resistance which it would otherwise offer to the passage of the ball through the palpebral fissure. This is far easier to describe than to perform, and repeated bungling attempts will inevitably lead to great eyeball injury. Ophthalmia is then greatly to be feared, followed probably by loss of sight.

followed by collapse of the whole eye, and its total destruction.

In other instances there may be no rupture, but there will be displacements of one or all of the vital parts of the eye, resulting in total blindness, and eventually in atrophy of the whole organ. The chances of successful treatment are remote, and nothing usually remains to be done but to remove the diseased eye.

Glaucoma, or dropsy of the eye, is a condition in which the eyes become greatly distended with an abnormal amount of fluid. The intra-ocular tension is much increased and the eyes seem to stare in a blank kind of way, whilst sight is partially or entirely lost. The cause is not well understood, but it is thought in some cases to be associated with tuberculosis of the eye, and in others to be due to over-secretion of the humours combined with an inability of the excess to find any exit.

Treatment is very unsatisfactory, and, like that of any other serious eye disease, must be left to the expert.

Inverted Eyelids, or Entropion.—The eyelids themselves are unduly turned in towards the eyeball, a condition very common among dogs.

CAUSES.—Entropion may arise in consequence of shortening of the conjunctiva between the lid and the eyeball through wounds or inflammatory processes. Eczema or mange affecting the eyelids are sometimes exciting causes, as may be, also, chronic or acute conjunctivitis. But by far the greatest number of cases of entropion are hereditary, and, curiously enough, they are most frequently found among the Chows. It is a great

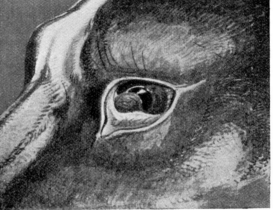

Tumefaction and protrusion of the Harderian gland.

mistake to breed from an animal which is, or has been, afflicted with the malady unless one is sure that the cause was traumatic and not hereditary.

SYMPTOMS.—Owing to the irritation of the cornea which invariably arises, there is a good deal of watering and tenderness of the eye, accompanied by photophobia (fear of light). Lachrimation may, however, occur as a result of the imperfect closure of the eyelids, thus permitting tears to escape over the brim of the lower lid, instead of effecting their retention and ultimate discharge via the lachrymal duct. In very severe or old-standing cases, corneal opacities, or even ulcerations, may be provoked, which in the absence of treatment may

Illustrating corneal opacity of the dog's left eye.
(From *Kirk's Canine Distemper.*)

594

TWO FAVOURITES.

It is often said that the Eskimo dog is dangerous and not suitable for the home. It is really nothing of the kind, if properly treated.
Carol Lombard, the film star, is only one of many American people who have Eskimo dogs as pets.

Photo]   [Douthwaite.

Whilst the Eskimo dog is used for shooting, one often meets with dogs of different types entirely distinct from the wolf-breed or from the Samoyed type. They also do good work in the snow.

probably lead to ophthalmia and quite possibly complete loss of sight.

TREATMENT.—Nothing will remedy the condition except an operation, the principle of which is the shortening of the eyelid and the consequent withdrawal of its free edge from the eyeball. It is therefore essentially a case for the surgeon.

Everted Eyelids, or Ectropion, is the reverse of entropion, one or both lids, in this case, hanging away from the eyeball and revealing a red, raw-looking pocket. The lower lid is usually implicated and some amount of inflammation and discharge of tears is probably occasioned. The remedy is again operative. This condition is a characteristic of bloodhounds, in which breed it would apparently seem to be an essential and sought for character.

Protusion of the Haw.—The haw, *membrana nictitans*, or third eyelid, is a semi-lunar fold of membrane arising from the inferior and inner angle of the orbit and resting upon the eyeball. It is strengthened at its margin by a thin cartilage and is covered in about two-thirds of its extent by a fold of conjunctiva. So frequently may both haws be seen fully protruded over the eyes of dogs, that everyone is familiar with their existence and appearance.

The function of this membrane appears to be partly that of scavenger to the eyeball, over the surface of which it sweeps, clearing away dust and remoistening the cornea so far as it can reach. Its thickened base, deep in the orbit, is in contact with a pad of fat, which

upon retraction of the eyeball, is pushed forward, taking with it the haw. This is the mechanism of its movement.

It is not infrequently observed that a dog will exhibit the membranes well over its eyes for many days, without any apparent reason. The latter, too, is often difficult to ascertain. It is definitely known, however, to occur in cases of anaemia, debility, wasting disease, starvation, foreign bodies and tumours in the orbit, conjunctivitis and keratitis. It may not necessarily occur in all such cases. Some disturbance of the sympathetic system may occasionally be responsible.

Any condition causing the eyeball to recede into its orbit is, for this very reason, responsible also for protrusion of the third eyelid.

Such protrusion may become a source of great annoyance to the dog by interference with sight, whilst the squint-eyed appearance of an animal so affected renders it very ugly.

The application of astringent, sedative and antiseptic lotions is called for, which, in combination with tonics and fattening foods internally, may cause this eyelid to resume its normal position. Should failure result, the haw must be surgically removed.

The *membrana nictitans* are not uncommonly the seat of benign or malignant tumour formations, particularly of tubercular or cancerous origin.

Tumefied Harderian Gland.—Now and again one is asked to see dogs which have, as the owners explain,

Photo]   [E.N.A.

THE FUR TRADER.

During the winter months the fur trader depends largely upon the dog for transport purposes. Show points are of no importance in this case, work and obedience being of foremost importance.

"a lump in its eye". On the inner surface of the third eyelid is situated the gland of Harder, and for some reason or other this gland occasionally becomes swollen or tumefied, thus in some instances causing the haw to protrude, or becoming itself exposed (dislocated) beyond the free margin of the haw. The most certain cure is surgical excision under local anaesthesia. Eye-washes of various kinds have often been tried, but generally without useful result.

Conjunctivitis.—Inflammation of the conjunctival mucous membrane which lines the eyelids. It is an exceedingly common condition in dogs; in fact, in all animals, the conjunctiva seems to be especially vulnerable to congestive or inflammatory processes because of its great sensibility to external or internal

redness, swelling and tenderness of the membrane, with an abnormal flow of tears in the early stages. The latter symptom is often more apparent than the former, though, as the condition increases in severity, the inflammatory phenomena are also augmented, whilst the mucous discharge becomes muco-purulent or even purulent.

Generally there is great irritability of the eye, which the animal denotes by incessantly rubbing its face on the ground or with its paws. There is more or less fear of light and marked resistance to clinical examination. Discharge continues to run down the cheeks and, after some time, begins to excoriate and render hairless the areas over which it pours.

Photo]   E. M. Joyce.

A DIFFERENT TYPE.

At one time the Eskimo dog was crossed with the Newfoundland, and many of these dogs show this strain clearly. The dogs here shown are of this breed and are working in the Antarctic

impressions, and its ample blood and lymph supply. There are two forms recognized, viz. simple conjunctival catarrh and acute purulent conjunctivitis.

CAUSES.—Systemic infections are often ushered in by catarrh of the conjunctival mucous membranes, a fact which is well and frequently exemplified in cases of distemper. Mechanical and chemical influences of every description are variously responsible for the condition. Exposure to cold and rapid winds, as experienced by dogs which are allowed to ride in cars with their heads out of the windows, is a ready means of inducing its onset. One or both eyes may be affected, and age appears to exert no influence upon the incidence of the disease. In distemper the malady is usually bilateral.

SYMPTOMS.—Like catarrh of other mucous membranes, conjunctivitis is accompanied by increased

TREATMENT.—The first procedure is to discover the cause and, if possible, remove it. The second important point is to ensure that no discharges are permitted to remain long in contact with the eye. The collyria which may be employed for irrigating the eye are very numerous, but it is thought to be a safe plan to discourage the use, by amateurs, of any but the simplest and most harmless preparations, such as boracic acid 10 per cent solution, chinosol 1 in 1000, or permanganate of potash 1 in 4000. Prior to the instillation of any agent, it is an excellent idea to bathe the eye generously with a fairly warm solution of boracic acid to reduce the pain and inflammation. Some precaution against self-mutilation should be taken, or one's best endeavours may be undone in a few moments. If the case is severe, keep the dog in semi-darkness and do not permit it to lie before a fire.

Dog suffering from severe conjunctivitis wearing a shade to protect the eye from strong light, dust, and further injury.

The acute purulent type of conjunctivitis may be a sequel to the simpler catarrhal type. Occasionally it may even occur in young puppies, either before or soon after their eyes have opened. If it occurs before the eyelids have parted for the first time, the pus is imprisoned and the sight is nearly always destroyed. The grounds for believing that this type has a bacterial origin are very strong, and the fact that it so frequently accompanies distemper supports that view. The thick and almost caseous secretions which are thrown out are very excoriating, and, unless frequently removed, will set up great irritation of the skin and damage to the eyeball. The pus dries about the eyelids into scabs, sticks to the lashes and successfully glues all parts together unless vigilance is exercised by the nurse and the parts kept clean. Sometimes the condition is so painful that the patient refuses food, loses weight, and becomes very depressed. Ophthalmia and/or blindness may supervene, and death is not unknown.

Adopt the home remedies advised for catarrhal conjunctivitis, and if this seems to have no good effect, seek professional advice.

Glass Eyes.—Occasionally the injuries sustained by a dog's eye are so serious that there is no alternative to excision of the eyeball. This operation is not at all rare, but it is more seldom that owners think it worth while to go to the expense of having a glass eye fitted. This is, however, perfectly feasible, and excellent matches of dogs' eyes are obtainable. The dog so treated is generally an aristocratic member

Pug dog whose left eye has been replaced by a glass substitute.

of canine society which accompanies its mistress—when permissible—at all the functions she attends. But a one-eyed dog would perhaps offend delicate tastes, and the little dog must have its good looks restored. Accordingly, some two or three months after the real eye has been removed, and when all inflammation has subdued, a glass eye is obtained and inserted. It takes some little time for the dog to become accustomed to it, however, and it has not infrequently happened that just when the party is exclaiming how wonderful it looks, little Fido gives one scratch with its paw and leaves a guinea's worth of good glass eye on the hearthrug.

It is essential to accustom the dog to wearing it by graduating the amount of time it is left in from an hour or so to many hours, or even twenty-four hours; but at least once in twenty-four hours it should be removed for a while for cleansing purposes. The better plan is to remove it each night and replace it in the morning.

Nystagmus.—Oscillation or rolling movements of the eyeballs. This is a curious and rather alarming symptom, which is generally seen only in very serious maladies or immediately prior to death. The eyeballs oscillate in a jerky manner, from side to side or in a circular motion, a phenomenon which is accompanied generally by great disturbance of the whole nervous system, such as may be manifested by a fit, delirium, chronic convulsions, or coma. The cause is assumed, in some cases, to be cerebellar disease, internal-ear disease, or intoxication. In the writer's experience, the last-named has always been the cause, although the source of the intoxication may have varied. The curious palsy so commonly associated with acute uraemia is accompanied by nystagmus, which symptom does not cease until the excess of urea in the blood is diminished. It occurs also in attacks of eclampsia, and quite commonly in cases of chloroform poisoning, i.e. just prior to death from chloroform inhalation pushed to excess.

So far as treatment is concerned, there is no specific, but but one must endeavour to ascertain the cause and this cannot be done by a layman. If there is kidney disease, steps must be taken to treat it without delay. If it is due to chloroform poisoning, the appropriate antidotes must be administered.

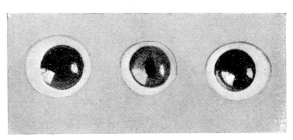

Types of glass eyes for dogs.
(From *Hobday's Surgical Diseases of the Dog and Cat.*)

[Keystone.

Photo]

A HARD LIFE.

It is a cold and hard world in which these strongly made Eskimo dogs carry out their work. This picture comes from Labrador and shows a team on the trail in a mountainous district.

F

FORGING AHEAD.
FORGING AHEAD.
An Eskimo dog-team belonging to the N.W. Mounted Police on an icy trail during the winter 1931–32.

F. = Fawn.

Faeces.—The excrement, or undigested residue of the food, discharged by the bowels. In the dog they are light or dark in colour, and soft or hard in consistence according to the prevailing circumstances, e.g. type of food consumed, its quantity, and the rapidity of its disposal. Dogs usually have two or three motions in twenty-four hours, but the amount of faeces passed at each evacuation will again depend upon the quality and quantity of food consumed.

A dog fed on biscuit and other vegetable food will pass larger motions than the dog fed on meat. Ellenberger estimated that a dog fed on cereal foods would pass 20 per cent of the amount eaten, whilst the same dog nourished with meat would void only 12 per cent by weight of the ration. The consumption of bones renders the faeces very pale and chalk-like, whilst meat causes them to be very dark. Many medicines produce an alteration in the normal colour of the faeces, and we find that iron, bismuth and calomel turn them black. Excessive secretion of bile turns them yellow or brownish-yellow; grass makes them green; and a bread-and-milk diet produces yellow motions. (*See* BLACK MOTIONS.) The unpleasant odour of faeces is due to the presence of a crystallizable body from indigo known as indol, and another body called skatol, which is produced from the decomposition of proteins. When the fat consumed is undigested, owing to an absence or inadequate supply of bile, the faeces are intensely disagreeable.

In a state of ill-health, we find the faeces are much altered, for in diarrhoea they may be very thin and watery; in enteritis and colitis they may be slimy, or coated with gelatinous mucus; frothy when there is fermentation and gas formation; clay-like in jaundice; black and pitch-like in cases of haemorrhage from the stomach and small bowels, or stained a bright-red in Stuttgart disease or in proctitis, etc., etc.

Fainting, or syncope, is an attack characterized by loss of consciousness and inability to stand, which occurs quite suddenly and usually passes off in a minute or two. It is due to anaemia of the brain caused, probably, by sudden and temporary interference with the action of the heart. This in turn is sometimes brought about by shock following severe injury or by fright; but in dogs, fainting occurs mostly among the aged animals which have weak or fatty hearts. Racing Greyhounds which have any cardiac defect will sometimes faint near the termination of a race.

When fainting occurs, give the animal plenty of fresh air, cool the feet by placing them in, or douching them with, water, and arrange the head at a lower level than that of the heart, so that circulation

Traversing the Beaver River, Yukon.

Photos by courtesy]   *[Douthwaite.*
ALWAYS AT WORK.
A very fine team of Eskimo dogs making its way over a passage between dents in the Beaver River.

Photo]   *[Keystone.*

THE DOGS OF THE "HEADLESS" PEOPLE.

Not so long ago there existed a legend that the people of the North of Russia were headless. This story was probably due to the fact that they covered their heads completely with their coats. Here are seen men with their teams wending their way amongst the snow, the sledges heavy with goods, and their heads entirely covered, as of yore.

in the brain is restored. Remove or loosen the dog's collar and massage the region of the heart. When it is able to swallow, a dose of brandy or whisky in water may be given; or sal volatile would be equally useful if any were at hand. If such attacks occur more than once, the patient should obviously be guarded with care against over-exertion of any kind, or against shocks. A purgative, in the first instance, will be beneficial, followed by a course of heart tonics for one or two weeks.

Photo]   *[E.N.A.*
A LONG JOURNEY IN FRONT OF THEM.
In the North-West Territories the Eskimo dog takes the place of the horse in winter time and undertakes long journeys along the countryside, of which the above is a typical example.

Fall.—The official term for the long, loose hair overhanging the faces of certain breeds, e.g. the Yorkshire Terrier.

Fallopian Tube, or Oviduct.—The bitch has two Fallopian tubes, one on each side of the body, forming a communication between the extremity of the uterine horn and the left and right ovary respectively. The Fallopian tube is not actually attached to the ovary, but it has a wide, fimbriated, funnel-shaped extremity which rather effectually encircles the ovary. When the Graafian follicles of the latter body arrive at its surface and rupture, the ova are set free, but are caught in the funnel of the Fallopian tube down which they commence their journey. It is here that they are met and fertilized by the male spermatozoa.

Inflammation of the oviducts is known as salpingitis.

Faradic Current. (*See* TREATMENTS, ELECTRICAL.)

Farinaceous Foods are vegetable foods such as wheat, rice, dog biscuits, potatoes, and, in fact, all cereals containing starch. Farinaceous means "of the nature of flour or meal; starchy or containing starch".

Fat, Storage of.—When the amount of fat consumed, or the amount of food convertible into fat, is greater than is required for the immediate needs of the body, the surplus is stored up in various parts of the anatomy as a reserve supply. The latter is called upon during any long period of illness, or if the amount of work imposed upon the dog becomes greatly increased, or if food is for any reason withheld.

The body, in fact, lives upon this store of fat until it is exhausted. The supply of nutriment is then taken on by the various glands, which become much diminished in size as a consequence. After that, the muscular system is drawn upon, and finally the blood yields a limited food supply. Dogs have been known to live in this way for as long as four weeks, but at the point of death they were mere skeletons. Provided that water is given, a dog might live even longer than four weeks. If glucose or albumen were added to the water, life could be sustained for a much longer period. Fat is generally stored about the kidneys, in the mesentery, under the skin, between muscles, or among the muscle fibres, and often around the heart. (*See also* EMACIATION.)

Fatty Degeneration.—Globules of fat becoming deposited in the cells of a tissue. The cells affected are made to atrophy owing to the pressure exerted upon them. Fatty degeneration is common in the liver and kidneys, and particularly in the heart. The cause is unknown, except that it has been observed to follow chronic phosphorus poisoning.

Favus. (*See* SKIN DISEASES.)

Photo]   *[E.N.A*
A POWERFUL TEAM.
Sixteen Eskimo dogs, the property of Mr. Leonard Seppals. This team won the 20th All-Alaska Dog Derby, which has become one of the greatest, most interesting, and exciting events of the country.

Feather.—The fringe of hair at the back of the legs; a term also applied to body-hair in long-haired breeds.

Febrifuge.—A medicinal or other agent employed to reduce abnormally high temperature. A cold bath will temporarily act in this way, but the febrifuges employed for dogs are generally drugs, such as aspirin, salicylate of soda, quinine, aconite, alcohol, the purgatives and diuretics, etc.

Choice must depend upon the case, as in one instance stimulation might be required such as would be afforded by brandy or whisky; in another instance a sedative like aspirin would give better service, especially as this is also an anti-rheumatic. Quinine reduces temperature partly because of its power to hinder bacterial life, and partly as a result of the slowing down of metabolism.

Feed—(Diminished desire to); and FEED (Increased Desire to): (*See* FOODS AND FEEDING.)

Felted.—Having a matted coat.

Femur.—The longest bone in the dog's body articulating above with the hip joint, and below with the bone called the tibia at the stifle joint. The femur is very commonly fractured and is particularly difficult to set owing to the mass of muscular tissue which practically surrounds it.

Fertilization. (*See* EMBRYO.)

Fever.—A dog suffering from a fever is regarded merely as having an elevation of temperature. In other words, it is "feverish". In the majority of cases, fever is merely a symptom or accompaniment of some well-recognized disease; but it may be encountered entirely alone, that is to say, it appears not to be secondary to any other condition, which

Photo]   [*Douthwaite*
VARIOUS TYPES.
A mixed team of Eskimo dogs, belonging to the Royal Canadian Mounted Police Detachment at Bache Peninsula.

renders its origin exceedingly obscure. The medical profession recognizes a malady among humans known as P.U.O., which means "Pyrexia of unknown origin." Veterinary surgeons also find apparently healthy dogs sometimes running a temperature even as high as 105°. There is nothing else about them which gives any clue as to its cause, and when the affected dogs have been subjected to enforced rest, the fever subsides.

Any bacterial infection of the body may give rise to fever. Infection of the blood (which is normally sterile) will rapidly produce alarming fever.

Inflammation of any organ or tissue, such, for instance, as nephritis, pneumonia, pleurisy, metritis, and hosts of others, are accompanied by low or high temperature according to their severity and extent. Chills and colds which do not occasion, as a rule, inflammation of any particular organ, are nevertheless frequently ushered in with feverishness which is manifested by shivering attacks, sometimes dry, hot nose, thirst, and lassitude. Later, appetite fails and there may be constipation, increased rapidity of respiration, and a quickened pulse. These phenomena denote a state of fever, and a closer examination of the animal is necessary to discover the underlying cause of the condition.

The normal temperature of the dog is 101° F., but in feverishness this may rise to any degree up to about 105°. On somewhat rare occasions it may reach 106° or 107°, but these are becoming dangerous temperatures. Cases have been known in which dogs' temperatures have reached even 108°, but unless a diminution is quickly effected, the animal is likely to die. (*See* THERMOMETER.)

TREATMENT.—The dog must be removed from draught, cold, damp or exposure of any kind. In fact, a ready way of reducing fever is to produce sweating. As dogs do not sweat via the skin, we can at least induce them to perspire in their own way,

Photo]   [*Douthwaite*.
OFF AGAIN.
The same team as is shown in the top picture is here seen leaving the Peninsula at full speed.

By courtesy]   "BEVERLEY RHEA".   *[E. C. Ash.*

In the 'eighties Mr. W. R. Bryden, of Beverley, was a breeder of Field Spaniels. They were not all, as this picture shows, so long in body as was then the fashion.

i.e. via the lungs, by applying warm clothing. Febrifuges may be given at regular intervals (*see* FEBRIFUGE), and for the dog, aspirin is very valuable. The bowel action must be attended to, preferably with saline laxatives such as Epsom salts.

Fibroma.—A benign tumour composed of fibrous tissue. This type of growth has a hard consistence and definite outline, and is commonly encountered in the mammary glands of the bitch. (*See* MILK GLANDS AND TUMOURS.)

Fibrous Tissue.—The tissue of which ligaments and tendons are composed. It is an exceedingly strong and tough substance arranged in long, closely packed fibres. Fibrous tissue, either of the white or yellow elastic variety, is found abundantly throughout the body and enters into the formation, in greater or lesser extent, of almost every part.

Fibula.—A long, slender bone lying between the hock and the stifle joints of the hind limb. An X-ray photograph of a fractured fibula will be found under the heading of FRACTURES.

Fiddle-headed.—Long, gaunt and narrow in the head.

Field Spaniel.—In writing of the present-day Field Spaniel, one cannot do better than quote the words of the late Theo Marples, Esq., F.Z.S., in *Our Dogs*, August 3, 1923 :

"A rationally built Field Spaniel—that is to say, a dog of medium height on leg, a little lower on the leg than the Springer and a little longer in the body, with its long and beautifully chiselled head, square fore-face, and intelligent expression—a well-balanced dog throughout, active and alert —is a most beautiful example of the Spaniel family, whose architecture, head (beaming with intelligence), substance, coat, and contour, all spell UTILITY."

The Field Spaniel is one of the handsomest of the sporting Spaniels. Its larger proportions give it the dignity that the Cocker can never attain, and it has more nobility of expression than the Springer.

By nature the Field is usually sweet and kindly,

and it often has a touch of humour which makes it an ideal companion.

The more compact body which present-day Field breeders have achieved make it a very suitably sized dog for rough shooting. It can gather a hare or pheasant easily and yet it can comfortably work under bushes and brambles.

In selecting a puppy, care should be taken to avoid one with an amber eye, as this entirely destroys the thoughtful expression. Depth of muzzle is also a point of importance and must be combined with length of fore-face. A deep short muzzle is undesirable, savouring of the Sussex, but a snipy one is anathema. Height of dome is to a certain extent controlled by the set-on of the ears ; a high-placed ear will give an appearance of flatness to a rounded skull.

The ears, which must be lobular, should never be set on higher than the eye level. Excessive throatiness is objectionable, and a long neck is a necessity to enable the dog to use its nose when going at a good pace.

If the shoulders are badly placed the dog will be out at elbows and develop a rolling gait, which is a hindrance to its work.

The length of a Field Spaniel's body, whilst greater in proportion than that of the Springer, should never be length for length's sake. It is essential that it be well coupled or it will lose power in the hindquarters.

The average height at shoulder is from 17 to 18 ins., and average length of dog from the occiput to base of tail about 27 ins.

The weight is seldom as low as 35 lb. and averages round about 45 lb.

The Field Spaniel Society, which was inaugurated in 1923, issued the following standard of points :

Head and jaw, 15 ; eyes, 5 ; ears, 5 ; neck, 5 ; body, 10 ; forelegs, 10 ; hindlegs, 10 ; feet, 10 ; stern, 10 ; coat and feather, 10 ; general appearance, 10. Total, 100.

DESCRIPTION OF THE FIELD SPANIEL.

HEAD.—Should be quite characteristic of this grand sporting dog, as that of the Bulldog or

By courtesy]   "BARUM KING".   *[E. C. Ash.*

In the 'eighties the craze was for long bodies on short legs and this resulted in dogs difficult to use in the field. "Barum King" is an example of the longer body.

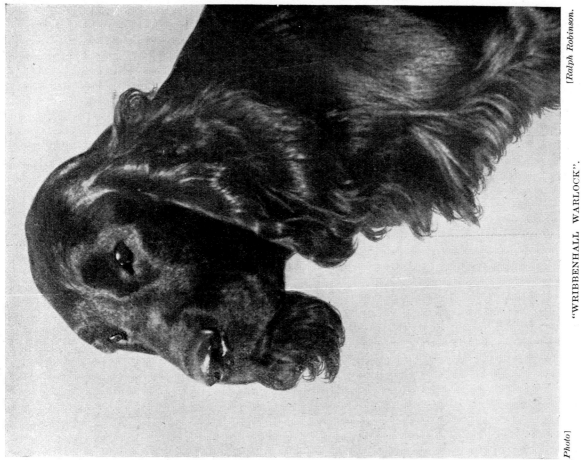

[Photo]   [Ralph Robinson.

"WRIBBENHALL WARLOCK".

Mr. Mortimer Smith and Field Spaniels always come to mind together, because of the success of the "Wribbenhall" Kennel and the excellent type of his dogs. Mr. Mortimer Smith's "Warlock" has a most attractive head, suggesting exceptional intelligence.

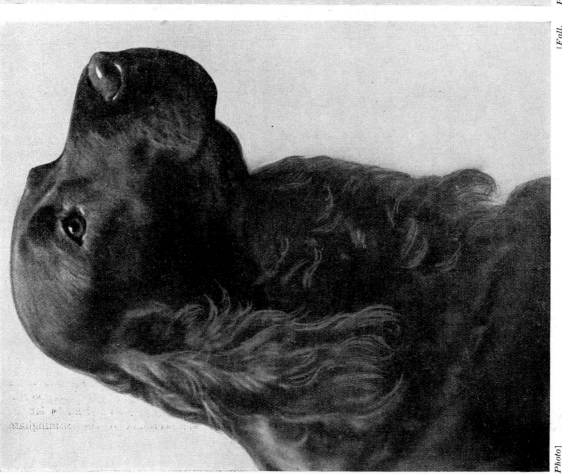

[Photo]   [Fall.

WOODBELL PERFECTION".

"The beautiful head of a spaniel" are words often used to denote the exceptional charm. Mr. Owen's dog certainly fills the bill.

Bloodhound; its very stamp and countenance should at once convey the conviction of high breeding, character and nobility; skull well developed with a distinctly elevated occipital tuberosity, which, above all, gives the character alluded to; not too wide across the muzzle; long, lean, never snipy or squarely cut, and in profile curving gradually from nose to throat; lean beneath the eyes, a thickness here gives coarseness to the whole head. The great length of muzzle gives surface for the free development of the olfactory nerve, and thus secures the highest possible scenting powers.

EYES.—Not too full, but not small, receding or overhung; colour dark-hazel or brown or nearly black, according to colour of dog. Grave in expression and showing no brow.

EARS. — Moderately long and wide, sufficiently clad with nice Setter-like feather and set low. They should fall in graceful folds, the lower parts curling inwards and backwards.

NECK.—Long, strong and muscular, so as to enable the dog to retrieve his game without undue fatigue.

BODY.—Should be of moderate length, well ribbed up to a good strong loin, straight or slightly arched, not slack.

NOSE.—Well developed, with good open nostrils.

SHOULDERS AND CHEST.—Former long, sloping and well set back, thus giving great activity and speed; latter deep and well developed, but not too round and wide.

BACK AND LOIN.—Very strong and muscular.

HINDQUARTERS.—Strong and muscular. The stifles moderately bent, not twisted either in or out.

STERN.—Well set on and carried low, if possible below the level of the back, in a straight line or with a slight downward inclination, never elevated above the back, and in action always kept low, nicely fringed with wavy feather of silky texture.

FORELEGS.—Should be of fairly good length, with straight, clean, flat bone, and nicely feathered, immense bone is no longer desirable.

FEET.—Not too small; round, with short, soft hair between the toes; good strong pads.

COAT.—Flat or slightly waved, and never curled. Sufficiently dense to resist the weather, and not too short. Silky in texture, glossy and refined in nature, with neither duffleness on the one hand or curl or wiriness on the other. On the chest, under belly and behind the legs there should be abundant feather, but never too much, especially below the hocks, and that of the right sort, viz., Setter-like. The hindquarters should be similarly adorned.

COLOUR.—This Society maintains that the Field Spaniel should be a self-coloured dog, viz., a Black (as it was originally some sixty years ago), or a "sport" from black, i.e. liver, golden-liver, mahogany-red, roans; or any one of these colours with tan over the eyes, on the cheeks, feet and pasterns. Other colours, such as black and white, red or orange, and white, etc., while not disqualifying a dog (providing the architecture is correct), will not be considered so desirable, since it is the aim of the Society to make a clear distinction between the Field and Springer Spaniel.

HEIGHT.—About 18 inches at shoulder.

WEIGHT. — From about 35 lb. to 50 lb.

GENERAL APPEARANCE.—That of a well-balanced, noble, upstanding sporting dog; built for activity and endurance. A grand combination of beauty and utility and bespeaking of unusual docility and instinct.

By courtesy]   *[G. M. Smith.*
CH. "WRIBBENHALL WATERHEN".
Mr. G. Mortimer Smith, a most successful owner of Field Spaniels, has had many famous dogs, including the very beautiful "Waterhen" shown here.

It is generally accepted that the Field Spaniel and the Cocker came from the same original stock, the blacks having been bred from a cross of the Sussex and the old-fashioned Cocker of Devon and Wales, the small ones remaining Cockers and the larger ones becoming Fields. For many years Cockers and Fields were produced in the same litter.

"Stonehenge" was of this opinion, and in *The Dogs of the British Islands*, 1882, he gives a scale of the points of the Field Spaniel under the heading of "The Modern Cocker".

His general description of the dog was extraordinarily similar to that of to-day, only "the length of the Spaniel should be rather more than twice his height at shoulder", which at the present average of 18 ins. at shoulder would produce a dog more than one yard long!

The oldest known breeder of Black Fields seems to have been a Mr. Footman, of Lutterworth, Leicestershire, who had supplied them to Mr. F. Burdett, who was secretary to the Birmingham

FOXHOUNDS.

This exceptionally fine painting of Foxhounds by J. Emms is the property of Mr. Walter Hutchinson, M.A., F.R.G.S., etc., Editor-in-Chief of the "Dog Encyclopaedia" and many other important Part Works. The picture shows some members of a pack on their sleeping bench, and by their sides rests the hard-bitten game Terrier which, when the fox goes to earth, has the job of turning it out again.

Dog Show This would be in the 1850's. After the death of Mr. Burdett his dogs became the property of Mr. Jones, of Oscott, and Mr. Phineas Bullock, of Bilston, Staffs., who won with his dogs, according to "Stonehenge", from 1861 onwards for ten years with great regularity. "Stonehenge" deplores the long, heavy ears on the dogs from these kennels, so that we can now see the beginnings of the Field Spaniel head.

During his successful show career, Mr. Bullock started in the fancy Mr. J. Jacobs, of Newton Abbot. This gentleman, using the Sussex-bred dog "Bachelor", standardized his Fields to the long, low type, and was for some years unbeatable

in the show ring, his best dogs being "Kaffir" and "Zulu" by Ch. "Bachelor".

Mr. Jacobs gave up breeding when an attempt was made to raise the variety a little on the leg. (This effort was bitterly fought by the old-time judges, but a more active type of Spaniel gradually developed.) Good prices were obtained at that time, Mr. Jacobs obtaining £1,500 for the last twelve dogs he sold.

In 1890 the late Mr. Moses Woolland purchased from Mr. Jacobs several blacks, including Ch. "Squaw", who, at the age of twelve years, bred him a litter. Mr. Woolland's prefix "Bridford", and Mrs. Woolland's "Newbarn", were the hallmark of beautiful black Field Spaniels. "Bridford

Photo] FIELD SPANIELS. *[Guiver*
Two attractive representatives of the breed, "Nobel Bang" and "Nobel Blackie", the property of Mr. R. R. Kelland.

Photo] *[Keystone.*
YOUNG, BUT SENSIBLE.
Common sense is a characteristic of all Spaniels and can be detected in the expression of even the very young members of the family. The Spaniel, although a sporting dog, is also a popular pet.

Bobbie" was great-grandsire of "Magellan", himself a pillar of the breed and sire of the famous "Bridford Marquis". Almost every Field Spaniel alive in 1934 had "Marquis" blood. He sired "Arlington Duke", whose son, "Wardleworth Marcus", another valuable stud force, brings us nearer to our own times. Ch. "Wribbenhall Waiter", Ch. "W. Waitress", Ch. "W. Whitewash", Ch. "W. Waterhen", Ch "W. Wetbob", were also in the direct

1873, the year before Mr. Jacobs founded his kennel.

"Alonzo" was a liver-roan dog and won many times at Curzon Hall, Birmingham ; he sired the liver-roan Ch. "Fop", which was the grandsire of "Alva Dash", a liver white-and-tan, the property of Mr. J. W. Robinson.

Undoubtedly "Alonzo" was the cornerstone of the coloured Fields, almost all the coloured winning

These Spaniels were bred on the continent and are not shown here to represent type, but because of the remarkable expression on their faces. Presumably, they are mother and child.

line. Contemporary with Mr. Woolland was Mr. H. E. Gray, of Merthyr Vale, who also specialized successfully in blacks, purchasing many of Mr. Woolland's best specimens. Mr. Gray bred "Lord Dunnohoo" (K.C.S.B. 842C), sired by "Hindley Black Prince", ex a bitch of the Bridford strain. "Lord Dunnohoo" was the sire of "Magellan" (K.C.S.B. 473F).

The coloured Field Spaniels were championed by Dr. Spurgin, one of the few gentlemen of his time to appreciate the beauty of this variety. Dr. Spurgin bred "Alonzo" (K.C.S.B. 2098) in

dogs about the end of last century being descended from him. "Alva Dash" inherited his great-grandsire's powers and stamped his qualities on the breed. His great-grandson, "Coleshill Climax", was the sire of many winners, including "Trumpington Dax", "Trumpington Dora", and "Shillington Rona".

The Matford kennel, owned by Mr. H. Trimble, was a very strong force. From the mating of "Trumpington Dax" and "Matford Rose" came a host of champions, including "Matford Punch" and "Matford Scout", which had a considerable influence on the Field of to-day."

CH. "WRIBBENHALL WAITER".

This excellent type of Spaniel, owned by Mr. G. Mortimer Smith, shows what is required in this breed. Long bodies are not now deemed desirable. Excessive length and lowness interfere with the dog's activity and represent faults that are seldom seen to-day.

"WOODBELL BRIGAND".

The Field Spaniel should be a useful dog as well as a beautiful one. The coat, as seen above, may be slightly waved but it must never be curly. This dog should be compared with the one shown above. Note that in the breed the ears should be set low.

A BEAUTY.

Champion "Wribbenhall Whitewash" is certainly an outstanding Field Spaniel bitch. At one time blacks were the rage, but to-day red-and-white, or black-and-white are favoured. Flecking adds greatly to their beauty.

A GOOD DOG.

A full-length portrait of Mr. Owen's "Woodbell Perfection". On page 605 is shown a head study of this interesting dog.

Ch. "Wribbenhall Whitewash", the only coloured Field to become a champion since the War, was in the line of "Matford Scout" and straight back to "Alonzo".

The War caused a sharp break in the activities of Field Spaniel breeders, and dealt the breed a blow from which even in 1934 it had made but a partial recovery.

The late Mr. John Budge, fortunately for the breed, kept his enthusiasm, and to his "Wardleworth Marcus", grandson of "Bridford Marquis", the blacks owe an enormous debt. He was sire of "Darland Doctor", one of the soundest pillars of the modern type Field, as he bred both show dogs and field trial winners. "Nobel Ballistite", his son, was the most notable example, winning at trials in competition with all varieties of Spaniel

Though much has been said of show dogs, there have always been sportsmen who have kept these dogs purely for shooting purposes Unfortunately, they have rarely taken the trouble to register their dogs at the Kennel Club, so that it is difficult to find any record of them.

Mr. P. Elliott Scott was successful at several trials just before the War with "Besford Bustle" and "Besford Beauty", the latter winning also at shows.

It must also be remembered that whereas the old-time champions had only to prove their worth at shows, no Spaniel can now become a champion without satisfying the judges of a field trial that they are capable of performing their proper functions as gun-dogs.

The best dogs since 1920 have been "Woodbell Bobby", Ch. "Field King", "King's Revival", "Woodbell Marquis", and "Woodbell Perfection" (all of which, through "Matford Dusk", were

Photo]   *[Guiver.*
A NOTED JUDGE AND BREEDER.
Lady Kitty Ritson is as well known in the dog-world as in social circles. She is here seen exercising a beautiful Finsk Spets, in which breed she specializes.

descendants of "Matford Scout" and "Trumpington Dax"). "Black Prince", "Darland Doctor", "Roy of Packwood" and "Nobel Ballistite", through "Wardleworth Marcus", are of "Bridford Marquis" blood.

Ch. "Wribbenhall Waiter", Ch. "W. Waitress", Ch. "W Waterhen", "W. Warlock" Ch. "W. Whitewash", "Wardleworth Libby", and "Wribbenhall Worritt" combine both these strains. "W. Worritt", a daughter of "Black Prince", won a challenge certificate and also at two field trials before she was sold to America.

Ch. "Nobel Black Satin" and "Nobel Tatters", two bitches who did much winning, came of a different strain. Bred by Mr. Caldwell, of Bromsgrove, they come through Ch "Brownhill King" from Mr Jacobs' "Bachelor III" and Ch. "Squaw".

Two-thirds of the Field Spaniels that are bred are purchased by people who have no interest in either field trials or dog shows, so that the number registered at the Kennel Club is comparatively small. The Field is not of a type which shines at field trials It does not make the spectacularly swift display in which the field trial-bred Springer and Cocker specialize. However, it will maintain a steady consistency throughout the longest day, painstakingly working in front of the guns and bringing its game up to hand in an unassuming manner which has endeared it to sportsmen through out the greater part of a century.

Field Trials.—Competitions which are held for testing the working capabilities of sporting and utility dogs. (See TRIALS.)

Fighting Dogs.—(See DOG FIGHTS.)

Finnish Laika.—Finnish Laiki (the plural of Laika—a Russian word, derived from the word "Lai", which means "barking"), just as the Samoyeds, belong to the group of Nordic Spitzen, which latter are, of course, fox-like in appearance. The Finnish Laika looks more like the jackal than the fox, and in Finland this Laika is considered to be a product between a fox and a dog, though

eyes are slanting, rather light in colour. The muzzle is very fox-like, and the nose is black. The ears are large, erect, and carried rather forward. Although the chest is narrow, it is deep, and the shoulders are very long. The back is moderately long, and the loins tucked up. The legs are straight, the feet hare-like, and the hindquarters are well-formed. The tail is bushy and carried

FINSK SPETS.
A most excellent picture, of "Noita" showing what the Finsk Spets ought to be like. They cannot be mistaken for any other breed yet they show clearly that they are related to the Spitz family.

the pupil of the eye of the fox is elliptical, whereas that of the dog is circular.

In Finland this dog is used on black game and hares, at which it gives voice by "starting" them. In appearance, the Finnish Laika is small, long-coated, elegant, and its mistrustful expression reminds one of the Alsatian when the latter faces a stranger. The skull is not very large between the ears, and there is a pronounced "stop". The cheeks protrude but little, although they appear to very much, but this is due to the fact that the head is rather thickly covered with hair. The

quite downwards in repose ; otherwise it falls over the back. The coat is Pomeranian (Spitz)-like, with good under-coat. The colour is red, with white chest and white markings, intermingled with grey or black hair. From time to time one meets with an almost entirely black Finnish Laiki.

Finsk Spets.—Sometimes called the Finnish Cock-eared Hunting Dog and the Barking Bird Dog, this represents a unique breed which until comparatively recently was found as a pure breed

FINSK SPETS "HALLO AARO UKINPOIKA".
The head of Mr. L. S. Taylor's dog is very typical indeed. Some, however, are even more fox-like in head formation and expression.

only in its native land, Finland. Even now there are not many of them in other countries, partly because they are not prolific breeders, and partly because so few people have had an opportunity of appreciating their virtues.

The pure-bred Finsk Spets is the descendant of a dog which was, thousands of years ago, the companion of the ancestors of the Finns, when these lived in small clans in their primeval forests, subsisting on the results of their hunting and fishing. These dogs were their constant companions and helpers, assisting in the hunting of all kinds of forest game, from bear down to squirrel, but mainly birds.

The march of civilization brought strangers, and with them other breeds, which got crossed with the native dog, and as the tribes moved North so their dogs went with them. Hence, the pure Finsk Spets were only to be found among the tribes inhabiting Northern Finland, Lapland, and the settlements of the Finnish tribes in Russian Carelia. Towards the end of the nineteenth century, interest in kennel matters and breeding began to take shape, and a few Finnish sportsmen, whose business or pleasure took them North, realizing the many virtues this breed possesses, brought specimens home.

Photo]   *[L.N.A.*
THOUGHTFUL.
Mrs. F. Pink's Finsk Spets, "Sarumcote Kiho Peikho", seen at
Cruft's Show in 1934, appears to be thinking hard.

As time went on, their popularity increased, the Finnish Kennel Club drew up a standard, and, as the result of experience gained, revised it in 1927 as follow :

HEAD.—Medium sized and dry ; forehead somewhat arched, forehead angle distinctly evident.

NOSE.—Narrow, dry ; tapering evenly seen both from above and from the sides. Nose-wart deep black.

LIPS.—Compressed and thin.

EARS.—Cocked, pointed, fine-hairy, extremely mobile.

EYES.—Medium sized or larger ; lively, preferably dark.

THROAT.—Springy ; in the males it seems fairly short by reason of the thick hair, in females it is of medium length.

BACK.—Straight and strong.

CHEST.—Deep.

BELLY-LINE.—Slightly drawn up.

SHOULDERS.—Comparatively upright.

FEET.—Elbow, steady and straight ; hindfeet strong ; hock comparatively straight. Paws preferably somewhat round.

TAIL.—Is curled right from the root intensely in a bow forward, downward and backward pressed against the thigh. Straightened out, the caudal vertebrae generally reach as far as the hock angle.

Photo]   *[G. Denes.*
FROM BUDAPEST.
This delightful dog is a pure-bred Finsk Spets of Hungarian
ownership. Compare the head with the other examples shown.

By courtesy]   Rusty.   *[Sir Edward Chichester*

SOMETHING NEW.

"Rusty", a Finsk Spets, was imported by Sir Edward Chichester, Bart. At first the appearance of this dog caused no little comment, and great interest was aroused in the breed. Although it belongs to the great Spitz family, it is more fox-like than any of the other members. The dog above shown is reproduced from a painting by Dorothy Hallett.

COAT.—Hairy coat on head and feet, with the exception of the back parts of the latter, short and lying down; on the body somewhat upright; on back of neck and body stiffer. The hair on the back parts of the thighs long and bushy. The same applies to the hair on the tail. The bottom layer of hair short, soft, thick and light-coloured.

COLOUR. — On back brownish-red or yellowish-brown, preferably clear; at the sides of the ears, cheeks, lower jaw, chest, belly, inner sides of feet, as well as the back hair of the thighs and the lower layer of hair on the tail, of a slightly lighter colour. A white colour is allowed on chest and paws, also black on the lips, and a few hairs here and there on the back, stiff and with black points.

TOTAL IMPRESSION. — Body almost square. Shoulder height and length of body in males 42–48 cm., in females 38–45 cm.

Pose lively. The whole behaviour of the dog, and particularly so its eyes, ears and tail, show liveliness.

The characteristic features of the Finnish Cock-eared Dog are their interest in hunting, boldness and fidelity. They are also used when shooting birds.

FAULTS.—Fleshy head. Blunt nose. Ears sloping at an acute angle forward toward the forehead-line, to the sides or against one another; nor must

the ears be slack at the points, or have long hairs inside. Yellow and "wall-eyed" eyes. Elbows turned inwards. Too pliable wrist and hock. Slack or too curly tail. Too soft, too short hair, lying against the skin, or locky. Dirty or too motley colour. Spurs are unbecoming.

This description, coupled with the accompanying illustrations, show the Finsk Spets to be a particularly beautiful and symmetrically built dog. Their splendid red coat reminding one of a red fox, their bushy tail (or brush) curled artistically over the back, and their keen and alert expression, together with their graceful movements, all combine to make a most attractive whole. From the day the cubs are born they appeal to all dog-lovers and, being sharp and playful, children adore them, and as by nature they are very clean and tidy they make ideal pets. When very young, the cubs possess soft fur of a greyish colour and very close, which gives them the appear-

Photo] 　　　　　ATTRACTIVE　　　　 *[G. Denes.*

Another Hungarian example of a very beautiful Finsk Spets, although it has not the typical fox-like expression one usually associates with this breed.

ance of a soft ball of fur. Cleanliness is a very strong characteristic of this breed—they just hate to be dirty and are very cat-like in the way they clean themselves. Faithfulness and bravery are also very strongly developed, while they possess a powerful homing instinct, many remarkable stories being told of their long treks home.

The Finnish sportsman uses his Finsk Spets

After a painting by [*Dorothy S. Hall*

"TOMMI" AND "HAMMON".

Two remarkable Finsk Spets, the property of Sir Edward Chichester, Bart., who is mainly responsible for the popularity of the breed in England. "Hammon" is the sire of "Tommi".

almost entirely for shooting birds, principally black game and capercailzie, and Field Trials are now held. The hunting is carried on only in the forests, where the dog ranges through the brushwood searching for the bird at a suitable distance from the hunter. When disturbed, the bird usually rises in front of the dog and settles in a tree. By the aid of its very keen scent and other faculties, the dog follows, and, having located its bird and made sure of it, it sets up a fine ringing bark to inform its master where it is, so that he can get near enough to shoot. Points taken into consideration under these conditions are keenness, power of endurance, obedience, ability to track and follow the bird, and, if it flies on, keeping in touch,

By courtesy]					[E. C. Ash.
CANINE HISTORY.
Here is Mr. L. Allen Shuter's famous dog, "Darenth", which played so great a part in improving the breed of Retrievers.

and manner of barking ; while it is considered a fault to search for and bark at all other kinds of game than birds.

Except for possibly an odd specimen, their introduction in Britain dates from about 1927, when Commander Sir Edward Chichester, Bart., was on a shooting and hunting expedition in Scandinavia, and, being very greatly attracted by them, imported a brace and, later, an unrelated

stud dog. He exhibited occasionally among the Foreign Dogs, but circumstances prevented him developing as much as he would have liked. However, he enlisted the sympathies of some enthusiasts, among them Lady Kitty Ritson (who became so fascinated with them that in 1933 she journeyed to Finland to see them for herself in their native surroundings, coming back more keen than ever), and Mr. Lionel S. Taylor, of Prestatyn, who, having bred as far as possible from the stock available, imported a fine brace. With one or two other imported specimens there is now sufficient really good stock to build up the breed. Their popularity grows daily, more breeders becoming interested. Greater progress would have been made, but these dogs are not very prolific breeders, the usual number in a litter being three or four, though Mr. Taylor had two or three fives, and one litter of six, a record in Britain and extremely rare in Finland.

So much progress was made that a Club was formed to further the interests of the breed, with Sir Edward Chichester as President, supported by Lady Kitty Ritson, Mrs. Moulton, Mr. Lionel S. Taylor and others.

By courtesy]					[E. C. Ash.
FLAT-COATED RETRIEVER.
Mr. Allen Shuter's Ch. "Horton Rector", the sire of Mr. H. Reginald Cooke's Ch. "Grouse of Riverside", a winner of the St. Neots Open Stakes.

Fistula.—An abnormal channel leading from some cavity, organ, or other part of the body to the surface. It may lead from the rectum to the skin surface in consequence of an anal abscess having burst outwardly as well as inwardly ; or due to the presence of a foreign body in the lower bowel. When a fishbone is swallowed and becomes arrested somewhere in the gullet, it not infrequently sets up an abscess which forces its way to the surface, eventually to rupture. The channel between the oesophagus and the skin is a fistula.

Another very common fistula in dogs is that which arises in consequence of disease of the fourth premolar tooth. A discharge forms and makes its way to the nearest point on the skin's surface which, in this case, is midway between the eye and the angle

temperature from some other cause, or by excitement, fatigue, shocks, sexual stimulation, and large amounts of food given at one time. Occasionally there seems to have been no predisposing cause for an attack, and one never really can foresee when one might occur.

SYMPTOMS.—True epilepsy is characterized by a definite loss of consciousness. Without preliminary warning the dog suddenly sits down or falls to the ground and manifests the usual signs of convulsions, i.e. rapid champing of the jaws producing a frothing of saliva, running motions with all four legs, rigidity of muscles alternating with violent exercise of same, staring eyes and dilated pupils ; and sometimes there is an involuntary evacuation of faeces or urine, or of both. After a minute or two, in mild attacks, the

AN OLDER TYPE.
Here indeed is a very remarkable type of Retriever, suggesting its Newfoundland ancestry, with the coat then known as "wavy-coated" but now commonly termed "flat-coated"

of the mouth. This condition is known as a dental fistula.

The treatment is essentially surgical, the cause first having to be removed. In all cases the curative procedure is tedious and even difficult, entailing curetting and cauterizing, as well as irrigation.

Fits.—(*See also* CONVULSIONS, PARTURIENT ECLAMPSIA, HYSTERIA).

Fits, Epileptic.—Epilepsy is a chronic nervous disorder characterized by fits, or attacks in which there is loss of consciousness with a succession of tonic or clonic convulsions. It is a common malady among dogs.

CAUSES.—The actual cause is not really known, although the disease is recognized as being hereditary in many cases. There must, however, be a degeneration of nerve cells in the brain or cord, and animals which are so affected, or born susceptible, are rather easily made subjects of a seizure by an elevation of

body becomes quiescent, consciousness returns, and the animal rises very unsteadily to its feet, looking around in a dazed fashion.

In still milder cases, the animal may lose consciousness for a few seconds only, and show no worse additional symptoms than slight muscular tremors and frothing at the mouth. It then gets up, apparently all right.

In severe attacks, however, the dog may shriek out as though in pain, fight violently, and thoroughly exhaust itself, thus rendering recovery a very protracted process and leaving the patient exceedingly weak.

Dogs may live a number of years as epileptics if the attacks are not frequent or severe, and in such cases the fits should not occur more often than about once a week or even less. But chronic affections may suddenly become acute, and the attacks may recur even two or three times in a day.

Unless the attacks can be cut short or prevented

[Cassell's Book of the Dog

CH. "WORSLEY BESS".
Another noted Flat-Coated Retriever of the days before the development
of the narrow head. "Bess" was the property of Mr. Reginald Cooke.
(From a painting by Maud Earl.)

altogether, it is obvious that a serious degree of exhaustion will be bound to follow, and the termination will, in most of such cases, be death during one of the paroxysms.

TREATMENT.—There is, unfortunately, no specific or curative treatment for true epilepsy. When a dog has been definitely diagnosed as a subject of epilepsy it is probably kinder, and certainly more economic, to have it painlessly put to sleep. Such dogs cannot even be kept for breeding purposes, as the malady is hereditary. So soon as an attack seems imminent, or is in its commencement, one should loosen the collar, apply cold water to the poll and back of the neck, and remove any obstacle in the room against which the dog might injure itself. Such dogs do not bite nor show any kind of vicious tendency. They are not cognizant of what they are doing at all, and have to be protected against themselves. In a little while the animal recovers, and should be left lying quietly on the floor, the room meanwhile being darkened and all noises suppressed. Do not even talk to the dog or pet it in any way. Brandy, etc., is contra indicated.

If the attacks are becoming rather too frequent, a course of sedatives should be prescribed, and in all cases any exciting factor must be carefully avoided. Large meals must never be given, nor should the dog be permitted to become constipated. The diet must be light, nourishing and varied, so that advantage may be taken of all the vitamins contained in different foods. Vitamin B is of particular value and is found largely in wheat, rice, egg-yolk, and ox liver.

Fits, Epileptiform Convulsions. — Fits or convulsions may occur in dogs which so resemble the attacks seen in true epilepsy that they are designated as "epileptiform". The very fact that they occur only once or twice, instead of recurring at intervals throughout life, is a reliable distinction, and serves to show the owner that the seizures are amenable to treatment.

It is better to ascribe the causes of epileptiform convulsions as due to worm infestations of the bowels, parasitic affection of the ear, cutting of the teeth, intense hot sun, temporary head injuries, and auto-intoxication (*which see*). The home treatment is similar to that for true epilepsy.

Flag.—The tail of a Setter, Retriever, etc.

Flat-Coated Retriever.—This member of the Retriever group was originally known as the "Wavy-Coated Retriever", by reason of its jacket showing what is termed by the fair "a permanent marcel wave". But as the variety progressed, so did the coat "flatten out", until at last the original denomination was abandoned in favour of that by which this dog is now known.

There can hardly be a doubt as to the origin of the Flat-Coated Retriever—and, incidentally, of that of the Labrador—both breeds having been evolved from the same source : namely, the Lesser Newfoundland dog, and, in some cases, from the smaller dog of Chesapeake Bay.

The lumber ships plying between St. John's and various British ports used to bring with them dogs of these types, for which they found a ready market ; especially among gamekeepers, who imagined—and rightly too—that they would make excellent housedogs and efficient bodyguards when their masters were on night duty and poachers were on the prowl.

But they soon discovered that these animals possessed remarkable scenting powers ; were very keen on game and were amenable to discipline. But they were heavily built and cumbersome, and not as well balanced as might be desired.

Some of these gamekeepers, therefore, started to improve matters by crossing these imported dogs with various gun-dogs.

Photo]   [Sport and General.

"DASH OF RIVERSIDE"
It is no wonder that this breed became so popular. Mr. H. Reginald Cooke's beautiful dog.

ONE OF THE OLD TYPE.
Some say that these powerfully built Flat-Coated Retrievers were too heavy and prefer the more lightly built dog of to-day.

CH. "HIGH LEGH BLARNEY".
One of the most famous of all Flat-Coated Retrievers, owned by Mr. H. Reginald Cooke. The painting by Maud Earl is one of her
finest works. It shows "Blarney" holding a grouse.

Matings with Spaniels were not as successful as had been hoped, so resort was had to Pointers and Setters. The desire was to preserve the black coat as being more suitable than any other. In the issue thus produced, were types more or less constant, which respectively provided the nucleus of the Labrador (where a Pointer was used) ; and that of the Wiry or Flat-Coated Retriever (where the Setter cross has been resorted to).

A fair number of the original members of the family bred, as above described, were scattered

Kennel Club, of which he became the first President and Chairman of Committee.

Having an unbounded faith in the merit of "Zelstone"—as proved in the field and in the dog's prospects as a sire—his owner gathered together a select kennel of matrons and began at once to breed a strain of Flat-Coated Retrievers which held its own with the gun, or on the show bench, for many years.

From one of these bitches was produced "Moonstone", a dog which stood out from all his

Photo] [Sport and General

AT FLAT-COATED RETRIEVER TRIALS

Major H. L. A. Swann's 'Kennett Ruth'', having retrieved the game that has fallen on the other side of the road, returns with it to the guns in the spinney Roads are often a nuisance on shooting days because of the crowd likely to collect as sightseers.

about in districts adjacent to the ports entered by the lumber ships, which had introduced the original Newfoundland stock ; but it was some time before these were recognized as a separate breed. The first dog to attract individual notice was one "Ben", but evidence of his having been successfully exhibited is wanting.

Nevertheless, this dog was—if such chronicles as are available are accurate—the sire of "Zelstone", a dog which lovers of the breed have universally accepted as the "Adam" of the established breed.

He was the property of the late Sewallis Evelyn Shirley, of Ettington Park, Stratford-on-Avon (at one time Conservative Member for Co. Monaghan), who was mainly instrumental in founding the

contemporaries in point of quality symmetry balance, action and type.

The writer awarded the highest honours to "Moonstone" when, as a puppy, he made his *début* at the Kennel Club's show at the Crystal Palace. This was the first of "Moonstone's" successes, but not the last ; for he went from triumph to triumph, and, indeed, was never beaten on the show bench. Moreover, he had the reputation of being invaluable to the gun, with the physical advantages commensurate with his executive ability. At stud, too, he proved himself an outstanding success. Probably the pedigree of every champion of the breed to-day, as in the past, can be traced, either in tail male or female, to "the immortal Moonstone".

Photo] WATERFOWL. [*Sport and General.*

Retrievers are excellent workers both on land and in water. Like most dogs, they are powerful swimmers and use their brains.
Above is seen a Flat-Coated type retrieving from a pond.

Photo] BY THE POND. [*Sport and General.*

Wounded wild fowl will sometimes hide away amongst the reeds and rushes, or may even remain below the water, hoping to escape
detection. Perhaps just the tip of their beaks may be seen above the surface. Above, a Flat-Coated Retriever recovers the "shot".

2D

It was one of "Sloe's" offspring which was the first bearer of the "Black" distinction. An unfriendly cat had deprived this "Black Cloth" (as he was named) of his left eye ; but, even so, he was deemed good enough to win "first and challenge prize" at Birmingham, and, moreover, eventually he annexed Championship honours.

A SNAPSHOT.

Heads of two Flat-Coated Retrievers that have been sired by "Boy of Riverside" (dam unknown). Sent by Miss M. Wood, an entrant to our photographic competition.

But it was his son, "Black Drake", which became such a power in Flat-Coated Retriever circles ; whereby hangs a story which is worth recording. "Black Cloth's" owner, having come across a particularly impressive bitch, whose pedigree went back to "Zelstone", without any intermediate in-breeding, arranged with her owner a union with Ch. "Black Cloth". In the event of success, the former was to have first choice of puppies, the latter second choice, and so on alternately.

In due course there were seven whelps, of which one appeared to be more hearty and promising than the rest, so this unit entered the "Black" kennels and became known as "Black Drake".

Another of the same litter passed to Mr. Reginald Cooke. This was a smaller puppy, but of exquisite quality, and one which eventually proved himself to be the best of the breed that had appeared since the days of "Moonstone". Up to now,

the "Blacks" had been predominant, and had practically swept the boards at the leading shows. But when "Black Drake" and "Wimpole Peter" (as Mr. Cooke's puppy had been named) met at Cruft's, the "Black" flag was lowered, and "Drake's" litter brother held the trump card for some years. In fact he, and he only, stood in the way of his bigger brother ever becoming a full champion. "Black Drake", although (on this occasion) beaten on the bench, became a sire of outstanding brilliance.

His services were in constant demand throughout the length and breadth of the land. No matter what the quality or antecedents of his succession of mates, each produced at least one offspring which took high honours on the bench or in the field. Often, every whelp in the litter became a prize-winner. On the other hand, "Wimpole Peter" was a comparative failure at stud, for he never succeeded in siring anything which approached his own high quality.

But Mr. Cooke's kennel flourished, and for a time was a serious menace to the position erstwhile occupied by the "Blacks". Then, joining in the fray, came Colonel Legh, of Legh Hall, Mr. Vincent Davies, and others, among whom were many enterprising and intelligent gamekeepers, who gallantly supported the breed, then enjoying its halcyon days and popular favour. But the same invaluable "Ettington blood" still ran in the veins of each of the ruling lights of the Flat-Coated Retriever *coterie*.

Then certain breeders came to the conclusion that the foreface

Photo] [*Keystone*

STRANGE, BUT TRUE.

"Fanny", a Flat-Coated Retriever belonging to Mr. J. Smart, of Rossie, Fifeshire, has developed a great fondness for its master's ferrets, frequently carrying them about. They do not seem to mind the unusual method of transport.

A HANDSOME QUARTET.

Miss Phizacklea with four of her "Atherbram" Retrievers, all of which are prize winners. The three in front appear to be of exceptionally good type. Whereas until recently women breeders did not go in for large dogs, to-day they do so to a considerable extent, and are holding their own against the sterner sex, who once had the monopoly in this field.

and jaws of the Flat-Coated Retrievers were too short to enable them to retrieve a hare or a pheasant in style and comfort. With this view in mind they tried to lengthen the face by introducing Borzoi blood to their polyglot Flat-Coats; the pedigrees of which contained names foreign to the hitherto jealously guarded Ettington records.

The products immediately displayed narrow skulls and long forefaces, giving to the whole head a "coffin-like" structure and aspect.

The old-established judges were unwilling to recognize this new type, but in time the resistance broke down. New judges took the place of the old, and the Flat-Coated Retriever became a breed with long narrow heads and weak muzzles. Some "old-time" breeders and exhibitors gave up the breed altogether, but a few held on and eventually succeeded in putting the "coffin-headed" dogs in their proper place, "below the salt"!

But the damage had been done, and it took generations of careful breeding to eliminate the traces of this destructive experiment; to which also is attributed, by many, the decline in the popularity of the Flat-Coated variety, and the apotheosis of the Labrador.

But in 1932, at Cruft's, it seemed as though a recovery was approaching, for an entry of over one hundred and seventy was secured, but unfortunately this betterment did not continue and failed to be progressive.

At the ensuing Kennel Club's Show at the Crystal Palace there were only nine entries, though the appointed judge was an expert of high repute. This falling off was inexplicable, and the early extinction of the "Flat-Coat" as a breed was sadly prophesied. It was not until "Cruft's 1934" came round, with the writer (who had officiated two years previously) again sporting "the judicial badge", that yet another welcome

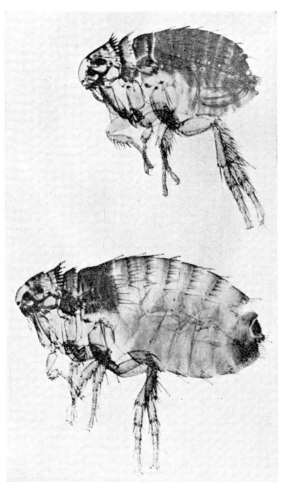

Photo]   [J. F. Stirling.
FLEAS (*Ctenocephalus canis*).
Above: male. Below: female. Note the comparatively huge and powerful hindlegs, which enable the insect to propel itself several hundred times its own height into the air.

resuscitation of the "Flat-Coat" was manifested. A fine entry—distinguished by both quantity and quality—giving promise of renewal of the popularity of one of the most beautiful, intelligent, and loyal and affectionate of all our resplendent gun-dog breeds.

DESCRIPTION OF THE FLAT-COATED RETRIEVER.

GENERAL.—A dog of moderate size, somewhat of the Setter type (especially that of the Red Irish Setter) with liberty and length; though as regards the latter, it is more suggestive than actual, for the measurement from the point of the withers to the "set on" of the "flag" or stern is (where a typical unit is concerned) the same as the former point to the ground.

Note.—This measurement also holds good as regards the Labrador; though at first glance the latter appears to be much squarer and shorter in the back than the Flat-Coat. The height at the shoulder of the latter is about 23–25 ins. in dogs, and 19–22 ins. in bitches.

COLOUR. — Usually a whole black. A small star of white on the chest is permissible; but white on the limbs or head is fatal.

Note. — Chocolate-coloured puppies often appear in litters, the parents of which are of the orthodox black hue. Such are elegible to compete on equal terms with their own kin. It is difficult to account for this variation, but it is apparently a hereditary peculiarity, and is evidently due to some mysterious atavistic influence.

It is a strange thing that though these chocolate-tinted Flat-Coats are of fairly common occurrence, no other colour is to be met with in the breeding of this Retriever. The mating of black Labradors, whose immediate parents and forebears were of the same hue, often results in the production of yellow, golden, or almost white stock, but seldom, if ever, chocolate. This would seem to

Photo] "STAINTON SPINNER". [*Fall.*

Mr. T. H. Moorby specializes in sporting dogs, and the dog shown above is a soundly built youngster from his kennel, and is of a type that may be expected to do well both in the field and on the bench.

Photo] "BETTY OF RIVERSIDE". [*Fall*

The name "Riverside" stands for some of the very best in Flat-Coated Retrievers, referring as it does to Mr. H. Reginald Cooke one of the leading breeders and authorities on the breed.

suggest that some of the original dogs of the North-West, which were mated with British Pointers, were of the Chesapeake Bay variety, individuals of which are frequently yellow or golden.

POINTS OF CONFORMATION.

HEAD.—This should be of fair length. The skull flat on top and moderately broad between the ears, which are of fair length and falling closely to the cheek. When extended, the tips should reach to the outer corner of the eye. The cheek itself should be flush and not showing undue prominence of the cheek-bones. The foreface of moderate length. The length from the occiput to the inner corner of the eye should be the same as from the latter point to the end of the nose, which should be of fair size, a deep black, with fairly open nostrils. Jaw, strong and perfectly level, with the lips and flews well braced; teeth strong and white; eyes placed rather wide small, but not too deep-set. A round, pedunculated (i.e. prominent) eye is very undesirable. The colour of the iris is a deep, rich brown, but not sloe-black! Its expression should be highly intelligent and altogether affectionate and benevolent. A light eye is objectionable, a yellow one fatal!

NECK.—Fairly long and well moulded; set symmetrically into oblique shoulders which are not overloaded with muscle, and which work with piston-like and rhythmic regularity.

CHEST.—Moderately broad and forming a deep brisket, on which the legs, in action, impinge.

FORE RIBS.—Strong, and only slightly rounded.

BACK RIBS.—Rather more "sprung", but not "barrel-like"; and well "ribbed-up".

COUPLINGS.—(I.e. the space between the last back rib and the stifle) should be of not more than three or four inches in measurement. "Open" couplings are highly objectionable. The stifle itself well bent.

BACK.—Strong and level, nicely rounded at the quarters, which are powerful and well muscled in the thighs, second thighs and gaskins.

HOCKS.—Bony; fairly bent and comparatively close to the ground.

TAIL, "STERN" or "FLAG".—Of moderate length (from "set on" to point of hock) and well feathered. A long "flag", curling or "ringing" at the extremity, is a terrible disfigurement. Where it exists, the

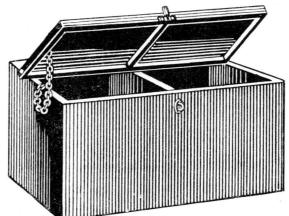

A strong airtight bin for storing biscuits and meal.

temptation to curtail it is acute, and many owners have transgressed a rule which, in the main, is well justified. Detection of such mutilation entails disqualification of both dog and exhibitor. The flag should be carried gaily, on a level with the back.

LEGS.—Straight, with plenty of bone, which is carried down to the feet; the knees of fair size, flat and neither "standing over" nor "back"; the pasterns strong, but springy enough to "give play" when the dog is "pulling up", or "on the turn".

FEET.—Large; the toes close and well knuckled up; but they, too, should be pliant enough to spread suddenly when required to do so, as is often the case where the dog is sent to retrieve a wounded, but still active, hare or rabbit, or a "jiggering" pheasant or partridge.

COAT.—Smooth and fine, but showing a denser under-coat. It should be glossy and rather soft to the touch, but not silky. Nothing shows up that indefinable and desirable attribute "quality" in a Flat-Coated Retriever more resplendently than a coat which is diligently well-groomed and "strapped" until it catches the high lights.

Flat-sided. — Flat in the rib area when viewed from in front.

Flatulence.—The presence of an abnormal amount of gas in the alimentary canal.

CAUSES.—There is always a certain amount of bacterial fermentation going on in the bowels, but in consequence of certain circumstances this may be increased. Gases of various kinds are evolved from the decomposition of foodstuffs, particularly of the vegetable elements, and if a dog receives an unusual amount of green vegetable there will be proportionate increase of flatus. A similar thing accompanies indigestion and constipation and diminished peristalsis, whilst the gases evolved in consequence of the consumption of sulphur, will not only be increased in amount but very obnoxious.

SYMPTOMS.—Severe flatulence may cause acute pain, and although we do not know the feelings of the dog, we do know that in human beings the feeling of fullness or of heartburn arising from flatulence is very distressing. Occasionally, intense colic is set up, when the animal is extremely restless, lying down and getting up very frequently and roaming about the room in an aimless way; it looks round at its flanks, arches the back, and may stand stiffly and more or less motionless.

In other cases, nothing much in the way of a symptom is noticeable other than the frequent passage of flatus (wind) which at times is most objectionable.

Photo] [*E.N.A., & P. Popper.*

THE RIGHT AND THE WRONG WAY.

The above pictures illustrate how one should and how one should not feed dogs or puppies. It is always better to allow each dog its own plate or dish. It prevents fighting and timidity at feeding times, which causes dogs hurriedly to bolt their food. When puppies are allowed to eat out of one vessel it should be a long rather than a round trough.

Photo] A FAMILY MEAL. [Mondiale.
Young Alsatians being taught by their mother to take solid food. Puppies learn to feed by tasting from their mother's dish and very soon eat enough to require far less milk.

TREATMENT.—The first procedure is to administer a purge; then prescribe a course of intestinal antiseptics to reduce bacterial life, and administer a liberal daily supply of charcoal in tablet or biscuit form. (*See* WOOD CHARCOAL.) Omit all vegetable foods, and feed for a time on fresh meat and fish. See that the dog is well exercised.

Fleas.—A degenerate form of two-winged insect. On dogs, the flea—*Pulex serraticeps*—is very common, and is of much larger dimensions than *Pulex irritans* which affects man. Unlike the louse, a flea has a complex life cycle, going through the various stages of egg, larva and pupa, to perfect insect. The large white eggs are not usually laid on the dog's body, but are deposited by the female between the floorboards, or in the dust collected in the corners of the kennel; and from these there eventually emanates a small, dirty-white maggot which as a rule assumes the pupal stage in a cocoon in about two weeks' time. After a lapse of a further fortnight the perfect insect is reached, and so the cycle continues. The flea has no wings, but possesses very powerful hindlegs, which enable it to jump several hundred times its own height. It has the ability to both pierce and suck its host, and is entirely parasitic. The flea is flattened laterally and has three pairs of legs. *Pulex serraticeps* is distinguished from *P. irritans* by having two rows of bristles just behind its head. As a general rule, each species confines its attention to its particular normal host, but dog fleas may be found on humans and *vice versa*.

It has sometimes been observed that the female flea will climb to the tips of the dog's hairs and deposit her eggs loosely in the coat. The dog has only then to shake itself to scatter these eggs in every direction, and in this way they reach the kennel floor (or carpets of the owner' residence) and every other place or article with which the dog comes in contact. Realizing these facts, then, one should appreciate how useless it is to attempt to eradicate fleas merely by treating the dog.

As the flea is parasitic in the last stage only, to rid a dog of this pest, therefore, it is not only necessary to exterminate the adult insect, but thoroughly to treat the kennel and other surroundings of the dog with some agent which is lethal to all the stages of the flea's metamorphosis.

When fleas exist on a dog, the fact will be quickly realized by finding little black particles of excreta among the hairs, and it often happens when searching, that one misses a view of the actual offender, since the flea is as nimble as he is cunning, and rapidly avoids the area of disturbance.

Should a nursing mother have fleas, it is useless to rid her of them unless all the puppies are simultaneously treated. The best plan in such a case is to bath the bitch, and, whilst she is drying, search each puppy separately for the few fleas they have, and then dust into their coats one of the many efficacious powders which are now on the market. Pyrethrum powder to be effective *must* be fresh. If it cannot be obtained in this condition, some other powder must be employed.

The symptoms set up by fleas are frequently mistaken for mange, eczema, ringworm, etc., and it behoves anyone who attempts a diagnosis in skin diseases to search always for the probable parasite involved, before essaying a definite opinion. There are some very good shampoos available for eradicating fleas, most of which will completely rid the dog of its trouble within ten minutes. A good method of repelling the flea is to wipe the dog's coat over occasionally with a paraffin rag ; or to spray the coat with oil of citronella. The bedding should be boiled, baked or burned, and all sleeping-boxes scrubbed out with boiling water and disinfectant.

Flews.—The pendulous lips on the upper jaw of some dogs. Also the inner corners of the lips.

Flies.—The ordinary house-fly is a constant menace to the health of the dog, as it carries disease of all kinds not only from point to point within the establishment, but from one establishment to another.

Flies settle on every conceivable kind of filth, germ-laden or otherwise, and then most likely settle on and walk all over the dog's food. There seems no possible doubt about the spread of disease through this medium, and it behoves every breeder or proprietor of kennels to adopt every possible method of reducing the number of flies in his kennels. Flit and other lethal agents may be frequently sprayed against flies wherever they are seen ; fly-papers should hang everywhere, and glass or wire fly-traps should be in abundance. Fumigation with formalin will clear them out of a building quite effectively, the dogs, of course, having been previously removed.

All old bedding, excrement, and other offal should be at once deposited in an incinerator rather than be allowed to collect and encourage the breeding of flies. Particularly is this important in sick kennels, where all discharges, bloodstains, or droppings may be charged with pathogenic bacteria, which only need the agency of flies to broadcast them on a wholesale scale.

Foetus.—The unborn offspring of an animal. The foetus is therefore still in the uterus, and it only becomes known as such after the first month of gestation. Prior to that it is referred to as an embryo. (*which see.*)

Follicular Mange. (*See* Skin Diseases.)

Fomentation.—The treatment of local parts of the body by warm or hot and moist applications. It may consist of wringing cloths out in hot water and laying them over the bruised part, or of spraying or bathing the part. To have any real effect the act should be continued for a considerable time, as a matter of a mere five minutes or so hardly allows the hair to become properly wet, let alone causing any relaxed condition of the skin and its cutaneous blood-vessels. Half an hour or more of treatment several times daily would be more appropriate for the relief of sprains, bruises and other injuries. The ripening of abscesses can be greatly expedited by means of hot fomentations frequently applied.

Photo]   *[Ralph Robinson*
GREAT TEMPTATIONS,
Dogs are by nature inquisitive, more especially when they are young. Before a dog is trained, food not intended for it should be kept well out of its way.

Foods and Feeding.—The selection and apportionment of a dog's daily ration is a matter deserving of the utmost attention, yet is one which is probably the least understood by the rank and file of dog owners. It is not yet realized—even in these days of enlightenment—what a profound bearing food has upon the growth, immunity to disease, and general health of a dog.

Meat as a Food.—Many people have adopted the belief that meat as a food should be rigidly withheld from a dog; that it causes worms, fits, savage character, and conduces to the contraction of distemper. Others will be found to have acquired the fixed notion that a dog needs an abundance of green vegetable; while some consider that a diet of odds and ends from the kitchen (no matter what they may be) affords quite the best-balanced food; yet another class believes in feeding nothing but dog biscuits and meals.

The writer considers meat to be the only rational and obvious food for canines, no matter of what age (after weaning) or of what breed. The very fundamental fact that a dog is a carnivore, or meat-eating animal, is constantly lost sight of.

Nobody would dream of feeding a horse on meat or on biscuits, or a cage-bird upon fish; so why select vegetables and starches for a flesh-digesting dog? That the dog is, in fact, a member of the carnivora is readily proved by an examination of its alimentary tract. Beginning with the mouth, we find its teeth are designed essentially for killing, tearing and breaking. They have no flat opposed surfaces which could be utilized for grinding, as may be seen in the ox, horse, or man. The stomach is comparatively large and the intestinal tract short, all of which factors are characteristic of flesh eaters. The dog in its natural or wild state lives by preying upon other animals, in the pursuit of which it perforce travels many miles daily. It does not consume cereals, nor is its food cooked, and probably the only other substance eaten is green grass. Yet what healthier type of dog exists than the wild specimen?

It is said that domestication has changed the dog's character and has necessitated the substitution of a mixed or almost wholly farinaceous diet for the natural flesh one. The author of this article cannot, however, acquiesce in this view for, in reality, the only change which has taken place in the domesticated dog is its abandonment of the hunt, or its realization that its food is automatically provided and need not be sought. This, in turn, of course, has led to the lack of that strenuous exercise which formerly was so instrumental in keeping the animal strong and healthy. It has been proved over and over again that if one will only afford his dog a sufficiency of real exercise he can do no better than to feed it upon meat, almost to the exclusion of all other foodstuffs.

In Defence of Meat.—Let us analyse the charges brought against the feeding of dogs with flesh. First, the astounding statement that it conduces to distemper. Distemper is a specific infectious disease, which means that it is caused by a particular and definite germ or virus, even as is tuberculosis.

Such a germ cannot be found, and never has been found, in the flesh of the ox, horse, or sheep. Flesh, therefore, does not convey the contagium. The only other way in which meat could encourage the onset of distemper is its presumed lack of nutriment, or its inability to supply the tissues with material essential for making good the wastage caused by metabolism.

Such an idea is, of course, absurd, as there is no more sustaining or stimulating food known than that of the protein variety. One can unhesitatingly assert that the dog which will resist infections in the highest degree is the one that is systematically fed on meat from the day it is weaned.

Secondly, we hear that the consumption of flesh causes worms. No sound ox- or horseflesh ever contained the eggs or larvae of worms, and therefore could not possibly infect a dog with the adult parasites. On the other hand, if one gives lungs, liver, brains, viscera or other offal to a dog, especially if it be uncooked, then there is a risk of setting up some verminous infestation. By flesh, however, one alludes to muscular tissue and not to offal.

From time to time it is asserted that flesh-fed dogs become savage, but it is doubtful if there has ever been an authentic case of such an occurrence. Such an eventuality might have been surmised because in some particular instance a dog developed a vicious temperament. Yet are we to attribute a nervous or unfriendly character in a dog to the fact that it may have had some meat to eat? If so, what of the many thousands of tractable, peace-loving dogs which, to one's certain knowledge, subsist almost entirely upon flesh.

The fact that some dogs exhale a disagreeable body odour is often attributed to the meat diet afforded them, and in this case it must be admitted that such a possibility exists; but even this depends upon other circumstances, as, for instance, the amount of exercise taken daily, the activity or torpidity of the bowels, and the quantity of the ration. An excess of food of any kind will cause a dog to smell disagreeably, as will the inability of the bowels, through constipation, to rid the body of effete material; or the lack of stimulation of the other eliminative channels (lungs, skin, and kidneys) through general body inactivity. Unpleasant doggy odour may also arise in consequence of sarcoptic or follicular mange, digestive derangement, distemper, and other abnormal conditions of health. So that one is not justified in jumping too hastily to conclusions.

Different Kinds of Meat.—What kind of meat should I buy? is a question very frequently asked. Shall it be beef, horseflesh or mutton? The simplest answer to this query would be "Buy beef". Yet such a simple answer does not meet all cases, and qualifications will be necessitated by varying circumstances. The town-dwelling owner of one or two dogs, for instance, will have no difficulty in obtaining sound shin of beef, which usually costs anything from 4d. to about 9d. per lb. Butchers' pieces are also obtainable at prices varying from 3d. to 6d. per lb., but these often include masses of pure fat, pieces of gristle, and other somewhat objectionable material. Neck of mutton is offered in many districts at a figure as low as 2½d. per lb., and it is very valuable for the feeding of a number of animals, for it can be boiled with a small proportion of potato or rice, onion and salt, into a most palatable and sustaining stew.

It is not suggested that such a diet should be adhered to daily, but it can profitably be occasionally included in the week's menu. Other kinds of meat sometimes given to dogs are sheeps' or bullocks' heads, paunches, lights, rabbits, and fish. A good deal of flesh and nourishing broth can be obtained from the boiling down of heads, and it is a good plan to add a proportion of rice or pearl barley to the water in which meats are boiled. Oatmeal, broken biscuit,

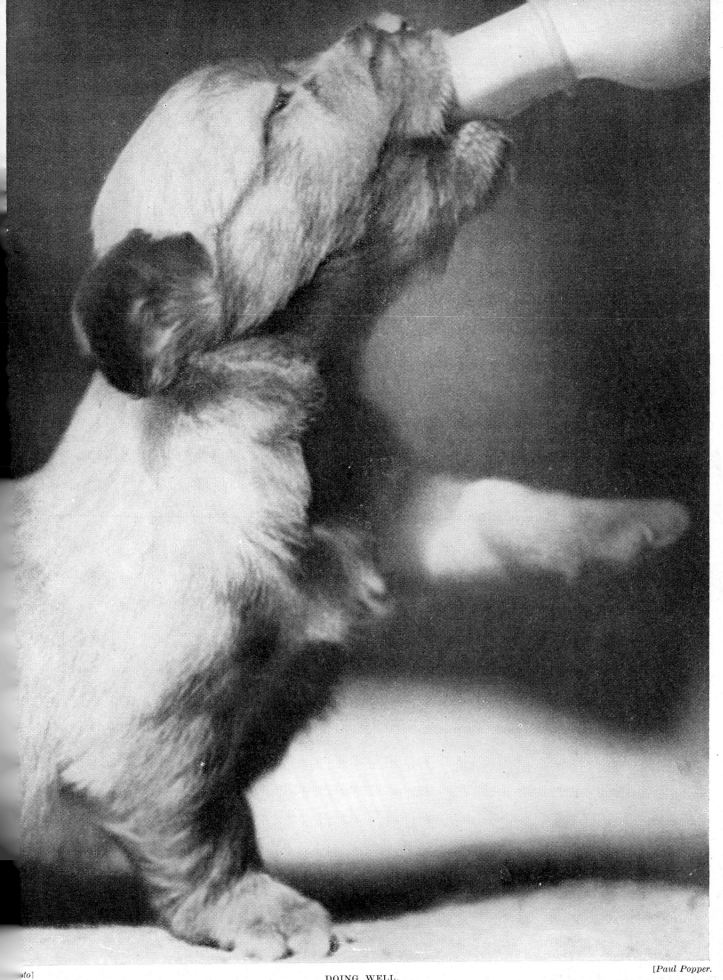

DOING WELL.

The use of a baby's feeding-bottle is quite a simple method for feeding a puppy. Anyway, this young Skye Terrier appears to be enjoying its meal.

or wholemeal bread may occasionally be substituted for rice, as occasion arises.

Liver is often greatly relished by canines, but is considered of small value as a food, indigestible, laxative, and perhaps somewhat liable to convey the eggs of parasites unless well cooked.

The Value of Bones.—The supply of bones to dogs is almost essential, not because of any particular food value obtained from them, but because it is really necessary to give employment to the teeth. This is an important matter, inasmuch as the almost (if not wholly) incurable dental disease known as pyorrhoea is the result of disuse of the teeth and gums. The gums will only keep hard and healthy, and the teeth tight in their sockets, if pressure is exerted upon them. Thus, whether one adopts biscuit or meat as an animal's main ration, these must be offered in such a condition that the dog is obliged to masticate them.

The safest bones are the ribs and shin bones of beef, leg bones of sheep, and other equally large and non-splinterable bones. Small chop bones, rabbit or chicken bones and some fish bones are potential sources of trouble ; they not only may become lodged across the mouth or gullet, but their needle-like spicules (after they have been broken up) are likely to injure or even perforate the stomach or intestines.

Raw or Cooked Meat ?—Shin of beef may be fed raw or cooked, and it is wise to vary the dog's food by giving it sometimes uncooked and at other times prepared. Raw meat probably contains more nourishment than cooked meat, because its contained vitamins are said to become destroyed in the process of heating.

Horseflesh.—Horseflesh was at one time very largely purchased for the feeding of dogs, and particularly of packs of hounds. Nowadays the town-dweller will, however, find that sound horseflesh commands a price averaging about 8d. per lb., thus often being more expensive than foreign beef. Masters of hounds are usually obliged to rely upon the local knackerman for their supply of dog meat, and whilst some are favoured in the cheapness and maintenance of their supplies, others find that the acquisition of a sufficiency is as difficult and uncertain as the cost is high. The disadvantages of horseflesh, as compared with beef, are that it seems to possess poor keeping qualities, and is more prone to cause a dog to smell unpleasant than is beef.

Milk.—Many dogs are very fond of milk, and in spite of the many extraordinary prejudices against it, milk is a very useful and fattening food for either adult or puppy. It is an excellent plan to encourage a dog's taste for milk, because when the dog may have no appetite for solids, milk will sustain it for long periods.

The stupid notion that milk causes worms is wholly untrue. Its greatest danger possibly is that it may be obtained from a cow suffering with tubercular mastitis ; but the human being shares with the dog any such risk as this, and so long as we consider milk good enough for our own consumption, it will be good enough for the animal.

VEGETABLE FOODS.

There are several useful vegetable foodstuffs which may be utilized in the canine dietary. Among the best known are oatmeal, barleymeal, rice, cornflour, arrow-root, and brown bread ; of green vegetables there are onions, leeks, carrots, spinach, cabbage, and grass. The first two meals are not often utilized as feeding products, although if given occasionally and sparingly would no doubt be quite satisfactory.

Rice is in common use, but must be thoroughly boiled and mixed with the day's meat ration. The unpolished variety is that which is invariably recommended because it is in the natural external coat of the seed that the vitamins are found.

Cornflour and *Arrowroot* are used mostly for their astringent properties in cases of diarrhoea. Arrowroot gruel may be prepared by adding one tablespoonful of arrowroot to half a pint of sweet milk and half a pint of boiling water. A little extra sweetening may be effected by adding loaf sugar. This is a good drink for dogs suffering from irritable bowels.

Bread of any kind is inclined to be harmful to the dog in many ways, and especially to puppies ; but if there is reason to use it, then the brown or wholemeal variety is the kind to choose.

Onions or Leeks may be very profitably boiled up with other articles of a dog's diet, and seem to be beneficial and well relished. They supply just that proportion of anti-scorbutic elements required for combating, or rather preventing, the development of skin and blood disorders. *Cabbage* or *Spinach* may in small quantities be used in the same way and for the same purpose. The dog, when free, finds his own vegetable, namely green grass, of which he consumes quantities.

Grass consumption very frequently is followed by sickness, the vomit consisting of mucus and grass in which round worms have often become enmeshed. This occurrence has quite commonly been observed.

Potato is not recommended as a suitable food for dogs. It appears to conduce to eczema, indigestion and flatulence.

Dog Biscuits.—Foremost among the farinaceous foods come dog biscuit, of which there are innumerable varieties and makes. It would be invidious to single out any particular biscuit, as the products of all the well-known firms of biscuit manufacturers are probably of equal excellence. A dog biscuit lends itself admirably to the inclusion of much worthless rubbish which may easily pass undetected ; indeed, some of the inferior and almost unknown brands of biscuit contain only the lowest class of meat such as gristle, tendon, or flesh from which all nutriment has been expressed in the manufacture of meat extracts, etc. They include also a good proportion of ground bone, sweepings of granaries and other deleterious rubbish. Thus it is imperative to purchase only from reliable and well-established firms whose manufactures have proved their worth.

The majority of dog biscuits are a combination of protein, carbohydrate, and mineral matter, and they alone are quite able to supply all the necessities of life (except water) ; yet the writer would not for a moment advocate their exclusive use, for he considers fresh meat to be an absolute necessity.

It is interesting to note that quite a variety of biscuits is obtainable, among the list of which we find cod-liver oil, charcoal, oatmeal, meat, and plain meatless biscuits ; there are also small pocket biscuits, puppy cakes, and larger, harder cakes for the big breeds of dogs. In addition, there are various kinds of meals or crushed biscuits, some pepsinated, others containing molasses.

Biscuit meals may be fed dry, or may be scalded with a small quantity of hot milk or soup until they become just crumbly moist. They should never be made into a wet mash.

Sometimes it is convenient to mix with such meal a proportion of meat, and perhaps a very little cooked green vegetable. When a dog is a shy feeder of

DOG'S OWN BAKERY.

The famous Great Dane kennels at Send, Surrey, are believed to be the only kennels in England to have their own bakery, where an experienced baker is kept busy all the year round, making biscuits for the hundreds of dogs

biscuits, it is expedient to so combine his biscuit with his meat that he cannot separate them, and is obliged to eat the mixture if he takes any at all.

Unsuitable Foods.—There exists an irresistible desire in some homes to give the house-dog all kinds of artificial and unnatural edibles solely because the animal begs for them. It is not infrequently that one is told of a dog's extraordinary partiality for pastry, dough-nuts, tea, chocolate, sugar-candy, and a hundred and one other articles which are wholly unnatural for a dog and usually most indigestible. The more a dog's taste for sweetstuffs is cultivated the more it will beg for them, and the more it begs for them the greater supply it receives. In time the animal becomes obese, out of condition, easily fatigued, perhaps constipated, with a foul breath and a general body odour. It has lost its real appetite for normal food, and is a subject of chronic indigestion. Most likely, too, the blood will rid itself of waste products through the skin, and we shall find the dog a chronic sufferer of skin disease.

When to Feed.—Regularity in feeding is very essential as it teaches the dog to expect its meal at a certain hour. The number given in a day must depend upon circumstances, and a hard and fast rule cannot be laid down. The average healthy adult dog should, however, generally receive one full meal per day, supplemented by a light breakfast. Digestion is slow in the dog, and many hours must elapse before the stomach is once more empty and able to deal with a new supply of food.

The majority of dogs need, and probably receive but one meal a day. This will be offered at varying times according to the use to which the dog is being put. If it is a yard-dog or one which it is desired should be wide awake at night time, then the principal meal will be given about midday. Sleep will probably ensue during the remainder of the afternoon, but by the evening digestion will be more or less complete and the dog alert

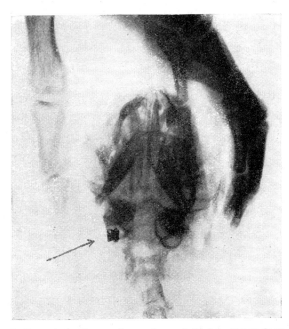

Radiograph showing an air-gun slug embedded in the neck of a small dog. Human fingers are seen encircling the dog's skull.

A pet dog should receive its big meal in the evening. Sporting field-dogs during the season should also have one meal per day, and that in the evening.

Many dogs seem to have little inclination for much to eat in the early morning, but for those which evince an irrepressible desire to feed, a handful of some kind of biscuit will usually suffice. Hard - working sheep - dogs, which travel many miles daily, often over rough mountainous tracks, require

A Greyhound's foot showing two minute pieces of granite-grit embedded in one of the pads.

very generous treatment and should be fed, if possible, more than once. In this case, however, it would be most unwise to give a substantial meal just prior to setting out upon a hard day's work, for blood which should accumulate in the viscera for the assistance of the process of digestion, would be diverted to the muscles of the limbs and body for the performance of work.

Toy dogs may, with advantage, receive two or three small meals in the course of twenty-four hours, and of as variable a nature as possible.

Quantity of Food per Day.—This is entirely governed by the circumstances peculiar to each case. A guiding rule has certainly been formulated, and very frequently it answers admirably; but so many factors have to be considered that one must really rely upon one's own discretion. The rule alluded to is that for each pound of the dog's body weight $\frac{1}{2}$ oz. of total food should be allowed per day. In other words, a 16-lb. terrier would receive approximately 8 ozs. of food in twenty-four hours. It may have 2 ozs. of it in the morning and 6 ozs. at night; or it may have it all in one meal.

This proportion has been found to work very well except in the cases of extreme weight. For instance, an 80-lb. dog would not need so much as 40 ozs. of food daily, and a 3-lb. animal would doubtless require a little more than $1\frac{1}{2}$ ozs. In these cases, as in those of pregnancy, convalescence after illness, growing puppies, suckling bitches, indolent dogs, hard-working dogs, etc., allowances must be made. An increased ration will obviously be necessary for a bitch suckling a litter, or for sustaining an animal through bitterly cold weather.

The proportion of proteins to carbohydrates must be regulated according to circumstances, but a broad principle may be adopted of giving well-exercised or hard working dogs a maximum proportion of meat.

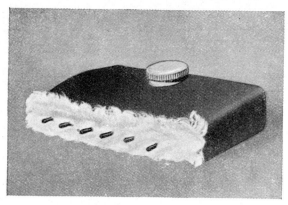

REPLACING NATURE.
Tee's artificial foster-mother. Note the furry surround of the teats.
(From *Hobday's Surgical Diseases of Dog and Cat.*)

Dogs leading a less active life should have their total ration divided into flesh two-thirds, and other kinds of food one-third. Dogs having little or no exercise should receive equal proportions of meat and biscuits.

The following table of approximate quantities is one which is considered fairly reliable as a general guide: St. Bernards, Mastiffs, Great Danes, and dogs of similar size 2 to 4 lb.; Collies, Retrievers, Alsatians, and dogs of similar size, 1 to 2 lb.; Airedales, Chows, Bulldogs, and dogs of similar size, ¾ to 1½ lb.; Fox Terriers, Cairns, Scotties, and dogs of similar size, ½ lb.; Pugs, Poms, Pekingese, and dogs of similar size 4 to 6 ozs. Even such a table as this must necessarily be very elastic, for some of the largest dogs may need almost 5 lb. of food daily, whilst the most diminutive of the small breeds might be better off with less than 4 ozs.

Water Supply.—Clean water, in clean, unspillable dishes, should always be available to a dog. If a dog is fastened by a chain the water-trough should be so placed that the dog can just reach it.

There is no excuse for neglecting to supply water, but if one should be so remiss, the consequences may be serious for the dog.

FEEDING IN SICKNESS.

In treating disease, loss of appetite is one of the greatest obstacles with which one has to contend. A case often might do well if only the patient would continue to feed and thereby preserve its strength. Usually one has to use every artifice to get a sick dog to feed, though cases arise, of course, in which abstention from food for a while would be the wiser treatment.

Inducing a Dog to Feed.—Dogs may often be induced to eat everything offered if only their sense of greed can be aroused. This is usually and simply done by bringing another dog into close proximity of the food dish. To call the cat or pretend to fetch another animal, is often sufficient to produce the desired effect.

Waning appetites may sometimes be stimulated

by changing the diet and thus eliminating monotony. For instance, delicate feeders may be coaxed into eating cooked brains, sweetbreads, liver, high game, tripe, etc., even fish being often regarded as a delicacy when such has only very rarely been offered before.

In sickness the digestive powers are often enfeebled, and even if the animal will eat ordinary foods such as biscuits and meat, it may not be able to digest or assimilate them. In such cases special diets should be drawn up and be, as strictly as possible, adhered to. In illness it is usually necessary to feed small quantities at more frequent intervals. Most probably if the usual large meal were offered and consumed, it would be almost immediately vomited.

Food which is voluntarily eaten is worth far more than that which is forcibly given, and it behoves us to do all we can to keep the normal appetite in existence. Perhaps this end may best be attained by administering a course of tonics over a prolonged period. In all cases endeavour should be made to ascertain and eliminate the cause of the inappetence.

Various Sick Foods.—There is a fair variety of foodstuffs from which one may select those most suitable to the case. The following list comprises some of the most popular articles for sick diets: Boiled tripe, minced raw beef, cooked liver, sheep's brain, calves' sweetbreads, boiled fish, sardines, rabbit, chicken and its broth, beef-tea, milk with or without arrowroot or cornflour, egg and milk, milk puddings, and the many proprietary foods such as Virol, Bovril, Oxo, Valentine's Meat Extract, Armour's Meat Essence, many brands of dried milk, Benger's Food and Allenbury's Food, etc.

Milk is an ideal diet for the sick, and can in most

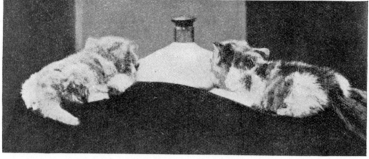

MODERN METHODS.
Ware's artificial foster-mother has saved the life of many puppies and kittens.
(From *Hobday's Surgical Diseases of Dog and Cat.*)

MOST UNUSUAL.
An Alsatian bitch, obligingly suckling six little pigs.

cases be quite easily digested and retained ; in addition, it contains all the tissue-building elements necessary for the sustenance of the system.

Foods in Special Complaints.—As a general rule in FEVERS but little food can be disposed of, and that little must be chosen with reference to its mildness and unstimulating qualities. Fish, eggs, meat juices, milk, and patent foods would thus be more suitable than beef or biscuit.

For DIARRHOEA, indigestible or irritant articles must be avoided. Rice boiled in plain water is excellent for a relaxed state of the bowels ; and cooked arrowroot or cornflour, with milk, are commonly used for the same purpose. Barley water to drink is also indicated.

In CONSTIPATION one avoids giving astringent foods such as the starches and their substitutes. Oily foods such as cream, salad oil, sardines, herrings, or the fat of meat, raw beef and liver, have also a stimulating and relaxing action. The proprietary preparation known as Virolax, containing 60 per cent paraffin and 40 per cent Virol, is not only an intestinal lubricant but also a valuable food.

When there is inflammation of the mucous lining of the bowels—ENTERITIS—the diet, during the early stage of it, should be confined to cold water, after which milk and barley water, or weak chicken or veal tea may be given in small quantities. Pepsin and pancreatin are organic extracts which may be added to the food either before it is ingested, or may be given along with it. Barley water is made by adding 2 ozs. of pearl barley to 2 quarts of boiling water. This mixture should be boiled until it has evaporated to half the original bulk. It is then strained and cooled. In DYSPEPSIA, peptonized milk is often of great service, and it is prepared by mixing a peptonizing tablet or powder in a quarter of a pint of cold water, adding this to a pint of fresh milk in a quart bottle, and placing the latter in a pan of water which has been heated to about 120° Fahr. The bottle should not stay in this heat for longer than ten minutes, and the milk should then be used at once. If it cannot be utilized, it should be placed upon ice or brought quickly to the boil in order to stop the action of the peptonizing ferment. In dyspepsia, great care should be taken not to overload the stomach. Small meals at more frequent intervals are the order. Starchy, rich, or fatty foods must be avoided. Fish is good, and chicken, scraped raw meat, sweetbreads, or tripe may be given.

Dogs suffering from DISTEMPER can only be dieted according to the particular symptoms obtaining in each case. As a general rule, however, they require as much strengthening food as possible in order to increase their resistance to the invading infection. When diarrhoea and dysentery are absent, benefit is derived from adding cod-liver oil (with or without malt extract) to the dietary.

In ACUTE RHEUMATISM the diet should consist almost entirely of milk, and even in convalescence meat should be given only very sparingly. Sugar should be avoided and starches greatly reduced in quantity. Small amounts of wholemeal bread, oatmeal, or rice may be allowed ; whilst boiled cod or other coarse fish are permitted.

ECZEMA is a disease largely brought about by wrongful feeding, and it is not uncommon to find that a complete change of diet will be all that is necessary to effect a cure. Usually, it appears to be the excess of starches and sugars which predisposes to eczematous skin eruptions, thus the wholly biscuit-fed dog is more frequently a sufferer than the animal which eats a generous proportion of flesh daily. Very small quantities of well-boiled green vegetable or onion added to the food are often helpful, but must not be given in excess.

For dogs subject to CONVULSIONS, an unstimulating dietary is essential, such as the proprietary meals and biscuits ; fish ; Benger's and other foods ; etc. Red meat is contra-indicated.

SEVERE VOMITING, as occurs in acute gastritis, is probably one of the most difficult conditions with which to contend so far as concerns the diet, for whatever is swallowed seems almost immediately to be rejected. In such cases great care must be exercised in selecting only those articles of diet which exert the least irritant effect, which are digested with the greatest ease, and which can be retained.

Probably the food which most nearly answers to this description is egg-albumen. If raw white of egg is placed upon a plate and cut across in all directions by a knife and fork, it will be found that the long tenacious strings will become separated or broken up, thus permitting them to be mixed with ordinary cold water or barley water.

Milk, on the other hand, may be entirely and immediately rejected on account of an excessive acid secretion curdling it into hard, indigestible clots. Curd formation may be considerably diminished by the addition of Benger's Food to the milk ; or by diluting the milk with lime water or barley water— one-third of either to two-thirds of milk. Milk may be mixed with soda water or with ice, which sometimes act as effective antemetics. Whey is very beneficial in cases of weak digestion, gastritis (*which see*), etc., and is made by heating a pint of milk to about body temperature and adding a teaspoonful of essence of rennet. Break up the curds and strain off the whey through muslin.

Forcible Feeding.—If the dog has lost all inclination for food, it is hardly wise to commence its forcible administration immediately ; better far to coax the animal by offering little pieces of food out of the hand, and by tempting it with a variety of dishes, preparing oneself to be satisfied at first with the small amounts voluntarily taken. Of course, refusal to feed cannot be countenanced indefinitely, as a dog very soon loses strength and condition if not nourished ; therefore, having allowed two or three days' fast, and the alimentary tract having had a perfect rest, we must then proceed to administer food artificially.

Usually, forcible feeding means the administration of liquid nourishment via the mouth, which is the most commendable method. Probably in the first instance pure milk will suffice, or a new-laid egg may be beaten up in it ; to this a little port wine may be added for cases which seem to require an alcoholic stimulant. Beef tea, soups, broth with the yolk of an egg in it, extract of meat, small quantities of minced raw meat, are all very good diets for sick animals.

Of the proprietary foods there is an extensive choice, and of them all Virol has a high value, containing, as it does, bone marrow and malt extract. Brand's Essence of Beef is also very excellent, and as a food for dogs, should be warmed until liquefied, then given with a spoon.

Benger's, Allenbury's, and many patent foods— much as those containing phosphates—are beneficial and reliable, and some splendid results have accrued in nervous cases from the use of Sanatogen.

Eatan is a comparatively new concentrated food which has been well spoken of. There are very

"ROMPISH" "REMEDY" "REVEL" "RADIENT"

GONE AWAY ON!

After a painting by Cuthbert Bradley. The master, E. A. V. Stanley, is seen riding his "Boots" up with the Woodland Pytchley pack. Fox-hunting is a British national sport and greatly followed all over the country. Men, women and children ride to hounds, and the sport provides much employment and leads to the breeding and sale of hunters, apart from the help it brings to farmers, for whom it opens a good market for the very best oats, hay, and straw.

[Capt. E. A. V. Stanley.

numerous brands of dried milks available and suitable for sick dogs, amongst the best known of which are Lactol, Glaxo, Virol and Milk, and Milkal.

Rectal Feeding.—It may happen, of course, that in some cases the administration of food by the mouth becomes impossible or undesirable owing to excessive weakness, sore throat or mouth, poor digestion, or vomiting, when recourse must be had to rectal feeding. This may be accomplished in two ways, viz. : (1) Clysters ; (2) Suppositories ; but in the case of either the layman would be well advised to seek the services of a vet.

FEEDING THE PUPPY.

Puppies are weaned at the age of about six weeks ; but some precocious pups will much earlier show a marked inclination to take food other than their mother's milk. It is well to take advantage of any such tendency, for the mother is thereby saved a great proportion of the drain upon her strength and constitution. It does not follow, of course, that because a puppy has learned at four or five weeks to consume food prepared for it, it must necessarily cease to suckle its mother. It is better in fact that it should not entirely cease to do so. The bitch knows by natural instinct when her offspring should commence to forage for themselves.

Saucers of cows' milk with added cream, or of Lactol, Glaxo, or Puppilac, may be offered the puppies in the early stages of weaning, allowing the youngsters to be with the mother several times during the day and stay with her the whole of each night. As time advances they are allowed access to the dam perhaps only twice during the day, and later, once only. Eventually, they enjoy her company during the night only.

During this transitional period their prepared food takes on gradual changes. Having commenced with fortified cows' milk, they go on to Lactol or some other dried milk, thence to well-boiled oatmeal

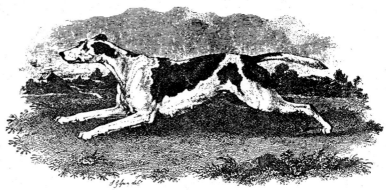

"MERKIN".

Col. Thornton (see *The Book of the Greyhound*) owned "Merkin", and offered to race her against any hound for 10,000 guineas. The drawing is by Sawrey Gilpin.

and milk, later to Spratt's Pepsinated Puppy Meal, Melox Food, or some other meal, with fresh milk or gravy poured over, and when finally weaned they may commence the consumption of finely minced raw beef. Meat is not started until the pups are six or seven weeks of age, from which time the quantity allowed gradually increases until the additional milk diet is almost dispensed with. Spratt's Weetmeat may now be alternated or incorporated with the minced flesh, for this is a meal which is very rich in frame-building elements and which, apparently, does not entail the least strain upon the most delicate puppy digestion.

One of the greatest mistakes that amateurs make is to dilute cows' milk with water in the belief that it is too rich or too strong for an unweaned puppy. This erroneous belief is evidently based upon the generally accepted theory that "milk is a perfect food in itself". The bitch's milk *is* perfect for the puppy, cow's milk ideal for the calf, and so on ; but cows' milk is not by any means perfect for the pup, since it is three times weaker than the milk of a bitch.

In order, therefore, to render cows' milk practically identical with bitches' milk, one may proceed as follow : (1) Slowly evaporate cows' milk until so much water has been driven off that only one-third of the original bulk remains ; or (2) one may heat a breakfast cup of cows' milk to *near* boiling point and then shake in 2 ozs. of full-cream dried milk, afterwards vigorously shaking or stirring.

If puppies are given unlimited quantities of cows' milk under the impression that they are bound to thrive well, the result may be tragic.

Puppies are easily taught to lap, for their noses have only to be dipped into the saucer of food a few times in order to impress upon them that the process is pleasant and satisfying. Care is necessary to ensure that nothing is given to the dam

AN OUTSTANDING HOUND.

Lord Coventry's "Rambler" (on left), was considered to be one of the best Foxhounds in England. It was entered in 1873. The dog on the right is "Marksman", which was entered in 1874. The original painting is by C. Lutyens.

CUBBING.

Before fox-hunting starts in all seriousness, early Meets are held at which the stock is thinned down and the foxes are dispersed. These early Meets go by the name of Cubbing, and the Fife Foxhound Pack is seen on its way to the first draw.

WOODLAND PYTCHLEY HOUNDS.
A picture showing a couple of Captain E. A. V. Stanley's Hounds—"Wallflower" and "Tragedy"—when he was master of the
Woodland Pytchley Kennels in 1910.

which might be eaten by, and prove injurious to the offspring.

Plain milk, polished rice, and bread-and-milk are unsuitable foods for growing dogs, as they contain too little of the essential ingredients and may predispose to rickets, etc. In order to grow a good bony frame, especially in dogs of the larger breeds, an abundance of bone-growing salts must be furnished. Growing dogs thrive best on animal nutrients—raw meat, bones and blood. Milk may be discontinued at the eighth to tenth week, and there is nothing to gain by withholding meat at this period. On the other hand, no attempt should be made to induce a puppy to eat solids until after the suckling period is over.

From the age of about ten weeks to four months, puppies should be fed three times a day at regular intervals ; after this age two daily feeds are sufficient. Many adult dogs receive only one meal a day, but this is quite optional and must be left to the discretion of the owner.

Increased Desire to Feed.—Increased appetite, i.e. an excessive craving for food, may be due to pure greed, the animal not really feeling hungry, but wishing rather to eat everything it sees lest some other animal might get it. Or it may be due to some previous starvation ; or to large demands being made upon the body, such as in the case of nursing mothers ; or to diabetes ; or to intestinal parasites (which are a well-known cause of gluttony) ; or to dyspepsia.

But hard work must never be forgotten as a means of creating abnormal appetite, and any dog —such as the working sheep-dogs—which gallop miles over the hills, must be very liberally fed.

Diminished Desire to Feed.—The causes of diminished or entire loss of appetite could hardly be enumerated. In general, this accompanies any constitutional disease, pain, injury, or fever, but at times seems to have no ascertainable cause whatever.

An unwillingness to feed must not be confused with lack of appetite. Quite often a dog may be very hungry but fears to eat because of some painful lesion in the mouth or throat. In such cases, it will be noticed that the dog *takes an interest* in the food set down, in that it stands near the dish, watches it and smells it, and may even pick up a portion only to drop it without mastication or swallowing. The mouth should be examined for ulcers, pyorrhoea, loose teeth, sore tongue, sore throat, etc., etc.

When it is definite that the dog is off colour and its appetite has become capricious in consequence, it is advisable to use every artifice to induce it to take a little solid food at frequent intervals. The tit-bits offered should be somethng unusual and very tasty ; and if the dog has nasal catarrh, involving some diminution of the sense of smell, then the morsels should have a strong scent : hare, partridge, pheasant, sardines, etc., etc. (See FAT, STORAGE OF ; DEPRAVED APPETITE.)

Foot.—The dog's foot comprises four toes, each being composed of three bones or phalanges. The claw is situated on the terminal or third phalanx. There is a large centrally-placed cushion-like pad radiating in front of which are four smaller pads—one beneath each toe. These five pads take the weight of the dog, none being imposed upon the carpal pad or "stopper", as this is situated behind the wrist. The carpal pad does, however, come into action when the rapidly moving dog is attempting to stop itself, and we often find this pad badly injured in coursing and track-racing Greyhounds. Once they become torn they heal with difficulty, and the best treatment has appeared to be complete removal.

A dog has a fifth or rudimentary toe on the inner aspect of its foot, also placed off the ground, and generally on the forefeet only. This is known as the dew-claw which possesses no useful function. On the contrary, it is generally a great nuisance, and in well-conducted kennels it is removed during the first week of puppyhood.

The swellings which form between the toes have been described under the heading of CYSTS, and the abnormalities of the claws such as ingrowing nails, inflamed claws, etc., were referred to under CLAWS.

Eczema of the Feet.—Moist eczema of the foot is not at all rare in dogs, and affects the solar surface of the foot between the pads ; and also sometimes between the toes. The skin, in this condition, is very red and generally moist, examination of which is usually resented. The condition causes marked lameness, and the dog continually licks the affected foot and perhaps holds it off the ground. A cooling astringent lotion is required to harden and heal the lesion, such as lead lotion or alum solution. The foot might, with advantage, be totally immersed in it for ten or fifteen minutes at a time. Between treatments the foot should be protected from the ground, and the dog should be purged and receive a course of alterative medicine.

Abnormalities of the Pads.—Eczema sometimes affects the horny pads, causing an under-running of the most superficial or horny layer. The latter will be found peeling off at the edges, revealing a raw-looking surface beneath. This is vulgarly known as "sweaty foot". Great lameness results, but under treatment as advised for *Eczema of the Feet* resolution soon results.

Corns have been dealt with under that heading.

Cracked pads are common, and the writer has not been able to trace the cause in many instances. It is certain, however, that for some reason or other the pads become very dry and brittle, when comparatively large and deep fissures appear. Pressure upon these fissures causes pain, and walking is only performed lamely. The curative appears to be the application of a liberal coating of antiseptic jelly such as carbolized vaseline, or any other agent having a softening influence, as glycerine and carbolic or zinc ointment. A square of oiled silk is then wrapped around the foot and a gauze bandage superimposed.

Injuries to the pads may be caused by rapid or prolonged travel over short stubble, treading on broken glass, or upon upturned tintacks or barbed-wire, and treading in quicklime or acids. Very painful injuries may result from these causes, and the treatments almost suggest themselves.

Knocked-up Toes are a common sequel to racing, whether it be after a rabbit, an electric hare, or during the coursing of a real hare. Apparently there is severe sprain of the external ligaments, and probably of the capsular ligament of the second or third joint A synovitis is the frequent result, following which there is an accumulation of fibrinous tissue or membrane around the joint. The synovial membrane itself becomes thickened, and there is an increased secretion of synovial fluid. Occasionally the inflammation of the joint becomes chronic and is associated with cicatricial contraction, the net result being that the affected joint appears swollen, hard, and nodular. In some cases, for a dog to race in this condition causes pain and lameness ; in other instances it does not, and

TWO FOXHOUNDS.

Two very fine Hounds of about 1903, as painted by G. Paice, showing Mr. Edward E. Barclay's (M.F.H.) "Colonist" and "Cardinal".
They belonged to the Puckeridge Pack.

nothing remains but permanent thickening around the joint. Actual cautery (*which see*) has been tried for the cure of this condition, but the writer's experience is that surgical excision is the quickest, most economic and surest treatment.

Broken Toes.—Dogs with toes affected in the manner described under *Knocked-up Toes* are sometimes submitted to X-ray examination.

In the great majority of cases all that is seen in the radiograph is a great increase of peri-articular thickening, but in some few one may detect fractures of the digital bones. Sometimes small particles of bone are broken off, and in other instances the bone may be split from end to end. So far as racing Greyhounds are concerned, it is more economical to amputate the broken bone than to wait several weeks for union to take place, for even if this occurs, one is not able to forecast whether racing will not cause lameness.

Foreign Body.—A solid which grows in or upon, or which gains entrance to any part of an animal's anatomy, and being strange or abnormal to such situation, is a foreign body. It may be that the latter takes the form of a piece of coal dust or an oat husk gaining access to the eye ; or a thorn penetrating the foot ; or a bullet piercing any part of the body ; or it may be a portion of bone which, having become broken off and no longer forming a living or useful part of the whole, then becomes a foreign body. A pathological growth is, similarly, a body foreign to the normal anatomy, and often exerts even more serious consequences than do the simpler bodies. An accidentally swallowed ball, stone or bone is a foreign body, as also is a stone which forms in one or other of the organs as a result of disease, e.g. cystic calculus.

The general effect of the entrance of foreign bodies is, first, some discomfort or pain, followed by inflammation (unless they are extracted) and finally by abscess formation. It is Nature's method of eliminating the offending substance, for with the escape of pus—when the abscess bursts—comes the foreign body. It sometimes happens that the new body is so wedged in that it cannot move, even after abscess rupture, and, unless a surgeon is in charge of the case, the layman plays a waiting game in the hope that the place will heal up. Whilst the foreign body is still *in situ*, however, the wound never will heal up and a fistula is formed (*which see*).

Following comminuted fractures, in which small sequestra of bone become entirely detached from their normal positions, these particles die and act as irritants unless and until they are entirely removed.

Swallowed bodies, incapable of being digested or passed out, will set up inflammation of the bowels, then, later, ulceration and possibly perforation. The latter might very probably lead to peritonitis and death of the animal.

X-radiography is extremely useful in detecting deeply placed solids whose presence cannot be ascertained by clinical examination. For instance, we publish two radiographs herewith, in one of which will be noticed a lead slug, shot out of an air-gun, which penetrated a small dog's neck. In this case, rather peculiarly, the wound healed and there was nothing further noticed to cause anyone to suspect a foreign body, except a somewhat stiff movement of the neck. X-ray revealed the cause at once, which was removed.

The other picture is of a greyhound's foot. The dog had been unaccountably lame for over a month, and no reason could be assigned. A radiograph showed that two small foreign bodies were embedded in the pad of the third digit (shown at the arrowhead) the pad being much more swollen than its fellows. An incision was made and the two bodies removed. They proved to be pieces of granite.

Formalin or formaldehyde is a very powerful disinfectant which readily evolves a pungent gas. It has also a great property of hardening tissue with which it comes in contact. It has internal and external uses, in the former case being employed by the mouth in cases of Stuttgart disease or haemorrhagic gastro-enteritis, and as an intestinal antiseptic to allay bacterial fermentation. It may be injected intravenously against septicaemia, or profuse haemorrhages.

Externally it forms a constituent of some lotions for the healing and hardening of ulcers, sloughs and infected wounds generally. As a fumigant, it is very valuable. (*See* DISINFECTION.)

Foster-Mothers.—A bitch or other female which provides orphan puppies with their sustenance. When a bitch whelps it is not at all an uncommon occurrence for her to die at or very soon after the act. She may have an exceedingly difficult parturition necessitating great delay and possibly instrumentation. Unless the latter is very skilfully performed (and sometimes even though it is), there is a considerable risk of peritonitis, and death. Short of dying, she may be very ill, and quite unable to take any interest in her whelps.

For these and other reasons, there are many occasions upon which it would be highly desirable —if not absolutely necessary—to obtain the services of a foster-mother.

The wise breeder generally makes enquiries, some weeks before parturition, as to the whereabouts of a bitch likely to be in milk when he needs her. It is, indeed, not unknown for breeders of valuable dogs to keep valueless mongrels whose oestral periods coincide, in order that two bitches may whelp at once. Then, should anything unforeseen occur to the pedigree bitch, her pups are put to the mongrel, and the common puppies are probably destroyed. There are people who make a regular business of keeping common bitches, all whelping at various times, in order that other breeders may hire them. The fee ranges from 30s. to 63s. weekly.

A suckling cat can often be induced to take to very small puppies if they are put with her in the dark and as unobtrusively as possible.

It becomes increasingly risky to put little puppies to strange mothers if they are more than three or four days old. The writer has seen youngsters, so transferred, die from apparently no other reason than that the new mother's milk disagreed with them and caused profuse diarrhoea. There is, of course, always a possibility that the foster-mother may savage the orphan puppies, push them out of her bed, or refuse to allow them to feed.

If a strange foster-mother is brought in, one should exercise extreme caution with regard to its state of health. She really should be carefully examined by a veterinary surgeon. The ideal procedure would be to have her in isolation and under strict observation for a week prior to the day she is required. The bitch

AT WORMLEY.

A very characteristic picture indeed, taken when the Hounds are going off to the covert to find their fox. In the background can be seen men waiting by the gate to let the Hounds through. Note how the Hounds are holdin[g] their tails up—a sure sign of eager anticipation.

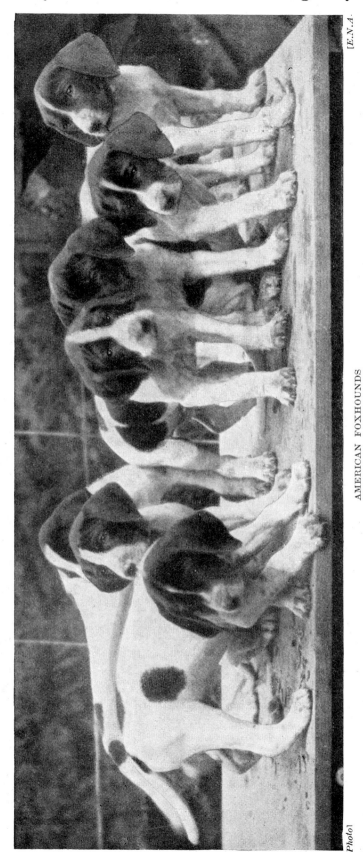

Note their legs and feet.

Some of them look promising.

AMERICAN FOXHOUNDS

A group of Foxhound puppies taken in New York, probably, if not certainly, descended from the English Foxhound.

Photo]

may then be admitted freely to the house or kennel; and if she has any pups of her own, these should not be removed simultaneously with the addition of the other pups. They may, however, be gradually abstracted so soon as one is sure that the bitch has taken kindly to the new puppies.

It is not at all unlikely that just when one finds great need for a foster-mother, none can be obtained any-where. In such cases, one has to fall back upon artificial types of foster mother, of which there are several. We illustrate two kinds on page 636, but the construction of all are more or less on the same principle, viz.: a large con-tainer for the warmed and specially prepared food, leading from which are numerous rubber teats. Some of the latter have fur arranged about them, although this is really quite unnecessary.

A little patience and perseverance is often essential in teaching the pups how to feed from artificial mothers. One tries to get the teat into a puppy's mouth, at the same time expressing a little of the milk; and once the pup finds that food can be extracted in this way, it will continue at it without further trouble.

Foxhound.—Fox-hunting origin-ally followed stag-hunting, but the fox was in those days looked upon as vermin, and a fox-hunt, instead of constituting a sporting chase, was merely a scouring of the country by a great company of horse and foot men, for the extirpation of an animal then held to be destructive. The method of killing was by nets surrounding a covert or part of a wood, and any method was thought good enough to destroy the fox.

Gradually, however, fox-hunting became a recognized sport, and the big landed proprietors of the day kept packs of hounds for that object. Originally, the kings of England held all the hunting rights in the Royal Forests, and permitted local land-owners, by charters, to hunt the fox and hare, but hardly ever the red deer.

Records exist of the packs of hounds kept many generations ago by the Earl of Yarborough (Brocklesby), the Earl of Fitz-william (Milton), Lord Fitzharding (Berkeley), the Duke of Beaufort (Badminton), the Duke of Rutland (Belvoir).

In the days of King Canute it was ordered that all dogs, except the very small breeds, should be so maimed that they could not chase deer and suchlike animals in the Royal Forests. This mutilation took the form of the cutting of knees, the amputation of a claw, the cutting out of the ball of one foot, and this apparently was carried on until 1189, during the reign of Henry II.

Only those persons who received the royal permission or charter were permitted to keep uninjured hounds or dogs of the larger breeds.

When Foxhounds are so named in the many descriptions of hunting in the olden days one can only conclude that they were the type of hounds which were used to hunt the fox at that time. The larger-sized hounds were used for stag-hunting, the smaller type for fox- and hare-hunting.

The hounds of the St. Huberts or Talbots, brought over to England by the Norman invaders when they conquered England, were the foundation stock of the breed afterwards known as Southern Hounds.

The St. Huberts were celebrated as far back as the eighth century, when they were known as Flemish Hounds. The St. Huberts Monastery was in the Ardennes, the home of the breed. They were divided into two strains, the black and the white. They had wonderful noses, fine coats

Photo]   *[Sport & General*
EAGER FOR THE HUNT.
Behind a resisting grill, the Bedale Hounds are anxiously waiting to be let out, for it is a fine morning for hunting.

(usually black-and-tan), broad heads, and feathered sterns (like the modern Bloodhound, which is descended from them). They were slow hunters.

George Turberville, in Queen Elizabeth's reign, wrote *Art of Venerie*. Turberville dealt with French hounds, and as our English are all derived from them, it may be well to mention the breeds described in this book :

The White was used mostly for stag-hunting.

The Fallow was used for hunting all sorts of quarry, principally the stag.

The Dun, commonest breed, and would hunt any game.

The Black or St. Huberts is the hound that interests English people most, undoubtedly a forbear of the Bloodhound and Southern Hound. They were of many colours, which points to much crossing of other breeds.

Gervaise Markham, in his work, *Country Contentments* (1611), states that there were distinct breeds of hunting hounds :

The heavy and tall type, used in the West—Cheshire and Lancashire.

The middle size, used in Worcestershire and Bedfordshire, were of a lighter type and able to hunt faster in the more open parts of England.

The Northern Hound, bred in the North—Yorkshire, Cumberland, Northumberland—and in the open Counties. More slender and greyhound-like. Work and speed good, but lacked the low, deep notes of the heavier hound.

G. Paice
'03

"Bonnylass"

[By courtesy]

"BONNYLASS".

A good type of Foxhound bitch, from a painting by G. Paice, showing good shoulders, plenty of heart room and standing on well-built front legs. She was for many years a most active member of the Woodland Pytchley pack.

[Capt. E. A. V. Stanley.

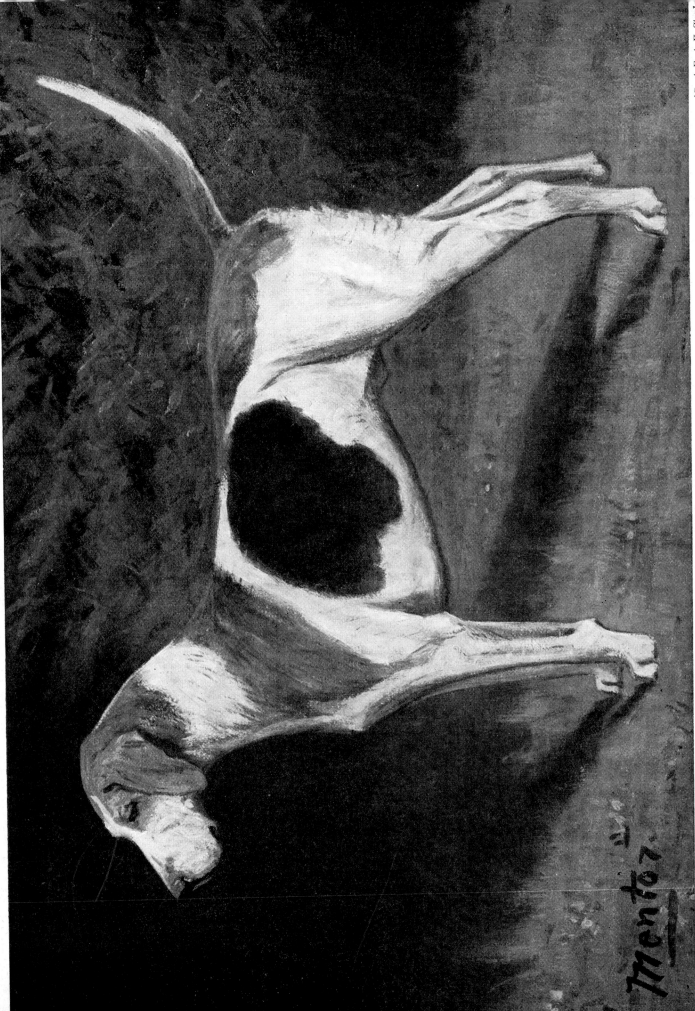

Markham's reference to the Northern Hound probably refers to Yorkshire Hounds, and possibly the foundation of the Earl of Yarborough's Brocklesby pack.

The Welsh Foxhound may be founded on the "Shaghaired Hounds", stated by Count de Canteleu to be the Bresse Hound of Eastern provinces of France. The coat was shaggy and of yellow or sandy-red colour.

It appears from Richard Blome's *Gentleman's Recreation* (1686) that by then a commencement had been made of crossing the various hounds then in existence, so as to obtain a faster variety, and for the better hunting of the fox, and so on until the breed became of a fixed type and produced the packs of Foxhounds that practically all the present packs of to-day throw back to.

After 1800, the pace began to quicken in the hunting field, and it was common to find the more venturesome taking the fences that came in their way at a gallop, whilst previously, if an obstacle looked too big, the field dismounted and led over.

The main points of conformation of the modern Foxhound are:

SKULL.—Broad.

NECK.—Long, but not thick. A short-necked hound is deficient in pace.

SHOULDERS.—Should show quality and no lumber. A shoulder with an excessive amount of fleshy conformation will prevent the hound from running up or down hill at top pace.

FORELEGS.—Full of bone, and the bone should reach right down to the feet and not taper off in any way.

TOES.—The toes of the feet should be close together, and not open. The writer is not greatly enamoured of the modern type of Peterborough Show catlike feet, but, being in the minority, must conclude that his opinion may be wrong. In his opinion, the catlike foot does not stand work over rough ground as well as the more unfashionable but slightly flatter foot.

GIRTH.—Deep, with plenty of heart room.

BACK.—Broad, and a hound should be well ribbed up; but there should be a fair space between the end of the ribs and the commencement of the hind-quarters, otherwise the hound will be deficient in stride, and therefore lack pace.

STERN —Should be well put on at the end of good quarters, and these quarters should in no way end abruptly and be of the type that houndmen term "chopped off behind". A curly stern, although unsightly, will not be detrimental to the hound's hunting qualities.

QUARTERS.—Full, and of great muscular proportions.

HOCKS.—Should be well let down, and the bone of the hindlegs (as in the forelegs) should continue all the way down to the foot, and not become light under the pastern.

The Foxhound on the Show Bench.—No regular classes are confined to Foxhounds at shows held under Kennel Club rules, though a few shows

Photo]   *[L.N.A*

QUITE FRIENDLY.

The Belvoir is one of the most important packs in England. Master Edward Grennall, like so many country-bred children, has not the slightest fear of Hounds and is here seen making friends with one of them.

take place annually confined solely to the breed, which are recognized by the Kennel Club. Peterborough Show always has pride of place, and the awards at this show, held early in July in conjunction with the Agricultural Show, are coveted by all M.F.H.'s.

There used to be good shows held at Reigate and Exeter. Both were great successes, but do not seem to have been revived since they were

best three bitches, and to the best couples. Such prizes are keenly contested for, and treasured by the walkers, and are presented at the lunch which follows the judging. It is extraordinary how frequently prizes are won by the same walker, which shows that care and looking to the comfort of the puppies earns its just reward.

Although the puppy is nominally walked as a rule by the master of the house, it is the mistress

Photo] [*Keystone.*
ON SHOW.
Foxhounds are seldom exhibited, except at special Hound Shows. At some Agricultural Shows a class is given for Foxhounds. "Wildair", seen above, won at the Cambridgeshire Show. Hounds are not accustomed to this sort of thing and if held on a lead photograph badly.

abandoned during the years of the Great War.

In 1933, besides the Peterborough, other shows were held at Aldershot and Middlesbrough, the former being held under the auspices of the Aldershot Command, the latter by the Great Yorkshire Agricultural Society.

Apart from these public Hound Shows, where representatives from many packs of hounds compete, every Master holds a puppy show of his own, when the entry for the next hunting season is judged by neighbouring masters and huntsmen. Prizes are usually allotted to the best three dogs and

or daughter of the home who is usually entitled to all the praise and congratulation.

Principal Diseases.—The principal disease that used to decimate Foxhound kennels was distemper, but now, since the "Field Distemper Cure" has been perfected, the mortality has decreased enormously.

The ailment commonly called "yellows" is very destructive, and has been the cause of the death of many a promising puppy whilst out at walk. The name of the disease is derived from the fact that the gums and whites of the eyes become

[Photo]   [Keystone

A TYPICAL SCENE.

The pack moves off, followed by the field.   A scene in Cheshire with the hunt leaving Tattenhall, near Tarporley.   The Hounds keep well together and the followers of the hunt at a respectable distance.

"WATCHFUL"

...time to get an even pack.

Capt. E. A. V. Sla...

a decided yellow colour. The origin is a chill that settles on the liver.

Foxhounds do not seem so prone to kennel lameness as Staghounds. This ailment will be dealt with when that breed's turn comes in this Encyclopaedia.

Since the War, a new disease has attacked kennels of hounds, namely, hysteria. As far as is known, there is a decided difference of opinion as to the cause and cure for this scourge. All sorts of remedies have been tried, but veterinary science has not yet located the cause of the trouble. It is hoped that a happy solution will come in due course.

number of bitches. Taking into consideration that to put on an average of twenty-five couples of young hounds each year, one must send out to walk one hundred couples, it can be well imagined that the breeding industry of a pack is of the utmost importance.

Of this one hundred couples, what with disease and accidents, only half can be counted on as being returned to kennels safe and sound, and of this fifty couples probably only half will survive and be of sufficient standard of looks, make and shape, to be good enough for being added to the pack.

These figures show how great the importance of friendly walkers of puppies are to the M.F.H., and

Pho'o]   [Sport & General.
A USEFUL LITTER.
A group of young Foxhounds bred by Lt.-Col. David Davies, M.P. They are by "Boaster" out of "Ullswater Melody", and represent a litter of Fell Cross Hounds.

The general constitution of the Foxhound is weak and feeble, and unless any ailment is caught in its infancy, it is difficult to save the patient.

The rounding of hounds' ears has become less general since 1920. The reason for cutting off the leather of the ear was to protect the ears against injury from brambles and thick undergrowth in the woods. The general appearance of the hound was also improved by this operation, as it gave the head a sharper and more alert expression.

Most packs tattoo a mark in either or both ears, which will enable the hound to be traced both as to ownership if lost, and as to the identity of the litter.

Maintenance of the Pack.—A pack of hounds is maintained by the yearly whelping of a large

what a deep debt of gratitude is due to them. Without the goodwill of the countryside in walking puppies, no pack of hounds could continue in existence for any length of time.

No Master who wishes to show his fields good sport will breed from any bitch or use a sire unless perfect in his or her work. Looks must be at a complete discount where work is concerned.

The time of year for pups to be born is of importance. If the bitches marked to be bred from will obligingly come into season soon after January 1st, then so much the better. The whelps will then be born in late winter or early spring, and so will be whelped early. Puppies whelped after June seldom do much good. They miss the warm summer months in their early infancy.

CAPT. M. J. KINGSCOTE, M.F.H.
A well-known character and a famous pack. Here is Captain Kingscote and the Cricklade Hounds at a Meet at Ashton Keynes.

The Foxhound in the Field. — Now comes the most important part of a Foxhound's existence, and practically the sole reason for its existence at all. The main points which a hound should have are nose, tongue, pace, constitution, general work, and last, but most important of all, drive.

NOSE he must have to be able to hunt and follow the line.

TONGUE is necessary to show that the hound is on the line, and, if alone in a wood, to throw its tongue and so bring the other members of the pack to it. A mute hound is an abomination, and should be drafted at once.

PACE.—It must be able to gallop after the fox and run up with the rest of the pack. To own a pack that run well together, it is necessary to draft any hounds that are faster than the rest of the pack, and so get away in front on their own. Others should be drafted that are not fast enough to run with the main body but keep hanging behind. Nothing is more heart-rending for a huntsman than to have the main body of the hounds, when a check has occurred, cast themselves back to a hound that is hunting the line some little way back and throwing its tongue lustily.

CONSTITUTION is necessary to be able to run up at the end of a hard day's hunting. A hound that is a half-day hound, by which is meant one that cannot run up in the afternoon, is of no use to anyone. A hound that is tired when the second horses are made use of should be drafted.

GENERAL WORK.—A hound must draw the coverts properly, and as soon as a fox is found, join up with all speed to those of its comrades that are on the line. It must cast itself when the line has been lost, and not stand waiting for the huntsman to help. A good huntsman will leave his hounds alone at a check for them to cast themselves, and only when this has been done, and still if the line has not yet been recovered, then will the huntsman come to the pack's aid. A hound must hunt the line together with the rest of the pack, and not run parallel, which fault is termed "skirting".

Photo]   *[Keystone.*
THE DUKE OF BEAUFORT'S PACK.
A meet at Westonbirt Girls' School at Tetbury, the only school in England where girl students are allowed to ride to hounds. They hunt regularly with this pack.

[*Sport and Gener*

THE WHADDON CHASE.

An interesting picture taken at the opening meet of this famous pack at Whitchurch, in Buckinghamshire. The fox has gone to ground and the hunt are apparently deciding whether to try and

Photo]

A "skirter" is of no use, and is a menace from getting on to the line of a fresh fox.

DRIVE.—A good Foxhound, by which one can say a good pack of hounds, must have drive, and by this is meant the pack must pursue the fox with no delay, and keep running on. A fox keeps travelling all the time. Until absolutely dead beat it will not lie down and so wait for the pack to work up to him. A slow pack with no drive could walk after a fox all day and still never catch it.

Some Outstanding Hounds.—It is difficult to name hounds of great note that can be recalled by memory, the trouble being not which to mention, but which to leave out, but in the writer's opinion the following have had as much or more influence on the present-day packs than any others : Pytchley, "Potentate" ; Brocklesby, "Rallywood" ; Meynell, "Whynot" ; Belvoir, "Dexter" and "Weaver" ; Grafton, "Woodman" ; Milton, "Rector" ; Lord Lonsdale's, "Sergeant".

Pride of place must be given to the Belvoir. There it is customary for dog hound after dog hound to be brought forward for inspection and

Photo] INNOCENCE ! *[Paul Popper.*
Young German Foxhound puppies, long before they know of foxes, or the sound of the horn or the rumble and clatter of horses' hooves.

admiration, and there seems no end to them whilst at most other kennels some six hounds may be paraded that earn the distinction of being considered as stallion hounds, and there is then a falling-off to nice but ordinary Foxhounds. At Belvoir the numbers seem inexhaustible, and their work in the field is as good as their looks warrant. Anyone who has tried to keep up with the Belvoir dog pack when they are running a fox on a good scenting day, will appreciate the pace and working qualities of this pack. As stallion hounds they are superb, and stamp their stock—the *sine qua non* of all good stallions—whether they be horses or hounds.

Nature and Sagacity of the Foxhound.—By disposition the Foxhound is affectionate and faithful to its natural master, the huntsman. By nature the breed are not quarrelsome amongst themselves in kennels, thought it may be that an old dog hound may find it necessary to put a younger one in its proper place and teach it a lesson in respecting its elders and betters.

If two packs join up whilst hunting a fox, and the time comes for them to be separated and go

Photo] *Sport and General.*
RATHER BORED.
A photograph of some of the West Norfolks, taken at a Meet at Petygards, near King's Lynn. The hounds are wondering and waiting. They are never so happy as when hunting.

Photo]   [Sport & General.

"DO YE KEN JOHN PEEL . . ."

Old-fashioned houses, elegant horses, eager hounds, scarlet coats and interested villagers—a memorable and typically English sight.
The picture shows a meet of the Avon Vale at the "Long's Arm," near Melksham, Wilts.

their respective ways, then watch each huntsman just ride his horse away from the two packs standing in the middle of the field. It is almost certain that if each huntsman is beloved by his hounds, then automatically the two packs will divide themselves, each following their own master.

One great peculiarity of the Foxhound is the easy manner and ability it has in finding its way home, if left out after a day's hunting. This can be easily under- stood if left out in its own home county, but cases are known where a hound has been sent away to another part of England by rail, and to another pack of hounds, then, after being left out, has found the way back to its old home kennels, frequently spending over a fortnight on the journey.

The writer can vouch for the following instance : In 1903 Capt. E. A. V. Stanley bought some hounds from the late Mr. Washington Singer, who was then Master of the South Devon Foxhounds. One of these hounds was unfortunately left out on the Quantock Hills in Somersetshire on its first appearance in the field. For about two weeks no news was heard of the lost one, and then, lo and behold, Capt. Stanley received a postcard from Mr. Singer's huntsman in Devon, saying the hound had arrived at his kennels that morning, and what should he do with it ? This hound had been sent to Capt. Stanley by rail, and had found its way back on foot across country to its old home. The distance from the kennels in Devon to the new owner's kennels in Somerset could not be less than seventy miles as the crow flies.

Fox Terrier (Smooth).—The Smooth Fox Terrier has been called the gentleman of the Terrier World ; it is aristocratic in the sense that its lineage can be traced back to the middle of the nine- teenth cen- tury, and there are photo- graphs in ex- istence of a dog called Jock, who won prizes at shows in the year 1862 and on- wards.

From time to time crazes arise, and in the doggy world differ- ent breeds suddenly be- come all the rage; but the Smooth Terrier always holds and maintains its position be- cause it is the ideal com- panion, a good house dog, not too large (being an average weight of about 17 or 18 lb.), not quarrel- some, but

Photo]　　　　　　　　　　　　　　　*[Sport and General.*

A NOTED PACK.

The Belvoir, one of the most important packs in England, is seen moving off after the Meet at Croxton Park, near Grantham. In the background is seen old Croxton Abbey.

ready to defend its master's and his own interests if attacked, even if its opponent is six times its own size.

An attractive trait in its character is its gentle- ness when a baby of the human race pulls and hugs it about, and the same dog, having a romp with the elder boy or girl of the family, will accommo- date them, and it is usually the human who cries enough, with the dog asking for the game to go on.

[Sport and General

Photo]

THE QUORN.

Another of Britain's leading packs of Foxhounds at the opening Meet of the season at Kirby Gate, Melton Mowbray, in Leicestershire. The Meet over, the Hounds were being taken to Burrough Hill, where a fox was certain to be found.

One could not say in justice to the breed that it is a noisy fellow, but it will give tongue and continue barking until satisfied the stranger to the premises has passed on, or a word of command from its master allows the visitor to enter, and then it will permit the visitor to pat and admire it.

The Smooth Fox Terrier is equally at home in a flat in a crowded city as in the country. Its gameness in killing vermin, such as rats, etc., cannot be equalled. It is used with the Hounds for drawing fox and will face a badger three times its own weight.

One constant source of annoyance to the lover and breeders of Smooth Fox Terriers is the nondescript type of terrier mongrel very often passed off to the layman by dog dealers as a Smooth Fox Terrier for one purpose and one purpose only — gain The result is that the breed does not get from the British public the credit for the outline, symmetry and beauty which the breed should command.

In the year 1876 certain gentlemen of the Fox Terrier Club met and laid down a standard of points for the breed. So well did they do their work that with just minor alterations the standard still stands good to-day and is universally adopted. Here are the points as laid down in those far-off days.

POINTS OF THE SMOOTH FOX TERRIER

HEAD.—The skull should be flat and moderately narrow, and gradually decreasing in width to the eyes. Not much "stop" should be apparent, but there should be more dip in the profile between the forehead and the top jaw than is seen in the case of the Greyhound. The cheeks must not be full. The ears should be V-shaped and small, of moderate thickness, and dropping forward close to the cheek, not hanging by the side of the head like a Foxhound's. The jaw, upper and under, should be strong and muscular, should be of fair punishing strength, but not so in any way to resemble the Greyhound or modern English Terrier. There should not be much falling away below the eyes. This part of the head should, however, be moderately chiselled out, so as not to go down in a straight line like a wedge. The nose, towards which the muzzle must gradually taper, should be black. The eyes should be dark in colour, small, and rather deep set, full of fire, life, and intelligence; as nearly as possible circular in shape. The teeth should be nearly as possible level, i.e. the upper teeth on the outside of the lower teeth.

NECK.—Should be clean and muscular, without throatiness, of fair length, and gradually widening to the shoulders.

SHOULDERS.—Should be long and sloping, well laid back, fine at the points, and clearly cut at the withers.

CHEST.—Deep and not broad.

BACK.—Should be short, straight and strong, with no appearance of slackness.

Photo]   THE PYTCHLEY.   *[Sport and General.*

Typically British indeed is the scene depicted above. It shows this important pack coming along a country road on a November morning near Newnham Hall, Daventry, in Northants.

Photo] [Paul Popper.

A GERMAN PACK.

A beautiful picture of silver birch trees and part of a German Foxhound Pack on their way to the woods. Foxhound hunting is very popular in Germany and Austria.

2G

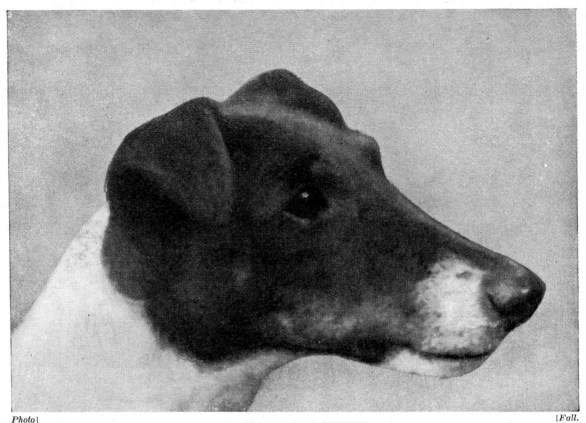

Photo] THE SMOOTH FOX TERRIER. *[Fall.*

The story of the Smooth Fox Terrier is one of the romances of the dog world. Some years ago the Smooth was the most important dog, and remained so until the Wire-haired Terrier became popular. Above is shown the head of Sir Robert Gooch's Ch. "Drungewick Peggy".

Photo] "SOLUS MINTED GOLD". *[Hedges.*

A smart head of a Smooth Fox Terrier. This one was exported to India, where Fox Terriers are great favourites. Smooth coats suit the climate.

LOIN.—Should be powerful and very slightly arched. The fore ribs should be moderately arched, the back ribs deep ; and the dog should be well ribbed up.

HINDQUARTERS — Should be strong and muscular, quite free from droop or crouch ; the thighs long and powerful ; hocks near the ground, the dog standing well up on them like a Foxhound, and not straight in the stifle.

STERN. — Should be set on rather high, and carried gaily, but not over the back or curled. It should be of good strength, anything approaching a "pipe stopper" tail being exceptionally objectionable.

LEGS.—Viewed from any direction. must be straight, showing little or no appearance of an ankle in front. They should be strong in bone throughout, short and straight to pastern. Both fore- and hindlegs should be carried straight forward in travelling. the stifles not turned outward.

"BROKENHURST STING".

This dog was born in 1877 and bred by Mr. H. Gibson. He was a son of the famous "Joe" out of the equally famous "Nettle", and weighed 16½ lb.

The elbows should hang perpendicular to the body, working free of the side.

FEET.—Should be round, compact, and not large. The soles hard and tough. The toes moderately arched, and turned neither in nor out.

COAT. —Should be straight, flat smooth, hard, dense and abundant. The belly and underside of the thigh should not be bare.

COLOUR. — White should predominate; brindle, red or liver markings are objectionable. Otherwise this point is of little or no importance.

SYMMETRY, SIZE AND CHARACTER.—The dog must present a general gay, lively, and active appearance ; bone and strength in a small compass are essentials, but this must not be taken to mean that a Fox Terrier should be cloggy, or in any way coarse—speed and endurance must be looked to as well as power, and the symmetry of the

THREE OF THE OLD SORT.

At the back stands Hyde's "Buffet"; on the left "Bristles", the property of Mr. S. E. Shirley, a Terrier with a wire coat and on the right Mr. F. Burbidge's noted Terrier, "Bloom". The above picture is reproduced from an old painting.

Foxhound taken as model. The Terrier, like the Hound, must on no account be leggy, nor must it be too short in the leg. It should stand like a cleverly made hunter, covering a lot of ground, yet with a short back, as before stated. It will then attain the highest degree of propelling power, together with the greatest length of stride that is compatible with the length of its body. Weight is not a certain criterion of a Terrier's fitness for

following points are what should be bred to. The head should be long and lean; the average length of the head on a dog 17 to 18 lb. measured with calipers is from seven to eight inches. Ears must be small and V-shaped with a good reachy neck, but the neck should not be thick, or, in other words, throaty. The feet should be small, with an appearance of standing right up on his toes. Shoulders should be long and sloping, well laid back, and

　　　　　　　　　　　　　　　　　　　　　　　　　　　　[C. H. Bishop.

CH. "DONCASTER DOMINIE".

The above photograph shows one of the great Terriers owned by Mrs. Bennett Edwards, a leading woman breeder of her time.

its work—general shape, size, and contour are the main points—and if a dog can gallop and stay, and follow its fox up a drain, it matters little what its weight is to a pound or so, though roughly speaking 15 to 17 lb. for a bitch and 16 to 18 lb. for a dog in show condition are appropriate weights.

POINTS.—Head and ears, 15; neck, 5; shoulders and chest, 10; back and loin, 10; hindquarters, 15; stern, 5; legs and feet, 15; coat, 10; symmetry, 15; making a total of 100.

As the standard to the lay mind might be rather technical in ordinary or common language, the

fine at the points. The chest and brisket should be deep but not broad. The back should be straight, short and strong, and when looked along should have a level top. The tail should be set on high and carried gaily, but a tail carried over the back is a bad fault. Hindquarters should be strong, with the thighs powerful, and when the dog walks it should move with perfect freedom. The coat should be straight, flat and dense, and a curly coat in a Smooth should be avoided at all cost.

A careful study of the above will assist the novice and beginner a great deal.

Photo] FANCY MEETING YOU! [*E.N.A.*

The Fox Terrier is found all over the world and is accustomed to all sorts of conditions and adventures. The one shown above, although only a recent resident on the Gold Coast, evidently is not at all afraid at meeting such a strange thing as an ostrich.

[E.N.A.

The owner must necessarily take precautions and protect his property accordingly.

This is the destructive age, when the puppy is full of mischief, looking out all the time for something to play with.

GROWING UP.

Photo]

becomes. In the excitement of the chase whilst working with ferrets it is uncanny to see how the Terrier knows when a rat is going to appear and when the ferret is coming out. Accidents, however, do happen, and many a ferret has met with an untimely fate through the over-excitement and keenness of the Terrier. The same applies to rabbiting, and a good day's sport can be enjoyed with a couple of ferrets and two good Smooth Fox Terriers.

The huntsman from the very early days of fox-hunting has always used a smooth dog or bitch for drawing a fox; in this work the size of the Terrier is very important. From time to time a raging controversy appears in the Canine Press on the correct size of the Fox Terrier, but again, the standard laid down so many years ago always answers the test, and very often when a leading kennel exhibits an outstanding specimen in all points but size, human nature being human nature, attempts have been made to justify the wins by that specimen, or why it should win, by the suggestion that size does not matter. It will be found, however, size is very important when a large Terrier tries to go to earth and fails to get in.

The same criticism applies to an undersized dog. There is nothing more disappointing than an undersized Terrier unable to stand up to a good day's work.

It is not always the Terrier that gets the best of the deal when working; an old buck rat will, when cornered by the Terrier, wrap himself round the dog's head and make a nasty wound, but this only ends in one thing for Mr. Rat, the death penalty, as it seems the bite from the rat only makes the Smooth more vicious, and the next arrival on the scene gets an even quicker despatch.

In badger digging the Smooth Fox Terrier excels, but for real hard work both for master and dog commend me to digging for badgers. Writing of badger digging recalls a story from Somerset.

A man wanted a dog for this purpose, and seeing some Smooth Fox Terriers advertised went to see them. They belonged to an old farmer. After fully inspecting the Terriers the purchaser's choice fell on a bitch, but he was very insistent in asking whether this bitch was game and would kill. After receiving several assurances and again repeating the question there was quite a long pause, and in the Somerset drawl there came from the seller of the bitch: "Maister, if the bitch was to meet the devil himself coming

MOTHERHOOD.

Motherhood is always delightful, and Fox Terrier puppies are great fun.　Three useful puppies with their mother, who is wearing an expression very often seen, as if to say "They are an awful nuisance, aren't they?"

up out of a hole, she would kill him."

The story goes to show how much faith the owner has in the gameness of the breed.

The same bitch, on being put into a dig for the first time, held on to a sow badger of about forty pounds weight and could not be turned away from her job despite any odds.

It has been said that the exhibition or show Terrier will not work, or will not be allowed to work in case it is spoilt for exhibition. This is not true, as breeders and exhibitors of Smooths welcome the opportunity of proving the worth of the breed, and, in addition, it adds to the value of the dog, especially in the eyes of some of the buyers abroad.

Photo]   WHAT IS THAT ?   [*Fall.*

Two of Capt. Crosthwaite's Terriers watching and listening (note the carriage of ear in the foremost dog and how the tail is held), ready to pounce into the hedge.

The difficulty is that the kennels cannot get the opportunity of working their dogs except in a very limited sphere.

To anyone desiring a pal and a guard without thinking of breeding or exhibiting, the Smooth Fox Terrier fills everyone's requirements no matter how exacting they may be. Prices for companion dogs of course vary, but at £2 10s. and upwards a prospective buyer will not find any difficulty in getting his or her requirements met by visiting a kennel or two in his or her immediate neighbourhood.

Fox Terrier (Wire).— The "Wire" has been aptly described as "the gentleman" of all Terrier breeds, and there is no doubt whatever that it is the dominant dog not only of this country but throughout the world.

As a show dog it has headed the list of Registration at the Kennel Club for a number of years—being equally popular with women exhibitors as with the men—in fact, many of the most beautiful

Photo]   RATS !   [*Fall.*

Two of the popular types of Smooth Fox Terriers, wearing an expression of excited anticipation. Who said "Rats"?

specimens produced have been bred and exhibited by the former.

The competition is extremely keen, and there are so many of super merit that at the great championship shows it is no uncommon thing for the leaders to change places under the leading authorities of the breed from week to week—this often is due to the perfect condition in which it is essential for them to be presented in the show ring —even a week will sometimes make just that little bit of difference in the judge's eyes as to whether the Terrier gains a first, second, third. or even minor position in the final "line up". There is no prettier picture than to look into the Wire Fox Terrier ring at any great show and to see these grand little fellows, and their equally keen, enthusiastic, and always thoroughly sporting owners. fighting desperately for supremacy.

must be a certain amount of difference of opinion in this matter. The generally accepted rule is that the body coat should be taken off six to eight weeks prior to a show, the skull left until about two weeks before the show ; the hair on the legs and quarters should be tidied, as necessary, with a fairly fine metal comb. Although combs with cutting edges are permissible for trimming, a much better effect is obtained by using the finger and thumb only.

Before starting the process, it is advisable to rub the terrier all over with ordinary whiting ; this has the effect of making it much easier to remove the unwanted hair. The whiskers in front of the eyes should be carefully combed forward and down, and, if too plentiful or bushy, they must be removed by plucking. This is particularly necessary under the muzzle and down to the brisket. It must be

Photo]   *[Stanley M. Ballance.*
THREE GREAT FRIENDS.
Mr. C. C. Walters, of the R.S.P.C.A. (Herts District), is a Terrier enthusiast, and is here seen with his two friends. The one, having had a game, pants in his arms, and the other is trying to get hold of the string and worry it. A photo taken at 1000th of a second.

The question of preparation for show is a very difficult one. Many experts have written at great length upon the subject, and much advice has been given as to the proper methods to be employed and as to the correct amount of coat which should be allowed to remain when exhibiting. The judge is the deciding factor, and his award is final, but as there are probably thirty different judges who have the awarding of Kennel Club Certificates during each year, it necessarily follows that there

plainly understood that trimming a "Wire" is not an easy matter at first ; it is only by experience and careful watching how the leading exhibitors trim their dogs that the novice can hope, in time, to compete successfully with the more experienced. The novice need never hesitate to ask questions of the exhibitors—they are all so splendidly sporting. Naturally, a very busy professional, who may have nearly a dozen exhibits at the show, has not much time to spare, but failing him, there are many amateurs—ladies and gentlemen—who will always be ready to try to help the genuine novice.

Shows are held in all parts of the country, full particulars of which can be obtained from the advertisements in the Canine Press ; also there will be found many advertisements of those with stock to dispose of. Here let a word of warning be given. Always go to a breeder of repute : by

its fellows in the show ring, accompany its master in any of his sporting activities, guard the house, protect the children (and it loves to share in their games), or be the faithful companion of the aged, it is at all times completely adaptable.

The "Wire" is cheap to keep, requires little and simple accommodation, and if one is really interested in this kind of dog, it will be found that the grooming of its coat is not a very serious matter—

"BOWES BREVITY".

This soundly built Terrier, bred by Mr. A. T. King, is a half brother to the noted Ch. "Petwick Cocktail", the property of Mr. H. L. Cottrill. "Brevity" is the sire of over 100 winners, including two champions, and was second best stud dog at the Wire Fox Terrier Show. Unfortunately, the dog having been tampered with, his show career was ended early, the culprit never being discovered.

doing otherwise you may find you are practising the "penny wise and pound foolish" theory.

It is not only as a show dog that the "Wire" is so popular—it is a dog which is suitable for every possible purpose that a dog can be useful for.

To begin with, it is a handy size and, whether trimmed or more or less in "the rough", it always has symmetry and carriage ; fearless, but not naturally pugnacious ; is to be found practically everywhere, and no wonder, for it has a delightful temperament, and whether its job in life is to beat

say ten minutes a day. Reasonable exercise must be given—preferably a walk on the road to keep its feet tight and its nails worn down. If possible it should have a good healthy gallop. This variety of dog should never be chained up.

The question of colour or markings is frequently discussed, but, as has been said, "a good horse cannot be a bad colour", so it is with the "Wire"—although the hound markings during recent years have become much more popular with both the general public and exhibitors.

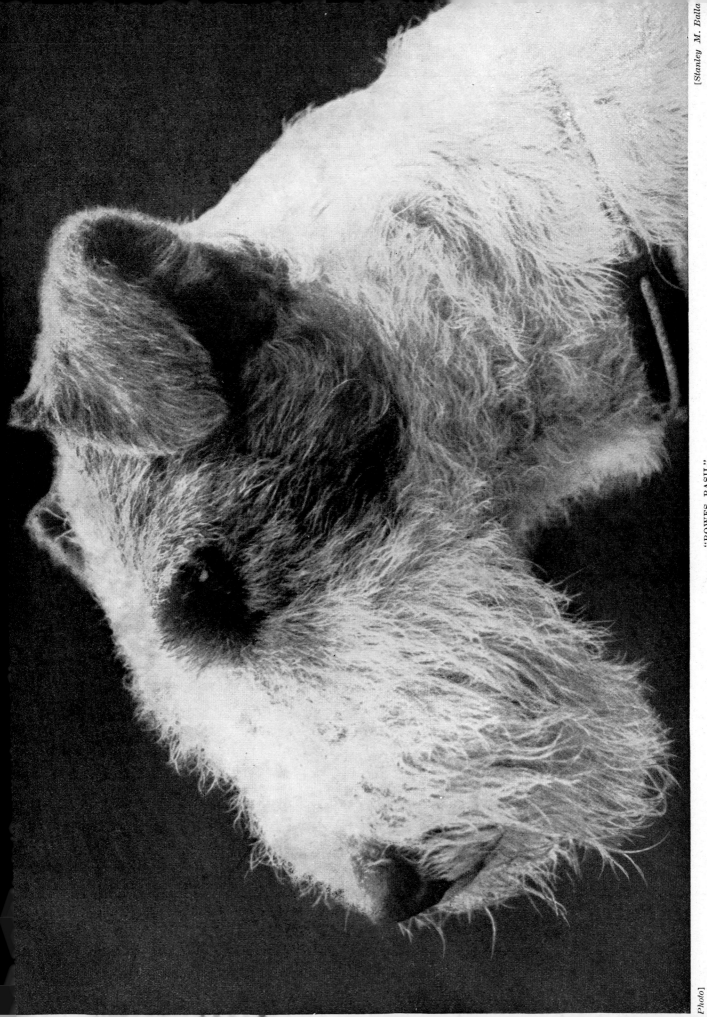

[Photo]

[Stanley M. Balla

"BOWES BASIL".

Bred out of a sister to "Bowes Brevity" (shown on page 676) by Ch. "Wycollar Wonder" it has been exhibited with considerable success. It was sold as a stud dog by its breeder, Mr. A. T. King, to Miss P. V. Lowe, and s

of its puppies at the home of Miss Lowe are seen on page 682. Its coat is rather long and rough, only because it needs plucking. Compare the head with that of "Bowes Brevity".

By courtesy]

[C. H. Bis...

CH. "DUSKY REINE".

In the early days of "Wires," Mr. Enfield showed the above dog, born in 1899, which was one of the best of the breed at that time.   Smooth-coated Terrier breeders (for "Smooths" were then in fashion) considered "Wir...
such as "Cracker", "Admiral", "Gleaner", and "Siren", the latter being shown on page 6

Those who decide to have a dog cannot go wrong in choosing a "Wire". It is best to obtain a puppy of about eight weeks, and a good specimen can be obtained from a reliable breeder for round about five guineas, or even less. A good dog will always be a joy to own, whereas one not quite so good may not find the same place in the owner's eyes or affection. Having acquired one of this breed, it is well to bear in mind a few simple rules which will add to the animal's comfort, and which,

to six months. An ample supply of drinking water should always be available, and the idea that a piece of sulphur in it is beneficial may be considered fallacious. If its condition needs sulphur, a little "flowers of sulphur" should be sprinkled on its food.

A small bed should be provided, and a good plan is to buy a box from the local grocer forabout sixpence. It is best to run a strip under it, about $\frac{1}{2}$-inch thick, to keep the bottom of the box just

By courtesy]   *[C. H. Bishop.*

CH. "DUSKY SIREN"

An outstanding type of Terrier brought to the front by Miss Hatfield, then living at Morden, and who exhibited at the same time the noted "Dusky Cracker". "Siren" was born in 1903 and was painted by Maud Earl. It is interesting to compare this dog with some of the champions of to-day, but it must be borne in mind that the above picture is from a painting.

if followed in a general way, will help to appreciate more fully the many and various virtues of which our little 'Wire" friend is capable. It should be remembered that it can never display these many virtues unless given a reasonable opportunity in puppyhood to develop them, and upon the owner falls much of the responsibility for seeing that the dog gets these opportunities. It should never be forgotten that it must have exercise, and that it must have worms. If acquired at eight weeks old, it should have been wormed once, therefore, when it is twelve weeks old, it should be wormed again—and then again between the age of five

off the floor, a 6-inch strip across the front to keep its bedding in (straw, wood shavings, or any old piece of rug), and another piece six inches wide across the front of the top, and it will then have comfortable sleeping accommodation. Fox Terriers will stand up to any amount of cold, but they hate draught or damp.

Feeding is really a very simple matter. Of course, fish, poultry and game bones should be avoided, also potatoes. Apart from this it may be fed on much the same lines as a healthy, growing child. If there are not sufficient table scraps available, a food known as "Terrier Meal" should

Photo]　　　　　　　　　　　*[Hedges.*

CH. "CRACKLEY SURETHING".

This Wire-hair Terrier is one of Mr. J. R. Barlow's stud dogs standing in 1934 at a fee of six guineas, which will give the reader some idea on this matter. He is a son of Ch. "Crackley Startler" and was bred by Mr. K. A. Knight. He was born in 1932.

be given. It is a mixture of meat and biscuit, to which should be added any bits of meat, gravy, and green vegetables that may be available. As an alternative, a fish's head, boiled thoroughly, will prove a most attractive addition to the biscuit.

It is not advisable to exercise the "Wire" by letting it run behind a cycle. If chastisement is necessary, one must be cruel to be kind—that is to say it is no use continually giving "gentle taps". If it requires punishment, just one which it will remember is far more efficacious, and, in the long run, kinder.

It will be appreciated that the subject of "Wire-hair Fox Terrier" is a very wide one, and, consequently, it becomes very difficult to deal adequately with the many aspects and the possible viewpoints of those who may read these lines. For instance, it is realized that some may be keenly interested to know what is best for a promising puppy ; others, who own a bitch, may wonder what is the proper course and how to make the usual arrangements for the mating ; and yet others may want to know how to deal with the litter of "prospective champions" when they arrive. The solution to all these problems is provided in other sections of this Encyclopaedia.

It is the generally accepted opinion of those

best able to judge that the standard of the Wire Fox Terrier has gradually and persistently improved during the past thirty years. Some photos of famous Terriers are included in this article, and whether it is the photographic art, the art of the "trimmer", or the improvement in the dogs themselves, must be left to the reader's own opinion, but the experts are agreed that the Terrier of to-day is a vast improvement upon that of earlier years. And this brings us to the question, "What is the origin of these little fellows ?" Well, frankly, there is very little really authentic information on the point of the origin of the Fox Terrier—which appears to be somewhat like "Topsy's baby"—wrapped in mystery !

As its name implies, it has always been primarily intended for use as "a ground dog", and it is quite certain that for the past eighty years or more it has always been the most favoured Terrier used by hunting men. It is a fact that it was not the same "gentleman" in those far-off days as it is to-day, but then, as now, it was always a gay, game dog, of hardy constitution and capable of going to ground.

There appears to be a general opinion amongst those who have been interested in the breed during

Photo]　　　　　*[Hedges.*

CH. "TALAVERA PEGASUS."

The dog on the left is one of Captain H. R. Phipps' Terriers. He was born in July of 1930 and is a son of "Beau Brummel of Wildoaks", one of Mr. and Mrs. Bondy's famous dogs, exhibited both in England and in the United States.

Photo]　　　　　　　　　　　*[Hedges*

CH. 'TALAVERA JUPITER".

This well-known Terrier is also the property of Captain Phipps, and was bred by its owner, the sire being Ch. 'Beau Brummel of Wildoaks", which has thrown some remarkable stock both here and in America.

hoto] [*Sport and General*.

"CHANDON COCKTAIL".

he Fox Terrier is a general favourite. Mrs. M. Feary has a kennel of "Wires", and this is one of her dogs making friends with Miss Jean Melville, the well-known

A FINE LOT.

These positively delightful puppies by "Bowes Basil", a head study of which appears on page 677, were bred by Miss P. V. Lowe. It is impossible, at the age of three weeks, to say if a puppy will prove a winner, ... may ... they may wob steady limbs.

the past fifty years or more, that the Fox Terrier existed a long time before the eighty years previously mentioned, but that it is during this later period that it has gradually become the "model of a good hunter" which it represents to-day. In those early days the Fox Terrier—judging from pictures to be seen at the Kennel Club—was a long-backed, thick-headed and bad-fronted fellow. The present-day excellences of the breed may be largely credited to the Fox Terrier Club which was formed in 1876, when a standard of points was evolved which has been rigidly adhered to ever since.

Whatever "outcrosses", such as Bull Terrier, might possibly have been resorted to originally, it is quite certain that nothing of the sort has been attempted during the past seventy or eighty years—except that a few years ago the experiment was tried of crossing the "Wire" and the "Smooth", with the intention of imparting more stamina to both varieties, and also to improve the texture of the "Wire" coat. In practice it was found to have very little advantage, and the experiment was

Photo]   [Hedges.
CH. "FOURWENTS ROCKET".
Owned by Miss Joyce Esdaile, this winning dog won the Fifty Guinea Challenge Cup for the best dog or bitch at the Fox Terrier Club Show in 1932. He is a tan-marked headed dog, excels in bone, apart from other good points and is a son of "Dogberry Barbed Wire".

Photo]   [Hedges.
"EDEN EXQUISITE".
It need hardly be said that the prefix "Crackley" stands for some of the very best in "Wires". This exceptionally good seven-and-a-half months old puppy was exported to the United States by Mr. J. R. Barlow. She has been considered one of the best bitch puppies seen.

not persisted in to any very great extent. The evolution of the Wire Fox Terrier has not been achieved without difficulties. At one time it was thought that the dog was gradually being bred too large, and certainly a number of dogs were exhibited which were too big. Then a reaction of opinion set in and it became the fashion to aim at a smaller type. As a result they became "too small and weedy", but in recent years this difficult question has not arisen. There is much more uniformity generally, and it is thought that the judges should receive all credit for this desirable state of affairs, although there is no doubt that the Fox Terrier Club and the Wire Fox Terrier Association have done wonderfully good work in looking after the many and varied requirements of our little friends. In the future it may be sagely left to these excellently managed Clubs to see that the "Wire" will maintain its position and its dignity, and continue to deserve the soubriquet of the "gentleman" of all Terriers.

POINTS OF THE WIRE FOX TERRIER

The following is the description of Points of the Wire Fox Terrier as adopted by the Wire Fox Terrier Association at a General Meeting held on February 12, 1913, at Cruft's Show, London. This description is mainly an amplification of the standard as laid down by the Fox Terrier Club, and the terms which are identical with

INT. CH. "GALLANT FOX OF WILDOAKS".
This great Terrier, one of the best of recent times, was born in December of 1929, a son of Ch. "Crackley Supreme" out of a noted matron, Ch. "Gains Great Surprise", owned by Mrs. R. C. Bondy of New York. The latter is the mother of Ch. "Beau Brummel of Wildoaks".

Photo]   *[Metcalf.*

CH. "THET TETRARCH".

A good upstanding Terrier, bred and owned by Miss L. M. Dixon. A son of Ch. "Eden Aristocrat", it was a January puppy of 1929. He goes back to "Crusader".

the standard are printed in italics. It is considered that this description, which has been drawn up, revised, and approved by many of the leading owners of Wires of the present day, will be of material assistance to the smaller owners and to the novice breeder.

NOSE.—*Should be black.*

FOREFACE.—Although the foreface *should gradually taper* from eye to muzzle and should dip slightly at its juncture with the forehead, it *should not* "dish" or *fall away* quickly *below the eyes*, where it should be full and well made up, but relieved from "wedginess" by a little delicate *chiselling*. Both upper and lower jaws *should be strong* and *muscular*, the *teeth as nearly as possible level* and capable of closing together like a vice—the lower canines locking in front of the upper—and the points of the upper incisors slightly overlapping the lower. While well-developed jaw-bones, armed with a set of strong, white teeth, impart that appearance of strength to the foreface which is so desirable in the Wire-haired variety, an excessive bony or muscular development of the jaws is both unnecessary and unsightly, as it is partly responsible

for the full and rounded contour of the cheeks to which the term "cheeky" is applied.

EYES.—*Should be dark in colour,* moderately *small* and not prominent, *full of fire, life, and intelligence ; as nearly as possible circular in shape,* and not too far apart. Anything approaching a yellow eye is most objectionable.

SKULL.—The top line of the *skull* should be *almost flat, sloping* slightly and gradually *decreasing in width towards the eyes,* and should not exceed $3\frac{1}{2}$ inches in diameter at the widest part—measuring with the calipers—in the full-grown dog of correct size, the bitch's skull being proportionately narrower. If this measurement is exceeded the skull is termed "coarse", while a full-grown dog with a much narrower skull is termed "bitchy" in head. The length of the head of a full-grown, well-developed dog of correct size—measured with calipers from the back of the occipital bone to the nostrils—should be from 7 to $7\frac{1}{4}$ inches, the bitch's head being proportionately shorter. Any measurement in excess of this usually indicates an oversized or long-backed specimen, although occasionally—so rarely as to partake of the nature of a freak—a Terrier of correct size may boast a head $7\frac{1}{2}$ inches in

Photo]   *[Metcalf.*

"FLORNELL SALOON".

A well bred dog by Ch. "Talavera Simon", a son of the noted champion "Fountain Crusader". He goes back on both sides to "Barrington Bridegroom", considered by many to be one of the best Fox Terriers in the breed. "Saloon" is owned by Mr. Jim Parkington.

Photo]   *[Metcalf.*

INT. CH. "THET TIMBER".

This outstanding dog was born in April of 1928. He was bred by Miss L. M. Dixon, whose kennel prefix is "Thet". His mother is "Simon's Dimple". "Thet Timber" is believed to hold a world's record as the only Wire Fox Terrier that is a champion of England, the United States and on the Continent.

[Dorien Le

A CANINE GENTLEMAN.

The Wire-hair Terrier is popular all over the world, and not only as a show dog or because it is as useful as a dog can be, but more probably because it is the most companionable of all canine breeds. Intelligent, resourceful, gifted with expressive features, it can make itself understood almost as plainly as if it had the power of speech.

length. In a well-balanced head there should be little apparent difference in length between skull and foreface. If, however, the foreface is noticeably shorter, it amounts to a fault, the head looking weak and "unfinished". On the other hand, when the eyes are set too high up in the skull, and too near the ears, it also amounts to a fault, the head being said to have a "foreign appearance".

EARS.—*Should be small and V-shaped and of moderate thickness*, the flaps neatly folded over *and dropping forward close to the cheeks.* The top

always be clean cut. A shoulder well laid back gives the long fore-hand which, in combination with a short back, is so desirable in Terrier or Hunter.

CHEST.—*Deep and not broad*, a too narrow chest being almost as undesirable as a very broad one. Excessive depth of chest and brisket is an impediment to a Terrier when going to ground.

BODY.—The back should be *short* and level, *with no appearance of slackness—the loins* muscular and *very slightly arched.* The brisket should be deep, *the front ribs moderately arched*, and

Photo]   THE DUCHESS OF NEWCASTLE.   [*Sport and General.*

Her Grace is seen at the Joint Terrier Show in 1930 trying to make her Terrier, "Cracknels Verdict of Notts", show itself a little better. No one understands the Terrier better than the Duchess, and the present position of the breed is greatly due to her influence. The dog won eight first prizes.

line of the folded ear should be well above the level of the skull. A pendulous ear, hanging dead by the side of the head like a hound's, is uncharacteristic of the Terrier, while an ear which is semi-erect is still more undesirable.

NECK.—*Should be clean, muscular, of fair length, free from throatiness*, and presenting a graceful curve when viewed from the side.

SHOULDERS.—When viewed from the front should slope steeply downwards from their juncture with the neck towards *the points*, which *should be fine.* When viewed from the side they *should be long, well laid back*, and should slope obliquely backward from points to *withers, which should*

the back ribs deep, and, of course, they should be well sprung.

The term "slackness" is applied both to the portion of the back immediately behind the withers when it shows any tendency to dip, and also the flanks, when there is too much space between the back-ribs and hip-bone. When there is little space between the ribs and hips the dog is said to be "short in couplings", "short-coupled", or "well-ribbed-up".

A Terrier can scarcely be too short in back, provided it has sufficient length of neck and liberty of movement. The bitch may be slightly longer in couplings than the dog.

686